Managing Information Technology in Multinational Corporations

EDWARD M. ROCHE

Macmillan Publishing Company
New York

Maxwell Macmillan Canada
Toronto

Maxwell Macmillan International
New York   Oxford   Singapore   Sydney

To Joe Ferreira

Editor: Ed Moura
Production Supervisor: Publication Services, Inc.
Production Manager: Aliza Greenblatt
Cover Designer: Publication Services, Inc.

This book was set in Garamond by Publication Services, Inc., and was printed and bound by Book Press.
The cover was printed by Phoenix Color Corp.

Copyright © 1992 by Macmillan Publishing Company, a division of Macmillan, Inc.

Printed in the United States of America

All rights reserved. No part of this book may be reproduced or transmitted in any form or by any means, electronic or mechanical, including photocopying, recording, or any information storage and retrieval system, without permission in writing from the Publisher.

Macmillan Publishing Company
866 Third Avenue, New York, New York 10022

Macmillan Publishing Company is
part of the Maxwell Communication
Group of Companies.

Maxwell Macmillan Canada, Inc.
1200 Eglinton Avenue East
Suite 200
Don Mills, Ontario M3C 3N1

Library of Congress Cataloging-in-Publication Data
Roche, Edward Mozley.
    Managing information technology in multinational corporations / Edward M. Roche
       p. cm.
    Includes bibliographical references and index.
    ISBN 0-02-402690-5
    1. International business interprises—Management—Data processing. 2. Information technology—Management. I. Title.
HD62.4.R64 1992
658'.05–dc20   91–42589
                                                                              CIP

Printing: 1 2 3 4 5 6 7   Year: 2 3 4 5 6 7 8

Preface

This book is intended to build a bridge between two different sets of literature and ideas. On the one side, it is concerned with the multinational corporation and the rather considerable amount of literature and academic thought developed over the past few decades regarding international business and its principal actor, the *multinational corporation*. This literature has many important themes of thought, its great debates, and an intellectual tradition that finds sustenance in the deeper currents of political economy and economic history. On the other side, I explored the management information systems (MIS) field to examine what we know about information technology, including telecommunications systems, with particular regard to how it is used in business and commerce. This field is relatively new—information technology is relatively new—and is, as yet, quite ill-defined. Although this gives it the chance to carry more flexibility than other academic disciplines, it still suffers from not having the deep well of tradition and history from which to draw its intellectual currents.

The MIS field sometimes reminds me of Japan during the Meiji period. Ideas were being imported from all over the world by the *ryugaku* trips overseas to absorb foreign knowledge. So it is with MIS, to which many of its proponents have come as intellectual refugees from other areas (many from the social sciences), bringing with them the myriad of methodologies, approaches, and values associated with those other fields.

MIS has also become the home to refugees from computer science as well, and this has produced what may be one of the strangest phenomena of the academic world—the circuslike specter of persons who have spent their lives studying a narrowly defined technical matter (such as artificial intelligence), now taking their place alongside their colleagues from finance, marketing, and the classical disciplines of business, and assuming the air that they actually have something relevant to say to MBA students regarding how they should operate a business. With such pedagogical absurdities, it has been easy to criticize MIS.

This book is a story of a young field, and an older field; of a highly theoretical field, and a field that despite the many long hours of toil put in by teams of obscurants and pedants, has yet to congeal into a fixed cosmology of navigable theories.

In some ways, the field of international business also suffers from ridicule from other fields. In many business schools, for example, international business is denied the status of being a separate department. Many of the more entrenched disciplines, such as the powerful finance departments and marketing departments, hold in many cases that international business should be taught within each discipline. Finance courses can teach aspects of international finance, and marketing courses can teach courses of international marketing. So why do we *need* to have separate studies in international business? By the way, the same argument is made regarding MIS— that those courses too can be taught within other disciplines.

This book then, is my attempt to bridge the disciplines of international business and MIS. Perhaps such a relationship is a genetically unpredictable marriage with little potential for offspring of significance, but it *does* fit in with the two major trends we see today: increasing internationalization of most economic transactions, and the worldwide growth of a massive technological infrastructure based on computer communications systems. My belief that these two trends represent important aspects of the near future is my underlying motivation for writing this book, for it is a phenomenon that I believe is both misunderstood by the information systems professionals in many multinational corporations, and also under-utilized in most of the world's business strategy classes. It should be more fully considered in the future, and I hope this book will help it to be.

The research has been difficult and slow, hampered by problems of access to multinational corporations (MNCs) and by fundamental theoretical problems, one of the most important of which is the correct empirical modeling of internationalization. It is hoped that in the future, more collaboration with overseas scholars, particularly in Japan and Europe, will increase the pace of research.

This book grew out of a multiyear effort to understand the strategic significance of computer and telecommunications systems in multinational corporations. As time went on, the research was eventually oriented toward six theoretical areas of inquiry, which may be thought of as "modules" of an overall theory. These included the following, which will later reappear to the reader as chapters herein.

1: Coordination of Headquarters/Subsidiary Relationships

The study of communications channels and control relationships between MNC headquarters and subsidiaries (and also between subsidiaries) has emerged as a distinct stream of inquiry. Researchers have examined types of information exchanged and have been particularly interested in what this indicates about decision making. New information technologies (electronic mail, voice mail, teleconferencing, digital facsimile, distributed processing, etc.) are changing the nature of communications within the MNC. In general, there is potential for more transparency in decision making, and considerably tighter coordination between headquarters operations and individual subsidiaries. In addition, intersubsidiary coordination may be enhanced as subsidiary-subcontractor or subsidiary-customer relationships are linked together with information systems.

2: Corporate Intelligence and (Market) Monitoring Systems

The literature on corporate intelligence has emphasized the need for the MNC to scan its environment for many types of information that can directly (or indirectly) influence its ability to do business. In addition to "standard" information on market trends and competitors, other areas of coverage usually include political developments, economic trends, host government policy, security threats (such as terrorism), and general cultural developments. This line of inquiry has the potential to relate closely to the considerable body of literature on Decision Support Systems (DSS). The heterogeneous nature of external information raises many important issues of how it can be handled through computer systems and how it can be collected (translated), synthesized, and communicated. A related area of inquiry concerns use of information technology in crisis management situations.

3: Information Technology-based FSAs (Firm-Specific Advantages)

Much of the research in international business has focused on why a firm becomes a multinational corporation. One important line of thinking holds that firms set up operations overseas because they have some type of advantage (a firm-specific advantage) in the target market. Advantages of capital or technology are two key examples, although there are also alternative reasons why firms set up overseas (i.e., government regulations, trade barriers, etc.). No one appears to have studied IT-based FSAs in the multinational. This research can build from the rich (and controversial) literature on "information technology for competitive advantage," sometimes called "strategic information systems." The concept of information systems becoming a "barrier to entry" has not been tested in the international arena (so far as I know) yet should be. In addition, it is clear that many "global" strategies (e.g., in manufacturing) would be utterly impossible without the (relatively) new developments in distributed processing and other technologies. For example, the Cadillac production of its Allante, in cooperation with Pininfarina of Turin, Italy, is tracked completely through an international information technology system.[1] However, the methods to understand what specific component(s) of competitive advantage are accounted for by global information systems (as opposed to marketing, technology, manufacturing, capital, or management skill and other advantages) are not well understood.

4: Internalization Theory

Internalization theory is used to explain (partially) the rise of the multinational corporation. It holds that a firm grows by internalizing economic transactions previously carried out on the open market. The firm can do them more efficiently than the market, and can thus make a profit (or extract economic rents). This theory has been built up particularly in regard to raw materials processing, manufacturing, and transportation, but not to the same degree (so far as I know) in regard to either information-intensive industries (banking, finance, insurance, publishing, etc.) or the internal information-based operations and functions of the general MNC (e.g., the information system of a manufacturing or raw materials processing firm). In terms of information systems research, as a very crude example, we could observe a large MNC turning to electronic mail and G-IV (digital) facsimile—all operating on its internal data processing network—in order to "internalize" postal and courier services that are available (less efficiently and more costly) on the open market, but this is a fringe pedagogical example, as we are really concerned with understanding the role of mainstream data processing. However, a more intriguing, and considerably more substantial, line of research examines the role of information technology in overall general internalization (not just of information transactions but of all economic transactions). It may well be that information technology is the single most important factor in explaining this phenomenon.

5: Host Country/MNC Relations

A vast amount of literature has emerged on host country and MNC relationships regarding bargaining power, the international division of labor, technology transfer and licensing, transfer pricing, and government-imposed barriers against the MNC. For example, technology transfer by the multinational corporation is called for in the United Nations code for investment.

---

[1] See Stephen Macaulay, "Cadillac: On Its Own—And Agressive," *Production*, 99(10), October 1987, pp. 74–76.

Preface

"Transnational corporations should contribute to the strengthening of the scientific and technological capacities of developing countries, in accordance with the established science and technology policies and priorities of those countries. Transnational corporations should undertake substantial research and development activities in developing countries and should make full use of local resources and personnel in this process.... Transnational corporations in their transfer-of-technology transactions, including intra-corporate transactions, should avoid practices which adversely affect the international flow of technology, or otherwise hinder the economic and technological development of countries...."[2]

A subset of this literature has examined the information technology aspects of this issue, particularly with respect to developed–developing country relationships (where information technology is seen as a negative force in helping the MNC take advantage of the "weak" developing country). In addition, issues such as the regulation and control of transborder data flow (building international computer networks across national borders) has been a major breeding ground for conflict between the MNC and host governments, where it was viewed as being a very significant nontariff barrier (NTB) to trade. Host country regulations against information technology extend well beyond transborder data flow: importation of computers, utilization of local programming, licensing of international database access, prohibition against private networks, and onerous database maintenance requirements—including stipulations the the MNC must operate data centers within the host country regardless of economic considerations—are a few of the other areas where host country/MNC relationships need study. Finally, there is the question of host country infrastructure and the FDI decision within the context of information technology. Some countries (e.g., Singapore) have undertaken specific investment programs in telecommunications facilities; they train computer operators, programmers and engineers specifically for the purpose of attracting the multinational corporation.[3]

6: Global Systems Development and Business Strategy

Given all of these considerations about information technology in multinational corporations, some practical advice and insight must eventually

---

[2] See ¶38 of UNCTC, *The New Code Environment*, (UNCTC Current Studies, series A, no. 16) (New York: United Nations, 1990) (ST/CTC/SER.A/16).

[3] Some countries appear to be investing in telecommunications infrastructure in order to attract MNCs, but others have restrictive policies that retard development of international computer communications systems, and thus the business prospects of any potential business considering foreign direct investment. For a survey of some of these issues, see Grady E. Means, and Beverly Bugos, "Global Views: The Road to Rio," *CIO*, 1(7), June 1988, pp. 16–19. The authors concentrate somewhat on the situation in Brazil, and report on a survey done by Coopers & Lybrand concerning some of these issues.

be turned over to the chief information officer (CIO) in charge of building and implementing these global systems. This problem can never be viewed as simply gaining an understanding of international telecommunications, cultural differences, or experience with very large-scale systems development projects. Instead, just as in the case of a domestic corporation, the CIO must grasp the overall drift and fabric of international business strategy. However, at this time, there is only a minimum of information available to the CIO on how to actually implement global information technology strategies consistent with the grand strategies of the multinational corporation, and I believe it is important to set forth what can be known in this area. Yet, even at the subterranean level of academia, there are many indications that developing global applications has many unique factors that must be studied, including language barriers, complex project coordination and management (e.g., across numerous time zones), information economics approaches to location of data processing resources, and identification of basic "models" of the process.[4]

The methodology to examine these modules involves a variety of techniques of information collection, analysis, and synthesis. From approximately 1984–1988, most of my research concentrated on the transborder data flow (TDF). During 1990, three surveys were conducted with MNCs to determine the geographical distribution of their underlying information technology infrastructure. The results indicated a strategy- and applications-independent tendency toward centralization. Elite specialized interview techniques were used to develop historical case studies of IT infrastructure creation and systems development in MNCs covering the 1950s to 1990s.

The case study part of this research started in the fall of 1989 with a meeting in Cambridge, Massachusetts, in which we set up lengthy day-long discussions with several companies regarding the problem-solving strategies they were finding successful in building global information systems. This meeting was followed by a further meeting in San Francisco in which we interviewed approximately 20 companies about their global strategies and how they were responding in building information systems.[5] At approximately the same time, we began a comprehensive review of international business literature and MIS literature to learn more about the history of the MNC, its administrative heritage, and the vast body of explanatory theories used to justify its existence.

---

[4]Some of the earlier research was done by Blake Ives, Sirkka Jarvenpaa, Marvin Manheim, and William Chismar on the MIS side, and by Candace Deans on the international business side, whose investigations predate the MIS research.

[5]See CSC Index, "Managing Global Information Systems," *Meeting Summary*, Regional Forum, Cambridge, Massachusetts, 1990.

I also conducted a series of interviews of management consultants in Booz-Allen & Hamilton and CSC Index to review actual assignments in building international systems and the lessons learned from them.

Compiling these case studies has helped immensely in gaining further understanding, although an eclectic approach has been used.[6] It is hoped that the general practitioner will be able to benefit from the case studies herein, each of which addresses a different problem.

Acknowledgments

I would like to thank some of my special mentors who have helped out in various ways over the past few years while this research was being conducted. These include Joseph Ferreira and Bradford Powell at the CSC Index Group in Cambridge, Massachusetts; Seymour E. Goodman at the Mosaic Group at the University of Arizona. (The Mosaic Group is a center for the study of international developments in information technology.) I should also like to thank my editors at Macmillan, Ed Moura and Vernon Anthony, who were a great inspiration. Finally, I would like to thank the reviewers who have helped in shaping the final draft. These include James Senn, University of Georgia; Yves Doz, Insead in Fountainebleau, France; John Dunning, United Nations Centre on Transnational Corporations, and University of Reading; Henry Lucas, New York University; Candace Deans, Wake Forest University; and finally, Cristiano Antonelli, University of Padua, Italy. A note of special appreciation should be extended to Mr. Michael Blaine of Ohio State University for help in setting up the overall structure of the book. These persons have helped immensely in their comments, some quite pointed, and I have benefitted from their thought leadership. I would also like to thank Melissa Madsen Blankenship of Publication Services, Inc. for her patience. Transportation of my library was provided by Wintersteen Trucking of Des Moines, Iowa. This book was prepared on a Macintosh Portable using Microsoft Word 4.00C.

---

[6]See John Van Maanen, "Some Notes on the Importance of Writing in Organization Studies" in *The Information Systems Research Challenge: Qualitative Research Methods*, James I. Cash and Paul R. Lawrence, eds., I, (Boston: Harvard Business School, 1989).

Contents

Preface		iii
Acknowledgments		ix
Part I: Administrative Legacy		1
1	The Multinational Corporation and Its Information System	2
	Summary	12
2	Back in Time	14
	The Change in the Balance of Global Competition	22
	Strategy and Information Structure	24
	The Explosion of Information Technology Options for the Multinational	29
3	Types of International Information Systems	33
	International Information Systems	34
	Transnational Information Systems	36
	Multinational Information Systems	36
	Global Information Systems	37
	Collaborative or Cooperative Information Systems	39
	Historical Centralization and Decentralization	42
	Summary	46
4	Multinationalizing the Computer	47
	Summary	53
Part II: Five Strategic Dimensions		55
5	The Distributed Enterprise	56

xi

6	**Headquarters-Subsidiary and Intersubsidiary Coordination**	65
	Ford Motor Company and the "World Car"	75
	Summary	82
7	**Corporate Intelligence Systems**	84
	Merck Corporation's International Financial Consolidation System	99
	Summary	108
8	**Information Technology-Based FSAs (Firm-Specific Advantages)**	109
	Tupperware Corporation and Building of the Tupperware Express International Ordering System	117
	Summary	124
9	**Internalization of Transactions and Economic Efficiency**	126
	Whirlpool Corporation: Merger and Internalization	134
	Summary	142
10	**The Problem of Host Country/MNC Relations**	144
	A Small Survey	160
	Summary	170

Part III:	**Computer Hegemony Lost**	173
11	**The Relentless Onslaught of Information Technology**	174
12	**The Global System of Industrial Alliances**	180
	AT&T's Entangling Alliances	183
	IBM's Global Reach	189
13	**The European Response to the "Threat" of IBM**	195
	ESPRIT and JESSI	197
	Fortress Europe	203
	Continued Weakness in Europe	211

14 Eastern Europe and the Dragon Kingdoms — 214

The Soviet Union — 215
The Dragon Kingdoms of East Asia — 218

15 Nihon no Computa no Yokozuna — 225

Yokozuna — 235

Part IV: Eight Strategies to Win — 237

16 Systems Development and Strategy Formulation — 238

17 Strategy #1: Informatize Strategic Alliances — 242

Discussion — 243
United Technologies Automotive — 253
Telecommunications Is a Major Problem — 257
Summary — 261

18 Strategy #2: Develop International Systems Development Skills — 262

Discussion — 263
The Skills Required — 269
The Philip Morris Corporation — 271
Summary — 279

19 Strategy #3: Build an Anticipative Infrastructure — 281

Discussion — 282
Syntex Pharmaceutical — 287
Summary — 295

20 Strategy #4: Tear Down the "National" Model — 296

Discussion — 297
Caterpillar Logistics — 305
Summary — 316

21 Strategy #5: Capture Residual Value — 317

Discussion — 318
Manufacturers Hanover Trust — 323
Summary — 329

22 Strategy #6: Exploit the Coming Liberalization in International Telecommunications — 330

- Discussion — 331
- Tele-vaulting the Berlin Wall — 337
- Summary — 344

23 Strategy #7: Homogenize Data Structures — 346

- Discussion — 347
- Imperial Chemical Industries, PLC — 349
- Summary — 356

24 Strategy #8: Globalize Human Resources — 358

- Discussion — 359
- Summary — 365

Part V: Postscript: Managing International Information — 367

25 The Multinational CIO* — 368

- The Administrative Heritage of the MNC — 373
- New Competitive Conditions — 375
- Re-engineering the MNC for New Competitive Conditions — 378
- The Challenge of Business Re-engineering — 379
- The Challenge of Global Systems Development — 381
- How the CIO Can Win — 382
- Use the Structure of Access to International Decision-making — 387

Appendix: Notes and Sketches for Understanding the Dynamics of International Information Systems — 391

- The Key Variables — 392
- Causal Dynamics and System-wide Change — 397

References — 401

Index — 447

---

*Chapter 25 was written with Brad Power, Joe Ferreira, and Adam Crescenzi.

PART I
ADMINISTRATIVE LEGACY

CHAPTER

1

The Multinational Corporation and Its Information System

The multinational corporation, ("multinational," "MNC"), one of the oldest economic entities, has its history tangled up with political and economic controversies of other historical ages, including the age of imperialism. There are still suspicions in some quarters that the multinational serves as an informal extension of economic and political power from its home country. The developing world has been even more reluctant to accept the multinational, particularly since the legacy of colonialism is still fresh in many people's minds. Information technology is a relative latecomer to this form of organization; it is a product of the last two decades, whereas the multinational is a product of the last two centuries.

Chapter 1 The Multinational Corporation and Its Information System

The multinational corporation is the greatest force shaping the world economy[1] — apart from the democratic renaissance currently sweeping through Eastern Europe, Africa, the Far East, and generally throughout the world, except perhaps Cuba. It is the multinational corporation that organizes most of the world's international trade and resource utilization. The amount of economic power contained in the world's multinational corporations is immense: "Five hundred and seventy-nine transnational corporations accounted for about one fourth of the world's production and range in size from $1 billion to $100 billion in sales, which is greater than the GDP of all but 15 of the largest developed market economies of the world. Half the total sales were accounted for by 67 members, one third of which were petroleum companies. Six developed market economies accounted for 500 of the transnationals, over half of which were located in one country, the United States."[2]

The multinational corporation creates and commercializes most of the world's newest and best technologies. It is the multinational corporation that uses the great international telecommunications infrastructure to move data and information around the globe in seconds; and it is the multinational corporation that uses most of the information technology produced in the world—and uses it in the most advanced applications. Nanus gives one of the earliest definitions of a multinational computer system: "A multinational computer system is any arrangement whereby one or more computers in one country are directly linked to other computers, data bases or computer users in one or more other countries."[3]

Hymer discusses some of the effects of international telecommunications and information systems (in particular, how they are used) and argues that they help in "imposing a hierarchical system" on weaker countries.

> ...The dependency relationship between major and minor cities should not be attributed to technology. The new technology, because it increases interaction, implies greater interdependence but not necessarily a hierarchical structure. Communications linkages could be arranged in the form of a grid in which each

---

[1] "Actually, MNEs [multinational enterprises] are not a recent phenomenon. However, it is only since the 1950s, and increasingly during the past decade, that international production has become a major factor—or possibly *the* major factor—in international economics.... Two factors, in particular, were responsible for this development. First, technological advances in communication and transportation facilitated the development of global business perspectives in an increasing number of enterprises and permitted the establishment of transnational unity in management policies and corporate organization." See Karl P. Sauvant, and Farid G. Lavipour, eds, *Controlling Multinational Enterprises: Problems, Strategies, Counterstrategies* (Boulder, CO: Westview Press, 1976), p. x.

[2] UNCTC, *Joint Ventures as a Form of International Economic Cooperation* (New York: United Nations, 1988), p. 5. For a good discussion of the historical view of this issue, see H. A. Innis, *Empire and Communications*, (Oxford: Clarendon Press, 1950).

[3] See Burt Nanus, Leland M. Wooton, and Harold Borko, *The Social Implications of the Use of Computers Across National Boundaries* (Montvale, NJ: AFIPS Press, 1973), p. 3.

point was directly connected to many other points, permitting lateral as well as vertical communications. This system would be polycentric since messages from one point to another would go directly rather than through the center; each point would become a center on its own; and the distinction between center and periphery would disappear.... Such a grid is made *more* feasible by aeronautical and electronic revolutions which greatly reduce costs of communications. It is not technology which creates inequality; rather, it is organization that imposes a ritual judicial asymmetry on the use of intrinsically symmetrical means of communications and arbitrarily creates unequal capacities to initiate and terminate exchange, to store and retrieve information, and to determine the extent of the exchange and terms of the discussion. Just as colonial powers in the past linked each point in the hinterland to the metropolis and inhibited lateral communications, preventing the growth of independent centers of decision making and creativity, multinational corporations (backed by state powers) centralize control by imposing a hierarchical system.[4]

These organizations are a force that will not be stopped in the foreseeable future, and they exist under an international system of arrangements that, although codified and made flexible in the immediate postwar period, have been around a very long time.[5] Before the United Nations system and its failed International Trade Organization[6] and its moderately successful General Agreement on Tariffs and Trade, and even before the League of Nations, it was these giant international trading companies, organized around corporate structures spanning across international borders, that were the most developed.[7] They were the engine of growth in world economic development, and in that process they many times acted as an instrument of national power,[8] with the excess baggage that implied, including imperialism,[9] racism, religious chauvin-

---

[4] See Stephen Hymer, "The Multinational Corporation and the Law of Uneven Development," *International Institutions*, p. 126.

[5] Willkins says "the rise of the multinational enterprise seems to have been directly associated with the shortening of distances by railroads and the steamships," and she is referring to the nineteenth century. See Mira Wilkins, "Modern European Economic History and the Multinationals," *Journal of Economic Literature*, pp. 575–595.

[6] The definitive history of the failure of the ITO is found in William Diebold, Jr., "The End of the ITO," *Princeton Essays in International Finance*, 16, October 1952.

[7] See Fernand Braudel, *The Mediterranean and the Mediterranean World in the Age of Philip II*, Vols. I and II. (New York: Harper Colophon Books, English translation 1972); Immanuel Wallerstein, *The Capitalist World-Economy* (Cambridge: Cambridge University Press, 1977); then, for those who have the time, the definitive book is Fernand Braudel, *The Structures of Everyday Life: Civilization & Capitalism 15th–18th Century* (Vol. 1), *The Wheels of Commerce: Civilizations & Capitalism 15th–18th Century* (Vol. 2), and *The Perspective of the World: Civilizations & Capitalism 15th–18th Century* (Vol. 3) (New York: Harper & Row, 1984, English trans., 1984).

[8] See "super critics" such as Holly Sklar, ed. *Trilateralism: The Trilateral Commission and Elite Planning for World Management* (Boston: South End Press, 1980).

[9] See Frank Shaker, "The Multinational Corporation: The New Imperialism?" *Columbia Journal of World Business*, November–December 1970, pp. 80–84.

Chapter 1 The Multinational Corporation and Its Information System

ism, and economic exploitation.[10] Svedberg describes the way in which colonial powers were used to enforce foreign direct investment and thus protect the multinationals in the poor developing countries of the world. This type of pressure has made the task of attacking the MNC easiest for its critics. For example, Svedberg concludes from his analysis of "enforcement ratios" (the share of foreign direct investment accounted for by the metropolitan country[11] as a ratio of a country's share of foreign direct investment) that regardless of the changing political situation, the multinationals have continued to play their tricks of domination in developing countries:

> The empirical results derived show a heavy overrepresentation (unilateral enforcement) in foreign direct investment by metropolitan countries in their former and present colonies.... In foreign investment, the enforcement in both 1938 and 1967 was the greatest for the dependencies of the smallest colonial powers, especially Portugal, Belgium, and Italy. Investments in domestic market-oriented sectors like manufacturing were more dominated by the metropolitan countries than the primary-producing, export-oriented sectors.... The cross-country examination of U.K. and French dependencies suggests that enforcement decreases, although very slowly, after a colony has gained political independence; even after 25 years the metropolitan overrepresentation is more than 100 percent.... The minuscule decolonization effect does not automatically signify that the (ex-)colonial powers have retained their dominant foreign direct investment position through neo-colonial influence, although this *may* be one of the explanations.... The colonial pattern of foreign investment may very well be perpetuated even in the absence of neo-colonial influence.[12]

There is still a great deal of debate regarding how much the multinational corporation can really help in bringing about technology transfer to the developing countries of the world. One analyst predicts that the initial effects will be negative:

> For [developing countries], the initial effects [of the new technologies] may be largely negative and could take the form of reduced exports of minerals and commodities; less international competitiveness for manufactured products because

---

[10]Much of the literature concerning the *negative* aspects of the multinational corporation is found in writers that have looked at international economic relations from the point of view of the developing world. Flash points such as South Africa provided powerful arguments against the multinational. See works such as Ann Seidman and Neva Seidman Makgetla, *Outposts of Monopoly Capitalism: Southern Africa in the Changing Global Economy* (Westport, CT: Lawrence Hill & Company, 1980); Giovanni Arrighi and John S. Saul, *Essays on the Political Economy of Africa* (New York: Monthly Review Press, 1973); S. B. D. de Silva, *The Political Economy of Underdevelopment* (London: Routledge & Kegan Paul, 1982).

[11]The "metropolitan country," many times called the "metropole," signifies the former capital country in the colonial systems that preceded the Second World War. The primary metropoles were Paris, London, Lisbon, and Brussels.

[12]See Peter Svedberg, "Colonial Enforcement of Foreign Direct Investment," *The Manchester School,* approx. 1980, pp. 21–38.

of increased automation and technological efficiency in industrialized economies; greater difficulty in locating industries based on, or using, new technologies because of infrastructure and other constraints; and reduced employment and income, following the initial introduction of new technologies and because of the above factors.[13]

Franko's analysis discusses "new forms" of direct investment in developing countries by multinational corporations and concludes they are related to trade protection policies and result from the competitive oligopolistic strategies of different multinationals.[14] The multinational corporation has long been the whipping boy of many political economists and revisionists, and has been accused of committing virtually every crime known to humankind, including genocide. Nussbaum's description of the early debates that took place within the League of Nations on cartels and other abuses of multinational enterprises demonstrates clearly that this debate is by no means a new phenomena.[15]

Mason describes the laundry list of complaints against international firms that have been developed by the nation-state:

> [International firms] restrict or allocate markets among subsidiaries and do not allow manufacturing subsidiaries to develop export markets; are able to extract excessive profits and fees because of their monopolistic advantages; enter the market by taking over existing local firms rather than developing new productive investments; finance their entry mainly through local debt and maintain a majority or up to 100 percent of the equity with the parent; divert local savings away from productive investment by nationals, hire away the most talented personnel, exhaust resources, and so on; restrict access to modern technology by centralizing research facilities in the home country and by licensing subsidiaries to use only existing or even outmoded technologies; restrict the 'learning-by-doing' process by staffing key technical and managerial positions with expatriates; fail to do enough in the way of training and development of personnel; affront the country's social customs or frustrate the objectives of the national plan; contribute to price inflation; dominate key industrial sectors; and answer to a foreign government.[16]

---

[13] See UNCTC, *Transnational Corporations and the Transfer of New and Emerging Technologies to Developing Countries* (New York: United Nations, 1990), pp. 2–3.

[14] See Lawrence G. Franko, "New Forms of Investment in Developing Countries by U.S. Companies: A Five Industry Comparison," *Columbia Journal of World Business*, 22(2), Summer 1987, pp. 39–56.

[15] See Helga Nussbaum, "International Cartels and Multinational Enterprises," in Alice Teichova, Maurice Lévy-Leboyer, and Helga Nussbaum, eds., *Multinational Enterprise in Historical Perspective* (Cambridge: Cambridge University Press, 1986).

[16] Mason describes the underlying reasons why nation-states impose these restrictions: "Nationalistic policies are designed to reduce the influence of and even dependence upon external forces. ...Such a policy has neither economic efficiency nor economic equity as its objective." See R. Hal Mason, "Conflicts between Host Countries and the Multinational Enterprise," *California Management Review*, 17(1), Fall 1974, pp. 5–14.

Chapter 1 The Multinational Corporation and Its Information System

He goes on to say, "This list is not exhaustive"! Unfortunately, his analysis does not touch on those nationalistic controls over foreign information technology and computer communications systems that have been another one of the significant responses to the multinational corporation.

The inherent conflict between the multinationals and the host countries in which they operate can spill over to the arena of telecommunications and data processing. This conflict is based on a set of different and basically opposed interests, as summarized by Robock: "Each multinational enterprise tries to maximize its goals on a supranational level. Each nation-state tries to maximize its goals on a national level. Inevitably, therefore, an inherent conflict potential exists between the multinational enterprise and the nation-state."[17] His major categories of reasons why the nation-state is restrictive are "political conflicts," concerns over balance payments, and employment considerations in the nation-state.

These conflicts between the multinational corporation and its environment have a strong effect upon how strategy is formulated. On the one hand, changes in most of the world's economy have forced companies to adapt to stronger international competition by developing a more coherent international strategy. On the other hand, as they have formulated these strategies, they have immediately encountered the many prejudices and barriers erected by different nation-states. This produces a type of complexity that does not exist for domestic firms, and it is particularly difficult for smaller companies.

Smaller corporations are now faced with many challenges in adapting and managing worldwide operations as the world's economy becomes more international. They must decide whether to adopt a national or an international orientation. Particularly corporations with little experience operating in the international environment must face the "ramping up" of competition at the international level. This is particularly the case for U.S. corporations, because they cannot expect the same level of support and protection from their government as can their colleagues in other countries.[18]

In developing its management strategy, a rapidly *internationalizing company* must constantly reconcile differences between the national and the international view.[19] For example, in terms of strategy, a *national* orientation

---

[17]See Stefan H. Robock, "The Case for Home Country Controls Over Multinational Firms," *Columbia Journal of World Business*, Summer 1974, pp. 75–79.

[18]Much of the *industrial policy* literature has shown how corporations have received a great deal of support from their governments. In the United States, however, government support—derisively called *hand-outs*—is looked upon with disapproval. In the case of Japan, see Chalmers Johnson, *MITI and the Japanese Miracle: The Growth of Industrial Policy, 1925–1975* (Stanford, CA: Stanford University Press, 1982).

[19]Some argue that corporate strategies can change quickly, a type of "strategic revolution." See Henry Mintzberg, "Crafting Strategy," *Harvard Business Review*, July–August 1987, pp. 66–75.

would focus on the operations within the boundaries of a nation-state, and on operations within a national market with a fixed arena of competition; whereas an *international* viewpoint would bring into play varying national policies and the complete variability they imply for the *modes of competition*—which, in any case, may be more fully controlled by the individual nation-state. This applies also to the varying conditions that must be faced by the information systems function, as pointed out by Palvia, Palvia, and Zigli.[20]

Cost analysis is also conditioned by this national versus international orientation. With a national orientation, cost is structured according to the dictates of a single national market with predictability and a body politic that can be politically influenced. With the international view, the first major international cost variations show up as technology availability, then labor costs, and now many other factors weigh against analyzing the cost basis of a business through the eyes of a single market or national experience. In addition, there is little if any legitimate political control or influence over the system of arrangements.[21]

In terms of the structure of the multinational corporation, the national versus international perspectives also play an important role. The national view results typically in a corporate center or headquarters that is responsible for national coordination of all major operational and strategic aspects of the corporation. Benoit attributes this in part to information technology:

> The rapid technical improvement and lower cost of communication and transportation, plus the computer and improvements in business management, have greatly improved the ability of managers to direct a larger volume of activity over a wider area transcending national boundaries. This has made it economical to enlarge the total size of the business operation which capable managers administer, so as to spread the cost of management over a larger number of units of output.[22]

The international view, on the other hand, is more highly variable, with stronger pressures for decentralization of major functions, particularly on a

---

[20] Shailendra Palvia, Prashant Palvia, and Ronald Zigli, "Global Information Technology Environment: Key MIS Issues in Advanced and Less-developed Nations," in Palvia et al., eds., *The Global Issues of Information Technology Management* (Harrisburg: Idea Publishing Group, 1992), pp. 2–35.

[21] Although international organizations, such as the United Nations Centre on Transnational Corporations, have been instructed by the UN General Assembly to draft a code of conduct on the behavior and activities of multinational corporations, this effort has had little impact on the international system. Drafting the code, however, has been a decade-long process requiring consensus on the part of many states that are otherwise not generally disposed to cooperate. We could therefore expect that the code will have perhaps some impact in the late 1990s.

[22] See Emile Benoit, "The Attack on the Multinationals," *Columbia Journal of World Business*, November–December 1972, pp. 15–22.

continent-by-continent or "regional" basis.[23] This type of decentralizaton is most often the result of national legislation.[24] At the same time, decentralization has been accelerated by technology options such as minicomputers, which are growing very rapidly in installed base,[25] and advances in telecommunications, which make it even easier to manage data across international borders.

Some writers have also discussed what they believe to be the operational advantages of decentralization. Mandell warns of the false assumptions of centralization of data processing:

> Much has been said about the economies associated with centralization of the data-processing organization in terms of manpower. We apparently forget that the increasing complexity of large-scale centralized systems requires that many people concern themselves with the system programs. Many authors concur in the belief that centralizing the data-processing organization leads to insolvable problems and increased game playing (negative work). Historically, computer centers have grown into empire-building enterprises where little senior-level management involvement can be found.[26]

Mandell then discusses the challenge of building distributed minicomputer networks. Using a decentralized network approach, "communications links can be structured to match organizational flows, thus requiring no change in existing operations. By matching the distributed computer modules with their associated functional elements, the system is more likely to be success-

---

[23]See David F. Feeny, Brian R. Edwards, and Michael J. Earl, *Complex Organizations and the Information Systems Function—A Research Study*, Oxford Institute of Information Management, Research Paper series RDP 87/7. Feeny et al. have discussed the role of decentralization in terms of information technology: "For organizations which are 'complex' in the sense we have defined, there is a strong trend to devolve such resources into the business units. The trend seems entirely appropriate, but we would stress that most of the benefits sought seem to be achieved as long as some of the resources are devolved: one-step transition from a centralized past to a decentralized future may be neither necessary nor desirable" (p. 19). They appear to see a movement in the multinational corporation toward decentralization of computing resources, but it is not clearly defined what they mean. The research in this monograph contradicts the concept of a trend toward a decentralization of infrastructure, but Feeny's logic could just as well be applied to applications migration, in which case it may be easier to make a case. The case of Grand Metropolitan PLC is discussed.

[24]For example, it is very common for the nation-state to require that a company actually manufacture within its borders as a condition for gaining entry to the market. Pharmaceuticals is a good example of a sector that frequently faces this problem.

[25]See, for example, a report on the growth prospects of Hewlett-Packard, a major scientific minicomputer and workstation vendor that for more than 20 years grew at an average compound rate of 20 percent. Dick Alberding, "A Company Study: Exploiting Your Competitive Edge," *Journal of Business & Industrial Marketing*, 2(2), Spring 1987, pp. 37–46.

[26]Steven L. Mandell, "The Management Information System Is Going to Pieces," *California Management Review*, 17(4), Summer 1975, pp. 50–56.

ful and useful." Mandell does, however, make a serious error in his analysis: "At present, it is debatable whether the distributed minicomputer network is superior technically, operationally, and economically to the multiaccess centralized information system. In the future, there will be no debate!" Of course, this debate is still raging, and even intensifying.

Some writers have given examples of the "networked organization" and the extreme type of decentralization that is possible, sometimes working to the advantage of business strategy.[27]

Although this heightened degree of international competition and trading is having effects in most countries of the world—at least those that have *relatively open* economies—its effects are felt differently in different parts of the world. For example, in East Asia[28] the major Japanese multinational corporations have been driven in their expansion by trading networks and the need to cross tariff barriers. Their relatively late success in setting up global enterprises has been met with tariff and nontariff barriers around the world, particularly in Western Europe, and their response has been to develop strategies to cope with this.

The role of nontariff barriers in influencing the development of multinational corporations is an old one: Hertner and Jones mention that

> It is now accepted that the firms which became multinational in the nineteenth century and afterward generally possessed some kind of "ownership-specific advantage," in the form of technology, marketing skills, access to financial sources or oligopolistic market structure...although the concept of "advantage" is imprecise. It has also emerged that many firms which became multinational before 1914 preferred exporting to, rather than investing in, foreign markets. This strategy, however, was blocked by a variety of "location-specific" factors. The spread of protectionism from the late 1870s was a major influence in this context, but patent legislation and *other non-tariff trade barriers* were also significant, and it is clear that no single "location-specific" factor explains multinational growth.[29]

Not suprisingly, the Japanese have adopted a strategy that was used earlier by the U.S.-based multinational corporations—they are setting up manufacturing plants to *jump over* the tariff walls.[30] In terms of their information systems, there are indications that many Japanese multinationals are copying

---

[27] See Patrick J. McGovern, "The Networked Corporation," *Chief Executive*, 57, April 1990, pp. 46–49. The writer presents a study of the International Data Group in Framingham, Massachusetts, and emphasizes that its strong degree of decentralization is critical in its ability to remain small, an attribute that does not match the mainstream multinational corporation.

[28] For economic reasons, this does not include the Peoples Republic of China.

[29] See Peter Hertner and Geoffrey Jones. "Multinationals: Theory and History," in Peter Hertner and Geoffrey Jones, eds. *Multinationals: Theory and History* (Aldershot Harts, England: Gower Publishing Co., Ltd., 1986), p. 10.

[30] This strategy was used in the interwar period, and even before World War I.

U.S.-style arrangements and using U.S. equipment.[31] The picture is not entirely rosy, however, as indicated by Bartlett and Yoshihara, who argue that the Japanese companies have a strong cultural mindset inhibiting them from top performance in some markets.[32] Kobayashi reported on studies that indicated that Japanese firms are very advanced in terms of planning, training, and supervising of managers overseas, but noted that Japanese multinationals do not do well in employing local staff in managerial positions.[33] There may be indication that some third-world multinationals, such as those in Hong Kong, which has a very open international telecommunications policy, are facilitated by "a high degree of communication with industrialized countries."[34] In terms of information systems, Hanada has discussed some of the problems Japanese multinational corporations have experienced in becoming truly "global" corporations.[35]

In the United States, on the other hand, the situation has been different. U.S. multinationals are presently in a state of change; many are experiencing rapid loss of market share, and many are searching for less expensive labor and production technology overseas. This has produced the famous "hollowing out" of the U.S. economy, which has been discussed so much in the press and in academic literature.[36] The European multinationals appear to be watching the 1992 situation to develop a European-wide strategy, although many do not have a history of having built up those skills. Booz Allen & Hamilton, Inc., a management consulting firm, has argued[37] that the U.S. multinationals operating in Western Europe are *better prepared* to cope with the impending internationalization in 1992 than are many of the indigenous European

---

[31]See Jeff Moad, "Japanese Pledge Allegiance to U.S. Information Systems Strategies," *Datamation* 34(4), February 15, 1988, pp. 43–49. This study examines the U.S.-based subsidiaries of Hitachi America, Nomura Securities International, and Sony Corporation of America.

[32]See Christopher A. Bartlett and Hideki Yoshihara, "New Challenges for Japanese Multinationals: Is Organization Adaptation Their Achilles Heel?" *Human Resource Management,* 27(1), Spring 1988, pp. 19–43.

[33]See Noritake Kobayashi, "Comparison of Japanese and Western Multinationals, Part I," *Tokyo Business Today*, 58(10), October 1990, p. 50.

[34]See Ian H. Giddy and Stephen Young, "Conventional Theory and Unconventional MNEs," in Alan M. Rugman, ed. *New Theories of the Multinational Enterprise* (New York: St. Martin's Press, 1982).

[35]See Mitsuyo Hanada, "Management Themes in the Age of Globalization—Exploring Paths for the Globalization of the Japanese Corporation," *Management Japan*, 20(2), Autumn 1987, pp. 19–26.

[36]It is interesting to note that the term "hollowing out" is a translation of a Japanese term. It was developed by the Japanese in their discussion of what has been happening to their *own* economy as a result of its own multinational corporations' shifting manufacturing resources away from Japan towards other Asian countries such as Thailand, Singapore, and Taiwan.

[37]See Booz Allen & Hamilton, Inc., *Europe 1992: Threat or Opportunity*, special report, New York, 1989.

corporations. They base their analysis on a survey conducted in conjunction with the Japanese economic newspaper *Nihon Keizai Shimbun.* Their reasoning is that the U.S. multinationals have been forced to operate in that mode all along, whereas many of the European firms have been conducting the bulk of their business behind national economic walls. Kremer has discussed how the 1992 situation will place new demands upon an information system in a multinational corporation.[38] He argues that the new system should be able to handle the operations of multiple companies and be able to process information in different currencies. Another key requirement is that it should be possible to access the system from throughout Europe, as well as from the rest of the world.

SUMMARY

These changes in the world's economy, in the changing receptivity to the multinational, in the growing internationalization of manufacturing and production, and in the strategies corporations must adopt in order to cope with these new realities all call for further investigation into the internal control systems of the multinational, and how its computer and telecommunications systems operate to help it manage. We can see that information technology is helping power this shift toward *accelerated internationalization,* which is forcing businesses all over the world to respond in different ways to market competition. This sea-change of new opportunity is opening up new avenues for the managers and strategists inside many multinationals, and there is no doubt some will eventually be able to take advantage of the new tools available. After all, multinationals have certainly done so in the past when other technologies came along. A long-term historical view, such as that proposed by John Dunning, indicates that successful economic enterprises have *always* been involved in *re-engineering their operating structures* to cope with changes in economic conditions and regulatory environments.[39] As a re-

---

[38]See Tony Kremer, "Europe 1992: Are Your Information Systems Going to Be Ready?" *Management Accounting,* 66(10), Nov. 1988, pp. 32–33. Kremer notes that there are more than 285 proposals being considered for bringing about the harmonization of the internal market in Western Europe and that most of these have the potential to influence how data-processing operations are set up and organized. He believes that as the market reaches a substantial level of harmonization, only those companies that have multicapable information systems available throughout the new Europe will be able to compete effectively.

[39]See John H. Dunning, ed., *Multinational Enterprises, Economic Structure and International Competitiveness* (New York: John Wiley & Sons, 1985); and John H. Dunning, ed. *The Multinational Enterprise* (London: George Allen & Unwin, Ltd. 1971). Note carefully: The historical periodization here is taken from Dunning. It is a useful tool to compare against corresponding developments in information technology.

sult, we can expect that they will continue to do so. But as we shall see, the promises made by information technology are more than made up for by the difficulties and barriers encountered in implementation. Technology may be new, but the multinational is not, at least as a form of economic organization, and it is this *oldness* that poses the most difficult challenge.

CHAPTER 2

Back in Time

The multinational corporation and international business have their beginnings in the Industrial Revolution and have gone through at least four distinctive periods since then. The traditions and ways of working of the MNC are called the "administrative legacy." Information technology has come only recently to the MNC and has given it power to operate in ways never before thought possible. Although many of the American MNCs were innovators in the use of information technology, we have seen the global balance of economic and technological power shift decisively against the United States. This has left the once-proud American multinationals at competitive risk at a time when the possibilities for global strategies based on information technology are wider than ever.

Chapter 2 Back in Time

The current environment is the product of a long chain of developments in international business.[1] Teichova states that "the quantitative evidence shows the phenomenon is new.... Without an acknowledgement that multinational companies have a history and in turn have affected history, a deeper understanding of long-term trends impinging upon our time cannot be gained."[2] Her data shows the tremendous growth of multinationals during the post-war period.

Numbers of Foreign Manufacturing Subsidiary Firms Established or Acquired by Parent Companies

Period	US	UK	Continental Europe	Europe (incl. UK)	Japan	Total	No. of companies per annum
Pre-1914	122	60	167	227	0	349	—
1914–18 (WWI)	71	27	51	78	0	149	21
1920–38	614	217	361	578	4	1,196	63
1939–45 (WWII)	172	34	44	78	40	290	41
1946–58	1,108	351	377	728	21	1,857	143
1959–67	2,749	1,111	993	2,104	247	5,100	566

Franko traces the spread of European multinational corporations and begins with an 1815 investment by the Belgian steel company Cockerill in Prussia.[3] Dunning has an even longer historical perspective. His analysis reaches back into history to the beginning of the international enterprise. He divides the history of international business into five phases: Phase I reaches from the industrial revolution to approximately 1870; Phase II reaches from 1870 to 1914,[4]

---

[1] The business history side of this discussion is based on the work of John Dunning.

[2] See Alice Teichova, "Multinational in Perspective" in Alice Teichova, Maurice Lévy-Leboyer, and Helga Nussbaum, eds., *Multinational Enterprise in Historical Perspective* (Cambridge University Press, 1986). Table from p. 364.

[3] See Lawrence G. Franko, "Patterns in the Multinational Spread of Continental European Enterprise," *Journal of International Business Studies,* pp. 41–53. It appears there was a great deal of trade in most sectors, except telecommunications.

[4] According to some researchers, "historical research now suggests that international production was both absolutely and relatively more important before 1914 than at any time until at least the 1960s." Quoted in John H. Dunning, John A. Cantwell, and T. A. B. Corley, "The Theory of International Production: Some Historical Antecedents" in Peter Hertner and Geoffrey Jones, eds, *Multinationals: Theory and History* (Aldershot Harts, England: Gower Publishing Co., Ltd., 1986).

the outbreak of World War I; Phase III is the interwar period, from 1919 to 1939; Phase IV is the first part of the postwar period, from 1945 to 1965; and Phase V is the most recent part of the postwar period, from 1965 to 1985.

Although Dunning goes to great lengths to describe the major business events during these phases, he does not describe or analyze the information technology used during these phases. If these two factors are combined, the resulting analysis clearly indicates that the present information technology strategies of the multinational corporation are a result of an *inherited structure* that was in place long before information technology began to make a significant impact upon the economic system. Bartlett and Ghoshal discuss the concept of "administrative heritage" (although not in relation to the information system of the multinational corporation). They write, "A company's organizational capability develops over many years and is tied to a number of attributes: a configuration of organizational assets and capabilities that are built up over decades; a distribution of managerial responsibilities and influence that cannot be shifted quickly; and an ongoing set of relationships that endure long after any structural change has been made. Collectively, these factors constitute a company's *administrative heritage*."[5] They also discuss how the "internationalization history of a firm also influences its administrative heritage." The term I will use in this book is *administrative legacy*.

Phase I, lasting from the industrial revolution until approximately 1870, might be called the ancient regime of international business. This was the first era in which technology was traded internationally to any significant extent. There was little activity on the part of the multinational enterprise. However, there was much expatriate direct investment, particularly by European immigrants into the United States. During this period, information technology was just beginning to make an impact on how business was conducted. At the end of this period, the telegraph was starting to spread from country to country in Europe, primarily along the routes of railroad construction. The structure of international communications was to follow the patterns of international commerce, and this basic pattern holds even today.

Chandler argues that the successful multinationals that expanded "were the first to recruit the management teams essential to exploit the new high speed, high volume production technologies that were made possible by the coming of modern transportation and communications".[6] He characterized these as "first mover advantages" that resulted in such an advantage that "the

---

[5]See Christopher A. Bartlett and Sumantra Ghoshal, "Managing Across Borders: New Strategic Requirements," *Sloan Management Review* Summer 1987, pp. 7–17.

[6]See Alfred D. Chandler, Jr., "Technological and Organizational Underpinnings of Modern Industrial Multinational Enterprise: The Dynamics of Competitive Advantage" in Alice Teichova, Maurice Lévy-Leboyer, and Helga Nussbaum, eds, *Multinational Enterprise in Historical Perspective* (Cambridge University Press, 1986).

pioneers continued to dominate the resulting global oligopolies for decades." Without the ability to move information and data, the multinational would not have grown at all.

Phase II, lasting from 1870 until 1914, the outbreak of the first world war, might be called the "Golden Age." During this period, the multinational enterprise grew from infancy to adolescence. During this period, new technologies required more hierarchical forms of governance for efficient exploitation. There were advances in the organizational, transport, and communications technologies. Other technologies advanced as well. For example, the internal combustion engine, the electric generator, the use of volume production, and the creation of interchangeable parts all characterized this very formative period in international economic history. During this period, the United States led the world in development. There were many lasting innovations that are with us even today. The development of branded consumer goods, the transportation of tropical agricultural products, and the widespread mass production of metal products all characterize this period. However, in spite of the advances taking place in so many areas of the economy, information technology developments, still limited essentially to the telegraph, progressed comparatively slowly until the telephone started to develop. The telegraph advanced, but the telephone started to grow in importance. The telephone started to increase the "velocity" of information flow, particularly in business.[7] There was, however, little new in the way of data-processing technologies. The picture that emerges, then, is a period of rapid transformation in business and technology, but a comparatively lesser development on the side of information technology.

Phase III, from 1919 to 1939, is the interwar period, from World War I to World War II.[8] This was the period of the great tariff wars that posed formidable barriers to international commerce. In general, the economic climate for international direct investment was less congenial. The total stock of foreign capital rose by 75 percent during this period. The tariff barriers and other restrictions fueled a high growth in the number of foreign affiliates of manufacturing companies, particularly in developed-market countries where import controls were restricting international trade flows. During this time, there was a general intensification of industrial concentration, a more oligopolistic market structure emerged, and there was a great deal of increase in the transaction power of the multinational firm.[9] On the technology side,

---

[7]See Ithiel de Sola Pool, *The Social Impact of the Telephone,* Doctoral Thesis, University of Chicago, 1952.

[8]Eugene Weber calls this period the "Second Forty Years War" in Europe.

[9]One of the critical insights of Dunning was that the multinational firm grows by "capturing transactions." This means that as the firm grows, it becomes more horizontally and vertically integrated. More and more economic activity is subsumed and controlled by the multinational corporation.

the global telex system was extended greatly and used as the primary operating mechanism for "imperial" control of foreign operations of companies. Computers and data-processing equipment were still not available. Although reasonably reliable, telex was expensive and as a result was severely limited in terms of the amount of information that could cost-effectively be transmitted from one country to another.

Phase IV, from 1945 to approximately 1965, might be thought of as the "American Century," because it represents a time when the United States was at its peak in the postwar period. This period saw the greatest increase in the rate of international production. Dunning estimates this as half as much again as world trade. This was when the technological hegemony of the United States reached its peak. With the strong liberalizing trend set by the General Agreement on Tariffs and Trade (GATT), international commerce flourished. A shortage of dollars forced U.S. firms to service foreign markets via foreign production rather than by exports. In the early 1960s, 187 of the largest U.S. multinational corporations were setting up more than 300 new manufacturing subsidiaries in Europe each year. These manufacturing investments were substitutes for exports rather than part of an international marketing strategy. The currency situation was forcing this type of response on the part of the multinational corporation.

Finally, the information technology picture began to change rather dramatically. At the end of this period, the first "large" mainframe computers began to appear. The IBM 360 with its more flexible operating system replaced the 1401. Top management attention regarding information technology was stimulated to a level that would not be repeated again until the mid-1980s.[10] In spite of the high level of attention, in retrospect we see that during this period the results from application of information technology were limited to harvesting of easy repetitive operations that could be done repeatedly by the computer. Much literature regarding the emerging "information society" appeared during this period.[11]

Phase V, which is dated from 1965 to 1985, might be termed the "multipolar system" due to the high degree of internationalization that took place. Multinational corporations from countries other than the United States came on very strong in the world economy, and the Japanese economy revived from World War II. This period saw a slowing down of the rate of increase in MNC activity. On the other hand, there was tremendous acceleration in the extent of technological creation and dissemination. By the late 1970s, Japan was

---

[10] It was during the mid-1980s that the great amount of focus on "use of information technology as a competitive weapon"—much of which was later determined to be sheer hucksterism—gained top management attention. For the most part, during the 1970s, information technology languished in the back rooms, away from top managements' attention.

[11] This included some of the first examinations of the threat to individual privacy and security posed by the computerized society. See the numerous works of Alan F. Westin.

rapidly advancing in computer and robot technology, consumer electronics, and optics. The United States was rapidly advancing in microchip production, biotechnology, and general information technology. A rapid industrialization of Asia was taking place, and people began to write about a "shift in the center of the world from the Atlantic to the Pacific."

During this period, the final period immediately preceding our current times, information technology developed dramatically. Remote processing and the rise of the minicomputer accelerated the complete penetration of information technology throughout businesses. The debate about centralization and decentralization started because telecommunications was providing the data-processing "center," a conduit with which to reach out to many different locations simultaneously. At the same time, smaller computers allowed departments or other groups to bypass the centralized data-processing group altogether. John Diebold, in a seminal but not well-known book, discussed how information technology would begin to transform organizational structure.[12] The use of information technology in the multinational corporation began to allow a greater amount of information to move from the remote corners of the globe back to headquarters. Instead of being sent by telex, this information could now be sent with batch uploads of information. This type of activity intensified. In general, the pattern was developed within the multinational whereby mostly financial reporting data was transferred to headquarters through the information technology infrastructure.[13] Some information seems best left in the local subsidiary, particularly concerning payoffs.[14] For the most part, this type of relationship between the "center and the periphery" stuck throughout the 1980s, after which it began to change as transmitting higher volumes of more varied data and information around the world throughout the multinational corporation became easier and more technologically feasible.[15]

---

[12]John Diebold, *Business Decisions and Technological Change* (New York; Praeger Publishers, 1970).

[13]See Merwin H. Waterman, "Financial Management in Multinational Corporations: I", *Michigan Business Review*, Jan. 1968, pp. 10–15; also Merwin H. Waterman, "Financial Management in Multinational Corporations: II", *Michigan Business Review*, March 1968, pp. 26–32. Waterman distinguishes several of the key dimensions in financial reporting in the multinational corporation. He includes "investment justification", "special exchange risks", "financial controls", "working capital problems", "management of cash", "income administration and dividend policy", and different management strategies for loans.

[14]See Wolfhart Kasparek, "Auditing Multinational Operations: Foreign Commissions," *Internal Auditing*, 3 (3), Winter 1988, pp. 60–64, for a discussion of using computer records to uncover fraud. For a look at the use of computer-assisted auditing techniques, see Wolfhart Kasparek, "Interaction with Local Internal Auditors, *"Internal Auditing*, 3, (4), Spring 1988, pp. 67–70.

[15]The "center and periphery" is a term taken from dependency theory showing a subservient relationship between the controlling entity and its overseas branches. This refers more properly to the relationship between developing countries and their former metropoles.

However, the fact that the multinational was operating in foreign environments made the task of collecting and processing information more difficult than would be the case if a domestic corporation expanded, even if the domestic was larger and more complex.

> The major effects of operating multinationally on the business enterprise can be meaningfully analyzed as to their impact on the organization of the enterprise and its decision-making processes and techniques. Such operations differ from purely domestic operations primarily concerning distance, time, and additional variability of the operating environments.[16]

The rise of the "automated multinational" had significant implications for the organizational structure and the management of information technology. According to a United Nations study, the Long-Wave theorists argued that the emergence of the "new micro-electronics technologies" helped explain the rise of Japan and the Republic of Korea in the postwar period and more important, pointed to the need for multinational corporations to reassess their management and structuring of information:

> Micro-electronics and related data technologies remain the acknowledged driving forces of the new cycle, constituting a different techno-economic paradigm expected to define the path of future industrial development. Current economic uncertainties are seen as resulting from a mismatch between, on the one hand, prevailing patterns of social behavior and institutional structures that were shown by the previous paradigm and, on the other hand, the dynamics of the new micro-electronics-based paradigm. *Thus, established patterns and structures must change to meet the needs of the new micro-electronics-based paradigm in order to stimulate a new round of global economic expansion.*[17]

According to the study, "the nature of current organizational innovations inherently contradicts the logic and principles of the mass-production model that served as the basis for the post-World War II, economic preeminence of the United States."

Utilization of information technology has been a key element in making possible the development of entirely new international business strategies. The new options that have become available in the 1980s and have started to change the complexion of international competition include the following:

- *Global inventory management.* Manufacturing firms on a worldwide basis are finding that information systems are useful for managing inven-

---

[16]See Thomas H. Bates, "Management and the Multinational Business Environment," *California Management Review*, 15(3), Spring 1973, pp. 37–45.

[17]See UNCTC, *New Approaches to Best-Practice Manufacturing: The Role of Transnational Corporations and Implications for Developing Countries* (UNCTC Current Studies, ser. A, no. 12, New York: United Nations, 1990). (Emphasis added.)

tory at the global level even though this management requires tight timing and logistics capabilities.[18] In most cases, it appears that the resources spent on the development of the information system are more than paid off by improvements in turnover velocity and also by reduction in safety stocking levels. These new systems also help a great deal in providing better customer satisfaction.[19] Greene discusses how the new opportunities in global manufacturing have raised major challenges for computer software and hardware vendors, and how new products are being made available.[20]

- *Worldwide sourcing of components and raw materials.* In manufacturing, the concept of worldwide sourcing for components and raw materials has been developed with the aid of information technology spanning the globe. This type of "global sourcing" also takes place in information-intensive industries (such as trading), in which information technology allows companies to be linked to obtain 24-hour-per-day access to sources of vital economic information. Information as well as raw materials or components can be "sourced". Narasimhan, for example, argues that whether a multinational corporation adopts a centralized, decentralized, or matrix organization depends upon the number and types of suppliers with which it is conducting business, and that the matrix form is needed when it is dealing with a few very powerful suppliers or if there is a need to obtain high volumes of strategic supplies.[21]

- *Decentralized R&D collaboration and design.* Electronics firms, petrochemical firms, pharmaceuticals, and others are finding that electronic mail, teleconferencing, and high-speed networks are vital for global co-ordination of their research and development efforts. This appears to be particularly important when key designs must be adapted to various national markets.

---

[18] For an early study of information systems for linking logistics systems across international borders (with Western Europe) see Arnoldo C. Hax, "Planning a Management Information System for a Distributing and Manufacturing Company," *Sloan Management Review*, Spring 1973, pp. 85–98.

[19] See the United Technologies Automotive and Ford Motor Company case studies included in this book.

[20] See Alice H. Greene, "Globalization: Reality or Trend?" *Production & Inventory Management Review & APICS News*, 9 (12), December 1989, pp. 24–25. She emphasizes that the information infrastructure in the global corporation must integrate operations both across product lines and across geographic regions of the world.

[21] See Ram Narasimhan and Joseph R. Carter, "Organisation, Communication and Co-Ordination of International Sourcing," *International Marketing Review*, 7 (2) 1990, pp. 6–20. They argue, however, that from a communication and coordination point of view, the matrix form of organization is much more difficult to organize and operate.

THE CHANGE IN THE BALANCE OF GLOBAL COMPETITION

In the most recent decade, after the beginning of the 1980s, the world experienced two dramatic changes in the role of information technology and the global strategies of multinational corporations. The balance of power decisively shifted, and this shift was against the United States.[22] Beginning in the 1960s and early 1970s, the power of the Japanese companies gradually increased to the point that by the end of the 1980s, Japanese multinational corporations created and controlled most of the innovative and leading-edge technology and were in many cases vastly competitive and profitable in spite of the fact that many had come late onto the scene with various degrees of help from Japanese industrial policy.[23] Japanese manufacturing power came on the scene remarkably late to attack mature markets, many times with little or no support from the Japanese government, including MITI. The export drives of some companies that later became greatly successful were actively opposed by the Japanese government. Nippon Electric Corporation (NEC), the world's largest producer of semiconductor devices, was told bluntly by the Japanese government that it should avoid going into the computer sector. NEC now has the largest market share in the small computer market of any company in Japan, although it has been less successful in overseas markets with its information technology. Another example is Honda. Although Honda is highly successful in the U.S. market today (it has achieved the highest consumer rating of any automobile several years in a row), it entered the U.S. market in the 1960s, when the automobile market was highly capital-intensive and also mature. In addition to its engineering genius, Honda achieved success by innovative changes in the distribution channels. However, Honda was violently opposed by the Japanese government, and never received any help at all in its export drives. Honda was and still is considered to be an "outcast tribe," not part of the Japanese establishment. However, this has not seemed to hurt Honda, which has managed to attract some of the best engineering talent and run circles around its Japanese competitors in terms of innovation. *Car and Driver* said in its reviews of the Honda Accord: "There is nothing wrong with the Accord... absolutely nothing."

---

[22]This was written before the Persian Gulf War, in which the United States and the Allies scored a historic victory using the technologies of the "electronic battlefield." This gave everyone a temporary illusion that the United States was once again a superpower, as it was from the military point of view, but it did little to stop the decline of the computer sector and other high-technology industries.

[23]See Hugh Patrick, ed., with Larry Meissner. *Japan's High Technology Industries: Lessons and Limitations of Industrial Policy* (Seattle: University of Washington Press; and Tokyo: University of Tokyo Press, 1986).

On the European side, the preoccupation with the eventual unification of Europe under the Treaty of Rome and other factors, including the strength and endurance of the nation-state, prevented all but a handful of European multinational corporations from emerging as particularly strong either economically or technologically. Europe continued to lag behind in technological innovation, although certain national policies, notably the French telecommunications policy, resulted in the creation of highly vibrant and advanced infrastructures. France was the world's first country to convert all of its telephone system over to digital technology. It has been highly criticized because of the loss-making character of its Minitel program to distribute videotext service to the entire French population. However, this criticism may, in retrospect, be short-sighted because on the positive side is the very major contribution of creating an infrastructure that will add value to many other information transactions in the future. This value cannot be reliably calculated or estimated. As the Japanese rose in power and as the Europeans remained more or less stagnant, the American multinational corporations faced a relative diminution of their power, in sync with the relative decline of the United States.

The result of this is a continuing shift in the balance of power between the multinational corporations from the different national blocs: East Asia, Western Europe, and North America. This shift of power toward a more multipolar world has come at a time when there is also a falling away of single solutions to complex problems involving information technology. This new situation of intensified competition has been met by different strategies on the part of the multinational corporations from the different blocs. The U.S. multinational corporations appear to have developed first in the postwar period and to have worked toward a decentralized model of national "host government" country cooperation, and to have been a carrier of a strong "egalitarian" culture in management. European multinationals, on the other hand, have in general been more acutely aware of international trading issues because of their longer historical traditions. Many of the multinationals we see today have roots that go back centuries, to previous ages of history. This cannot be said for the bulk of the U.S. multinational corporations. In addition, in comparison with the U.S. cultural "model" of the multinational corporation, many of the European firms were able to take advantage of a certain degree of cultural homogeneity in management. Homogeneity made it possible to effectively increase the degree of decentralization on a global scale without sacrificing the predictability and risk control needed in such giant economic undertakings. Because the leaders of the satellite locations of the company had the same "behavioral patterns," they were more predictable and thus could be more loosely controlled. We will see later that this had an effect on the types of information technology systems that were put into place.

Fannin and Rodrigues discussed the changing organizational structure of the multinational corporation during the 1970s and 1980s and observed that the expansion to global markets was producing several types of responses.

Companies were simply replicating their home market strategies overseas, taking separate approaches in each national market (as IBM was famous for doing), or developing global approaches that were integrated for the world as a whole.[24]

The Japanese multinational corporations, on the other hand, have come onto the scene in the postwar period relatively late. The "Japanese invasion" has been led by the trading companies, which existed before the war. In contrast to many of the European multinationals, Japanese multinationals have tended to remain *highly centralized* in their managerial control and decision making. Some have argued that this is due to the Confucian nature of the Japanese tradition, but there are also a few counterarguments to this idea. The Korean *chaebols* (multinational corporations) are also infused with a high degree of Confucian thinking, as are the Chinese corporations. However, Chinese multinational corporations, and companies in general, tend to be organized around families, and this appears to place a type of *organic limitation* on the ultimate size and scale of operations they are able to achieve. Korean multinationals, on the other hand, appear to have characteristics of both the Japanese and the Chinese models. Although they are often dominated by a single family, they are organized in a way similar to the Japanese corporation and appear to grow accordingly beyond the scope possible by the Chinese model. In any case, since all three groups have strong Confucian backgrounds, but different organizational structures, there appears to be no single "Confucian model" to explain the type of decision-making structures of the East-Asian multinational corporation.

STRATEGY AND INFORMATION STRUCTURE

Comparing Dunning's periodization of MNC history with the information technology available at the time in each stage provides enough evidence to suggest that, except in the very newest corporations, the IT function of the MNC has been required to *overlay* the *pre-existing structures* and traditions of the corporation with its present information technology infrastructure. The organization of work and the logical flows of information of the MNC were well in place and operating extensively *before* information technology had a tremendous impact on the firm.

In the 1960s, at the dawn of the mainframe era, it was possible to have *only* a polycentric pattern of data processing in a multinational corporation because even the most powerful mainframes were incapable of coordinating data across international borders (even if the telecommunications system had

---

[24]See William R. Fannin and Arvin F. Rodrigues, "National or Global? Control vs. Flexibility, *Long Range Planning*, 19 (5) October 1986, pp. 84–88.

allowed it, which it did not). The response of the multinational was to place a mainframe computer in the headquarters of each country in which it operated, assuming it was a large enough operation.

An example of the prevalence of centralized assumptions is found in Zani. His analysis of competitive advantage for computing systems is based entirely on assumptions about centralization. He writes:

> New breakthroughs in communications, such as microwave and satellite data transmission systems, have the potential to reduce dramatically the cost of long-distance data transmission. The introduction of these new systems and others that can be developed will stimulate the growth of computer utilities by drastically reducing the communication costs. This will allow computer utility suppliers to take advantage of large computers that can service more sweeping geographic markets.[25]

Later in the 1970s, as the minicomputer came into play and as mainframes became more powerful, it was possible to have smaller minicomputer-based installations in less important areas, tied together into a regional center run by more powerful mainframes. For example, a typical pattern might be for a MNC to have a major data-processing center in London or Brussels, with a few minicomputers "feeding" the center with information from other countries in Europe. This produced a regiocentric pattern. At the same time, remote batch uploading of information files on an ad hoc basis through the telecommunications network became popular, so the corporate mainframes, particularly those at headquarters, started to adjust toward a pattern of "listening" to reports from the overseas subsidiaries.

With the 1980s came the personal computer era, resulting in a massive increase in computer literacy and the rise of "end-user computing." With improvements in telecommunications, such as the widespread availability of packet-switched networks, the ethnocentric model of data processing became possible. It became easier for information to be uploaded quickly to the mainframes at corporate headquarters; for many firms, these linkages were kept on around the clock with the international provision of "real time on-line" transaction-processing systems operating across international borders.

In the 1990s, should trends continue, we will see more global applications in which multinationals are able to move and process their data where it is needed, without any worry about the type of platform on which it is being processed. Personal computers, workstations, minicomputers, and mainframes will be working together in a type of cooperative processing that will centralize those data and applications needing centralization and decentralize those that need a strong point of presence in the field, and that will tie them all

---

[25] See William M. Zani, "The Computer Utility," *California Management Review*, Fall 1970, 13(1), pp. 31–37. It is interesting that he discussed the American Airlines case about a decade before it became more popular in MIS circles.

together with an integrated, virtually private telecommunications network. There will be both centralization and decentralization at the same time.

In the human resources area, for example, it is very difficult to implement a global centralized system. In addition to the general problems associated with building international telecommunications linkages and ensuring equipment works properly, for example, there is the different nature of each national market, and these variations can confuse an information system. Morgan writes about computerized systems that will not work properly because in some countries people have only one name, and most systems must use both a first name and a last.[26] There are also major problems associated with privacy and transborder data flow regulations in that personal confidential information regarding citizens must be telecommunicated internationally in a global human resources management system, *infra*.

A study of the data-processing arrangements in Grand Metropolitan PLC, a highly decentralized company, revealed that electronic mail was one of the most important "glues" helping to coordinate various overseas divisions and subsidiaries.[27]

Reck provides a view of the information system of the multinational corporation that involves the use of a "mixed mode" in matching architectures against corporation strategy. He discusses an *imperialistic* or centralized type of system for financial systems, a *multidomestic* system for marketing to be able to respond to each national situation, and a *global* system for manufacturing that ultimately must be coordinated from a single location.[28]

Reck's analysis and others appear to recognize that the information-systems function in the MNC appears to have inherited large centralized architectures that have been clustered near headquarters. We can conclude that in the early stages, information technology had the effect of helping the corporation to *centralize within geographical regions* but to *decentralize on an international scale* (See Table 2.1).

Now the centralized ethnocentric and polycentric architectures inherited from past decades are begging to be integrated. What has been possible in business strategy for quite a while is at last becoming possible on the

---

[26]See Patrick V. Morgan, "International HRM: Fact or Fiction?" *Personnel Administrator*, 31, (9) September 1986, pp. 42–47.

[27]See Anonymous, "Helping People Work More Effectively," *I/S Analyzer*, 25(12), December 1987, pp. 1–12. For an example of how the CCITT X.400 electronic mail standard can be used to overcome standards-related transborder data problems, see Donald E. Ross, "The Way to Handle Electronic Messages" *Infosystems*, 34(2), February 1987, pp. 64, 66.

[28]See Robert H. Reck, "The Shock of Going Global," *Datamation*, 35(15), August 1, 1989, pp. 67–70. Reck recognizes the strong challenge faced by IS executives in "going global" but recommends several steps that can be taken to align strategy with information technology systems.

TABLE 2.1 Evolution of Computer Technology and Development of the Geocentric Model of Data Processing in the Multinational Corporation

Generation of Information Technology[a]	Time Frame	Computer Architectures	MNC Information Technology Infrastructure
First Mainframe Era	1960s	Centralized. No remote processing.	Limited telecommunications and processing capacities of the technology forces firm to adopt a polycentric type of infrastructure. Data centers are typically set up in each country as needed.
Minicomputer Era	1970s	Multiple small systems. Beginning of remote batch processing and summary uploading or information to the corporate mainframes. Inflexible leased-line networks.	Regiocentric processing develops as batch movement of updated information becomes possible. Networking of minicomputers between different countries on a regional scale is possible.
Personal Computer Era	1980s	Rise in end-user computing. First of some international systems. Proliferation of packet-switched networks.	Ethnocentric model becomes possible with vast improvements in telecommunications linking together the greatly increased number of end-users with corporate mainframes, even internationally.
Second Mainframe and Supercomputer Era	1990s	Improvements in telecommunications and distributed processing make global systems possible. Virtual private networks.	Geocentric applications appear in some industries in which information is cooperatively processed at many levels of the organization as needed.

[a] In his discussion of the changing role of information technology in multinational settings, Chorafas gives the following generations: first generation, 1952–1958; second generation, 1958–1964; third generation, 1964–. See Dimitris N. Chorafas, "Computer Technology in Western and Eastern Europe," *Columbia Journal of World Business*, May–June 1970, pp. 61–66.

technology side, but if the costs of large systems development projects and their frequent catastrophic failure are any indication, firms may find it much easier to rearrange their business and product strategies than to redevelop their international information systems.

An alternative periodization is provided by Robinson, who discusses the "Postwar Decade" up to 1955, when the United States was the dominating force in the world economy and in world politics; "The Growth Years" (1955–1970), when there was an increasing realization of the "political impact of the firm's operations overseas"; and the "Time of Trouble" (1970s), when the Group of 77 appeared and began to attempt getting a global redistribution of wealth. He ends with the "New International Order" and dates it from 1980 onward, arguing that it is characterized by "the entire sphere of international business...being heavily politicized, both at home and abroad." Regarding the present era, he writes:

> One suspects that the main profit generator in international business lies increasingly in an efficient and accurate international information system which has the capacity to ascertain almost instantaneously and on a 24-hour-a-day basis where the cheapest capital is to be found, where the most appropriate technology is available, where skilled people can be hired, where the lowest priced goods are or can be produced—and, on the demand side, where the opportunities to employ these resources most profitably are located and how to do so. In such cases, profit is generated from selling access to the information system or from stimulating flows, not from dividends arising from investment in fixed assets.[29]

According to Robinson, in the future the "guts" of multinational corporations "will be international information networks and data banks."

A hint to the growing global concern regarding the social and economic effects of information technology and international telecommunications systems comes from Dordick in his discussion of the "emerging world information business."

> The desire for a new world economic order is now paralleled by the demand for a new world information order. Nations far advanced in the information era are also the most economically successful and, quite understandably, want a free flow

---

[29]See Richard D. Robinson, "Background Concepts and Philosophy of International Business from World War II to the Present," *Journal of International Business Studies,* Spring/Summer 1981, pp. 13–21. He (correctly I believe) places the first developments in transnational computing in the immediate postwar era, which he calls the growth years: 1955–1970. He writes: "A number of the larger U.S.-based international firms became multinational in the sense that they moved toward fashioning globally integrated production and marketing systems, whose development begged central control. Such control became increasingly feasible in that, over time, international expertise appeared in headquarters and international communication systems were fashioned. New communication technology and jet air travel facilitated the move" (p. 14).

policy for international information. Nations that are informationally and economically poor desire the means to protect their information resources at least long enough to develop the technology and institutions necessary for capitalizing on them.[30]

Douglas analyzes how five multinational corporations in the United Kingdom are using their internally generated information resources and selling them to the outside as a separate form of business, although these "information subsidiaries" create only a small fraction of the revenues of the business.[31]

Heininger traces the arguments that criticized the effects of multinational corporations on developing countries:

> The process of political independence of a great number of developing countries and their mounting struggles for economic independence, from the early seventies, were accompanied by growing insight to the effect that transnational corporations were in many respects obstacles in the path of full independence."[32]

We can imagine, then, that the multinational corporation we see today is the result of years of transformation, and its use of information technology has come after the fact in terms of its organizational structure. It has caused different social and economic effects wherever it has taken root, and has a strong "corporate culture" that is intimately tied to its history.

THE EXPLOSION OF INFORMATION TECHNOLOGY OPTIONS FOR THE MULTINATIONAL

This new situation has come into being just as the options available through information technology have exploded. The intensified competition among the different multinational corporations finds a greater variety of information technology tools available for use in corporate strategy than at any time in the past. During the 1950s, when the world was just emerging from World War II, when the various postwar international institutions were just starting

---

[30] See Herbert S. Dordick, "The Emerging World Information Business," *Columbia Journal of World Business*, Spring 1983, pp. 69–76.

[31] See Alison Douglas, "Information: A New Multinational Industry?" *Multinational Business*, no. 2, Summer 1987, pp. 37–39.

[32] See Horst Heininger, "Transnational Corporations and the Struggle for the Establishment of a New International Economic Order," in Alice Teichova, Maurice Lévy-Leboyer, and Helga Nussbaum, eds., *Multinational Enterprise In Historical Perspective* (Cambridge University Press, 1986). He writes that "the turnover figures in 1980 of 382 leading transnational corporations accounted for more than 28% of the GNP of all western industrial states and all developing countries and for about 60% of all trade between those countries."

to become effective, and when land in Shinjuku was going for pennies, the bureaucracies and control structures of the multinational corporations were primarily running on paper-based systems developed in the eighteenth and even seventeenth centuries, and little had changed since then. Information technology was in its experimental state and computing was not having a significant effect on business operations or strategy. During the 1960s, as the postwar recession of the 1950s ended, as Europe and Japan recovered, as the United States became *relatively weaker*, and just as European intellectuals began to discuss the role of U.S. multinationals in Europe, it was the emergence of mainframe computing that was taking all of the attention on Park Avenue.[33] There was an emerging high visibility to data processing, but the actual business impact was not yet that significant.

It was during the 1970s, when the world experienced its first modern oil crisis, and when U.S. companies began to lose their competitive edge, that information technology literally exploded with new options, such as departmental minicomputers, and improvements in storage devices and displays. Centralization in data processing was being challenged just as the postwar economic system was starting to buckle. This economic chaos and explosion in information-technology options intensified in the 1980s when many of the Japanese companies became dominant in their particular arena. The U.S. production-technology lead was permanently lost in automobiles, semiconductor memory, and in many other critical technologies, including new materials. The U.S. deficit widened to uncontrollable amounts. With a national debt greater than that of Mexico, Argentina, and Brazil combined, the United States became the poorest country in the world as measured by the amount of debt per capita, yet it continued to spend on foreign aid, military development, and social programs. The crash of 1989 pushed the economic system near a panic collapse as the world economy continued its binge of takeovers and leveraged buyouts. This acceleration in the pace of business change was helped perhaps by the rapid proliferation of information technology to the end-user level. The rise of microcomputers made it possible to model leveraged buyouts on one's desk, and end-user computing, complex workstations capable of modeling artificial intelligence, and expert system environments pushed the management of information and its supporting technology into new domains. The trend toward noncentralized systems continued, and yet mainframes became even more powerful, and supercomputers, minisupercomputers, superminicomputers, and supermicrocomputers, proliferated at a blistering pace.

Many multinational corporations moved even more strongly toward matrix management, and the strong trend toward decentralization, which was

---

[33] IBM was able to attract a great deal of attention when it opened its showroom on Park Avenue.

given a boost by what was happening with information technology, began to lead the corporation toward a "crisis of connectivity." The applications available on an international basis proliferated. Breakthroughs in telecommunications made many of the notions of classical data-processing *locational economics* obsolete as companies such as Citibank proved that processing could be removed from metropolitan areas and transferred through telecommunications to remote low-cost areas of the world, and that programming and systems development could be done remotely in places such as India. The development of software-programming shops set up in developing countries and their use of telecommunications has been studied by the World Bank.[34] Developments are also taking place on a rapid scale in other parts of Asia, such as Hong Kong, where companies such as COL, Ltd., are writing efficient back-office software for banking.[35] Nye, in his discussion of the impact on world politics, emphasized how telecommunications has drastically changed the prospect for the multinational:

> What distinguishes the modern multinational enterprise from the large international corporations of earlier centuries is its global management strategy, made possible by the technology of modern communications.[36]

As a result, the MIS function began to be swamped with questions about the "value" of the massive investments in information technology as the amounts came to account for *almost one-half* of all capital investments being made.

As of the 1990s we are well on our way to seeing the center of the world's economy move to East-Asia, with the yen perhaps replacing the dollar, and waves of new East European immigrants flooding into Western Europe looking for jobs at any price, with perhaps a "Fortress Europe" emerging after 1992. As the multinational corporations manage this transition to an even more destabilizing environment, their share of world production is likely to increase, particularly given the renaissance under way in Eastern Europe and the economic openness this might imply, and we may therefore see the continued large-scale globally coordinated production and quasi-private economic

---

[34] Much of the software-manufacturing industry in the developing world is operated on a "branch plant" basis, many times with use of remote processing. Developments in the software industry are found in Robert Schware, "The World Software Industry and Software Engineering: Opportunities and Constraints for Newly Industrialized Economies," World Bank Technical Paper Number 104, Washington, D.C.: 1989.

[35] See World Bank, "Computer Bureau: Beating the Odds," *Asian Finance*, 15(9) September 15, 1989, COL is one of the two computer processing bureaus in Hong Kong.

[36] See Joseph S. Nye, Jr., "Multinational Corporations in World Politics," *Foreign Affairs*, pp. 153–175.

planning that many have feared.[37] In this environment, workstations will work with mainframe capacities, and Integrated Services Digital Network (ISDN) will turn every telephone circuit into a data highway for as-yet-unknown purposes.[38] Will there be a complete loss of central control? Will entirely transparent standards for data processing and telecommunications emerge?

Past the year 2000 we should begin to see world-scale efficiencies in production and continued focus on developing countries and their peculiar needs. Supercomputer power will be available on a laptop, and telecommunications with extremely high bandwidth through technologies such as the Synchronous Optical Network (SONET) will make information in many different media forms available everywhere. These shifts will completely change the nature of data processing, bureaucratic structure, and information control in the multinational corporation. There will never be stability or rest for the information system function.

---

[37] A persuasive argument explaining how the multinational corporation has played a key role in East-West trade and how this is so is found in Leon Zurawicki, "The Cooperation of the Socialist State with the MNCs," *Columbia Journal of World Business*, Spring 1975, pp. 109–115. According to his argument, MNCs have three main advantages: They have a technology edge that is attractive to socialist countries, they are able to undertake very large contracts with the socialist government acting as the other partner, and they are able to pursue global strategies and better qualified to be more flexible in working with socialist countries.

[38] For a look at the many telecommunications-based services of the new "global village" see Karen Wright, "The Road to the Global Village," *Scientific American*, March 1990, pp. 83–94.

CHAPTER

3

Types of International Information Systems

The plethora of information systems located in many different geographical locations and supporting various types of enterprises and organizations can be divided into several families according to their fuctions and internal structure. Although this is a useful exercise in some cases, it is only a preliminary step in comprehending the phenomena in its entirety. Some systems are based on the older, pre-computer age administrative arrangements found in the 1940s and 1950s. Others are newer and have a more independent pedigree. We might observe two processes of transformation: the reorientation of older information systems into a more global alignment, and the gradual supplanting of older information systems with entirely new arrangements dependent upon shared systems and various information brokers.

The violent combination of political events, changing economies, increased competition among different multinationals and their national economies, and the explosion in the information technology available to use as a tool for survival has resulted in the development of several types of international information systems. Not all systems are alike. Some are centralized, some distributed. Some are owned and operated by a single corporation; others are cooperatives. Some are "outsourced" configurations, or commercial systems that act as intermediaries between the different multinationals. The classification of international information systems is a fuzzy business, but the systems can be categorized according to their ownership (either single or multiple) and their purpose (collaborative or single-purpose). Given these dimensions of classification, we can identify several families of systems (Figure 3.1).

INTERNATIONAL INFORMATION SYSTEMS

International information systems are a general class of computer networks that operate in more than one nation-state. General international systems can be distinguished from more specific systems through their linkage to functionality, the sole limiting criteria being the providing of informational support to transactions that originate in one nation-state and terminate in another. The architecture of international systems is not fixed, but rather may be either centralized or decentralized on an international basis. In this type of information

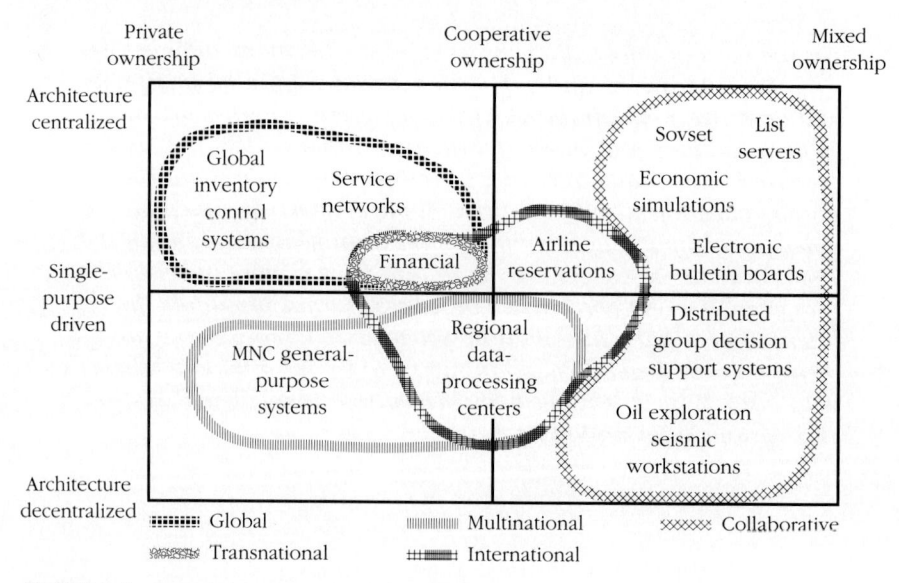

FIGURE 3.1 Families of Information Systems

system, the important element is the existence of data crossing international borders in support of a transaction, typically trade and commerce data.[1] However, the nature of the trade, once it is made, limits it within the national border of at least one host nation-state.

It has been reported, for example, that Xerox Corporation uses a centralized location for monitoring its photocopy machines, which are placed at customer sites. This system enables Xerox to anticipate maintenance requirements for the individual machines connected to Xerox central. The system also works in monitoring machine use for purposes of billing. Also, Wal-Mart uses a completely centralized system to monitor more than 1,300 stores directly, thus giving executives an almost real-time view of inventory levels and sales volume.[2] Porsche has a similar system to link together its 328 dealers in the United States using IBM System/38 minicomputers.[3] In the garment industry, LeviLink, operated by Levi Strauss & Co., links together customers so they can order inventory.[4] These types of uses for information technology will become even more strongly reflected in the global operations of multinational corporations, although few are currently taking full advantage of this arrangement.

In discussing centralization in the multinational corporation, Sauvant writes:

> The degree of centralization varies, depending on the specific corporate functions involved. It is usually strongest in the central areas of finance; budget preparation (particularly the planning of investment expenditures); product planning, design, and development; sourcing, purchasing, and rationalization; and pricing. Affiliate autonomy is usually highest in the area of salaries and personnel policy at the lower level.[5]

---

[1] See E. J. Novotny, "Transborder Data Flows and World Public Order: Law and Policy Problems in Controlling Global Computer Communication Technology," Doctoral thesis, Georgetown University, 1985, and E. M. Roche, "The Computer Communications Lobby, the U.S. Department of State Working Group on Transborder Data Flows and Adoption of the O.E.C.D. Guidelines on the Protection of Privacy and Transborder Data Flows of Personal Data," Columbia University, Ph.D. thesis, 1987.

[2] See Paul Konstadt, "Into the Breach," *CIO*, 3 (11), August 1990, pp. 71–73.

[3] See Jim Petroff and Marie Petroff, " 'Porsche Quality' in Application Design," *Systems/3X World*, 15 (9), September 1987, pp. 42–52.

[4] See Brenton R. Schlender, "How Levi Strauss Did an LBO Right," *Fortune*, 121 (10), May 7, 1990, pp. 105–107. In 1985, Levi increased sales by 31 percent, but *profits went up five times!* However, like most situations, it is not possible to attribute this *directly* to information technology.

[5] See p. 49 of Karl P. Sauvant and Farid G. Lavipour, eds., *Controlling Multinational Enterprises: Problems, Strategies, Counterstrategies* (Boulder, CO: Westview Press, 1976), pp. 39–78.

TRANSNATIONAL INFORMATION SYSTEMS

The transnational information system is slightly different in that it supports transactions that take place without reference to national borders. A good example would be foreign exchange systems or other forms of international trade in equities. In these systems, the "market" is really an electronic fiction. It does not exist within the confines of any particular nation-state; instead it exists as a worldwide *informational transaction space* that operates as an entity in itself. Foreign exchange traders in New York, Frankfurt, Hong Kong, and Tokyo may be interacting with each other at all times of the day through the transnational information system. The architecture of these types of systems tends to be decentralized, relying heavily on a teamwork configuration of minicomputers, packet-switching networks, and data-processing intermediaries such as Reuters, Telerate, or Quotron. Transnational systems, of course, are international in nature, but their transactions are not tied down to any particular geographical locations.

MULTINATIONAL INFORMATION SYSTEMS

A multinational information system, frequently called the "United Nations Model"[6] of data processing, is characterized by the linking together into a loose confederation of different data-processing centers located in different countries.[7] This is the typical arrangement we find today in most multinational corporations where, because of both the historical technical limitations of information technology in the 1960s and 1970s and the legal and regulatory requirements involved in doing international business, the multinational corporation has tended to set up separate but duplicative data-processing centers in each country where they do business. These architectures are, of course, decentralized, and data processing and applications are decentralized, *not* distributed.[8] Although changing, (toward *global?*), these systems have been set up for the purpose of supporting a full range of computational activities within the confines of each location where activity takes place. In some cases this is because of efficiency, in others because of regulatory controls,

---

[6]Although it can be shown that there are many serious disadvantages to the UN Model of data processing, particularly in terms of obsolete technology, inefficiencies, redundancy, and other wasteful factors, this is not meant to be a stab at the reputation of the United Nations itself.

[7]This is not to deny an increasing trend toward integration that accelerated in the 1980s.

[8]Decentralized applications means that the same function, such as payroll, is processed at each computer location; distributed applications take place by operating across an entire data-processing network.

Chapter 3   Types of International Information Systems   37

and in other cases because of technical limitations. But regardless of the factors involved, the multinational system is one of the more common types for today's multinational corporation.[9] It has evolved within the context of the multinational corporation, which existed long before information technology, and as a result has been organized to take on the structural characteristics of the the business operation, which generally has been set up with autonomous or semi-autonomous operations within each nation-state.

GLOBAL INFORMATION SYSTEMS

By the end of the 1980s, global information systems were developing rapidly, particularly within the context of multinational corporations. Global systems are characterized by the distribution of integrated applications throughout the entire information-processing system, regardless of the country in which it is operating. Dyment has argued that as the multinational corporation "evolves" to a global configuration for its information-technology infrastructure, it carefully manages several types of control information, including management accounting information (i.e., financial control reports), tactical information (i.e., general managerial operations), information regarding taxation and other types of administrative compliance with national regulations, and information relating to various critical functions and strategies of the multinational.[10] Although the infrastructural architecture of these systems appears to bear a tendency toward centralization, it is possible to use distributed architectures; yet the distribution of applications access must be homogeneous throughout the entire system. Information accessed and processed in one country must be equally accessible in another country.[11] Sauvant has distinguished *physical* access to data and *functional* access to data, the latter being associated with the use of transborder data flows and telecommunications systems to obtain access to remote databases.[12] The development of global systems, at least in

---

[9] We have ignored here other types of specialized multinational systems found in police or military work. There is not enough data for this, and, in addition, the installed base is considerably smaller than that found within general commerce.

[10] See John J. Dyment, "Strategies and Management Controls for Global Corporations," *Journal of Business Strategy*, 7 (4), Spring 1987, pp. 20–26. According to Dyment, all of this information should be carefully merged into a performance measurement system.

[11] This assumes that it is the type of application, such as spare parts, which must of necessity take place in several different countries.

[12] See Karl P. Sauvant, "Trade in Services: The Impact of Data Techniques," *Information Age*, 11 (1), January 1989, pp. 37–39. According to Sauvant, the increasing ability to move data internationally has been responsible for accelerating the "tradeability" of services on an international scale.

international business, has been driven by the need to coordinate transactions in more than one or two countries simultaneously. In an old-style international system, transactions are coordinated one at a time; in a multinational system, transactions are coordinated within each nation-state with reporting of summary information to a centralized control point, typically corporate headquarters. However, in a global system, an individual transaction may have relevant aspects that link data processing in several countries simultaneously. Examples are large logistics systems that operate in many different countries simultaneously, or multiple sourcing manufacturing and assembly operations in which both the inputs and outputs of plants located in different regions of the world must be coordinated in real time. In the manufacturing environment, these systems should be seen within the context of flexible manufacturing as well as interorganizational linkages.

> The development and diffusion of flexible manufacturing cells/flexible manufacturing systems are receiving greatest attention now, but major advances are taking place in other areas. Those include linking CAD with computer-directed machining operations (known as CAD/CAM), CAD links into computer-based inventory control and purchasing systems, and the linking of all three (inter-sphere automation) via computer-integrated manufacturing (CIM). Integration has not stopped there, however, since the possibility of electronic communication links has opened up a variety of opportunities for electronic links between suppliers, producers and customers in design, production scheduling, purchasing, shipping and other areas.[13]

A practical example of this is the use of CAD/CAM systems linked from the United Kingdom to the United States by the Instron corporation. This linkage simplified the creation of design standards and documentation, but there are hints that a price had to be paid in terms of training and the creation of new forms of coordination between departments that were accustomed to acting autonomously.[14]

Global systems are relatively new to the international environment because they have been made possible only through the technical advances in networking and computing that occurred in the 1980s; as a result we can expect that more and more systems will tend in this direction. For example, much of the value lost because of the inefficiencies and redundancies in

---

[13] See *New Approaches to Best-Practice Manufacturing: The Role of Transnational Corporations and Implications for Developing Countries,* UNCTC Current Studies, Series A, No. 12, p. 11 (New York: United Nations, 1990).

[14] See Anonymous, "Ideas & Applications: Intercontinental CAD/CAM," *Systems International,* 15 (1), January 1987, pp. 19–20.

multinational systems might be recovered by engaging in a type of strategic centralization or regionalization, and today several major firms are engaged in this practice.

COLLABORATIVE OR COOPERATIVE INFORMATION SYSTEMS

Another type of system involves sharing or intermediary-type functions that tie applications together and yet achieve a purpose not specific to any given user. The world's international airline reservation system is cooperative in nature in that it is paid for from the funds of many different companies and is used by all of them together. The world's interbank transfer mechanism, SWIFT,[15] also acts as a type of cooperative between many of the world's banks. In addition, many companies that provide intermediary or interorganizational services such as electronic document interchange[16] operate as shared resources, similar to utilities, among different organizations, that all have essentially different purposes in using the system. Some types of collaborative research systems are found in the oil exploration industry, where analysts linked together over international borders work together to analyze seismic data from many different locations, work usually done on high-powered workstations linked over great distances using wide-area networks.[17] Even the hallowed legal profession is beginning to use information technology to link offices overseas to handle the problems of multinational corporate clients.[18] Finally, some types of group decision-making systems, groupware, or collaborative research systems[19] have a similar nature, although they may be centralized from an architectural point of view and, in terms of their applications distribution, may be quite similar to a global system. Nevertheless, according to purpose specification, they are highly distinct. Table 3.1 classifies information system usage according to business, research, or academic orientation.

---

[15] The Society for Worldwide Interbank Financial Transfers.

[16] The General Electric Information Services Company (GEISCO), and many value-added network carriers such as Tymnet or Telenet would be good examples of this.

[17] These are local area networks linked with LAN bridges operating over international borders. For a case study of TRW, Inc., of Cleveland, Ohio, and TBG Holdings NV of Monaco, and their use of private wide-area networks to coordinate the operations of geographically distributed business, see Eddy Goldberg, "Users Call on WANs for Far-Reaching Business Needs," *Computerworld,* 21 (13A), April 1, 1987, pp. 57–62.

[18] See Robert M. Smith, "Overseeing Foreign Counsel: The In-House Lawyer's Role," *International Financial Law Review,* 5 (9), September 1986, pp. 24–25.

[19] This is a very highly specialized type of research system at the leading edge of development. One cannot be sure of the future of these types of systems.

TABLE 3.1 Types of International Systems[a]

Topology	Architecture	Economics of Growth	Historical Genesis
		Business Orientation	
International	Centralized (including super-computing); polycentric.	Early growth by being an overhead support function for general international transactions. Growth based on efficiencies of data processing, and not by other factors, such as general business operations.	The earliest forms of data processing, reminiscent of use of telex at earlier stages of international business. In nonbusiness settings, systems developed piecemeal linking together specific applications in 1960s and 1970s.
Global	Centralized but with exceptions. Optimized according to data-processing efficiencies, rather than in order to conform to national regulations (which have become weaker in many cases).	Growth by concentration of data-processing activities into a single location. Rationalization of transaction coordination across many different countries.	Made possible by computing and telecommunication advances that allow linkages of applications on a worldwide basis. Product of late 1980s (although some experimental work earlier).
Multinational/Regional	Separate repetitive and duplicative data-processing centers in each country in which the system operates; regiocentric.	Probably inefficient. High degree of redundancy in applications and database location, including extra equipment and personnel costs.	Growth under conditions of national regulations that encouraged autonomy of business operations in each country. Also, privacy regulations and other administrative controls on data processing produced a tendency toward multiple data centers.

Research and Development, Academic Orientation

Collaborative	Centralized, but with very high peripheral access. Also, some variations are composed of networked high-powered workstations.	The experimental nature of these systems means they are not economic, but are rather in an investment stage. Their payoff may not be assured. However, for interorganizational systems, their range and scope of operations is dependent upon charging for each transaction. They must work according to this basis.	Relatively recent development made possible by advances in collaborative software, including database architectures, and hardware, particularly high-powered workstations that yield distributed architectures.
Transnational	Polycentric; many with distributed applications and databases.	Growth according to need for rapid transactions. Many set up on competitive basis against other, similar systems in order to steal transaction volume.	Developed in response to changes in the world's marketplace, particularly in the financial services area.

[a]There are several ways to categorize international systems: according to infrastructure, according to applications distribution and nature, or according to purpose.

41

HISTORICAL CENTRALIZATION AND DECENTRALIZATION

Except for the very newest corporations,[20] multinationals of today have been required to overlay their present information-technology infrastructure on the *pre-existing* structures and traditions of their corporation. This does not mean simply that information technology has been physically placed in the same buildings and offices that may have been within the property of the multinational corporation before information technology came on the scene in the 1960s. But the critical fact is that the *ways of working* and the *logical flows of information* and other bureaucratic systems of the multinational corporation were well in place and operating extensively *before* information technology had a tremendous impact. Information technology, its systems and way of working, is a relative latecomer to the multinational corporation. It is this fact that may be the most important element determining how information technology is best used.

The information-systems functions within the multinational corporation have inherited large centralized architectures that have been clustered near the headquarters of the corporation, which is also typically centralized, at least in critical functions such as finance. Because the computer architectures available to the multinational in the 1960s were typically centralized around the mainframe computing environment, we may say there was a general match between the available information-processing infrastructure and the control methods of the multinational. This implies that since the multinational had a central command center—the corporate headquarters—placing the bulk of data-processing resources there tended to enhance the power and influence of the headquarters and 150 helped to further concentrate critical corporation information resources.

A counter-argument to this might be that at the time information technology started to have a significant impact, many of the multinational corporations were effectively *decentralized* for many if not most of their operating functions and information flows. This line of argument would posit that the introduction of the mainframe's essentially centralized environment was not a good match for the decentralized structure of the multinational. This argument would help explain why mainframe computing and medium-sized computing resources were placed in different national locations. The information technology had the effect of helping the corporation to *centralize within geographical regions* but *decentralize on an international scale*. The counter-

---

[20] Some few Japanese corporations created in the postwar period such as Honda and Sony might fit into this category. Since they are too "new," there is no doubt they did *not* have to impose their information technology infrastructure over an old set of structures and traditions determined by events in a previous age. This discussion is a generalization regarding the MNC as an abstract form and is not referring to specific MNCs.

counter-argument to this would be that although it is true that many multinational corporations were developing along highly decentralized models, there were certain applications and set flows of critical corporate information that had to be processed at the central headquarters. Under these circumstances the buildup of a large-scale mainframe computing environment was a reasonable match for the structure and internal operating characteristics of the multinational corporation, as far as critical information flows were concerned. A typical flow of information that associated with this argument would be *financial information.* We have seen that the international flow of financial information is one of the most important aspects of management control and reporting within the multinational corporate structure.

For most U.S.-based multinational corporations, there have been relatively low levels of internationalization of the information-technology infrastructure, depending on how this is measured.[21] In spite of this, a popular model of the decentralized multinational corporation has emerged, but this was not driven by information technology, its capabilities, or its promise:

- *Much of the available information technology did not work so well internationally in the early years.* The inability of the early stages of information technology to work well internationally was driven by the lack of advancement in telecommunications, particularly at the international level. Availability of international leased lines was relatively rare until the 1970s, and even then were not in wide-scale use. In addition, the availability of packet-switched public X.25-based data networks did not accelerate until relatively recently. Another popular international application, electronic data interchange (EDI),[22] is now (at the beginning of the 1990s)

---

[21] The empirical measurements (presented later) show that regardless of the global operating strategies of the U.S.-based multinational corporations, much of their *information technology infrastructure has remained centralized.* This is shown through a variety of empirical measurements. Also, pay careful attention to the methodological notes that detail possible sources of error in these measurements and the resulting conclusions.

[22] For a look at EDI, see Anne E. Skagen, "Nurturing Relationships and Enhancing Quality with Electronic Data Interchange," *Management Review,* February 1989, pp. 28–32. Cash and Konsynski develop a basic framework for examining interorganizational systems. James I. Cash, Jr. and Benn R. Konsynski, "IS Redraws Competitive Boundaries," *Harvard Business Review,* March–April 1985, pp. 134–142. Mascarenhas describes and classifies interorganizational linkages that might exist between firms. He describes *migrations, transportation links, political agreements, tax treaties, currency ties, organizational linkages* (which would include computerized linkages such as EDI), *colonial ties, cultural ties, ideological ties,* and *informal interorganizational links.* He suggests that "given the excess number of possible linkages relative to the limited capacity of executives, the loss of historical knowledge as experienced executives retire, and the unsystematic and ad hoc use of linkages in current management practice, there is a real need and opportunity for developing data banks. These data banks would compile a vast number of linkage patterns which could readily be sorted and retrieved as decision aids in strategic decision making." See Briance Mascarenhas, "Transnational Linkages and Strategy," in *International Strategic Management,* Anant R. Negandhi and Savarta Arun, eds. Lexington, MA: Lexington books, 1989.

beginning to surface as a major player. In 1988, the research firm Input forecast that EDI would grow by 147 percent per year until 1992, but it warned against transborder data flow problems and other government restrictions.[23] This is in contrast to Snapp's assessment of drags on EDI penetration caused by problems with cultural differences, ambiguities over legal interpretations of the validity of EDI messages, and differences in standards shown by the fact that some companies were developing their own systems.[24] The early versions of SNA and other networking arrangements simply did not make it easy for the information-technology infrastructure to operate efficiently at the international level until well into the 1980s. For many multinational corporations, "international" data-processing operations were limited to batch uploads of standardized and limited-volume information on perhaps a monthly basis.[25]

- *As a result, few information-technology projects have been managed on a truly international basis.* The result of this was that information technology grew up within the multinational corporation as a series of "islands" within different nation-states. Each country where a multinational did a significant amount of business typically had a data-processing center, but this center was typically much smaller than the operation found at the corporate headquarters. Each regional or national center would then act as a type of *centralized environment* for the subbranches of the multinational within the nation-state. Many times this type of arrangement was driven by national legislation instead of by any type of formalized planning or analysis. The role of national legislation within the data-processing strategies of multinational corporations has not been adequately addressed. It has had a very great role in changing the *boundaries of locational economics* for finding the optimum location of data-processing centers. For example, rules on *transborder data flow* and maintenance of the privacy and confidentiality of name-linked data can force a multinational to place a data center in a country where it would not otherwise wish to. In addition, some countries—Brazil might be cited as one example, although it is by no means alone—might *require* that all related business data processing be performed *within national boundaries,* and this requirement might be made a *condition of doing business.* Only a handful of persons have attempted to calculate the economic ef-

---

[23]See Victor S. Wheatman, "Just Getting Started," *Software,* 8 (4), March 1988, pp. 52–58.

[24]Cheryl D. Snapp, "EDI Aims High for Global Growth," *Datamation,* International Edition, 36 (5), March 1, 1990, pp. 77–80.

[25]There was no talk of the type of global instant data processing that is talked about today with cash machines, point of sales information, and companies such as Benneton being touted as taking "strategic advantage" of this type of information technology application.

Chapter 3 Types of International Information Systems

fects of these regulations.[26] If one asks whether the data-processing structure of the multinational corporation is centralized or decentralized, then the answer is *both*.

- *Instead, information technology has simply been mapped onto the preexisting multinational corporate structure.* Since the existing structure of the multinational corporation was already fixed to a great extent when information technology came on the scene, as information technology first went into the multinational, it did little if anything to alter the corporate structure. It did not transform the organization. In the early stages, information technology did not have the technical power to radically alter the way work was done, except for the simple automation of repetitive tasks; and even if it had, there would have been a great deal of resistance to these changes because information technology was not well understood.

- *The ultimate result is that information technology follows, and doesn't lead, the multinational corporate strategy.* There is evidence, as we might suspect, that given the weak state of information technology in the early stages, information technology was not a cutting-edge technology of change. It followed, rather than determined, corporate strategy. There are major questions today regarding whether or not this is still the case. There appear to be only a few examples where information technology strategy leads.[27]

---

[26] For an examination of the economic effects of transborder data flow regulations see Manuel Werner, "Transborder Data Flows: A Cost Benefit Analysis," *Canadian Banker*, 93 (5), October 1986, pp. 36–39. Also, a model for calculating the effects is found in M. Jussawalla and C. W. Cheah, *The Calculus of International Communications: A Study in the Political Economy of Transborder Data Flows* (Littleton, CO: Libraries Unlimited, 1987). Earlier work is found in Meheroo Jussawalla, *The Analytics of Transborder Data Flows*, Conference paper at Second World Conference on Transborder Data Flow Policies, Rome, June 1984. An outline method of calculating the effects is found still earlier in McCaffery, Seligman & von Simson, Inc, *Impact of Transborder Data Flow Legislation: Corporate Case Studies*, August 1979 (mimeo). A study of the effects, including economic effects, of transborder data regulations is found in Edward J. Regan, *Emerging Transborder Data Flow Issues and Their Impacts on International Banking*, Master's thesis Stonier Graduate School of Banking, 1984.

[27] As a hypothesis we might suggest that the financial services sector provides a good number of examples of information technology leading the development of corporate strategy. It is certainly easy to show the critical nature of the relationship between the information resources that are available to the corporation and the actual performance of employees, such as traders, who are completely dependent on the information systems for generating corporate profits and income. Under these circumstances, the corporate strategy is centered around developing the best information technologies to support their workers. There is an implicit assumption that better information technology will create better income for the company. A related assumption is that

(*continued*)

SUMMARY

The multinational corporation is one of the most powerful forces shaping the world economy, although in many cases it is trying to live down its past history of association with colonialism. Its history goes back to the nineteenth century, but its information technology goes back only to the 1960s. The earliest types of information technology were scarcely capable of meeting the coordination and control requirements of the multinational, which was by the 1950s and 1960s firmly in place. It was only during the 1970s when more electronic linkages at the international level became possible, that information technology began to play a more significant role in the development of the multinational.

The result is that the pre-existing administrative heritage of the multinational corporation received the wave of information technology but was not necessarily changed by it. Several different types of international information systems have developed, including international systems, transnational systems, global systems, and collaborative systems. The development of each of these has been conditioned by the peculiar combination of national regulations, multinational strategies, and the technologies available at the time. Regardless of the outcome of the struggle between the administrative heritage and the explosive force of computerization, the result will have a very great effect on international relations and the world's economic system.

---

if a company lags behind in its adoption of leading-edge technologies, then its income will suffer. In areas such as program trading, there is also a clear relationship between the data-processing capabilities developed in-house and the profit or loss of the firm. In this case, programming trading systems is like two groups designing chess-programming algorithms for play against each other, except that there is considerably more money involved in Wall Street trading. It is also reasonable to assume that other *information-intensive* industries would have similar problems, particularly industries that create and distribute only information, such as news retrieval services or database services. Under these circumstances, the development of the information technology infrastructure and the delivery mechanism would be *synonymous* with the development of the corporate strategy. These questions would provide an interesting line of research to a person who is doing sectoral-specific studies.

CHAPTER

4

Multinationalizing the Computer

Another way to examine the role of information technology in the multinational corporation is to look more closely at the relationship between organizational structure and strategy. Generally, the information structure of the MNC should match its organizational structure. We see this parallel emerge when the information systems of world headquarters, regional headquarters, and national headquarters are examined. This three-layer division of the information system gives the first approximation of the relationship between the multinational corporation and the computers that support its operations.

The study of use of information technology in MNCs is fraught with difficulty and ambiguity regarding the type of measurement system to use and the types of relationships that must be examined. Many questions are raised, and they fall in three classes: the assessment of the information-technology infrastructure in the MNC; the relationship between international business strategy and international use of information technology; and methodological questions that arise when one is attempting to calibrate realistic empirical referents uncovering the relationship between business strategy and information technology on such a broad geographical scale. How do we define the IT infrastructure of the MNC? How do various national barriers, including legal and regulatory controls, influence the development of the information-technology infrastructure in the MNC? And what is the relationship between the information-technology infrastructure and the business strategy of the corporation? What is a representative way to measure the information-technology infrastructure of the multinational corporation? What are the data elements that are collectible and provide valid insight into the distribution of information-technology resources on a global scale?

The consensus appears to be that the structure and nature of the international technology system in the MNC is driven by the strategy of the corporation, rather than the other way around. King (1985) pushed the emerging idea that the structure of the international information system can be driven by the general international strategy of the MNC. Hedlund's (1984) study of four Swedish MNCs discussed the "manpower and more international experience to be really able to utilize the international information system," thus further subliminating the role of information technology.

If the information-technology infrastructure is a reflection of the administrative arrangements of the MNC, and if those arrangements in turn are driven by the strategy of the firm as it copes with its environment, then much analysis turns upon the overall business strategy and the external conditions that play the largest part in its development. Dance's (1969) study of General Electric demonstrated how external factors such as government pressure (the 1950 consent decree), *force majeur* (the devastation of Western Europe by World War II), changing market size (the Common Market), and others all exerted strong pressure against the strategy of the MNC. Doz (1980), in three in-depth case studies and further interviews with seven other MNCs, studied the way in which the MNC must balance "between the *political imperatives* of responding to host governments' industrial policies and the *economic imperatives* of maintaining a competitive position worldwide." The structure of the MNC then becomes determined by the external factors it meets in its environment, not the least of which is national sovereignty and its manifestation through government control and interference. Behrman (1969) discussed this balance between national sovereignty and the interests of the MNC—the exercise of national sovereignty frequently results in encumbrances on the activities of the MNC. Poynter (1982) discusses the "political risk" of host government interference with the MNC, particularly in the less-developed countries. Das (1981) gives a detailed explanation of how "the competitive advantage which the MNCs have had as a result of their worldwide integration of resources will greatly decrease as a result of the regulatory controls that are being imposed on MNC operations in the host countries." Lecraw's (1983) study of several major variables shows that the competitive advantage of a MNC changes "in response to factor and product market conditions" at the local level. Rugman (1980) argues that such major strategic decisions as FDI occur as a result of barriers to international trade coming from host countries.

The greatest barriers to international operations of the MNC include controls on the information-technology infrastructure. Since the information-technology infrastructure of a MNC involves many computer systems linked over international borders by a complex web of telecommunications systems, the nation-state has many opportunities to indirectly hinder the operation of the MNC by controlling the flow of information and data. Brewer (1983) discusses controls on electronic transfers of funds. Nanus (1978) discusses government controls on computer systems. Samiee (1983, 1984) reviews the problems encountered by MNCs in moving data from one country to another through their information-technology systems. Sauvant (1983) explains the rationale of these restrictions and how they work from the point of view of the developing countries. Poynter (1982) also discusses how developing countries erect special restrictions against MNCs. Roche (1986) shows how international business fought vigorously in international forums to forestall draconian limitations on international computer networking and transborder data flow. Shrivastava[1] and Grieco[2] discuss the policies adopted by India in building up its computer industry, and Adler[3] discusses the process in connection with Brazil.

These and others have confirmed much of the idea that the external environment determines the structuring of the MNC, including its investment strategy, its location of subsidiaries, and how its subsidiaries report and communicate with headquarters (Figure 4.1). This causal chain exists because the business structure of the MNC, as well as its administrative and computer and telecommunications infrastructure, is organized on a global, regional, and

---

[1] He argues that there is a "dualistic technological structure of economic development." He introduces the concept of "adaptive technological innovation," which is a type of technology transfer that is more suited to the level of the country into which it is being injected. See Paul Shrivastava, "Technological Innovation in Developing Countries," *Columbia Journal of World Business*, Winter 1984, pp. 23–29.

[2] Joseph M. Grieco, "Between Dependency and Autonomy: India's Experience with the International Computer Industry," *International Organization*, 36 (3), Summer 1982, pp. 609–632.

[3] Emanuel Adler, "Ideological 'Guerrillas' and the Quest for Technological Autonomy: Brazil's Domestic Computer Industry," *International Organization*, 40 (3), Summer 1986.

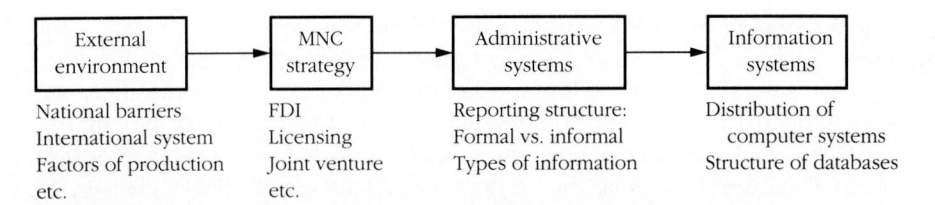

FIGURE 4.1 Causality Chain Determining Information-Technology Infrastructure

```
External          MNC         Administrative     Information
environment  →   strategy  →   systems       →   systems

National barriers       FDI              Reporting structure:    Distribution of
International system    Licensing        Formal vs. informal        computer systems
Factors of production   Joint venture    Types of information    Structure of databases
etc.                    etc.
```

local basis (Figure 4.2). The world headquarters of a MNC usually has a large data-processing center that is linked to other data-processing centers around the world located both in regional headquarters and in each national site of the corporation.

Writing from the perspective of MIS, George and King (1990) performed an extensive literature review and distinguished four arguments regarding the relationship between centralization of data processing and the centralization of decision-making power and administrative organization in a firm. Their analysis of organizations was not intended to be applied to an international environment, but their four classifications of effects can be extended to form a series of hypotheses regarding how information technology might affect the decision-making arrangements in MNCs. The effects are as follows: (1) IT leads to centralization of decision-making authority; (2) IT leads to decentralization of decision-making authority; (3) IT has no relationship with decision-making

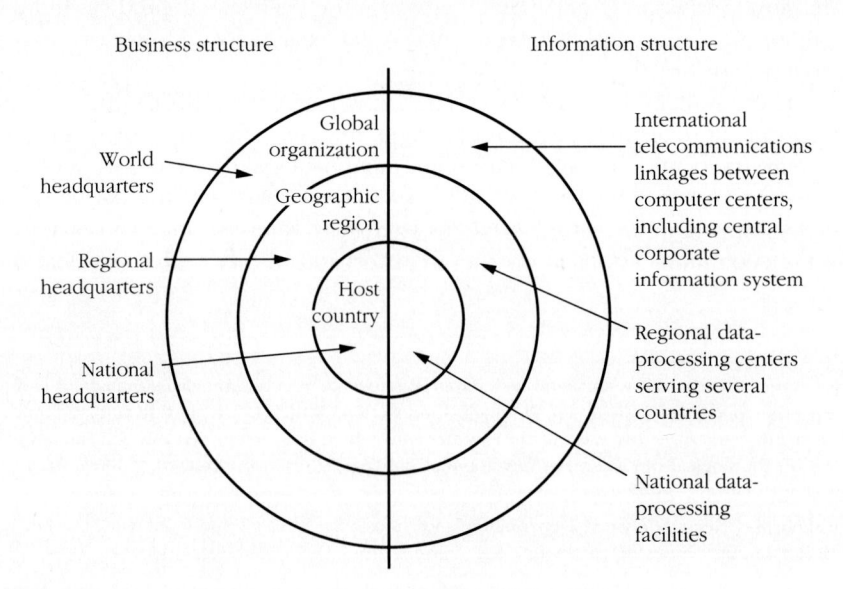

FIGURE 4.2 Business Structure and Information Structure

distribution; (4) the relationship is reversed—the decision-making authority determines the centralization or decentralization of the information system. If the MIS perspective is to agree with the international business perspective, then option 4, that the effect is reversed, must hold. George and King quote Laudon (1974, 1985) as supporting this thesis; however, it is for entirely different reasons, since Laudon's study is of data processing in public services in the United States.

Table 4.1 extends this line of hypothesis further by using the Perlmutter (1969) and Chakravarthy and Perlmutter (1985) classifications of MNC structure to generate assumptions about international information-technology infrastructure, as an extension of what we know about business strategy, structure, and the resulting communications patterns.

If the business strategy classifications[4] could be shown to produce a parallel information-technology infrastructure, then the extension of the analysis is consistent throughout the causal sequence: from environment, to strategy, to administration, and finally to information-technology structure.

In some ways, it does not matter how any particular MNC being considered arrived at its current configuration. Some have argued that since some MNCs are relatively new on the world stage, it is impossible to discuss them in terms of historical development. Take, for example, a new Japanese transplant factory in the midwestern United States. How can such a new organization possibly have an administrative heritage? How can one discuss its development of information technology utilization patterns in terms of a long-term perspective? If one attempts to do so, then surely the logic is flawed.

The answer to this observation is that although the company under consideration may be new, the forces involved in its establishment are not, and in most cases the companies were set up based on preexisting models of headquarters and subsidiary relationships. Japanese transplants, for example, are part of the long heritage of the industrial culture of Japan. This culture determines the conditions into which information technology is placed.

The multinationalization of the computer then becomes a process of adapting technology to culture, administrative structure, and ways of working

---

[4]These classifications also have a parallel to the Fischer and Behrman's (1980) four styles of R&D coordination in transnationals: "absolute centralization" (commitment is imposed by the parent on the subsidiary), "participative centralization" (commitment is reached as a result of negotiation between parent and subsidiary, where the parent decides and the subsidiary gives advice or proposes another decision), "supervised freedom" (commitment is established by subsidiary's decision, and the parent may express opinion or make suggestions), and "total freedom" (commitment is established by the subsidiary and automatically accepted by the parent). Their research demonstrated that the inclusion of new product research in overseas laboratories changes depending on the market orientation of the multinational corporation. They distinguish "world market," "host market," and "home market" orientations. See Jack N. Behrman and William A. Fischer, *Overseas R&D Activities of Transnational Companies* (Cambridge, MA: 1980), Oelgeschlager, Gunn, & Hain, p. 17.

TABLE 4.1 Strategy and Structure for Information Systems

	Typology (Chakravarthy & Perlmutter)		Hypotheses (Roche)	
Profile	Strategy	Structure	Communications	Information-Technology Infrastructure
Ethnocentric	Global integrative	Hierarchical product divisions	Hierarchical, with headquarters giving high volume of orders, commands, and advice	Centralized data processing at headquarters, with global database and real-time online processing of information from any location
Polycentric	National responsiveness	Hierarchical area divisions, with autonomous national units	Little communication to and from headquarters and between subsidies	Strongly independent data-processing centers in each host country, with no applications integration or real-time access to corporate headquarters
Regiocentric	Regional integrative and national responsiveness	Product and regional organizations tied through a matrix	Both vertical and lateral communication within region	Centralized data processing within geographic regions (such as Western Europe), with ties to world headquarters
Geocentric	Global integrative and national responsiveness	Network of organizations	Both vertical and lateral communication within the company	Large, centralized systems and integrated cooperative or distributed data processing

within the multinational corporation. Whether the information processing is clustered at headquarters, in large megacenters organized to cover entire regions of the world, or in many different satellite centers around the world, we can be sure that this arrangement has been driven much more by environmental considerations, administrative heritage, and business strategy, than by technology or its optimization.

SUMMARY

The information-technology infrastructure of the multinational corporation should reflect the business strategy being pursued. If the global market were perfect and if there were no national barriers impeding flows of information and adoption of technology, then this would no doubt be the case. We can see a relationship between the global, regional, and national organization of a multinational corporation in its information system. Large data centers at headquarters might support global operations. Companies may also build various "megacenters" in different regions of the world, such as Europe, to manage all operations there. Finally, within each nation-state where the multinational corporation is doing business, we see a hierarchy of mainframes, minicomputers, and terminals or workstations. This type of arrangement supports different databases at each level. This, then, is the relationship between information technology and the organization and structure of the multinational corporation, but it is unclear how much this tells us about underlying business strategy.

PART II
FIVE STRATEGIC DIMENSIONS

CHAPTER 5

The Distributed Enterprise

There are at least six major dimensions of information technology in multinational corporations. These dimensions are tied up with the formal strategic thinking of the multinational corporation, but they have specific attributes that give important lessons for systems development and guidance of the information-technology function. Information technology plays a critical role in coordination between headquarters and subsidiaries and also among subsidiaries of the multinational corporation; it provides the computing and telecommunications infrastructure for corporate intelligence, reporting systems, and market-monitoring (environmental scanning) information systems; it may give the multinational corporation specific competitive advantages in some cases; it helps to radically reduce the cost of economic transactions within the multinational; and it plays a very important part in relationships with host governments.[1]

These critical functions to a great extent have always been important operational elements of the multinational corporation. However, with the advent of computerization, and the exponential growth in the power and complexity of infomration systems, many of the operations within the multinational that were heretofore manual and paper-based in nature have become absorbed into the computing system. This encapsulation of key functional elements in the multinational is one of the driving forces behind today's events. On top of this sea tide of internal change, today's multinational is constantly facing the challenge of mergers, corporate restructuring, and market chaos.

---

[1] The intent of this monograph is *not* to set forth a new theory of the role of information technology in the modern multinational corporation, but rather to examine many of the classical and received theories of the multinational corporation and to extract what implications they might have for use of information technology and automation.

Chapter 5 The Distributed Enterprise

These changes mean that today's MNC is facing many structural changes in the international business environment. Very rapid advances in the substance of business—new processes, new materials, new manufacturing techniques, new distribution and marketing channels, and other innovations—are all combining to force MNCs to constantly reexamine and update their strategies. In addition, the current end of the GATT[2] and GATS (General Agreement on Trade in Services) negotiations will open up the world trading system even more to MNC operations, expanding further the arena of global competition.

One of the fastest growth areas in the world's economy is services. These are highly information-intensive, and as a result, they rely heavily upon the use of computer and telecommunications technology. Foreign direct investment in services has been skyrocketing:

> By the mid-1980s, about 40 per cent of the world's total FDI stock of about $700 billion (about $300 billion) was in services, compared to approximately one quarter at the beginning of the 1970s and less than 20 per cent in the early 1950s. Moreover, FDI in services has increasingly become the most dynamic part of the growth of FDI in general. More than half of total investment flows of about $40 billion annually were in the services sector during the first half of the 1980s, of which no less than two thirds were in finance- and trade-related activities.[3]

The technological developments in international computer-communications systems are posing great challenges for international negotiations in the Uruguay Round because they are changing how services are delivered, as well as the general relationships between countries and between multinational corporations and the countries in which they operate. Compiling a great deal of information on the prospects of international trade in telecommunications services, the Uruguay Round report concludes in part by stressing the prospects for reassessment of policies on the part of host countries and the international community.

> Pressures for a reassessment of policies are further shown by several factors, including the growing realization that the efficiency of the service sector and, particularly, that of producer services, is an important factor influencing the efficiency of an economy as a whole; constraints relating to capital availability for developing countries since the early 1980s and to the need for technology (or expertise, especially in modern, knowledge-intensive services); increased tradability of certain services (as a result of the increased use of data services), which makes some restrictions on the establishment of foreign affiliates obsolete or less effective; and the support, especially of principal home countries, for an international framework for trade in services which would facilitate the rapid expansion of

---

[2]Some are writing that the OECD will gradually replace the GATT, which is considered in some quarters too slow and too dominated by developing countries to carry out the task at hand.

[3]UNCTC, *Joint Ventures as a Form of International Economic Co-operation* (New York: United Nations, 1988), pp. 12–13.

their service corporations internationally, since such expansion is viewed as a source of growth and structural adjustment.[4]

Other arguments hold that the operations of multinational service corporations in developing countries can be of great benefit to the host country by "injecting a dose of competition into the service markets of developing countries."

> Technological developments, that is, the advent of transborder data flows through the convergence of computer and telecommunication technologies, may change fundamentally the situation described above. By permitting instantaneous, long-distance interactive transactions via transnational computer-communication systems, transborder data flows make it possible for certain services to be produced in one place and consumed in another.... In extreme cases, that is, in industries which are very information-intensive, some foreign affiliates may be reduced to terminals in which data are merely entered (for example, insurance or travel information), while most of the value (for example, risk calculation and fare construction) is added elsewhere. This would represent a complete reversal of the situation which currently characterizes foreign service affiliates. It would be a development which, if it occurs, could have profound effects on the character, impact, and level of FDI in services. In consequence, the mechanisms of technology transfer by transnational service corporations or of diffusion of technologies (through training of personnel employed in foreign affiliates or turnover of trained personnel) may become less relevant.[5]

In the banking sector, it is realized that providing computer cash management facilities to the key client base, which is increasingly composed of multinational corporations, is critical to competitive advantage. This type of service is often based on a direct electronic link between the client and the bank itself, all mediated through the information system.[6] This is also seen in large banks such as Citibank, which for decades has been working hard to build an effective global strategy.[7] These new factors in the business environment

---

[4]UNCTC, *Transnational Corporations, Services and the Uruguay Round* (New York: United Nations, 1990), p. 19.

[5]See Commission on Transnational Corporations, *Impact of Transnational Service Corporations on Developing Countries: Report of the Secretary General*, Doc. E/C.10/1991/6, February 20, 1991 (New York: United Nations, 1991).

[6]See Deborah Miller Shure, "Upgraded Cash Management Fills Demand for Timely Info," *Bank Systems & Equipment*, 23 (6), June 1986. For a study of global banking information systems, see Ajay Mookerjee and James Cash. *Global Electronic Wholesale Banking* (London: Graham E. Trotman, 1990), esp. Figure 3.7.

[7]For more details on Citibank, see David Lascelles, "Banking on Boulevards to Build the Business," *Financial Times*, July 24, 1991, p. 8. As of 1991, Citibank was operating 1,680 branches "only a third of which (551) are in the U.S. Of the rest, 682 are in Europe (mainly Germany, Belgium and Spain), 195 in Asia and Japan, and 252 in Latin America." According to the article, Citibank is working at linking all its cash machines and branches into a single global network. For a general perspective that touches on banking's investments in information technology, see Alfred Kenyon and Shiv Sahai Mathur, "The Development of Strategies by International Commercial Banks," *Journal of General Management*, 13 (2), Winter 1987, pp. 56–73.

Chapter 5 The Distributed Enterprise 59

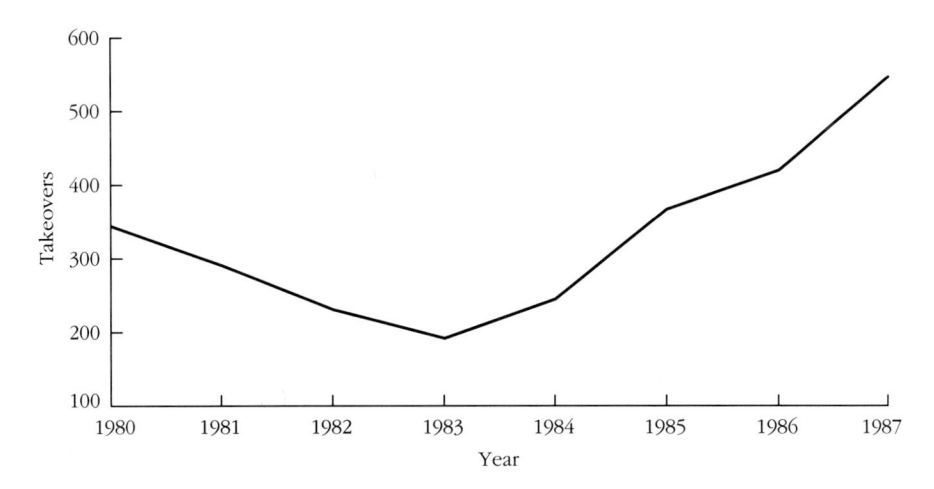

FIGURE 5.1 Takeovers in the United States by Foreign Companies

have been driving the MNCs to adopt new forms of competition. The number of international mergers and acquisitions[8] has increased greatly: there were more than 300 in 1989 alone, and the pace is increasing.

Between 1980 and 1987, there were approximately 1,114 foreign takeovers by United States companies that scooped up operations abroad (Figure 5.1). Most (314) were in the United Kingdom, followed by Canada, which supplied 239 targets during this period. There also were 95 in West Germany and 88 in France. The United States also received investment from abroad. In 1987 alone, there were 1,328 transactions, of which 547 were acquisition and merger situations, 63 were equity increases, 99 were joint ventures, and 321 were new plants or plant expansion moves. No one seems to know what type of transactions the other 388 were.[9]

The situation was different in Latin America, where during the 1970s, governments had taken many steps to limit the ability of "foreign" multinational corporations to operate in their markets:

---

[8] See Brent D. Wilson, "The Propensity of Multinational Companies to Expand through Acquisitions," *Journal of International Business Studies* (nd), pp. 59–65. Wilson concluded that "U.S.-based multinationals on average have a higher level of diversification in their subsidiaries than multinationals based in other countries." He also stated that "the Japanese tend to invest more in LDCs" and that "firms with a lower ratio of pre-1960 implantations were more likely to acquire subsidiaries." He noted that "on average the Japanese multinationals acquire a significantly lower percentage of subsidiaries than do those firms based in the remaining countries."

[9] The number of takeovers in the United States by foreign companies by year is given as 1980, 344; 1981, 291; 1982, 231; 1983, 192; 1984, 245; 1985, 367; 1986, 420; and 1987, 547. See UNCTC, *The Process of Transnationalization and Transnational Mergers*, UNCTC Current Studies, Series A, No. 8 (New York: United Nations, 1989), pp. 26, 27, 31, 32.

Most Latin American governments, from Mexico to Chile, enacted special laws and procedures and set up administrative bodies to deal with transnational corporations and their investment and technology transactions. One of the main features of those policies and laws was the emphasis placed on preventing the takeover and domination of local enterprises by foreign investors. Fade-out formulae, incentives for joint ventures and new contractual forms were adopted with the explicit purpose of protecting and mobilizing domestic entrepreneurs. Takeovers, and the incorporation of restrictive business practices in technology agreements, were prohibited or discouraged by specific regulations. Local credit, royalty payments and transfer prices were also regulated.[10]

Acquisitions allow the MNC to enter new markets, solidify its position in certain critical technologies, acquire distribution channels, and so on. International partnerships have also proliferated, particularly in high-capital and R&D-intensive fields such as aerospace, information technology, biotechnology and pharmaceuticals, and automobile manufacturing. Caves argues that "MNEs tend to be found in research-intensive sectors, and there is evidence that they consciously allocate their R&D activities around the world to best advantage [as] R&D is pulled toward the parent's headquarters by the needs of efficient supervision and scale economies in the R&D process itself, dispersed toward the subsidiaries by the advantages of doing developmental research close to the served market."[11] The creation of international "mega companies" covering large areas of the high-technology spectrum has again raised challenges for the MNC. Wortmann found, however, that German multinationals were rapidly increasing the internationalization of their R&D and were actively transferring much of it overseas.[12]

The complicating factor in this picture is the role of information technology. Each acquisition requires a rethinking and occasional reenginering of the information system in the multinational corporation. Willner's examination of how Citibank was acquiring branches overseas revealed that most local processing could be done on simple personal computers with spreadsheets, but that the back-end functions of the bank could be easily linked into a regional or home office.[13] Wright confirms the need to study "computer-

---

[10] UNCTC, *Measures Strengthening the Negotiating Capacity of Governments in Their Relations with Transnational Corporations* (New York: United Nations, 1983).

[11] Richard E. Caves, "Multinational Enterprises and Technology Transfer," in Alan M. Rugman, ed., *New Theories of the Multinational Enterprise* (New York: St. Martin's Press, 1982).

[12] Michael Wortmann, "Multinationals and the Internationalization of R&D: New Developments in German Companies, *Research Policy*, 19 (2), April 1990, pp. 175–183.

[13] Eric Willner, "MIS in Banking: Keep Branch Systems Simple," *Computerworld,* 22 (33), August 15, 1988, p. 70. Willner discusses the use of microcomputers in running "downsized internal programs," which are lean and mean "consumer" versions of systems operating on the main application system of the bank.

Chapter 5 The Distributed Enterprise 61

based information systems for multinational firms" and mentions specifically "information transfer in international business," which includes "financial information systems of multinational firms" and "information transfer."[14] Dymsza emphasizes the need to be aware of "the impact of changing technology... more widespread use of computers in a wide range of business activities" for managers.[15] Czinkota's Delphi study of 30 executives in international firms also highlights concern with computer and telecommunications systems, at least in the financial sector.[16]

Many writers have discussed the important role of information technology in the operations and strategies of the MNC. Perlmutter mentioned telecommunications as a factor making possible "geocentric" enterprises.[17] Nanus predicted many of the effects that are written about widely in the press today, including the ability to "coordinate... operations effectively across national boundaries."

> The marriage of computers and telecommunications has freed the systems designer from geographic constraints on the location of input, output and processing elements so that the manager is now able to distribute data processing capability on the basis of convenience and need. However, as management information systems freely traverse national boundaries, new problems and opportunities are created for the managers of multinational firms.[18]

He noted that:

> In addition to coordination, rapid and effective information flows can assist decentralized local units to compete more effectively and to take better advantage of the scarce managerial talents available to them. Multinational computer systems also permit the corporation to increase its maneuverability in negotiations with government, labor, suppliers and customers, and to increase its ability to react quickly to uncontrollable shifts in the environment.

He also discussed host country relations, effects on distribution of R&D, headquarters-subsidiary reporting relationships, transborder data flow issues, as well as corporate intelligence functions. Considering that this article was

---

[14] Richard W. Wright, "Trends in International Business Research," pp. 109–123.

[15] See William A. Dymsza, "The Education and Development of Managers for Future Decades," *Journal of International Business Studies*, Winter 1982.

[16] Michael R. Czinkota, "International Trade and Business in the late 1980's: An Integrated U.S. Perspective," *Journal of International Business Studies*, Spring 1986, pp. 127–134.

[17] Howard V. Perlmutter, "The Tortuous Evolution of the Multinational Corporation," *Columbia Journal of World Business*, January–February 1969.

[18] Burt Nanus, "The Multinational Computer," *Columbia Journal of World Business*, November–December 1969. See also Burt Nanus, "Business, Government and the Multinational Computer," *Columbia Journal of World Business*, Spring 1978, pp. 19–26.

written in 1969, it was far ahead of its time, as it was based on a book that had been written even earlier.

The use of international information-technology systems is also seen as critical in the creation of corporate intelligence. Root discusses the "surprise-intensive" nature of the international environment, which calls forth the need for careful monitoring on the part of the MNC.[19] Dymsza mentions the role of "computerized information systems" in helping the MNC cope with environmental change.[20] Kennedy shows the linkage between "external environmental analysis and strategic planning."[21] However, Eells complains that the "communicational strategy" is "not adequately conceptualized."[22] Mascarenhas discusses the "four strategies" of "control, flexibility, insurance, and prediction" in terms of corporate intelligence systems.[23] Similarly, Ghoshal and Kim discuss corporate intelligence and "environmental scanning" in six large Korean firms.[24] We know that the information-technology infrastructure of a MNC carries this corporate intelligence data throughout its worldwide operations.

A wider body of research has examined the dynamics of the relationship between the headquarters of the MNC and its subsidiaries, which has implications for the shape of the information-technology systems. Cray studied 57 subsidiaries of 34 American MNCs with operations in two European states, England and France. He noted the presence of a "fully integrated computer system linking several countries" and how it plays a role in headquarters/subsidiary coordination."[25] The use of information technology appears to be a "bureaucratic" instead of a "cultural" control system, as seen by Baliga and Jaeger.[26] Jaeger discussed "cultural control systems" that replace

---

[19] Franklin R. Root, "Some Trends in the World Economy and Their Implications for International Business Strategy," *Journal of International Business Studies*, Winter 1984.

[20] William A. Dymsza, "Trends in Multinational Business and Global Environments: A Perspective," *Journal of International Business Studies*, Winter 1984.

[21] Charles R. Kennedy, Jr., "The External Environment–Strategic Planning Interface: U.S. Multinational Corporate Practices in the 1980s," *Journal of International Business Studies*, Fall 1984, pp. 99–108.

[22] Richard Eells, "Multinational Corporations: The Intelligence Function," *Columbia Journal of World Business*, November–December 1969.

[23] Briance Mascarenhas, "Coping with Uncertainty in International Business," *Journal of International Business Studies*, Fall 1982.

[24] Sumantra Ghoshal, "Environmental Scanning in Korean Firms: Organizational Isomorphism in Action," *Journal of International Business Studies*, Spring 1988, pp. 69–85. This is related to earlier work with Kim. See Sumantra Ghoshal and Seok Ki Kim, "Building Effective Intelligence Systems for Competitive Advantage," *Sloan Management Review*, Fall 1986, pp. 49–58.

[25] David Cray, "Control and Coordination in Multinational Corporations," *Journal of International Business Studies*, Fall 1984.

[26] Alfred M. Jaeger and B. R. Baliga, "Control Systems and Strategic Adaption: Lessons from the Japanese Experience," *Strategic Management Journal*, 6, 1985, pp. 115–134.

these "bureaucratic control systems" in the MNC, implying that Japanese-style or "Type Z" companies might rely on weaker information-technology systems to maintain their control.[27] Mascarenhas discussed how "the use of communication between country-subsidiary managers, the use of impersonal methods, and the use of personal communication are higher than the use of other coordination methods and communication patterns."[28] The types of communication studied include "direct communication between managers of different country subsidiaries," "communication with a manufacturing staff group," and "communication with a line manager in the formal hierarchy higher than the country subsidiary manager." Tappan shows how information technology can be used in international project management in MNCs.[29] There is no doubt that information technology forms the nervous system linking headquarters with subsidiaries, but we do not know how this relationship is structured or balanced, particularly as regards the extent of decentralization.

Many writers have studied the centralization/decentralization issue in the MNC and have tried to identify which factors are most important in determining the shape of the MNC. These factors also would appear to relate strongly to the "shape" of the information-technology infrastructure. As early as 1984, Raptis and Collins warned of the problems faced by the multinational corporation in managing the information linkages between its headquarters and subsidiaries. They suggested that companies could adopt a policy of "decentralization with strong control" as a managerial guideline.[30] Pucik and Katz argued that in order to have effective decentralization of the information technology function, a great premium must be placed on human resources management to cope with both the "social" and and "technical" information systems in the multinational corporation.[31] Behrman and Fischer discuss how and why R&D is distributed through the MNC and why it might be moved away from the headquarters to the subsidiaries.[32] Picard interviewed executives of 56 U.S. subsidiaries of European MNCs to study the "organization and communi-

---

[27] Alfred M. Jaeger, "The Transfer of Organizational Culture Overseas: An Approach to Control in the Multinational Corporation," *Journal of International Business Studies*, Fall 1983.

[28] Briance Mascarenhas, "The Coordination of Manufacturing Interdependence in Multinational Companies," *Journal of International Business Studies*, Winter 1984, pp. 91–106.

[29] See David S. Tappan, Jr., "Project Management of the Future," *Columbia Journal of World Business*, 20 (4), 1985, pp. 27–29.

[30] They argued that prepackaged software was incapable of meeting the needs of such a situation. See George Raptis and Joanne Collins, "Managing Multinational Information Systems," *Management Accounting*, 67 (7), January 1986, pp. 14, 29, 81.

[31] Vladmir Pucik and Jan Hack Katz, "Information, Control, and Human Resource Management in Multinational Firms," *Human Resource Management*, 25 (1), Spring 1986, pp. 121–132.

[32] Jack N. Behrman and William A. Fischer, "Transnational Corporations: Market Orientations and R&D Abroad," *Columbia Journal of World Business*, Fall 1980.

TABLE 5.1 Information Technology Functions and the Role of Subsidiary Data Centers in the Transnational Corporation

Function of IT	Location of Corporate Data	Predominant Direction of Information Flow: HQT ⇔ SUB	Role of Subsidiary Data Centers
Headquarters-subsidiary coordination	Integrated but with centralized control	⇐ ⇒	Provides port and interfaces for incoming and outgoing corporate data and ensures correct interfunctional distribution of control information
Corporate intelligence systems	Centralized	⇐	The subsidiary data centers act as "feeders" into the environmental scanning system
Internalization	Integrated, shared control	⇐ ⇒	Extends efficient processes into the subsidiary and maintains minimum transaction processing costs
Firm-specific advantages	Decentralized	⇒	Specific aspects of IT are projected into the host country in order to obtain advantages in the market.

cation" patterns between the headquarters and the subsidiary.[33] Bartlett and Yoshihara show the relationship between the forms of international communication and the success of the firm in adapting to new conditions.[34]

All of these different ideas and streams of thought can be reduced to five dimensions of information technology in the multinational corporation, which are detailed in Table 5.1. They are discussed in detail in the following chapters.

---

[33] Jacques Picard, "Organizational Structures and Integrative Devices in European Multinational Corporations," *Columbia Journal of World Business*, Spring 1980.

[34] Christopher A. Bartlett and Hideki Yoshihara, "New Challenges for Japanese Multinationals: Is Organization Adaption Their Achilles Heel?" *Human Resource Management,* 27 (1), Spring 1988, pp. 19–43.

CHAPTER 6

Headquarters-Subsidiary and Intersubsidiary Coordination

One of the most important roles for information technology in the multinational corporation involves transmission of information among its different organizational parts, usually scattered around the world. All types of data and information are contained in the constant flow, and the telecommunications system acts as a giant nervous system for management at headquarters to know what is going on in the subsidiaries and to ensure that their controls and guidance are transmitted efficiently to the field. In a large manufacturing company, such as Ford, the coordination needed at the international level is great, involving as it does financial information, manufacturing control and design information, and a formidable logistics system.

The study of control relationships for communications channels between MNC headquarters and the subsidiaries (and also among subsidiaries) has emerged as a distinct stream of research. Researchers have examined types of information exchanged and have been particularly interested in how this indicates where decisions are made (i.e., where the real power lies).

However, new information technologies (electronic mail, voice mail, teleconferencing, digital facsimile, distributed processing, etc.) may be changing the nature of communications within the MNC. In general, there is potential for more transparency in decision making and considerably tighter coordination between headquarters operations and individual subsidiaries. In addition, intersubsidiary coordination may be enhanced as subsidiary-subcontractor or subsidiary-customer relationships are "informated."

The economic size and sophistication of the multinational corporation does not automatically imply that its use of information technology is more sophisticated, particularly in terms of the way it achieves coordination among different units of the enterprise. Gremillion's study of 64 units of the Forest Service could find no significant correlation between size and information systems use.[1] One can only speculate about the extra problems that are faced by the multinational corporation because it must operate in the international environment.

According to Kogut, Porter places the information technology system within the category of "support activities" and distinguishes "configuration" and "coordination" as follows: "*configuration* refers to where the various links of the value chain are located. *Coordination* refers to how like or linked activities performed in different countries are coordinated with each other."[2] Lodge describes EDS and General Motors as an example of the use of computerization for forming linkages along the value-added chain between manufacturers and suppliers.[3] Hayes and Wheelwright's analysis of the value-added chain, which they call "the commercial chain" in manufacturing, includes (1) raw material producers, (2) material fabricators, (3) component parts producers, (4) manufacturers/assemblers, (5) wholesalers/distributors, (6) retailers, and

---

[1] Lee L. Gremillion, "Organization Size and Information System Use: An Empirical Study," *Journal of Management Information Systems*, I (2), 1984, pp. 4–17. He bases his study on the assumption that "increases in organization size are usually associated with increasing problems in communications and coordination. The theoretical basis for this relationship is the inevitable increase in communications complexity stemming from the increased number of organizational members" (p. 5). He observes that "the relationship between organizational size, other characteristics of the organization, its members, and its environment, and its use of computer-based information systems appears to be complex, perhaps more complex than earlier studies have indicated" (p. 16). One can only imagine the problems posed by the multinational corporation.

[2] Bruce Kogut, Book review of *Competition in Global Industries, Sloan Management Review*, Winter 1987, pp. 73–76.

[3] George Lodge, "The American Corporation and Its New Relationships," *California Management Review*, Spring 1989, pp. 9–24.

Chapter 6   Headquarters-Subsidiary and Intersubsidiary Coordination   67

(7) consumers.[4] An example of a smaller network based on System/3x architecture is found in a case study of the Crosby Group, Inc., a manufacturer of oil fittings operating in the United States, Canada, and Europe.[5]

Kogut discusses "information arbitrage" as one of the four opportunities that might be exploited by the multinational corporation.[6] To Kogut, this is the process of "scanning world markets to match sellers and buyers," and it can be a great advantage in the global strategy of the multinational corporation. He also notes (p. 37):

> The failure to develop systems tied to the global strategy of the firm may well reflect the significant costs attached to a *sophisticated information system* that supports the management of planning and control and human resources. One suspects, however, that the benefits of such a system have not been fully specified in terms of balancing the centralized coordination of the multinational network against the maintenance of local subsidiary responsiveness. [Emphasis added.]

Porter describes the development of coordination capabilities in multinational corporations and points out the role that information technology is playing in that process:

> The ability to coordinate globally has also risen markedly in the postwar period. Perhaps the most striking reason is falling communications costs (in voice and data) and reduced travel time for individuals. The ability to coordinate activities in different countries has also been facilitated by growing similarities among countries in marketing systems, business practices, and infrastructure.... Pioneering global competitors also stimulate the development and growth of international telecommunication infrastructure.... There are also signs of globalization in some service industries as the *introduction of information technology creates scale economies in support activities and facilitates coordination in primary activities*.... Communications and coordination costs are dropping sharply, driven by breathtaking advances in information systems and telecommunication technology. [Emphasis added.][7]

Brandt and Hulbert concluded that "home offices clearly need to give more thought and planning to their information systems" for reporting from subsidiaries, but that "merely increasing the information flow without regard to quality will not improve the relationship." They noted that "in many firms some type of special 'international information system' was urgently needed to coordinate and control the constant flow of communications." Their re-

---

[4]Robert H. Hayes and Steven C. Wheelwright, *Restoring Our Competitive Edge: Competing through Manufacturing* (New York: John Wiley & Sons, 1984), p. 276.
[5]Dave Powell, "Case Study: Implementing an International S/3X Network," *Systems/3X World*, 14 (7), July 1986, pp. 26–32.
[6]Bruce Kogut, "Designing Global Strategies: Profiting from Operational Flexibility," *Sloan Management Review,* Fall 1985, pp. 27–38.
[7]Michael E. Porter, "Changing Patterns of International Competition," *California Management Review,* XXVIII (2), Winter 1986, pp. 9–40.

search also indicated that the more complex the organization, the more likely the multinational was to "experience greater communications systems problems."[8]

In his analysis of manufacturing rationalization, Yves Doz points out some of the informational difficulties he found in a two-year study of multinational corporations: "The company itself is often in a poor position to detect overall competitive pressures... [because] predominance of a national orientation can lead to decay of central management... [and the] absence of systematic exchange of information about specific products and markets between national subsidiaries."[9]

In discussing the theory of location and the multinational enterprise, Buckley says that "the increased communications flows in an internal market may bias high communications cost activities towards the 'centre'—usually towards the source country where critical activities are focused on the head office."[10] This factor will have a strong impact on location. As we will see later on in this monograph, the empirical measurements that were taken did indicate a tendency toward centralization in data processing and its supporting international telecommunications infrastructure linking subsidiaries with headquarters locations. Some studies of competition among cities emphasize that by adopting investment policies that make available in the infrastructure state-of-the-art telecommunications facilities, such as fiber optic networks, some geographic locations are able to gain a competitive advantage over others in attracting high-technology investment.[11] Ireland, for example, has been promoting itself as a "data processing" location for multinational corporations operating in the European Community.[12]

---

[8] William K. Brandt and James M. Hulbert, "Patterns of Communication in the Multinational Corporation: An Empirical Study," *Journal of International Business Studies*, September 1976, pp. 57–64. Their study focused on Japanese, North American, and Western European multinationals and their reporting to Brazilian subsidiaries. Also, they did not study information technology systems, but all types of communications, both formal and informal, from the subsidiary to headquarters and back. Interestingly, they found that Japanese multinationals appeared to have greater communications problems than those of other nationalities.

[9] Yves L. Doz, "Managing Manufacturing Rationalization within Multinational Companies," *Columbia Journal of World Business*, Fall 1978, pp. 82–94.

[10] Peter J. Buckley, "A Critical View of Theories of the Multinational Enterprise," in Peter J. Buckley and Mark Casson, eds., *The Economic Theory of the Multinational Enterprise* (New York: Macmillan, 1985).

[11] Joyce Elam, Dan Edwards, and Richard Mason, "How U.S. Cities Compete through Information Technology: Securing an Urban Advantage," *Information Society*, 6, 1990, pp. 153–178. See also Peter G. W. Keen, "Telecommunications and Organizational Advantage," Conference paper in "Global Competition and Telecommunications Colloquium," Harvard University Graduate School of Business Administration, May 1–3, 1991.

[12] Stephanie Cook, "Ireland Moving to Become Integral Part of Transatlantic Connection," *Data Communications*, 14 (13), December 1985, pp. 68, 70. By 1985, approximately 30 percent of Ireland's exchanges were digital, using the Ericsson A.X.E. central office switches. Ireland was also engaged in establishing its first public packet-switched network.

Chapter 6 Headquarters-Subsidiary and Intersubsidiary Coordination 69

In his study of the coordination of manufacturing interdependence in multinational corporations, Mascarenhas examined three communications patterns: (1) direct communication between managers of different-country subsidiaries, (2) communication with a manufacturing staff group, and (3) communication with a line manager in the formal hierarchy higher than the country subsidiary manager (for example, a regional manager or a global product manager).[13] His results indicate that as the multinational corporation attempts to get tighter coordination between headquarters and subsidiaries and also among subsidiaries, the amount of communication required increases substantially. Of particular interest is his analysis of interpersonal communications, which appear to be good for relieving tensions and ironing out problems. He concludes:

> Although the use of impersonal methods of coordination is extensive in multinational companies, with increasing manufacturing interdependence there appears to be a shift in coordination mix toward the use of system-sensitive members, personal communication, *communication with central manufacturing staff group, and communication between country subsidiary managers*. The shift toward these coordination methods and communication patterns suggests the importance of socializing organization members to build a system-sensitive outlook. [Emphasis added.]

From the point of view of developments in information technology, the results are puzzling. Mascarenhas conducted his study in the early 1980s, when the capabilities of global telecommunications networking were still in a relatively developmental stage. In addition, his measurements did not make specific reference to the computing system. Technologies such as voice mail, facsimile, teleconferencing, and, in particular, electronic document interchange within the context of coordination, or even the development of global applications designed to manage global manufacturing operations were not considered. Very few multinationals had advanced systems at this time. Had the information-technology system and its communication patterns been measured, a slightly different picture would have emerged. The overall trend would probably indicate an increasing dominance of the computing system, particularly if the actual amount of data and information flowing through the system were measured.

Jelinek and Golhar point to the close relationship between manufacturing and information technology and communications systems: "Technological developments in the miniaturization of electronic components, in integrated computerization and in communications system design are radically transforming the interface between manufacturing and strategy."[14]

---

[13] Briance Mascarenhas, "The Coordination of Manufacturing Interdependence in Multinational Companies," *Journal of International Business Studies*, Winter 1984, pp. 91–106.

[14] Miriann Jelinek and Joel D. Golhar, "The Interface between Strategy and Manufacturing Technology," *Columbia Journal of World Business*, Spring 1983, pp. 26–36.

Bartlett and Ghoshal have argued that "while goods flows could be coordinated through formalization, and resources flows through centralization, critical information flows [are] much more difficult to manage." They point out the need to "move strategic information and proprietary knowledge around the company much more quickly." They state that "while some routine data could be transferred through normal information, much of the information was so diverse and changeable that establishing formal processes was impossible,...[leading to the] encouragement of informal communications channels."[15]

From the point of view of information technology, the assertion appears out of synch.[16] The complex infrastructure of information technology provides adequate means for both formal and informal communication, and there is no reason to believe that somehow this informal communication takes place independent of the information system. However, their observation that "strategic information appears in many different parts of the world" fits in squarely with the long tradition of corporate intelligence and the need to acquire information from overseas operations.

Their view of the "mind matrix" is an information system in which the company can "channel information in a way that (shifts) the balance of power" and in which all persons in the company have a clear understanding of, "identification with, and commitment to the corporation's objectives, priorities, and values." They point to a type of arrangement in successful multinationals in which values of centralization and decentralization are mixed depending on the purpose, and this agrees with the idea that different computing applications should be distributed to match strategy: "Instead of deciding the overall roles of product, functional, and geographic management on the basis of simplistic dichotomies such as global versus domestic businesses or centralized versus decentralized organizations, many companies are creating different levels of influence for different groups as they perform different activities."

This vision agrees with that of Guterl, who discussed how multinational corporations are changing to nonhierarchical matrix or "network-type" organizations to allow them to respond faster to changes in the competitive environment:

> This theory holds that a multinational corporation should be managed not through a vertical chain of command but as a vast network of employees who are *linked*

---

[15]Christopher A. Bartlett, and Sumantra Ghoshal, "Managing across Borders: New Organizational Responses," *Sloan Management Review*, Fall 1987, pp. 43–53.

[16]The only possible explanation is that their definition of the "information system" is narrow. If they are focused on structured applications, such as inventory control, their assertions make more sense. However, if one considers the entire scope of the information and its capabilities for supporting both formal and informal communications, a discrepancy emerges. However, we do know that designing information systems that handle unstructured informal data and communication is much more complex than systems for structured data.

together by an extensive communications system and united by a clearly articulated corporate vision.... A networked company is one in which all employees in all parts of the world create, produce and sell the company's products through a carefully cultivated system of interrelationships. [Emphasis added.][17]

Gates and Egelhoff's study of centralization observed that "the global communications systems of MNCs...may be the most important forces shaping the pattern of centralization in MNCs today" and found noticeable differences between European, Japanese, and U.S. multinationals in terms of their use of centralization. They write that "European and UK MNCs tend to decentralize as the relative size of their foreign operations increase, but this tendency was not apparent in U.S. MNCs...[and this might] suggest that large U.S. MNCs with large foreign subsidiaries might be pursuing a more global marketing strategy than other MNCs." Their study examined three major functional areas and examined the degree to which they were handled on a centralized basis: marketing functions, manufacturing functions and financial functions.[18] In another study, Egelhoff used a model of "cybernetic control" and applied it to multinational corporations.[19] He defined cybernetic forms of control: as

---

[17] Fred V. Guterl, "Goodbye, Old Matrix," *Business Month*, February 1989, pp. 32–38.

[18] They found generally that complexity—as measured by foreign product diversity, product modification differences between subsidiaries, extent of outside ownership in foreign subsidiaries, and extent of foreign acquisition—was negatively correlated with centralization in marketing, manufacturing, and finance; in other words, these factors push the firm toward more decentralization. See Stephen R. Gates and William G. Egelhoff, "Centralization in Headquarters-Subsidiary Relationships," *Journal of International Business Studies*, Summer 1986, pp. 71–92.

[19] William G. Egelhoff, "Patterns of Control in U.S., UK, and European Multinational Corporations," *Journal of International Business Studies*, Fall 1984, pp. 73–83. See also William G. Egelhoff, "Strategy and Structure in Multinational Corporations: A Revision of the Stopford and Wells Model," *Strategic Management Journal*, 9 (1988), pp. 1–14. Here Engelhoff analyzes five types of organizational structures of the multinational corporation: international divisions, area divisions, product divisions, product divisions/area divisions matrix structures, and product divisions/area divisions mixed structures. He added a third contingency variable to the Stopford and Wells model, producing a model incorporating level of foreign product diversity, percentage of foreign sales (the Stopford and Wells variables), and percentage of foreign manufacturing (which Engelhoff argues must be added as a third improtant variable). Stopford and Wells argued that as the multinational corporation expands abroad, it progresses from the use of autonomous subsidiaries to an international division structure and finally to a global structure (p. 28). Their analysis discussed how two key variables, foreign sales as a percentage of total sales and foreign product diversity, influences the organizational structures developed by the multinational corporation. They show how the development of a firm can take two paths, which they label α and β. The α type multinational moves toward a form of organization based on worldwide product divisions as the number of products diversify and sales increase. The β type firm, however, moves toward the use of an area division structure as the amount of foreign sales increases but product diversity stays low (p. 65). See John M. Stopford and Louis T. Wells, Jr., *Managing the Multinational Enterprise: Organization of the Firm and Ownership of the Subsidiaries* (New York: Basic Books, 1972).

follows: "The general model of cybernetic control contains 3 basic elements: (1) a measuring unit which monitors some activity or output; (2) a comparing unit which evaluates and compares the measurements against some standard; and (3) an intervening unit, which provides feedback, when necessary, to adjust the activity or process producing the outputs." His results uncovered a strong contrast between European and American multinational corporations in the way they are controlled:

> Control in U.S. MNCs tends to measure more quantifiable and objective aspects of a foreign subsidiary and its environment, whereas control in European MNCs tends to measure more qualitative aspects.... Control in U.S. MNCs requires more precise plans and budgets to generate suitable standards for comparison. Control in European MNCs... requires a higher level of company-wide understanding and agreement about what constitutes appropriate behavior and how such behavior supports the goals of the subsidiary and parent.... Control in U.S. MNCs requires larger central staffs and *more centralized information processing* capacity to make the necessary comparisons and generate the necessary feedback. Control in European MNCs requires a larger cadre of capable expatriate managers, who are willing to spend long periods of time abroad.... Control in European MNCs requires more decentralization of operating decisions than does control in U.S. MNCs... [and] favors short vertical spans or reporting channels from the foreign subsidiary to responsible positions in the parent. [Emphasis added.]

The role of the regional office of the multinational is seen by Grosse as very closely related to the need to "improve the functioning of the firm's internal market for information flows between the region and the home office" so that they can "serve as a conduit of information from customers/suppliers in the region to the home office."[20] Thus the regional headquarters is a type of information machine helping to manage the information processing of the multinational as a whole.

Priel distinguishes five aspects of communications between headquarters and subsidiaries, including content (depends on problems), texture (depends on personalities), procedures (depends on means used), direction (depends on relationships), and timing (depends on processing rate). He notes:

> It is often mistakenly asserted that the most important function of communications is controls. This misunderstanding stems from the fact that conveying information is often confused with the exercise of controls. Although information may trigger off controls, it is not a prerequisite to that effect. Control may be exercised through detailed planning and by establishing check-points and benchmarks in advance. However, feedback is required to ascertain whether controls are effective,... and this is where communications apply.... Objectives must be *cor-*

---

[20] Robert E. Grosse, "Regional Offices in Multinational Firms," in Alan M. Rugman, ed., *New Theories of the Multinational Enterprise* (New York: St. Martin's Press, 1982).

related, functions must *collaborate* and activities must be *coordinated*. Finally, people must be led to *cooperate*.[21]

Schollmanner points out the disadvantages of "an organization structure based on splitting domestic and international operations" including "failing to preserve a high degree of organizational cohesiveness...which can lead to fragmentation of the planning effort, intracompany politicking, interdivisional strains and...coordination difficulties." His research indicated that the data "refutes the idea that with an increasing magnitude of the international business activities a firm would shift its organizational structure from a domestic orientation to an international division approach and, finally, to a global approach." He emphasized the need for top management to "institute a uniform information system." His analysis led him to conclude that "there is little evidence that a global orientation to the design of a multinational firm's organization structure is superior to the international division concept or vice versa."[22]

Alpinder traces the balance between centralization and decentralization in a multinational over time as it proceeds through the stages of internationalization proposed by Franko: (1) export, (2) initial manufacture, (3) foreign growth, (4) foreign maturity, (5) stable growth, and (6) political and competitive threat. Alpinder finds that "at the early stages of foreign growth, an international division seems to be the prevailing form of organizational structure" and that the use of the "world-wide product division" form "is characteristically found in MNCs at the height of overseas growth, slightly before foreign maturity is attained." He argues that the product division form "offers a means for an effective flow of product knowledge and market information throughout product divisions" and that the "combined geographic-international structure... is representative of organizations that have mature and standardized product lines for which marketing rather than production or technology is the critical variable." According to his data, "67 per cent of the firms do not practice a management philosophy advocating extreme centralization or decentralization of decision making." His measurements of "corporate involvement in design and provision of operating and auxiliary functions" revealed that for data processing, approximately 50 percent showed high involvement of corporate headquarters. In terms of control and supervision, his data revealed somewhat of a bias toward centralization. He is able to show the change in the balance between centralization and decentralization as the multinational grows:

---

[21] Victor Z. Priel, "Some Management Apsects of Multinational Companies," 1974/4-5, pp. 45–68.

[22] Hans Schollhammer, "Organization Structures of Multinational Corporations," *Academy of Management Journal*, September 1971, pp. 345–365. His study examined the organization relationships between corporate executives and the general managers of overseas operating units in multinational corporations. His variables included both single and multiple reporting relationships with direct line authority, nominal line authority, and coordinative authority.

As the MNC transverses the continuum from low to high centralization, the provision of certain staff services diminishes and then advances... as MNCs increase the number of their foreign subsidiaries, they may adopt a more centralized management system. When this occurs, management is pulled from functional areas such as employee relations and is transferred to other areas in response to initial corporate expansion needs. However, as growth continues, more personnel are hired to fill the functional areas that were originally depleted. The corresponding rise in (centralized control) occurs as these functions are returned to the general framework of corporate staff services.[23]

Doz and Prahalad emphasize the importance of information flows throughout the multinational corporation as one of the "3 closely interrelated tasks" needed for maintaining a balance between effective strategic decisionmaking and responsiveness to local (i.e, host country) conditions.[24] They note:

> The purpose of data management tools is to control which information is gathered systematically by the members of the organization; how such information is aggregated, analyzed, and given a meaning; how, in which form, and to whom it circulates; and how it is used in major decisions. *Data management tools would, therefore, include not only information systems, but also measurement systems, strategic planning processes and resource allocation procedures....* To support both responsiveness and integration perspectives, information systems have to create a dual focus; accounting data, as well as strategic data, must be aggregated both by country and by product (or activity) to allow to bundle and unbundle activities for analytical purposes and to support both the perspective of integration (a portfolio of countries within a business) and that of responsiveness (a portfolio of businesses within a country). [Emphasis added.]

For an example of how an X.25 network was used to link together IBM 3090s at headquarters in the United Kingdom with international distributors in the heavy equipment and tractor industry, see an examination of Variety Corporation.[25]

The leading thinkers in the academic world about global strategic control in the multinational corporation have recognized the role played by informa-

---

[23] Guvenc G. Alpander, "Multinational Corporations: Homebase-Affiliate Relations," *California Management Review*, XX (3), Spring 1978, pp. 47–56.

[24] The other two tasks are "creating the conditions for a consensus among key managers on important decisions" and "managing relative power among managers." See Yves Doz and C. K. Prahalad, "Patterns of Strategic Control within Multinational Corporations," *Journal of International Business Studies*, Fall 1984, pp. 55–72.

[25] The study is found in Paul Korzeniowski, "X.25 Connections: Variety Satisfied with INS Board," *Network World*, 4 (12), March 23, 1987, pp. 17–18. Since the firms were using SNA in an IBM environment, one would normally expect that leased lines would be used, at least in the mid- to late-1980s. Although X.25 networks are sufficient, they are clearly less efficient in terms of data communications than direct leased lines. From the UK headquarters, the system was intended to link together 35 distributors. For another discussion of the advantages of X.25, including the fact that it may be considerably more easy to implement with the PTTs in Europe, see Dave Weatherby, "Worldwide VANs," *Systems International*, 14 (12), December 1986, pp. 73–74.

tion technology. The information infrastructure of the multinational provides the nervous system through which reports from subsidiaries are transmitted to headquarters, and through which commands are sent back out into the field by the headquarters. There are, of course, many informal means of communication, particularly between the top layers of management in the multinational, but this is increasingly being absorbed by the newer technologies of the information-technology system.

In the following example of a large information system used to coordinate the activities of one of the world's largest automobile manufacturing companies, many of the ideas expressed by academic researchers are put into practice.

FORD MOTOR COMPANY AND THE "WORLD CAR"

Ford is one of the "Big Three" automobile manufacturers in the United States. Like most folklore in the U.S. automobile industry, the relevant terms and categories changed rapidly during the 1980s. The "Big Three" are no longer the "Big Three," as competition from Japan has accelerated the hollowing out of the automobile manufacturing base in the United States. Although American manufacturers have held on to some of their market share, when Asian-produced automobiles marketed domestically under the U.S. company's logo are taken into consideration, this hollowing is even more pronounced. Much of the once-proud U.S. automobile industry is becoming a marketing and distribution channel for Asian manufacturers.

This has placed tremendous strain on U.S. producers to reduce costs, increase innovation, and shrink the new car development and introduction product cycle. As a company that had to respond to these pressures, Ford developed the "world car" in the 1980s. The "world car" concept involves an attempt to make a car that, with small modification, will sell in many different national markets of the world. The world car is produced using the cheapest components available, regardless of their sourcing.[26]

> It is not possible...to evaluate the cost savings implicit in the use of these highly automated, capital-intensive techniques, nor to assess whether they would render uneconomical existing assembly-line technologies in the developing countries. ...These new techniques further increase the economies of scale inherent in automotive manufacturing, and they thereby force manufacturers to expand the markets for each model and/or major part and component. One major consequence of this development has been the production of the so-called world car. This is a basic vehicle which incorporates all the innovations mentioned above

---

[26]UNCTC, *Transnational Corporations in the International Auto Industry* (New York: United Nations, 1983), pp. 23–24. The report mentions the high costs of creating a new car: "Ford's new Escort world car...cost $US 3 billion to develop and launch; British Leyland's "metro" cost $650 million; General Motor's X-cars cost $2.5 billion and its J-cars $5 billion."

and is produced for world markets. It is slightly adapted to local conditions and it uses common components which can be produced on massive scales in different plants.... For most firms it is likely that manufacturing operations will be spread globally.

This accomplishes some important objectives for the manufacturer: It drives down the cost of manufacturing the car and it reduces the number of components worldwide through standardization, thus lowering the need for different parts stores in different countries.

Ford is continuing to move toward the capability to perform basic product development on a worldwide basis. This strategy is based on standardization of mainstream products. For example, Ford has taken steps to reduce the 10 versions of a 4-cylinder engine it manufacturers in different locations around the world to 2 versions. It has made a platform world car of its Tempo-Topaz group. In the future, it can do the same with its Taurus-Sable-Granada platform and with the many versions of its 6-cylinder engines it now produces worldwide.

The benefits from this type of strategy are clear. The use of worldwide sourcing allows Ford to conduct purchasing on a worldwide basis. This effectively increases the amount of competition among subcontractors and allows Ford to drive down supplier costs. In addition, engineering and testing can be concentrated into fewer locations through creation of "centers of excellence." The corporate simplification that results from these strategies helps Ford reduce the product cycle (there are fewer national variations to cope with).

Although Ford corporate strategists have studied the idea of global manufacturing strategies—producing different parts of the car in different areas of the world—this is still in the raw feasibility stage. The sales function appears to resist a change to a worldwide basis.

There are both advantages and disadvantages to this type of international strategy on the part of Ford. There are clear advantages in the way of cost efficiencies available through the type of costcutting and economy measures made possible by global rationalization of various functions, such as design. Why design a part 10 times in 10 different countries when a part satisfying the needs of all locations could be collaboratively designed *only once* in a single location? The disadvantage to this type of arrangement is that in striving to produce a single "world car," the company may ignore local variations needed for different national markets. This could ultimately hurt sales.[27]

---

[27] Some have argued that the Japanese manufacturing firms are moving in the other direction. That is, they are moving toward the ability to customize their cars to an even greater extent for each national market they are attempting to sell into. In a sense, this ability for customization of small manufacturing runs in order to be able to address the peculiarities of each national market might represent the "ultimate" in flexible manufacturing systems. See Alan Altshuler et al., *The Future of the Automobile: The Report of MIT's International Automobile Program* (Cambridge: MIT Press, 1984). See also any work by Cusumano, who has concentrated on understanding Japanese manufacturing techniques, particularly in the use of software.

Implication for Informations Systems Strategy

The information systems function at Ford has approximately 6,000 people worldwide. As Ford has moved toward a strategy of globalization, the IS department has responded with new strategies of its own. It is clear, however, that IS is *not* leading the global strategy of Ford; rather, IS is responding to a strategy that has been determined *elsewhere* within the corporation.[28]

In terms of the strategy to rationalize the design and engineering of new automobiles, the Ford IS team has tried to "get out in front of the global programs." For example, it has developed a second data communications network dedicated to the linking of computer-aided design (CAD) workstations and tools worldwide. This network runs parallel to the regular data communications network, which is used for regular applications in the different data centers around the world. The IS management at Ford considers it a very important move to take a lead role in linking the CAD workstations, since this is in clear support of the geographically decentralized but rationalized design and engineering strategy adopted by the leadership in the corporation.

Ford faces several challenges in attempting to rationalize its international information-technology infrastructure. Although it is crucial that changes be made, according to IS management, these changes will be "evolutionary and not revolutionary." The IS management also appears to value a management-by-consensus approach to high-level strategic planning for information technology. Although it is clearly important to make quick progress on the various "global" inititiatives under way, the IS management team at headquarters strives for common agreement on the direction to take in attempting to develop the global economies of scale in data processing that are so essential. For example, when making decisions about adoption of common systems versus promoting the unique character of a "local" system, Ford places the "burden of proof" on the local side. Unless a convincing case is made for maintaining or building in system uniqueness, the pressures for standardization are high.

---

[28] For a study of the information system in a small European car manufacturer, Volvo, see John Lamb, "Volvo's Net Gains," *Datamation,* International Edition, 33 (19), October 1, 1987, pp. 76 (1)–76 (9). Lamb reports that Volvo relies on overseas sales for 85% of its income. Its data processing operates in an SNA environment with 25 mainframes linking more than 20,000 terminals located in 10 different data centers. Volvo uses more than 500 private leased lines for this network. Volvo also uses DEC equipment and has approximately 200 VAX processors with about 3,000 workstations. The communications part of this organization is run by a 10–person network board, which sets policy and makes decisions. More details of the Volvo system are found in Rob Wyder, "Volvo Finds VTAM to Be the Key to Its In-House Electronic Mail," *Data Communications,* 15 (10), September 1986, pp. 193–199. The electronic mail system operates at about 350,000 transactions per day as of 1986, with approximately 15,000 users. Data transmission is over 9.6 kbps and 14.4 kbps lines. Volvo uses Memo software for its electronic mail system.

At this time, Ford has avoided adopting a common processing strategy for all of its applications.[29] For example, Ford has decided to create a worldwide supplier database, with the objective of giving top-level management the ability to "comparison-shop" for components around the world. For example, a carburetor produced in Korea might be compared with one produced in Mexico, in Western Europe, or in some other location. This type of comparison shopping done on a regular basis for every possible sourcing decision clearly entails a great potential for savings by Ford, given the volume of manufacturing.[30]

Of particular interest is that Ford has decided *not* to "globalize" either order-processing or dealer systems. For the dealer systems, there is a clear logic in this decision. The sharing of information among local dealers on a global scale is probably not enough to justify building a worldwide system. In terms of the order-processing systems, the picture is not so clear. Particularly in companies that have very large spare parts operations, a highly centralized solution is sometimes preferable. If, for example, a centralized order-processing system were combined with a centralized inventory control system, the result would be a great deal of potential synergy. As Ford moves more and more toward its concept of a global car for a global market, there may be pressures to change the order-processing system. The view of IS management is that this is a "long-term" issue.

In their study of the automobile industry, Kaplinsky and Hoffman estimated that centralization would result in a 50 percent reduction in work in process for machined parts, with inventory being cut from 120 days to 40 days in a European company. Their estimates were similar for other parts of the automobile industry: inventory reductions of 72 percent for transmission cases, 98 percent for machined parts, 60 percent for shafts, and 40 percent for cams; a reduction of 70 percent in work in process for brake shoes, 80 percent for clutches, and 40 percent for transmissions; and a cut from 1 month down to 1 day for seats.[31] Such changes, driven by information technology, may be the only hope for a company suffering from the Japanese attack.

---

[29] It is interesting that the global corporate strategy does not appear to imply that the information technology strategy will also be global. A single strategy at the corporate level appears to break down into many different individual strategies for the IS function as it divides up what to centralize and what to decentralize. This is a fundamental concept.

[30] There is a counter-argument to this: Global sourcing may result in further "hollowing out" of the U.S. industrial plant. It might also be resisted by those economic blocs, such as the European Community, that require certain levels of "local content" (which should be renamed "regional content") to qualify for tax and tariff benefits.

[31] Raphael Kaplinsky and Kurt Hoffman, *Driving Force: The Global Restructuring of Technology, Labor, and Investment in the Automobile and Components Industry* (Boulder, CO: Westview Press, 1988).

In its adoption of an information-technology strategy, Ford IS management has learned some important lessons. They believe that it is critical to get top management to endorse a global strategy and the principles that will guide its implementation. They do however, face a key constraint: The IS group must avoid changing the basic structure of the corporation.

Building the Ford Common Manufacturing System

In its effort to rationalize production on a worldwide basis, Ford is now in the process of placing a common manufacturing system into plants around the world. Various aspects of the international nature of the problem have caused problems for the IS management teams in charge, including physical separation, culture differences, and language differences.

The physical separation of the different plants around the world makes the practical logistics of managing global projects staggering. Travel time can wear down a team, time zone differences make interactive communication and coordination difficult, and it is difficult to get a true vision of the "big picture." In addition, any IS department involved in building international systems must face the inevitable culture and language problems inherent in an international undertaking. Language problems can clearly lead to miscommunication not only of facts, but of subtle signals such as anger, humor, and urgency.

The effect of these factors is to rob Ford IS executives of the ability to reach the quick consensus that might be needed occasionally. The building of consensus is viewed as critical to globalization efforts. In addition, problem identification is important for working out the details of any implementation. According to Ford IS management, "not everyone has the temperament to deal with the unique aspects of global IS management." At Ford, those who cannot work in this environment are moved to other locations, sometimes within the firm.

The Worldwide Engineering Releasing System and the Worldwide Sourcing System and Global Supplier Database

Engineering releases occur when the product or component design department hands over the technical design details to the manufacturing engineers. Although an automobile company changes its models yearly, engineering releases, often involving changes that are invisible to the consumer, occur very frequently, and the automobile manufacturing is improved step by step. The engineering release system is at the core of the product development and innovation cycle for Ford.

Ford's engineering release system was started in 1983 and has taken approximately six years to reach full operation. It is a reasonably large system. For example, in the United States, Europe, and Mexico, approximately 10,000 to 12,000 persons access the system regularly. The database is operated in the United States, which gives the advantage of having only one set of code in a single location. This facilitates updating information, applications development, and maintenance of the database. The engineering release system involved approximately $70 million in investment and a three-year development program. Roll-out was scheduled for 1991.

According to plans, the large core system will be replaced with an infrastructure of six local systems. These systems will interact with the main core system, which will retain its function as home base for the satellite systems. The justification for this lies in the need to handle the creation of global products. These products will be engineered in several different locations, but distribution of the design and engineering specifications will be from the core system. Each of the satellite systems will support on-line capability for users. Additional task forces have been formed to speed development of the project for roll-out, but the project is facing obstacles.

One of the key problems inhibiting full development of a worldwide engineering release system is the need to get agreement from the different parts of the world involved. Developing the convincing arguments needed to produce a consensus concerning the next steps to take in a project can sometimes be difficult. IS is in the center of a complex development and engineering process being coordinated on a worldwide basis. Getting agreement from the different parts of the information systems function is time-consuming and difficult. Why is this the case?

The IS management team believes that one key factor behind this difficulty is the *absence of a worldwide line manager* for engineering. In their opinion, if there were a worldwide line manager who provided support to the IS team, it would be easier to reach the agreement required for faster planning and implementation of the system. Lack of this support makes it more difficult to manage the consensus among the far-flung parts of the information technology function.[32]

The development of the engineering release system has taught IS management at Ford a few important lessons. The most important is that all of the players involved must understand that development of *common systems* is important across the corporation, even when systems in the past have been developed behind national barriers.

Another nagging problem for development of a common international system involves *training of users*. Training has been made many times more

---

[32] This theme surfaced repeatedly throughout the interviews: The geographical distances involved and the clashing cultural characteristics of the players makes it difficult to reach consensus on projects, and this difficulty slows down the development process. It would be an interesting series of studies to measure the development of *essentially equally complex* information-technology projects both within a country and internationally. This type of field study would help isolate the *specifically international factors* hindering development of global systems.

difficult because it must now be done in five languages instead of only one. In this particular effort, the IS team has found it useful to "put the user in charge."[33]

The Worldwide Sourcing System and Global Supplier Database for the Purchasing Function

In the mid-1980s, Ford started in earnest to develop worldwide sourcing for the Tempo-Topaz lines of automobile. This decision by top management was based on considerations other than what the resulting information strategy would be. As a result, the information function was forced to "scramble" to build the system. In the development of the system, "there was no time for the long-term view," according to Ford sources. The objective was to build the system to meet minimal requirements and to be sure that the organization learned from the experience.

As the next generation of the system comes into being, the global supplier database is being developed. The Europeans are taking the lead in the development process.[34] The system will be arranged so that each relevant part of the world has a duplicate copy of the database, with updates done on a frequent, regular basis. Ford sees many potential benefits flowing from this system.

The global supplier database is being implemented in two distinct phases. The first phase will see the integration of information on the production suppliers, those companies and subcontractors directly feeding the manufacturing process. The second phase will see integration of nonproduction suppliers into the system.

The chief benefit of the overall system is the economic advantage of having global sourcing.[35] According to Ford, the system will assist in developing and maintaining world-class quality at the local level. The most serious ob-

---

[33] It could be that this is an abrogation of duty because of the difficulties in coordination of worldwide training. Another explanation is that decentralization of training efforts may allow the specific pedagogical characteristics of each national culture to come to the front, thus enhancing the learning experience. I lean towards the latter hypothesis.

[34] This kind of "lead system," in which lead responsibility is placed in different parts of the IS function depending on which group has knowledge to successfully lead the development effort, has been seen in other multinational corporations. It appears to be one international information-technology strategy that works.

[35] Although it is no doubt possible to estimate the benefits to Ford from utilization of worldwide sourcing, in the end it is difficult to tell whether this will make a difference in the long term viability or profitablity of the company vis-à-vis competition, particularly that from the Far East. However, within the narrow context of cost/benefit analysis, the system appears to offer a substantial advantage in terms of reduction of the competent costs for automobiles.

stacle confronting the Ford IS team has been the reconciliation of business practices among the different parts of the company located in distant parts of the world. The interviews also uncovered some difficulties in showing the benefits to Europeans, but this was not elaborated upon.[36]

It appears that the move toward global systems has made the IS team at Ford aware of the need for *common planning* in building the infrastructure and architecture of their world system. One example of this occurred in the office automation infrastructure. The European operations had standardized on Wang equipment, whereas the U.S. operation had decided around 1985 to standardize on IBM equipment. To consolidate the system into an infrastructure that would operate globally, it was necessary to build bridges between the two types of systems. This has resulted in a significantly higher need for ongoing maintenance and has sacrificed some flexibility of the applications that are available. On the other hand, with the CAD system, there was no preexsiting bias involving two such different vendors. As a result, the IS function came out better in implementation of the global strategy. "We were lucky on CAD," remarked one executive.

SUMMARY

Information technology is used to coordinate the functions of headquarters and subsidiaries. It allows the many types of information flowing from headquarters to the subsidiaries to be controlled and used in the planning process. Also, central deposits of information can be used to keep standardized records. In addition, subsidiary-to-subsidiary information flows are common in worldwide manufacturing enterprises and may also be coordinated through information technology.

The Ford case shows how information technology can help in meeting the needs of global competition. The essetial function of a global information system is to reduce manufacturing costs. Large multinationals in manufacturing must consider the entire world as a single market, subject to variances in different areas of the world. For some purposes, such as engineering designs, a globally centralized application is the best approach. On the other hand, applications used heavily by groups in host countries or in subsidiaries are

---

[36] There were several instances during the course of this research when European attitudes toward information technology were mentioned. A superficial view of the data presented indicates that making the case for improvements in information technology may be far more difficult in Europe than in other parts of the world. This would be another fertile area for comparative research into attitudes toward information technology on the part of business executives in different parts of the world.

best suited for remote rather than central processing. However, some factors stand in the way of global centralization.

The world's telecommunications systems still do not allow the building of globally integrated networks, so many are built separately, on an application-by-application basis. Standardization is a great headache at every level: hardware, software, data elements, procedures, and so on. Moreover, multinationals do not generally have a management structure in place that makes it easy to build efficient global information systems, and forming one may create frustration. Finally, efficient global systems may involve not only internal information, but information related to suppliers and customers, although this has not been frequently mentioned in the business literature.

CHAPTER

7

Corporate Intelligence Systems

With some rather famous exceptions, such as the Bank of Credit and Commerce International (BCCI), all multinational corporations have a headquarters somewhere, the halls of which are populated by the most elite managers, responsible for making decisions that will affect the business as a whole. Like generals in battle, these managers need timely and accurate information to assess how their strategies are working out and to learn about the intentions and actions of their enemies, the competitor companies. An important function of the information system in a multinational is to help supply this information. However, for a large organization this is a difficult task, not unlike true government or military intelligence operations. Information must not only be collected, but it must be accurately processed and transmitted to the right decision maker in order to have maximum impact. Many types of information must be considered — economic, political, environmental. The Merck case concerns the reporting of financial information and the difficulties encountered in setting up an efficient global system.

The literature on corporate intelligence emphasizes the need of the MNC to scan its environment for many types of information that can directly (or indirectly) influence its ability to do business. In addition to "standard" information on market trends and competitors, areas of coverage might include political developments, economic trends, host government policy, security threats (such as terrorism), and general cultural developments. Famous consultants such as Kenichi Ohmae have argued that the revolution in communications technology has made it far easier for the multinational corporation to operate on a global basis and to make decisions based on information from all major markets, giving it the ability to plot a global strategy and simultaneously adjust to local markets.[1]

This line of inquiry relates closely to the considerable body of literature on executive support systems (ESS) and, to a lesser extent, on decision support systems (DSS). The use of DSS to help the multinational corporation choose target countries for marketing, to help in tactical planning, and to aid in implementation of management decisions is discussed by Iyer, who studied the Onan Corporation.[2] The heterogeneous nature of external information raises many important issues concerning how it can be handled through computer systems and how it can be collected (translated), synthesized, and communicated.[3] A related area of inquiry concerns the use of information technology in crisis management situations. Skyrme argues that the key activities that can benefit from the development of a corporate intelligence function include marketing support operations, planning of all types, development of corporate strategy, and development of a deep understanding of the market being served.[4]

Douglas and Wind discuss in great detail why there are a great number of factors making it impracticable to have a globalized marketing strategy that ignores national differences, they discuss the "certain conditions" under which a global strategy may be used. Besides "the existence of a global market

---

[1] "Managing Your Oyster," *Economist*, 313 (7626), October 28, 1989, pp. 78–79. Ohmae, who can always be counted on for a controversial and counter-intuitive answer, argues that the Japanese multinationals may have come closest to perfecting management of global corporations.

[2] Raja K. Iyer, "Information and Modeling Resources for Decision Support in Global Environments," *Information and Management,* 14 (2), February 1988, pp. 67–73. Although this is a relatively small corporation, one assumes that some of the implications should apply to larger multinationals.

[3] See Robin Roberts and Anna Hickling, "Computer Integrated Management?" *Multinational Business,* 2, Summer 1989, pp. 18–25. Their analysis revolves around how the information can help the multinational corporation cope with complex decisions involving multiple countries, markets, business trends, and changes in customer base. The information system must be able to accommodate multiple communications channels within the organization, as well as multiple systems and multiple functional databases, according to the authors.

[4] For a case study development of a corporate intelligence function based on the Porter model of the value chain, see David J. Skyrme, "Developing Successful Marketing Intelligence: A Case Study," *Management Decision,* 28 (1), 1990, pp. 54–61.

segment" and "potential synergies from standardization," they mention the need for "the availability of a communication and distribution infrastructure to deliver the firm's offering to target customers worldwide."[5] For a study of marketing information systems, see McLeod.[6]

Beauvois begins his analysis of the corporate intelligence function with a comparison between government and corporate intelligence:

> Every morning the President reads through a thick sheaf of secret-situation reports prepared by specialists in the State Department, the C.I.A., and other government agencies that give him a summary of the latest political and economic developments the world over.... While the President and his counterparts in London and Paris are studying intelligence reports, the heads of large international corporations... are also studying political, economic, and business information that affects their world operations. Today international intelligence is as essential to international business as it is to governments.[7]

Beauvois warns of the danger of making misinformed decisions—"long-range planning cannot be carried out in the best corporate interest.... Management decisions affecting personnel (fail to recognize) local business practices and ethics"—and then goes on to describe the different types of intelligence that should be collected by the multinational corporation. He includes preparation of background reports, economic intelligence on the "basic strengths and weaknesses of a country's economy" and "analysis of the local business framework... [including] the investment climate... [and] current legislation," political and social intelligence on matters such as "the local political and social climate, the government's policies, and the administrative structure of the country," and analysis of the current situation particularly as regards rapid economic and political change. He recommends the creation of an "intelligence coordinator" within the multinational firm.

---

[5]Susan P. Douglas and Yoram Wind, "The Myth of Globalization," *Columbia Journal of World Business*, Winter 1987, pp. 19–29. They write: "Improvements in telecommunications and in logistical systems have considerably increased capacity to manage operations on a global scale and hence facilitate adoption of global standardization strategies. The spread of telex and FACS (*note:* they are referring to facsimile systems) systems, as well as satellite linkages and international computer linkages, all contribute to the shrinking of distances and facilitate globalization of operations. Similarly, improvements in transportation systems and physical logistics such as containerization and computerized inventory and handling systems have enabled significant cost savings as well as reducing time required to move goods across major distances" (p. 24). They also note the existence of national differences in "the physical and communications infrastructure" that can interfere with having a "global strategy" (p. 25).

[6]Raymond McCleod, Jr. and John C. Rogers, "Marketing Information Systems: Their Current Status in Fortune 1000 Companies," *Journal of Management Information Systems*, I (4), Spring 1985, pp. 57–75.

[7]John J. Beauvois, "International Intelligence for the International Enterprise," *California Management Review*, 1960–1961, pp. 39–46.

Chapter 7 Corporate Intelligence Systems

If we take the definition of intelligence from the *Dictionary of United States Military Terms for Joint Usage,* as quoted by Ransom, and substitute *competitors* for *foreign nations,* then we have a reasonable working definition of corporate intelligence:

> Intelligence: The product resulting from the collection, evaluation, analysis, integration, and interpretation of all available information which concerns one or more aspects of *competitors* or of [their] areas of operations and which is immediately or potentially significant to planning.[8]

It is interesting that Ransom argues that "80 per cent or more of intelligence raw material in peacetime is overtly collected from nonsecret sources such as newspapers, libraries, radio broadcasts, business and industrial reports" (p. 20). This probably means that for a multinational corporation, the vast bulk of corporate intelligence will come from similar sources, and that the use of covert means and "spies" may be even more limited than in the case of national governments. Ransom gives an idea of the tremendous volume of documents that are processed through the information system of the CIA including, in 1960, "thousands of different intelligence documents each week in numbers of copies running into the tens of thousands... [with] newspapers, books, maps... being acquired on the average of 200,000 pieces per month." The information is then added into the computer information system of the CIA.[9] He discusses the role of computerization in the intelligence process:

> The CIA continues to experiment with systems for effective indexing, storing, and retrieving of this mountain of classified information, using punched cards, microphotography, and automated data-processing. Although automation has undoubtedly been incorporated to a degree into the process, an electronic library will be unlikely to serve as a substitute for competent human judgment at many of the crucial steps in the intelligence process. And a pressing problem of more recent years has been that of trying to make the information storage and retrieval systems compatible among the various separate agencies of government.[10]

One of the problems with a corporate intelligence system in an organization as vast as the multinational corporation concerns the sheer amount of

---

[8]See Harry Howe Ransom, *The Intelligence Establishment* (Cambridge, MA: Harvard University Press, 1970), pp. 7–8.

[9]Ransom writes that "the open literature is catalogued and filed centrally in the CIA library according to the Library of Congress classification system. The secret documents go through a different process and constitute a major management problem: their volume fluctuates, their formats vary enormously, their length and quality also vary as does the degree of secrecy to be accorded them" (p. 39).

[10]Ransom also discusses the dangers of having a poor indexing system and the attendant problems in the information retrieval process (pp. 39–40).

information that must be processed. It is not simply a matter of collection. All writers seem to agree that collection is understood, as are the vast amount and high variety of information that must be covered. The analysis of intelligence is another problem, and that too is discussed. But what about *distribution* of the intelligence and its *integration into decision making in the appropriate place within the multinational?* Surely it is not simply a question of collecting all of the information at the center (headquarters) of the multinational and making decisions in a single location. Rather, the intelligence must be channeled to the appropriate place within the vast superstructure of the multinational where the decisions are made. An approach to this problem is found in Kilmann and Ghymn in their proposal for a "strategic intelligence system," abbreviated SIS, which is based on the use of their "multivariate analysis, participation, and structure" (MAPS) methodology. This methodology, which relies on a series of detailed regressions, analyzes the relationship between the incoming information and the structures of the subunits of the multinational and the tasks (decisions) of the different managers. Application of this methodology helps the multinational become an "organic organization" better able to cope with the ambiguities and uncertainties of its environment.[11] Contractor (1986, p. 84) lists the many considerations at the host-country level that face a multinational doing business in the country. He mentions "economic nationalism, protectionism, transport costs, local culture, local standards, and entrenched domestic firms."

Attanasio sees competitive intelligence as "a formal information system that allows management to make informed decisions in satisfying the rivalry for consumer patronage. [It] formalizes information for tactical and strategic management." He argues that it is most likely to be used by "operational managers of various disciplines."[12]

Ghoshal and Kim argue that "environmental intelligence is rapidly becoming a major source of competitive advantage in an era of global competition among firms that are increasingly similar in technological and managerial competencies and in the size and scope of their operations." They discuss the many types of information that might serve as sources for "environmental in

---

[11] Ralph H. Kilmann and Kyunjgh-Il Ghymn, "The MAPS Design Technology: Designing Strategic Intelligence Systems for MNCs," *Columbia Journal of World Business,* Summer 1976, pp. 35–47.

[12] Dominick B. Attanasio, "The Multiple Benefits of Competitor Intelligence," *Journal of Business Strategy,* May/June 1988, pp. 16–19. He describes the object of competitor intelligence: "The prime objectives of competitive intelligence are (1) identifying a direct competitor's weaknesses and, thereby, providing possible new market share opportunities; (2) anticipating a competitor's market thrusts; and (3) reacting more quickly and effectively to changes in the market itself" (p. 16).

formation." They lament that "business intelligence... is rarely used for actual decision making," although they present a very limited amount of information to substantiate this point.[13] Hamel and Prahalad also call for development of "a competitor focus at every level through widespread use of competitive intelligence."[14]

A former intelligence official writing about corporate intelligence systems describes the "intelligence cycle" as consisting of forms of "three basic operations: (1) collecting and reporting; (2) information processing and dissemination; and (3) intelligence analysis and forecasting." It is observed that "for the most part, U.S. industry has not committed itself to the development and use of business intelligence systems." Herring argues that "corporations worldwide are looking for new ways to achieve a competitive advantage and to counter aggressive domestic and foreign competition. By creating and then using a modern business intelligence system, corporations can accomplish those objectives."[15]

Hout, Porter, and Rudden in their study of global multinationals make a few observations regarding organizational structures. They note that "no one organization structure applies to all of a company's international businesses... [as] organizational reporting lines should probably differ by country market depending on that market's role." They believe that "organizational reporting lines and structures should change as the nature of the international business

---

[13]Sumantra Ghoshal and Seok Ki Kim, "Building Effective Intelligence Systems for Competitive Advantage," *Sloan Management Review*, Fall 1986, pp. 49–58. The article also hits on consultants: "Even consultants, though many exist to provide such information, are not very effective since they generally provide information that is stale and inappropriate for immediate business purposes." The writers also present some puzzling statements such as "external intelligence becomes most effective when it becomes a widely shared organizational Gestalt." In addition, there is virtually no discussion of the information-technology systems that support this creation of useful information. However, the article makes a solid point about the need to examine how much information is used and its relationship to decision making.

[14]See p. 67 in Gary Hamel and C. K. Prahalad, "Strategic Intent," *Harvard Business Review*, May–June 1989, pp. 63–76. They call for the following actions: "Create a sense of urgency,... develop a competitor focus at every level through widespread use of competitive intelligence,... provide employees with the skills they need to work effectively,... give the organization time to digest one challenge before launching another,... establish clear milestones and review mechanisms" (pp. 67–68). They provide several case studies of Japanese companies.

[15]Jan P. Herring, "Building a Business Intelligence System," *Journal of Business Strategy*, May/June 1988, pp. 4–9. He discusses a wide range of classes of information, including "markets and customers; industry structure and trends; political, economic, and social forces; competitor capabilities, plans, and intentions; corporate security threats; and technology developments and sources" (p. 8). For a look at government intelligence, see Lyman B. Kirkpatrick, Jr., *The U.S. Intelligence Community: Foreign Policy and Domestic Activities* (Boulder, CO: Westview Press, 1977).

changes...[so that] when a business becomes global, the emphasis should shift toward centralization."[16]

Richelson distinguishes five steps in the intelligence cycle: (1) planning and direction, (2) collection, (3) processing, (4) production and analysis, and (5) dissemination. He presents a detailed description of the problem in 'managing information access and analysis." He describes the entire classification system, which by no means would be practical for use in any but the very largest multinational corporations, and then only in a considerably shortened form.[17]

Rugman's analysis of how a multinational uses information and how it must change to cope with new incoming information concludes:

> The strategies required for success in a changing international environment all require that the MNE cope with the costs of information about key environmental factors such as political risk, foreign exchange risk, government policy changes, and so on. The successful MNE has an excellent information appraisal and planning system that allows it to make scientific predictions about the influence of changes in environmental factors on its operations.[18]

Rugman believes that only with correct handling of information internally can the multinational take advantage of the firm-specific advantages in the markets in which it is operating, including the use of information in negotiations with host governments.

Using the analysis provided by Ransom concerning U.S. intelligence community, we can distinguish three types of intelligence that might be used by

---

[16] Thomas Hout, Michael E. Porter, and Eileen Rudden, "How Global Companies Win Out," *Harvard Business Review,* September–October 1982, pp. 98–108.

[17] Jeffry Richelson, *The U.S. Intelligence Community*, 2d ed. (Cambridge, MA: Ballinger, 1984). This study contains a very detailed examination of the way intelligence works within the U.S. intelligence community.

[18] Alan M. Rugman, "Multinationals and Global Competitive Strategy," *International Studies of Man & Organizations*, XV (2), pp. 8–18. In an extensive study of the role of information, he discusses the types of information used in the information system: "In addition to head-office forecasting of political and country risk, constant monitoring of the host-nation environment of subsidiary managers can provide vital information and help in appropriate revision of corporate strategy. The internal market of the MNE can be reversed, that is, information can also flow from the subsidiaries to the parent company, where strategic planning is undertaken....Both environmental and internal variables [must be considered].... The environmental variables consist of the economic, political, cultural, and social factors relevant in both the home and host nations served by the MNE." He notes that "the managers of the internal communications network of the MNE must screen out superfluous environmental information from its monitoring agencies and be competent enough to extract all relevant changes, spot key trends, and advise on new opportunities as they arise." (Compare Herring's analysis of the intelligence cycle.) The only key shortcoming of the analysis is the Rugman has no indication about the type of information technology used in this type of corporate system. However, his analysis can be extended to provide a powerful framework for analyzing information technology utilization (pp. 17–18).

Chapter 7 Corporate Intelligence Systems

the multinational corporation: (1) strategic intelligence, (2) tactical or operational intelligence, and (3) counterintelligence.[19] Roughly speaking, strategic intelligence is analogous to the "environmental scanning" described by Kim and Ghoshal and would involve a large amount of external information. Tactical or operational intelligence is analogous to careful analysis of internal information within the multinational. Counterintelligence operations are related to a type of security strategy in which the multinational acts to protect its trade secrets from falling into "enemy" (i.e., competitor) hands. Ransom's analysis of the intelligence process includes several steps: collection, evaluation and production, and dissemination. Ransom's work is still relevant today, since few multinationals appear to have corporate intelligence systems much more advanced than what the U.S. government had in the early postwar period.

One of the most computationally intensive techniques of analyzing external information is content analysis. Heuer discusses the concepts of content analysis as applied to intelligence examination of foreign political leaderships. This type of analysis might be used in assessing the political environment of the multinational corporation, although host government reactions and signals in most countries of the world may be much clearer than the Kremlinology problem described by Heuer.[20] Maintenance of an "events data base for analysis of transnational terrorism" is described by Mickolus.[21]

Hilsman distinguishes three types of intelligence—intelligence as information, "intelligence as knowledge," and "intelligence as organization"—and

---

[19] Harry Howe Ransom, "Central Intelligence and National Security" (Cambridge, MA: Harvard University Press, 1959), pp. 12–13. He was writing before the time of major impact of the computer, and it is interesting to note his concern with the "indexing" problems in keeping track of the information collected. Kirkpatrick notes that the United States has had a national intelligence system only since 1947. See Lyman B. Kirkpatrick, Jr., *The Real CIA* (New York: Macmillan, 1968). An interesting look at early developments is found in Rhodri Jeffreys-Jones, *American Espionage: From Secret Service to CIA* (New York: Free Press, 1977). A discussion of "communications intercept," "electronic intelligence" (ELINT), "radars for intelligence collection" (RADINT), "nuclear-test-detection methods," and "photoreconnaissance" is found in Herbert Scoville, Jr., "The Role of Technology in Covert Intelligence Collection," in Robert L. Brorsage and John Marks, eds., *The CIA File* (New York: Grossman, 1976), pp. 109–124. For a developing-country view, see David W. Conde, *CIA: Core of the Cancer* (New Delhi: Entente Private Limited, 1970). For an interesting look at early Europe and the United States in revolutionary times fighting against the British, see Monro MacCloskey, *The American Intelligence Community* (New York: Richards Rosen Press, 1967).

[20] Richards J. Heuer, Jr., "Content Analysis: Measuring Support for Brezhnev," in Richards J. Heuer, Jr., ed., *Quantitative Approaches to Political Intelligence: The CIA Experience* (Boulder, CO: Westview Press, 1978).

[21] Edward F. Mickolus, "An Events Data Base for Analysis of Transnational Terrorism," in Richards J. Heuer, Jr., ed., *Quantitative Approaches to Political Intelligence: The CIA Experience* (Boulder, CO: Westview Press, 1978).

discusses each within the context of the foreign policy establishment of the U.S. government.[22] However, his analysis can be directly applied to today's multinational, which faces the same challenges in handling its information about the competitive environment.

The need for flexibility in the information systems of a multinational seems to increase for financial and accounting control systems as the complexity of the organization increases.[23] This can be inferred from Brownell's study of Australian subsidiaries of U.S. companies and their "environmental complexity and dynamics."

> In a world of perfect information, there would be no uncertainties about the present and future intentions, capabilities, and activities of *your competitors*. Information, however, is bound to be imperfect for the most part. Consequently, the *corporate intelligence function* can at best reduce the uncertainties and construct plausible hypotheses about these factors on the basis of what continues to be partial and often conflicting evidence. [Emphasis added.][24]

There is no doubt, however, that intelligence is turning into an information-technology-intensive form of activity. According to Robert Butterworth, "Analysis will benefit from new techniques for mathematical inference, more flexible computerized aids for exploring hypotheses and patterns, more

---

[22] Roger Hilsman, "Intelligence through the Eyes of the Policy Maker" in *Surveillance and Espionage in a Free Society* (New York: Praeger, 1972), pp. 163–177. For a racy look at the role of intelligence in creating a so-called invisible government, see David Wise and Thomas B. Ross, *The Invisible Government* (New York: Random House, 1964). Wise and Ross never seem able to explain why the intelligence community working underneath the executive branch is somehow illegitimate. Their discussion that it forms an "invisible government" that "is shaping the lives of 190,000,000 Americans" is a bit shrill.

[23] Some organizations with limited geographical activities can, however, use a narrower band of software. For an example, in accounting software used where markets have similar accounting procedures, see "The Solution from Down Under," *Management Accounting*, 69 (4), April 1991, p. 52. The article refers to a software package called *Solutions 6*. Some have argued that many of the software houses are not acting quickly enough to create multicurrency software packages for use in the post-1992 European environment. There is a misconception that since most firms operate from the United Kingdom, there is need for software that is adequate for that environment and nowhere else. See Adele Ward, "Practice Management: Geared up for 1992?" *Accountancy*, 107 (1171), March 1991, pp. 119–120. The key factors for such software seems to be multiple languages, multiple currency capabilities, ability to meet different international financial regulations, and ability to create a great variety of different reports that might need to be generated in different national environments. The pressures for 1992 seem likely to force many multinational firms to move towards a single accounting and financial system for their organizations (if they have not done so already). See Candice Goodwin, "Financial Software: Some Hard Choices," *Accountancy*, 107 (1171), March 1991, pp. 114–118.

[24] Peter Brownell, "The Role of Accounting Information, Environment and Management Control in Multi-National Organizations," *Accounting and Finance*, May 1987, pp. 1–16.

interpretive guidance from visitors and émigrés, and new analysts trained by those who produced the critical insights of the past."[25]

Yoshino distinguishes several types of information that help the multinational control its global operations, including "environmental data (political, social, and economic), competitive data (real and potential), and internal operating data (both quantitative and qualitative)" and warns that "it is dangerous to delegate overall intelligence functions solely to foreign affiliates." He concludes that "the most challenging area in designing an international intelligence system lies in analysis of data by headquarters staff for effective control and planning."[26]

Fannin and Rodrigues distinguish three types of multinational approaches, "home market oriented," "multi-domestic," and "global"—and discuss the role of information control. They point out a weakness in the information control of the multi-domestic organization:

> Information about the multinational environment tends to be the result of adding together information collected by individual market units on their national markets. Such an information system does not look at the "global environment" created by the transfer of resources across national borders. Opportunities and threats arising from these environments may be missed by the process of monitoring domestic environments unless a special monitoring unit is established at the corporate headquarters.[27]

They recommend the creation of a "dual monitoring strategy where detailed analysis is made of both the global market and individual national markets," the creation of "corporate task forces," and the "development of organizational flexibility... to share information."

Bates warns that "if today's business enterprise is to perform successfully in this environment they must be cognizant of what changes in their organization are required and how to make decisions based on broader, perhaps less reliable, but substantially more information in ways that are useful, workable, and not overly expensive considering the value of the output."[28]

In his discussion of different planning approaches, Schollhammer observes that "planning in a multinational corporation is inherently decentralized." His analysis indicates that strategic corporate planning should be tightly integrated with the information system of the multinational corporation:

---

[25] Robert Butterworth, "Collection," in Roy Godson, ed., *Intelligence Requirements for the 1990s: Collection, Analysis, Counterintelligence, and Covert Action* (Lexington, MA: Lexington Books, 1989), pp. 31–42.

[26] M. Y. Yoshino, "Toward a Concept of Managerial Control for a World Enterprise," *Michigan Business Review*, XVIII (2), pp. 25–31.

[27] William R. Fannin and Arvin F. Rodrigues, "National or Global? Control vs. Flexibility," *Long Range Planning*, 19 (5), 1986, pp. 84–88.

[28] Thomas H. Bates, "Management and the Multinational Business Environment," *California Management Review*, XV (3), Spring 1973, pp. 37–45.

> Planning must be used as a strategy...to create a framework for a communications system which insures that all parts of the organization are striving towards the same set of over-all objectives and in their pursuit are using policies which are beneficial for the corporation as a whole rather than individual parts of it.... In view of the recognized need for intimate knowledge of the local environmental conditions, the bottom-up planning cycle requires that the long-range local objectives and related plans be first established by the individual operating units.... These plans gradually filter upward in the organizational hierarchy; each high level makes its plans based on all levels under it until the combined intelligence becomes the input for formulating the objectives.[29]

His analysis of the types of variables that must be considered in the intelligence collection and analysis cycle includes country-related variables, product-related characteristics, and company-related variables.

In his extensive analysis of corporate intelligence systems in multinational corporations, Alex Murray identified several key types of information that should be collected and analyzed to help in the decision process. These included legal, cultural, political, market structure, and economic information. According to Murray, these types of information can be used to assist several managerial functions, including planning, organizing, staffing, motivating, control, and communications. In addition, each of these factors should be considered separately within the major functional divisions of the multinational, including manufacturing, sales, finance, and organization. The multinational corporation "usually requires global information...[on] scientific topics, market opportunities, financial considerations, and environmental risks." Murray's analysis also confirmed what might be called the "classic" problem in intelligence—how to summarize and synthesize the massive amounts of data collected into meaningful information for high-level decision making. He writes:

> The value of information was usually found to be inversely correlated with quantity. Information processing concerns itself primarily with information refinement and reduction. In the international companies surveyed the information hierarchy roughly corresponds to their organizational hierarchy, and as information is directed towards the top echelons it is quantitatively reduced. It should be mentioned, however, that many executives felt that it was not always qualitatively upgraded for decision-making purposes.[30]

---

[29] Hans Schollhammer, "Long-Range Planning in Multinational Firms," *Columbia Journal of World Business*, September–October 1971, pp. 79–86.

[30] Alex J. Murray, "Intelligence Systems of the MNCs," *Columbia Journal of World Business*, September–October 1972, pp. 63–71. "Telex and telephone services are increasingly being used ... The technology utilized by different international companies to disseminate, store and retrieve information varies from manual operations to highly sophisticated on-line data devices. These collect and feed itemized inputs directly to processing computers which, in turn, reproduce and forward information to decision centers. The size and international involvement of the user company were the criteria determining the level of organization of their information system."

Chapter 7 Corporate Intelligence Systems   95

Murray also emphasizes the difference between information collected from outside the multinational and information from inside. One interesting observation is that "part of the company information processing functions have been taken over by a number of international intelligence research services."

Keegan analyzed the growing need of the multinational corporation for information about its environment. He distinguishes "human sources" from "documentary sources" and "perception sources," by which he means actual surveillance of foreign sites. He argues that "90 per cent of the information acquired by direct perception of physical phenomena occurs while executives are traveling abroad." A final source of corporate intelligence is "surveillance and search," which is a more concentrated form of environmental scanning that takes place after the multinational has identified specific targets of inquiry upon which to focus. His approach to corporate intelligence emphasizes the human element and careful planning of the information collection process.

> As business organizations spread around the world, the extent and complexity of information essential to their success will grow geometrically. Accelerating the progress of communication technology will be helpful but the essential consideration will be the nature of the intelligence that is transmitted. An orderly and comprehensive flow of information on activities in any part of the world will require the same careful planning as the production, distribution and personal phases of the business.[31]

If Keegan is right that "viewing, monitoring, and investigation, which together generate 96% of the important external information acquired by executives, receive considerably less attention than does research, which generates only 4%," then there seems to be a gross misappropriation of resources in the multinational regarding corporate intelligence functions. In addition, it indicates a lax attitude and very poor discipline regarding the systematic collection of intelligence information.

It is interesting to note that some seasoned observers of the international business scene believe that multinational corporations have been used by

---

[31] Warren J. Keegan, "Acquisition of Global Business Information," *Columbia Journal of World Business*, March–April 1968, pp. 35–41. He says that "human beings (provide) 67% of all important information acquired by the executives [in his survey]. ... Documents are the source of only 27% of the important external information received by executives. The bulk (60%) of these documents are publication and information service reports from outside the company. Letters and reports from inside sources account for the remaining 40%. Direct perception is the source of 6% of the information acquired by executives." In a later article, Keegan discussed the role of information flows and functional control and structure in the multinational corporation. He shows the connections among the headquarters, international division, regional headquarters, and country subsidiaries with their associated functional staff functions at each level, including research and engineering, production, finance, and marketing. See Warren J. Keegan, "A Conceptual Framework for Multinational Marketing," *Columbia Journal of World Business*, November–December 1972, pp. 67–76.

governmental intelligence agencies in the collection of information in foreign environments. Joseph Nye writes: "And there can be little doubt that the U.S. government has on occasion been able to use wittingly and unwittingly, the information-gathering capacities of global corporations domiciled in America for intelligence purposes."[32]

Doz highlights the need for and importance of quality information reaching the top of the managerial hierarchy. He writes in his study of power systems and telecommunications companies:

> The quality of the information that reached the top and the way in which it was used were important for top managers to exercise their choice and rule over differences of opinion in a constructive way. The use of administrative tools by top management can thus be seen largely in terms of gaining the right information and using it for motivating and directing lower-level managers.[33]

Kim examines the role of information-gathering activities of general trading companies within the context of transactions analysis. His analysis led him to conclude that the information systems of the trading companies allow them to act as powerful intermediaries for smaller firms unable to properly process information on an international scale.[34] He emphasizes the critical importance of gathering marketing intelligence and other information in providing this service.

> In the initial stage, trading companies act primarily as purchasing and sales agents. Hence, the development of a suitable marketing information system assumes importance. To develop a sophisticated marketing intelligence network, trading companies should employ people in the field and incorporate state-of-the-art communications. Trading companies that have fine-tuned their skills for the gathering of information about market needs will be able to source and supply the needed goods expeditiously.... [The result is] economies of scale ... in information gathering.

Becker's analysis of the emerging global consumer culture, which is based on immediate availability of information on a worldwide basis with virtually no lag times, raises interesting questions for the multinational.[35] Obviously, if the

---

[32] Joseph S. Nye, Jr., "Multinational Corporations in World Politics," *Foreign Affairs*, pp. 153–175.

[33] Yves L. Doz, *Government Control and Multinational Strategic Management: Power Systems and Telecommunication Equipment* (New York: Praeger, 1979), p. 251. The management pyramid appears on p. 247.

[34] Kim calls this process "transactional intermediation." See W. Chan Kim, "Global Diffusion of the General Trading Company Concept," *Sloan Management Review*, Summer 1986, pp. 35–43. For a study of the development of export trading companies in the United States, see Daniel C. Bello and Nicholas C. Williamson, "The American Export Trading Company: Designing a New International Marketing Institution," *Journal of Marketing*, 49, Fall 1985, pp. 60–69.

[35] Helmut Becker, "Is There a Cosmopolitan Information Seeker?" *Journal of International Business Studies*, September 1976, pp. 77–89.

multinational is to compete successfully in highly consumer-oriented markets, its information-handling process must be very rapid and very flexible in terms of its connections with overseas firms for information reporting purposes.

One example of this type of system is discussed by Mulqueen, who reviews how I.M.S. International uses 16 data-processing centers, accessible through direct dial-up or public packet-switched networks, to collect and analyze international information on 18 different national markets. It provides information on sales of drugs, beauty aids, veterinary products, and livestock and poultry feed. It has 128 kbps satellite linkages between London and Frankfurt, and it also is a large user of T-1 facilities. Its online database service is made available and delivered electronically throughout the world.[36]

When Kennedy went back to reexamine the environmental scanning and intelligence-gathering operations of multinational corporations after the shock of the Iranian revolution, he found that "although there has not been a significant quantitative increase in the rate of institutionalization of external environmental analysis by large U.S. multinational corporations during the last 5 years, qualitative changes are certainly more prevalent. External environmental assessments have a much greater impact on decision making by top management."[37]

Dymsza presents a complex model of global strategic planning in which environmental scanning and intelligence collection provides a key ingredient in "evaluation and projection of national and regional environments."[38] Just as Dymsza's strategic planning process calls for a "periodic revision and recycling

---

[36] John T. Mulqueen, "Research House Crosses Oceans and Continents to Track Drug Sales," *Data Communications*, 17 (6), June 1988, pp. 92–96. The article also notes that many sales representatives of different companies use the database from their own homes via modems. Another interesting problem in decentralization is found in a company that has an essentially distributed and decentralized *headquarters* with fairly tight control over subsidiaries. For a look at Warner Communications, which is split between the East and West coasts, see Rebecca Hurst, "Directing Communications at Warner," *Computerworld*, 21 (36A), September 9, 1987, pp. 41–43. As of 1987, Warner's data-processing budget was approximately $2.23 billion annually. For a study of the decentralized environment of the accounting and consulting firm Peat Marwick Mitchell (PMM), see "Network Unites European Offices," *Systems International*, 15 (6), June 1987, p. 26. PMM uses Wang VS equipment with Wang Office software. Peat Marwick has 36 offices in 14 countries throughout Europe, and its network was linking six of the offices as of 1987. The offices are using the European Client Record Information Service (ECRIS), which is a multinational auditing capability offered to clients. ECRIS is based on software from Computer Automated Business Systems, an Australian software company. The Brussels data center controls the network.

[37] Charles R. Kennedy, Jr., "The External Environment–Strategic Planning Interface: U.S. Multinational Corporate Practices in the 1980s," *Journal of International Business Studies*, Fall 1984, pp. 99–108.

[38] William A. Dymsza, "Global Strategic Planning: A Model and Recent Developments," *Journal of International Business Studies*, Fall 1984, pp. 169–183. He includes several classes of data and information to be collected, including political, economic, sociocultural, regulatory, technological, and business. It is unfortunate that he does not discuss the types of information systems that might be used to deliver this data to its correct location.

of the strategic plan," the model of internationalization proposed by Johanson and Vahlne emphasizes a constant feedback loop between knowledge about the external environment and decisions to continue with expanding international operations of the firm.[39]

One of the dangers of any intelligence system is that it can develop a systematic bias toward prevailing views that becomes hard to change. There is also the continual problem of "imperfect information," as pointed out by Schlesinger.[40] In addition, there is a problem of where to place the monitoring software, as discussed by Kasparek, who was concerned about auditing overseas subsidiaries and how this could be accomplished with computer-assisted audit techniques (CAAT).[41]

The role of information systems in relaying information from the environment to the decision-making complexes of the multinational corporation has been recognized as being very important. No one is able to explain exactly how this can be done, given the great diversity of types of information and the difficulty in channeling it to the correct decision makers, but everyone agrees that it *should* be done. In some ways, corporate intelligence systems may be thought of as miniature versions of government intelligence systems, and unfortunately, they may face some of the same problems: collection of too much information and inability to process it into the clear, concise recommendations for decisions: distortion of data and information; and the creation of institutional biases that might become established and then be undermined at a strategic moment.

---

[39] Jan Johanson and Jan-Erik Vahlne, "The Internationalization Process of the Firm: A Model of Knowledge Development and Increasing Foreign Market Commitments," *Journal of International Business Studies,* September 1977, pp. 23–32.

[40] See comments by James Schlesinger in Tyrus G. Fain, Katharine C. Plant, and Ross Milloy, eds., *The Intelligence Community: History, Organization, and Issues* (New York & London: R. R. Bowker Company, 1977), pp. 45, 251. The report also provides a glossy discussion of the role of information technology in the production of intelligence: "The systems of storage and retrieval developed by OCD (Office of Collection & Dissemination) were unusually effective for that time and the Office began to gain recognition throughout the intelligence community. In 1955, OCD was renamed the Office of Central Reference to more accurately reflect its Agency-wide responsibilities. In 1967, OCR was renamed the Central Reference Service (CRS). Today, CRS can offer intelligence analysts throughout the community some of the most sophisticated information storage and retrieval systems to be found anywhere in the world" (p. 246).

[41] Wolfhart Kasparek, "Applying Computer-Assisted Audit Techniques Overseas," *Internal Auditing,* 3 (2), Fall 1987, pp. 64–68. Kasparek discussed how to locate the auditing software: either keeping it on the mainframe of the facility being audited, setting it up at the auditing office of the nearest subsidiary, or using remote access to the headquarters auditing software via telecommunications linkages. For a look at some of the communications problems associated with auditing in developing countries, with comments on the role of information technology, see Robert G. Gillespie, "Auditing Concerns in Developing Countries," *Internal Auditor,* 45 (5), October 1988, pp. 27–30. Gillespie also discusses the cultural problems involved, particularly as they concern local management in the subsidiary.

MERCK CORPORATION'S INTERNATIONAL FINANCIAL CONSOLIDATION SYSTEM

Merck Corporation is one of the largest and most successful pharmaceutical companies in the world.[42] It has been selected as the "most admired" U.S. corporation several years in a row. Besides making hefty profits, Merck has provided incalculable service to developing countries free of charge. For example, it gives away a drug that stops river blindness, a particularly horrible disease that has plagued sub-Saharan Africa for generations.[43] It is a $5 billion dollar company, number 1 in the world. It has 10 products that each bring in more than $100 million in sales per year, and it has 2 or 3 products that bring in more than $1 billion per year.

Approximately 47 to 52 percent of Merck's sales are overseas, depending on the exchange rate. Approximately 70 percent of these overseas sales are made in Europe (France, England, Italy, Spain, Portugal, and other countries). Its drugs are sold at an approximate 70 percent markup, which is needed to recoup the very high costs of research and development.

As a drug company, Merck faces intense regulation in each market in which it conducts business. Each country has a different and highly restrictive regime for managing the legal drug trade. This regulation has a great impact on the prices that Merck is *allowed* to charge. In many national markets, the largest customer is the national health service, which purchases large amounts of drugs to dispense to patients of the plan. Negotiations with these national health services determine the prices that Merck will charge. The high degree of variability among countries and their markets forces Merck to tailor its business activities to each market. For example, in Europe, Merck has 13 subsidiaries.

This regulatory and business operations structure drives the information technology support system. In the 1990 Computerworld Premier list, Merck was ranked as "the most effective user of information systems" in the drug market. At the time it was reported, Merck had an information systems bud-

---

[42] For a global study of the drug industry, see UNIDO, *Global Study of the Pharmaceutical Industry* (Vienna: United Nations, 1980). For an examination of the role of multinational corporations in the international pharmaceutical industry, particularly as it applies to developing countries, see UNCTC, *Transnational Corporations in the Pharmaceutical Industry of Developing Countries* (New York: United Nations, 1984). The UNCTC report reviews developments in Argentina, Brazil, Columbia, Costa Rica, Egypt, India, Kenya, the Republic of Korea, Malaysia, Mexico, Sierra Leone, and Thailand. It also reviews the various barriers to entry found in many developing countries.

[43] Before Merck's discovery, river blindness was so widespread that it had actually become part of the "culture" of many tribal groups in sub-Saharan Africa (around Niger). The population had become so used to becoming blind at the age of 6 or so that its entire structure was premised on this disease. Merck's drug literally gives sight to millions of people and will awaken to a new and richer life. There is no way to measure the beneficence of this act on the part of Merck.

get of $185 million and was employing approximately 1,000 MIS professionals. Merck is a heavy user of computers in the drug development phase, using them for molecular modeling and crystallography. In 1989–1990, Merck installed an IBM 3090 supercomputer. In the 1980s, Merck had been one of the first companies to equip its sales force with portable personal computers.[44] Merck uses a great deal of automation in its manufacturing. It was reported in 1989 that Merck used an automated line to package 240 bottles per minute for a physician's sample pack of two new drugs in a "one-by-four" packaging designed by Merck.[45]

According to Merck, it has a "United Nations" type of organization in its information systems function: it has separate IS departments in each country. The "United Nations" model refers to a type of multinational organization that has specific replicable units in each country. It is very different from a business in which a single unit or function serves many different countries simultaneously. We see in the case of Merck that although a single organization, perhaps for Europe as a whole, might be more efficient, regulatory structures prevent this from happening. Hout, Porter, and Rudden distinguish what they term a *multidomestic* firm and a *global* firm.[46] They use the term *multidomestic* in the same way Merck uses "United Nations model" and point out that "in *multidomestic* industries a company pursues separate strategies in each of its foreign markets while viewing the competitive challenge independently from market to market... [whereas] a *global* industry... pits one multinational's entire worldwide system of product and market positions against another's." The larger of these departments, or *satellites,* has approximately 40 to 50 MIS professionals.

The financial reporting structures of Merck are tightly controlled. It is one of the most profitable multinational corporations in the world, although it has not formed its own internal bank, as some other multinational corporations

---

[44] For details about the reward, see Glenn Rifkin, "Tight Lips, Laptops and Supers Help Merck Shine," *Computerworld,* section 2, October 8, 1990, pp. 62–63. Another analysis of the Computerworld Premier 100 companies concluded that the "faith" in information systems displayed by the corporation is proportional to its profitability. See Michael Sullivan-Trainor and Joseph Maglitta, "Top IS Users Soar above Tough Times," *Computerworld,* section 2, October 8, 1990, pp. 6–9.

[45] See Bruce R. Holmgren, "All-New Line Automates Sample Packs for Doctors," *Packaging,* 34 (8), June 1989, pp. 66–71.

[46] Thomas Hout, Michael E. Porter, and Eileen Rudden, "How Global Companies Win Out," *Harvard Business Review,* September–October 1982, pp. 98–108. The concept also appears, although without specific reference to data processing, in Christopher A. Bartlett and Sumantra Ghoshal, "Tap Your Subsidiaries for Global Reach," *Harvard Business Review,* November–December 1986, pp. 87–94.

have.[47] Each month, 89 financial reports arrive at Rahway, New Jersey, from the various overseas locations of the company. It takes Merck approximately three weeks to close its books for the preceding month.[48] It is necessary for Merck to get this information before it can to formulate financial strategy.[49]

Prior to this, the consolidation process was manual. The various subsidiaries around the world would create their local reports and then use facsimile to transmit these to headquarters. After the summary reports arrived in Rahway, they would go through data entry and consolidation. The format of the incoming reports was not entirely standard, which produced the need for a great deal of manual accounting work at headquarters. A staff was set up to handle this job. This process was essentially manual in spite of the great investments that had been made in information technology in the past.

To simplify this process, management decided to work toward building an information system that would link headquarters with the satellite locations. This would be done by uploading the reports from the field to headquarters. A high-level task force was appointed to solve this problem. After much study and more than one year, the team developed a system to achieve this. Un-

---

[47] David Fairlamb, "Multinationals Open In-House Banks," *Dun's Business Month,* 127 (5), May 1986, pp. 54–56. Toyota is one multinational that has opened its own bank.

[48] There are reports that some companies are able to close their books much faster. For example, General Electric is able to close in less than 72 hours, even on a world-wide basis. Arvai reports that some multinational corporations are using BASIC programs running on personal computers to prepare data at regional offices before sending it on to the mainframes at corporate headquarters. He argues that in some cases, this is an efficient alternative to other, more primitive forms of financial reporting. In the case of Merck, however, we see that this type of option did not work very well. See Ernest Stephen Arvai, "Eliminating the Lag in International Reporting," *Information Strategy: The Executive's Journal,* 3 (2), Winter 1987, pp. 43–44. A review of software to support microcomputer-based reporting to corporate headquarters in multinational corporations is found in "Financial Management: Micro Control in Large Corporations," *Business Software Review,* 5 (9), September 1986, pp. 17–19. The article reports on a product from International Management Reporting Services (IMRS). For a positive review of this type of software, see James A. Perakis, "Consolidation Software," *FE: The Magazine for Financial Executives,* 2 (9), September 1986, pp. 31–32. For a discussion of cash management in the multinational corporation using an international in-house system, see Leon J. Level, "Meeting the Needs of Multinational Corporations," *Journal of Bank Research,* 16 (4), 1986, pp. 254–257.

[49] For a study of the use of information systems in creating global financial strategy for multinational corporations, based on creation of a "model-based multiobjective decision support system (MODSS)," see Hyun B. Eom and Sang M. Lee, "A Large-Scale Goal Programming Model-Based Decision Support for Formulating Global Financing Strategy," *Information and Management,* 12 (1), January 1987, pp. 33–44. The system is designed to help manage and calculate trade-offs among different financing options involving foreign exchange, capital structure, and extraneous risks, such as political problems.

fortunately, it would require rewriting code at each location. Their solution called for an aggressive programming effort that was beyond the capability of the number of team members allocated for this project. In addition, the particular approach selected would require constant recoding, and the number of programs would proliferate.

The problem lay in the preference for building a "supersystem" at headquarters that was capable of dealing with the incoming format of each of the different subsidiaries reporting. It was estimated that creation of this system would have taken approximately $500,000 on the conservative side.

An additional complication was that the subsidiary satellite locations did not all have the same type of equipment. Some of the locations had IBM S/36 and others S/38, which is slightly more advanced.

As realization spread of the impending problems, a new management team was brought in to assess the situation. The new team quickly realized that the situation was impossible. In order to meet the schedule, the team would have had to use eight people to write more than 700 programs in eight weeks. This was highly unlikely considering the time it had taken just to write a simple program to handle only a portion of the requirements.

The new management of the project realized that the original team had invested a great amount of time and effort into the solution they had come up with. There would be a great deal of demoralization and frustration if the effort was quashed at the start, and this frustration could lead to outright rebellion.

The new management then divided the team into two parts. One-half was assigned to continue working on the old approach, and the other half was assigned to work on an alternative solution (which won out in the end). The alternative solution was based on a Lotus 1-2-3 type of program that would work with a database-type application. Only 40 programs were required, and they were written in RPG and were far less complex. This was a great simplification over the original plan, which required more than 700 programs of much greater complexity.

The second solution was based on the S/36 architecture, which was less advanced than the S/38 but was a common architecture. Programs and applications developed on the S/36 would run on the S/38, but not the other way around. The S/38 platform was more sophisticated and ran better software, but the S/36 was a "common denominator" among the platforms available. When the idea of using the common denominator came up, there were complaints that the solution would "not be using the full capabilities of the S/38." In addition, the software would also operate on a PC. From the point of view of the locations that were operating S/38s, the solution proposed would amount to "running inferior software on a superior machine." On the surface, this appeared to be a waste of computing capacity.

The counter-argument to this was that using an application common to all of the machines would radically reduce the amount of coding required to get the operation up and running. Because of its simplicity, this solution quickly won out. Not only was it easier to manage, but the first "solution" was incapable of being implemented because of the tremendous coding and programming required.

Additional savings were realized when the time for installation came. The packets of the new program were simply mailed to each of the locations, with instructions for use. After a few hours on the phone during the initial setup phase of troubleshooting, the systems were up and running. This was a very different outcome than would have resulted if a programming team were required to go out to each remote location and practically customize a package. In addition, should changes to the system be required, much of this could be done centrally in Rahway.

The second team immediately realized that the Rahway operation could be very quickly simplified, eliminating the need for much of the manual accounting work that was required for consolidation. In effect, it would be possible to achieve one- or two-day consolidations using a modification of the linkages between the remote S/36s and the machines in Rahway. However, this could have taken away work from some of the persons on the accounting staff who had built a career on knowing how to reconcile the different types of statements from around the world. When it was realized that the information technology system could replace much of the administrative function of these people, then the issue became more *political* in nature. The project was killed.

Highlights of the Merck Approach

This example from the rich history of Merck Corporation carries some important lessons:

- *Historical autonomy and the inheritance of incompatible equipment.* The existence of different types of equipment in the various satellite IS installations posed problems for Merck, particularly during the initial stages of the design process, when the failed solution was created. This experience emphasizes the importance of having standardized equipment throughout the international operations of a company. It may be that because of the *historical autonomy* of the subsidiary installations, it was easy for incompatible types of equipment to proliferate.[50]
- *Use of a common denominator.* Selection of the S/36 for the base solution points out an important strategy for coping with the inherited

---

[50] In the absence of a pressing need or application designed for consolidated international operation, it is easy to see how the various units of the multinational would grow apart and adopt different types of equipment over time.

incompatibility of equipment. Even though it was not the most advanced equipment available, the reduction in performance was balanced against the need to write different types of code to accommodate the variety of equipment.[51]

- *Primacy of line management.* After the initial installation of the S/36-based solution, the team identified a next step that clearly would have improved efficiency. This idea, however, was quashed by the accounting and financial group, which actually stood to benefit the most. In the face of this opposition, there was little that the IS team could do.[52]

- *Difficulty of international logistics.* This case also points out the high-profile role that international logistics played in building an application that requires a significant amount of systems integration and yet is also highly geographically distributed. This is an enduring factor in the development of international information systems.

Several other interviews[53] conducted at the Merck Corporation produced additional insights and "nuggets" pointing the way toward "best practices" in operating an international information system in a multinational corporation.[54]

- *End-user interfaces are best designed first in Spanish.* The Merck IS team decided that in developing end-user interfaces for standardized applications that must be delivered in several different languages, the end-user application screens would be developed *first* in Spanish. Why? Because Spanish is "more wordy" than other languages and therefore takes up

---

[51] One criticism of the analysis of international computing developments is the need to distinguish phenomena and solutions that are *inherently international* from solutions that *can have international application*. In the case of Merck, the use of the S/36 as a common-denominator platform for the application could have been adopted in either a domestic or an international situation: therefore one could question the *international validity* of the lesson. On the other hand, the difficulty of international logistics puts stronger pressure in favor of such a solution, and the complexity of the problem at the international level means that a higher payoff will come from taking this path in the search for a solution.

[52] The IS team responsible for solving the problem was constrained by the line management, which was unprepared for change.

[53] A second set of interviews was conducted at the Merck headquarters with the director of international operations for the information systems department. In addition, the director of Western European marketing and operations (not an IS function) was interviewed to investigate attitudes toward use of information systems.

[54] At the time of these interviews, Merck had just been voted the most admired large corporation in the United States *for the third year in a row*. Under these circumstances, it is doubtful that the organization is propagating many poor practices in its use of information systems.

more room on the screen. As a result, when the screen is reinterpreted into other languages, the new translations always fit with room to spare.

- *1992 should be considered for the introduction of a single point of ordering for Western Europe.* The prospects of a single European market has both positive and negative implications for Merck. There is little expectation that "suddenly" the market for pharmaceuticals will become unified. However, Merck sees several opportunities for Europe-wide systems. One point of concern is the development of a centralized single point of ordering for all of Europe. This is *not* driven by information-technology considerations, but rather by the prospects of having Europe-wide distributors emerge in the new European environment. Merck sees the possibility of distributors linking up across European borders. In addition, there are many factors to consider on the information systems side. For example, what is the ideal architecture of such an arrangement, and what is to be the emerging relationship between the national organizations and the centralized ordering organization? Also, what will be the technological relationship? Merck's emerging view is that a type of *distributed processing* will allow both a centralized and a decentralized architecture to exist simultaneously, thus avoiding political problems between the new entity and the national entities.

- *Transborder data flow of name-linked data is a "manageable" problem.* Being a pharmaceutical company, Merck is concerned that movement of name-linked data may prove a hindrance to the transfer of testing data. Merck notes that this problem is "particularly acute" in the Scandinavian countries, which appear to have the strictest legislation regarding transborder flow of personal data. Although this problem was significant in the 1970s, Merck has more or less routinized the solution. Each time this type of transborder data flow must take place, Merck gets the proper and required permissions of the relevant national authorities. However, there is undoubtedly an extra cost of doing business associated with this requirement.[55]

- *There is an advantage in moving towards a standard platform (the AS/400).* As mentioned earlier, Merck has many installations with different models of minicomputers, including the S/34, S/36, and S/38. Merck

---

[55]On the other hand, it is doubtful that this cost is significant in the grand scheme of things, particularly for a company such as Merck, which spends millions if not billions of dollars per year simply in conducting advanced research on new products.

has generally stuck with IBM for its production equipment.[56] Since IBM introduced the AS/400, Merck has been giving serious consideration to upgrading all of the S/3x machines to the AS/400 platform. This would greatly simplify the development of future applications.[57]
- *There may be a shortage of Japanese-qualified MIS employees.* The interviews revealed that there may be a shortage of American-educated MIS employees who can operate effectively in the Japanese language and culture.[58]
- *Applications are developed only if they are unavailable from outside sources.* One of the ways in which Merck minimizes its effort and frees up scarce human resources to tackle the really difficult problems is by judiciously purchasing as much as possible in the way of applications from the outside. Merck avoids creating applications that are available from the outside. They do not "reinvent the wheel," even if this outside purchasing may result in somewhat higher costs. Merck IT executives noted that the scope of required development activity has been changing dramatically. It is simply not necessary to develop as many applications as in the past.[59]
- *Multilingual applications are developed by bringing together employees from different locations.* Merck's approach to developing a global application is similar to that of other companies interviewed.[60] When it is necessary to bring together talent, such as speakers of different languages

---

[56]For Merck's research and development laboratories, it is using a Cray supercomputer and many VAX machines. However, it is preparing now to introduce an IBM supercomputer (probably a 3090 extended). It has also used Sun workstations for modeling biochemical molecules and also for expert system and artificial development purposes.

[57]If, however, the future applications had to merge the S/36, S/34, and S/38 applications into a new system, then running the new application on the AS/400 may not prove to be such a great advantage. However, any new applications developed would more than likely be chosen with a preference to running on the AS/400, and over time these applications will push out the older applications. In addition, many conversion and upgrading tools are rapidly becoming available to help in the process of migrating the S/3x series application to the AS/400.

[58]This observation lends further evidence to the hypothesis that MIS skills are highly variable from one country and region of the world to another. This is an interesting subject for further MIS research.

[59]In the past, for example, Merck developed many of its own programs for manufacturing. Control of process machines, robotics, and automation were developed in internal laboratories to speed up and revolutionize manufacturing of pharmaceuticals. Now, the IT management notes, the same programs are available almost "off the shelf" from commercial vendors. In creating these applications in the past, however, Merck was able to benefit from competitive advantage and efficiency in its manufacturing operations.

[60]Tupperware, for example, uses a similar approach.

used in the end-user interface, Merck moves these teams together into a project. Merck observes that the fact that these teams are international in nature does not seem to change the basic process much, or complicate or slow down the decision-making process. The relevant team members from different countries are assigned different parts of the problem, much as if they were working in the same office. In contrast to the "lead system,"[61] Merck coordinates this activity centrally.

- *Subsidiary IT installations are given complete autonomy as long as they satisfy centralized corporate reporting requirements.* Merck indicates that a rather loose type of management style towards subsidiary MIS installations may be in order. "As long as the foreign MIS operation satisfies its reporting requirements [for financial and inventory information], they are given complete autonomy in all other matters." This allows each of the national organizations to take advantage of the software and applications available in their national markets. Payroll, for example, is an application best handled at the national level because of the constant changes in taxation and other requirements that are unique to the host country. If, for example, a firm attempted to respond to these changes on a centralized basis, the situation would quickly become intolerable because the headquarters IS team would have to monitor and respond to changes generated by each national arena. The complexity would be too great.[62]

It is interesting to note that at approximately the same time Merck was developing in-house this financial control system, with all of the special variations required for operation within its own company, vendors on the outside were responding to what was perceived to be a growing market need for

---

[61] The *lead system* refers to the appointing of lead teams in a single national market, which are then put in charge of developing a standard application for the entire multinational corporation. The lead team is chosen based on how advanced they are in solving the problem. For the purpose of the project, then, the different national groups report to the lead team. This is supposed to save approximately 25% of development costs.

[62] This is an important argument for *decentralization of portfolio selection and operations.* Giving this great degree of autonomy to the various satellite operations allows the central IS function to concentrate on its most critical task: consolidating the financial reporting systems as well as inventory and sales data. All of the other functions, such as personnel, are handled at the local level. This type of arrangement takes a great deal of pressure off the central-headquarters IS function. It is intuitively the most efficient way to operate. More research is needed to determine if this type of arrangement is used in other multinational corporations. In addition, it would be interesting to find a situation in which this type of arrangement was *not* optimum. What, then, would be the guiding circumstances that turn this logic on its head?

multilanguage and multicurrency software.[63] However, this type of software is not expected to be available and widely used until well into the 1990s.

SUMMARY

It appears more research and analysis need to be done to better learn how to build corporate intelligence systems that take advantage of new advances in information systems.

- More case studies are needed on corporate intelligence systems that handle more complex information, such as external political and economic events coverage.
- Methods of handling information need to be studied to learn how to automate what in most companies is undoubtedly a haphazard process.
- A better understanding is required of how new database techniques (filing, indexing, retrieval, distribution) can be used to handle heterogeneous information more efficiently.
- Additional analysis may help to determine how best to staff, operate, and manage a corporate intelligence function.

Today's multinational corporation cannot expect to equal the intelligence-gathering power of governments and, most agree, should not engage in covert activities, at least on the political side. It is also a safe assumption that a multinational may encounter some of the same problems as intelligence agencies but not be as well staffed to cope. The classical problems involve collection of too much information, difficulties in retrieving information once it builds up, complexities of performing accurate analysis, and the ever-present problems of getting the critical information to the appropriate decision maker in time for the person to take effective action.

---

[63]Commercial software that is capable of doing electronic funds transfer, automatic translations between different currencies, and different arrangements for tax reporting within different countries is reported on by Arthur J. Tobias, "Multinationals Spearheading Worldwide Financial Thrust," *Software Magazine,* 8 (7), May 1988, pp. 64–70. Tobias notes that the newer financial packages allow for integrated communication and access between different applications databases. This is a great improvement, but the Merck case raises a red flag regarding this type of effort, particularly if the interfaces are difficult to construct or require a great degree of customization. A discussion of automatic machine translation for documents in the accounting industry is found in David C. Yang, "Machine Translators: Accounting Applications," *CPA Journal,* 60 (11), November 1990, pp. 8, 10.

CHAPTER

8

Information Technology-Based FSAs (Firm-Specific Advantages)

The concept of the FSA comes originally from the international business literature, and its purpose is to explain why a corporation takes the trouble of setting up business in a foreign land. Having a specific advantage can be a powerful reason for making an investment. On the MIS side, many have examined the use of information technology for competitive advantage and we see, therefore, that the MIS argument can be merged with the international business argument to focus on information technology-based firm-specific advantages. There has been very little, if any, thought given to what importance information technology has in determining whether or not a multinational corporation should invest in a foreign country. In the case of the Tupperware Express system, we see the merging of many different national data processing centers into an effective global system with a result being a definite improvement in the competitive force of the company.

Much of the research in international business has focused on why a firm becomes a multinational corporation. Why should a company engage in Foreign Direct Investment (FDI)? One important line of thinking holds that firms set up operations overseas because they have some type of advantage (a Firm-Specific Advantage) in the target market. Advantages of capital or technology are two key examples, although there are also alternative reasons why firms set up overseas (i.e., government regulations, trade barriers, etc.). Bain[1] identified four types of specific entry barriers against multinational corporations attempting to set up operations in a foreign market: (1) scale-economy barrier, (2) product-differentiation barrier, (3) absolute-cost barrier, and (4) capital-requirement barrier. In each of these categories, it is easy to see how information-intensive industries could be adversely affected by national regulations, such as transborder data flow controls, which in effect change the cost of inputs into the value-added process of the firm.

No one appears to have studied IT-based FSAs in the multinational. This research can build from the rich (and controversial) literature on information technology for competitive advantage, sometimes called "strategic information systems." The concept of information systems becoming a barrier to entry has not been tested in the international arena (so far as I know), but should be. In addition, it is clear that many global strategies (e.g., in manufacturing) would be utterly impossible without the (relatively) new developments in distributed processing and other technologies. However, the methods for analyzing what specific component(s) of competitive advantage are accounted for by global information systems (as opposed to marketing, technology, manufacturing, capital, or management skill and other advantages) are not well understood.

Earl[2] has reviewed the many frameworks that discuss the use of information technology for competitive advantage and has created a "framework of frameworks" that can be used to diagnose which framework works best for a given situation of analysis. His awareness frameworks are aimed at "executive appreciation and understanding of the strategic potential and impact of IT" (p. 2), his opportunity frameworks "are explicitly designed to be analytical tools which lead to firm-specific strategic advantage opportunities and/or clarify business strategies in order to demonstrate options for using IT strategically" (p. 7), and his positioning frameworks are "tools to help executives

---

[1] Joe S. Bain, *Barriers to New Competition: Their Character and Consequences in Manufacturing Industries* (Cambridge: Harvard University Press, 1956). See also W. Chan Kim and R. A. Mauborgne, "Becoming an Effective Global Competitor," *The Journal of Business Strategy*, January/February 1988, pp. 33–37. Although this is not a review of information-technology issues, they mention "(1) local economies of scale, (2) product differentiation, (3) switching costs, (4) access to distribution channels, (5) cost disadvantages independent of scale, and (6) local capital requirements" as the "six major sources of barriers to entry, each of which can influence an MNC's decision of whether a direct or indirect global competitive strategy should be pursued" (p. 36).

[2] Michael J. Earl, "Exploiting IT for Strategic Advantage—A Framework of Frameworks," Oxford Institute of Information Management, Research paper RDP 88/1, 1988.

assess the strategic importance, the particular character, and the inherited situation of IT for their business" (p. 15). These frameworks have never been applied to the multinational corporation, but should be.

Behrman discusses the role of proprietary technology in the multinational firm and believes that it may be "so sophisticated that the parent will not release it to outsiders."[3] Gardner and Vambery review the complex accusations that have been made by developing countries against the multinational corporations. They appear to attack the position of the Group of 77:

> It ignores all the contributions that MNC's made to the economic growth... including the transfer of both basic and advanced technologies and the discovery and development of natural resources which may be their most important revenue sources. Among the issues to be investigated are: the opposition by MNC's to the renegotiation of concession agreements, the unwillingness of MNC's to accept exclusive jurisdiction of host country domestic law in cases of compensation on nationalization, appeals to governments of the country of origin to intercede with the host government during conflicts, excessive outflow of funds, the failure to generate sufficient foreign exchange revenues for the host country; takeovers of locally owned companies by MNC's and *limiting the flow of information to host country government to facilitate the regulation and control of the multinational corporations.* [Emphasis added.][4]

Caves discusses the way in which control over information can give advantage to a multinational firm engaged in "horizontal"[5] investments overseas, although he was writing before information technology played a major part in the international operations of multinational corporations. Caves discusses control over information as one of the advantages of the firm: "any advantage embodied in knowledge, information or technique that yields a positive return over direct costs in the market where it is first proven can potentially do the same in other markets without need to incur again the sunk costs asso-

---

[3] Jack N. Behrman, "Transnational Corporations in the New International Economic Order," *Journal of International Business Studies*, Spring/Summer 1981, pp. 29–42. He writes: "these companies are likely to be characterized by sophisticated technology, which is continually changing and probably capital intensive. Where it is not capital intensive, the technology can be disaggregated, but it is so sophisticated that the parent will not release it to outsiders." Behrman is not discussing the use of information technology specifically, but his framework can be applied to any proprietary technology controlled by the multinational corporation in a national market. In terms of information technology, many proprietary in-house developed applications would fit this criteria.

[4] Richard N. Gardner and Robert G. Vambery, "Progress Towards a New World Economic Order," *Journal of International Business Studies,* Fall 1975, pp. 11, 14.

[5] Richard E. Caves, "International Corporations: The Industrial Economics of Foreign Investment," *Economica,* February 1971, pp. 1–27. Caves defines "horizontal" investments as those in which a firm invests abroad to set up manufacturing in a product which it already makes in its home country (e.g., automobile manufacturing); whereas "vertical" investments are characteristic of a reach down the value-added chain (e.g., a steel company invests overseas in order to get access to raw materials).

ciated with its initial discovery." He also sets forth a fundamental distinction between the information controlled by the local firm and the information that can be controlled by the multinational, arguing that it is necessary for the multinational to have some proprietary advantage:

> The native entrepreneur always enjoys an advantage over a foreign rival from his general accumulation of knowledge about economic, social, legal and cultural conditions in his home market and country. The foreign firm...investing abroad must not only enjoy enough of an information advantage in its special asset to offset the information disadvantage of its alien status; it must also find production abroad preferable to any other means of extracting this rent from a foreign market.[6]

Caves also notes that "the relatively high fixed costs of securing the information necessary to undertake a foreign investment predispose the small firm to settle for licensing."[7] In some of his later studies, Caves bypasses the information issue, probably because the sources of data he was working with did not carry any information regarding this aspect of the operations of the multinational.[8]

On the other hand, the probing vision of Ohmae's "borderless world" seems to suggest that as global communications become more and more advanced, the advantage that a firm might gain from control over communications is weakened. He argues that "in the past, there were gross inefficiencies—some purposeful, some not—in the flow of information around the world. New technologies are eliminating those inefficiencies, and, with them, the opportunity for a kind of top-down information arbitrage—that is, the ability of a government to benefit itself or powerful special interest at the expense of its people by following policies that would never win their support if they had unfettered access to all relevant information."[9]

Using Buckley's "critical" analysis of different theories of the multinational corporation,[10] some of the specification advantages that a multinational cor-

---

[6] Ibid, pp. 4–5.

[7] Ibid, p. 7.

[8] Richard E. Caves, "Causes of Direct Investment: Foreign Firms' Shares in Canadian and United Kingdom Manufacturing Industries," *The Review of Economics and Statistics,* 1974, pp. 279–293, and Caves, "Multinational Firms, Competition, and Productivity in Host-Country Markets," *Economica,* May 1974, pp. 176–193.

[9] This view of the "global village" with "instant communication" is found in the "borderless world" of Kenichi Ohmae. If Ohmae is right—and he is writing as an intuitive futurist with special reference only to developed countries—then this would imply that the information advantages that could be held by the multinational in a host country could be weakened by the advent of efficient global communications. Kenichi Ohmae, "Managing in a Borderless World," *Harvard Business Review,* May–June 1989, pp. 152–161.

[10] Peter J. Buckley, "A Critical View of Theories of the Multinational Enterprise," in Peter J. Buckley and Mark Casson, eds., *The Economic Theory of the Multinational Enterprise* (New York: Macmillan, 1985), pp. 1–19.

poration might have in a foreign market might be classified as falling within the "Hymer-Kindleberger" tradition, as Buckley calls it.[11] Buckley's assessment of the Kindleberger approach lists the specific advantages that might be mastered by a multinational in a foreign market, "including access to patented or 'proprietary' knowledge... and skill differences embodied in the firm."[12] Another major advantage mentioned in the Kindleberger theory is "internal and external economies of scale, including those arising from vertical integration." It is clear that these ideas were not generated with an analysis of information technology in mind, or of its effects. However, we can suggest an analysis of automation effects within the context of the Hymer-Kindleberger tradition. The information-technology infrastructure can clearly help a firm control proprietary knowledge, particularly if its skill in handling information is higher than that of the competitors (or of the host country government). A second major way in which information technology is used is in facilitating the sophistication of vertical integration in the firm, which may lead to the economies of scale that are necessary for successful foreign direct investment according to the Hymer-Kindleberger tradition. The use of information technology can also help enhance the "ability of a multinational to forecast," which Buckley sees as "one of the major competitive skills," although he argues that the concept of firm-specific advantages is "a short-run one" that explains the internationalization process at only a single point in time.

Buckley also discusses the Product Cycle Model, which he abbreviates as "PCH," developed by Raymond Vernon.[13] Under this model, a new product is created in one country where the firm has an "innovation-based oligopoly" because of control over the technology. As the innovation matures, price competition and scale economies become more important. As production expands, consumption of the product spreads overseas and rises until it becomes more

---

[11] Hymer was Kindleberger's student at MIT. According to Dunning and Rugman, 'the great contribution of Stephen Hymer's seminal dissertation [1960] was to escape from the intellectual straightjacket of neoclassical-type trade and financial theory, and move us towards an analysis of the multinational enterprise (MNE) based upon industrial organization theory." John H. Dunning and Alan M. Rugman, "The Influence of Hymer's Dissertation on the Theory of Foreign Direct Investment," *AEA Papers and Proceedings,* 75 (2), May 1985, pp. 228–232. Unfortunately, it appears Hymer was deficient in internalization theory.

[12] Dunning describes the Kindleberger argument as being a type of "monopolistic competitive theory" "expressed in terms of net advantages MEs or their affiliates possess over indigenous firms...[including] an easier or cheaper access to knowledge and information" (p. 314). John Dunning, *The Determinants of International Production* (Lausanne: IRM, 1988), pp. 289–331.

[13] Dunning describes the Vernon thesis: "The Vernon thesis argues that the production of many new products and processes, first discovered in one country, is later transferred to another by a variety of means, one of which is through affiliates of the innovating firms. This assumes that the innovating firms both create new markets, and supply these markets initially from a domestic and then from a foreign location and, in so doing, they may induce a certain response from other firms and create a market structure which may influence future locational decisions." John H. Dunning, *The Determinants of International Production* (Chichester/New York: Wiley/IRM, 1988), p. 310.

profitable to manufacture in foreign markets to maintain the advantage. Again, these insights into the expansion of multinational business were not developed in connection with studies of the use of information technology. However, they can be used to understand advantages that might accrue to a multinational that has an innovation advantage in use of automation. Theoretically, if a firm has a great advantage in its use of information technology, then it could expand into foreign markets and reap economic rents from exploiting this advantage. The only example that comes to mind is the experience of Citibank in the Netherlands where the innovative cash management and treasury management services it provided to corporate customers gave it a great advantage over local banks (such as Rabobank) and enabled it to gain market share.[14] Like other innovations in the Vernon hypothesis, innovations in the use of information technology can decline in value as other firms master the same technique and develop similar systems. Most of the *craft* in the use of information technology is not patentable, although it is obviously proprietary to a firm, and we would expect, therefore, that the advantages would deteriorate faster than for other types of innovation advantages. We must recall that Vernon's thesis was referring to technological innovation such as patentable products or processes. To a certain extent, Casson hints at the nature of information-based advantages and how they must be maintained by secrecy, since they cannot be patented:

> Where know-how is concerned, information about the product quality is difficult to separate from the information which constitutes the product itself. The *proprietary value of the information* can only be protected by enforcing a right of exclusion, and in the absence of patent protection a right of exclusion can be enforced only by secrecy. [Emphasis added.][15]

It is interesting to note, however, that Giddy argued that the produce cycle theory was insufficient to explain the strategies of multinationals. "New products, such as digital watches and disposable razors, are sometimes introduced abroad almost at the same time as at home...much of the international

---

[14]For a review of how computer and telecommunications systems are changing the basis of competition in the financial services industry, see Paul Shrivastava, "Strategies for Coping with Telecommunications Technology in the Financial Services Industry," *Columbia Journal of World Business*, Spring 1983, pp. 19–24. He writes: "Computers and telecommunications technology are jointly revolutionizing the Financial Services (FS) industry worldwide....[the] communicative nature of financial transactions makes FS organizations especially susceptible to advances in information processing and communications technology."

[15]Mark Casson, "Transaction Costs and the Theory of the Multinational Enterprise," in Peter J. Buckley and Mark Casson, eds., *The Economic Theory of the Multinational Enterprise* (Macmillan, 1985), p. 36. Casson also discusses the role of information and "psychic distance" between buyer and seller in "General Theories of the Multinational Enterprise: Their Relevance to Business History," in Peter Hertner and Geoffrey Jones, eds., *Multinationals: Theory and History* (Aldershot Harts, England: Gower Publishing Co., Ltd., 1986), p. 49. It would be interesting to speculate about "psychic distance" and its effects on the economics of the multinational given teleconferencing.

Chapter 8 Information Technology-Based FSAs (Firm-Specific Advantages)

investment of multinational firms, particularly in the raw materials industries, seems to have little to do with the product life cycle," he writes.[16]

Hayes and Wheelwright, however, attack some of the traditional "advantages" which come from vertical integration. They discuss the "classical" case for vertical integration. Within the context of information flows, they argue, costs can be reduced through "greater efficiency by coordinating the design, production, and marketing of both the end product and its components as a single system"; control can be enhanced by "better measurement of, and hence increased influence over, management performance because of access to information that otherwise would not be available..., freer communication and more cooperative behavior, since upstream and downstream operations are now members of the same organization...[and] increased control over the product quality, delivery time, and price charged by the in-house supplier."[17] However, they attack these assumptions:

> *Vertical integration may also impede information transfer, even though increased information may now be available to the firm.* In the buyer-seller relationship of independent firms, selected focal points exist for the contact and passing of information among the two organizations. Following a vertical integration step, such focal points may increase in number and become blurred, making it even more difficult for design engineers and manufacturing managers to assign priorities to the information coming to them. [Emphasis added.] (p. 295)

Vernon revisited the product lifecycle hypothesis and concluded that the effects of newer communications systems, in conjunction with the rising development of Japan and Western Europe after the immediate post-war period, *weakened* the applicability of his hypothesis. The effect of the global communications system in creating a "global scanner" multinational[18] tended to make the playing field more level, and increased the level of competition. The development of the level playing field

---

[16] Ian H. Giddy, "The Demise of the Product Cycle Model in International Business Theory," *Columbia Journal of World Business,* Spring 1978, pp. 90–97.

[17] Robert H. Hayes and Steven C. Wheelwright, *Restoring Our Competitive Edge: Competing Through Manufacturing* (New York: John Wiley & Sons, 1984).

[18] Raymond Vernon, "The Product Cycle Hypothesis in a New International Environment," *Bulletin,* pp. 255–267. Vernon noted that "the hypothetical global scanner, of course, is not to be found in the real world. The acquisition of information is seldom altogether costless; and the digestion and interpretation of information always entails cost. The typical patterns of behavior that one observes in the real world reflect that fact" (p. 262). This led Vernon to conclude that "as we search for a hypothesis that would replace the product cycle concept as an explicator of the trading and investing behavior of the innovating multinational company, a simple variant such as that of the global scanner will not take us very far. Global scanning is not costless, even when a network of foreign subsidiaries is already in place; costs of collecting and interpreting the information, as the firm perceives those costs, may not be commensurate with its expected benefits...so the day of the global scanner...is not yet here. Nevertheless, even if the global scanner is not yet the dominant model,...the power of the product cycle hypothesis is certainly weakened."

weakened a critical assumption of the product cycle hypothesis, namely, that the entrepreneurs of large enterprises confronted markedly different conditions in their respective home markets...[and with] *communication [being] virtually costless between any two points of the globe; information, once received, is digested and interpreted at little or no cost [in the hypothetical global scanner multinational]* ...the global scanner, therefore, would be in an advantageous position as compared with those firms without such a scanning capability. [Emphasis added.]

His conclusion is that "the product cycle concept continues to explain and predict a certain category of foreign direct investments...although it no longer can be relied on to provide as powerful an explanation of the behavior of US firms as in decades past, it is likely to continue to provide a guide to the motivations and response of some enterprises in all countries of the world."

Camillus makes a distinction between "technology-driven" and "market-driven" strategies of multinational corporations, arguing that the multinational corporate strategy should be tailored "to the basic driving forces underlying product and industry life cycles." He argues that "product and industry life cycles are propelled by either technological or social change, or a combination of these." Camillus draws a distinction between developed and developing countries when he points out that "the product or industry life cycle may be driven differently in lesser developed countries (LDCs) than in the more developed countries." Depending on the type of strategy being adopted, the structure of the planning and control system within the multinational must change:

> Organizations that adopt a technology-based strategy have to ensure that their structure, planning and control system and management style are consistent with the imperatives of technology as the distinctive competence.

King discusses the role of information technology in giving an "information-based comparative advantage" in the firm. He notes that Drucker predicted that "knowledge would become the 'central capital' and the critical resource of the economy—in other words, that information technology would become the driving force for growth in business and industry." King believes this change is driven by the new economics of computers, which are becoming cheaper, and by fundamental changes in the business environment (deregulation in particular), market fragmentation and demand for "customized and specialized products," and by "shifts in cost, quality, and time requirements for products," all of which place a premium on the information processing capabilities of the firm.[19]

Clemons and Weber have taken a different approach to the question of FSAs. Their research took as a unit of analysis the entire London stock ex-

---

[19] William R. King, "Information Technology and Corporate Growth," *Columbia Journal of World Business,* Summer 1985, pp. 29–33.

change and demonstrated how its transformation to screen-based trading gave the exchange as a whole competitive advantage over other rival exchanges, such as Paris and Milan.[20]

Sarathy's analysis of the critical factors in building a competitive general trading company emphasizes, at least in part, the critical role played by information technology and communications systems in helping to make the deals necessary to keep the trading company in business:

> An ability to obtain information rapidly so as to be able to react to it quickly and in a timely fashion is what distinguishes Japanese trading companies. Technological developments in satellite communications and high-speed data transmission, and reduction in the costs of using such networks, mean that new competitors need to quickly develop equally efficient data networks. Shared networks and the possibility of renting valuable data bases... mean that the importance of scale economies with regard to communication networks might be declining. Such developments make more viable the emergence of smaller trading companies that specialize in technologically complex products and after-sales services.[21]

Although writers in the international business literature have discussed generally the concept of informational advantages for a firm, they have not specifically discussed the role of information technology. They often refer to patents, copyrights, or other specific types of technical *knowledge* rather than to information. However, there is no doubt that by extending their theory—which is used to explain what type of advantage a multinational can get in the local market of a host country—to include the role of information technology, it is possible to imagine new forms of strategic advantage. But has anyone seen a multinational corporation entering into a specific country's national market *specifically because* it possessed an information technology advantage? Perhaps there are one or two examples, but it appears that this is a strategy for the future and not for today.

TUPPERWARE CORPORATION AND BUILDING OF THE TUPPERWARE EXPRESS INTERNATIONAL ORDERING SYSTEM

The world's plastic industry is concentrated in the United States, Japan, and a few countries of Western Europe. It is a complex industry with upstream and

---

[20] Erik K. Clemons and Bruce W. Weber, "London's Big Bang: A Case Study of Information Technology, Competitive Impact, and Organizational Change," *Journal of Management Information Systems,* 6 (4), Spring 1990, pp. 41–60.

[21] Ravi Sarathy, "Japanese Trading Companies: Can They Be Copied?" *Journal of International Business Studies,* Summer 1985, pp. 116, 119. His notion of "economies of scale in communications networks" is not readily understandable.

downstream products used in a variety of ways. Olefin cracking of petroleum produces propylene which goes into bulk thermoplastics. It also produces ethylene which can be used to create vinyl chloride and the ever-popular polyvinyl chloride. Ethylene can also be processed into polyethylene. Aromatic refining produces benzene which works with ethylene to create styrene and the polystyrene so popular in packing materials. There are a lot of thermoplastics created in the world, considering the difficulty in disposing of them in an environmentally safe manner. The 1976 production of thermoplastics was 31.2 million tons and by 1985 this had risen to 47.5 million tons per year.[22] Tupperware is one of the downstream users of these plastics.

Tupperware is the world leader in the area of plastic kitchen storage systems doing business worldwide in over 35 countries, with 17 plants located in North America, South America, Europe, and the Pacific. The concept of Tupperware has been rated as one of the most innovative breakthroughs in the history of product design.[23] The company which is headquartered in Orlando, Florida, does approximately $1 billion in sales annually. In addition to kitchen storage products, the product line is expanding into toys, and home entertainment products in the form of plastic glassware and serving pieces. Tupperware products are sold solely through the home party system, supported by a network of independent Tupperware dealers and distributors.

The key to understanding Tupperware's business is to know the role of the mold in the manufacturing process.[24] Tupperware molds are expensive both to manufacture and move from one location to another. Each mold is hand-made and takes more than one-half year to produce. There is typically only one mold per product. After a mold is created, it is expected to last for many years. Tupperware provides a lifetime guarantee for all of its products. Once the molds are in operation, they generally produce a new product every 15 seconds. The production rate can be between 4 to 32 products per minute, depending on the complexity of the product being manufactured. Some complex products can require the use of as many as 25 molds for each copy of the product.

---

[22]See UNCTC, *Transnational Corporations in the Plastics Industry* (New York: United Nations, 1990).

[23]See Jeremy Myerson, "Ten out of Ten," *Management Today,* June 1990, pp. 96–101. Other products included in the review are the fountain pen, the kitchen knife, the Filofax, and electric table fans.

[24]According to the UNCTC report, the "main high-pressure moulding techniques...[are] (a) compression moulding...the method of moulding a material in a confined cavity by applying pressure and usually heat; (b) transfer moulding...a method of forming articles by fusing a plastic material in a chamber and then forcing a mass into a hot mould where it solidifies; (c) injection moulding ...the process of forming a material by forcing it, under pressure, from a heated cylinder through a sprue [runner, gate] into the cavity of a closed mould; (d) blow moulding...a method of fabrication in which a heated parison is forced into the shape of a mould cavity by gas pressure" (p. 43).

There are many older Tupperware products which continue to be large sellers even many years after they are first introduced into the market. Tupperware produces approximately 300 products. The "core" products account for approximately a million in unit sales per year. Each year, Tupperware produces approximately 15 to 25 new products. In order for this to happen, Tupperware must create 45 to 75 new molds per year. This is a very large investment. When a product does not sell as intended, the mold is mothballed in case it might be valuable either in another part of the world or several years later when consumer philosophy has changed.

On the other hand, out of all the new product introductions, Tupperware creates one or two products which sell rapidly and generally exceed by a great number the ability of the molds to produce for the demand. It is primarily these products that make up for the lost investment in the products which do not sell as well.[25] The good-selling products account for approximately two to three million unit sales per year, in contrast to the core products, which are stable at approximately a million unit sales per year.

A key problem being faced by Tupperware is that it is completely impossible to anticipate the demand for the good-selling products.[26]

This raises significant problems for Tupperware. When good-selling products are discovered, Tupperware must be ready to supply the demand. Otherwise, they risk alienating their independent distributors. According to Tupperware management, selling Tupperware products is a "highly emotionally charged business." Some research shows that salespersons must have a high perception of the public image of their activity in order to do well, and this is very important in the Tupperware case.[27] Utility, pricing, and many other traditional factors associated with mass consumer goods do not appear to play a large part. It is the unpredictable tides of emotion which do more than anything else to determine sales.[28]

---

[25] In a sense we could say that Tupperware is something like a pharmaceutical company which invests heavily in R&D for years in the hope of finding a single super drug upon which the entire company can live. The difference, however, is that in the case of a drug, much testing can be done during the regulatory process *before* the investment is made in the complex and expensive manufacturing process. On the other hand, in the case of Tupperware, the rather expensive investment must be made in the mold *before* the company can really be sure whether or not the product is a "hit" in the market. This perhaps makes the Tupperware more risky.

[26] Tupperware management, realizing the critical nature of this problem, have tried a number of methods to anticipate hot products, but has met with no success. Pre-testing, consumer surveys, and other standard techniques have all been tried and found lacking in predicting hot products.

[27] For a study which includes analysis of Tupperware salespersons, see Thomas R. Wotruba, "The Relationship of Job Image, Performance, and Job Satisfaction to Inactivity-Proneness of Direct Salespeople," *Journal of the Academy of Marketing Science,* 18 (2), Spring 1990, pp. 113–121.

[28] This is the view of Tupperware management from the interviews. If management is correct, then there is not likely to be any reasonable way for them to predict sales. It is not unreasonable to assume that Tupperware management has given this phenomenon careful thought and is correct in its analysis.

Tupperware's computing and telecommunications resources are distributed worldwide. Their activities are managed directly by the company headquarters. The computing hardware consists of a large IBM mainframe located at headquarters, with a mixture of mini and micro computers distributed worldwide. The minis and micros include equipment from IBM, Digital, Wang, NCR, Compaq, Apple, and miscellaneous PC clones.

Information technology has until recently supported the normal day-to-day accounting, order processing and distribution functions in a very classical fashion. The company has recognized that in order to continue to survive in the 1990s, it must increase its ability to react quickly, to maintain and improve its margins, and to bring more and more innovative products into the marketplace at a faster pace. In addition, since sales levels are directly related to the active dealer force, the company must be able to track the performance of the sales force in a timely manner. It is in these functional areas that the use of information systems has lately been focused.

Until recently the worldwide businesses were run independently. As each of these businesses evolved through various levels of sophistication and developed at different growth rates, problems began to be encountered in their ability to respond to sudden changes in the demand. To satisfy the market and still contain operating costs, the company was reoriented to operate much more on a worldwide basis. The initial emphasis of this shift in direction was placed on worldwide sourcing of product, raw materials, and the central coordination of the sharing and movements of molds around the world. To accomplish these objectives effectively, it would be necessary to create a worldwide information systems infrastructure, including a responsive telecommunications network, and a portfolio of distributed applications, including order processing, distribution, mold data and tracking, and associated accounting systems.

As with most problems in the information systems arena, the issues focused on people and management of information. In terms of overall systems architecture, Tupperware found itself operating about a dozen data centers in different parts of the world. It realized that in order to improve its ability to forecast changes in demand for fast-selling products, it would have to substantially improve its ability to coordinate market and sales data information on a global basis. It was clear that a new type of arrangement, based on closer cooperation and real-time or near-real-time sharing of data between these geographically dispersed data centers, would be needed. Using stand-alone or semi-autonomous operations in data centers would no longer be sufficient to meet competitive needs, and yet the different national practices, languages, and entrenched systems posed a formidable barrier to bringing these different data centers together.

The IS management at Tupperware faced two major challenges. First, it had to make an accurate estimation of the resources required to implement its worldwide system. Second, Tupperware had to learn how to organize, staff, and operate a project which on a local basis would have been relatively easy,

Chapter 8 Information Technology-Based FSAs (Firm-Specific Advantages)

but on an international basis, with so many countries, cultures, and time zones involved, would be considerably more difficult.

In order to solve this problem, Tupperware IS management first began to develop a technical strategy which related as closely as possible to the business objectives of the company. The underlying philosophy in the technical effort was "to keep it as simple as possible." After the technical strategy was developed, the next step was to estimate the cost and human resource estimates needed for accomplishing the project. Management approval of the underlying systems as well as the resource costs was needed from *each* of the involved business units. This approval was sought *after* the basis presentation to top management was approved. The next step was to staff and set up the project teams in all of the concerned units. When this was done, the IS management team set up a project management and control system to facilitate scheduling, review of progress reports, and resolution of any potential conflicts between different systems, development teams, or between managers with different views of the same problem.

The solution was arrived at by bringing together the key interested parties from around the world. A conscious decision was taken to ensure a good balance of information systems' technical skill combined with a strong knowledge of the business and its problems in each geographical location, particularly in Western Europe, where it operates 13 major data centers.

Once this was accomplished, the next step was to set up a planning team to solve the problem and develop the specifications for the new system. At this point, the IS team at headquarters brought together professionals from many of its data centers around the world. If appears that this was a skillful political move as well as sound systems development practice. Tupperware expected that once the overseas IS managers were made part of the process, they would eventually show stronger support when they returned to their home data centers in their new role as "systems missionaries." They would thereby serve the useful purpose of helping prevent the outbreak of conflict between the headquarters operation and its subsidiaries. The second purpose in adopting this approach was more routine in nature. It was to ensure that any special technical considerations arising from the subsidiary data centers would be properly taken into consideration at the earliest possible stage of the systems development process.

Several brainstorming and problem-solving sessions resulted in an EDI-type of solution which would involve the definition of transactions moving between locations and would require interface standards between different pieces of equipment. After this basic strategy and direction was agreed upon, the core IS management team divided up the project into a series of teams which would then go to each geographical location and build the standard interfaces and transaction systems that were needed to handle the processing of orders and the other associated functions, particularly inventory.

There were both technical and managerial advantages to using the EDI approach. For example, by concentrating on interfacing each system to a common EDI standard, the development work could be done with the local staff familiar with the system. It was not necessary to bring in outsiders for that effort, and thus the "pride of ownership" of the local system managers and operators was preserved. In addition, since each machine was interfacing to a single standard, the total number of interface problems was reduced.[29] Instead of building its own international network to handle the flow of EDI transactions, Tupperware decided to use public store and forward services.[30] This also helped in simplifying the task.

The project was implemented over a period of a year, with project teams working at each of the key locations. The total project staff consisted of approximately 30 information-systems and business-systems specialists. Each business unit was responsible for developing and monitoring its own work plans under guidelines established by the corporate project coordinator.

In carrying out this plan, Tupperware management faced several problems. One of the foremost problems was that communication between the various work groups was made more difficult by language barriers. The groups were located around the world, spanning at least six major time zones, and using English as a second language in most cases. In ensuring the success of this project, a strict project management strategy was adopted. Local project plans were consolidated by the project coordinator and weekly reviews of progress were conducted via teleconference with all key personnel. Regular sessions were held to discuss requirements and design specifications. In addition, periodic review sessions were set up at key check points as team members met face-to-face to review status and revise project plans.

With a well-planned mix of written, teleconferencing and face-to-face meetings, the misconceptions and the differences in culture and local objectives were minimized to allow for a successful implementation.

Tupperware has been able to harvest many benefits from this project implementation. According to Tupperware's internal estimates, the benefits associated with the project were more than 8 times the costs, as measured by the increased sales that resulted from the system. These benefits were accounted for by the ability to reduce costs, to negotiate worldwide raw material contracts, to source production at low cost locations, and to respond better to potential product shortages through more effective utilization of worldwide production capacity. In terms of psychological benefit, the teamwork that was

---

[29] Without this type of approach, Tupperware would have been saddled with the task of interfacing many different types of equipment with each other. This is clearly more complex. Given five types of machines, only five interfaces would need to be developed. However, without a common standard, dozens or even more interfaces would have to be developed and maintained.

[30] Tupperware IS management stated that it had experienced debilitating delays with the EDI service provided by GEISCO (The General Electric Information Services Company). As a result it moved as quickly as possible to build a system based on the X.25 packet-switched network standard.

built up through the intensive project review and planning processes has resulted in a greater sense of comradeship among the employees.

After GEISCO stopped carrying the EDI traffic (see footnote 30), the Tupperware Express system was able to process orders on a worldwide scale almost instantaneously. The company was able to harvest a 50 percent cost production in this function. Since the corporation is now "operating globally," it is able to optimize manufacturing and distribution costs. In addition, the global inventory and order-management system gives Tupperware the ability to respond quickly to hot products when they "catch fire" in different parts of the world. For example, if a product suddenly "catches fire" in Korea, Tupperware might be able to supplement its supply from manufacturing centers located in other parts of the world. The inventory system is able to detect a hot product faster than at any time in the past, thus giving the company more time to plan its response.

Both shipping and supply can now take place on a global basis. In addition, the ordering system gives a great boost to the sales side, which operates to a very great extent by independent distributors.

By all indications, the Tupperware Express project was a success. The IS management is able to demonstrate clear advantages to its implementation. In terms of what IS management did to handle the project, and the way in which various challenges were met, we might draw the following lessons:

- *Interface to a common standard instead of between different machine types.* What is clever about the solution adopted is that in making the various machine types interface to a common interface, Tupperware avoided forcing any of the technology into an obsolete status. Tupperware was also able to maintain its eclectic collection of equipment located in different places around the world. In addition, this solution produces proportionally greater savings in terms of systems effort the greater the variety of machine types.
- *Maintain local ownership and pride.* In the implementation of the Tupperware Express system, the decision to interface the satellite systems to a common *lingua franca* was critical in allowing the information-system employees at the satellite locations to continue using their expertise on *their* systems. This decision can be contrasted with a strategy in which a centrally developed system is imposed upon the satellite locations in order to have a consistent system throughout the company.
- *Develop consensus with satellite managers, then use them to implement the system.* The process of planning and building consensus appears to provide important lessons for international information-system management. Rather than the emerging strategy being a result of a central plan being imposed on the satellites, the information officers from the satellites were brought into the process from the very beginning. After agreement was achieved, these same employees were used to implement the system in the satellite locations.

The teamwork and the elimination of personal and cultural barriers resulting from the intensive brainstorming sessions undoubtedly played an important role in helping the company navigate the rough passage of the implementation phases. Even though during that phase of the project the different principals were interacting with one another at very long distances, the fact that they had been through a series of intensive brainstorming sessions together provided an important element of "human fabric" which sustained the group and eased communications.

- *Information systems can help alleviate, but not solve, many problems.* The most critical factor in the Tupperware business is the unpredictable nature of the hot product: how it is structured and how information systems need to respond. No available information-technology strategy even comes close to having as large an impact on the business as do the production, distribution, and operation of the plastic injection molds used to manufacture the product.

Given this situation, the best the IS function could do was to improve the global communication system first to identify quickly the hot products as soon as they "caught fire," and, second, to provide an ordering infrastructure that would accelerate product delivery to the large army of independent distributors. This was an important achievement.[31]

SUMMARY

The information technology-based firm-specific advantage has not been well-tested on either a practical or theoretical level.

- It is doubtful we will find many examples in which IT-FSAs were the most important factor for a multinational corporation making a decision to invest in a host country.
- We may expect to find examples in the financial services sector, owing to its inherent information intensity and a changing and more permissive international climate.
- Everyone agrees that control over proprietary information can in itself constitute a great advantage for the multinational corporation, particularly as regards the markets in a host country.
- Some believe that the increasing transparency and efficiency of the world's telecommunications system will tend to erase any competitive advantage some multinationals have had in processing their information.

---

[31] It is, of course, highly *reactive* in nature. This is clearly not a case of IS leading the strategy of the organization, but rather of providing a concrete and realistic contribution to the critical operations of the business.

Chapter 8 Information Technology-Based FSAs (Firm-Specific Advantages)

The Tupperware Express case demonstrates that multinationals need to work toward building globally competitive information systems, even if their old systems are dispersed and not well-organized.

- The information-systems function may be able to take advantage of a strong installed base, providing it is able to weld them together into a global system.
- The systems development function at the international level is difficult, time-consuming, expensive, and requires a great deal of skill to pull off effectively.
- Electronic document interchange techniques can be of great help in fitting together noncompatible information systems.
- Information systems can be used to solve severe business problems that originate in other parts of the corporation.

CHAPTER

9

Internalization of Transactions and Economic Efficiency

The most fundamental and common use of information technology is to raise transactional efficiency within an organization. Things happen faster, record-keeping is easier, and the cost per transaction is lowered, thus generally raising productivity, at least according to this measure. This is not the place to delve into the raging debate in which some Neanderthals are claiming that there is no increase in efficiency simply because they cannot measure it. What concerns us is the relationship of information processing to the theory of the multinational and the degree to which this relationship might explain why the MNC expands as it does abroad. Much writing has focused on "internalization" theory, but little has explicitly examined the role played by information technology. The Whirlpool and Philips merger case demonstrates some of the almost terrifying problems faced within the information technology function as a global merger takes place, and it is charged with developing a strategy to "internalize" the processing of information.

Chapter 9 Internalization of Transactions and Economic Efficiency

Internalization theory is used to explain (partially) the rise of the multinational corporation. This theory holds that a firm grows by internalizing economic transactions that were previously done on the open market. The firm can do them more efficiently than the market, and can thus make a profit (or extract economic rents). This theory has been built up particularly with regard to the processing, manufacturing, and transportation of raw materials, but not to the same degree with regard to either information-intensive industries (banking, finance, insurance, publishing, etc.) or to the internal information-based operations and functions of the general MNC (e.g., the information system of a manufacturing or raw materials processing firm).

In terms of information-systems research, as a very crude example, we could observe a large MNC turning to electronic mail and G-IV (digital) facsimile—all operating on its internal data processing network—in order to "internalize" postal and courier services which are available (less efficiently and more expensively) on the open market. However, a more intriguing (and considerably more substantial) line of research examines the role of information technology in overall general internalization (not just of information transactions but of all economic transactions). Information technology may well be the single most important factor in explaining this phenomenon, but you would not be able to discern this from the international business literature.

Armen and Demsetz discuss the concept of basic firm efficiencies as being a "consequence of the flow of information to the central party ... [in which] the firm takes on the characteristic of an efficient market in that information about the productive characteristics of a large set of specific inputs ... can be more efficiently ascertained than by the conventional search through the general market."[1]

Buckley defines internalization as follows:

> The thrust of the concept of internalisation is that the actions of firms can replace the market or alternatively can augment it. The explanatory power of the concept

---

[1] Armen A. Alchian and Harold Demsetz, "Production, Information Costs, and Economic Organization," *The American Economic Review* (nd), pp. 777–795. They state: "Conceiving competition as the *revelation and exchange* of knowledge or information about qualities, potential uses of different inputs in different potential applications indicates that the firm is a device for enhancing competition among sets of input resources as well as a device for more efficiently rewarding the inputs" (p. 795). They add that "Whether or not the firm arose because of this efficient information service, it gives the director-employer more knowledge about the productive talents of the term's inputs, and a basis for superior decisions about efficient or profitable combinations of those heterogeneous resources. In other words, opportunities for profitable team production by inputs already within the firm may be ascertained more economically and accurately than for resources outside the firm.... Efficient production with heterogeneous resources is a result not of having better resources but in knowing more accurately the relative productive performances of those resources" (p. 793).

rests on an analysis of the costs and benefits to the firm of internalising markets, particularly markets in intermediate goods.[2]

He discusses the various advantages a multinational corporation has in this process, including the "increased ability to control and plan production and in particular to co-ordinate flows of crucial inputs" and "avoidance of uncertainties in the transfer of knowledge between parties which may exist in the alternative [market] solution"—both aspects of internalization that are linked to use of information technology. In any logistics system, or tracking system that involves management of inputs into the firm, the information system plays a major role. Additionally, advanced technologies, such as teleconferencing, electronic mail, voice mail, digital facsimile, and other information technology-based international communications technologies, can be advantageous in reducing the difficulties in transferring knowledge throughout the corporation.

Casson reviews the theory of internalization within the multinational with examples of "specialisation in market-making," and "specialisation in risk-bearing" where "prior to contract, the allocation of risk between the two parties will depend upon who takes the initiative in making contact, communicating specifications and opening negotiations." In his review of the importance of information in "quality control and backward integration," Casson notes:

> *Information* about product quality is generated naturally as a joint product of the production process and accrues in the first instance to the person supervising production. The costs of quality control may be reduced significantly by drawing upon this *information* instead of replicating its discovery at a subsequent stage. [Emphasis added.][3]

It is interesting to note, however, that some of the most successful quality control information programs appear to contradict Casson's suggestion. For example, Toyota's Lexus quality control program uses Very Small Aperature Terminals to link each dealer to a centralized computer database with direct links to Nagoya in order to report immediately any problems with quality. Although this appears to contradict the assertions made by Casson in this specific instance, the overall concept of internalization theory appears to stand because Toyota has internalized vast amounts of transnational information flows which for other companies competing with Toyota are still externalized. Casson hints

---

[2]Peter J. Buckley, "A Critical View of Theories of the Multinational Enterprise," in Peter J. Buckley and Mark Casson, eds., *The Economic Theory of the Multinational Enterprise* (New York: Macmillan, 1985) pp. 1–19. An interesting observation that comes out of examining Buckley's analysis is that each of the contending schools presenting a theory of the multinational firm has an aspect which can be applied in some way to information technology.

[3]Mark Casson, "Transaction Costs and the Theory of the Multinational Enterprise," in Peter J. Buckley and Mark Casson, eds., *The Economic Theory of the Multinational Enterprise* (New York: Macmillan, 1985), pp. 20–38.

Chapter 9 Internalization of Transactions and Economic Efficiency   **129**

at the type of advantage achieved by internalizing communications (although in a slightly different context) and describes the advantages that might accrue to the multinational that is able to internalize communications costs so that when a customer approaches, it can carry out the same transaction with lesser costs than using the external market.

> *The cost of international communication* may be relatively great to the buyer, particularly if he does it only occasionally and therefore lacks expertise. It may be cheaper, and certainly less costly to the buyer, *if international communication is internal to the firm.* [Emphasis added.][4]

In the context of explaining the "extent and pattern of international production," Dunning discusses the ownership-specific O advantages which are balanced against location-specific L advantages in influencing where production takes place.[5] He notes that if the L advantages favor the host country, then production is likely to be internationalized. However, this is based upon O advantages of which he distinguishes two types. The first is "exclusive or privileged possession of intangible or tangible assets which gives the owner some proprietary advantage in the value-adding process of a particular product." A second type involves "the ability of a firm to coordinate, by administrative fiat, separate but interrelated (productive) activities better." It appears that this line of thought was part of an attack against "most neo-classical theories of trade...[wherein] no account is taken of international production, since factor inputs are assumed to be immobile."[6] Although Dunning and Buckley were writing before information technology was perceived as having a major effect on the internal operations of multinational firms—at this time, firms were still engaged in occasional remote batch processing, and rarely across

---

[4]Mark C. Casson, "Transaction Costs and the Theory of the Multinational Enterprise," in Alan M. Rugman, ed., *New Theories of the Multinational Enterprise* (New York: St. Martin's Press, 1982), pp. 33, 37.

[5]John H. Dunning, ed., *Multinational Enterprises, Economic Structure and International Competitiveness* (Chichester: John Wiley & Sons), pp. 6–8. A more precise analysis which sets forth his ideas in connection with other streams of economic thought is found in John H. Dunning, "Trade, Location of Economic Activity and the MNE: A Search for an Eclectic Approach," in Bertil Ohlin, Per-Ove Hesselborn and Per Magnus Wijkman, eds., *The International Allocation of Economic Activity: Proceedings of a Nobel Symposium Held at Stockholm* (London: Macmillan, 1977), pp. 395–418. He introduces the concept of the "economic agent" which is responsible for carrying out international business transactions.

[6]John H. Dunning and Peter J. Buckley, "International Production and Alternative Models of Trade," *The Manchester School*, 1977, pp. 392–403. Dunning and Buckley discuss some of the advantages exercised by U.S. multinationals during the mid-1970s: "the U.S. may have an advantage in the production of knowledge, but when this can be transmitted to other countries with U.S. enterprises, what would otherwise be a location specific advantage becomes an ownership specific advantage. Advantages which, due to the immobility of inputs, would be location specific in the absence of international production become ownership specific when direct foreign investment occurs" (p. 398). They went on to conclude that "our results emphasize the distinction between

(*continued*)

international borders—the fundamental concept applied to information technology would imply that *information technology might be used to export location-specific advantages overseas,* thus creating an *ownership-specific* advantage in a foreign market. Dunning and Buckley appear to be aware of this possibility, particularly in technology-intensive firms.[7]

These ideas immediately bring into question the role of information technology in helping to make the internal transactions of the multinational firm more efficient. Is it possible for information technology to make the processing of internal business transactions so efficient that it beats the market and gives the corporation an advantage over all other firms in a particular market? A United Nations report studying the automobile manufacturing industry discusses the effects automation will have on internalization and the ability of subcontractors to compete:

> The increasing scale of operations and the high costs of product development will not only affect vehicle producers but also component manufacturers. Auto firms may increase or decrease the extent of buying out of components depending on economies of scale and whether independent suppliers can keep up with the pace of technical change. Increased automation may permit the economic internalization of processes previously subcontracted to smaller firms. However, those suppliers who can keep abreast of scale/technology changes and are able to match the international growth of their customers can benefit significantly from developments under way in the auto industry.[8]

We know that as the *reach* of the information technology infrastructure increases, transactions are speeded up and therefore their costs plummet.

---

endowments specific to firms and those specific to particular locations. We also distinguish between economies of scale at a *plant* level, best represented by a pure plant scale variable and exploited at a given location, and those economies which are derived from the size of the *firm,* such as technical know-how [the product of R&D expenditure], human capital inputs and the advantages of internalising economic activities. These latter variables are not location specific, and, therefore, the inclusion of industries comprising firms which are relatively technology intensive and/or vertically or horizontally integrated across national boundaries, tend to weaken the explanatory power of hypotheses based solely on location specific endowments" (p. 401).

[7]See Buckley's attack against a Japanese approach to internalization theory in Peter J. Buckley, "Macroeconomic versus International Business Approach to Direct Foreign Investment: A Comment on Professor Kojima's Interpretation," *Hitotsubashi Journal of Economics,* 24, 1983, pp. 95-100. Buckley is defending internalization theory, which appears to have been subjected to a considerably different interpretation in Japan. He published another more extensive comparison between the "Reading School" (where he had evidently studied with John Dunning) and the "Japanese Approach" (which referred to the work of Kojima and Ozawa) in Peter J. Buckley, "The Economic Analysis of the Multinational Enterprise: Reading versus Japan?" *Hitotsubashi Journal of Economics,* 26, 1985, pp. 117-124, in which Kojima and Ozawa's discussion of "the role of traders [*sogo shosha*] as information networks, reducing uncertainty in transactions whilst appropriating the rewards" (p. 118) was reviewed in a critical light.

[8]UNCTC, *Transnational Corporations in the International Auto Industry* (New York: United Nations, 1983), p. 24.

Can the effects of information technology *in comparison with other proprietary advantages* of the multinational yield a significant advantage?

The internalization of firm transactions is also discussed by Belassa, whose study of the European Common Market demonstrated that "trade creation has resulted largely from intra-industry specialization in manufacturing, which brings benefits through the exploitation of economies of scale...[and that] further gains can be obtained through the rationalization of production in response to intensified competition in a wider market."[9] In other words, Belassa found evidence that the breaking down of the trade barriers in Western Europe allowed firms to internalize their own trade to a greater extent to achieve economies of scale.

It is interesting to note that a major debate ensued between Buckley, Kojima, Ozawa, Imai, and Itami regarding the application of internalization theory to Japanese *sogo shosha*. The Japanese side maintains that internalization theory does not apply to what they see as a unique type of organization which is very information intensive in its operations. Ozawa writes:

> Now, in order to remove the uncertainties of foreign supplies of industrial resources and to cope with shortages of labour and land, surplus capital began to be exported to other countries in which these productive factors existed in abundance, culminating in a gush of direct foreign investment from Japan that started in the late 1960s.[10]

Although the discussion does not touch upon the specific aspects of the information-technology systems used in the *sogo shosha,* there are many discussions of information flows and control over information processing within the firm. The Japanese seem to believe that the specific nature of the control

---

[9] Bela Balassa, "Trade Creation and Trade Diversion in the European Common Market: An Appraisal of the Evidence," in *The Manchester School,* pp. 93–127.

[10] Ozawa argues that the monopolistic theory (that firms expand overseas when they have a monopoly position which they can exploit) "is not quite appropriate to explain the recent Japanese experience: it does not help explain why Japanese enterprises, small as well as large, suddenly and simultaneously took on multinational characteristics in the late 1960s, even though most of them at least initially had not yet, by Western criteria, quite reached the stage at which they evolved naturally into multinational corporations." Terutomo Ozawa, "International Investment and Industrial Structure: New Theoretical Implications from the Japanese Experience," *Hitotsubashi Journal of Economics,* pp. 72–92. See also Mason's comments on the Kojima thesis: "My own findings indicate that there is not all that much difference in ownership patterns when comparing Japanese and American firms producing the same products. Where the product is a high technology product such as electronics, assemblies, semiconductors, and to some extent automobiles, the Japanese seem to be as likely as American firms to hold a substantial majority ownership or even 100% ownership. The attitudes are also similar." R. Hal Mason, "A Comment on Professor Kojima's 'Japanese Type versus American Type of Technology Transfer,'" *Hitotsubashi Journal of Economics,* February 1980, pp. 42–52. For further reference, see Sadayuki Sato, "Japanese Multinational Enterprises: Potential and Limits," *Japanese Economic Studies,* Fall 1980, pp. 68–85. Sato attacks the idea of considering Japanese multinationals as being different from European or American multinationals—in other words, Sato attacks the Kojima thesis.

of information in the *sogo shosha* provides a unique advantage, but that the nature of this advantage is different from the "classical" internalization advantages described by the Reading School. These differences revolve around the "institutional backgrounds" of the Japanese multinationals. Buckley argues that control over information within the *sogo shosha* can be a type of internalized competitive advantage just like control over other forms of technology and know-how on the part of multinationals in other sectors.[11] Gray later continued the argument and pointed out:

> It is quite possible that DFI (Direct Foreign Investment) is capable of generating better informational flows among different units of the same corporation than between two firms of different national origins communicating at arm's length. Other externalities which transcend the scope of arm's-length markets could involve the willingness of MNCs to transfer technology and to introduce new products to foreign markets. Such efficiency-enhancing effects of DFI result from intra-firm trade when economies of vertical integration and *information flows* tend, partially at least, to offset the impediments to international trade comprised by transportation costs, tariffs and non-tariff barriers and *inadequate informational linkages*. [Emphasis added.][12]

This may be one of the most extensive discussions of information processing advantages in the multinational corporation.

---

[11] Buckley quotes Yannopoulos as saying that the "use of specific information in a confidential manner has a great deal in common with the international merchant banks from Western economies" and "there are differences among countries in the availability of information inputs characterised by high communication costs." [See G. N. Yannopoulos, "The Growth of Transnational Banking," in M. Casson, ed., *The Growth of International Business* (London: George Allen and Unwin, 1983).] However, Buckley acknowledges that "the *sogo shosha* do operate internal markets in brokerage and information activities...the extensive trading network and reputation as honest brokers are non-transferable assets giving them opportunities to effect 'net combinations' and earn a return" (p. 121). Buckley notes the work by Kojima and Ozawa [I. Kojima and T. Ozawa, *Japan's General Trading Companies: Merchants of Economic Development* (Paris: OECD, 1984)] and writes that they "emphasise the mix of market and organisational 'principles' in the operation of *sogo shosha* and point to the crucial role of control over information of the companies which they describe following Williamson as 'information impactedness'." [O. E. Williamson, *Markets and Hierarchies: Analysis and Anti-Trust Implications* (New York: Free Press, 1975).] Buckley tries to bridge the different points of view by saying that this "exactly parallels the activities of (non-Japanese) multinationals in keeping core skills under total control. In the case of *sogo shosha* these core skills are knowledge of trading opportunities, margins and brokerage/arbitrage possibilities. In traditional multinationals they are technology or marketing based" (p. 121). A view of how the internal control systems within Japanese companies, including multinationals, is *cultural* rather than *formal/bureaucratic* is found in Alfred M. Jaeger and B. R. Baliga, "Control Systems and Strategic Adaption: Lessons from the Japanese Experience," *Strategic Management Journal*, 6, 1985, pp. 115–34. No one has investigated what this might mean for consideration of the information systems.

[12] H. Peter Gray, "Multinational Corporations and Global Welfare: An Extension of Kojima and Ozawa," *Hitotsubashi Journal of Economics*, 26, 1985, p. 129. This appears to be one of the earliest recognitions of the critical role information (and, by extension, the supporting computer and telecommunications infrastructure) can play in internalization in the multinational corporation.

In his review of the "appropriability theory," Calvert discusses Magee's work, which focuses on the role of the creation and control of information in multinational enterprises. This concern with "the neoclassical ideas on the private appropriability of the returns from investments in information" rests upon the assertion that "valuable information is generated by MNCs at five different stages: new product discovery, product development, creation of the production function, market creation and appropriability." What is of key interest is that it appears that "sophisticated information is transferred more efficiently via internal channels than by market means." According to this argument, most information is created in new and innovative firms, and considerably less is created in mature firms.[13] Rugman emphasizes that "the costs of internalization depend on, first, the organization of an effective communications network within the MNC and, second, the additional costs of social distance and political risk associated with entry to an unfamiliar foreign environment."[14]

One wonders what the role of information technology, which is rapidly improving its efficiency in the multinational corporation, would be in reducing transactions costs. If there were a rapid change in efficiency, then competitive advantage might be gained. However, in terms of internalization theory and analysis of transactions within the multinational, there could be a very major effect as well. Teece found that there are two major ways to explain foreign direct investment (FDI) by multinationals in overseas locations. The first concerns "locational forces," and urges the multinational to set up operations in different markets. The second is "explaining governance costs [or, equivalently, the transactions costs] associated with placing these production activities under common administrative control, rather than letting markets mediate transactions between stand-alone business units." Teece argues that in the process of vertical integration in the multinational, the costs of "governance," which is abbreviated GC, are different between the licensing option and the decision to set up operations overseas. Whether the GC of licensing is greater than the GC of FDI depends on the "complexity of knowhow." More complex problems require greater GC for licensing, so the FDI option is used. If information technology could significantly change the costs of coordination and transactions, and if Teece's theory is correct, then it would change the

---

[13] A. L. Calvert, "A Synthesis of Foreign Direct Investment Theories and Theories of the Multinational Firm," *Journal of International Business Studies,* Spring/Summer 1981, p. 49. Also see S. P. Magee, "Technology and the Appropriability Theory of the Multinational Corporation," in Jagdish Bhagwati, ed., *The New International Economic Order* (Cambridge MA: MIT Press, 1976), and Magee, "Multinational Corporation, the Industry Technology Cycle and Development," *Journal of World Trade Law,* July/August 1977, pp. 399–421.

[14] Alan Rugman, "Internalization and Non-Equity Forms of International Involvement," in Alan M. Rugman, ed., *New Theories of the Multinational Enterprise* (New York: St. Martin's Press, 1982), p. 10.

ratio between licensing and FDI, probably in favor of licensing.[15] In other words, improvements in information technology and its ability to process efficiently the inner transactions of the multinational corporation can have a great effect on the underlying structure of the multinational, in addition to changing the general cost base of the firm.

The concept of internalization theory holds that economic transactions made within the multinational corporation can be done cheaper than transactions on the open market, and this helps explain the growth and geographical reach of the firm. The multinational corporation is like a large organizing blob which oozes out into the world's economy and digests (internalizes) economic transactions, thus locking them away under its control. If one examines the international business writing, the role of information technology is less clear. Obviously for sectors such as financial services, it would be difficult to argue that information technology plays anything but *the* critical role in international operations. However, we find information technology at virtually every transaction point within the multinational corporation, and we can conclude that it is the chief enabler of more efficiency and internalization within the multinational firm.

WHIRLPOOL CORPORATION: MERGER AND INTERNALIZATION

The appliance manufacturing industry in the United States has become relatively concentrated in the past few years. By 1986, approximately 80 percent

---

[15]David J. Teece, "Technological and Organisational Factors in the Theory of the Multinational Enterprise," in *The Growth of International Business*, pp. 51–62. Teece also discusses the role of know-how and information in the multi-product firm. He argues that without specialized control over information and the ability to use it to produce different products in the firm, economies of scope of the enterprise are not automatically generated. He writes: "Knowhow may also display some of the characteristics of a public good in that it can sometimes be used in many different non-competing applications without its value in any one application being substantially impaired. ...Accordingly, although knowhow is not a pure public good, the transfer of proprietary information to alternative activities is likely to generate scope economies if organizational modes can be discovered to conduct the transfer at low cost. In this regard, the relative efficiency properties of markets and internal organization need to be assessed. If reliance on market processes is surrounded by special difficulties—and hence costs—internal organization, and in particular multiproduct enterprise, may be preferred....The basic conclusion is that economies of scope do not provide a sufficient raison d'etre for multiproduct firms. There are likely to be numerous instances where economies of scope can be captured by an economy of specialized firms contracting in the marketplace for the supply of common inputs. Nevertheless, there are important instances where multiproduct firms will be needed to capture scope economies...(1) where the production of two or more products depends upon the same proprietary knowhow base and recurrent exchange is called for, and (2) when a specialized indivisible asset is a common input into the production of two or more products." David J. Teece, "Economies of Scope and the Scope of the Enterprise," *Journal of Economic Behavior and Organization,* 1, 1980, pp. 223–247.

of the appliance industry, worth about $11 billion annually, was controlled by four companies, including General Electric, White Consolidated Industries, Maytag, and Whirlpool. Refrigerators accounted for 25 percent of all appliance sales.[16] The industry is characterized by strong competition, and, in the late 1980s, by a move to improve quality in line with competitors. In 1987, Whirlpool and General Electric both offered to replace any faulty appliance.[17] In the late 1980s, Whirlpool started a strong and aggressive period of growth with the acquisition of KitchenAid and also a kitchen-cabinet business. From 1982 to 1986, Whirlpool grew from $2.3 billion to more than $4 billion per year in net sales.[18] It had been supplying Sears with Kenmore appliances since before the First World War, and by the late 1980s depended upon Sears for 37 percent of its sales, including automatic washing machines, gas and electric dryers, residential trash compactors, vacuum cleaners, refrigerator-freezers, and room air conditioners. Unfortunately, this dependence was being threatened by a change in the marketing strategies of Sears, which itself was facing many problems and competitive threats.[19] By the early 1990s the Whirlpool Corporation constituted a leading manufacturer of major household appliances, including home laundry appliances (which accounted for 34 percent of net sales), home refrigeration and room air-conditioning equipment (39 percent), and other household appliances (25 percent). It also produces or provides other products and services for home[20] and industrial use accounting for 2 percent of net sales. The kitchen cabinet business was added to the portfolio of businesses for a short while. However, Whirlpool divested itself of all assets in this area 18 months ago.

---

[16]See Zachary Schiller, "Appliances: Turning Up the Heat in the Kitchen," *Business Week*, Industrial/Technology Edition (2958), August 4, 1986, pp. 76, 78. This heated competition is indicated by advertising expenditures. In 1985, Whirlpool was ranked 135th in the United States. It spent $41.7 million with $14.5 million allocated for network television. See Anonymous, "Second 100 Leading National Advertisers: Wellcome Foundation/Whirlpool Corp./F. W. Woolworth Co./Zale Corp.," *Advertising Age*, 57 (56), November 3, 1986, pp. S64–S65. Its advertising stayed the same, at $62 million, in 1986, but began to shift its emphasis away from general promotion to a stronger focus on specific brands. It still ranked 135th in the United States. See Anonymous, "The Second 100 Leading National Advertisers: Whirlpool/Wickes Cos./Winn-Dixie Stores/F. W. Woolworth Co./Zayre Corp.," *Advertising Age*, 58 (50), November 23, 1987, pp. S49–S50.

[17]See William J. Hampton and Zachary Schiller, "Why Image Counts: A Tale of Two Industries," *Business Week*, Industrial/Technology Edition (3002), June 8, 1987, pp. 138-140.

[18]See Michael A. Verespej, "Whirlpool's New Kitchen Recipe," *Industry Week*, 234 (6), September 21, 1987, pp. 56, 58.

[19]See H. Lee Murphy, "Sears Bullish on Brands," *Advertising Age*, 58 (47), November 2, 1987, p. 28.

[20]The major household appliances include home laundry appliances, such as automatic washing machines and gas electric dryers; home refrigeration and room air-conditioning equipment, including refrigerators and refrigerator freezers, upright and chest freezers, room air conditioners, and dehumidifiers; and other household appliances, including electric freestanding and microwave ovens, and residential trash compactors. These appliances are primarily sold under brand names which are commonplace to most consumers.

Its factory in Clyde, Ohio, is the largest of its type in the world, measuring about 1.5 million square feet, employing 3,500 people as of early 1991, and costing about $162 million to construct. It is operated with a heavy amount of automation with robotic assembly and extensive use of automation programs.[21]

Whirlpool sales are in excess of $6 billion annually. Roughly two-thirds of sales are domestically generated. The company employs 30,000 people throughout the world.

The appliance manufacturers in 1987 accounted for more than $6.5 billion in parts and materials purchases from subcontractors and suppliers, and Whirlpool launched a Total Performance Supplier award to help tighten up its supplier relationships in order to improve quality and lower materials costs.[22] By 1988, Whirlpool was purchasing 500,000 tons of steel per year with 10 percent coming from foreign suppliers.[23] Product research had indicated that appliances were similar in working components everywhere in the world, and Whirlpool worked hard to purchase as many component suppliers as possible. In the spring of 1991, Whirlpool reported that it had been working hard to redefine its procurement strategy for the electronics side of its components. It was trying to force its suppliers to stay at the very leading edge of the technology.[24] It upgraded its Clyde plant with a $175 million overhaul, thereby drastically improving quality.[25] It was reported that by early 1991, Whirlpool had improved its quality by more than 40 percent above the levels that had taken more than 30 years to reach.[26] At the same time, Whirlpool restructured into seven business units, with one each focused on Whirlpool, KitchenAid, and Kenmore appliances. Unfortunately, 1987 and 1988 were not the best financial years for Whirlpool as profit margins dropped 25 percent, with net income $192 million in 1987 being down 4 percent from 1986. Return on equity was below 15 percent, which many consider to be a danger sign in this industry. Whirlpool toughened up and began to work aggressively at cutting costs.[27]

---

[21] See Anonymous, "Factories of the Future: Electrolux Corp.; General Dynamics Corp.; Whirlpool Corp.; Bader Meter Inc.," *Industry Week,* 236 (6), March 21, 1988, pp. 34–42.

[22] See Shirley Cayer, "Buyers in the Appliance Industry Thrive in the New Global Market," *Purchasing,* 104 (4), April 14, 1988, pp. 46–51.

[23] See Shirley Cayer, "Building a World-Class Supplier Base Is the Number-One Priority," *Purchasing,* 104 (4), April 14, 1988, pp. 52–55.

[24] See Shirley Cayer, "Develop a Supplier; Own the Future," *Purchasing,* 110 (8), May 2, 1991, pp. 57, 59.

[25] See Stephen Kindel, "World Washer: Why Whirlpool Leads in Appliances, Not Some Japanese Outfit," *Financial World,* 159 (6), March 20, 1990, pp. 42–46.

[26] See Gary S. Vasilash, "A Big Job. A Big Plant. An Enormous Challenge," *Production,* 103 (2), February 1991, pp. 42–46. One of the key elements of the manufacturing strategy was to attain as many economies of scale as possible through consolidation of production.

[27] See Wendy Zellner, "A Tough Market Has Whirlpool in a Spin," *Business Week,* Industrial/Technology Edition (3050), May 2, 1988, pp. 121–122.

Whirlpool's headquarters are located in Michigan. Its principal plants are located throughout the United States, with two overseas. U.S. based plants are located in Arkansas, Arizona, Colorado, Illinois, Indiana, Kentucky, Michigan, Mississippi, North Carolina, New Mexico, Ohio, South Carolina, Tennessee; international plants are located in Canada and southern Europe. Spare parts are handled by a single worldwide operation located in Indiana. The extent of international operations is indicated by Whirlpool's distribution channels. Appliances are sold through independent distributors and co-owned sales branches in major U.S. cities. Whirlpool has minority interests in concerns making appliances in Mexico, Canada, and Brazil, and provides advice and assistance to foreign manufacturers for fees based on sales.

In January 1989, Whirlpool greatly increased its international presence by acquiring 53 percent of Philips' major appliances division, located in the Netherlands. The announcement was made at a grand party in Cannes, France, the site of the yearly film festival, which had been temporarily taken over by 2,000 dealers brought in for the occasion. This move was interesting in light of the reported over-capacity in the market of about 25 percent at the time, and a bout of price-cutting in the air as dealers fought out the battle in the market. Philips and Whirlpool promised to "bring quality to life" as the keynote slogan of the announcement.[28] One of the Philips plants, Bauknecht, which produces 500,000 dishwashers per year and holds an 8 percent market share in the West German market, is a major focus along with other facilities located throughout Europe. Philips was the number two manufacturer of white goods in Europe and Whirlpool was the number two manufacturer in the United States. Whirlpool paid $350 million for 53 percent of Philips' appliance business, with an option to buy more later. Theoretically, this would give Whirlpool the secure manufacturing base it needs to take advantage of the post-1992 environment in Europe.[29] The combined operation would have annual sales exceeding $4 billion per year,[30] and Whirlpool planned on capitalizing in Europe on its quality management system, which had been perfected in its Ohio operations.

In some sense, this expansion was one of the only available courses, as the American market was flat, and only the European market showed potential for growth. Ninety-eight percent of all the washing machines manufactured in the United States were manufactured there, and the strong "heartland" manufacturing base had benefited from 40 years of constant expansion in the post-World-War period. The U.S. market appeared saturated, but the European market was 25 percent larger and growing by 4 percent per year. However,

---

[28] See Christopher Parkes, "Unknown Warrior," *Business*, March 1990, pp. 90–92.

[29] See Zachary Schiller, "Whirlpool Plots the Invasion of Europe," *Business Week*, Industrial/Technology Edition (3068), September 5, 1988, pp. 70, 72.

[30] See John J. Kendrick, "Whirlpool's World Market," *Quality*, 27 (12), December 1988, pp. 18–20.

Whirlpool and Philips faced strong competition in Electrolux which had a 20 percent share of the market and was extensively represented throughout the continent.[31] Later on, France's Thomson Company, also a manufacturer of appliances, would be sold to General Electric in a counter-move to Whirlpool.[32] By 1990 it was reported that profits had risen by 14 percent in 1989, despite a 3 percent fall in overall sales. Whirlpool was still facing problems in some markets, such as Brazil, where the economy was taking a nose-dive, although by the late summer of 1991, it was reported that the Brazilian market had been responsible for a significant amount of Whirlpool's profits. In addition, environmental changes such as the Montreal protocol on the use of chloroflourocarbons (CFC) meant that Whirlpool would have to begin to redesign its numerous models for the reduced energy savings available from using the more environmentally sound hydrochlorofluorocarbons (HCFC) 123 and 141b to be used in foam insulation.[33] Whirlpool also cosponsored an exhibition with Frank Lloyd Wright in 1990 to emphasize its commitment to good design.[34] By March 1991, it was designing items specifically aimed at special groups, including the aged, in spite of its massive move into manufacturing volume for individual components.[35] It was offering products in braille, with operation manuals being made available in large type and also in audiocassette formats, and it stood as the *only* U.S. manufacturer with a complete recovery and recycling process for chlorofluorocarbons.[36] Whirlpool was also making its service manuals available on optical disk CD-ROM.[37] Combined with the washers and dryers it was selling through the Sears' Kenmore labels, Whirlpool was controlling more than 50 percent of the U.S. market.[38]

---

[31]See Thomas A. Stewart, "A Heartland Industry Takes On the World," *Fortune,* 121 (6), March 12, 1990, pp. 110–112.

[32]See Anonymous, "Europe's White-Goods Industry: Going Through the Wringer," *Economist,* 317 (7680), November 10, 1990, pp. 80–81. This acquisition was in spite of the downturn in the global market taking place at that time. Electrolux was predicted to lose 10 percent of its workforce within two years, although all of the European manufacturers were eagerly eyeing Eastern Europe as a potential new market.

[33]See Robert D. Leaversuch, "Total Redesign of Refrigerators Now Is Inevitable," *Modern Plastics,* 67 (10), October 1990, pp. 68–73.

[34]See David Finn, "Good Design Is Good Business," *Marketing News,* 24 (24), November 26, 1990, p. 9.

[35]See Norman E. Remich, Jr., "High Tech Wins Vote of Mature Consumers," *Appliance Manufacturer,* 39 (3), March 1991, pp. 62–63.

[36]See Terry Goldston, "Whirlpool's Whirlwind of Introductions," *Dealerscope Merchandising,* 33 (2), February 1991, pp. 68, 72.

[37]See Maura J. Harrington, "Optical Discs Move into Reach," *Computerworld,* 25 (17), April 29, 1991, p. 48.

[38]See Steve Weiner, "Growing Pains," *Forbes,* 146 (10), October 29, 1990, pp. 40–41.

Most of Whirlpool's domestic (U.S.-based) computing is centrally managed out of Benton Harbor, Michigan, for manufacturing, sales, and engineering.[39] All manufacturing plants employ computer technology to receive and transmit information to and from the central site. The plant's computer equipment supports local manufacturing requirements, including materials, production, and inventory. Manufacturing schedules are produced daily at the central site and downloaded to local computers nightly. The parts operation in Indiana is supported by its own data processing facility on site. International locations have data centers and employ the necessary staffing to support applications and equipment utility centers. Engineering applications include computer-aided design (CAD) technology which is located throughout the major domestic manufacturing areas and in the research and development centers in Michigan. Computing facilities in Europe are being studied at this time to ascertain the inventory of hardware, software, and applications, and their primary uses. Canadian, Mexican, and Brazilian operations run their own data centers.

Telecommunications and networking for inter-location data, voice, facsimile, graphics, and text are managed by a central group from headquarters. By late 1990, Whirlpool was engaged in switching over to a more sophisticated fast packet network linking together eight key nodes through T-1 facilities. Prior to this, Whirlpool had been using 19.2 kbps analog lines and 56 kbps digital leased lines for its network. The new arrangement, using the NET IDNX bandwidth management technologies, was projected to offer four times the capacities at the same cost as the use of leased lines in the past. The T-1 links and their supporting equipment had the capability of automatically rerouting around a failed node with a second or two, another vast improvement over the past. The use of a mesh topology between five Whirlpool data processing centers allowed this new network to do load levelling and to make the best use of the IDNX capabilities.[40] The responsibilities for international connectivity is a function of this group. Increased focus is being directed toward the implementation of enhanced networking capabilities.

---

[39] There is an interview with Richard D. Koeller, Vice President of Information Technology at Whirlpool appearing in David Ludlum, "The Value of Ad Hoc Partnerships," *Computerworld,* 24 (16), April 16, 1990, p. 76, in which he discusses the role of consultants in the formulation of the Whirlpool information-technology strategy.

[40] The IDNX multiplexers are supplied by Network Equipment Technologies Inc. and allow complete integration of all types of information into a single telecommunications channel, including voice, computer-generated data, and videoconferencing. Both a PBX as well as mainframe FEPs can be directly connected to the bandwidth manager. See Paul Desmond, "T-1 Network Keeps Watch Over Itself," *Network World,* 7 (53/v8n1), December 31, 1990/January 7, 1991, pp. 1, 6. For a detailed discussion of the role of bandwidth management technology in large SNA-based backbone networks, see Edward M. Roche, *Telecommunications and Business Strategy* (Homedale, Ill.: Dryden Press, 1991), especially the chapter on vendor solutions.

Whirlpool has aggressively sought to increase the role of information technology in its company, and in so doing has expanded its use from the traditional administrative areas to a more positive role with regard to research and development of new products, sales analysis and forecasting, and product evaluation. As mentioned earlier, Whirlpool has been a world leader in adaptation of factory automation in its Clyde plant. Another important function that has been added over the past five years involves order processing and distribution systems. In this area, Whirlpool has been a leader in linking sales branches and even customers for daily transfer of data and information through the network. The role of information technology has grown tremendously and is now critical to even the most general business operation.

A new challenge has been posed by the new strategic direction of the company, which involves expansion to markets outside the United States. As the U.S. market has been flat, this has become increasingly necessary should the company wish to maintain growth rates. The blistering rate of change has not been particularly easy on the old-time employees of the company. The new era of global competition has opened up what to many seems to be a new era of instability. Whirlpool's acquisition of Philips' European operations has put further strain in the human fabric as new relationships have to be worked out with new people arriving from outside the company, unfamiliar with its corporate culture, and bringing with them a cultural baggage of their own.

The need to understand the European acquisition in terms of the evolving structure of information technology poses a challenge to management. The IS management at Whirlpool sees several problems in this regard:

- *Working effectively with Europeans.* The IS management team foresees difficulties in working with Europeans. It is unsure what challenges will emerge in this regard, and seems to be unprepared for them at the time of this research. What are the best techniques and skills to use? These are the principal questions facing the IS management team.[41]
- *Weaning Philips away from its former parent company.* Since the takeover process does not run its course overnight, Whirlpool can be expected to face a series of adjustments in "digesting" its new company in Europe.[42] This must happen at several levels of the organization. It is

---

[41] It is not surprising that Whirlpool management has reservations about working with Europeans in the "new international environment" that their company has entered. Since up to this point, Whirlpool has worked almost exclusively with Americans in building their information systems, their experience base in the international environment is lacking. One would guess that the IS team will begin the process with the experiences it has developed in Brazil and Canada. This set of skills—to the extent that they are resident in the IS organization—will provide the foundation for working in Europe.

[42] This can be expected to cause a great number of internal conflicts and political turf battles between the companies. Depending on the levels of management skill being utilized, these conflicts can range from being either debilitating or liberating.

reasonable to expect that the overall management strategy and business structure will define the *reaction space* made available to the IS function. On the other hand, it is also reasonable to expect that IS will be incapable of playing a leading role in this regard.

- *Lead times in building networks in Europe.* Since the IS management team is aware of the need to build a comprehensive global system linking together their different locations around the world, it is concerned that building data communication networks and integrated networks will be much more difficult, expensive, and troublesome than accomplishing the same in the United States. It is unsure exactly how to proceed, and may not be ready for the heightened regulatory experience which it is going to work through in putting together an integrated worldwide system.[43]

- *Assessment of information technology requirements on an international basis.* In planning out its strategy, the Whirlpool IS management must conduct a worldwide inventory survey of its information-technology base. This survey will include *both* the old Whirlpool base and the new equipment which was purchased as part of the acquisition of Philips. Without this information, it will be impossible to begin the comprehensive planning process that will be required should IS attempt to build an effective worldwide system for data processing.[44]

- *The telecommunications environment is different internationally.* As companies expand at the international level, they must face a highly variable telecommunications environment. Those companies that are in the early stages of internationalization may face greater difficulties and uncertainties than more mature companies. In any case, the types of services, the conditions under which those services might be purchased, and the general level of flexibility available to the IS function, are highly variable from one international environment to another. Learning to cope with this uncertainty is a critical skill.

- *Assumptions regarding the availability of technology must be reexamined at the international level.* There *may* be a relatively higher level of

---

[43] In the survey that accompanies this research, uncertainty over telecommunications appeared near the top of the list. The many different telecommunications problems, such as transborder data flow, standards, protocols, and others, all appeared to be causing significant unease in the minds of IS management in a variety of corporations.

[44] The author repeats the observation that academic research might do well to focus on what happens to the information-technology function when its organization is involved in an international merger and acquisition. One could hypothesize that if assessments were made of both domestic *nation-state-bounded* M&A's in comparison with *international* M&A's, then one would find a greater degree of complexity and difficulty in adjusting by the international situations. The reasons might lie in the higher probability of different types of equipment, in the higher probability of different types of application portfolios, in the logistical aspects of the problem, or in other factors.

variability of information-technology platforms at the international level.[45] Certainly this is the case for Whirlpool. As part of its expansion overseas, it is going to have to cope with what might be a highly diverse information-technology base upon which it must build its applications. The type of environment encountered and the various combinations of equipment and other factors may force the company into adopting a recruiting drive in a relatively scarce human resources market.[46]

- *Information technology may be less likely to play a competitive advantage role internationally.* The IS management team at Whirlpool stated clearly that they have *not* found any examples within their company when the role of information technology was to get competitive advantage for the corporation. There is no evidence here to suspect that information technology will play an even greater role on an international basis.

SUMMARY

The internalization of transactions in the multinational corporations is a central explanation of the growth of the firm.

- Internalization is based on early ideas of expansion of the firm in general and has been extended to include analysis of multinational corporations.
- Although internalization has provoked great debate within international business circles, there has been virtually no consideration given to the role of information technology in the process of internalization.
- It is clear that in many important administrative areas of the multinational, information technology can play a critical role in reducing transaction costs.
- Considerably more thought needs to be given to quantification and measurement of internalization effects to determine the overall relevance of the concept; information-technology systems generally keep good enough internal records to form the basis for this analysis.

The Whirlpool and Philips case shows the type of internal trauma in the information-technology function that may result from an international merger, taken for reasons of grand strategy.

---

[45]This is another hypothesis that might be examined by academic researchers. The only way this might be determined is through intensive survey and examination of the installed base on a country-by-country basis. In addition, it is important to understand the situation within specific industrial sectors as well as at the individual company level.

[46]This is another hypothesis that might be examined in future research on international computing.

- We know of no cases in which the top management of a multinational takes into consideration the information-technology implications of a merger.
- It is clear that in such cases, the information-technology function does not play much more than a minor role in setting overall corporate strategy — it follows the strategy once it has been adopted, and must pick up the pieces and patch together any needed information-system changes.
- As the operation of the new merged multinational develops over the coming years, we can expect to see power struggles within the data processing function take place between Europe and Ohio, and these will be particularly acute when it is time to rationalize and streamline.

CHAPTER

10

The Problem of Host Country/MNC Relations

At the root of the great controversies in the post-war period has been the high level of starvation and inequality in the world. How does this relate to the management of information technology in multinational corporations? Host countries, particularly developing countries, have seen the multinational corporation as an instrument of power for its home (headquarters) country. Everyone remembers the more famous examples such as ITT in Chile, but on every level countries have taken steps to ensure that foreign multinationals are brought under domestic control. Controls over the amount of equity that can be held by foreign multinationals, imposition of certain performance requirements, extraction of guarantees regarding the treatment of national labor, are all examples of the conditions that host nations impose upon the multinational. These controls also extend to the multinational's use of information systems. Controls over international telecommunications (transborder data flows) have been highly publicized, but there are other more subtle controls as well. However, in spite of these controls and pressures, we find that in the early 1990s, there are strong indications that multinationals have not transferred and distributed technology and decision-making authority as they were asked to do.

Chapter 10 The Problem of Host Country/MNC Relations

A vast amount of literature has emerged on host country and MNC relationships, especially regarding examination of bargaining power, the international division of labor, technology transfer and licensing, transfer pricing, and government-imposed barriers against the MNC. Mason, for example, discusses the problems in technology and observes that "differences in capital to labor ratios are not as great as might be expected when the developing countries' manufacturing sectors are compared with the same sectors in advanced countries... [This might be explained by] technological fixity of production processes, distorted price relationships in factor markets, etc." His view of the central problem is that the host countries "desire technology [from the multinational] but wish not to become dependent upon an externally controlled force."[1] The ways to achieve technology transfer vary from sector to sector. For an analysis of technology transfer from multinational corporations to developing countries in the construction and design engineering industry, we might look at a report from the United Nations Centre on Transnational Corporations, which distinguishes between two types of technology transfer, "embodied" and "disembodied": "Disembodied technology transfer concerns the transfer of information through the medium of documents, design drawings, patents, discussions, seminars and technical training and education.... Embodied technology transfer concerns transfer through various planning and contracting devices. These consist of provision of services such as preparation of feasibility studies or of engineering designs, execution of projects on a turnkey basis, training of technical staff to operate the completed plant... until full production by an indigenous workforce is achieved." The report also indirectly mentions the use of computers in these firms: "the transnational contractors... [use] more sophisticated technology" to gain a foothold over the firms in developing countries.[2] Providing details about how multinational banks transfer technology to developing countries, another United Nations study says that "in some countries, the reluctance of transnational banks in introducing new banking technology is also evident, as in the introduction of a simple technology such as automated teller machines."[3]

A subset of this literature examines the information-technology aspects of this issue with particular reference to relationships between developed and developing countries. This literature views information technology as a negative force helping the MNC take advantage of the "weak" developing country.

---

[1] See R. Hal Mason, "The Selection of Technology: A Continuing Dilemma," *Columbia Journal of World Business*, Summer 1974, pp. 29–34.

[2] UNCTC, *Transnational Corporations in the Construction and Design Engineering Industry* (New York: United Nations, 1989), pp. 50–51.

[3] UNCTC, *Transnational Service Corporations and Developing Countries: Impact and Policy Issues*, UNCTC Current Studies, Series A, No. 10 (New York: United Nations, 1989), pp. 40–41.

Although much of the literature deals with problems between developed and developing countries, it is by no means limited to that. For an examination of the relationships between the United States and Canada, of how fears are raised in Canada at the prospect of a liberalization of the free trade agreement between the two nations, and of how that might harm the autonomy and power of U.S. subsidiaries in Canada, see the study by Baranson.[4]

The balance of information and data held in the transnational corporation subsidiary can influence how the host country, particularly a developing country, strengthens its hand in negotiations and aids its own industries. This is known to apply to patents and intellectual property,[5] but can also be extended to include the general balance of information between the national authorities and the transnational corporation.

> A second main line of policy—in addition to the strengthening of policy towards restrictive business practices...is aimed at increasing the host country's bargaining power through improved information-gathering and dissemination and improved evaluation capability.[6]

A United Nations study observed that "there is the question of regulating entities that operate across national boundaries and are able to escape the jurisdiction of individual countries...[and that] decisions taken by transnational corporations can lead to sudden changes in the production of their affiliates in different countries, without necessarily taking into account the interests of host countries." The report covers the problem of how multinational corporations dominate the world markets in primary commodities and how they "retain an overwhelming control over their marketing and downstream processing." It also reviews one of the information-specific advantages of the multinational corporation: "the growing importance of timely information about world market conditions gives transnational corporations a special advantage over producers in individual developing countries."[7] The UNCTC report also contains a great deal of information regarding the use of transfer pricing in the multinational corporation, a practice that is impossible without sophisticated international information systems.

---

[4]See Jack Baranson, "Multinationals and Free Trade: The Implications of a US-Canadian Agreement," *Multinational Business* (3), 1986, pp. 7–16.

[5]Some problems with counterfeiting are discussed in Michael G. Harvey and Ilkka A. Ronkainen, "International Counterfeiters: Marketing Success Without the Cost and the Risk," *Columbia Journal of World Business,* 20 (3), Fall 1985, pp. 37–45.

[6]See Department of Social and Economic Affairs, *The Acquisition of Technology from Multinational Corporations by Developing Countries,* Doc. No. ST/ESA/12 (New York: United Nations, 1974), p. 46.

[7]UNCTC, *Transnational Corporations and International Trade: Selected Issues* (New York: United Nations, 1985), pp. 1–15.

Chapter 10 The Problem of Host Country/MNC Relations

Fowler sets forth the principal reason why the business environment overseas is complicated by the relationships with host countries:

> There is no international law applicable to business because there is no supranational authority to issue and enforce it. Thus the conditions and circumstances of entry and the regulation of the operations of the subsidiary, affiliate, or branch of a multinational corporation chartered in a given country are subject to the laws of the country where it operates. National sovereignty covers corporations as well as people.

He concludes that "the prospect for an improving institutional environment for multinational companies depends primarily on the willingness of potential host countries as a matter of national policy to forego voluntarily the exercise of extremes of nationalism."[8]

One should not assume that the relationships between the multinational corporation and the host government are static. There is ample evidence to suggest that as the multinational gets more deeply involved, the host country's attitudes change.[9]

Das concludes that the many restrictions that are placed on the multinational by host governments will decrease the competitive power and economic efficiency of the firm. In his study of MNCs in India, he argues that "the competitive advantage which the MNCs have had as a result of their worldwide integration of resources will greatly decrease as a result of the regulatory controls that are being imposed on MNC operations in the host countries."[10]

India and IBM fought for a long time over the ability of IBM to set up a wholly owned subsidiary in India, which the Indians did not wish to permit. Eventually, IBM began to slip back into India, once the Indian government signed a letter of understanding that no IBM technology would be transferred

---

[8] Henry H. Fowler, "National Interests and Multinational Business," *California Management Review*, Fall 1965, pp. 3–12. (Fowler was a U.S. Secretary of the Treasury).

[9] A good example of this is a study of Chrysler corporation in the United Kingdom. The UK government first didn't wish it to enter the market, then eventually ended providing subsidies. See Stephen Young and Neil Hood, "Multinational and Host Governments: Lessons from the Case of Chrysler UK," *Columbia Journal of World Business*, Summer 1977, pp. 97–106.

[10] Ranjan Das, "Impact of Host Government Regulations on MNC Operations: Learning from Third World Countries," *Columbia Journal of World Business*, Spring 1981, pp. 85–90. He studied more than 877 private sector companies in India. Das presents some interesting observations regarding how the information system will change as host country regulations become more entrenched: "As host country regulations become increasingly predominant in influencing an affiliate's decisions on capital investment, product introduction and withdrawal, logistical planning, pricing, recruitment of employees, etc., the traditional performance evaluation system based on conventional reports will no longer be useful in evaluating the affiliate's management. New systems for management appraisal will have to be designed based on qualitative analysis and nonaccounting measures of performance."

from India to the USSR.[11] Wang discusses the sensitive role that international business may play in transferring computer technology to developing countries, and laments that COCOM restrictions have made it very difficult to conduct business with China. He writes: "even an Apple personal computer ran into problems because it embodied a part or device which was considered sensitive. An entire product line or turnkey plant might have to be redesigned so that certain items could be avoided and the level of technology lowered."[12] This type of restriction would have a great effect on the types of computers a multinational corporation might use within Chinese borders. It is an example of an internationally imposed barrier to trade that does not originate with the host country.

In his discussion of the effects of the multinational corporation on balance of payments of host countries, Stobaugh mentions some of the chief criticisms that have been levelled at the multinational. He mentions the use of "inter-company transfer pricing to avoid taxes," "the use of intercompany loans or extension of intercompany credit to avoid monetary restraints in the host country," and "the engagement in currency speculation which weakens a nation's reserves." He seems to hint that as the power and sophistication of information technology grows, it will be easier for the multinational corporation to engage in these (and many other) practices:

> Heightening this need for international agreement is the rapid increase in communications and transportation combined with the increasing capabilities of electronic computers, which give the multinational enterprise headquarters a growing ability to operate the enterprise as an organizational whole rather than as a number of somewhat independent subsidiaries.[13]

In some developing countries, particularly those in which there is a high degree of inflation and economic uncertainty, the information-systems department is required to develop applications to prevent the chaos that could conceivably occur. For a study of the situation in Mexico, and of the functioning of the clearing system between banks, much of it hosted on personal computer systems, see Griffiths and Robertson.[14]

---

[11] See Maggie McLening, "Big Blue Tiptoes into India," *Datamation,* 32 (7), April 1, 1986, pp. 54–58. It remains to be seen what the eventual situation will be in India, although one would suspect that, with its booming software industry, it will eventually find it of great advantage to work more closely with IBM. In late 1991, IBM finally reached an agreement to enter the Indian market to produce personal computers.

[12] N. T. Wang, "United States and China: Business Beyond Trade—An Overview," *Columbia Journal of World Business,* Spring 1986, p. 7.

[13] Robert B. Stobaugh, "The Multinational Corporation: Measuring the Consequences," *Columbia Journal of World Business,* January–February 1971, pp. 59–64.

[14] Susan H. Griffiths and Nigel J. Robertson, "Mexico: A Progress Report," *Journal of Cash Management,* 8 (4), July–August 1988, pp. 21–24. The situation is very difficult when there is a major currency devaluation, as was the case with Mexico in the mid-1980s.

Boddewyn and Cracco argue that the "political game in world business" can bring opportunities in disguise. They classify the reasons why countries take "nationalistic" actions against the multinational as being based on "national interest," "national sovereignty," and "national identity." The nation-state (host country) in which the multinational is operating may have many different goals that are not the same as the goals of the multinational, including "reduction of unemployment," "training of managerial talents," "training of skilled workers," "limitation of foreign personnel into managerial and highly technical positions," "representation of nationals on board of directors," and "development of local personnel up to 100%."[15] It should be added that the protection of the domestic telecommunications in many host countries is often responsible for the barriers to computer networking that are experienced by the information-technology function of the multinational.

Gabriel believes that the relationship between the host government and the MNC does not always have to be one of hostility: "conflict between multinationals and host countries is not inevitable.... in almost all cases, constructive adaptation can reconcile the fundamental interests of the multinational corporation and those of the host country's government and business community."[16]

Host country relations can be further strained when the multinational itself becomes a direct instrument of national power and is used by its home country to enforce foreign policy in the host country. Nye and Keohane give the examples of the United States forbidding IBM to sell computers to France in order to prevent France from developing nuclear capability, and of the controls over exports to such "enemy" countries as mainland China and Cuba.[17]

In an extensive analysis of how governments act to control the multinational corporation, Doz developed a theory of bargaining power in which the resources of the multinational corporation are matched against the

---

[15]Jean Boddewyn and Etienne F. Cracco, "The Political Game in World Business," *Columbia Journal of World Business,* January–February 1972, pp. 45–56. They suggest several "offensive measures" including the need to "recognize the role private enterprises are expected to play in the nation's development," "appoint a top executive to handle government relations," "make it a point to participate, preferably through a local trade association, in the making and application of public economic policy in the host country," and "behave as a good citizen concerned with the achievement of the goals of the country." They also suggest defensive measures: "limit vulnerability, just as is done with market. Adopt a low profile. Develop local allies among suppliers, customers and those dynamic elements—private and public—who appreciate the presence of progressive firms. Learn what makes foreign policy makers and administrators tick and develop a public relations campaign surrounding it."

[16]Peter P. Gabriel, "Adaptation: The Name of the MNCs' Game," *Columbia Journal of World Business,* November–December 1972, pp. 7–14.

[17]Joseph S. Nye, Jr. and Robert O. Keohane, "Transnational Relations and World Politics: An Introduction," *International Organization,* 25 (3), 1971, p. 341. They define "communication, the movement of information, including the transmission of beliefs, ideas, and doctrines" as one of the "four major types of global interaction."

resources and political-economic objectives of the host country. This work was developed in conjunction with a study of multinationals in the power systems and telecommunications equipment business. Possible host government goals might be to control a national monopoly, to protect either nascent or senescent national industries, or to turn around a failing company or sector. Doz shows that, under some circumstances, it is possible to have a form of cooperation between the entering multinational and the host government, if the MNC adopts a policy of being responsive and can bring proprietary knowledge into the host country.[18]

One of the difficulties in meeting host country demands is that the operations in a specific host country must strike a balance between the demands of the specific national market and the needs of the multinational as a whole. Doz, Bartlett, and Prahalad argue:

> The most difficult challenge management faces is administrative: the structuring of the company's internal decision-making process to allow the organization to sense, interpret, and respond to tensions, and the resolution of the often contradictory demands for global competitiveness and national responsiveness.... The complexity of critical decisions varies substantially between a company with a single business in a few foreign markets, and a diversified company operating in a large number of national environments. Not only is there likely to be an increased need for coordinated management approach in the latter situation, but top management will be less able to maintain a detailed understanding of the substance of the numerous complex decisions central to the company's successful operations.[19]

Although not an analysis of information technology systems per se, De La Torre's analysis of the bargaining which takes place between host governments and the multinational corporation brings out the critical role of information in determining the net benefits to the host country from foreign direct investment. De La Torre believes that "in international business negotiations access to relevant information is paramount" and notes the work of the United Nations Centre on Transnational Corporations as working toward helping developing countries regain the informational balance between themselves and the multinational corporations.[20] As this argument is extended into the 1990s, with the continued great impact of information systems in the multi-

---

[18]Yves L. Doz, *Government Control and Multinational Strategic Management: Power Systems and Telecommunication Equipment* (New York: Praeger, 1979), p. 42. An elaboration of the model is found in Yves Doz, *Strategic Management in Multinational Companies* (Oxford: Pergamon Press, 1986), p. 97.

[19]Yves L. Doz, Christopher A. Bartlett, and C. K. Prahalad, "Global Competitive Pressures and Host Country Demands: Managing Tensions in MNCs," *California Management Review,* Spring 1981, XXIII (3), pp. 63–74.

[20]José De La Torre, "Foreign Investment and Economic Development: Conflict and Negotiation," *Journal of International Business Studies,* Fall 1981, p. 24.

national and the continued lagging behind on the part of many countries in building up their data-processing infrastructures and capabilities, this problem will continue to exist, for computer systems can deny outside access to critical information. The problems with infrastructure have been pointed out in a United Nations study focused on developing countries:

> The rapid development of the electronics sector... is essential both from the viewpoint of creating new employment opportunities and of developing competitive skills and capability in a period of rapid technological change. These arise both from infrastructure constraints, such as inadequate and irregular power supply and inadequate communication facilities, and from severe shortages of trained personnel, particularly programmers, limited availability of hardware, including repair and maintenance facilities, little software capability and a scarcity of packaged sector-specific software of direct relevance in particular country situations.[21]

According to research done by Heitzman, one can find in many developing countries a lack of public interest in information technology and an uncomfortable dependence upon the multinational corporation as the key means of technology improvement in the country. Heitzman observes that a situation characterized by high population growth and low capital formation leads to this dependence.[22]

There is some evidence presented by Dunning that the multinational corporation transfers technology to the host country and can help improve its productivity in the export of research-intensive products.[23] Dunning points out that "at the point of entry, this bargaining weapon is in the host-country hands; once they are established the power (not least the power of withdrawal) passes to the MNE's."[24] We might suggest that, in terms

---

[21] UNCTC, *Transnational Corporations and the Transfer of New and Emerging Technologies to Developing Countries* (New York: United Nations, 1990), p. 61.

[22] James Heitzman, "Information Systems and Development in the Third World," *Information Processing and Management,* 26 (4), 1990, pp. 489–502. His research includes India, Pakistan, Sri Lanka, and Bangladesh; he observes that there is a general tendency away from large centralized projects toward "down-sized" regional projects within developing countries.

[23] John H. Dunning, "United States Foreign Investment and the Technological Gap," in *Conflicts of Interest in Agricultural and Industrial Policies* (nd), pp. 364–406. He records that "it would appear that the transference of knowledge—particularly enterprise-specific knowledge—from the United States to Europe by way of American direct investment in research-intensive industries has contributed in no small measure to the reduction in the technological *usage* gap" (p. 403). In terms of Western Europe, he demonstrated that "between 1954 and 1964, those countries which most improved their competitive position in the export of research-intensive products, relative to the United States, also attracted the greatest expansion in foreign (and in particular United States) investment and/or had the largest proportion of patents taken out by foreign (and in particular by United States) firms" (p. 398).

[24] John H. Dunning, "Some Conclusions and Policy Implications" in Dunning, ed., *Multinational Enterprises, Economic Structure and International Competitiveness* (Chichester: John Wiley & Sons, 1985), p. 428.

of providing telecommunications infrastructure to the MNC, changes initiated by the host country can change the economics of computing and thus the underlying assumptions regarding the best L advantages for placement of data-processing facilities. In addition, this may act as a type of non-tariff barrier or impediment to trade for the multinational. At best, arbitrary increases in the cost of data processing act as an indirect tax on the multinational.

One result of this is shown in a survey by Coopers & Lybrand who found that most CEOs do not have a clear idea of what an operational global system is, and that case studies indicate that many countries, such as Brazil, have highly restrictive policies regarding international computer communications systems.[25] As several keen observers have noted, this policy toward information technology was not new, a similar policy having been adopted in 1953 for a government monopoly on oil drilling and refining, and on all aspects of the telecommunications networks in 1962.[26] The policy was reported to have resulted in very rapid growth in manufacturing of computer equipment in Brazil and generated creation of approximately 150 nationally owned informatics companies in Brazil.[27]

Sauvant discusses the role of international computer networking and transborder data flow in connection with multinational corporations and their relationship with developing countries. His research indicates that there is a trend toward "greater specialization and centralization in the internal organization and decision-making structures of transnational corporations" and that "the transnational intrafirm division of labor within the corporate computer-communication system often allocates input-output or very simple processing functions to facilities located in developing countries." He seems to support the location advantage thesis: "the information advantage of transnational corporations may place domestic enterprises at a competitive disadvantage, thus hindering the emergence of indigenous capacities in host countries. This last factor also bears directly on the bargaining position of

---

[25] See Grady E. Means and Beverly Bugos, "Global Views: The Road to Rio," *CIO*, 1 (7), June 1988, pp. 16–19. The report sees indications that some developing countries are recognizing that it is in their benefit to loosen up restrictive practices in this area, and to provide critical infrastructure. Colson argues that the Brazilian computer industry owes its rapid growth to the highly interventionist industrial policy controlled by the Secretaria Especial de Informatica, which ceased to exist in 1990. See Frank Colson, "New Perspectives on the Brazilian Computer," *Multinational Business* (4), 1985, pp. 1–9.

[26] See Anonymous, "More Market Reserves in Brazil," *Multinational Business* (4), 1986, pp. 25–27.

[27] See Anonymous, "Information Technology in Brazil—The National Firms Take the Lead," *Multinational Business* (3), 1986, pp. 33–35, for an analysis of the 1984 informatics law and the First National Plan for Information and Automation.

these corporations vis-à-vis states and groups within states (e.g., trade unions)."[28]

However, the advantages of the multinational firm might appear nightmarish from other points of view. In his discussion of the corrosive effects of the information technology of multinational corporations on the host country in which business is being conducted, Schiller argues that the new telecommunications networks make it even easier for the multinational corporation to ignore the desires, needs, and interests of the host country, particularly if it is a developing country with little power:

> The transfer of authority from the national state to the transnational entity is continuing, and, indeed, accelerating. This is so partly because the transnationals are the chief beneficiaries and employers of the new information processes and instrumentation.... With powerful intra-company global communications networks at its disposal, the transnational enterprise today is in a position to make production, investment, funds transfer and related decisions on a global scale. There is no reason why the MNC's global considerations should be in accord with the plans or perceived needs of any one of the many nation states in which the MNC is active.[29]

Schatz reviews the demands coming from developing countries for a better "balance" in flows of information.[30] The problem of imbalances in the flows of information and processing power of multinational corporations is highlighted in the question of remote sensing, the process whereby data from satellites passing over developing countries is analyzed without the express consent of the country from which the data is taken. The use

---

[28] Karl P. Sauvant, "Transborder Data Flows and the Developing Countries," *International Organization,* 37 (2), Spring 1983, pp. 359–371. I am not sure that his conclusion regarding movement of data entry functions to developing countries is as widespread as he suggests, although there is ample evidence that some companies are doing this in claims processing and chit processing for credit cards; however, these are specific types of industries and may be special sectoral exceptions. For example, one knows of no cases in automobile manufacturing, chemicals, electronics, and so on. In an earlier work, Sauvant distinguished three major types of channels through which the home country cultural system influences that of the host country. He is writing in reference to what he defines as the "business subculture". He distinguishes (1) ownership and management control of parent enterprises and foreign affiliates, (2) ownership and management control, and (3) organizational dependency or imitation content. In Sauvant's model, the multinational corporation has both indirect and direct influence on the host country. Karl P. Sauvant, "The Potential of Multinational Enterprises as Vehicles for the Transmission of Business Culture," in Karl P. Sauvant and Farid G. Lavipour, eds., *Controlling Multinational Enterprises: Problems, Strategies, Counterstrategies* (Boulder, CO: Westview Press, 1976), pp. 39–78.

[29] Herbert I. Schiller, "The World Crisis and the New Information Technologies," *Columbia Journal of World Business,* Spring 1983, pp. 86–89+.

[30] Willie Schatz, "Communications: Airing the Issues," *Datamation,* 32 (2), January 15, 1986, pp. 30–35.

of remote-sensing data in mineral and petroleum prospecting and exploration, and in management of agricultural, forestry, and water resources, is characterized by this inequality because only the most sophisticated multinational corporations have the computing horsepower needed to analyze the data effectively. However, since the satellites are passing by at great altitudes in outer space, there is little countries can do in controlling this extraction of data.[31]

It should not be surprising that countries would wish to control their foreign trade relations by regulating multinationals, particularly if these countries are relatively weak militarily. Holsti discusses the changing concept of national security from military and political security to economic security:

> The textbook literature of international relations of the 1950s and 1960s implicitly or explicitly declared that politics, conceived as the search for security, power, and prestige, were a domain largely separate from economics, or argued that security was the proper sphere of foreign policy, while the maximization of welfare values was the concern of domestic politics. The rebirth of international political economy as a subfield of international relations has reopened the question.[32]

The ultimate extension of the power struggle is suggested by Keohane and Ooms in their discussion of how the multinational corporation will possibly affect the entire world economy. They approach the problem of multinational to host country relations from the point of view of political science, and indicate that much of the concern about multinationals on the part of host countries involves a search for *economic security*. The controls placed over multinationals can be seen as an attempt by developing countries to ensure better economic development and advantage. Keohane and Ooms also discuss the "possibility that multinational enterprises may become truly international—corporations without countries." The result of such a

---

[31] This problem is highlighted in UNCTC, *Transborder Data Flows: Transnational Corporations and Remote-Sensing Data* (New York: United Nations, 1984).

[32] Kal J. Holsti, "Politics in Command: Foreign Trade as National Security Policy," *International Organization*, 40 (3), Summer 1986, pp. 643–671. He discusses the policies of Japan and Finland as they searched for security under the hegemony of both the United States and the U.S.S.R. Instead of concentrating on military power, they tried to develop their economic power as a means of guaranteeing their security. See also Michael Mastanduno, "Trade as a Strategic Weapon: American and Alliance Export Control Policy in the Early Postwar Period," *International Organization*, 42 (1), Winter 1988, pp. 121–217. See also Walter E. Schirmer, "American Alternatives in an Era of Free Trade," *Michigan Business Review*, March 1968, pp. 8–19, which calls for continued technological leadership in the United States as a way for U.S. multinationals to withstand the rigors of freer world trading regimes.

development, of course, would be that they would be beyond the control of any single nation-state.[33]

In terms of developing countries and the New International Economic Order,[34] Behrman touches upon the role the multinational firm might exercise in control of information and data, and how it might be a disadvantage to the host country, resulting in "pressure for information disclosure."[35]

Kim's analysis seems to indicate that the multinational corporation should "be designed to enhance political responsiveness to the host government as the level of competition increases" and that, depending on the level of competition within an industry, the type of response, as well as how the response is handled internally within the firm, should change. He argues that as competition changes from the "turbulent to the intensive stage ... it may make sense to increase strategic integration between head office and subsidiary ... [and the] mode of communication and decision making will change from 'top-down' [unilateral] to 'interactive' [bilateral]."[36] In other words, as competition intensifies, the communication between the host government, subsidiaries, and headquarters will intensify.

---

[33] Keohane and Ooms note that "Political scientists have been very slow to realize that their descriptions of international relations in terms of power, the use of force, and struggles for security and status were inadequate insofar as they failed to comprehend the increasingly important role of economic activities and relationships in world politics. As long as international politics was seen largely as a politico-military struggle between two contending blocs representing different social systems, it hardly seemed necessary to focus attention on global economic transactions except insofar as they were directly relevant to that struggle." Robert O. Keohane and Van Doorn Ooms, "The Multinational Enterprise and World Political Economy," *International Organization,* 26 (1), Winter 1972, pp. 84–120.

[34] The NIEO was a movement on the part of the developing countries in the late 1970s and early 1980s to use various international organizations, such as the United Nations system, to redistribute resources on a global scale. A cynic would argue that the movement was little more than a type of glorified international "global socialism" in which entire countries were to be treated as recipients of aid. A more generous view would emphasize the contribution made in the debate toward bringing to the forefront of the world's attention the plight of many countries in dire need of some type of aid. It may be surprising to the reader that these debates eventually spilled over to the strategies used by multinationals in their planning for computerization of their subsidiaries in the developing world. In some cases, the training of local personnel in data processing became an important host-government demand which had to be met as a condition of doing business.

[35] Jack N. Behrman, "Transnational Corporations in the New International Economic Order," *Journal of International Business Studies,* Spring/Summer 1981, pp. 29–42. He notes that "Pressure for information disclosure by companies is rising, and despite the fact that many governments have extensive control over the companies and require substantial reporting, what is wanted more than host country information is an understanding of how the companies operate in other countries, so that each government feels that it is being treated equitably" (p. 39).

[36] W. Chan Kim, "Competition and the Management of Host Government Intervention," *Sloan Management Review,* Spring 1987, pp. 33–39.

Louis Wells noted how innovations developed in one country can be "leaked quickly to other countries through the communication network of the multinational enterprise," and warned that "if decisionmaking is highly centralized, governments are likely to feel increasingly threatened; they might respond by lashing out at the multinational enterprise, or they might try to reach agreements with other governments in order to control the new entity that is escaping the jurisdiction of individual governments."[37]

Encarnation and Wells' later study discussed the different strategies that many countries, including developing countries, were using to strike bargains with multinational corporations. It appears that by the mid-1980s, rather than being seen an enemies, many multinational corporations were seen as being very beneficial for host-government economies. The "storm over the multinationals" had subsided, restrictions had changed to inducements.[38]

In 1989 Franko confirmed some of Wells' theories when he found that the smaller and second-ranked oligopolists in their specific sectors tended to accept minority or 50 percent–50 percent joint ventures in their overseas investments.[39]

Heenan and Keegan have studied the emergence of third-world multinationals and argued that they hold the key to development for many poor countries, but that some governments are erecting barriers against them, thus retarding their own development.[40] Vernon-Wortzel and Wortzel discuss the competitive strategies of multinationals from developing countries and conclude that they need to pay attention to rapid absorption of new technologies if they are to survive in the markets of the industrial world.[41]

---

[37] Louis T. Wells, Jr., "The Multinational Business Enterprise: What Kind of International Organization?" *International Organization,* XXV, 1972, pp. 447–464. Wells is writing before the establishment of the United Nations Centre on Transnational Corporations, which attempted to do some of the very things he suggested here.

[38] Dennis J. Encarnation and Louis T. Wells, Jr., "Sovereignty en Garde: Negotiating with Foreign Investors," *International Organization,* 39 (1), Winter 1985, pp. 47–78.

[39] Lawrence G. Franko, "Use of Minority and 50–50 Joint Ventures by United States Multinationals During the 1970s: The Interaction of Host Country Policies and Corporate Strategies," *Journal of International Business Studies,* 20 (1), Spring 1989, pp. 19–40.

[40] David A. Heenan and Warren J. Keegan, "The Rise of Third World Multinationals," *Harvard Business Review,* January–February 1979, pp. 101–109.

[41] Heidi Vernon-Wortzel and Lawrence H. Wortzel, "Globalizing Strategies for Multinationals from Developing Countries," *Columbia Journal of World Business,* Spring 1988, pp. 27–35. According to the authors, these multinationals, which they call MEDECs (Multinationals from Developing Countries) "to a significantly greater extent than MNCs, use third party distributors and depend significantly on their distributors to push their products.... [Their] overseas subsidiaries are usually much smaller than those of MNCs." These conclusions would indicate that developing-country multinationals have considerably different information-technology requirements, and face considerably different barriers than are faced by multinationals from developed countries.

Chapter 10 The Problem of Host Country/MNC Relations

Gomes-Casseres shows how the eventual development of the multinational is determined both by the desire of the multinational to lower its transaction costs and thus achieve efficiency, as well as by the policies of the host government.[42] If it were the case that information technology and international linkages through telecommunications systems were being used by the multinational to get the greatest lowering of costs of internal transactions, then this would be a logical place for the restrictive nation-state to apply pressure. This type of restriction would be consistent with the Gomes-Casseres model.

Vernon argues that the multinational corporation has been used by different nation-states to pursue "beggar-thy-neighbor policies" because when they "try to attract multinational enterprises through tax exemptions or credit subsidies, they are often aware that their success will mean the diversion of facilities from some other national jurisdiction."[43]

If the multinational faces difficulties at the national level, the problem may be even more complicated at the international level. Robinson reviews how international organizations such as the OECD, the European Economic Community, and the United Nations have each adopted various policies and "guidelines" which regulate the multinational corporation at the international level. If there is any possibility of the multinational corporation becoming a "stateless" economic enterprise, without control of any single nation-state, then Robinson's analysis demonstrates clearly that even without control from *individual* nations, the multinational will face regulatory control from the international community. Robinson argues that in Europe, for example, the multinational has faced at least three major challenges: a democratic challenge in which labor law and "industrial democracy" have risen to the top of the public agenda; a capitalist challenge in which control over cartels and various forms of nationalization and protection for nationalized industries has changed the competitive playing field; and a "competitivity" challenge in which the activities of the multinational become subject to the various policies aimed at making Europe "more competitive," and in which international political issues, such as apartheid in South Africa, are considered. He writes:

> The emergence of the political constraint on Western multinationals has not been sudden.... [It] amounts to a quiet revolution in the values and rules governing business and its role in society.... [and] is paralleled by a decline in the capitalist

---

[42] Benjamin Gomes-Casseres, "Firm Ownership Preferences and Host Government Restrictions: An Integrated Approach," *Journal of International Business Studies,* first quarter, 1990, pp. 1–22. In his model, the general level of restrictiveness was based on the degree to which the host allowed joint ventures with its borders. There is no specific reference to information systems or to the non-tariff barriers in information technology and telecommunications that might be used by the host nation.

[43] Raymond Vernon, "Multinational Enterprises and National Governments: Exploration of an Uneasy Relationship," *Columbia Journal of World Business,* Summer 1976, pp. 9–16.

ethic to which big business... has itself contributed. The individual stockholder, the link to the democratic base from which capitalism emerged, has now been largely effaced in his function of control of business management... The decline of traditional forms of business control is part of a broader picture in which the decline of the capitalist ethic is a recurring leitmotif.... The hierarchical and centralised structure of multinational company decision-making has thus come under attack.... economic liberalism has become 'unidentified' with the European democratic mainstream. In the process, multinationals, from having initially been an acceptable—even perhaps logical—economic expression of the Western political system, have instead come to be a prime object of democratic criticism.[44]

Frederick argues that the many restrictions and "codes of conduct" being imposed on the multinational corporation have a moral foundation. They form a "deontological norm" based in principles of human conduct and embody "respect for persons, respect for community integrity, respect for ecological balance, and respect for tested human experience in many spheres of life."[45]

Lindell's study shows numerous examples of how the father country of the multinational rather than the host country might use controls over exports and other regulations to carry out its foreign policy. In this case, the multinational becomes the extension of the foreign policy of the father country.[46] Cao, for example, describes the non-tariff barrier effect of the French *Plan Calcul* which made it more difficult for French firms to purchase foreign computer equipment. He also touches upon a similar situation that existed, although in a different form, in Japan.[47]

Finally, there is the question of host-country infrastructure and the FDI decision within the context of information technology. Some countries (for example, Singapore) have undertaken specific investment programs in telecommunications facilities and in training of computer operators, programmers, and engineers specifically for the purpose of attracting the MNC. These moves by Singapore are representative of a larger class of actions that countries have taken to attract various industries and their multinational corporations, including high-technology firms and computer manufacturers. Miller, for example,

---

[44]John Robinson, *Multinational and Political Control* (New York: St. Martin's Press, 1983), pp. 225, 226.

[45]William C. Frederick, "The Moral Authority of Transnational Corporate Codes," *Journal of Business Ethics*, 10, 1991, pp. 165–177.

[46]Erik Lindell, "Foreign Policy Export Controls and American Multinational Corporations," *California Management Review*, XXVIII (4), Summer 1986, pp. 27–39. He gives many examples of control over computers to states such as the Soviet Union and South Africa (before the Botha reforms). A similar problem comes up with U.S. laws forbidding its multinationals, even those operating from a country such as Canada, to trade with Communist China. See I. A. Litvak and C. J. Maule, "Guidelines for the Multinational Corporation," *Columbia Journal of World Business*, July–August 1968, pp. 35–42.

[47]A. D. Cao, "Non-Tariff Barriers to U.S. Manufactured Exports," *Columbia Journal of World Business*, Summer 1980, pp. 93–102.

lists more than 25 specific incentives offered by governments in order to attract the computer industry to locate within their national borders. He notes that "in the vast majority of cases in this study, incentives did not materially influence the decision to locate a plant in a region. Within regions, the picture is somewhat different, as company managements have investigated incentive packages of similarly placed countries quite carefully."[48]

In addition, an issue such as the regulation and control of transborder data flow (building international computer networks across national borders) has been a major breeding ground for conflict between the MNC and host governments. Most MNCs see controls over TDF as being very significant non-tariff barrier (NTB) to trade. Dordick argues:

> Domestic information policies concerning computing and communicating are intertwined with international politics. The emerging information society is a global one; while political tensions appear not to be lessening, a single telecommunications world is emerging.... [T]he international debate concerning transborder data flow is, in essence, a debate about international trade in telecommunications and information products and services.... Nations are seeking entrance to this new international trade regime and developing strategies that will maximize their opportunities.

Dordick noted that "multinational corporate operations require worldwide, round-the-clock communications and global networks for banking, air traffic control, travel reservations, news and trade."[49]

Mascarenhas gives an example of a French bank having difficulties processing German data outside of Germany.[50] Jenkins discusses the problems multinational corporations face in setting up data networks in the German environment, such as onerous requirements, excessive delays in getting approval, high costs, and problems with the licensing of types of software that can be used as well as with controls over what type of data can be transmitted. This situation, Jenkins argues, leads most multinationals in Europe to choose public packet-switched technology for their operations.[51] Jenkins describes similar delays and problems encountered in the United Kingdom. Host-country regulations against information technology extend well beyond transborder

---

[48] Robert R. Miller, "Computers," in Stephen E. Guisinger and Associates, eds., *Investment Incentives and Performance Requirements: Patterns of International Trade, Production, and Investment* (New York: Praeger Special Studies, 1985).

[49] Herbert S. Dordick, "The Emerging World Information Business," *Columbia Journal of World Business,* Spring 1983, pp. 69–76. The most comprehensive study published on transborder data flow appears to be Karl P. Sauvant, *International Transactions in Services: The Politics of Transborder Data Flows* (Boulder, CO: Westview Press, 1986).

[50] Briance Mascarenhas, "Transnational Linkages and Strategy," in Anant R. Negandhi and Arun Savarta Arun, eds., *International Strategic Management* (Lexington, MA: Lexington Books, 1989).

[51] Avery Jenkins, "Communications: Networks in a Strange Land," *Computerworld,* 21 (36A), September 9, 1987, pp. 25–30.

data flow: import of computers, utilization of local programming, licensing of international database access, prohibition against private networks, and onerous database maintenance requirements (including stipulations that the MNC must operate data centers within the host country regardless of economic considerations) are a few of the other areas where host country–MNC relationships need study. Many of these regulations are described by Wunder.[52] Guynes et al. sum up the various national concerns that drive restrictions on transborder data flow, but note that in addition to the OECD Guidelines, the GATT has taken some steps in helping to improve the ability of firms to utilize international telecommunications.[53]

The relationship between the multinational corporations and the host countries in which they operate has always been a major problem, not only in developing countries but also in advanced countries. This problem arises because of a divergence of interests: the country is interested in economic development and protection of its national and economic sovereignty, and the multinational is interested in conducting business and making profits. Some writers have extensively analyzed the power-bargaining relationships between these two parties. There have been many disagreements in the area of information technology as well. Controls, both direct and indirect, over how information technology is used, over the structure and administrative regulation of data bases, and, in particular, over the utilization of telecommunications services, have all combined to complicate matters for the information-technology function.

A SMALL SURVEY

In part to examine how multinational corporations distribute their information systems from one country to another, we took a small survey that attempted to make measurements. The results are imperfect, and are intended merely as an incentive to further research, but if they are correct, they indicate strongly that multinationals *do not* distribute the bulk of their computing resources.

---

[52]Bernard J. Wunder, Jr., "International Commerce in Telecommunications and Information Products," *Columbia Journal of World Business,* Spring 1983, pp. 62–67. Wunder writes: "Among the protectionist barriers that have been proposed or employed are: (1) discriminatory taxes or tariffs on the international transfer of information, (2) pricing the local telecommunications services that our firms need at levels greatly exceeding relevant costs, (3) imposing novel or otherwise exclusionary technical standards on telecommunications and data processing vendors and users, (4) requiring that domestic information and transactions be processed only in the home country, and (5) denying foreign enterprises entry outright."

[53]Jan L. Guynes, Stephen C. Guynes, and Ron G. Thorn, "Conquering International Boundaries That Restrict the Flow of Data," *Information Strategy: The Executive's Journal,* 6 (3), Spring 1990, pp. 27–32.

Frankly speaking, the author hopes this data is wrong and that, therefore, multinationals are in fact helping transfer technology and skills to host countries to a considerably greater extent than indicated here.

The initial contact with the MNCs was through a survey, which had two parts. Part I was formed using some of the issue-analysis questions of the Deans (1988) survey of U.S.-based MNCs.[54] Part II was intended to identify the geographical distribution of data-processing activities. The survey was sent to approximately 200 corporations in the fall of 1989. The questionnaire was mailed to the CIO or head of MIS of major U.S. multinationals. Most of the firms did a fairly good job of completing the questionnaire, although one or two did not answer all the questions, particularly the questions in part II that examined the geographical distribution of data-processing resources on a global basis. Preliminary analysis was completed in December 1989. A second copy of the survey was mailed to a wider group in early 1990, along with a limited mailing to various corporations in Western Europe. No Japanese multinationals have been included in the survey.

The index of internationalization provides a quick reference guide, indicating the balance of power between home country-based data processing and international data processing, and shows the type of data received (See Table 10.1). This index was calculated by taking the number of data-processing centers located outside the home country and dividing it by the number of centers within the home country.[55] A plot of the number of countries in which the firm is doing business against the index of internationalization of data processing, shown in Figure 10.1, does not reveal a clear pattern or relationship, except that most firms operate in 50 countries or less.

The analysis of international topology involved the selection of six indicators: the index of internationalization, the distribution of DASD, MIPS, data-processing centers, and employees; and the geographical distribution of the MIPS/Employee ratio.

- *DASD*—the amount of Direct Access Storage Devices, measured in gigabytes for each geographical region.
- *MIPS*—the processing power within each geographical region, measured by equivalents of millions of instructions per second.

---

[54] See Candace P. Deans et al., *Identification of Key International Information Systems Issues in the U.S.-Based Multinational Corporations,* Working Paper in Management Science DOR G-89-02, 1988, Division of Research, College of Business Administration, University of South Carolina. Some of this research also appeared later in C. P. Deans et al., "Key International IS Issues in U.S.-Based Multinational Corporations," *Journal of Management Information Systems,* 7 (4), Spring 1991.

[55] For example, if the firm had 5 centers inside its home country and 1 center outside its home country, then the index of internationalization would be calculated as 1/5, in other words, .2 index. If a firm has 2 centers in its home country and 2 outside, the ratio would be 2/2, or 1.0.

TABLE 10.1 Index of Internationalization and Scope of Firm Operations

Company	Sector	Number of Countries in which It Operates	Internationalization Index for Information Technology
CGE Distribution	Distribution sector in France	10	.083
Raychem Corporation	Specialized chemicals and materials	40	.971
Oxy	Petrochemicals	15	.80
Storage Technology	Computer peripherals	7	.857
Teleco Oilfield Services	Petroleum and natural gas exploration	15	.334
Honeywell	Computer and control systems	90	.412
Bank of America	Financial services	45	.6
Chevron Information Technology	Information services for Chevron, Petrochemicals	96	.187
British Petroleum	Petrochemicals	70	.90
Whirlpool	White goods	6	.23
Merck	Pharmaceuticals	132	.857
United Technologies Automotive	Automobile parts	11	.36
Phillips Petroleum	Petrochemicals	115	.466
Kraft General Foods	Food	22	1.0
Tupperware	Plastic containers	30	.84
Syntex	Pharmaceuticals	25	.83
Premark International	Diversified	100	.49
Sonoco Products	Petrochemicals	19	.75
Pirelli Informatica	Tire manufacturing	29	.571
Abbott Laboratories	Pharmaceuticals	45	na
Levi Strauss	Jeans	50	.54
Marion Merrell Dow	Chemicals	20	.4
Sonat Offshore Drilling	Oil exploration	30	na
FMC	Manufacturing	35	.218
James River	Paper	5	.167

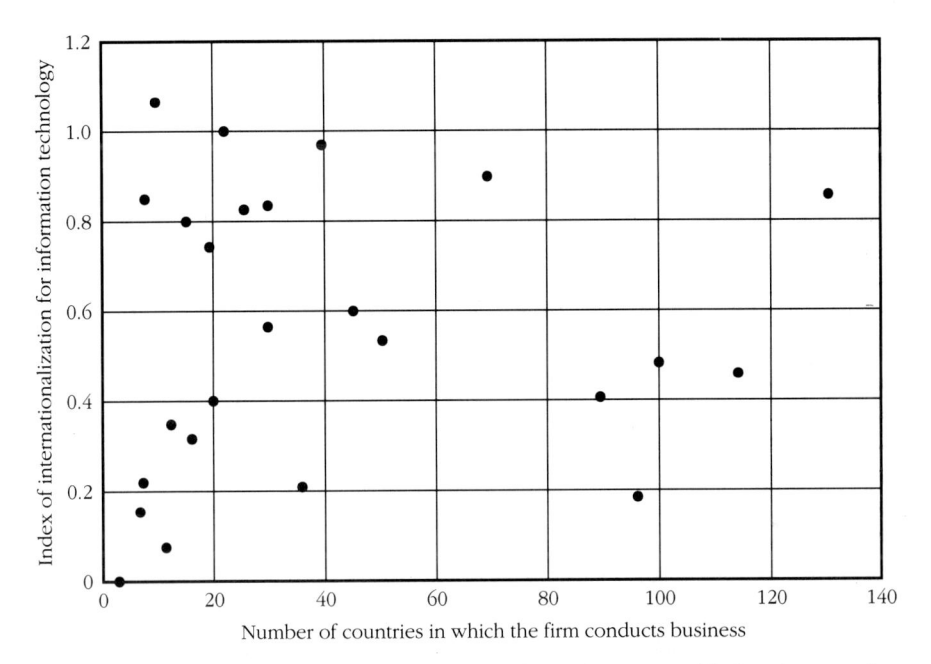

Chapter 10 The Problem of Host Country/MNC Relations 163

FIGURE 10.1 Index of Internationalization for Information Technology and the Number of Countries in Which the Firm Does Business

- *Centers*—the number of data-processing centers in each of the geographical regions.
- *Employees*—the number of corporate employees in each geographical location.

The analysis used four indicators, each of which was distributed over nine geographical regions of the world: North America, South America, Western Europe, Eastern Europe, Japan, Other Asia, Middle East, Africa, and Australia/New Zealand.

Distribution of Data Centers and MIPS

The distribution of data centers for the TNCs in this sample[56] shows a concentration in the developed countries. The great bulk of data centers are located within either North America or the EEC. As can be seen in Figure 10.2, TNCs

---

[56] In each of these figures, the names of the TNCs providing data is withheld as a condition for being given access for the study.

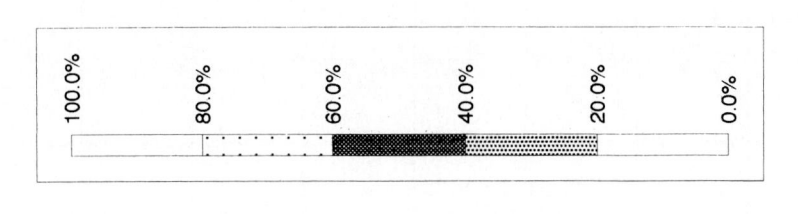

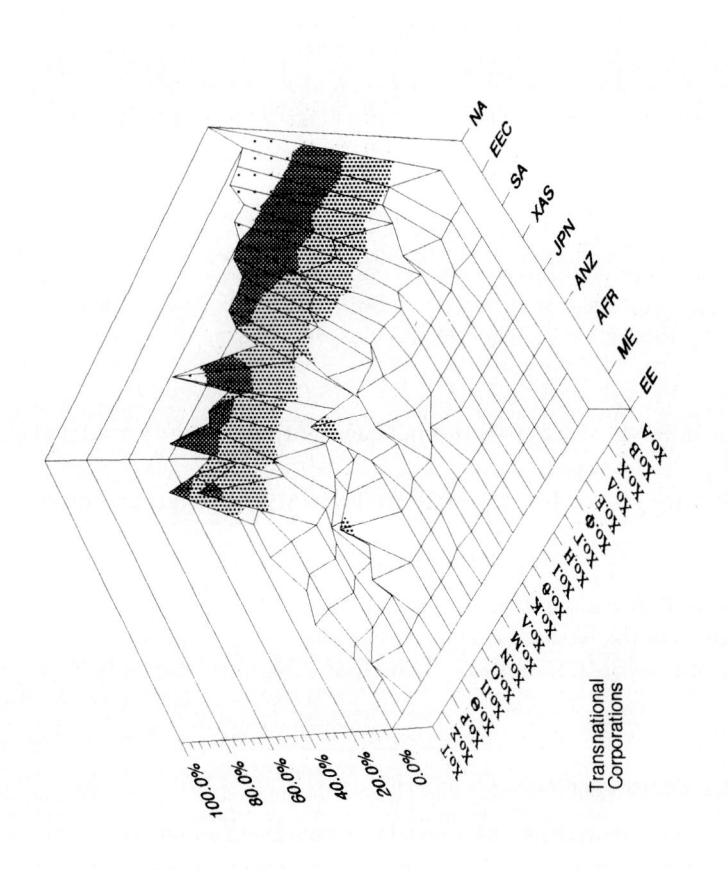

FIGURE 10.2 Distribution of Data Centers
NA: North America XAS: Other Asia (not Japan) ME: Middle East
EEC: European Economic Community ANZ: Australia/New Zealand AFR: Africa
JPN: Japan SA: South America EE: Eastern Europe

164

Chapter 10   The Problem of Host Country/MNC Relations   **165**

have data centers[57] in other parts of the world, including Asia outside of Japan, Africa, the Middle East, and so on, but the general level is significantly lower than in the core developed areas of the world.[58]

Examination of the distribution of MIPS, which is a better indicator of where real data processing is taking place, shows an even stronger tendency to concentrate resources in North America and the EEC. As with the distribution of data centers, there is noticeable activity in other parts of the world, with the exception of Eastern Europe, but this is small in comparison to the concentration at the "center" of the system (see Figure 10.3).

Internationalization of Infrastructure

When all four of the key variables are considered together, it is possible to see a contrast that might not be generally expected, as it is neither completely centralized nor decentralized. The results, as shown in Table 10.2, indicate that the level of internationalization for MIPS and DASD appears significantly lower than that for Employees and data Centers.[59] The lowest average is for DASD, which represents the "corporate memory" of the transnational corporation. This implies that the TNCs are keeping the bulk of financial and other records in their home countries. The same balance is seen in MIPS. These two variables, DASD and MIPS, combined together provide a strong indication of the relative geographical balance of the information-technology infrastructure in the TNCs sampled here.

In contrast, the level of internationalization for Employees and data Centers is higher. Certainly the four variables are not in balance. Also, there can be no question about the relationship between DASD (corporate memory) and data Centers. The concentration of power for data processing, with all that implies in terms of decision making, is focused in the home country. The TNCs have many data-processing centers located outside their home country, usually a minimum of one in each of their subsidiaries, but these centers control considerably less infrastructure.

When the four variables are plotted together for each of the TNCs in the sample, then the relationship becomes more clear. This is done after sorting

---

[57] Note that in Figures 10.2 and 10.3, the number of TNCs reporting is slightly different due to uneven availability of data.

[58] In this particular sample, concentration in Japan is low, reflecting the need to include Japanese TNCs in future studies.

[59] For each of the variables—Centers, Employees, DASD, MIPS—that might be thought of as representing *information processing resources,* a distribution was calculated as a percentage so as to eliminate as far as possible problems that might occur in interpretation of data on such different TNCs. This data was then averaged for each of the variables across all of the firms responding. The matrix was then sorted by this average, resulting in a general sequence of Centers-Employees-DASD-MIPS as indicative of a *descending* level of internationalization.

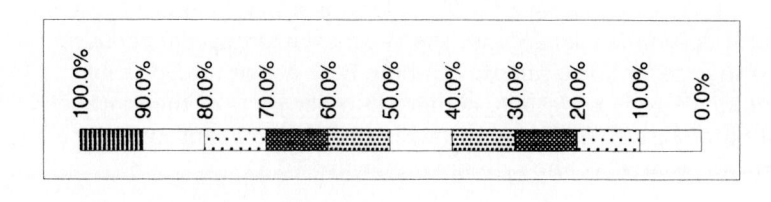

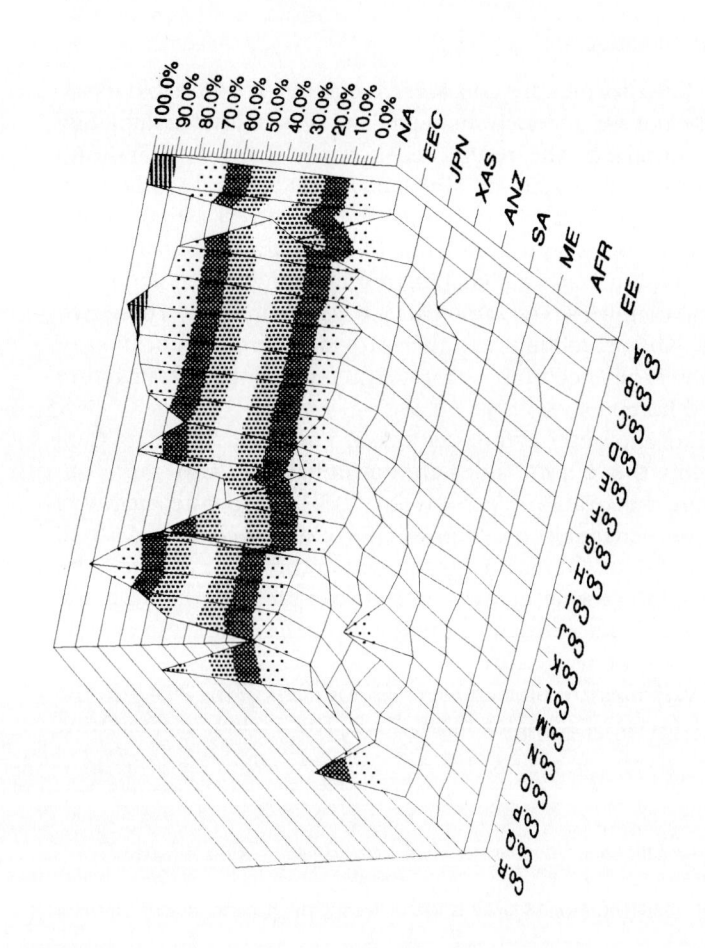

FIGURE 10.3 Distribution of MIPS
NA: North America XAS: Other Asia (not Japan) ME: Middle East
EEC: European Economic Community ANZ:Australia/New Zealand AFR: Africa
JPN: Japan SA: South America EE: Eastern Europe

TABLE 10.2 Average Level of Internationalization

Variable	Percent of Internationalization
MIPS	36
DASD	28
Employees	41
Centers	60

the individual company data according to descending averages. In Table 10.2, we can see that the level of internationalization for Centers is the highest, followed by Employees. DASD and MIPS appear to resist being internationalized. Although the TNC is operating large global data-processing networks, as indicated by the distribution of data Centers, it is keeping the bulk of its computer technology at the center of its system.

Figure 10.4 presents a general topology of the information-technology infrastructure of multinational firms. An analysis of this general topology of the firms yields the following conclusions about the geographical distribution of computing resources in these multinationals:

- The DASD and MIPS factors seem on the whole *resistant to internationalization* in comparison with the distribution of employees or distribution of data-processing centers.
- Firms seem to be highly variable in their patterns of infrastructural distribution, and there does not appear to be a sectorally based explanation of other ascertainable reasons from the present data.
- This appears to imply that although the firms have very widely dispersed global operations, they tend to hoard their corporate "memory" (i.e. DASD) and real processing power at the center of the corporation. In other words, they are centralized.

These results correspond roughly with the data presented by Gross, who examines the installation of data-processing centers in five regions of the world. His analysis shows that by 1980, North America had between two and three times the installed base of Western Europe, and Japan was equal to all of Eastern Europe.[60]

---

[60] There are some adjustments to be made because of differences in calculations of costs, but Gross' data shows at 1980: North America $82.4B, Western Europe $35.8B, Eastern Europe $16B, Latin America $3B, Japan $6B, and All other $6.7B. These were projections at the time. He predicted that by 1980, Japan would have the second largest data-processing establishment in the world. He could not have known that by the end of the 1980s, Japan would be number one in manufacturing computer equipment. Andrew C. Gross, "World Computer Markets," *Columbia Journal of World Business,* Spring 1974, pp. 13–23.

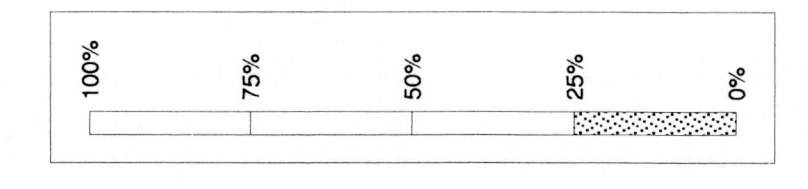

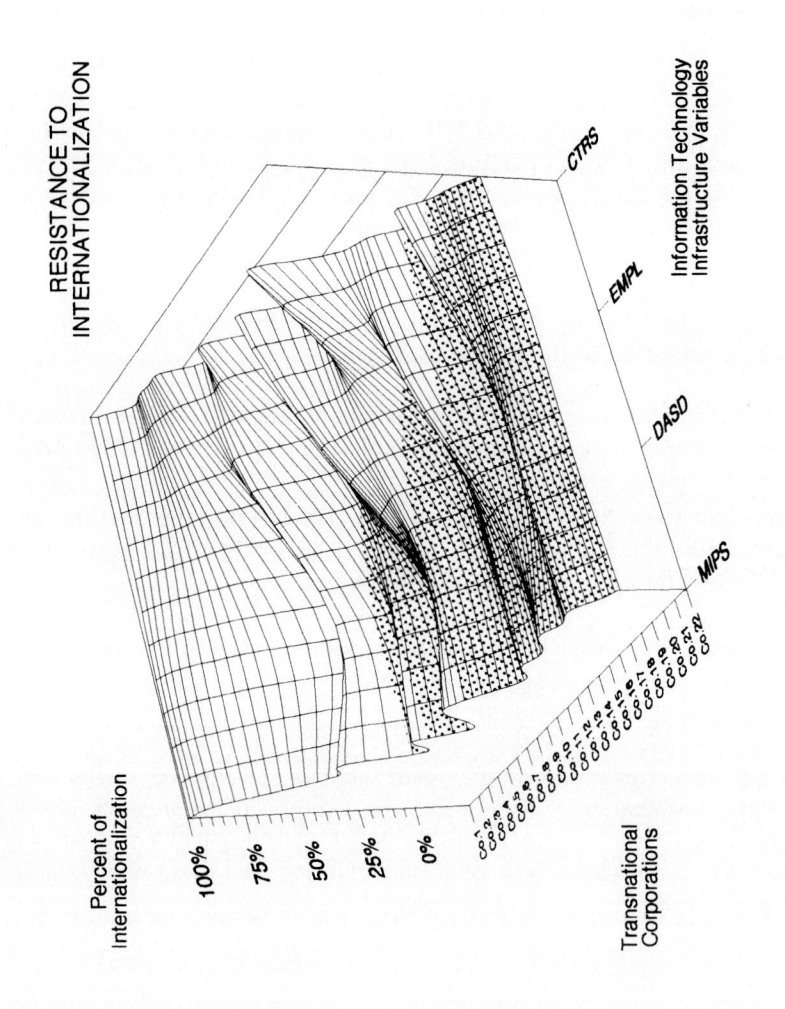

FIGURE 10.4 General Topology of MNC Information-Technology Infrastructure

Chapter 10 The Problem of Host Country/MNC Relations 169

Although there are sources of error in the data,[61] the research generates a few preliminary conclusions and calls forth some questions about the data analysis, the selection of empirical referents, and the design for further research aimed at understanding the global information-technology strategies of multinational corporations. It is difficult to see any relationship between the topologies of the information-technology infrastructure and the corporate strategies of the multinational corporations, except that the MNCs operate globally and tend to "hoard" the bulk of their databases and information processing at headquarters.

It appears that regardless of the strategy or sector of the multinational corporation, there is a tendency to maintain and operate a predominantly centralized information-technology system, with the bulk of its operations in developed countries. It is true that multinationals have many data-processing centers located around the world in their subsidiaries, including locations in developing countries, but these centers on the whole are relatively *under-*

---

[61] There are many ways in which this type of research might be improved in the future. First, improve and expand the selection of empirical referents. There may be other referents that are useful to collect and that might complete the picture. These might include telecommunications, LANs, distribution of terminals or work-stations, etc. It would also be useful to know the location of data (not just hardware, as was measured by MIPS and DASD). Knowledge of the updating frequencies of databases, the distribution of different functions, and a mapping of generalized access patterns and their geographical distribution would build up the data picture. A sample of major applications, rank-ordered by size or consumption of computing resources, followed by a study of their geographical distribution of the user base, would give a much more "business function" picture. This would perhaps show a strong contrast to the distribution of hardware resources (i.e., DASD and MIPS), and be much more easily traceable to strategic business functions (i.e., sales, marketing, R&D, etc.).

Second, improve accuracy of data. Another problem with the data is that many of the respondents are obviously estimating much of their data, and it is doubtful that any but a handful of corporations actually have this type of data easily accessible at a high level of detail. Data accuracy might be improved by asking for data on a country-by-country basis, but this would greatly increase the amount of data requested and would make it impossible to collect this data using traditional survey methods. For identification of some of the more sensitive ranges—such as those found for the MIPS/employee ratio, using an iterative process for the topological mapping—more sophisticated statistical procedures should be used, assuming it is possible to obtain a larger sample. The issue-identification section is generally weak because there may be interpretation problems with the data. Also, due to sample size, the precision of the rank ordering of the issues is weaker than it appears; this, too, can be rectified through analysis of a larger sample of firms. We do not understand why the data did not agree with Dean's results. This analysis lumps together firms operating in very different economic sectors, with different histories and strategic orientations.

One of the most obvious improvements to this research would be to increase the size of the sample. At the same time, a stronger focus on applications would help provide deeper insight into MNC strategies for global use of information technology. At the same time, it may be useful to increase the variety of empirical referents and the statistical sophistication of the analysis.

computerized. If "information is power," the power is being held at the corporate center of the multinational, at least insofar as this is indicated by measurements of the underlying infrastructure.[62]

SUMMARY

Information technology is an important part of understanding the relationship between host countries and multinational corporations.

- At the core of the debate, questions of technology transfer reflect on how the multinational distributes its information-technology system.
- Although governments have many means through which they control the business activities of the multinational within their national boundaries, this control often extends to important parts of the information system, and may occasionally represent a substantial barrier to trade.
- Some regulations and practices by nation-states force the multinational to adopt technologically inferior or economically less efficient solutions to their international data-processing requirements.
- The dependence the multinational has upon its information-technology system within each host country may change the bargaining relationship between the two parties. This may be one reason why multinationals are reluctant to transfer some technology to developing countries, but we have no direct data on this.

Preliminary measurements of the global distribution of information-technology infrastructure indicate that regardless of their strategy, multinationals tend to keep the bulk of their data processing in their home country.

- This centralization of the information-technology system "matches" the administrative structure of many multinationals, which are controlled managerially from the center of their system.
- There are several applications that are "naturally centralized including corporate intelligence, financial reporting, and some engineering matters. However, there are an equal number of applications that are "naturally" decentralized, and yet the infrastructure remains essentially centralized.

---

[62] For a study of the relationships between control systems and information flows see J. Karimi and Benn Konsynski, "Globalization and Information Management Systems," *Journal of Management Information Systems,* 7 (4), Spring 1991.

- The core of the data-processing infrastructure appears less easy to distribute than data centers, which are evidently accessing corporate systems using remote terminals.
- Understanding the global distribution of *applications* is a very different problem from understanding infrastructure, and will probably eventually yield a different pattern, as applications are far easier to distribute through international telecommunications.

PART III
COMPUTER HEGEMONY LOST

CHAPTER

11

The Relentless Onslaught of Information Technology

Franko presaged the decline of the economic power of the West, or at least of the United States, in his analysis presented in 1978. He demonstrated how many of the global trends had changed and how the changing attitudes toward business found in the West were having a severe impact on the relative economic strength of the national economies. Measurements of the strength of U.S.-based multinationals showed that they were participating less and less in the global economy (although they were still quite strong). Franko wondered if the anti-business attitudes and the fact that economic priorities were placed on factors such as ecology and social rights would mean that multinationals would eventually "feel more at home abroad."[1] All of these assertions concerning the loss of hegemony and the decline of the West have come in the wake of a massive onslaught of technological development and proliferation of information technology on a worldwide scale. No part of the world, particularly the West, can continue to count on having exclusive control over superior information technology in the future, and this will inevitably weaken the relative competitive strength of its multinational corporations.

---

[1] Lawrence G. Franko, "Multinationals: The End of U.S. Dominance," *Harvard Business Review,* November–December 1978, pp. 93–101.

Chapter 11 The Relentless Onslaught of Information Technology

What began in a small, limited part of the world, has now spread, as have so many other technologies, to the remotest portions of the globe.[2] The concept of the computer, being an essential element in business, has spread as well. This rapid proliferation has been powered in great part by the economic efficiency in data processing and bureaucratic operations that has been achieved through information technology. The many economic assumptions about processing information that existed before the computer have now all been revised. This proliferation has gone through at least two distinct phases, and, even as I write, we are entering into the third phase.

The development of information technology first started in small patches, dominated by a fabric of different companies, each pursuing its own economic motives. This first phase saw the initial development of information technology in the electronics industry in the United States, powered in great part by the high level of research and development sponsored by the military-industrial complex, although Americans love to dispute this and adhere to the cowboy-on-the-range myth about entrepreneurship, ignoring the obvious benefits of larger R&D organizations.[3] The market was also rather substantially penetrated by IBM, which focused more heavily on civilian business applications. Other companies in the United States as well as in Europe began to develop computers at approximately the same time, but were never as successful as IBM and the other American corporations. This situation continued to develop until it reached Phase II, which is characterized by the increase in the amount of joint technological collaboration between different information-technology firms located in many different parts of the world. Joint ventures, shared research and development, co-development of critical technologies, and an incredible increase in the amount of licensing, all characterize this period.

International computing developments had their start in the United States and spread rapidly to other parts of the world. Early production was supported through research grants from the U.S. military, which was interested in any possible war-time applications. The incredible expenses associated with

---

[2] Tilton contrasts the entry barriers for the semiconductor industry in Japan, Europe, and the United States: "the market structure of the semiconductor industry in Europe and Japan differs markedly from that in the United States. In the latter country, entry barriers have been low, many new firms have entered the industry, and a few have risen to become industry leaders. In Europe and Japan, entry barriers have been high. Although some new firms have entered the industry, they are not numerous, they have not become industry leaders, and they have not played an important role in diffusing new technology" (p. 164). See John E. Tilton, *International Diffusion of Technology: The Case of Semiconductors* (Washington, D.C.: The Brookings Institution, 1979). For an assessment of the complex trade-related issues, see OECD, *The Semiconductor Industry: Trade Related Issues* (Paris: Organisation for Economic Co-Operation and Development, 1985).

[3] Some business schools, such as the University of Arizona, have gone so far as to set up "Entrepreneurship Programs" that continue to express faith in this myth of the small-time businessman.

Eniac and Univac[4] and related computers based on vacuum tubes meant that only the highly speculative capital supplied by the government was capable of maintaining the basic research and development necessary to get the job done. Miller and Alic review the high capital requirements of advanced semiconductor design and manufacturing and note that finding access to capital is one of the most important elements of success in competitive survival.[5] The early success of IBM is well known[6] and, according to the more generous accounts, was based on marketing genius and sensitivity to the customer, particularly in the area of rapid and dependable service. According to considerably less generous accounts, the success also came through industrial espionage, sabotage, market collusion, theft of commercial secrets, and general oligopolistic practices that tended to bilk the customer out of very large amounts of money—particularly in the way of upgrades.[7] The computer industry in the United States followed the same path as the automobile industry: at first there were many players in the market; then a shake-out left only a few standing. At one time RCA, General Electric, Univac, Remington, and others were heavily involved in producing computers. It was by no means clear at this early stage that IBM would gain the success it eventually did.

Gradually, however, the market thinned out, leaving only a single dominant player, IBM. By the 1934 Consent Decree, ATT, supported by the greatest concentration of engineering talent ever assembled in Bell Laboratories, was kept out of the information-processing business. This development, although a great legal victory for the bureaucratic slugs in Washington, may not have been wise from the point of view of industrial policy, as we learned in the 1980s when neither ATT nor IBM appeared capable of meeting the competition of companies that had computer and communications products combined into single product lines. These companies, many in Japan, were the product of a less restrictive regulatory environment which supposedly resulted in less competition, but which in fact increased it dramatically on a world scale.[8]

---

[4] See J. Diebold, ed., *The World of the Computer* (New York: Random House, 1973).

[5] Robert R. Miller and John A. Alic, "Financing Expansion in an International Industry: The Case of Electronics," *International Journal of Technology Management,* 1 (1, 2), 1986, pp. 101–117.

[6] See M. Killen, *IBM: The Making of the Common View* (Boston: Harcourt Brace Jovanovich, 1988); J. Maisonrouge, *Inside IBM: A Personal Story* (New York: McGraw-Hill, 1985); J. Vernay, "IBM France," *Annals of the History of Computing,* 11 (4), 1989, pp. 299–312.

[7] For a very critical analysis, see R. T. DeLamarter, *Big Blue: IBM's Use and Abuse of Power* (New York: Dodd, Mead & Company, 1986).

[8] A relatively positive view is contained in J. Tunstall, *Communications Deregulation: The Unleashing of America's Communications Industry* (Oxford: Basil Blackwell, 1986). In contrast, see C. R. Kraus and A. W. Duerig, *The Rape of Ma Bell: The Criminal Wrecking of the Best Telephone System in the World* (Secaucus, NJ: Lyle Stuart, 1988), who see the break-up of the phone company as a great national tragedy. Many of the constitutional issues are covered in I. de Sola Pool, *Technologies of Freedom* (Cambridge, MA: Harvard University Press, 1983). See also G. R. Faulhaber, *Telecommunications in Turmoil: Technology and Public Policy* (Cambridge, MA: Ballinger, 1987).

As the importance of information became evident to the various other developed nations around the world, they made moves to develop their own information technology. Since they had only a fraction of the market space in the United States, and a very much weaker military-industrial complex, many of these states were forced to promote a very high role for government intervention in the technology development process.

The result of this dilemma was the creation of so-called "national champions"—computer manufacturers that were specific to individual nation-states but that were supported by the nation-state through a variety of measures, the most significant of which were government purchasing and subsidy. It is foolish to underestimate the effects of government purchasing on the computer industry as so many rigid free-marketeers are wont to do.[9] Government control over not only its military budgets, its vast public data-processing sector (extending as it might down to the state and local level in many countries and indirectly even to the United States), as well as the indirect control exercised over a large research establishment with many laboratories, all engaged in the purchase of computing equipment, can almost always provide a market large enough to help a struggling computer industry survive. French R&D establishments for the most part are "encouraged" to purchase French computers.

In Western Europe[10] the governments of France, England, and, to a lesser extent, West Germany, realized the long-term economic importance of information technology and as a result began various programs to encourage its development. However, Hayes argues that "by 1965, the year IBM announced its new 360 series, the battle along conventional lines was effectively over," and that the critical problem with the European vendors was that they focused too much on national markets that were too small in themselves to sustain a computer industry:

> Most European computer companies unfortunately defined their niches geographically—that is, a national boundary—rather than according to a particular computer market, and thus tended to try to offer too broad a range of equipment.

---

[9]There is considerable literature on the formation of various national computer industries and the role of governments therein. For the United States, see K. Flamm, *Targeting the Computer: Government Support and International Competition* (Washington, D.C.: The Brookings Institution, 1987). Also see K. Flamm, *Creating the Computer: Government, Industry, and High Technology* (Washington, D.C.: The Brookings Institution, 1988). For a perspective on Western Europe, see M. Sharp, ed., *Europe and the New Technologies: Six Case Studies in Innovation and Adjustment* (London: Frances Pinter Publishers, 1985). J. C. Derian's *America's Struggle for Leadership in Technology* (Cambridge, MA: MIT Press, 1990) does much to compare the U.S., Europe, and Japan.

[10]In the early post-war period, Europe was divided into two sections, from approximately 1945 until 1989. Gabriel briefly discusses the adaptation challenges faced by multinational corporations such as IBM in Western Europe. Peter P. Gabriel, "Adaptation: The Name of the MNCs' Game," *Columbia Journal of World Business*, November–December 1972, pp. 7–14.

As a result they were unable to achieve the necessary "critical mass" in any one niche; they divided their forces and were conquered, one by one.[11]

It was noted that in 1986 IBM's success in Europe was due to its policy of becoming "European" in terms of personnel.[12] In 1985, the IBM World Trade Europe/Middle East/Africa Corporation, headquartered in Paris, had sales of $14 billion. It seemed to have overcome the dangers of picking the wrong top personnel to manage its overseas installations. DeYoung emphasizes the critical nature of picking the best top management for the multinational, particularly as regards abilities to deal with foreign markets and different cultures. There is a premium on this type of talent, regardless of the other factors behind the MNC's operations.[13] In 1985, IBM accounted for 39 percent or $13.4 billion of the European computer market, with the other top 25 companies in Europe accounting for $34.5 billion taken all together, and those European sales accounted for 27.7 per cent of IBM's worldwide sales.[14] IBM was maintaining separate operations in each European country.[15] Nevertheless, the government policies that were adopted had an impact on U.S. companies doing business in Western Europe. Gabriel, for example, discusses the problems this caused for companies such as IBM: "Faced with IBM's dominance in this market, European governments are fostering the creation of a European computer industry through overt subsidies and favored treatment of local computer

---

[11] Robert H. Hayes, "Europe's Computer Industry: Closer to the Brink," *Columbia Journal of World Business,* Summer 1974, pp. 113–122. He describes the dilemma faced by the European computer manufacturers: "They are too small compared with U.S. competitors, and have spread themselves too thinly. While government support appears to be increasing, the ante is also going up. Their ability to finance themselves continues to deteriorate. Their primary revenue generator, medium-sized computer CPUs, will be the slowest growing segment in the industry the rest of this decade [Hayes is writing in the mid-1970s]. The most rapid technological change today is occurring in semiconductors—an area where Europe lags far behind the United States and Japan.... The fastest growing market segment today, and probably in the future, is the minicomputer segment. However, minicomputers are heavily wedded to semiconductor technology and this segment is coming under attack from semiconductor manufacturers—largely U.S.-based" (p. 120).

[12] See the comments of the Vice-Chairman of IBM, Kaspar V. Cassani in Robert Wrubel and Charles Gaffney, "Men of the Year: Philip E. Benton Jr.; Kaspar V. Cassani," *Financial World,* 157 (25), November 29, 1988, pp. 34–40. Discussion of use of sales joint ventures or other types of affiliates in foreign markets where the multinational needs to overcome cultural and language barriers is found in Edward R. Koepfler, "Keys to Growing a Global Strategy (Part 2)," *Systems/3X & AS World,* 17 (5), May 1989, pp. 141–142.

[13] H. Garrett DeYoung, "In Search of the New European Manager," *Electronic Business,* 16 (23), December 10, 1990.

[14] See Paul Tate and Linda Runyan, "Europe's Elite," *Datamation,* 32 (15), August 1, 1986, pp. 34–39.

[15] See Michel Faucon, "A U.S. Multinational in Europe: Politics and Freedom of Operations," *Vital Speeches,* 52 (22), September 1, 1986, pp. 695–698.

manufacturers.... [I]t is difficult to expect IBM under these circumstances to sustain its extraordinary rate of growth in Europe."[16]

The governments of Western Europe engaged IBM in a terrific legal battle which eventually forced it to give out information on its equipment that would enable clone makers or plug-compatible manufacturers to meet standards more quickly.[17] In the United Kingdom, International Computers Limited (ICL) was the preferred company, given a large number of preferred government-purchasing contracts[18] through research and development laboratories, the military, and public service, which was quite large and growing under the socialist-oriented labor government.

The first wave of information technology was carried overseas by a few merchants, especially IBM. This was a great and amazing period for the United States, which at the time was pioneering many new technologies. IBM found ready customers in the multinational corporations operating overseas, and proceeded to set up data-processing centers around the world, most of which are still in place a quarter of a century later. One must assume that the early success of U.S. multinationals operating overseas, particularly in Europe, was due at least in part to their use of information technology and the superior form of organization that it promised. This is, however, only speculation, for we all know that the data to support or deny such a proposition has long since faded from the scene.

Nevertheless, there is strong reason to believe that there was a connection. U.S. multinationals at that time represented in some ways a new form of industrial organization, and the computer quickly began to play a role in its propagation. As long as the U.S. vendors of information technology remained strong and unchallenged, it is safe to assume that U.S. business could reap the benefits. Unfortunately, the challenge quickly arose.

---

[16] Peter P. Gabriel, "Adaptation: The Name of the MNC's Game," *Columbia Journal of World Business,* November–December 1972, pp. 7–14.

[17] For details of the settlement, see J. Patrick Raines, "Common Market Competition Policy: The EC-IBM Settlement," *Journal of Common Market Studies,* 24 (2), December 1985, pp. 137–147.

[18] At this time, government purchasing was covered under the GATT, but states were still able to get a great deal done through this mechanism of subsidy, however skillfully applied.

CHAPTER
12

The Global System of Industrial Alliances

Another phase of the global development of information technology is characterized by a strengthening of industrial alliances between leading vendors and partners in overseas markets. The strong role of AT&T and IBM in the postwar world shows the importance of industrial alliances in the formation of global strategy. Although in most cases the creation of various alliances is a sign of strength, it also can be interpreted to indicate weakness. The strong vendor is able to operate alone, and the vendor forced into various alliances also loses some freedom of action.

As phase I ended, phase II continued earlier developments in a second wave of international collaboration between different manufacturers of computer technology. This collaboration began first with the rise of the Newly Industrializing Countries (NICs) and their integration at the lower levels into the worldwide system of manufacturing. The NICs had concentrated on manufacturing of components as subcontractors for the major vendors.[1]

According to a United Nations study

> During the late 1960s and throughout the 1970s, there was a significant redeployment of electronics manufacturing to certain countries in south-East Asia and, to a lesser extent, the Caribbean. This redeployment has been largely confined to the assembly of consumer electronic products and semiconductor devices.... [D]uring the 1970s...foreign direct investment is the principal form of manufacture and point-of-sale assembly in facilities oriented towards domestic markets, but in catering for the export market it shares the major role with sub-contracting arrangements.[2]

However, the "computer shakeout"[3] in which the number of dominant vendors began to shrink and change complexion was the inevitable result of, among other factors, the liberalization of world trade under the General Agreement on Tariffs and Trade (GATT). Just as it had become possible for IBM to manufacture and market its information technology in many countries outside the United States, so too did it become possible for computer manufacturers of other countries to attempt penetration of the U.S. market and thereby attack the soft underbelly of IBM.[4] The era of intensified competition

---

[1] Some writers called Taiwan a "nation of order-takers."

[2] UNCTC, *Trends and Issues in Foreign Direct Investment and Related Flows,* ST/CTDC/59 (New York: United Nations, 1985), p. 76.

[3] See S. T. McClellan, *The Coming Computer Industry Shakeout: Winners, Losers, & Survivors* (New York: John Wiley & Sons, 1984) for an analysis of different waves of consolidation in the computer industry. See also Gary E. Willard and Arnold C. Cooper, "Survivors of Industry Shake-Outs: The Case of the U.S. Color Television Set Industry," *Strategic Management Journal,* 6, 1985, pp. 299–318. Willard and Cooper studied the survivors in the color television industry in the United States and concluded that "the variables emphasized in traditional economic theory, relative costs and prices, did not seem to play a major role in distinguishing survivors from non-survivors.... There were strong indications that differences in 'corporate culture' between parent and subsidiary may have had an important influence on survival."

[4] This is the exact same strategy that was pursued by the Japanese as they launched their successful bid for the copier market against Xerox, which at the time (late 1970s and 1980s) was suffering under the short-sighted, unimaginative and ultimately destructive control of the cost-accounting profession ("bean counters") that had transferred in bulk from the Ford Motor Company (where they had also wrecked the company). See G. Jacobson and J. Hillkirk, *Xerox: American Samurai* (New York: Macmillan, 1986). Even as late as 1986, Xerox was looking for a way to diversify from the copier business into office automation. To this writer, the failure of Xerox is one of the most puzzling business mysteries of this entire century. See Michael Skapinker, "Xerox Searches for Life Beyond Boxes," *International Management,* 41 (6), June 1986, pp. 24–30.

heated up considerably in the 1980s, particularly as the Europeans weakened and as the Japanese strengthened, coming in as they did at both the high and the low end of the market.[5]

But as the intensification of competition was driving the computer manufacturers to fight against each other in various national markets, the economics of semiconductor manufacturing was forcing them to cooperate. The cost of bringing a new semiconductor memory chip to the market kept increasing to the point where it was beyond the financial capacity of all but the very largest vertically integrated manufacturers, all of which were Japanese except IBM.[6]

In addition, the gradual specialization of component manufacturing meant that, for many key technologies, the most efficient manufacturing occurred in only a few places in the world, many in East Asia. Weak vendors, particularly the Europeans, were forced more and more to source their technology there, the result of which was a shift in the competitive emphasis to component-level systems integration and more careful control over marketing and relationships with the customer further down the business chain. Some of the most successful European computer manufacturers—Apricot and Amstrad are examples—conducted the great bulk of their business by extensive utilization of subcontracting organizations based in East Asia.[7]

The result of all these forces—the increased requirement for resources, the dominance of component manufacturing in only a few countries, the increased interpenetration of markets by the major vendors—resulted in a situation where by the end of the 1980s, a system of industrial alliances was being formed. The weak were merging together to protect their survival against the

---

[5]A good early competitive analysis is given in W. H. Davidson, *The Amazing Race: Winning the Technorivalry with Japan* (New York: John Wiley & Sons, 1984).

[6]See Daniel I. Okimoto, T. Sugano, and F. B. Weinstein, *Competitive Edge: The Semiconductor Industry in the U.S. and Japan* (Stanford University Press, 1984); Verner, Liipfert, Bernhard and McPherson, Chartered, *The Effect of Government Targeting on World Semiconductor Competition: A Case History of Japanese Industrial Strategy and Its Costs for America*, Cupertino Semiconductor Industry Association, 1983; F. Warshofsky, *The Chip War: The Battle for the World of Tomorrow* (New York: Charles Scribner's Sons, 1989); J. Botkin, D. Dimancescu, and R. Stata, *Global Stakes: The Future of High Technology in America* (Cambridge, MA: Ballinger Publishing Company, 1982); J. C. Derian, *American's Struggle for Leadership in Technology* (Cambridge, MA: MIT Press, 1990); G. Gregory, *Japanese Electronics Technology: Enterprise and Innovation* (New York: John Wiley & Sons, 1985); M. Moritani, *Japanese Technology: Getting the Best for the Least* (Tokyo: Simul Press, 1982). A comprehensive picture of Japanese industrial policy is found in H. Patrick and L. Meissner, eds., *Japan's High Technology Industries: Lessons and Limitations of Industrial Policy* (Seattle and London: University of Washington Press, 1986).

[7]It is perhaps unfair to use the term "computer manufacturer" or "computer vendor" (although that is still more accurate) to describe the activities of these personal computer merchants in the same context as one discusses IBM or Fujitsu or the other great vendors. "Minivendor" might be a better term or even "microvendor."

strong, and the strong were buying out the weak in order further to consolidate their control over the market.

AT&T'S ENTANGLING ALLIANCES

AT&T entered into a strategic alliance with Ing. C. Olivetti & C. SpA in June 1986 to manufacture personal computers and low-end office equipment. This strategy would allow AT&T to continue to concentrate on high-end data networking while using Olivetti for low-end computing products, thus saving investment costs.[8] Olivetti was hoping through this deal to gain access to the giant U.S. market so as to "overtake Apple" for the number two position in sales, and celebrated with $7 million stock issues to its employees that were evidently well-received.[9] Olivetti also made a deal with Triumph-Adler to get about 50 percent of the European typewriter business, but observers noted that Triumph-Adler had lost money for more than 10 years in a row.[10] By 1987, Xerox had canceled an order for 40,000 personal computers "for exchange rate reasons" and it was clear that jumping into the Cambodian killing-fields of IBM-compatible personal computers had not been very successful. By 1989, Olivetti was reporting an 11 percent drop in net profits of $254 million garnered from $6.1 billion in sales.[11] By 1990, Olivetti was well into establishing a record of continuing declines in profits, stemming primarily from very stiff Japanese and American competition; some observers wrote that Carlo De Benedetti was losing his grip on his large $15 billion empire.[12] In November of that year, it was announced that the Olivetti workforce would be cut by 13 percent and that assets would be sold off.[13] First-half profits had fallen by more than 40 percent as growth in personal computers in Europe fell from 24 percent to only 4 percent, which is even less than the general replacement market.[14] Olivetti was getting $115,000 per employee but its competitors were getting $221,000 per person on the payroll.

---

[8] See Alan Alper, "AT&T Focuses on Data Networking in Cost-Cutting Strategy," *Computerworld,* 20 (45), November 10, 1986, pp. 98, 102.

[9] See Anonymous, "Italy: Olivetti Is Reaching Out for the Apple," *Euromoney,* September 1986, pp. 393, 397.

[10] See William C. Symonds, Thane Peterson, John J. Keller, and Marc Frons, "Dealmaker De Benedetti," *Business Week,* Industrial/Technology Edition (3013), August 24, 1987, pp. 42–47.

[11] See John Rossant and Thane Peterson, "Can Cassoni Get Olivetti off the Slippery Slope?" *Business Week,* Industrial/Technology Edition, (3109), June 12, 1989, pp. 99, 102.

[12] See Anonymous, "Can Carlo Come Back?" *Economist,* 315 (7652), April 28, 1990, pp. 69–70.

[13] See John Rossant, "As Profits Plunge, De Benedetti Cries 'Basta,'" *Business Week,* Industrial/Technology Edition (3190), December 3, 1990, p. 52.

[14] See Anonymous, "Going Solo: Olivetti," *Economist,* 317 (7683), December 1, 1990, pp. 78, 80.

AT&T and Olivetti

The original deal had seen AT&T buy 25 percent of Olivetti for $260 million.[15] By 1987, the Data Systems Division of AT&T was losing $700 to $1 billion per year and sales of the Model 3B minicomputer were low, as UNIX-based office systems had not "taken off" and there were rumors of AT&T slicing off the computer division to stop the losses.[16] In the early 1990s, AT&T turned its big guns toward NCR. At about the same time, Olivetti introduced the LSX 3000 model of the 32-bit minicomputer based on Motorola 68000 processors, which was in direct competition with AT&T's 3B model minicomputer. The new LSX 3000 could handle up to 192 users simultaneously and process about 9 MIPS, all of which made it perfect for the small office environment.[17] It was based on the Open System Architecture (OSA) instead of the standard AT&T Unix. Many writers saw this as a slap in the face at AT&T, although Olivetti said it was going to continue to market both lines of equipment.[18] However, the new LSX 3000 was to be sold in the U.S. market not by AT&T but by Bunker Ramo which was an old-line company in the U.S. well-connected with the financial services sector.[19] In 1989, Olivetti purchased ISC Systems Corporation, which was a systems integration specializing in the banking automation market. ISC was soon merged with Bunker Ramo to form ISC-Bunker Ramo.[20] Its strategy of vertical markets and heavy use of systems integrators and value-added resellers (VARs) started to become visible. Olivetti was working with more than 100 VARs in Europe and 40 in the United Kingdom alone, all of which accounted for sales of more than 90 million lire in 1987. Olivetti spent a great deal of time training and working closely with VARs, and was relying on them as the critical element in marketing its LSX 3000 minicomputer.[21] Two years later, in 1990, Olivetti had jumped onto the Intel 80486 bandwagon, but was facing strong competition and being squeezed on the one hand by cheap Asian manufacturing of components and peripherals, and on the other hand by the basic process of innovation in systems and software taking place

---

[15]See Steven Solomon, "More Rabbits, Please, Signor De Benedetti," *Forbes,* 139 (5), March 9, 1987, pp. 114–118.

[16]See Jean S. Bozman, "Will AT&T Hang It Up?" *Computerworld,* 21 (28), July 13, 1987, pp. 95, 101.

[17]See Tim Gouldson, "Olivetti Reveals Global Push," *Computing Canada,* 13 (25), December 10, 1987, pp. 1, 6.

[18]See Michael Faden, "Olivetti: Biting the Hand That Feeds It?" *UNIX Review,* 6 (2), February 1988, pp. 14–23.

[19]See Janette Martin, "As Mini Supplier, Olivetti Recasts Its Identity—Again," *Datamation,* International Edition, 34 (1), January 1, 1988, pp. 17–18.

[20]See Barbara Berkman, "After AT&T, Olivetti Eyes U.S. Vertical Markets," *Electronic Business,* 15 (15), July 24, 1989, pp. 17–18.

[21]See Sarah Aryanpur, "Olivetti Ups the Value of Its Resellers," *Systems International,* 16 (8), August 1988, p. 13.

Chapter 12 The Global System of Industrial Alliances   **185**

in the United States.[22] The 486 machine got good reviews and there was talk of steady 15 percent growth in 1991.[23] At the same time, Olivetti released a 80386 machine, the P800, which was developed with ISC/Bunker Ramo and was aimed at the finance market. The new machine was a "tower case" type with a lot of room for expansion of peripherals, and was touting compatibility with IBM's OS/2 v.1.2, again a far distance from Unix.[24]

Olivetti in 1986 was the market leader in Europe with its M24 model clone of the IBM personal computer, although there were rumors that AT&T's UNIX/Xenix operating system would soon replace MS/DOS.[25] No one had expected the effect Windows would have on the market. AT&T invested $260 million in 1983 and gained 25 percent of a joint-venture company with Olivetti in Italy.[26] In exchange, Olivetti Italy made a marketing and sales agreement with AT&T, thus hoping to get better access to the giant U.S. market. The resulting joint-venture then controlled 80 percent of Olivetti Japan, which in turn had a joint venture relationship with Toshiba, which put up the other 20 percent to capitalize the company. Toshiba was also supporting a sales and marketing agreement with AT&T to sell the American-made equipment in the Japanese market. The Olivetti Italy group also had a joint venture with Acorn microcomputers in the United Kingdom in which it had invested $11.3 million in exchange for 49.3 percent of the equity.

Olivetti had been working hard on continuing to develop its information-systems line, such as the M60 minicomputer, which was supported by a comprehensive accounts production software package called COMPASS, capable of generating 26 different reports on up to 300 clients.[27] Olivetti was working hard at providing superior customer service through organizations such as its National Network Centre in Canada, which provided a real-time dispatch capability for servicing of its minicomputers, heavily used in the Canadian finance sector.[28] The Canadian organization was also concentrating on third-

---

[22]See Anonymous, "Olivetti: Going for Broke," *Economist,* 314 (7638), January 20, 1990, pp. 76, 78.

[23]See Martin Slofstra, "In Conversation: Harvey Coleman, Olivetti Canada," *Computing Canada,* 16 (22), October 25, 1990, p. 13.

[24]See Victor R. Garza and Tracey Capen, "Olivetti is Tops in 25-MHz 386 Performance," *InfoWorld,* 12 (33), August 13, 1990, p. 84.

[25]See Nancy Pocock, "Succeeding in the IBM-Compatible Market," *Data Processing,* 28 (5), June 1986, pp. 247–250.

[26]Much of this discussion of industrial alliances is based on Economic Commission for Europe, *The Telecommunication Industry: Growth and Structural Change* (New York: United Nations, 1987). This study is recommended reading for understanding the world's telecommunication industry and its interlocking structure of corporate alliances.

[27]See Malcolm Cole, "Olivetti Offers a System for the Busy Practice," *Accountancy,* 97 (1113), May 1986, pp. 139–141.

[28]See Eden Raine, "Hardware Maintenance: Monitoring by Olivetti Gets Results," *Computing Canada,* 12 (12), June 12, 1986, p. 17.

party maintenance contracts and distribution of software to pump up revenue in Canada which amounted to C$127 million in 1986, of which C$23 million was in maintenance.[29] An aggressive maintenance operation in Europe won Olivetti contracts such as Barclays Bank, at which it managed to replace 270 separate maintenance contracts with a single $56 million comprehensive contract.[30] Olivetti Canada was also busy marketing the Acorn computer optical database unit, Acorn being 80 percent owned by Olivetti.[31] By 1988 it was reported that the Olivetti File-Net Document-Image processor was selling well, and was being used by very large financial companies such as The Investors Group of Winnipeg, which had a document pile growing at the rate of over 100,000 pieces per month.[32] The Britannia Building Society also adopted the system, including the giant 64-platter optical "juke box" unit.[33]

AT&T and the Spread of UNIX

In addition to its work with the multi-faceted Olivetti, AT&T was also operating several overseas subsidiaries in which it had a 75 percent to 100 percent equity position, including AT&T Consumer Products Private Ltd. in Singapore, UNIX Europe in the United Kingdom, its brother UNIX Pacific headquartered in Japan, and AT&T Microelectronics, which was operating in the Federal Republic of Germany, Singapore, and Thailand. AT&T also worked with SGS in Italy in a joint venture in bipolar circuit technology, which focused on research and development, and technology exchange between the partners. SGS was operated by Pasquale Pistorio who had been trained at Motorola. Its 1987 merger with Thomson changed it from the world's twenty-third largest chip maker into the twelfth largest, and it was concentrating on Application Specific Integrated Circuits (ASICs).[34] It was also conducting innovative marketing operations at its plant in Phoenix, Arizona.[35] It also made a critical move in purchasing Inmos from Thorn EMI in 1988, and attained $1.1 billion in sales

---

[29]See Gordon Campbell, "In Conversation: John Kernick," *Computing Canada*, 13 (10), May 14, 1987, p. 11.

[30]See Michael Blanden and Gavin Shreeve, "Minding the Business," *Banker*, 140 (767), January 1990, pp. 19–20.

[31]See Barbara Sherman, "This Database Has Visual Info on the U.K.," *Computing Canada*, 13 (19), September 17, 1987, p. 28.

[32]See Anonymous, "Gain Control of the Paper Environment," *ComputerData*, 13 (2), February 1988, pp. 12–13.

[33]See Anonymous, "Britannia Leads the Way," *IMC Journal*, 25 (3), May/June 1989, pp. 15–18.

[34]See William C. Symonds, Thane Peterson, and Jonathan B. Levine, "An Italian Chipmaker Shows the Way," *Business Week*, Industrial/Technology Edition (3000), May 25, 1987, pp. 134, 136.

[35]See Sylvia Tiersten, "SGS-Thomson's Soup Cans Are 'M'm, M'm Good,'" *Electronic Business*, 15 (4), February 20, 1989, pp. 30, 32.

and a 26 percent annual growth rate in 1988.[36] Inmos was the developer of the famous "transputer," which had captured only 2.4 percent of the 32-bit microprocessor market. By 1988, 125,000 units were shipped, a relatively modest volume, yet it was being considered as the foundation for a new type of supercomputer, financed by the Eureka project.[37]

Besides the UNIX Pacific and Olivetti Japan/Toshiba operations, AT&T's Japan strategy was developed further. In 1985 it entered into a 50–50 joint venture with a consortium of 16 Japanese companies to create Japan Enhanced Network Services (ENS). It was also working with the venerable Ricoh company in Japan to manufacture telephone equipment, with 51 percent of the joint venture owned by AT&T and 49 percent owned by Ricoh.[38] Interestingly enough, AT&T also had a $57 million joint venture for mainframe computers with Fujitsu of Japan, which held 60 percent of the operation.

AT&T Gets Lucky in Korea

In Korea, AT&T worked with Lucky-Goldstar to form Gold Star Semiconductor and Gold Star Fiber Optic, the products of which we later saw in the Olympic games hosted in Seoul. Lucky was one of the large Korean business group conglomerates, called *chaebol,* which have dominated the Korean landscape in the postwar period. It is run by the Koo and Huh families who control about 26 percent of the equity. Lucky is known for generous employee benefits, but experienced labor problems in 1987 like most other large companies in Korea.[39] Lucky's move into semiconductor manufacturing was made in parallel with other *chaebol* that through different joint ventures, licensing arrangements, and other relationships with companies such as Texas Instruments, Intel, Vitelic and Zilog, have helped Korea rapidly build its manufacturing capabilities.[40] Being a conglomerate, Lucky is a major player in other sectors such as steel, in which it held tenth place in world production in 1988.[41] Unfortunately, Korea was struck with a series of labor problems in the late 1980s that led to 20 percent increases in pay raises per year for a while,

---

[36] See John Shutt, "SGS-Thomson's Ambitious Calendar," *International Management,* 44 (6), June 1989, pp. 55–57.

[37] See Valerie Rice, "SGS-Thomson Hopes to Bring Life to Inmos' Transputer," *Electronic Business,* 15 (17), August 21, 1989, p. 57.

[38] Ricoh's founder had proved to be a great inspiration to the psychological fight for the recovery of Japan. The early years of postwar reconstruction in Japan were a time when an individual could make a difference, and many did.

[39] See Mark Clifford, "Corporate Democracy Pays Dividends," *Far Eastern Economic Review,* 138 (47), November 19, 1987, pp. 84–85.

[40] See Tekla S. Perry, "Semiconductors Go to Korea," *IEEE Spectrum,* 24 (12), December 1987, pp. 34–38.

[41] See John Gittelshohn, "The Business Guide: Driving and Driven," *Business,* March 1988, pp. 130–134.

resulting in a stream of criticism of the *chaebol*, including barbs aimed at management quality at the top levels.[42] By 1990, it was reported that the Korean economy was slowing down to an annual GNP of only 10 percent and that the large trade surplus that had been built up from 1986 to 1988 had tumbled into a deficit situation. The labor-wage explosion had resulted in a *doubling* of wages since 1987, and an additional shock came from an appreciation of the Won against the U.S. dollar by 11 percent.[43] Lucky was not so lucky at this time. By 1990, its sales growth was chopped in half and it had reportedly suffered particularly hard from the currency appreciation of 14.8 percent by that time. There were also rumors about problems with the quality of components and parts.[44] In a desperate search for export markets, Korea turned to the USSR and set up two-way trade deals amounting to $1.2 billion in 1990, projected to rise to $10 billion by 1995. Korea was getting access to raw materials, and the USSR was getting valuable expertise in manufacturing of consumer goods.[45] However, by the end of 1990, the labor unrest had subsided, wage raises had been throttled from 25 percent annually to only 18 percent, and GNP was rising by 8 percent per year. Some of the rapacious speculation that had gone into real estate was also cooling its heels.[46] Perhaps in response to criticism, the Koo family, which had ruled Lucky for so long with an iron hand, loosened control and decentralized some responsibility to front-line managers grouped into three executive committees, and profits jumped 35 percent in 1990.[47]

AT&T and Companies

With Philips of the Netherlands, AT&T worked on a joint venture in mobile telephones, and also formed APT of the Netherlands, which set up a manufacturing plant in the United Kingdom.

The joint venture work continued in an endless circle: work on personal computers with Convergent Technologies of the United States, work in

---

[42]See Anonymous, "South Korea's Conglomerates: Do or Be Done For," *Economist,* 313 (7632), December 9, 1989, pp. 74, 79. and also Michael Breen and Erwin Shrader, "South Korea: Going Through a Rough Patch," *Asian Business,* 26 (6), June 1990, pp. 38–52.

[43]See Tim Jackson, "South Korea: An Impromptu Performance," *Economist,* 316 (7668), August 18, 1990, pp. S5–S20.

[44]See Geoff Crane, "Ailing Goldstar Needs Strong Medicine," *Electronic Business,* 16 (16), August 20, 1990, pp. 67–70.

[45]See Mark Clifford, "Friends in Need: South Korean-Soviet Trade Begins to Blossom," *Far Eastern Economic Review,* 149 (38), September 20, 1990, pp. 86–87.

[46]See Laxmi Nakarmi and Robert Neff, "South Korea: Can This Tiger Burn Bright Again?" *Business Week,* Industrial/Technology Edition (3190), December 3, 1990, pp. 56–57.

[47]See Laxmi Nakarmi, "At Lucky-Goldstar, the Koos Loosen the Reins," *Business Week,* Industrial/Technology Edition (3200), February 18, 1991, pp. 72–73.

systems integration with Electronic Data Systems, and work with Chemical Bank, Bank of America, and Time in the area of home banking. By 1990, the systems-integration market in the United States was a very fast growing sector, accounting for $6 billion in revenues in 1989, with predictions of rises to $17 billion by 1994.[48] In the United Kingdom, AT&T announced a purchase of Istel ltd., a small systems integrator. The new service was aimed at helping multinational corporations in Europe set up effective networks, including those with EDI capabilities.[49] AT&T worked with Corning Glass of the United States in a joint venture for manufacture of the fiber optics which would eventually carry the super high speeds envisaged by the Synchronous Optical Network (SONET) standard. There was also work with Compañía Telefónica National de España and a $200 million joint venture for manufacturing of semiconductors through AT&T Microelectrónica de España.

All of these joint ventures and corporate alliances were further supplemented on the services and switching equipment side. For example, AT&T worked in a joint partnership with British Telecom in improving its network. BT owned 50 percent of BT&D Technologies, a $150 million joint venture with Du Pont of the United States working on opto-electronic components. BT also owned ITT Dialcom in the United States for supply of electronic mail. Both British Telecom and AT&T Communications were working with Kokusai Denshin Denwa Co, Ltd. of Japan in creating digital networks.

AT&T Communications' work with Philips of the Netherlands promised to provide many useful linkages into the European environment. Philips was working on modems with its subsidiary TRT in France, which was manufacturing terminals in a joint venture with La Radiotechnique. It owned TDK in Germany and also had a joint venture in direct broadcasting systems with Thomson of France. Philips was also operating a joint venture with Control Data Corporation of the United States called Optical Storage International. AT&T continued to move to take over NCR, which itself had been a significant force in international computer technologies.[50]

IBM'S GLOBAL REACH

The system of foreign alliances being operated by AT&T was paralleled by the International Business Machines Corporation. IBM had made a heavily

---

[48]See Norman G. Litell and Richard Munn, "Service Providers Expand Their Horizons," *Datamation,* 36 (12), June 15, 1990, pp. 196–197.

[49]The messages to be used included EDICT and AT&T Mail which is a commercial mail product offered by AT&T. See Barbara N. Berkman, "Istel: AT&T's Key to Open European Markets," *Electronic Business,* 16 (14), July 23, 1990.

[50]For background on NCR's European operations, see Peter Spooner, "Management Hot House," *Chief Executive,* March 1987, pp. 16, 18.

publicized move into telecommunications with acquisition of 66 percent of Satellite Business Systems in 1975. The idea at the time was to use SBS to provide private high bandwidth telecommunications linkages for private networks, presumably for some of IBM's largest customers. A decade later in 1985, IBM got about 30 percent of MCI Communications Corporation, an alternative long distance carrier, which in turn took over parts of SBS. At about the same time, in 1984, IBM took 23 percent of Rolm corporation, a large manufacturer of Private Branch Exchange (PBX) equipment. IBM invested in a joint-venture arrangement with Intel for manufacture of microprocessors, it created a Value-Added Network (VAN) service with Merrill Lynch of the United States, it worked on Local Area Network (LAN) technology with Sytek of the United States, and it worked with British Telecom for creation of a financial network to aid the financial district of London. British Telecom was also working with McDonnell Douglas of the United States in the VAN market, and eventually went on to purchase Tymnet. BT, which was working with Du Pont of the United States in manufacturing of opto-electronic components, also purchased Mitel, the troubled Canadian PBX manufacturer, one of the chief competitors to Rolm. The Canadian computer industry has never been particularly strong except for a few players such as Northern Telecom. Foran observes that most Canadian companies in this sector are very small and work on seeking niche markets.[51] By the early 1990s, it was clear that some of these arrangements were not working out as intended. IBM was having problems depending on Intel for microprocessors in the personal computer market, where it had lost ground since its original entry in 1981. Its work with Rolm never reached the promise that had been so lauded in the press. Rolm and IBM products had been distributed through 50 sales offices in the United States and 24 sales regions.[52] In December 1989, IBM sold the manufacturing and development assets of Rolm to Siemens. IBM subsidiaries in Europe began to distribute and market Siemens-manufactured PBXs, and the Rolm arrangement gave Siemens immediate access to the U.S. market, thus making it the largest PBX manufacturer in the world, ahead of AT&T.[53] The new company, Rolm Systems Inc., would be a joint venture between IBM and Siemens and would contain about 5,000 persons in its Florida location.[54]

---

[51] Marjorie Foran, "The Canadian Computer Industry: Factors Affecting Government Policy," *Optimum,* 18 (4), 1987/1988, pp. 79–99, 107.

[52] See Richard A. Kuehn, "Sorting Through the Siemens-IBM Deal," *Business Communications Review,* 19 (2), February 1989, pp. 91–92.

[53] See Elizabeth Schultz, "Siemens, IBM Join Forces to Tackle Tough PBX Problems," *Telephony,* 215 (25), December 19, 1988, pp. 10–11. See also Anonymous, "Rolm's New President Discusses IBM-Siemens Deal," *Business Communications Review,* 19 (2), February 1989, pp. 10, 12 for a discussion of the details of the organizational relationships.

[54] See Byron Belitsos, "IBM's Rolm Deal: A Smart Move," *Computer Decisions,* 21 (3), March 1989, pp. 27–29.

At about the same time, IBM got rid of its investment in MCI Communications, and set up a company to conduct PBX research and development with Siemens, causing some worry in the Rolm user base, which was after all quite significant.[55] Rolm had been unprofitable for IBM. It was ironic that NEC of Japan, one of IBM's fiercest rivals, was dependent for distribution of its switches in the U.S. market on Tel Plus Communications, which was a subsidiary of Siemens Information Systems (the U.S. subsidiary) and was focusing on the interconnect market.[56] Both companies made announcements of benevolent intention towards Rolm in that IBM would continue to provide enhancement for ISDN capabilities to the Rolm 9751, which was a type of communications controller, and Siemens would move features from its Hicom and Saturn equipment into the Rolm product line.[57] The announcement came only one week after announcements were made on the 9751 PBX line, including T-1 and ISDN interfaces.[58] The use of ISDN interfaces for the PBX would help both Siemens and IBM develop a new set of applications based on Automatic Number Identification (ANI), itself based on Switch-to-Computer (SCL) linkages, to provide the new class of services called Computer Integrated Telecommunications Systems (CITS).[59]

The Merrill Lynch system petered out, helped along by the programmed trading crash of 1987.

The wholly owned subsidiary, IBM Japan Ltd., built a corresponding system of industrial alliances on the island of Shoguns. By the late 1980s, IBM Japan in its own right was considered to be one of the largest computer companies in the world, with sales in 1986 of $6 billion. IBM Japan employed about 20,000 workers there and was number one in installed base of large main-

---

[55] See Bob Brown, "IBM, Siemens Carve Up Rolm Operations; IBM/Siemens Deal Leaves Some Rolm Users Worried," *Network World,* 5 (51), December 19, 1988, pp. 1, 6, 41.

[56] See Bob Brown, "IBM/Siemens Pact May Aid PBX Rivals," *Network World,* 5 (52), December 26, 1988/ January 2, 1989.

[57] See Elisabeth Horwitt, "Rolm Users Look to Siemens," *Computerworld,* 23 (3), January 23, 1989, p. 4. See also Anonymous, "Siemens and IBM Offer Each Other a Helping Hand," *Business Communications Review,* 19 (1), January 1989, pp. 8–14.

[58] See Paul Desmond and Bob Wallace, "IBM Refines NetView, Closes Siemens Deal," *Network World,* 6 (33), August 21, 1989, pp. 1, 6, 58. The 9751 model 10 was about a 25 percent improvement in price/performance from the previous model and was designed for installations of 100 to 150 lines. See Elisabeth Horwitt, "IBM Tweaks Rolm; No Siemens," *Computerworld,* 23 (33), August 14, 1989, p. 10.

[59] See Mary Johnston-Turner, "Strengthening the PBX-Computer Bond," *Network World,* 7 (32), August 6, 1990, pp. 37–39, 49. The article notes that the state of Pennsylvania has outlawed this practice of ANI. Rehin classifies CITS into three groups of applications, including call centers, desktop applications, and application in data processing, although he uses the term "Computer-Supported Telephony Applications" (CSTA) instead. Adam Rehin, "Calling on CSTAs," *Telephony,* 219 (23), November 26, 1990, pp. 26–34.

frames with 32.6 percent of the market.[60] By 1988, however, it was sliding, with 1986 sales dropping 4 percent, and blame being placed on its reluctance to emphasize the microcomputer and work-station side of the market in deference to its position in mainframes.[61] It was hoping that its Personal System/55 Model 70 with OS/2 would help penetrate the market that saw NEC having a 51.3 percent share, followed by Fujitsu and then IBM Japan. Kurita reports that NEC had 90 percent of the 16-bit market, but the PS/55 was based on the 80386, which is a considerably faster chip.[62] In 1985 it took a 50 percent position in Nippon Information and Communication (NI&C) along with the other partner, the giant Nippon Telegraph & Telephone Corporation (NTT), which was the AT&T of Japan. NEC also worked with AST in Japan for providing VAN services along with the partners, Cosmo 80, and the large industrial empire of Mitsubishi. Like Xerox, IBM would gradually come to rely more and more on its Japanese subsidiary.

If AT&T had walked into Europe through its operations conducted with Philips of the Netherlands, which in an earlier century had taught Matsushita how to manufacture batteries and light bulbs, IBM's entry into the world of industrial alliances and joint ventures in Western Europe was through Italy. In 1984, IBM Italia, the wholly owned IBM subsidiary, took a 49 percent interest in Seias for research and development purposes. Seias was owned indirectly by Italtel, through its subsidiary STET, which owned Selenia Elsag, which in turn took a 51 percent interest in Seias. Interestingly enough, Italtel was related to the Fiat subsidiary Telettra, which had taken 48 percent in a joint venture with Mediobanca to be called Telit. Italtel, the Italtel Societa Italiana Telecomunicazioni SpA, had been a sleepy and unprofitable manufacturer of telecommunications equipment until the arrival of Marisa Bellisario in 1981, whose first step was to cut the workforce there by one-third.[63] She had found that Italtel was losing more than $200 million each year, was over-staffed, and was manufacturing technology that was outmoded and irrelevant to the future.[64] Italy's best-known female executive immediately started work on a digital public switching system with GTE and Telettra, thus forming Italcom.

---

[60] See Charles P. Lecht, "IBM Japan, Superperformer, to the Rescue," *Computerworld,* 21 (12), March 23, 1987, p. 17.

[61] See Joel Dreyfuss, "IBM's Vexing Slide in Japan," *Fortune,* 117 (7), March 28, 1988, pp. 73–77. Dreyfuss reported that IBM had acquired a reputation for "arrogance" in the Japanese market, which is one of the world's most demanding markets.

[62] See Shohei Kurita, "The PC Market in Japan: Where's IBM?" *Electronic Business,* 14 (10), May 15, 1988, pp. 56–57.

[63] See Anonymous, "Italtel Keeps Her Suitors at Bay," *Telecommunications,* International Edition, 21 (10), October 1987, pp. 218–220.

[64] See David Finn, "High-Tech Woman at the Top," *Across the Board,* 25 (7–8), July/August 1988, pp. 11–17.

Telit was formed from a merger with Telettra. Italtel had been a subsidiary of the Instituto per la Ricostruzione Industriale (IRI), which had lost money for 13 years in a row.[65] AT&T and Italtel began a full-scale alliance in 1989, involving research and development, manufacturing, and joint marketing. AT&T had purchased 20 percent of Italtel, and the Italian government-owned STET group purchased a 20 percent stake in AT&T Network Systems International BV.[66]

Telettra also took 10 percent in Litel Communications of the United States, and was working on joint research and development with the French group Jeumont-Schneider. Telettra also entered the digital cellular mobile radio systems market through ANT Telecommunications of West Germany, which was owned by Robert Bosch GmbH. It is interesting that both Italtel and Telletra were working in joint ventures with GTE of the United States, Telletra in the area of radio telephony. GTE owned GTE Telenet, a VAN provider in direct competition with both MCI mail and Tymnet. GTE Telenet in 1986 invested in Ace-Telemail International in Japan in cooperation with Intec Inc., part of the giant Sumitomo Corporation. (The manufacturing giant NEC is part of the Sumitomo group.) GTE Telenet also entered into a 50–50 joint venture in long-distance systems with United Telecommunications of the United States. GTE in the United States also set up a joint venture subsidiary with Ferranti of the United Kingdom for manufacturing there. This complemented the GTE subsidiaries set up in Brazil and Canada. The linkages of GTE did not stop there. GTE was working with Fujitsu,[67] which held a 49 percent stake in the U.S. IBM-compatible mainframe manufacturer, Amdahl. Fujitsu was also working in a joint venture with Siemens of West Germany, which was selling much of the Fujitsu equipment at the high end of the market. Siemens, in turn, owned 80 percent of a GTE and Siemens joint venture set up in 1986 for manufacturing of transmission and switching equipment. GTE took the rest of the equity, along with its subsidiaries in Italy, Belgium, and Taiwan. Surprisingly, Siemens also took a position in a technical research and development agreement in 1985, aimed at studying public switching systems. Its partners included Plessy of the United Kingdom, Alcatel of France, and Italtel, which, as pointed out, was busy working with IBM in a variety of areas.

---

[65] See Anonymous, "Italian Economy: Privatisation in Fits and Starts; Rome Fiddles While the Economy Burns," *Economist,* 306 (7539), February 27, 1988, pp. S28–S34.

[66] See Anonymous, "The Strategic Alliance of AT&T and Italtel: Why Two Telecommunications Heavyweights Joined Forces," *Mergers & Acquisitions,* 24 (4), January/February 1990, pp. 70–71.

[67] Fujitsu appears to be somewhat of an "untraditional" company for a Japanese multinational corporation. Its successful sponsorship of the Japan-American Management Institute in Hawaii, and also its cross-cultural atmosphere in its U.S. operations, puts it in contrast with many other Japanese multinational corporations. For a view of Fujitsu's corporate culture see Art Gemmell, "Fujitsu's Cross-Cultural Style," *Management Review,* 75 (6), June 1986, pp. 7–8.

The system of global alliances set up by AT&T and IBM with their numerous counterparts overseas have helped shape today's structure of opportunities for utilization of information technology by multinational corporations. Many of these actions were motivated by such factors as the desire to cross national boundaries and penetrate different national markets. It is true that these alliances are making more options available to multinationals, but they have also tremendously complicated operational control and strategy formulation for the vendors. Nevertheless, their competitors have been pursuing the same game.

CHAPTER

13

The European Response to the "Threat" of IBM

Part of the shock felt in Europe after the devastation of World War II consisted of the realization that U.S. multinational corporations had an exceedingly strong position within the European economies. The form of organization of the multinationals and the way they were managed made some Europeans shudder. The expanding role of computerization was an additional element fostering the sense of competitive advantage felt by the Americans. As the years went by, the space race between the USSR and the United States and later the rise of Japanese technology seemed to emphasize the pivotal and central role of technology in national economic success. The multinational corporation as it competes on a global scale must have available to it the newest and most advanced technologies; and yet for European multinationals, there were fears that they would not have a vendor as strong as IBM upon which to call for help. Behind the scenes in the postwar period, a blistering array of industrial and technological alliances were being played out as companies jockeyed for position on the shifting sands of innovation.

France launched the *Plan Calcul* aimed at building up a data processing industry similar to IBM.[1] Although at the time IBM was making great inroads into the French market, it managed to survive through clever diplomacy. The French envisioned a multi-faceted development programme that could create a competitive industry. We know that this plan eventually failed: By the end of the 1980s, the companies created (Bull, CII, etc.) were on their knees begging for technology handouts from the stern Shoguns in Minato-ku, but when the Plan was launched, in the early 1960s, there was no evidence it would fail.[2] By spring 1991, Groupe Bull, protected by government subsidies, was reporting losses of $1.2 billion, and it seemed that no European computer maker was making any real progress toward open systems, as had been their professed strategy.[3] Siemens Nixdorf Information Systems AG was planning on developing software applications to run on top of its Sinix operating system which had been derived from Unix V, and Groupe Bull was working with the Open Software Foundation on a Distributed Computing Environment which would be open to other vendors. Both were trying to sign up different software vendors to co-develop applications to be released in the 1992–1993 period.[4] After all, an interventionist government policy had been reasonably successful with the national transportation network, with atomic and nuclear power, with jet aircraft, and so on—so why could a nation not create a viable computer industry? And why shouldn't it? The reasons for failure are great and varied: the continual drain of national resources competing in the national agenda against more powerful social forces such as the workers in the inefficient French automobile industry; the inadequate size of the market which, even though an entire country, was not large enough to support the economies of scale necessary for manufacture of components and systems with competitive cost/performance; and probably, although this is difficult to know, the failure of proper organization and discipline in research, the result being too slow development in a technology where time is everything.

Even after the various national development plans in Western Europe were failing in a big way—and this had become very obvious by the mid-1980s if not sooner—the residual nature and impulse toward national pro-

---

[1] An assessment and history of the French policy is provided in J. M. Quatrepoint, J. Jublin, and D. Arnaud, *French Ordinateurs de l'affaire Bull à l'assassinat du Plan Calcul* (Paris: Editions Alain Moreau, 1976).

[2] See P. E. Mounier-Kuhn, "Bull: A World-Wide Company Born in Europe," *Annals of the History of Computing,* 11 (4), pp. 279–298, who wrote a history of Bull.

[3] See Anonymous, "Spare the Rod and Spoil the Child," *Economist,* 319 (7703), April 20, 1991, pp. 63–64.

[4] See John Desmond, "Siemens, Bull Seeking Openness," *Software Magazine,* 11 (6), May 1991, pp. 23–25.

grammes[5] was still emphasized at the European Community level through the Jessi, Eureka, Esprit[6] and other European-wide projects such as the 5 year $616 million Alvey research program in the United Kingdom[7] aimed at spurring the development of information technology. There was to be a "New Europe" which would once again regain the center of the world's stage and shake off the shackles which had been wrapped around its shoulders in the immediate postwar period.[8] The Europeans realized that if they could only band together and overcome cultural and historical differences, then they would be able to overcome their technological inferiority gap. For example, in digital switches, they would immediately control 25 percent of the world market if they built a single integrated product.[9] Much research was being coordinated through organizations such as Europe's largest research establishment, the Centre National de la Recherche Scientifique, and was supplemented by generous tax breaks and subsidies for research.[10]

ESPRIT AND JESSI

The European Strategic Programme of Research and Development in Information Technology (ESPRIT) was set up as a series of five subprograms, each of which was subdivided into research and development components. The subprograms were concerned with development of office automation systems, new types of logic programming, studies in the use of expert systems,

---

[5]A comparison of various national industrial policies is found in Office of Technology Assessment, *International Competitiveness in Electronics,* OTA-ISC-200 (Washington, D.C.: U.S. Government Printing Office, 1983), Chapter 10.

[6]See Lynn Krieger Mytelka and Michel Delapierre, "The Alliance Strategies of European Firms in the Information Technology Industry and the Role of ESPRIT," *Journal of Common Market Studies,* XXVI (2), December 1987, pp. 231–253. The research shows the nature and number of linkages between AEG, Thomson, STET, Plessey, GEC, Nixdorf, CGE, Philips, Siemens, Olivetti, STC, and Bull. They concluded that the ultimate success of the program is "uncertain."

[7]For the United Kingdom, see Department of Industry (UK), *A Programme for Advanced Information Technology: The Report of the Alvey Committee* (London: Her Majesty's Stationery Office, 1982). See also K. A. Frenkel, "The European Community and Information Technology," *CACM,* 33 (4), 1990, pp. 404–411, for a European perspective. See also Mary Wilkinson, "State Cash Helps British Electronic R&D Catch Up," *Electronic Business,* 14 (7), April 1, 1988, pp. 71–72.

[8]See Marnix L. K. Guillaume, "Risk Managers Face 'New Europe,'" *National Underwriter,* 94 (28), July 9, 1990, pp. 9, 39–41.

[9]See John Parry, "Survival of the Biggest," *International Management,* Europe Edition, 45 (9), October 1990, pp. 56–59.

[10]See Raymond Boult, Alexander Dorozynski, Ted Katauskas, Skip Derra, Bob Keeler, Robert Cassidy, and Colleen Davis, "Salute to French Technology," *R&D,* 32 (11), November 1990, pp. 78–113.

leading-edge manufacturing of microelectronics, and creation of leading-edge software.[11] Other programs included Research for Advanced Communications in Europe (RACE) for studies of advanced telecommunications (including definition and creation of switched broad-band ISDN), as well as the Basic Research in Industrial Technologies (BRITE) program, which by 1987 had more than 100 serious research projects funded and operational,[12] forty percent of which were being operated by either universities or research institutes.[13] The RACE program was aimed at developments in telecommunications based on high-speed fiber optic systems such as broadband ISDN that would allow video telephones, television, radio, and data to move over the same networks employing the very high-speed Asynchronous Transfer Mode (ATM) standard.[14] The RACE program was divided into five areas of research, including standardization, wideband systems, mobile telecommunications, videocommunications, and general broadcasting, which included HDTV.[15]

The HDTV market had been dominated by Japan through its equivalent of the BBC, NHK (Japan Broadcasting Corporation), which had invested more than $300 million in HDTV over the past 15 years. The HDTV market was expected to top $25 billion by the year 2000.[16] The Europeans were willing to throw away all of the Japanese research and develop their own standard under the ESPRIT program, simply for the purpose of manufacturing their own equipment.[17] The EUREKA 95 HDTV project was a $240 million effort to develop a receiver based on the multiplex analog component (MAC) standard, which could be received on old receivers as well, thus not requiring everyone to purchase a new television. The Japanese effort to get their technically advanced standard adopted at the International Consultative Radio Commit-

---

[11]See Alan F. Smeaton, "Information Retrieval Research and ESPRIT," *Journal of the ASIS,* 38 (1), January 1987, pp. 21–22.

[12]See William Dawkins, "E. E. Approves $6.2-Billion Plan for Research," *Europe* (271), November 1987, pp. 22–23.

[13]See Karl-Heinz Narjes, "Policies and Experiences of International Organizations for the Promotion of Enhanced Interaction Between Industries, Universities and Other Research Organizations," *Technovation,* 9 (2, 3), June 1989, pp. 241–248.

[14]See Adrian Morant, "From ATM to ERBIUM in European Optics," *Telephone Engineer and Management,* 94 (16), August 15, 1990, pp. 62–68.

[15]See Roland Huber, "The Role of Information Technology and Telecommunications in Promoting Economic Development in the European Community," *International Journal of Technology Management,* 2 (3, 4), 1987, pp. 501–514.

[16]See Jay Ramasastry, "The Road to HDTV," *Satellite Communications,* 12 (4), April 1988, pp. 33–35.

[17]See Ronald K. Jurgen, "High-Definition Television Update," *IEEE Spectrum,* 25 (4), April 1988, pp. 56–62.

Chapter 13 The European Response to the "Threat" of IBM

tee (CCIR) meeting in 1986 was beaten back.[18] The Europeans planned on developing techniques of transmitting HDTV on limited bandwidths associated with earlier generations of television, and were determined, through their Eureka EU-95 project, to prevent the Japanese from taking over their market.[19] The definition of the HD-MAC standard meant to keep out the Japanese was being pioneered by Philips and Thomson.[20]

The research accelerated quickly. By 1989, it was reported that ESPRIT had resulted in a seven-fold increase in international research agreements from the years 1983 to 1986; this was expected to supplement the predicted $58 million software market in 1992, up from only $25 million in 1987, based on a doubling of the hardware market from 1980 to 1985 up to $38 billion.[21] The ESPRIT program developed into a very broad-ranging research program including such areas as

- Load management and electricity distribution with expert systems[22]
- Compression techniques for sending full color video images over the 64 kbps channels that were being used by ISDN[23]
- Object-oriented approaches to engineering databases[24]
- Transputers capable of gigaflop float-point calculations[25]
- The Cathedral system for more efficient computer-aided design of VLSI microprocessors[26]

---

[18]See Philippe Guichardaz, "Europe's Challenge in HDTV," *Europe* (283), January/February 1989, pp. 18–19.

[19]See Barbara Berkman, "Europe's 1995 HDTV Goal: A Standard of Its Own," *Electronic Business*, 16 (16), August 20, 1990, pp. 44–45.

[20]See Jane Sasseen, "Television Jousts with Japan," *International Management*, Europe Edition, 46 (2), March 1991, pp. 37–39.

[21]See Nigel Tutt, "Europe's Computer Industry Prepares for 1992," *Europe* (284), March 1989, pp. 23–24.

[22]See T. Wittig and G. C. Koukoulis, "Expert Control," *Systems International*, 14 (11), November 1986, pp. 23, 26.

[23]See Roy H. Vivian, "DPCM Studies Using Edge Prediction and Adaptive Quantisation Laws for the Transmission of Still Pictures over the ISDN," *Microprocessing & Microprogramming*, 21 (1–5), August 1987, pp. 141–150.

[24]See D. P. Soupos Christodoulakis and C. Zaroliagis, "The Implementation of a Software Engineering Database Using Desk-Size Computing Resources," *Microprocessing & Microprogramming*, 21 (1–5), August 1987, pp. 383–389.

[25]See M. R. Hey, "Transputers and Computational Physics," *International Journal of Technology Management*, 2 (3, 4), 1987, pp. 541–543.

[26]See Chris Price, "Esprit de Corps," *Systems International*, 16 (1), January 1988, pp. 33–34.

- An experiment named SelFac to transmit custom-designed on-demand newspapers to readers with a home facsimile[27]
- The CARLOS and CACTUS projects for easing transfer of data between different types of equipment[28]
- The Portable Common Tool Environment (PCTE) for a new more open kernel to be used in software engineering environments that would eventually be free of the UNIX operating system[29] and would aid CASE tools in providing a set of interface specifications for linking tool standards[30]
- The ESPRIT project 881 FORFUN General Language for System Semantics (GLASS), for description of a greater number of attributes of analog and digital systems in an executable script helpful for circuit design,[31] such as for VSLI, which needs description of both hierarchy and regular structures[32]
- The Large Scale Pilot Exercise (LSPX) trial of the Obviously Required Nameserver (THORN) project, which would support the CCITT X.500 standard for vastly distributed environments[33]
- A Project Integrated Management System (PIMS) for complex project management that would use a Knowledge Acquisition Documentation and Structuring (KADS) methodology[34]

---

[27] See Philippe E. Maeght and Anton W. Jolkovski, "Selective Facsimile: The Electronic Text Medium of the 21st Century?" *Computer Networks & ISDN Systems,* 14 (2–5), 1987, pp. 155–158.

[28] See Don Cochrane, "Easing the Migration into the Future of Communications Technology," *Computer Networks & ISDN Systems,* 14 (2–5), 1987, pp. 323–329.

[29] See Malcolm Verrall, "PCTE—The Kernel of Software Engineering Environments," *Microprocessing & Microprogramming,* 24 (1–5), August 1988, pp. 161–165.

[30] See Herbert Weber, "From CASE to Software Factories," *Datamation,* 35 (7), April 1, 1989, pp. 34–36, 52. The PCTE project lasted from October 1983 to April 1988. See also C. De Groote, "PCTE—A Remarkable Platform," *Information & Software Technology,* 31 (3), April 1989, pp. 136–142. PCTE was eventually migrated into PCTE+, which was more independent of the UNIX operating system. See David Robinson, "Enhanced Environment," *Systems International,* 18 (6), June 1990, pp. 28–29.

[31] See Jozef A. De Man, "Designing Digital Systems with a Function Language," *Microprocessing & Microprogramming,* 24 (1–5), August 1988, pp. 227–232.

[32] See H. Oolman, M. Seutter, and C. van Reeuwijk, "GLASS, a Language for Analog and Digital Circuit Description, and its Environment," *Microprocessing & Microprogramming,* 27 (1–5), August 1989, pp. 267–271. See also Jozef De Man and Johan Vanslembrouck, "Transformational Design of Digital Circuits," *Microprocessing & Microprogramming,* 27 (1–5), August 1989, pp. 273–278.

[33] See Steve Kille, "The THORN Large Scale Pilot Exercise," *Computer Networks & ISDN Systems,* 16 (1, 2), September 1988, pp. 143–145. See also Christian Huitema, "The X.500 Directory Services," *Computer Networks & ISDN Systems,* 16 (1, 2), September 1988, pp. 161–166.

[34] See Ton De Jong, Robert de Hoog, and Guus Schreiber, "Knowledge Acquisition for an Integrated Project Management System," *Information Processing and Management,* 24 (6), 1988, pp. 681–691.

Chapter 13 The European Response to the "Threat" of IBM

- A European Local Integrated Optical Network project to link LANS with metropolitan networks[35]
- A Primary Rate ISDN OSI Office Facilities (PROOF) project to define the standards and procedures for interconnection of LANS with ISDN networks[36]
- Research on neural networks partially financed by Siemens, which had spent $3.36 billion in research concerning product and systems development[37]
- The ESPRIT number 1588 SPAN project to develop a model parallel architecture that would integrate both numeric and symbolic processing,[38] to be helped along by the Parallel Architectures Research language (PARLE) procedural programming language[39]
- A P1085 ESPRIT project to use transputers to strengthen the Edinburgh concurrent supercomputer[40]
- A "supernode" computer also using transputers from Inmos linked together without intervening memory[41]
- A Design Metrics Evaluator (DEMETER) project under 1257 MUSE for automatically assessing software quality[42]
- The ATHENA software maintainability tool that was being designed to measure constantly readability, volume, modularity, complexity of data structures, and other factors[43]

---

[35] See Angelo Luvison, "An Approach to Multi-Service Business Networks," *Telecommunications,* International Edition, 22 (11), November 1988, pp. 44–54.

[36] See Bharat Patel, "PROOF: Interconnecting ISDN and LANs," *Telecommunications,* International Edition, 23 (10), October 1989, pp. 49–54.

[37] See Andy Rosenbaum, "Siemens Restructures R&D to Be Closer to End Markets," *Electronic Business,* 15 (6), March 20, 1989, pp. 60, 62.

[38] See Peter A. Rounce, Ken Chan, Stuart Mackay, and Kevin Steptoe, "VLSI Architecture Research Within the ESPRIT SPAN Project," *Microprocessing & Microprogramming,* 26 (2), June 1989, pp. 139–152.

[39] See Eugeniusz Eberbach, Stephen C. McCabe, and Apostolos N. Refenes, "PARLE: A Language for Expressing Parallelism and Integrating Symbolic and Numeric Computations," *Microprocessing & Microprogramming,* 27, (1–5), August 1989, pp. 207–214.

[40] See Sandro L. Fornili, "You Don't Need Big Computers to Run Complex Simulations," *Research and Development,* 31 (11), November 1989, pp. 68–74.

[41] See Richard Evans, "Parallel World of New Superpower," *International Management,* Europe Edition, 45 (10), November 1990, pp. 58–60.

[42] See U. B. Helling Heitkoetter, H. Nolte, and M. Kelly, "Design Metrics and Aids to Their Automatic Collection," *Information & Software Technology,* 32 (1), January/February 1990, pp. 79–87.

[43] See D. N. Christodoulakis and C. Tsalidis, "Design Principles of the ATHENA Software Maintainability Tool," *Microprocessing & Microprogramming,* 28 (1–5), March 1990, pp. 183–189.

- A Computer-Aided Design Interfaces (CAD*I) project to create a reference architecture for the Computer-Integrated Manufacturing Open Systems Architecture (CIM-OSA) project[44]
- A Metrics Educational Toolkit (METKIT) project to encourage the use of software metrics in the European software industry[45]
- The world's first machine designed to manufacture the 64 megabit microchip[46]

Some had complained that the European approach to research and development had some fatal flaws. Diebold pointed out that most innovation in the United States had been driven by individual entrepreneurs and not by megaprojects.[47] Others noted that the weakness of the European approach under ESPRIT lay in its lack of focus, and a severe fragmentation of the financial outlay.[48] Hoffman argued that this was characteristic of European policies in general, even in the broader economic sphere, which had been characterized by slow growth, structural unemployment, and too much inflation.[49] Writers such as Berger, on the other hand, continued to see ESPRIT as one of the keystones of the continued integration of Europe and its emergence as a world power.[50] Some research tended to support a large role for government and public research consortia in promoting development of world-class leading-edge technology.[51] Other observers maintained that the central reason that European computer manufacturers, the "national champions," had been unable to compete with the Asians and the Yanks was their inability to control costs and to move away from slow growth markets.[52]

---

[44] See E. A. Warman, "Integration Revisited—An Appraisal of the State of the Integration of CAD," *Computers in Industry*, 14 (1–3), May 1990, pp. 59–65.

[45] See Robin Whitty, Marin Bush, and Meg Russell, "METKIT and the ESPRIT Program," *Journal of Systems & Software*, 12 (3), July 1990, pp. 219–221. Also see Martin E. Bush and Norman E. Fenton, "Software Measurement: A Conceptual Framework," *Journal of Systems & Software*, 12 (3), July 1990, pp. 223–231, which discusses the two-dimensional classification scheme being used, and Meg Russell, "International Survey of Software Measurement Education and Training," *Journal of Systems & Software*, 12 (3), July 1990, pp. 233–241.

[46] See Richard Evans, "ESPRIT Evades the Soft Option," *International Management*, Europe Edition, 46 (1), February 1991, pp. 58–61.

[47] See John Diebold, "The Changing Information Environment: Suggest Future Directions," *Vital Speeches*, 55 (5), December 15, 1988, pp. 138–145.

[48] See Anonymous, "The E. C.'s Research and Technology Development," *Europe* (282) December 1988, pp. 28–30.

[49] See Stanley Hoffmann, "The European Community and 1992," *Foreign Affairs*, 68 (4), Fall 1989, pp. 27–47.

[50] See Wolfram G. Berger, "Establishing the European Internal Market: Implications for Information Technology," *International Journal of Technology Management*, 3 (6), 1988, pp. 631–641.

[51] See Todd A. Watkins, "A Technological Communications Costs Model of R&D Consortia as Public Policy," *Research Policy*, 20 (2), April 1991, pp. 87–107.

[52] See Anonymous, "System Failure," *Economist*, 310 (7593), March 11, 1989, p. 70.

Jessi was formed in 1990 as a partnership of European companies, with the exception of IBM, in recognition of the fact that the European semiconductor industry was in third place in the world and was capable of supplying only 38 percent of its own European market demand. With a budget of $4 billion, Jessi was planning to create a 0.35 micron device by 1996, with production of 4 megabit memories in 1990, 16 MB in 1993, and 64 MB in 1996. By June 1990, Jessi had decided to join forces with Sematech, the consortium operating in the United States with essentially the same purpose, in order to exchange both membership and common databases.[53]

FORTRESS EUROPE

The 1985 agreement to collaborate on public switching systems between Plessey, Italtel, Alcatel, and Siemens represented one of the many efforts put forward in the 1980s to spur development and utilization of information and telecommunications technologies in the European Community. Euro-centric thinkers never ceased to point out that the promise of a "Fortress Europe" would constitute the largest market in the world, and the prospect of an emerging Euro-Techno complex was exemplified by this type of collaborative arrangement. Unfortunately, half a decade later, this venture appears to have made little progress worth mentioning, however laudable it might have seemed at the time. On the other hand, five years is not much time when one is considering the development or homogolation of public switching systems and their replacement in a market characterized by much equipment having life-spans of between one-quarter and one-half of a century. Siemens began to work with U.S. West Information Systems through its subsidiaries, FirsTel Information systems and Interline Communication Services, to pursue military contracts in the United States as it had done in Europe, by operating the Autovon private network for the U.S. military using its KN4100 distributed control system.[54] By 1986, Siemens was reporting that sales in the U.S. market had increased by 24 percent, amounting to $2.2 billion, which was twice the figure for 1982. It was working with Intel Corporation in producing an application specific integrated circuit (ASIC) for use in factory environments.[55]

The Plessey situation in the United Kingdom had long been burdened by problems with the development of the new generation of switches based on the System X provided by GEC in a joint-venture arrangement. Eventu-

---

[53] See Barbara N. Berkman, "Can the Barons of Jessi Save Europe's Chip Makers?" *Electronic Business*, 16 (5), March 5, 1990, pp. 42–47; and Anonymous, "New Technologies," *European Trends*, (3), 1990, pp. 56–60.

[54] See Sharon Scully, "No Deal on EWSD," *Network World*, 3 (8), April 28, 1986.

[55] See Frederic A. Miller, "Siemens: A European Giant Comes Alive in the U.S.," *Business Week*, Industrial/Technology Edition, September 1, 1986, pp. 68H–68I.

ally, Northern Telecom of Canada began to supply Olivetti of Italy with PABX equipment along with Intercom and Plessey. Northern Telecom was also working with Plessey's supplier, GEC. Plessey's subsidiary, Stromberg Carlson Inc. in the United States, entered into a joint venture with Mitsubishi International Corporation to provide cellular mobile telephone service in the United States through Astromet. At about the same time, Plessey invested in Telenokia of Finland, which was providing mobile telephones in corporation with Matra of France. Matra was working on videotext with Tymeshare of the United States, which was purchased eventually by British Telecom, and was a great competitor of GTE Telenet. Matra also worked with Boeing Aerospace Company of the United States and with British Aerospace. In 1986 it took 20 percent of CGCT Communications in France, which was owned by CGCT and was manufacturing private telephone equipment.

The "Euro" technical research and development agreement on public switching systems was supported by another French competitor, Alcatel, formed from CIT Alcatel and Thomson Télécommunications, which had taken a 10 percent share in the Olivetti PABX group along with Plessey.

Alcatel

Alcatel NV had been the product of a merger between Compagnie Generale d'Electricité (CGE) and ITT's telecommunications business which was worth more than $6 billion per year. The resulting merger in 1987 made Alcatel, which was set up in Brussels, the world's second largest supplier of telecommunications equipment behind AT&T. CGE owns 55.6 percent of Alcatel, and ITT owns 37 percent. Alcatel has operations in 110 countries, with annual sales of between $11 and $13 billion per year for 150,000 employees.[56] The merger started with losses of around 20,000 jobs.[57] The agreement gave ITT $902 million in cash from the deal, which was just as well since it was facing increasingly severe problems in Europe with the introduction of its System 12 digital switch, having no European government as a backer.[58] ITT sold more of its stake in the company in 1990, and continued its sell-off, as it had discovered they were worth more as separate companies than as a single entity.[59]

Alcatel operated two divisions in North America, including Alcatel NA in New Jersey and Alcatel Business Systems Inc, and was aiming in 1987 for a

---

[56]See Anonymous, "Alcatel—One Name, One Company," *Telecommunications,* International Edition, 21 (10), October 1987, pp. 146–147.

[57]See Leigh Bruce, "The new Alcatel Powerhouse: So Far, So Good," *International Management,* 42 (10), October 1987, pp. 45–53.

[58]See Terry Dodsworth, "ITT Adopts New Role in Europe," *Europe,* March 1987, pp. 22–23.

[59]See Brian Bremner, "It's a New Day for ITT's Rand Araskog," *Business Week* (3167), July 2, 1990, pp. 50–51.

Chapter 13   The European Response to the "Threat" of IBM   205

complete rethinking of its distribution channels.[60] In the U.S. market, it was selling fiber optic cables, different types of transmission equipment, and general business communications systems, knowing that within 10 years, less than 10 companies would still be in existence in the switching market.[61] In order to be one of the survivors, Alcatel was busy providing ISDN capabilities to its "Alcatel One" PBX, putting it in direct competition with AT&T and Northern Telecom.[62] It was doing the same in the Norwegian market, where it was taking advantage of its 13 research centers, and trying to sell ISDN capabilities to the Norwegian Telecommunications Administration.[63] In 1988, Alcatel was already operating innovative "technology transfer" programs with Austria.[64] It quickly moved into leveraging the advanced telecommunications industrial policy, which had been developed in France, to bank on further sales of its RCV-1G fiber optic system used for delivering fiber optics directly into each individual home, to eventually have broadband capabilities for telephone, television, data, and other functions.[65] In 1988 it had jumped into the IBM-compatible market with release of a vanilla 80386 computer with a few unique features, such as adding 32-bit busses and placing the BIOS into active ROM.[66] In Europe, it worked with Siemens to challenge the signaling system which had been proposed by the European Telecommunications Standards Institute (ETSI), keeping its eye on the European PBX market, which was expected to be $1 billion by 1993 for cordless PBX hardware alone and to carry an underlying growth rate of 13 percent increase per year until 1994.[67]

By the end of 1989, partially as a result of its recent reorganization, it was reporting a net income jump of 43 percent to $526 million,[68] and was work-

---

[60] See Pam Powers, "French Giant Alcatel Enters U.S. Picture," *Network World*, 4 (43), October 26, 1987, pp. 11–12.

[61] See Jack Gee, "The Bigger, the Better, Says Alcatel Chairman Suard," *Electronic Business*, 14 (22), November 15, 1988, pp. 62–67.

[62] See Elizabeth Schultz, "PBX Upgrades Travel the Bumpy Road to ISDN," *Telephony*, 215 (22), November 28, 1988, pp. 36–39.

[63] See Stephen McClelland, "Face to Face: Telecommunications Talks to Bjarne Aamodt," *Telecommunications*, International Edition, 24 (3), March 1990, pp. 73–74.

[64] See Herald Gessinger, Gunter W. Hasler, and Werner Hiller, "Technology Transfer Programme for the 5200 BCS Digital PABX," *International Journal of Technology Management*, 3 (1, 2), 1988, pp. 196–204.

[65] See Anonymous, "Can Fiber Slide Safely into Home?" *Telephone Engineer & Management*, 92 (10), May 15, 1988, pp. 106–108.

[66] See Patrick Honan, "Alcatel's 386: A Systems Approach," *Personal Computing*, 12 (5), May 1988, pp. 219–220.

[67] See John Williamson, "New Connections for the European PBX Industry," *Telephony*, 218 (26A), June 25, 1990, pp. 22–23.

[68] See Tim Harper, Paul Gannon, James Etheridge, and Johan Hallsenius, "The Datamation 100," *Datamation*, 36 (12), June 15, 1990, pp. 130–134.

ing hard with Siemens in various joint ventures to crack the Eastern European market which was estimated to be worth more than $150 *billion* in the medium term, with 60 percent of that being accounted for by the USSR.[69] By 1990, Alcatel was expecting its sales in Eastern Europe to more than double to $260 million, and was busy in China as well with the joint venture it was operating with Shanghai Bell, which had recently placed an order for 1,250,000 telephone lines.[70] In 1990, it was one of the only two vendors (the other was Fujitsu) demonstrating the successful interconnection of SONET standard OC-3 equipment carrying DS3 traffic. This was one of the first practical demonstrations of the American National Standards Institute (ANSI) T1X1 committee Synchronous Optical Network (SONET) standard, and showed clearly that Alcatel was pushing to be at the very front of the technology curve.[71] A study done by AT&T and Northern Telecom had indicated that using fiber optic cable with the SONET standard that transported the signaling information and overhead bits directly in the STS-1 frame would revolutionize end-user equipment and make obsolete the massive installed base of asynchronous standalone multiplexers and high-order digital cross-connects.[72]

When Alcatel took over 75 percent of Italy's Telettra, in late 1990, it immediately acquired 38 percent of the Italian transmission and 45 percent of the Spanish market, giving it a turnover of $1.2 billion, for a total of approximately the $11.1 billion turnover of AT&T, thus making it equivalent to the largest telecommunications company in the world.[73]

Alcatel was also working with Fairchild Industries in the United States, one of the pioneering semiconductor manufacturers, active in the satellite component and services business, and in a joint venture with Italtel in the area of videotext. Through its relationship with Compagnie Génerale d'Electricité (CGE) of France, Alcatel had a 60 percent interest in a holding company, the other 40 percent interest of which was controlled by Société Générale de Belgique and the Spanish group, Telefónica. This new holding company took 63 percent of another company which had 37 percent ownership from ITT Corporation of the United States.

---

[69]See Johathan B. Levine and Gail E. Schares, "The Last Gold Rush of the 20th Century?" *Business Week,* Industrial/Technology Edition, (3181), October 8, 1990, pp. 140H. (Note: as we go to print, it is clear the USSR will soon cease to exist.)

[70]See John Marcom, Jr., "First Europe, Then the World," *Forbes,* 146 (10), October 29, 1990, pp. 134–135.

[71]See Kenneth Head, "A SONET Milestone for the History Books," *Telephony,* 219 (25), December 10, 1990, pp. 24–27.

[72]See E. V. Hird, "Transmission/T1: Sacrifices in the Name of Simplification," *Telephone Engineer and Management,* 95 (1), January 1, 1991, pp. 43–47.

[73]See Anne-Marie Roussel, "Top of the World," *International Management,* Europe Edition, 45 (11), December 1990, pp. 48–51.

Other Players

The diversity of financial arrangements and the transnational nature of most of the alliances boggle the mind; there are so many of these alliances that it is difficult to imagine anyone speaking any longer of "national" industries. How can an industry or company be "national" in light of so many interlocking relationships at the financial, technological, and services level?

Northern Telecom of Canada had partnerships with Sperry Univac, Data General, and Digital Equipment Corporation (DEC), and supplied PABX equipment to Olivetti in Italy and to GEC in the United Kingdom. It worked with Nokia in Finland, which controlled much of Luxor in Sweden. The Japan Communications Satellite Planning Company in Japan was a joint venture with 40 percent ownership of C. Itoh & Company, the giant trading company, 30 percent owned by the aristocratic Mitsui & Company Ltd, and 30 percent owned by Hughes Communications of the United States, which was working with the French Thomson in satellites and was owned by Hughes Aircraft, part of the General Motors Corporation (which, by the way, owned Electronic Data Systems[74] mentioned earlier in connection with a systems integration joint venture with AT&T). Digital Equipment Corporation was active in the French market in creating PBX terminals servers and a special high-speed computer designed for specialized processing of financial transactions. Its Special Systems Centre (CSS) was located in Annecy, France and was charged with taking the lead with ISDN for DEC as a whole, given the highly advanced state of the French Telecommunications network.[75] Racal Electronics in the United Kingdom was working with Norsk Data in Norway in the field of artificial intelligence. Sumitomo Electric of Japan had licensed optical fibres in 1984 to Wacker Chemitronic of West Germany, where MBB was working with BMW, and Daimler-Benz had in 1985 taken 65.5 percent of Dornier and 56 percent of AEG, the electronics giant. The U.K. company Cable and Wireless, which had been responsible for developing so many of the major international telecommunications circuits, particularly at the beginning of this century, helped set up Mercury Communications to compete with British Telecom, invested in TDX in the U.S. market, and was a major player with Hong Kong Telephone. Marconi Communication Systems Ltd. of the United Kingdom had licensed

---

[74] EDS is famous for having rescued some of its employees from Iranian jails after the despotic Shah was overthrown. As of 1989, EDS was working on providing EDS*NET, a worldwide network for multinational corporations to use in operating their global systems. EDS*NET was reported to support 730 million transactions each month with a client base of 6,000 companies. It was using 1.5 mbps satellite linkages based on VSAT technology. EDS was helping General Motors in Europe connect electronically with its 2,000 suppliers. See Wayne Ekerson, "EDS Sows Seeds of Future Profit in Post-1992 Europe," *Network World*, 6 (38), September 25, 1989, pp. 33, 38.

[75] See Raymond Boult, "Competent Solutions," *Systems International*, 18 (4), April 1990, pp. 53–54.

automatic cross-connect equipment to Telecommunications Technology Inc. (TTI) of the United States.

Noh Bull

Bull of France was working with Philips of the Netherlands to manufacture memory cards while taking, in 1986, a major share in a research and development center operated in cooperation with Siemens of West Germany and ICL of the United Kingdom. At the same time, in 1986, Compagnie des Machines Bull took a major share in Honeywell Information Systems of the United States, which was partially owned by Honeywell and 15 percent owned by NEC of Japan[76] and was one of the major competitors to Fujitsu and IBM, both of which had been working with Siemens, the third partner of the joint R&D center. When Groupe Bull, Honeywell, and NEC's revenues were combined together, the figure was $9 billion, the third or fourth largest computer manufacturer in the world. The deal gave Groupe Bull 42.5 percent and NEC 15 percent in the company, with Honeywell retaining 42.5 percent, but with an option of reducing it to 19.9 percent within two years. Analysts reported that Honeywell had desperately wished to get out of the computer business, as indicated by the sell price of $175 million, which was estimated to be only one-third of what the division was actually worth,[77] more than $250 million less than book value.[78] Honeywell retained the U.S. Federal Systems Division, which was reported to be the only profitable portion of the business and was more in line with the traditional business of Honeywell.[79] It was expected that Honeywell would continue to purchase products from the new group, Honeywell Bull, for use in its systems and industrial integration work, including

---

[76]See Steve Gross, "Will Honeywell Bull Survive Its Inheritance?" *Electronic Business,* 14 (5), March 1, 1988, pp. 80, 82. The announcement included the news that 1,000 persons would be eliminated in manufacturing and 600 would be eliminated in marketing and sales. However, Gross reports on plans to hire 250 new software programmers. The company's factories in the United Kingdom were reported operating at only 50 percent of their capacity. The cash flow of the company was eventually saved by Jacques Stern who turned things from a $458 million loss in 1981 to a $45.2 million profit in 1984. See Leigh Bruce, "Corporate Turnaround: Bull Tackles the Yanks," *International Management,* 42 (12), December 1987, pp. 30–32. who reports on Stern's record in the turnaround in 1984.

[77]See Gordon Bock, Thane Peterson, and Patrick Houston, "Honeywell Beats a Retreat from the Computer Wars," *Business Week,* Industrial/Technology Edition (2977), December 15, 1986, p. 30.

[78]See Conna Raimondi, Rosemary Hamilton, Clinton Wilder, and James Connolly, "Honeywell Surrenders Info Group/New Company Freed from Distractions of Honeywell Goals," *Computerworld,* 20 (49), December 8, 1986, pp. 1, 6–7.

[79]See Cathy Hilborn, "Honeywell, NEC, Bull Join Forces," *Computing Canada,* 12 (26), December 29, 1986, pp. 1, 14.

Chapter 13 The European Response to the "Threat" of IBM

its large number of jobs for the U.S. Government, which now, of course, would begin to use Japanese mainframe computers, or at least parts of them.[80] In addition, the Honeywell-NEC Supercomputers Inc. (HNSX), based on Japanese technology, was now better positioned to threaten other supercomputer vendors such as Cray or ETA Systems, providing the U.S. market could get the bone out of its throat regarding purchase of Japanese supercomputers.[81] The traditional "top down" selling approach of Honeywell was no longer deemed most effective in the market for what some saw as potentially the world's third largest company after the buy out.[82] Instead, the new firm, Honeywell Bull, would make extensive use of third-party vendors and systems integrators to attach vertical markets in the United States, including health care, manufacturing, and state and local governments.[83] From an architectural point of view, users and industry analysts saw the opportunity for the three companies to offer a single architecture.[84]

ITT

The ITT situation was just as complex. Its European subsidiaries included FACE in Italy, Standard Telephon und Radio AG in Switzerland, Standard Radio och Telefon AB in Sweden, 60 percent of Standard Telefon og Kabelfabrik A/S in Norway, 85.9 percent of Standard Electric Lorenz AG in West Germany, Standard Electric Puhelinteollisuus OY in Finland, Standard Electric Kirk AS in Denmark, and ITT Austria. Standard Electric Kirk AS in 1986 entered into a computer network joint venture with Rovsing of Denmark. ITT's Belgium subsidiary, Bell Telephone Manufacturing Company, owned 39 percent of Teletas in Turkey, and 30 percent of Shanghai Bell Telephone Equipment Manufacturing Company in China, 60 percent of which was also owned by China Postal and Telecommunications Industry Corporation, and 10 percent by the Belgian Government. The 71 percent ownership of Standard Electrica SA in Spain was a joint venture with Compañía Telefónica Nacional de España, which owned 20 percent equity. In 1986, ITT had failed in its effort to promote the System

---

[80] See Alan Alper, James Connolly, and Clinton Wilder, "Honeywell Bull Born," *Computerworld,* 21 (13), March 30, 1987, pp. 1, 102.

[81] See Becky Batcha, "Three Vendors Give Cray Chase," *Computerworld,* 21 (41), October 12, 1987, pp. 99–106.

[82] See Jan Johnson, "Users Laud Honey of an Alliance," *Computer Decisions,* 19 (2), January 26, 1987, pp. 15–20.

[83] See Mike Bucken, "Groundwork for the Future," *Software Magazine,* 8 (14), November 1988, p. 41.

[84] See Susan Kerr, "Mergers: Are Three Heads Better than One?" *Datamation,* 33 (2), January 15, 1987, pp. 19–23.

12 digital switch in the United States, and had seen a fall in profits from $695 million in 1981 to just $294 million in 1985. Many analysts blamed its failure on very poor leadership at the top.[85]

The Swedish giant was also entangled in an octopus of financial and technological sharing arrangements that spanned the globe. It had manufacturing facilities throughout Europe and South America. It owned Datasaab in Sweden, was working with DEC of the United States in the banking sector, had leased 10 percent of the Elektrisk Bureau in Norway in 1986, and was also working with Sperry Univac of the United States in creating banking terminals. Sperry Univac and Burroughs formed Unisys in 1986. Ericsson also owned 51 percent of Intelsa of Spain, with the other 49 percent being owned by Compañía Telefónica Nacional de España. It was working in a joint venture with Isotech in the United States for creation of integrated voice and data telephones, had a joint venture with Shrack Elektronik AG of Austria, and gave licenses for switching systems to the Belgium company Ateliers de Constructions Électriques de Charleroi and to AG Hasler of Switzerland, which in 1986 had merged with Autophon S.A. ITT provided PBX equipment to Honeywell in the United States with which it had a 50–50 ownership investment in Honeywell Ericsson Development Company. Ericsson also had a 50–50 ownership of Ellemtel Utvecklings AB of Sweden, which was also owned by Televerket, the national telecommunications agency of Sweden and by Teli, also of Sweden. In the United Kingdom, Ericsson was a joint owner of Thorn Ericsson with Thorn EMI of the United Kingdom, which had invested in Inmos, the semiconductor manufacturer. Finally, Ericsson was operating a joint venture with Reynolds Metals of the United States for manufacture of fiber optic cables.

It appears that Corning Glass of the United States had emerged as a major player in the fiber optics market by this time. In 1973 it took 50 percent of Siecor, which was a joint venture with Siemens AG. Corning also operated a joint venture with British Cable and Plessey, and took 40 percent of Fibres Optiques Industries in France, owned jointly with Thomson-CSF and St. Gobain Pont-à-Mousson. It was also supplying Compagnie Lyonnaise de Transmission Optiques (CLTO) and CGE, running a joint venture in Italy with Pirelli, and conducting research with Sumitomo in Japan. It owned 65 percent of Telcor in Spain along with Compañía Telefónica Nacional de España, which had 35 percent and which also owned 49 percent of Cables de Comunicaciones in cooperation with General Cables of the United States, which owned 51 percent.

The list could go on forever, and can be found in all its depth and complexity when the reader stops to examine the industrial history of the information sector in the post-war period. The question that inevitably arises is: *Why?* Why did these companies form joint ventures? Why did they seek part-

---

[85] See Michael Gatermann, "ITT's Empire in Decline?" *Director,* 40 (3), October 1986, pp. 67–72.

Chapter 13 The European Response to the "Threat" of IBM

ners? Why did competitors cooperate in certain instances? The answers are as varied as the companies.

CONTINUED WEAKNESS IN EUROPE

At the pan-European nation-state level, promises of a considerably larger market, the ability to collect research funding from a European-wide budget, and the possibility of erecting subtle (and not so subtle) barriers against foreigners (particularly against the Japanese), all appeared to bode well for this effort. There were always calls for a Euro-Industrial policy that would cover computer and telecommunication systems, research and development, and all aspects of television and video.[86] Much of the debate in the political-economy field during this period revolved around the danger of the Japanese setting up "screw-driver" plants to manufacture within Europe so as to avoid the possible import taxes. The Europeans seemed to believe that this type of arrangement was not good for their economy, but the Japanese argued that they were forced to import most of the components for their equipment being assembled in Europe because they could not obtain the same supplies as in Japan. Epson was able to source only 30 percent of its raw materials and components from Europe.[87] The Western Europeans as a group seemed to be again falling into the trap of national development plans as they had before when they developed individual national policies. Again, there was success to count on in several other areas—the Airbus consortium and the new jet fighter consortium were examples of such success—and it was reasonable to expect that in information technology, it would be possible to develop a Euro-computopia. But technological development swept aside any hopes for Western Europe in this area as the relentless pace of competition between the Japanese and the Americans left the Europeans on the sidelines, with fine theories and lots of talk, but no significant breakthroughs.

The final blow came when ICL, one of the leading partners in the consortium, was sold outright to Fujitsu, and Apricot Computers, which had been producing high-powered workstations, was sold to Mitsubishi of Japan. Fujitsu's purchase of 80 percent of ICL was expected to hurt IBM in the Western European market that was supplying 37 percent of its revenues in 1989. Having a connection with ICL would allow Fujitsu to plan tariff-free manufacturing

---

[86]See Wisse Dekker, "Prospects for Collaboration and a Common Industrial Policy in Europe for the High-Technology Industries," *International Journal of Technology Management,* 1 (3, 4), 1986, pp. 297–307.

[87]See Dick Wilson, "Brother Ready to Raid Unified EC," *Asian Finance,* 16 (10), October 15, 1990, pp. 22–23.

in that market, which was growing rapidly.[88] There was thought, however, of kicking ICL out of the European Roundtable ESPRIT, which had been the focal point for creating an independent information-technology industry in Europe.[89] Plug-compatible mainframe vendors, such as the Amdahl corporation, 40 percent owned by Fujitsu, were also attacking IBM, and users were closing and consolidating data centers in favor of "downsizing" or adherence to "Open" (i.e., NOT-IBM) systems.[90] The purchase of ICL would give Fujitsu 10 percent of the European market, which was growing 30 percent faster than that in the United States. Fujitsu would now control the largest market share of any computer vendor in the United Kingdom's market, and would be poised to push aggressively forward with sales of the new arrangement with leading-edge Sun Microsystems to use its RISC microprocessors, thus being able to challenge the new generation of down-sized strategy being made available with IBM's RISC 6000 series.[91] There was at the time hushed talk of blackmail in the deal. ICL's parent STC[92] had evidently been desperately looking for a European partner for investment, as it was a major player in Eureka, the European-only research consortia, but the rumor was that Fujitsu had threatened to hold up supply of microelectronics and other components unless ICL gave in to being a subordinate lap-dog in Fujitsu's global strategy. Of course the rumors were denied, but doubt remains.[93] Like any other industry, computers can also have a dark side. In any case, Fujitsu now became the world's second largest computer company, with what it hoped would be an "insider's" track into the European market, where it hoped to concentrate on ICL's strengths in systems integration, European manufacturing and extensive marketing arrangements already in place.[94] Mitsubishi's purchase of Apricot

---

[88] See Richard Meyer and Sana Siwolop, "Fujitsu: The Samurai Have Landed," *Financial World*, 159 (19), September 18, 1990, pp. 46–50.

[89] See Elizabeth De Bony, "Japan May Find Closed Doors in Europe," *Computerworld*, 25 (9), March 4, 1991, p. 66.

[90] See Amiel Kornel, "Fujitsu Move Rattles Europe," *Computerworld*, 24 (32), August 6, 1990, pp. 1, 113. Kornel reports that British Telecom was consolidating 57 data centers into only 10 within two and one-half years.

[91] See Charles Smith and Tony Major, "The Stakes Rise: Fujitsu Set to Put Heat on IBM with ICL Takeover," *Far Eastern Economic Review*, 149 (31), August 2, 1990, pp. 46–47.

[92] At the time, ICL accounted for more than half of STC's turnover and profits. STC had purchased Computer Consoles in the United States in 1988 for $168 million and also Datachecker, which was purchased from National Semiconductor for $90 million. STC had also purchased Northern Telecom's UK business. See Charles Arthur and Sally Hamilton, "The Selling of STC," *Business*, November 1990, pp. 72–77.

[93] See Richard Evans, "Takeovers: Japan Moves in at Dawn," *International Management*, Europe Edition, 45 (8), September 1990, pp. 44–47.

[94] See Christopher McCooey, "From Competitor to European Insider," *Accountancy*, 107 (1170), February 1991, pp. 116–117.

Chapter 13 The European Response to the "Threat" of IBM 213

cost about $70 million and gave it a springboard to increase production by four times.[95] At the close of the 1980s it was becoming obvious that, in their desire to make all efforts to avoid domination by the Americans and their technology, the Europeans had maneuvered themselves into dependency on the Japanese for critical technology.[96]

Mytelka and Delapierre[97] concluded that although the situation in Europe naturally called for collaboration between European firms, the prospects for success were uncertain:

> Theories of regional integration lead us to believe that cross-investments within the enlarged market... are desirable from the perspective of both the firm, which can increase specialization and reduce costs through economies of scale, and the society which stands to benefit from the equalization of factor prices across member economies. In knowledge-intensive industries, however, the pace of technological change and the new modes of competition that have accompanied it put in doubt the inward-directed behaviour expected of firms in a common market.... The ultimate impact of the ESPRIT programme on the long-term viability of the European information technology industry is thus uncertain.

On the one hand, it is easy to criticize and browbeat the Europeans for failing to produce a viable computer industry and losing any hope of regaining a position as the center of innovation. Many of the industrial alliances appear to be little more than weakened European companies selling out and turning themselves into distribution channels for either American or Japanese system or component manufacturers. There is some evidence that, in many cases, the European partners found it easier to cut deals with non-Europeans than with their own. In spite of these problems, however, Europe stands as the third great center of technological excellence in the world, behind Japan and the United States. Other areas of the world, Eastern Europe and the East Asian area, were also developing during this period, although along completely different paths.

---

[95] See Richard Meyer and Sana Siwolop, "Fujitsu: The Samurai Have Landed," *Financial World,* 159 (19), September 18, 1990, pp. 46–50.

[96] The Financial Times reported that "The past 12 months have done nothing to allay fears that the European electronics industry is in inexorable decline. European markets for the principal products—semiconductors, computers, software and consumer electronics—are dominated by foreign-owned competitors." FT Supplement, "The FT European Top 500," January 11, 1991, p. 20.

[97] See Lynn Kreiger Mytelka and Michel Delapierre, "The Alliance Strategies of European Firms in the Information Technology Industry and the Role of ESPRIT," *Journal of Common Market Studies,* XXVI (2), December 1987, pp. 231–253.

CHAPTER 14

Eastern Europe and the Dragon Kingdoms

The responses to the rise of this new technology were different in other parts of the world. Africans did not resist the new technology and its effects; indeed, they clamored to receive more of it at the expense of various international development agencies. On the other hand, Latin Americans did resist, claiming that it would be necessary first to master the technologies on their own terms before allowing widespread implantation of foreign-dominated systems into the body fabric of their fragile societies, dominated as they were at the time by militarists and honchos.[1]

The Latin Americans were concerned about the effects of mass media, about the importation of cultural values through mass media and information technology. For example, they argue that the "consumer-oriented" society is not native to Latin America and has been imported through advertising in order to increase sales of multinational corporations. In Eastern Europe, the situation was driven by a state of permanent dependence upon innovation abroad. In the emerging states of East Asia, advances in the computer industry were driven by component manufacturing.

---

[1] For a study of the situation in Mexico, including the industrial structure of both the telecommunications and computer industries, see UNCTC, *Transborder Data Flows and Mexico* (New York: United Nations, 1991). The report details the conditions foreign corporations had to face in establishing manufacturing facilities for computer equipment in Mexico, including "a minimum of 51 percent Mexican capital" (p. 25). The report notes that "in 1980, Mexico had 3,311 microcomputers and 1,657 minicomputers and 69 mainframes. By 1984, those numbers had increased to 61,080 microcomputers and 5,210 minicomputers. The computer infrastructure in Mexico as of December 1986 consisted of 615 mainframes, 5,443 minicomputers, and 227,767 microcomputers. Of the latter, 36 percent were home computers, of which one third were IBM and compatibles" (p. 22).

In contrast to Latin America and its peculiar condition, the situation in Eastern Europe was different. The vast advances that had been made in information technology were locked behind the walls of the military-industrial complex, away from the eye and use of either the public or the consumer. The telecommunications infrastructure had remained terribly under-invested and the result was virtually no significant data transmission outside of the military sphere. The information society was a long way off, and yet in contrast to other countries of the world, research was progressing in some of the most advanced areas, such as artificial intelligence, supercomputing, and throughout the military complex.

THE SOVIET UNION

As the Brezhnev era came to a close, it was clear that the Soviet Union's seemingly impenetrable wall against the outside world was beginning to crumble. Information was seeping into the Soviet Union, and people became gradually aware of the wealth and prosperity of the West, regardless of the ills it held (crime, drugs, unemployment, racism, religio-chauvinism, etc.) It was the era of *samisdat*, the circulation of underground publications, as the early 1980s witnessed the rise of the personal computer. This new technology raised speculation about the effects of computerization on Soviet society, which was already approximately 20 years behind the times in terms of its applications base in the general economy. Chorafas called this the "computer-management gap." He writes:

> The Soviet Union and Eastern Europe are still so short of data-processing equipment and computers that the growth of management science has been significantly slowed. The USSR itself has very little computer equipment designed for management use. Large-scale systems do not seem to exist to any appreciable degree, and those extant do not seem to have been applied to industrial or commercial operations.[2]

It became fashionable later to talk of the role of information technology in Soviet society as a force for destruction of the Stalinist edifice that had been dominating everyone's lives through enforced bureaucratic rigidity. This line of argument stressed that electronic bulletin boards, telecommunication of information through the telephone network rather than through the postal lottery, and the new wave of thinking that personal computers would suppos-

---

[2]Dimitris N. Chorafas, "Computer Technology in Western and Eastern Europe," *Columbia Journal of World Business,* May/June 1970, pp. 61–66. He notes that the multinational corporation is changing: "Industrial focus [is] evolv[ing] from a one-product orientation to conglomerate diversification, geographical scope [is shifting] from national to international, time scales are increasingly accelerated, crucial questions, once production-oriented, are [becoming] research- and marketing-oriented, and procedures in information processing must accommodate to the fact that management itself changes from 'status quo' to a permanent state of development."

edly usher in, would lead to a loosening of the Stalinist yoke of repression. This type of writing peppered the popular and even academic press in the mid- and early 1980s. It was actually little more than a wish-transference from the Silicon Utopianists to the societies of Eastern Europe.[3] We have seen now that computers had little, if anything at all, to do with the social transformations in Eastern Europe. The social and economic forces for reform are far stronger than little electronic boxes on one's desk performing pascal calculations, word processing, and the like. Silicon Utopianism didn't work in the United States and it didn't work in Eastern Europe; yet it is very interesting to contrast the Silicon Utopianists' writing about Eastern Europe with the Latin American *dependenciatistas*. One side viewed information technology as essentially a great tool of repression; the other viewed it as a great liberating force. Which view is correct? How can the social effects of the same technology vary so greatly from one setting to another?

Dependency theory related directly to the structuralist theme and also raised the banner of cultural protectionism.[4] This banner was taken up by the revisionist historians, who saw the invasion of information technology as a type of electronic colonialism—a new way of enslaving countries into a type of subservience that they had just escaped as they moved toward independence. Information technology was viewed by these historians as a conscious and willful means to trick and exploit weaker countries, and computer technology and its associated technologies as little more than propaganda weapons to enslave the masses into a certain way of thinking and lifestyle.[5]

Under the cloak of Stalinism and centralized planning, giant computing enterprises were created that tried to emulate technological developments in the West. Within the Comecon structure of international economic relationships, a massive manufacturing and technology base was set in place, which effectively integrated computer production.[6] The computers were based on IBM architecture,[7] as were the computers being built in Japan, but there were

---

[3]The attitude seemed to be: "Why can't the people in Prague or Moscow use information technology like Southern Californians?"

[4]One wonders what type of cultural tradition the intellectuals were protecting. Why protect societies from outside influences and ways of thinking when the societies themselves are dominated by repressive tin-pan juntas or fading revolutionaries whose glories have been replaced in most cases with a police state?

[5]Much of this debate is covered in Eileen Mahoney, "Negotiating New Information Technologies and National Development: The Role of the IBI," Ph.D. thesis, Temple University, 1987. See also Vincent Mosco and Janet Wasko, eds., *The Political Economy of Information* (Madison: University of Wisconsin Press, 1988).

[6]For notes on the situation in Poland, see L. Łukaszewicz, "On the Beginnings of Computer Development in Poland," *Annals of the History of Computing*, 12 (2), 1990, pp. 103–108.

[7]See S. E. Goodman, "Technology Transfer and the Development of the Soviet Computer Industry," in B. Parrot, ed., *Trade, Technology and Soviet-American Relations* (Bloomington: Indiana University Press, 1985), pp. 117–140.

many differences. The components available for manufacturing the machines were not as advanced, and special techniques such as bit slicing had to be employed to get the same logical equivalence in operations. Also, the general *size* of many of the components and peripherals was very much larger and not as aesthetically pleasing, although still generally effective.

The critical difference in the USSR in terms of proliferation of information technology was that, first, the USSR faced severe restrictions on availability of foreign technology, restrictions implemented through Cocom aimed at inhibiting as forcefully as possible the ability of the USSR to make technical progress. Second, the essence of the centralized planning system, dominated as it was by the military-industrial complex, necessitated an avoidance of consumer acceptance of the technology. There was little "marketing" as we in the West know the term, taking place in Soviet enterprises; rather, this art consisted of fathoming the intricacies of inter-Ministerial politics and intrigues.

The result was a general lack of penetration of information technology throughout the consumer sector of the USSR—a fate shared by many material goods. The secondary effects of this were devastating: with no consumer market, there could be no economies of scale in manufacturing, no resulting fast trek down the price-performance curve, and thus no rapid proliferation of technology throughout the Soviet economy. By the end of the 1980s, with the Soviet Union reeling from the Eastern European renaissance, the Soviet computer industry was wondering how it would survive the rapid importation of foreign computer technology, and the Soviet government faced some hard decisions about whether to protect, and what type of model to adapt regarding this clearly important economic sector.

The basis of their problem lay in their inability to create a sustainable mechanism of innovation in high technology. In the computer field, the USSR followed the lead of IBM in terms of architecture. Their BESM and RYAD series of computers were created one generation after another, but were never as efficient as they always were following the technological lead of the United States. At the end of the 1980s, instead of being the size of teacups, 100 megabyte disk drives were the size of washing machines. The USSR was forced into a type of technological isolationism or autocracy because the West worked diligently to prevent the leakage of any technology into the Soviet Bloc. This effort lasted through the post-war period until the end of the cold war in 1990. Although other countries, as part of their national plans, had chosen to develop computerization in order to keep up with the technological developments in the United States, the USSR had done the same, but with the added element of military competition. It could be argued that the technological isolation or containment of the USSR was eventually effective. By the end of the 1980s, the World Bank's assessment of the Soviet economy emphasized that it was more similar to that of a developing country than to an industrialized country.

The COMECON system of economic cooperation and development also set in place a large coordination mechanism to build computers with distributed sourcing of both systems and various components. However, by the end of the cold war, the socialist system lay in ruins, and the massive infrastructure of coordination that had been put in place quickly crumbled.[8] It was the end of an era in Eastern Europe, and it signaled the potential end of the Soviet computer industry.

THE DRAGON KINGDOMS OF EAST ASIA

Developments in information technology also reached other areas of the world, approximately a decade later. In East Asia, the national leadership of the Four Dragons—Singapore, Hong Kong,[9] Taiwan,[10] and South Korea— embarked on a completely different strategy.[11] Instead of starting with bold national plans to foster the development of a massive mainframe-based computer industry as had been the case in the USSR, in Western Europe, and in

---

[8] For an overview of the status as of 1990, see Dimitry Chereshkin, Wladyslaw Turski, Tibor Vamos, A. Tomasz Jarmoszko, and Seymour Goodman, "National Information Technology Policies in East-Central Europe and the Soviet Union," *International Information Systems*, 1 (1), 1992.

[9] An example of a successful Hong Kong company moving into microelectronics is Semi-Tech Microelectronics (Far East). Semi-Tech started with a few people but by 1990 had 40,000 employees in 100 countries and annual revenues of $2.5 billion. Semi-Tech started out manufacturing microcomputers, but eventually purchased Singer sewing machines, and decided to use its expertise to improve Singer's product range. See Michael Selwyn, "Sewing Up the World," *Asian Business*, 26 (6), June 1990, pp. 60–62.

[10] For a study of the development of the semiconductor industry in Taiwan, see Massoud M. Sahhafi and Chin-Shu Davidson, "The New Age of Global Competition in the Semiconductor Industry: Enter the Dragon," *Columbia Journal of World Business*, Winter 1989, pp. 60–70. Their data shows that the United States began accumulating a trade deficit in semiconductor trade in 1981. The article contrasts the types of firms in Taiwan and Korea. In Korea, semiconductor manufacturing is done by very large firms; in Taiwan, small and medium-sized firms are used. The Taiwanese government has strong influence over the semiconductor industry through the Taiwan Semiconductor Manufacturing Company (TSMC). Sahhafi and Davidson write that "the overall semiconductor industry in Taiwan has a global rather than a multinational business philosophy— integrating R&D, manufacturing, management, and marketing function. In Taiwan, however, unlike in the developed nations of North America, Europe, and Japan, this integration is not a 'free enterprise' phenomenon. It is the result of a concerted and well-coordinated effort by the Taiwanese government." They note that "the success of South Korea and Taiwan in the industry results from two important factors—acquisition of foreign technology, and the government coordination and control of manufacturing, management, and marketing of semiconductors."

[11] For a review of computer communications development in the Pacific Basin, see Neil D. Karunaratne, "Information Technology and the Developing Pacific," *Telecommunications Policy*, 10 (2), June 1986, pp. 83–87. Karunaratne also discusses the possible effects on multinational corporations of what he sees as a considerably more advanced and liberal telecommunications regime in the area.

Japan, these countries took a more sober approach. Instead of starting at the top of the ladder with attempts to build a completely integrated computer industry, they started at the bottom. They began with simple component manufacturing and worked from the very beginning at integrating their manufacturing capabilities with the plans of the big companies. Even small companies such as the Chung Cheony Group in Bangkok, Thailand, were busy founding companies such as the Universal Digital Computer Company in hopes of building up more computer trade in Southeast Asia.[12] The success in Singapore was due to a clearly thought-out government policy introduced in 1979 involving technology development, subsidies for on-the-job training, and a generally heavy emphasis on development of human resources.[13]

This strategy was helped in no small way by the tremendous growth of the Southeast Asian economy, which posted a 35 percent per year growth in the computer market. This massive market was potentially the largest in the world because not only did it have people, it had money and commerce, something that the sad and liberalizing spectacle of Eastern Europe could not offer. The prospect of this large market was prompting Western computer manufacturers to alter their global strategies.[14]

Power supplies, displays, modems, components, assembly operations, disk drives, and so on—all these types of technology were rapidly transferred to East Asia, which, during the 1970s and 1980s, became the largest manufacturing center for much of this equipment.[15] As they climbed up the learning curve, and as technology advanced, these countries produced more and more sophisticated equipment. By the end of the 1980s, companies in the Four Dragons were busy producing multi-user personal computer-based systems with local area networks, file servers, and Intel-386 or even 486 chip set machines. They were well integrated into the general manufacturing plans of most world-class manufacturing vendors, and were beginning to export large amounts of equipment to the opening markets of Eastern Europe, where there was considerably less competition from the Japanese.

A type of specialization began to emerge among the Four Dragons. Singapore was creating a great number of hard-fix disk drives for data storage,

---

[12]See Joel Kotkin, "The Chinese Way of Business," *Inc.,* 9 (7), June 1987, pp. 66–70.

[13]See A. N. Hakam and Zeph-Yun Chang, "Patterns of Technology Transfer in Singapore: The Case of the Electronics and Computer Industry," *International Journal of Technology Management,* 3 (1, 2), 1988, pp. 181–188.

[14]See Coleen Geraghty, "Computer Vendors Re-Shape Product Strategy for Asian Market," *Asian Finance,* 12 (4), April 15, 1986, for a look at the new strategies of IBM, DEC, Prime, and Burroughs in the market.

[15]For example, see the case of Seagate Technology in Richard Brandt, "Seagate Goes East—And Comes Back a Winner," *Business Week,* Industrial/Technology Edition (2989), March 16, 1987, p. 94. Seagate had moved from $40 million in 1982 to $344 million in sales in 1984, only two years later! By 1987, sales were expected to reach $950 million. This was the only strategy Seagate could use to undercut the Japanese in the market.

and working on providing integrated computer services such as integration and consulting to the many service-oriented companies that Prime Minister Lee had systematically attracted to the small entrepot state; Taiwan was making rapid progress in developing national-level planning concerning the information-technology industry, with significant progress in manufacturing of all types of components, and even of their own machines, such as Acer, which were successfully entering various export markets, particularly in the United States.[16]

Emperor Shih of Taiwan Province

By 1988, Acer, founded by Mr. Stan Shih, had captured 2 percent of the world's personal computer market and had averaged growth of over 100 percent per year for the previous 12 years. Acer was hoping to top $1 billion in sales by 1990, and was spending 5 percent of its earnings on research and development, an amount that "went much further" because Taiwanese labor was cheaper.[17] Its 80386 personal computer, the Acer 1100, received good reviews in 1987, particularly because the U.S. subsidiary, Acer Technologies Corporation, promised to provide on-site service at no extra charge, and offered a free four-month repair guarantee, which was longer than that of other vendors in the industry.[18] By 1987, it was expected Acer's revenues would top $200 million, up from $36 million *only two years earlier,* even given the change of name (from Multitech) that had occurred due to a dispute with a similarly named company in the United States. Multitech had been known for developing the first Chinese language software.[19] Acer seemed attractive to foreign institutional investors, who had purchased 13 percent of the company in 1987 for about $16 million, in line with its plan to raise $40 million in capital by placing 10 percent of its equity through the Taiwan market.[20] By 1988, personal computers accounted for 80 percent of Acer's revenues, but there were plans to reduce that share to 50 percent when new products, such as

---

[16]For a contrarian point of view that downplays the role of the state, see Danny Kin-Kong Lam and Ian Lee, "Guerilla Capitalism and the Limits of Statist Theory: Comparing the Chinese NICs," working paper, W. Paul Stillman School of Business, Seton Hall University, 1991; and Danny Kin-Kong Lam, "The Myth of State-Led Industrialization: The Origins of Electronics Manufacturing in Taiwan," working paper, W. Paul Stillman School of Business, Seton Hall University, 1991.

[17]See Jonathan Moore, "Apple of Taiwan's Eye," *Far Eastern Economic Review,* 141 (28), July 14, 1988, p. 62.

[18]See Stephen Satchell, "Acer 1100: 386 Machine Offers Super Support at Super Price," *InfoWorld,* 9 (26), June 29, 1987, pp. 50–51.

[19]See Robert G. S. Welt, "The Taiwan Computer Industry—A Market at the Peak of Evolution," *OEP Office Equipment & Products,* 16 (109), Fall 1987, pp. 36–37.

[20]See Anonymous, "A Well-Worn Road to Dominance," *Economist,* 308 (7568), September 17, 1988, p. 76.

minicomputers, telecommunications devices, and various computer peripherals, were manufactured. Stan Shih was being called the "Emperor of Taiwan's Computer Industry."[21] In keeping with this strategy, in 1989 Acer released the Counterpoint, an X-Windows terminal, designed to work with the bit-mapped graphical interface designed at MIT, which was capable of working independently of processors and of displaying simultaneously different sessions from different machines. Sales of the X-Windows terminal were expected to top 600,000 units by 1990.[22] The MIT X-Windows system was seen as being a low-cost entry point for users who were interested in the "open" UNIX operating system, and Acer released another version, the Xebra 100, in mid-year 1989 to catch the wave of consumption.[23] By the end of 1989, Taiwan stood as the world's sixth largest manufacturer of information technology, and Acer was by far the largest company in Taiwan, with sales of over $740 million, and about 7 percent of the thick revenue stream now placed in advertising.[24] By 1990, Acer had struck a deal with the giant Texas Instruments to form Texas Instruments Acer Semiconductor Ltd., aimed at manufacturing one- and four-megabit DRAMs, with Acer controlling 74 percent of the joint venture, but with Texas Instruments having an option to raise its stake to 51 percent. A key factor in this deal was reported to be the desire to lessen the dependency of both companies on the Japanese.[25] To take advantage of the world's fastest growing computer market—Singapore, Hong Kong, the Republic of Korea, Taiwan, Thailand, and Malaysia—Acer started to develop a chain of AcerLand stores to market its products throughout that region.[26] Shih was intending Acer to be one of the world's top five personal-computer manufacturers by the year 2000, but by 1990, the world's growth and consumption of personal computers was already slowing. Yet information technology remained Taiwan's third largest foreign exchange earner.[27]

---

[21] See Philip Liu, "Emperor of Taiwan's Computer Industry," *Electronic Business,* 14 (20), October 15, 1988, pp. 96, 98.

[22] See Mike Seither, "Terminal Vendors Stake Out X-Window Display Territories," *Mini-Micro Systems,* 22 (2), February 1989, pp. 24, 26.

[23] See Sarah Keefe, "Into Low-Cost UNIX Through X-Windows," *Systems International,* 17 (7), July/August 1989, pp. 57–60.

[24] See Barun Roy, "Acer's Stan Shih: Against All Odds," *Asian Finance,* 15 (11), November 15, 1989, pp. 17–23.

[25] See Robin Agarwal, "TI-Acer DRAM Venture: Will This Marriage Survive?" *Electronic Business,* 16 (8), April 30, 1990, pp. 67–68. By this point, Acer's sales were reported at $494.7 million. See Stephen Lukow, Nobuko Hara, Marcia Stepanek, and Lew Young, "The Datamation 100: Ricoh; Seiko Epson; C. Itoh; CSK; Acer," *Datamation,* 36 (12), June 15, 1990, pp. 170–174.

[26] See Russ Arensman, "PC Makers Look to Asia for the Next Surge in Sales," *Electronic Business,* 16 (14), July 23, 1990, pp. 110–112.

[27] See Carl Goldstein and Julian Baum, "Taiwan: Acer in the Hole; the Chips Are Down," *Far Eastern Economic Review,* 150 (50), December 13, 1990, pp. 62–63.

In this respect, Taiwan had perhaps moved the furthest in terms of keeping up with technological developments and newer technologies. Its personal-computer industry was highly diverse and flexible. In 1989, the top 20 manufacturing firms were producing only slightly more than one-half of Taiwan's production, and the world's PC market had grown by 27 percent overall in the previous year as PCs started approaching the 100 million instructions-per-second rate predicted for the mid-1990s.[28] In late 1989 it accomplished the remarkable feat of designing, manufacturing, and bringing to market a lap-top computer within three months—an effort that must have meant many sleepless hours in various laboratories around the country. The Southeast Asia area was recognized by the major vendors as being the fastest growing in the world, as IBM released a special Korean version of its personal computer. Hong Kong developed rapidly in the late 1970s and 1980s, as its economy boomed with the rising speculation of the Japanese and others. The liberalizations under the aging Premier Deng had allowed Hong Kong to become the center of the SEZ Special Economic Zone strategy pursued by China in its opening to the West for technology. In this thrust toward the mainland, many "high technology"[29] industries set up in the SEZ's were controlled in Hong Kong, and often completely integrated with them; final assembly, design, raw materials sourcing, financing, and managerial organization would be provided by Hong Kong, and labor of other specialized value-adding processes would be provided by the firms that were set up in the Special Economic Zones.[30]

The Hermit Kingdom of Korea

In Korea, developments followed a path similar to Taiwan's and, to a certain extent, early Japan's. Much government and industry collaboration created a climate conducive to creation of the computer industry, and it was well understood in the leading government circles that higher-value-added activities were critical to the success of a country in its development process.

---

[28] See Bob Johnstone, "Asia: Technology—Into the Next Generation," *Far Eastern Economic Review*, 145 (35), August 31, 1989, pp. 48–54.

[29] In this context, the term "high-technology" or "Hi-Tek" industries is reserved for microelectronics and related technologies. In reality, on a worldwide comparative scale, the actual industries that were set up in China used outmoded technology, and were not "high-tech" at all in comparison to the leading-edge computer manufacturing going on around the Kanto Plane and Silicon Valley. There is, in fact, much evidence that China purposefully attracted older technologies in its modernization effort, primarily because the capital equipment could be purchased at considerably cheaper rates than for the newest items.

[30] Special Economic Zones are not unique to China; other countries have them as well, and operate them more successfully.

Korean firms followed the path of licensing their technology from the Japanese and Americans—the Europeans didn't have much worth licensing during this period—particularly at the component level, then working hard to produce finished goods, more complex integrated goods that would be mass-produced for a world market. Much of the Korean advantage in mass production during this period was based on simple labor cost advantages that both the government as well as the concerned industries were willing to use to the fullest to get things done. As a result, by the end of the 1980s, Korea was busy manufacturing printers, personal computers, power supplies, displays, even files servers. This industry was backed up with a considerable capability in manufacture of both merchant semiconductor and specialized Application Specific Integrated Circuits (ASICs). In addition, Korea worked hard at providing office furniture items suited to the "information age"—items such as wall partitions and office furniture with built-in capabilities for local area networks and extra power cables.[31] This effort was capped off somewhat during the Olympic games, when the Koreans showed off their advancement, including the massive amount of fiber optic cabling that had been put into place for specialized networking.

The Global System and the End of Phase I

The fall of Eastern Europe and the rise of the East Asian newly industrializing countries (NICs) presaged the end of Phase I of the global trend toward informatization of the world. The computer industry, which had been created in only a few centers of innovation in the West, could not be contained there. The rapid commoditization of equipment driven by the rapidly falling price-performance curves for information technology guaranteed that the technology would spread as had so many important technologies before it—steam, atomic power, genetics, the automobile, printing, and so on—to the point where it would become an integral part of all but the most ideologically backward economies.

The trading system that was put in place after World War II virtually guaranteed that it would be possible for agents of technology transfer and trade such as the multinational corporation to spread the technology to even the remotest corners of the earth. Finally, international commerce, heir to the shipping era, moved toward worldwide manufacturing, air transportation,

---

[31] See Edward M. Roche, "South Korea's Informatics Race," *Agora*, 9, 1984/3, pp. 12–14. Edward M. Roche, "Computer Communications in Korea," Mimeo, 1984, describes the early state of the Korean data-processing industry. See also Edward M. Roche, "Korean Informatics Policy," Academic Symposium on the Impact of Recent Economic Developments on U.S./Korean Relations and the Pacific Basin, University of California at San Diego, Graduate School of International Relations and Pacific Studies, November 9–11, 1990.

and global logistics, all of which drove the need for sophisticated information systems to support their activities further, the result being the further spread of the technology into different countries.[32] The vendors that had been accustomed to supporting their corporations inside the country where they had their base of manufacturing faced the task of supporting their customers as they expanded their worldwide operations. This required further expansion of their business, faced as they were with loss of market share in the absence of providing the ability to support their customers on a worldwide basis, and this in effect drove the world even further along the path toward global informatization.

The multinational corporation was able to benefit from these developments. At the same time that its business was becoming more integrated on a global basis, it was able to take advantage of information technology on a scale never before thought possible. In Eastern Europe, developments in information technology had been shielded behind a wall of official secrecy and were not made available to major economic and ecological organizations on the same scale as in the West. When the Berlin Wall fell, the economic and ecological backwardness of these socialist enterprises were laid bare for all to see. Most were being operated with information systems that were a quarter of a century behind.

In East Asia, the booming business in component and small-job manufacturing set the stage for the massive increase in international trade in the Pacific Basin, which in the mid-1980s exceeded that for other areas of the world. The rapidly expanding position of East Asia also hit hard against the Europeans and Americans. By the beginning of the 1990s, Japan was the world's largest manufacturer of information technology, and the smaller Asian countries were taking away most of the component manufacturing from the West, which was fatally weakened.

---

[32]It was reported in 1991 that United Parcel Service had spent $1.4 billion on computer technology to handle tracking of packages. All of the major players in the international courier business were doing the same, including DHL, Federal Express (which was a great innovator in the use of information technology for tracking), and TNT. See Anonymous, "Tracking: Customers Call the Tune," *Financial Times,* Financial Times Survey, Courier and Express Services, July 24, 1991, pp. iv–v.

CHAPTER

15

Nihon no Computa no Yokozuna

In the immediate postwar period, the countries of Western Europe, as well as Japan, attempted to build up national computer industries. The Europeans chose a path of protectionism combined with indirect and direct subsidies, particularly government purchasing agreements. It was a model that had worked for other sectors in their economies, but it ultimately failed because individual national markets are not large enough to sustain a computer industry. In contrast, the Japanese adopted a different approach that emphasized elements of controlled competition and rigorous performance requirements. This strategy worked, and it left Japan as the world's largest manufacturer of computer equipment by the beginning of the 1990s.

Note: Yokozuna is the Japanese term for the highest-ranking sumo wrestler. This chapter title translates as "The Japanese Computer *Yokozuna.*"

Amdahl had been forced to go to Fujitsu in order to get financial support for continued development of its massively integrated computer chips, although it insisted on purchasing components and peripherals from other vendors as well. Amdahl thus avoided being totally dependent upon Fujitsu, which was involved in a massive legal tangle with IBM over infringement of copyright and patents, a dispute that was inducing Fujitsu gradually to pull away from offering IBM compatibility.[1] This was supposed to leave more market room for Amdahl in the market for IBM plug-compatible equipment. In 1986 Amdahl was hoping to find a good market for the 3480 class machines that were made in Japan and designed to be compatible with IBM equipment and software.[2] By 1987, Fujitsu was reportedly supplying disk drives, processor components, and communications products to Amdahl, which was hoping that its new 5890 mainframe would continue to bring in substantial revenues. The 5890 was responsible for 75 percent of all Amdahl's revenues, which had risen by 10 times in the first half of the year.[3] It was reported in 1990 that the European users were moving toward more acceptance of plug-compatible machines, such as those produced by Amdahl.[4] The continuing legal battle with IBM tended to complicate product planning at Fujitsu because in order to continue to offer IBM-compatible equipment, it was necessary to know the technical characteristics of each new generation of equipment and then replicate it quickly enough to approach the market with a similar machine at a lower price. Fujitsu in turn supplied the German giant Siemens with mainframe computers for use in Mittle-Europa and then surprised everyone by purchasing complete control over the crumbling British computer manufacturer ICL. IBM entered into a joint research-and-development and manufacturing alliance with Siemens to produce very large-scale integrated 4-megabyte and 16-megabyte memory chips, a technology that had already been accomplished by the Japanese.[5] Siemens had to buy out the failing Nixdorf computer (although it waited until after the death of the founder). Nixdorf had been Germany's second largest computer manufacturer after Siemens, and had staked its commercial, as had so many others, on the success of the UNIX operating system. Nixdorf was put up for sale in December 1989, and the negotiations were completed in only 18

---

[1] See Lee Keough, "Amdahl Steps Out," *Computer Decisions*, 18 (25), November 4, 1986, pp. 34, 66.

[2] See Jeff Moad, "Tall in the Saddle," *Datamation*, 32 (22), November 15, 1986, pp. 52–60.

[3] See Jagannath Dubashi, "With a Little Help from My Friends," *Financial World*, 156 (20), October 6, 1987, pp. 26, 28.

[4] See Amiel Kornel, "Fujitsu Move Rattles Europe," *Computerworld*, 24 (32), August 6, 1990, pp. 1, 113.

[5] Nippon Telegraph and Telephone (NTT) announced a 16-megabyte chip in early 1988.

days.[6] The new company formed from the merger was Siemens-Nixdorf Informationssysteme AG (SNI), and was expected to have approximately $8.8 billion in information-systems revenues,[7] and a combined worth estimated at $61.1 billion, which cynics said was just a way for Siemens to eliminate one of its most stubborn competitors and appear helpful in the rescue of a company whose founder had suddenly passed away.[8] In the U.S. market, Siemens was concentrating on the banking and retail industry.[9] The new combination promised to make it easier for Siemens to enter the quickly developing market for Computer Integrated Telecommunications Systems (CITS), a technology that was already being worked on by DEC, AT&T, IBM, and other giants.[10] By 1991, SNI's business was still concentrated in Europe, which accounted for 90 percent of its operations and was reporting orders from the USSR for 300,000 personal computers.[11]

In France,[12] Bull and CII had combined as the *Plan Calcul* drifted into history and then worked out an alliance with Honeywell of the United States only to become dependent upon Nippon Electric Corporation (NEC), the world's largest semiconductor manufacturer, for supply of medium- and large-scale computers, as NEC had purchased most of Honeywell in the mid-1980s. NEC is a company that always had a policy independent of the rest of the market, fostered in great part by the personality of its leader, Dr. Kobayashi.

---

[6]See Barbara N. Berkman, "Rebuilding the House of Siemens on a Worldwide Foundation," *Electronic Business*, 16 (15), August 6, 1990, pp. 28–32. Berkman reports that at the time, Siemens had 1989 sales of $36 billion, with the U.S. market accounting for 11 percent of its total operations.

[7]See James Etheridge and Peggy Trautman, "The Datamation 100: Groupe Bull; Siemens; Olivetti; NV Philips; Nixdorf," *Datamation*, 36 (12), June 15, 1990, pp. 127–130.

[8]See Nell Margolis, "Computer Firms Set to Unite," *Computerworld*, 24 (40), October 1, 1990, p. 131.

[9]See Anonymous, "Nixdorf Bets on UNIX to Crack the U.S. Market," *Electronic Business*, 14 (5), March 1, 1988, pp. 84, 86.

[10]See Adam Rehin, "Calling on CSTAs," *Telephony*, 219 (23), November 26, 1990, pp. 26–34.

[11]See Tim Mead, "Siemens-Nixdorf's Wiedig: The Real Work Begins," *Datamation*, International Edition, 37 (3), February 1, 1991, pp. 64(7)–64(8).

[12]Doz, for example, studies the problems IBM encountered in the telecommunications sector in France. His interviews of IBM executives show the difficulties: "As soon as you cross the border from data processing to telecommunications everything becomes political. We are not interested in the number of jobs per se, but in technology problems. In the public sector you deal by political decisions not by economic balance and common sense. The technologies are converging between telecom and computers. The difficulty in both lies with component technology. The question for IBM is whether a company can protect its own technology. The answer is 'yes' in data processing, 'no' in telecommunications so far.... We would not accept a telecommunication equipment joint venture in which we would have to provide the technology. Telecom companies could use it to set up new competitors in data processing" (p. 267). Doz concluded that "the current government policies toward the telecommunication industry are outdated" (p. 273). See Yves L. Doz, *Government Control and Multinational Strategic Management: Power Systems and Telecommunications Equipment* (New York: Praeger, 1979).

Although in 1987 it held 55 percent of the personal-computer market in Japan, it had still not set up any manufacturing operations in Europe as had so many other Japanese companies.[13]

IBM was left as the only remaining U.S. manufacturer of supercomputers as Cray ran into financial difficulties and Control Data became another shipwrecked blip in history. AT&T also worked with Phillips in the Netherlands in several major areas of information technology until in 1989 it became obvious that Phillips could barely continue. Phillips announced it was giving up on attempting to manufacture several lines of semiconductors, particularly large-scale memory chips, as well as displays. The Europeans became even more concerned, as this announcement came within weeks of the Fujitsu/ICL buy-out. By the end of the 1980s, Western Europe had become a stomping-ground for Japanese and American competition and dominance. The only response from many of the vendors and "micro-vendors" was integration into the worldwide source and manufacturing system for information technology: Singapore for disk drives, Japan for memory devices and some displays, the United States for processors and operating systems, Korea for modems and some printers, France for knowledge of advanced telecommunications applications, the United Kingdom for financial applications, Taiwan for power supplies, low-grade components, and circuit boards, and so on.

These growing strategic alliances signaled one clear fact for the United States and its way of life—the end of hegemony. Not only was the United States declining as an economic power during this period—one of the greatest declines in history—but its control over information technology, to the extent we can say a nation as a whole controls something, was also diminished.[14] This became more evident as the giants of the computer industry, IBM and Digital, were having their knees chopped out from under them by the end of the 1980s. The position in which U.S. industry and its "way of life"—its software, its operating systems, its strategy, its type and pattern of utilization—was forever doomed. In its place stood a new and varied landscape as new vendors, primarily Japanese, grew in importance.

After the early developments in the United States,[15] several countries began working hard to develop their own information technology. The most significant turned out to be Japan, although, in the early 1960s, no one except

---

[13]See Michael Hergert and Robin Hergert, "NEC Corporation's Entry into European Microcomputers," *Journal of Management Case Studies,* 3 (2), Summer 1987, pp. 109–135, who write that NEC is famous for "aggressive marketing and ruthless price cutting."

[14]Many such as H. R. Nau, *The Myth of America's Decline: Leading the World Economy into the 1990's* (New York: Oxford University Press, 1990) see the U.S. economy as leading the world into the next century. Unfortunately this isn't going to happen in information technology.

[15]The early history of semiconductor manufacturing is documented in T. R. Reid, *The Chip: How Two Americans Invented the Microchip and Launched a Revolution* (New York: Simon and Schuster, 1984) and Robert Slater, *Portraits in Silicon* (Cambridge, MA: The MIT Press, 1987).

Chapter 15 Nihon no Computa no Yokozuna

real specialists could have guessed that the Japanese would soon dominate the technological landscape, regardless of the predictions of such observers as Rabino and Hubbard, who concluded that Japan would not be successful in manufacturing personal computers.[16] Having as they did already in place the hidden remnants of the giant *zaibatsu*,[17] which had supposedly been broken up, it was possible, but not particularly easy, for MITI to pull together enough engineering talent to encourage an electronics and computer industry. At the famous meeting between Shegero, the MITI minister, and IBM, the Japanese made it quite clear that in exchange for allowing access to the Japanese market, IBM would have to license some of its technology to the Japanese firms.[18] This was a period in which many American firms, glowing as they were in the early post-war bliss of economic and military triumph, were feeling very generous toward their little brothers, and as a result were licensing almost all of their significant technology.

The story of the Japanese success is well-known. Starting with JECC, the Japanese Electronic Computer Corporation, which was a type of government-subsidized leasing arrangement, the Japanese government began the process of creating a national *hinomaru* computer industry, which stands a quarter of a century later as the world's largest.

The single most important development was the rediscovery of German-Japanese industrial relations, which had been hidden from sight in the immediate post-war period.[19] In the computer field, Siemens acquired what

---

[16] See Samuel Rabino and Elva Ellen Hubbard, "The Race of American and Japanese Personal Computer Manufacturers for Dominance of the U. S. Market," *Columbia Journal of World Business*, Fall 1984, pp. 18–31. "After evaluating trends in the personal computer market and both American and Japanese marketing strategies in the last couple of years, it is our opinion that Japanese firms will not be able to penetrate the PC market in the near future (other than *perhaps* the portable computer segment) in a major way.... Japanese firms will have to face price competition from IBM, a late arrival, that already dominates a 35 percent share as well as the most recent entry by the giant AT&T.... Furthermore both Japanese and American manufacturers have to cope in an environment where the product life cycle is getting shorter and shorter, and a shorter product life cycle results in a shorter payback period.... It appears that by staying close to the consumer, by maintaining a stream of introductions, and by continuing to improve product design and product efficiency, the competitive lead of American companies will persist."

[17] For a view from the Japanese perspective, see Konosuke Matsushita, *Quest for Prosperity: The Life of a Japanese Industrialist* (Tokyo, Kyoto, Singapore: PHP Institute, Inc., 1988), and S. Kusumoto, *My Bridge to America: Discovering the New World for Minolta* (New York: E. P. Dutton, 1989).

[18] The definitive study of Japanese industrial policy toward the computer industry is M. Anchordoguy, *Computer Inc.: Japan's Challenge to IBM*, Harvard East Asian Monographs, 144 (Cambridge, MA: Harvard University Press, 1989). Writers such as C. Johnson, *MITI and the Japanese Miracle: The Growth of Industrial Policy, 1925–1975* (Stanford: Stanford University Press, 1982) did much to uncover the role of government in industrial policy.

[19] It is an interesting historical footnote that at the same time several strategic alliances between Daimler-Benz and Mitsubishi were announced involving no less than six strategic areas of high technology and research & development.

remained of Nixdorf and continued to cement its strategic alliance with the giant Fujitsu in medium-, mainframe-, and super-computers. Combined with the German-Japanese industrial alliances found in other areas of the economy, the Siemens-Fujitsu collaboration ushered in the beginning of a new age no longer dependent upon the development of technological leadership in the United States. Kono[20] argued that American and Japanese personnel and organizations were very different, but "the Japanese organization is more like *Gemeinschaft* than *Gesellschaft*.... [I]n the community organization, the belonging itself is a joy, members are united by mutual love and trust, and they help each other...." A new Deutschland-Nippon axis had been formed and the potential for disruption of the technological balance of power between different companies changed as much as had the disruption of the balance of power between states in the 1930s with the same dimensions in a *political* axis.[21] Writers such as Ferguson were calling for a "Euro-American *Keiretsu*" to regain control over developments in information technology.[22]

By the end of the 1980s, the West had lost its lead in information technology. Japan's superior ability to manage high-technology manufacturing exceedingly well,[23] to recruit the highest quality talent into government policy

---

[20] Toyohiro Kono, "Multinational Management," *Japanese Economic Studies,* Fall/Winter 1984–85, p. 35.

[21] It is interesting that as the cold war came to a close, many political scientists who had specialized in national security began to observe that a country's survival in the 1990s and beyond was no longer to be based on military power. They proclaimed that the "new" dimension of national security was "economic" security. This was hardly a new idea, but was proclaimed to be such by Ruggie, and this new security had a peculiarly *technological* dimension. Taken in this context, the increasing pace of German-Japanese collaboration could be seen as a genuine re-creation of the old axis of power. Insight into the underlying dynamics of why nations compete and cooperate with one another is found in John Gerard Ruggie, ed., *The Antinomies of Interdependence: National Welfare and the International Division of Labor* (New York: Columbia University Press, 1983).

[22] See Charles H. Ferguson, "Computers and the Coming of the U.S. Keiretsu," *Harvard Business Review* (4), July/August 1990. One wonders why we do not call for an American-Japanese Keiretsu—certainly it would be more powerful. This study contains a great deal of information about the Japanese *Keiretsu* (industrial grouping) system and how it has been used in the Japanese electronics sector.

[23] William H. Davidson, "Small Group Activity at Musashi Semiconductor Works," *Sloan Management Review,* 1982, pp. 3–14, gives an example of the "small group" system used in maintaining high levels of quality control in Japanese high-technology companies. On the other hand, Modesto A. Maidique and Robert H. Hayes, "The Art of High-Technology Management," *Sloan Management Review,* pp. 17–28+, shows that some of the best-managed U.S. multinationals are capable of doing as well as the Japanese, and not necessarily by adopting the same policies as the Japanese: "U.S. high-technology firms that seek to improve their management practices to succeed against foreign competitors need not look overseas."

Chapter 15 Nihon no Computa no Yokozuna

positions,[24] and to coordinate government-industrial relations had resulted in the ability to materialize the visions of the future, one of the most important of which was the "information society."

All these new technological arrangements for Phase II developed within the context of a massive proliferation of information on a worldwide scale. It was the spread of a technology which many argued changed the world and even led the global economy into a different Schumpeterian long-wave cycle, this time based on an entirely different (information) technology. This proliferation—driven by technical advances, the openness of a world trading system, and the movement toward international joint ventures and collaboration between industrial giants—has now developed over approximately one-half of a century.

Even though there was a great deal of analysis and writing on information technology, there was little to explain its functioning within different cultures and its integration into the world's system through its largest body of users— the multinational corporations. Much analysis of computing had been from a narrow perspective and primarily U.S.-based. Just as the *technology* had come out of the United States in the beginning, the bulk of the *analysis* of information technology also came first out of the United States and by the end of the 1980s was still dominated by research and scholarship from that country. The early U.S. dominance of information technology had led to early U.S. dominance of analysis[25] and it was only later, when we could observe activity in different countries, particularly France, aimed at understanding the effects of this new technology.

Roughly speaking, as the ability to manufacture information spread from Silicon valley to Europa and the Far East, schools of analysis followed. Interestingly, the variance in observation and research approach was much greater than for the manufacturing and design of the technology itself. For example, most of the Japanese companies built IBM-compatible machines designed to

---

[24]There is no affirmative action or quotas in Japan, and merit is based on examination rather than on race or minority status. This system, which is a true meritocracy, continues to provide superior talent to the highest levels in government bureaucracy. See S. Schlossstein, *The End of the American Century* (New York, Chicago: Congdon & Weed, Inc., 1989), and E. F. Vogel, *Comeback* (New York: Simon and Schuster, 1985). See also K. Azumi, D. Hickson, D. Horvath, C. McMillan, "Structural Uniformity and Cultural Diversity in Organizations: A Comparative Study of Factors in Britain, Japan, and Sweden," in *The Anatomy of Japanese Business*, K. Sato and Y. Hoshino, eds., (Armonk, NY: M. E. Sharpe, Inc., 1984), R. Clark, *The Japanese Company* (New Haven and London: Yale University Press, 1979), and M. Y. Yoshino and T. B. Lifson, *The Invisible Link: Japan's Sogo Shosha and the Organization of Trade* (Cambridge, MA: The MIT Press, 1986).

[25]Records of the International Conference on Information Systems show complete dominance by institutions and research groups based in the United States, as does much of the material from IFIPS and AFIPS. This general dominance is reflected in journals as well, although this picture began to gradually change.

mimic as closely as possible the operations of the complex IBM operating systems,[26] but their view of how information technology could be used within the Japanese context was very much more different, even utopian.[27] The French built various types of computers, but again their view of how information technology could be used had a completely different flavor, emphasizing as it did entirely new concepts, such as *telematique, informatique* and the like,[28] concepts which did not have their counterpart in the United States.

But in spite of the streams of analysis elsewhere, it was in the United States that the bulk of analysis was being done[29] and this was due in great part to the rapid advancements in information being made there—particularly in the way of applications, which were far more consuming of human intellectual resources than was the manufacturing of hardware.

The great stream of analysis which characterized intellectual activities in the United States rode on top of the most advanced technology, at least through Phase I. This technology was led by applications development that was far ahead of the rest of the world. In financial services, development of automatic clearing-houses and funds transfer systems, complex on-screen real-time trading and decision support tools, back-office processing of transactions, integrated customer databases, home banking, automatic teller machines, optical character-recognition equipment, as well as scanning and transmission of chit for billing, were only a few of the innovations that came from the United States in this period and spurred a complex line of research.[30] In the engineering field, developments including simulation and stress point analysis software, computer-aided design and computer-aided manufacturing, integrated inventory control systems, complex simulation, three-dimensional modeling, and automated layout systems, were examples of the rapid advances created in

---

[26] Several of the Japanese firms were caught stealing details of the operating systems and as a result have had to pay substantial royalties to IBM.

[27] See T. Kitagawa, "Creation of Industry and Culture in Establishing Full-Scale Information Societies in Japan," in H. Sackman, ed., *Comparative Worldwide National Computer Policies,* Proceedings of the Third IFIP TC9 Conference on Human Choice and Computers (Amsterdam: North-Holland, 1985); K. Kobayashi, *Computers and Communications: A Vision of C&C* (Cambridge, MA: The MIT Press, 1986); Y. Masuda, "Computopia," *Agora,* 11, 1985, pp. 40–41; Y. Masuda, *The Information Society as Post-Industrial Society* (Tokyo: Institute for the Information Society, 1988); or even some views in T. Moto-Oka, "Fifth Generation Computer Systems," Proceedings of the International Conference on Fifth Generation Computer Systems, Tokyo, October 19–22, 1981 (Amsterdam: North-Holland, 1982).

[28] Oswald Harold Ganley, *To Inform or to Control? The New Communications Networks* (New York: McGraw-Hill, 1982).

[29] Even if at times the gross bulk was greater, the quality may have been considerably lower.

[30] See H. C. Lucas and R. A. Schwartz, eds., *The Challenge of Information Technology for the Securities Markets: Liquidity, Volatility & Global Trading* (Homewood, IL: Dow-Jones-Irwin, 1989). See also Erik K. Clemons and Bruce W. Weber, "London's Big Bang: A Case Study of Information Technology, Competitive Impact, and Organizational Change," *Journal of Management Information Systems,* 6 (4), Spring 1991, pp. 41–60.

the United States before leaking abroad. Project-management software systems were developed for massive construction and systems-development projects. By the end of the 1980s "global" inventory control systems were operating, capable of calculating safety stocking levels for dispatch locations in many different parts of the world simultaneously. A computer in the middle of Ohio would be "informed" of the exact shelf location for a specific part being stored in Rotterdam or Sydney. At the same time, computer systems began to support manufacturing systems that were operating on a worldwide scale, employing sourcing from many different plant locations.

These were a few of the dynamic applications that powered the dramatic rise of information technology during Phase I and into Phase II. The first 40 years had been characterized by these rapid advances and the heavy amount of intellectual work needed to create these applications formed the conceptual foundation of the field.

It had been the United States which had hosted and supported most of the key research, as it made a herculean effort to maintain the balance of power in the post-war period, particularly through the Cold War, which it eventually won, just as it was being fatally weakened by military adventurism, economic mismanagement, failed social policies, self-destructive liberalism and misplaced guilt, and a rapidly disappearing industrial base.[31] This stream of research had been supported in large part by the military, which continued to push development of more advanced applications, materials, and technologies. For most of this period, patent registration information proved this out. High-energy physics, space exploration, nuclear weapons technology, guidance systems, the cruise missile, sub-sonic navigation and wave analysis, reconnaissance aircraft, smart bombs, fighter planes, invisible "stealth" aircraft, airborne radar, packet-switching networks, as well as intelligence collection and analysis systems based on ELINT[32] all contributed to the massive amount of state-of-the-art technology developed in the United States. Some of the work was very secret, but, when revealed, startled the world.[33] The result of this

---

[31] The essay by Lester Thurow sheds a great deal of light on the problems of American productivity. His conclusion is that the entire model of the firm must change if the U.S. economy is to survive. He writes that "If foreign firms invade the American market but American firms do not invade foreign markets, foreign firms will use secure home markets as bases from which they can pick off American firms in the American market. American firms will occasionally be defeated at home and will have no compensating foreign victories. In the world economy ahead of us, a firm that cannot compete successfully in foreign markets will not survive in the American market." See Lester Thurow, "Revitalizing American Industry: Managing in a Competitive World Economy," *California Management Review,* XXVII (1), Fall 1984. pp. 9–41.

[32] ELINT is an abbreviation for "Electronic Intelligence."

[33] During the Iraq peacekeeping operation, the United States began to unveil its stealth fighters (F-18) for the world to see. These craft were invisible on radar and fast. It was clear to the Europeans and others that their conception of fighter aircraft, such as the Pan-European fighter, were obsolete before they were even built. The United States, in spite of its massive economic crisis and corrosive racial tensions, had continued to pull ahead in the most advanced technologies.

large amount of research support on the part of the U.S. government, primarily through the military, but through other mechanisms as well (such as NSF), was a large-scale spin-off of many innovative technologies to the civilian sector. Examples of this include integrated circuits, various materials (Teflon, nylon, x-lon), and all types of electronic components. Not all of the creative work was adequately protected from piracy abroad because the international legal regime had difficulty in understanding the peculiar nature of semiconductor technologies.[34] Even the Fuzz-buster had its genesis in the fields of Southern England, where a team of MIT scientists were trying to understand how to defeat the German bombing missions.

The death of the UK computer industry had been more merciful and was characteristic of the situation in Europe as a whole. Starting with the difficulty in switching over from a public to a private network system in the late 1980s under the fading Thacherist regime, the United Kingdom had also abandoned any attempt to maintain a global computer industry. There was great innovation in pockets of intellectual circles revolving around Oxbridge. Coaxial thermography scanning technologies had been created in Britain along with a great number of other industrial and information-technology oriented innovations, but the step from laboratory to commercialization had eluded many of the innovators—a situation similar to the United States. The great British computer company, International Computers Limited (ICL), had been successful in building up a large installed base encompassing commercial and nationalized industries. A large part of the infrastructure was installed in the various public services, in keeping with the traditions of the previous Labor government, which insisted that public money be used to support the commercial activities of domestic corporations, particularly in high technology. However, by the end of the 1980s the British computer lay in ruins, with little profitability, lagging technology, and inability to expand into international markets, particularly continental Europe, which would have been the only real possibility, given the supposed opening of 1992. Many were predicting that by the end of the 1990s, only three or four European companies would survive.[35] The idea of a "Fortress *Computer* Europe" had failed miserably, and the Japanese were jumping over the trade barriers like the droves of Zulu at Roarks' Bluff, but this time the outcome of the battle would be considerably different.

---

[34]See Doria Bonham-Yeaman, "The United States' Leadership in Global Protection for Computer Chip Designs," *Columbia Journal of World Business,* Winter 1986, pp. 81–87. She writes: "Intellectual property protection for the semiconductor chip industry appears to address the industry's concerns better than does pure trade protectionism. Such specific protection of mask work designs under the Act can attack not only foreign abuse, but also any domestic abuse as well. In addition, a pure trade protectionist route could backfire on U.S. subsidiaries abroad which want to import products into the United States."

[35]See Jefferson Grigsby, "Europe: The Crisis of the Old Order," *Financial World,* 158 (24), November 28, 1989, pp. 60–62.

YOKOZUNA

By the end of the 1980s, the Japanese industrial complex for computerization was the largest and most successful in the world. Computers represented 20 percent of the GNP of the Japanese Sumo-sized economy, and MITI was continuing to take a strong thought-leadership position and move Japan toward highly complex inter-organizational networking.[36] It was reported that in the electronic sector, North American sales of $51 billion were 45 percent of the total market, whereas Asian sales of $20 billion accounted for 34 percent and European sales of $19 billion accounted for only 21 percent. However, revenue per employee in Asia as $35,000 above the U.S. average and more than $70,000 above the average for the European companies, a situation that would only lead to further decline in the West.[37] Japan had the best and most efficient manufacturing, the highest production of components, semiconductors, personal computers, and other parts of computers.[38] In contrast, the United States was continuing its rapid downward spiral, distracted by inter-Arab conflicts in the Gulf, and its once proud and arrogant companies were being forced into "co-development" of advanced technologies. By 1990, many were wondering if the downturn in the software industry from its "historical" growth rates of 20 percent to less than 15 percent in 1989 was the beginning of a decline in the United States in this industry.[39] AT&T was collaborating with Fujitsu Network Switching and Siemens Stromberg-Carlson in developing the Asynchronous Transfer Mode (ATM) for the high bandwidth switching systems of the future.[40]

---

[36] If Western companies believe that the present Japanese market presents a few severe barriers to entry against foreigners, one can only speculate what the situation will be like when the Japanese companies are linked together into a complex electronic web.

[37] See Bruce C. P. Rayner and Linda Stallmann, "The Electronic Business International 100," *Electronic Business,* 16 (21), November 12, 1990, pp. 86–91.

[38] See M. McLean, ed., *The Japanese Electronics Challenge* (New York: Technova/St. Martin's Press, 1982); F. Gibney, *Miracle by Design: The Real Reasons Behind Japan's Economic Success* (New York: Times Books, 1982); M. Kikuchi, *Japanese Electronics: A Worm's-Eye View of Its Evolution* (Tokyo: Simul Press, 1983); Moritani (1979), and Tatsuno (1990). An example of the government control on licensing is found in Majumdar, who discusses Texas Instruments and SONY: "Texas Instruments was permitted in 1968 to set up a joint venture with Sony, each firm holding 50% of the equity, on the condition that it would license its integrated-circuits patents to several local producers and also would limit its local production so that 90% or more of the Japanese market would be left for the licensees." Badiul A. Majumdar, "Industrial Policy in Action: The Case of the Electronics Industry in Japan," *Columbia Journal of World Business,* Fall 1988, pp. 25–33.

[39] Details on the software market are given in Harvey L. Poppel, "Software Stays at the Cutting Edge," *Datamation,* 36 (12), June 15, 1990, pp. 194–195.

[40] See Anita Taff, "Firms Unite to Form Plan for Broadband Offerings," *Network World,* 8 (12), March 25, 1991, pp. 2, 47.

There were fears that Japan's dominance of the consumer electronics market, which was increasingly dependent upon highly integrated semiconductors, would further increase its power over the computer sector. Huggins reported that U.S. companies were being cut out of sales by the Japanese in Southeast Asia, which had the world's highest growth rate.[41]

Japan had risen from the ashes of WWII. In the late 1940s and early 1950s, many Japanese were starving. It is this generation that powered the development of the modern Japanese economy.[42] They do not have the same easy lifestyle and approach characteristic of the Americans. For years the Americans and others smugly reassured themselves with a sugar-coated version of reality: the Japanese could only copy, they were not original, they could not create software, they didn't understand marketing, and so on.[43] It was a genuine series of last appeals for an economy on death row. The result was a gradual hardening of U.S. attitudes toward foreign technology, even though much of the technology had been originally created in the United States.[44] It was not the technology that was objectionable, but the fact that it was foreign. Perhaps the Americans just couldn't accept the idea of non-white, non-European peoples being superior in technology.

---

[41]See Lawrence P. Huggins, "Does the Asian IS Market Already Belong to the Japanese?" *Information Strategy: The Executive's Journal*, 4 (4), Summer 1988, pp. 31–34. Huggins notes that Korean workers "average 55 hours per week at $1.55 per hour," which is one reason, of course, that multinationals are investing in Korea and the Korean *chaebol* are doing so well. For a look at Apple's management of its workers, see Michel Perez, "Human Resources Policy in an Untraditional Company," *Benefits & Compensation International*, 15 (6), December 1985, pp. 19–20. However, even the hot-tub culture of California does not compare with the employee benefits in Europe. For a look at a Dutch multinational, Chrompack, and its rather liberal policies, see Theo Willems, "Mensgerichte Zakelijkheid" ("Employee-Oriented Yet Business-Like"), *Elan* 1 (3), March 1986, pp. 41–43. For an assessment calling for a loosening up of personal policy and formal managerial constraints in the multinational corporation see Roy Hill, "Why Managers Today Have a Tougher Task—of Managing Complexity," *International Management*, 41 (8), August 1986, pp. 22–24.

[42]However, for a probing and irreverent SCUD missile attack against the complacency of the typical Japanese, see Kenichi Ohmae, "Japan's Role in the World Economy: A New Appraisal," *California Management Review*, XXIX (3), Spring 1987, pp. 42–58.

[43]For an inside look at innovation in Japanese high-technology companies, see "New-Product Development," *Japanese Economic Studies*, Fall/Winter 1984–1985, pp. 72–103.

[44]Many writers criticize the various "Japan-o-phobes" who are upset with the success of Japan, and its economy, particularly in regards to high technology. As the Japanese success became greater, more and more cynical motives were attributed to their government and corporate leaders. See L. G. Franko, *The Threat of Japanese Multinationals: How the West Can Respond*, Wiley/IRM Series on Multinationals (Chichester and New York: John Wiley & Sons, 1983), or various works by people such as M. J. Wolf, *The Japanese Conspiracy: The Plot to Dominate Industry Worldwide—and How to Deal with It* (New York: Empire Books, 1983), who appear to many to be racists. There are also a great number of more balanced commentators who nevertheless take a very hard line against Japan, including C. V. Prestowitz, Jr., *Trading Places: How We are Giving Our Future to Japan and How to Reclaim It* (New York: Basic Books, Inc., 1989), and W. J. Holstein, *The Japanese Power Game: What It Means for America* (New York: Charles Scribner's Sons, 1990).

PART IV
EIGHT STRATEGIES TO WIN

CHAPTER

16

Systems Development and Strategy Formulation

The MNC of today is facing many challenges on many fronts. Regulatory changes, rapid introduction of technology, relentless pursuit of competition—all these factors make the environment difficult and uncertain. In the face of this, today's MNC is held hostage by its history of national operations in each country. As the 1980s developed, so too did other strategies, but information technology did not follow suit. In the 1990s, the situation is going to be entirely different. Information technology will come into its own in international strategy. The continued acceleration of change in international business conditions will drive this development. Those firms which have a very good sense of their use of information technology will be better able to cope with the increasing demands for advanced globally operating information-based applications in support of their business strategy. There are many levels to the challenges that must be faced. The management of human resources, the optimization of a highly complex technological infrastructure, the estimation and calculation of complex economies of scale with incorporation of tremendous sociological consequences, and the underlying difficulty of determining which applications can support the business—all of these levels must be faced, and in short turn. Without some way to address the different levels of challenge, it will not be possible to generate a coherent strategy. The following chapters discuss several important steps and strategies that the MNC CIO can take in pursuit of a successful operation to support the business.

Chapter 16 Systems Development and Strategy Formulation 239

Given the many different currents of thought touching upon the role of information technology within today's multinational corporation, it is clear that at least some practical advice and insight must eventually be turned over to the Chief Information Officer (CIO) in charge of building and implementing these global systems. This problem can never be viewed as simply gaining an understanding of international telecommunications, cultural differences, or experience with very large-scale systems-development projects. Instead, just as in the case of a domestic corporation, the CIO must grasp the overall drift and fabric of international business strategy.

However, at this time, there is only a minimum amount of information available to the CIO on how actually to implement global information-technology strategies that are consistent with the grand strategies of the multinational corporation. Yet, even at the "academic level," there are many indications that developing global applications have many unique factors that must be studied, including language barriers, complex project coordination and management (e.g., across numerous time zones), information economics approaches to location of data-processing resources, and identification of basic "models" of the process.[1]

De Meyer's survey of 14 multinationals found that in setting up global systems, it was critical to have an international network of communications between different development teams and parts of the business, but that in practice, this is very difficult to achieve.[2] He observes some of the advantages of creating a centralized office responsible for managing all communications and the role of certain individuals who operate at an international level within the firm. IBM's four major research laboratories located in the United States, Zurich, Switzerland, and Tokyo use an extensive amount of information technology to coordinate their efforts.[3]

The location of data processing resources throughout the infrastructure of the multinational corporation is no random issue, but one that should be linked to corporate strategy. Kogut's analysis of the use of the value-added chain in locating manufacturing resources might be applied. He argues that "a firm should locate its activities in those countries that possess a comparative advantage in terms of the relevant intensive factor... [and that] because

---

[1] Husian asks whether "we are developing applications in areas other than accounting and if not, how do we judge the relative value of new applications." Vincent P. Husian, "Rx for Top Management: A Periodic Checkup of EDP Operations," *California Management Review*, Spring 1972, XIV (3), pp. 31–37.

[2] Arnoud De Meyer, "Tech Talk: How Managers Are Stimulating Global R&D Communication," *Sloan Management Review*, 32 (3), Spring 1991, pp. 49–58. Also see Anonymous, "Multinational Management Strategies," *Multinational Business* (3), Autumn 1990, pp. 54–61.

[3] See John A. Armstrong, "Possible Dreams from IBM's Zurich Lab," *Across the Board*, 24 (5), May 1987, pp. 30–31.

countries differ in factor costs and the intensity of factor use varies along the value-added chain, the distribution of value-added activities between countries will tend to differ."[4] If one considers the factors of production that make up the components of an information system, then Kogut's capital/labor analysis would likely result in a pressure for regionalization and centralization of capital-intensive data-processing activities because the role of labor might be comparatively reduced. A second way to look at Kogut's analysis would be to ensure that the data-processing infrastructure is in alignment with the location of firm activities in the best strategic manner as the value-added chain is "broken across borders."

In Porter's analysis of the value chain, information technology would fit into the category of "firm infrastructure"—a system that is a "support activity" and that spans the entire length of the "primary activities" chain, including inbound logistics, operations, outbound logistics, marketing and sales, and service.[5] He argues that the type of competitive advantage changes according to the position along the value chain:

> Downstream activities create competitive advantages that are largely country-specific: a firm's reputation, brand name, and service network in a country grow out of a firm's activities in that country and create entry/mobility barriers largely in that country alone. Competitive advantage in upstream and support activities often grows more out of the entire system of countries in which a firm competes than from its position in any one country, however.

Fayerweather discussed "welding and molding world-wide operations into an integrated unit" as one of the three challenges that should be met by international business.[6]

Hymer believed that multinationals would inevitably be driven to centralize strategic decisions in regional coordinating centers and in corporate headquarters in the advanced countries.[7] However, Bartlett's discussion of

---

[4]Bruce Kogut, "Designing Global Strategies: Comparative and Competitive Value-Added Chains," *Sloan Management Review,* Summer 1985, pp. 15–28.

[5]Michael E. Porter, "Changing Patterns of International Competition," *California Management Review,* XXVIII (2), Winter 1986, p. 14. Porter has been so over-exposed in the academic media that it seems pointless to write further about him here. His insights are so fundamental that practically every writer in the field has been shaped by them.

[6]Fayerweather also discussed the "establishment of operations which are viable in highly nationalistic environments with particular attention to the ownership question and joint venture" and "development of local national executives for senior posts in overseas managements." John Fayerweather, "LRP for International Operations," *California Management Review,* 1960/61, pp. 23–35.

[7]See the summary of Hymer's testimony in Richard L. Barovick, "Congress Looks at the Multinational Corporation," *Columbia Journal of World Business,* November/December 1970, pp. 75–79.

the balance between centralization and decentralization has been extended into the realm of data processing by Gow,[8] who discusses factors such as the different geographic origins of multinationals as important elements. In the realm of data processing, flexibility should be used in assessing the balance between a centralized and standardized solution versus the requirements that all multinationals face in responding to local concerns of host countries and markets.

These observations point to the underlying relationship between the strategy and business operations of the MNC and its information system. To bring about changes in strategy requires a rethinking of the information structure of the firm, and to make significant changes in the computing and telecommunications system requires careful examination of firm strategy. This leaves the information-technology function searching for different strategies that may be useful in conducting a campaign.

The following chapters present eight different strategies that can be used to develop a winning environment in the 1990s. They are based on taking theories and ideas from international business and applying them to the understanding of international information systems.

---

[8] Kathleen A. Gow, "No Set Rules for Systems Design," *Computerworld,* 24 (40), October 1, 1990, pp. 98–99. She reports Bartlett as emphasizing that Japanese firms have a stronger tendency to accommodate local values and situations.

CHAPTER

17

Strategy #1: Informatize Strategic Alliances

The widely discussed concept of using the value chain to develop a strategy to link together information systems with customers and suppliers must be extended to the international environment. If your customers are implementing global strategies, then you must follow with your own. Technology must follow strategy, and linkages must follow globalization. The case of United Technologies Automotive shows how a supplier must follow the global strategy of its key customer, with significant implications for its international information systems.

DISCUSSION

One of the key organization and managerial breakthroughs in the past decade has been the development of linkages between firms.[1] This new type of arrangement has started to change the nature of international competition.

> An entirely new approach to the organization and management of production at the intra-firm and inter-firm level has emerged, [as a breakthrough] initially developed and cultivated within Japan but now diffusing to other countries, which stresses flexibility, quality and co-operation.[2]

These linkages are set up in support of the general strategy of the *multinational corporation*,[3] and inevitably drive the development of the information system. The Whirlpool case demonstrated some of the difficulties in rebuilding information systems linking together operations of highly diverse companies. The need to consolidate the data-processing infrastructure and its supporting data centers is most often driven by a series of strategic decisions made independent of the information-systems function. In retrospect, one could always argue that any merger or consolidation of different businesses needs to have input at the highest levels regarding the problems and challenges on the information-systems side. But the reality that must be faced by the CIO or equivalent is that this higher level input may be either obtained only at the very last minute in the process, after all the basic decisions regarding high-level strategy have already been made, or not at all. The worst possible situation occurs when the CIO is faced with a *fait accompli*

---

[1] See Deigan Morris and Michael Hergert, "Trends in International Collaborative Agreements," *Columbia Journal of World Business,* Summer 1987, pp. 15–21, for an examination of the "unprecedented increase in the use of international collaborative agreements" that were studied through the INSEAD database. They conclude that "agreements are most likely to arise between large corporations who are already multinational in nature," "the vast majority of collaborative agreements are between two partners," and that it is best if "cooperative behavior begins to occur very early in the product development cycle."

[2] See UNCTC, *Joint Ventures as a Form of International Economic Co-operation* (New York: United Nations, 1988). For a comprehensive analysis of this problem within the context of automobile manufacturing, including much empirical analysis and calculation of differences in productivity levels, see J. P. Womack, D. T. Jones, and D. Roos, *The Machine That Changed the World* (New York: Macmillan Publishing Company, 1990).

[3] See Colin Jackson, "Building a Competitive Advantage Through Information Technology," *Long Range Planning,* 22 (4), August 1989, pp. 29–39.

and is simply given the word from "on-high" with a minimum of advance notice, accompanied by a significant amount of pressure to "make it work, or else."

Arrow argues that one of the primary reasons that firms link together through upstream vertical integration is to get better control over information about supplies and their environment and thus reduce uncertainty: "It must be emphasized that the value of vertical integration is the information acquired about total raw material in production."[4]

Harrigan touches upon the role of information technology in helping support strategic alliances that "are becoming more widespread...due to... improved communications and computational power":

> Joint ventures are inevitable where such technologies are involved because, although expanded computing power and enhanced telecommunications capabilities promise that global coordination of a firm's factories will be possible, as yet, not one firm possesses all of the capabilities needed to deliver these systems. Cooperation will become routine in industries like these to maintain worldwide compatibility among data processing, factory-automation, and other "intelligent" devices.[5]

Contractor writes that for US multinationals, the joint venture is becoming a more popular form of investment. Contractor argues that the rationale for forming a joint venture is "uncertainty reduction, cost reductions through synergies and efficiences, and overcoming entry barriers to markets not served by the company."[6]

Auster discusses the "...improved information and communication systems (which) allow rapid global transactions" as being one of the environmental conditions facilitating the growth of ICL's (international corporate

---

[4]Kenneth J. Arrow, "Vertical Integration and Communication," in Walter P. Heller, Ross M. Starr, and David A. Starrett, eds., *Uncertainty, Information and Communication* (New York: Cambridge University Press, 1986), pp. 173–183. See also Kenneth Arrow, *The Limits of Organization* (New York: Norton, 1974).

[5]Kathryn Rudie Harrigan, "Strategic Alliances: Their New Role in Global Competition," *Columbia Journal of World Business,* Summer 1987, pp. 67–69+.

[6]Farok J. Contractor, "International Business: An Alternative View," *International Marketing Review,* Spring 1986, pp. 74–84. He does not believe, however, that this is necessarily the most efficient arrangement for conducting international business. He notes that "centralised control and full ownership of affiliates are important for efficiency and strategic direction in such corporations. On the other hand, economic nationalism, protectionism, transport costs, local culture, local standards, and entrenched domestic firms all are factors which encourage a link-up with a local company in order to serve the particular needs of the market or to obtain political permission to produce and tap natural resources."

linkages) which is roughly similar to joint ventures but of a slightly wider scope.[7]

In addition to the chaos and complexity raised by the need to merge together what might be entirely different systems,[8] the CIO must come face to face with what is usually the underlying rationale of mergers and strategic alliance—seeking "synergy" in operations. This means, in most cases, the elimination of redundancies throughout the operation in order to capture any internal economies that might be available. This is all sound and well-tried business logic, but it can have very difficult results for the CIO and his or her international planning teams, who are now faced with two aspects of a situation that makes their lives considerably more difficult. First, even the *general* merging of international data-processing operations poses serious challenges. Second, to do this in a context in which the corporation is actively engaged in a restructuring and "trimming-down" effort adds further complexity to the problem. One can only imagine the problems that might occur in the early stages of the systems-development life-cycle, when the systems-analysis and business-analysis teams from the information-systems function venture out into an entrenched bureaucracy that is in the process of being restructured, knows it, and probably fears the job-eliminating effects of the information system, even when this is not the intent of the particular project. Even without this psychological dimension of the situation, one would imagine that it is difficult to capture and codify the dynamics of the working procedures when the organization is undergoing restructuring.

Even under these circumstances, the information-systems function is forced to "muddle through" in formulating its response to the situation. Even with the fastest reaction time on the part of data processing, the nature of the change-management process dictates that it will be a year or even several years before benefits are felt. Even using very fast techniques such as prototyping or other tools for rapid systems development, a significant amount of lead time must be anticipated. Therefore, the information-systems function must begin the difficult process of making decisions and plans based on changing and incomplete data. It is a difficult problem, made even tougher

---

[7] Ellen R. Auster, *Columbia Journal of World Business,* Summer 1987, pp. 3–6. She mentions "the primary reasons firms enter joint ventures...[are] to circumvent trade and foreign investment restrictions and to enter new geographic markets; to develop regional know-how and cultural familiarity and expertise; to stimulate intertia laden internal organizational processes; to gain access to better quality or more cost efficient supplier networks, raw materials, or natural resources; to develop a labor force that is less costly; to use idle, or under-utilized equipment, and to increase economies of scale" (p. 4).

[8] Even merging systems that are provided on the same vendor platform can be difficult enough. If the underlying technical infrastructure is highly dissimilar, the problem becomes even worse.

by the international dimension of the multinational enterprise and the fact that these *international* alliances are for the most part relatively underdeveloped from the point of view of both the strategic business and the underlying technological infrastructure.

In strategic alliances, MNCs are typically highly under-computerized, particularly at the international level, because historically the information-systems function has faced a variety of both technical and regulatory barriers in building effective information systems. At the most fundamental level, companies faced the technical difficulty of building large international systems. One reason is the risk of having difficulties in getting cooperation at the local level with the joint-venture partner in handling and processing information. A United Nations study of the problems in managing international joint ventures emphasized the difficulties.

> Major differences with respect to the management processes between a transnational corporation and a national partner can lead to serious conflicts and the failure of a joint venture. United States and Western European transnational corporations often emphasize long-term strategic plans with objectives and strategies, annual or biannual operational plans, detailed and other budgeting, strategic and operations controls, periodic reports, *information systems* and monitoring of performance. They often strive to have joint venture affiliates adapt those types of managerial processes.... [T]he efforts of transnational corporations to impose such management systems may be resisted by national partners. When the transnational corporation believes that the imposition of key aspects of its planning, budgeting, control and organizational system is crucial for proper management of the joint-venture affiliate and strives aggressively to impose it, dissension arises between the partners. In time, this dissension, along with other differences in the management of the affiliate, can lead to its failure. [Emphasis added.][9]

Another factor is that the underlying possibilities were often limited by the available technology. At the political level, the multinational itself faced problems in building an effective relationship with host governments, and writers such as Doz built a fairly complex system of explanation for this phenomenon which took into consideration the balance of power between the MNC and the nation-state, as measured by control over technology and markets.[10] Although the great expansion in the role of the multinational in the

---

[9]See UNCTC, *Arrangements Between Joint Venture Partners in Developing Countries,* UNCTC Advisory Studies, Series B, no. 2 (New York: United Nations, 1987), p. 26. The study gives an example of problems encountered with a transnational corporation involved in a 50 percent joint venture in industrial machinery with a firm in the Republic of Korea. Controls over information systems should be written into contracts. "Management processes, including strategic and operational planning, [including] the control and *information systems*" [emphasis added] are listed as factors that should be included in the elements of a joint-venture agreement (p. 32).

[10]Yves Doz, *Strategic Management in Multinational Companies* (Oxford: Pergamon Press, 1986).

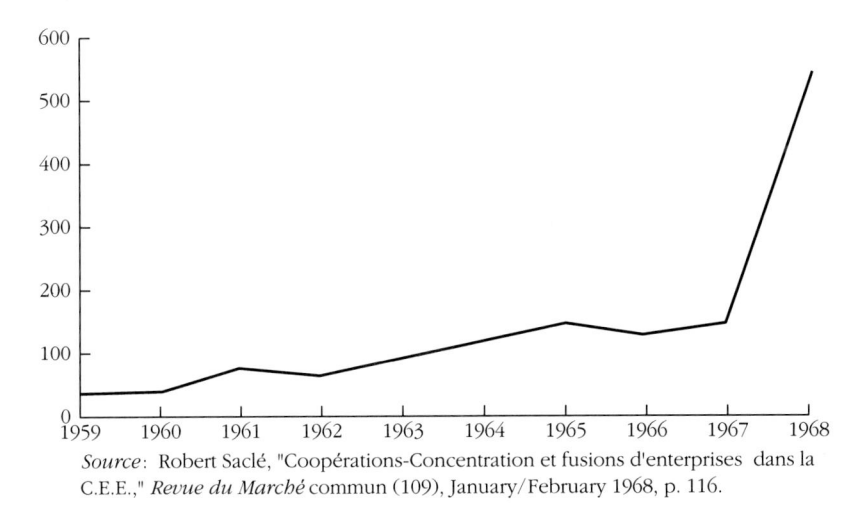

Chapter 17 Strategy #1: Informatize Strategic Alliances   247

Source: Robert Saclé, "Coopérations-Concentration et fusions d'enterprises dans la C.E.E.," *Revue du Marché* commun (109), January/February 1968, p. 116.

FIGURE 17.1 Growth in Transnational Link-ups

post-war period appears to indicate that whatever problems were encountered proved eventually to be solvable, there is an equally great amount of evidence detailing the specific barriers that were faced—and these certainly included technical barriers, particularly in the realm of international telecommunications, where the information-systems function of the MNC came face-to-face with an entrenched government bureaucracy and monopoly.

There are many political barriers as well as technical ones. On the political side, Feld discusses (within the context of Western Europe) barriers that inhibit the overall collaboration between multinationals. These include "divergent national laws setting technical standards for industrial products," problems reaching a European-wide system of patent law for intellectual and industrial property, differences over "common rules for a European company ...attitude [toward] the labor unions," and differences over "application of the antitrust provisions of the community treaties." Statistics from Robert Saclé, presented in Figure 17.1, show the growth in transnational link-ups from 1959 to 1968.[11]

In addition, a second set of barriers are more narrowly focused in nature and are targeted directly at the information technology and telecommunications systems of the multinational corporation. These barriers, such as they were, had a significant effect upon not only how multinationals built up their own internal systems, linking together headquarters and

---

[11] Werner Feld, "Political Aspects of Transnational Business Collaboration in the Common Market," *International Organization,* 24 (2), 1970, pp. 209–238.

subsidiaries, but also upon the range of possibilities they found at their disposal when building strategic *information-system* alliances at the international level.

In spite of the existence of different barriers, however, some of the earliest interorganizational systems were arranged as a type of international *cooperative* system. International cooperative information systems share many of the characteristics of any cooperative: they are shared among many different companies, their financing is supplied by a group-imposed set of user fees, their management and operations are shared through either a sub-contracting arrangement or through a jointly-held not-for-profit operating company. The Society for World-Wide Inter-Bank Transfers (SWIFT) and the SITA airline reservation system are two examples of large international information-processing cooperatives.[12] They are important pioneering efforts to build the infrastructure for interorganizational systems. However, they have certain common characteristics that preclude their general form being replicated in many other industries for many other applications. These early cooperative arrangements are highly specific in their application, and must be supported by a homogeneous user community. Without these two characteristics, the systems are not practical. There are, however, other types of *pseudo*-cooperative arrangements that have made significant progress.

One of these is Electronic Document Interchange (EDI), which is a technology based on the commercial provision of a virtual cooperative infrastructure. EDI systems allow the standardized transmission of commercial documents—shipment orders, invoices, and so on—through a time-sharing utility, which in some cases provides value-added services such as reformatting and speed/protocol conversion for the information being transmitted. This important advantage of EDI greatly facilitates the linking together of dissimilar data-processing platforms from around the world. Rather than having to build many different specialized interfaces between dissimilar systems, the task of systems development becomes greatly simplified. It is a type of computerized *lingua franca* between international systems, and as such can go far in promoting supplementary international business alliances of even a temporary nature. Rather than being required to build specialized computer interfaces on an application-by-application or relationship-by-relationship basis, a process that can be time-consuming and therefore costly, companies are finding it possible to use EDI services that act as a type of public utility in providing

---

[12]Johanson and Mattsson describe the application of transaction-cost theory to interorganizational systems. They point out the importance of *adaption* in which the parties learn how to work best with one another. They mention "information exchange" as an important part of the interaction in this process of adaption. See Jan Johanson and Lars-Gunnar Mattsson, "Interorganizational Relations in Industrial Systems: A Network Approach Compared with the Transaction-Cost Approach," *International Studies of Management and Organization,* XVII (1), pp. 34–48.

Chapter 17   Strategy #1: Informatize Strategic Alliances   249

this inter-firm linkage.[13] The fact that these services act as a type of common denominator provides many benefits in terms of ease-of-use and ultimately lower cost.

Korzeniowski reports that for Digital Equipment Corporation, the use of EDI systems has reduced the cost of processing purchase orders from $125 to $32 dollars per order and at the same time cut delivery time from five weeks to three days. He counted that more than 6,500 U.S.-based companies are using EDI as of 1989, and noted that the coming universal adoption of the United Nations EDI standard, called EDI for Administration, Commerce and Transport (EDIFACT), will greatly increase its international use in the 1990s.[14]

Carlyle reports that EDI, in cooperation with Structured Query Language (SQL), is emerging as one of the most important tools in bringing about "globalization" of the supporting information systems. He examined the strategies of American Standard Inc., Bache Group, Federal Express, Bethlehem Steel, and Du Pont & Co., and learned that although EDI is widely recognized by users as being important to increasing the efficiency of global information systems, there is some fear that this is not as widely recognized on the part of the vendors.[15]

However, being a common denominator, use of EDI can have certain limitations. One limitation may be legal liability; another a lack of capabilities. The question of legal liability arose early on in the United States. The degree to which the use of EDI can substitute for real paper-based trade documentation was more or less accepted early on, with a few limitations and caveats. The tougher question revolves around dispute settlement and liability. If an order processed through a public EDI system is fouled up, who is responsible for any damages which might occur: The public EDI service? The party that placed the order? The party that filled the order? If there is a dispute regarding where the order was improperly made, or where it was corrputed as it passed

---

[13]We could generalize and say that the first stages of this process of "public automation" took place when companies gave their customers terminals to directly access their information systems for processing trade documentation. Federal Express courier service, for example, is an early use of this technology. Other companies built specialized interfaces to move trade documentation and related data between closely related companies, a common example being between a manufacturing firm and its subcontractors who were providing supplies or components for assembly. The final stage of this process eliminates the need for building "private" linkages, and relies instead upon public utilities to accomplish the same purpose.

[14]Paul Korzeniowski, "International Software Trends: EDI—Overseas Signals Making More Sense," *Software Magazine,* 9 (4), March 1989, pp. 22–25. He notes that companies base EDI systems on either public value-added networks or on private dial-up linkages established between different business partners.

[15]Ralph Emmett Carlyle, "Managing IS at Multinationals," *Datamation,* 34 (5), March 1, 1988, pp. 54–66. His study also discusses the importance of opening good channels of communication within the IS function as it plans to improve the efficiencies of systems.

through the EDI system, or where it was received, how is this dispute going to be resolved? What are the rules of evidence? What is the legal status of a computer record that can be changed electronically? What type of auditing procedures must the public EDI provider make available in order to resolve a dispute of this type? Should it, for example, keep a record of all orders processed through the system? If it does this, what type of protection does it have to make over the data with which it is entrusted? How can it cope with conflicts of interest? Can it use the data obtained for any other purposes (e.g., for compiling mailing lists, or marketing lists for specialized marketing efforts)?

These questions are relatively straightforward, but what if the locus of the dispute is within the information system of one of the parties to the dispute? For example, party A claims it ordered 1,000 items and party B claims it ordered 10,000 items (which it shipped); should party B be able to subpoena evidence from the computer files of party A? If this is done, how can confidential trade data be protected? Should the public EDI provider be able to subpoena information from the same files? How can the judge or jury be sure that the original information within party A's computing system has not been altered? These speculations lead to the question of what type of auditing system the parties using an EDI system must be required to keep on file in case of a dispute. What, for example, is to prevent party A from going back into its own computer files and changing the copy of the original order from 10,000 to 1,000 and claiming that this was the original order? If this were the case, how would it be possible to verify this type of change? (Party B could also go into its system and change the 1,000 order to 10,000 and claim that this is what it received.) If the order was large enough and financially important enough, and the risk of financial loss to the company great enough, then it is easy to see how internal computer records would be altered after the fact to "prove innocence" on the part of the company.[16]

A second major disadvantage to EDI-type systems is their limitation. Standardized as they are around predefined documentation and specific types of relationships, they are no doubt able to take advantage of the ensuing efficiencies, but in so doing they lack flexibility. In order to get an advantage over competitors, assuming this is possible, it would be fruitless to rely upon standard utilities available to everyone else in the industry. Rather than being a source of competitive advantage, we are finding that EDI and similar interorganizational systems should be thought of as competitive *prerequisites.*

---

[16]No one enjoys thinking about their own information-systems operations being involved in such fraud, but this type of eventuality and its implications for EDI and interorganizational systems must be taken into consideration.

In the future, we can expect that even more sophisticated informational relationships will be needed to cement the business operations and strategies of multinational corporations and thereby get competitive advantage. These new relationships will be more complex and sophisticated than anything available currently through EDI. Although leadership of this type of application has shifted to Japan, and is clearly evident through developments such as the Information Network System (INS), which will link together the data processing of entire *economic sectors* of the Japanese economy using perhaps broadband ISDN systems, information-systems professionals in Western multinational corporations should not be blind to these developments. This and other types of comprehensive interorganizational networking strategies will include several new levels of sophistication that can be expected to appear in Japan, North America, and Western Europe. These are a few of the developments we are likely to see in the near future.

Shared Interorganizational Databases

In addition to the creation of standards, such as EDI, which are used to simply transmit data and information between different companies, we will see the creation of interorganizational databases. At the early stages these may be based on a type of cooperative data-processing model that is seen in utilities such as electronic clearing houses, airline reservation systems, and some EDI-providing services, but will extend to include more *value added* in the data-processing function. One example might include collection of marketing information, sharing of information that is important to analyze for the industry sector as a whole (e.g., latest financial and political information); other examples might include second-sourcing referrals being made automatically, and source-searching for suppliers given specific requests.

Creation of Separate Information-Processing Companies

We have found that, in the wave of mergers and acquisitions that swept Western Europe in the shadow of 1992, companies were resolving their data-processing problems by adopting a new alternative. Instead of taking the time either to continue to operate their respective data-processing operations separately, or giving the lead applications development to one of the partners (perhaps the most powerful one), companies were rather setting up separate data-processing companies, which had as their primary purpose the servicing of the new merged corporate entity. This type of solution might well become more common in the future, and it perhaps ushers in an era of increased autonomy for the information-systems function—the creation of a separate "data-processing island" located "off-shore" from the main corporate headquarters, dispassionately servicing the corporate needs from a respectable (and politically safe?) distance.

Joint Development of Strategic Applications

The development and utilization of EDI-type shared applications represents only an early stage in the increasing role of information technology in building strategic applications both between individual organizations and within groups of multinationals. As the role of shared databases, value-added services, and other information-sharing applications increases, we can expect to see greater development on a joint basis of strategic applications that will form the infrastructural backbone of entire industries. The arrangement of these development efforts will be driven by the need to achieve simultaneously economies of scale in data processing as well as efficiencies in the overall systems-development process. We would expect that in the earlier stages, these types of developments will take place between dominant and subordinate partners, such as between a manufacturer and its subcontractors or suppliers, but will eventually spread to encompass joint development efforts taken on a more equitable basis. In the case of Japanese industry, for example, we would expect to see further development of *keiretsu*-based strategic applications between industries having at first only semi-peripheral relationships; however, this type of arrangement and accompanying industrial structure can also be found in the large industrial groupings in Germany (bearing striking resemblance to some Japanese *keiretsu*).

Commercialization of International Applications

Another trend that will become increasingly evident involves the further global proliferation of international applications that are hosted on transnational information-technology infrastructures. This development will extend first from the proto-forms found in today's emerging information utilities, which are already available through public packet-switched networks wherever there are available nodes.[17]

All of these developments appear to indicate that the CIO in today's multinational corporation must work harder at defining and creating new informational relationships with customers and suppliers as well as with sector-specific organizations that will, through such informatization, further the general strategic business mission. The linking together of these relationships through either private or public EDI should be recognized as forming only the first step in a long-term process of increasing sophistication of these international linkages.

---

[17] Using both public packet-switched networks and the packet networks provided by various PTT organizations around the world, the reach of any computer is virtually global. The simple question remains the relative cost trade-off between data-communications cost and the superiority of the particular application that is being distributed. The rapid increase in transparency for international data communications, combined with the relatively rapid decrease in costs will mean that virtually any computer can become "global" in its applications.

UNITED TECHNOLOGIES AUTOMOTIVE

United Technologies Automotive is a manufacturer of parts and components for the automobile industry. It manufactures high-quality items such as electronic models. For Ford it supplies keyless door-locking mechanisms, for Cadillac the electronic turn-signal assembly, and for BMW several modules. It also supplies Honda. It maintains quality in manufacturing by extensive use of computerized statistical control procedures.[18] One of its major customers is the Ford Motor Company. The information-technology strategy of UT is being driven by its dominant relationship with Ford.[19] UT has approximately 130 manufacturing locations worldwide, and each of these locations must be linked together into the information system.

UT has worked hard to develop a system that is reasonably consistent from country to country, but it still faces several problems. One of the great problems is the *language barrier*. Since the information technology must extend from the processing center all the way down to the shop floor, where IT provides important manufacturing and scheduling data, it must be tailored to the individuals there. Since these individuals are local workers rather than the elite, educated, foreign-language-speaking managers found at the higher levels, there is a language barrier in the user interface to the various systems under consideration. This situation produces several problems:

- *System documentation may not be understandable.* If the end-user interface for the information system is going to be made available throughout the 130 plant locations, spanning many different countries, how is the multinational corporation going to handle the translation of documentation into the different languages required, providing that documentation is unavailable in all the needed languages? The further away one moves from the imperial languages of Europe—German and French—the less available documentation becomes.[20] Yet in order for the local employees effectively to operate the systems for manufacturing and inventory control and other functions, they must obviously have documentation available for consultation. What is the solution to this problem, asks the IS management team of UT.

- *Urgent error messages on the system may not be understood.* This language problem becomes even more severe when we consider a manufacturing environment. There, an urgent error message from the system

---

[18] See Mike Kaczmarek, "SPC Express," *Quality*, 28 (4), April 1989, pp. 58–59. SPC Express is the name of the quality control software UT is using.

[19] There are other examples of the subcontractor's information-technology strategy being driven or actually dictated and determined by a large customer on which it is dependent.

[20] How many documentation packets do you see in Portuguese, suitable for the Brazilian market?

must be immediately and clearly understood by the machine operator. Without this quick attention, problems could occur, even dangerous problems. The logical extension of this is that the end-user interface of each application used on the shop floor and in other lower level places should be translated into the local language of the employees. To rely on the English comprehension of the working population is not a viable course.

- *Even limited software programming may be impossible for the local workers.* Another factor related to the language barrier is that the *end-user programming advantages of object-oriented languages and 4GL's* is negated by the inaccessability of these programs in other languages. The effect of this is to shift more strain to the programming staff than would normally be the case in an English-speaking environment.[21]

In an interview, the IS management reported that six to seven years ago the outlook of the information technology function was "myopic." However, because of the international changes under way in terms of *globalization* of productions systems, such as at Ford, the IT team is learning more about "how to work well with other cultures."

UT is coping with how to organize the IS function to handle international problems. On the external side, it has made significant use of outside consultants in this process. Internally it has searched for persons who are able to work effectively in an international setting.

UT is only interested in working vendors who are able to give support for their products on a worldwide basis. This is critical in operations, and greatly simplifies the maintenance functions. For telecommunications, it has

---

[21] This hypothesis would be interesting for further international comparative research, using more sophisticated measurement techniques. The entire field of language barriers has not been adequately addressed in the MIS literature, although it should be. For further discussion on this, see Edward M. Roche, "Korean Informatics Policy," conference paper, Academic Symposium on the Impact of Recent Economic Developments on U.S./Korean Relations and the Pacific Basin, University of California at San Diego, Graduate School of International Relations and Pacific Studies, November 9–11, 1990. This research analyzed the language barriers faced by Korean data-processing professionals as they struggled to cope with the bridge between the programming side of affairs, all of which had to be done in English, and the end-user side of affairs, all of which had to be accomplished in Korean. In addition, IBM has extensively addressed this issue with its information technology. For example, the 5550 minicomputer series was designed from the very beginning for the Japanese marketplace. In addition, Lotus Corporation created a custom-tailored 1-2-3 program addressed to the Japanese market. Besides the ability to operate in the Japanese language, the Lotus program designed for Japan is able to reproduce the typical reporting and accounting forms found in Japan. This is a very great advantage for Lotus, and it has shown in terms of market share. In addition, the GDSS software developed at the University of Arizona was designed from the very beginning to be capable of working in several different languages. Feasibility studies are under way now for translation into Russian for use at Moscow State University.

no intention of building its own network. Instead, it is planning on probably buying network services from an outside vendor.[22]

United Technologies is moving toward an infrastructure that is both centralized and decentralized. Suprisingly, it has tended to decentralize financial control, and to a certain extent the utilization of software. However, it has attempted to weld together its manufacturing control into a centralized system.

As it moved toward its current strategy, the IS management team says that the transition toward global coordination of their 130 plants worldwide did not cause resistance on the part of the local IT executives "because it was handled correctly." As the system was rolled out, the various European IT executives were brought fully into the process and shown the advantages of moving toward a common type of system. Afterwards, when a basic agreement was reached, the strategy became mandatory for the corporation as a whole.

It took approximately three months to develop the system. United Technologies is using an AS/400 base with one to two basic software packages, including BPCS, used in 33 countries, and "Force Shift." The big challenge in software now is to supplement the relationship UT has with local manufacturing companies.

The process for reaching agreement on a basic strategy involved several steps. First, a meeting was set up to get a "validation or rejection" of the basic ideas. IT management called this a "reality check." Next, the team identified opportunities that are available to the company but have not been explored or exploited.

UT does not find hardware and software to be a problem within Western Europe: "Even consulting support is not a problem there." (This is a reference to hired programmers or analysts for short-term projects.) Of the three components of a system—hardware, software, and telecommunications—it is the latter that is clearly providing the most severe problems for United Technologies Automotive.

In the 1970s, the company moved toward a type of vertical integration oriented growth with a stream of acquisitions. United Technologies attempted to get a better control over its raw material suppliers. In addition, it moved toward outright purchase of new businesses. For example, it purchased Essex Wire Company. At the time, information technology was primarily characterized by a centralized system. This arrangement strongly emphasizes *financial control* rather than *manufacturing systems*. It was adequate to the business at that time.

---

[22]With operations at 130 sites around the world, it may not be suprising that the IS team is reluctant to begin the process of building its own private international network for data communications. The regulatory barriers would prove to be a tremendous drag on the effort. In addition, the international environment is still not ready to accept the most advanced forms of technology for telecommunications, such as voice/data integration. (Voice traffic is often held by state monopolies.)

During the 1970s, "information systems were allowed to languish." The IT function stopped reporting to the operating units and began reporting to the holding company. There was little, if any, change in the basic structure of the information systems during this period. The *financial systems* were kept more-or-less current, but the *manufacturing systems* were not developed to any significant extent.

In the 1980s, a great emphasis was placed on allowing plants to become more responsive to the customer. At this time, one of UT's dominant customers, The Ford Motor Company, started a move toward using *a single supplier* in each market.[23] As a result of this move, UT was forced into developing a new strategy, and the information system that had coasted through the 1970s began to change rapidly. In order rapidly to improve the manufacturing systems, United Technologies moved toward replacing its wide-ranging portfolio of systems as much as possible with packaged software. In addition, in order to work better with Ford, which wanted a *single worldwide point of contact,* UT moved toward a system that would take orders for components at a single location, then *auto-distribute* the orders to the appropriate manufacturing site at any one of the 130 locations around the world. The information-technology infrastructure that supported this new strategy is based on the IBM AS/400 distributed processing system using IBM's software, and a system of consolidation at the top level of the corporation.

In the 1990s, the IT management team at UT sees a movement toward a *closer relationship between the customer and the supplier* and a *heightened degree of communication within the firm* to support this strategy. This will involve *global networking* in order to make it easier to share engineering data—including CAD/CAM information—between different manufacturing locations of the firm. This will be particularly helpful because parts and components being manufactured tend to be the same in many different locations in the world. This type of exchange of information will probably take place on heavily networked engineering workstations. IT management planning calls for financial, manufacturing, and engineering data to be moved around the world in roughly equal proportions. They have estimated that it requires *less effort and complexity* to share financial than manufacturing data.

Engineering data will be *centralized in three locations* in the United States, in Europe, and in the Far East—probably the Philippines.

---

[23]This marked a difference in philosophy for Ford. Rather than spending time playing off one supplier against another, Ford management attempted to establish a better long-term relationship with a single supplier. The rationale for this transition was that with a closer relationship, it would be possible to actually exert more influence over the supplier. Other companies started to move in this direction as well during the 1980s. To a certain extent, it could be argued that this was in response to the tight relationships being discovered between Japanese manufacturing giants and *their* suppliers.

TELECOMMUNICATIONS IS A MAJOR PROBLEM

In setting up such a comprehensive global networking environment, United Technologies appears to have encountered major problems. The IT management team has said that it "can't get decent communications." There are problems with *high cost, delays,* and *quality* of the telecommunications circuits that are used. Western Europe is difficult in this regard. For example, UT has a design center in Germany and a manufacturing plant in Spain. There is no telecommunications network available to them which enables these two locations to be efficiently connected: "We are forced to use the Deutsche Bundespost with their protocols and we can't do it; no one can do it."[24] West Germany is not the only country to pose problems for United Technologies. In the Philippines, UT has experienced problems getting access to reliable *long-haul* networks. In Spain, UT's IT management reports that it takes *up to two years to get a new telecommunications line* for setting up a network. Needless to say, this type of unexpected delay severely strains any implementation effort.[25]

Even in a country that is not as advanced as West Germany, United Technologies is finding a more flexible situation. It is busy installing an international network that is approximately one-half satellite and one-half a terrestrial-based private network. This networking strategy is being driven by the difficulties UT is experiencing in updating files in Mexico. For manufacturing and production statistics, UT is experiencing difficulties of five- to seven-day delays in updating its master files. According to IT management, the most important form of international telecommunication right now is "sneaker net" for accounting and related information.[26]

The 1992 situation in Western Europe appears to provide the promise of an opportunity for cross-border labor movement of programmers and analysts.

---

[24]The Deutsches Bundespost is the PTT in West Germany, which both provides and controls the availability of telecommunications within Germany. It is considered to be inflexible and quite expensive. Private leased line networks are generally discouraged by the DB, and this has drastically changed the networking and telecommunications strategies of many multinational corporations doing work in Germany. In recent years, we have seen some indications that the DB is liberalizing, but if the UT case is to be believed, this "liberalization" has yet to have a significant effect on users as of 1990.

[25]This raises an interesting question for MIS research: *To what extent do international implementation efforts take more time than the same type of implementation that does not cross international borders?* This would be an interesting study, assuming the research could identify a series of pairs of implementation efforts that were *roughly equivalent* but were either international nor domestic in nature.

[26]"Sneaker net" is a slang expression referring to the use of couriers for transporting data stored on magnetic media across international borders. "Sneaker nets" are used when there is no available international telecommunications system reliable enough to transport the necessary data. ("Sneakers" are a type of plastic or rubber tennis shoe.)

According to UT executives, at this time, not all of the countries of Europe have an adequate skill base for information technology. They mention, for example, that in Portugal, it is not particularly easy to get the skills needed to run an effective IS operation. The IT management does not believe that the transition to a pan-European market will be as easy as the press claims and will pose serious challenges in the management of technology.

Lessons from United Technologies

The United Technologies situation is still evolving, driven by the changing philosophy of its major customer, Ford Motor Company. It is in the midst of building a "global" network, but has still not succeeded. We might suggest the following lessons from United Technologies Automotive:

- *The entire information technology strategy can be driven by your customers.* In the case of United Technologies, the information-technology strategy is being driven by its customer, and not by United Technologies. Although within UT, the IT function is leading the transformation of the corporation, this is being determined by the information-technology interface requirements of Ford, the largest and most powerful customer. It is perfectly reasonable to suspect that should UT not be able to respond to the changes "suggested" by Ford, the ultimate effect would be a diminution of market share.
- *International telecommunications are still a major headache, even in developed countries.* In its effort to link together 130 plant locations around the world, UT is encountering major problems with telecommunications. It is a surprise that even in developed countries, such as those of Western Europe, UT is encountering severe problems that in some cases are *more severe* than those faced in developing countries. This is because of the general regulatory environment and the inherent flexibility which, under certain circumstances, can be afforded by the liberally minded PTT in a developing country. IT planners would be foolish to assume that just because they are building a network in a developed country the networking problems are going to be significantly easier.
- *Building a central order-processing center may have advantages for worldwide management of production.* There may be a lesson in UT's effort to build a *single order point* for its entire worldwide operation. Although this is clearly motivated by its relationship with Ford, which will benefit from having such a relationship with one of its major suppliers,[27]

---

[27] For a discussion of a checklist in dealing with suppliers from an information-systems perspective, see James Morgan, "Welcome Booklet Contest: Ten Ways to Tell Suppliers What They Need to Know," *Purchasing*, 109 (3), September 13, 1990, pp. 80–84.

United Technologies believes that it will be able to harvest efficiency from this arrangement. Labor and bureaucratic effort will be reduced, and the coordination of manufacturing, inventory control, and related functions will become more efficient.

- *Information systems skills are in uneven supply around the world.* The availability of skilled personnel varies from country to country and from region to region. Although human talent is highly mobile, moving large numbers of persons around the world is in general more expensive and ultimately acts as a drag on the cost structure. It might be argued that telecommunications is making it easy to locate data centers wherever there is ample supply of labor,[28] but this view must be tempered by the need for local tailoring of applications, particularly at the end-user interface level.
- *Language can be a significant problem in international manufacturing systems.* If a multinational corporation is involved in manufacturing in a significant number of countries, it must inevitably cope with the need to generate factory-floor intelligibility of information technology and information systems at the lowest levels. Although many of the systems employees may be fluent in English and be generally educated, this is not as true for the line workers, who have been recruited based on excellence of other skills. Therefore, any global system may have significant parts of its database or other critical functions *centralized,* but its user interfaces must be *decentralized and multi-lingualized.*
- *Pressures towards centralization produce a trend toward packaged software.* Based on the experience of United Technologies, as the multinational corporation moves toward centralization of many information-systems functions that have historically been more decentralized, there is a greater pressure toward standardization of software packages and platforms.[29]
- *Will 1992 make Europe any more capable of accommodating the information-technology needs of multinational corporations?* There

---

[28]Source: comments of Dr. Peter G. W. Keen, Executive Affiliates Seminar, New York University, Stern School of Business, Information Systems Area Department, February 8, 1990.

[29]This standardization is probably produced by two important factors. First, implementation of any system in multiple units is easier if the actions to be taken in each location are *replicable* and can be handled quickly by a single team that is capable of quickly building up a learning curve for the implementation. A second factor is that as we move into the 1990s, there is undoubtedly a greater availability of standardized packages than in the past. This availability also shapes the trajectory of strategy chosen by the multinational corporation. Both of these hypotheses might be a subject of further investigation on the part of MIS researchers. The first part of the research would involve literally *counting* the number of packages available, and the second part would involve *matching* these new packages against the *requirement of multinational corporations* as determined by methodological techniques such as survey, interview, and literature analysis.

appears to be significant evidence that multinational corporations have not had an ideal information-technology enviornment within which to work in Western Europe. In particular, regulations on data flow and telecommunications infrastructural flexibility have inhibited many strategies. The move toward 1992 in Europe may not guarantee that these problems will magically disappear at the stroke of 12 on January 1, 1992, or even several years later. This is still an open question, and multinational corporations might watch the 1992 situation with this in mind.

- *Relationships between centralization and decentralization are changing, with different applications "exchanging positions."* The evidence provided by United Technologies might throw more gasoline on the fire of the debate about centralization and decentralization.[30] There is obviously no evidence provided by this case that "globalization" entails either. UT centralized its manufacturing environment for the purpose of ordering. In addition, there are indications that its financial control function, generally associated with a highly centralized posture in most corporations, moved toward a looser, decentralized type of posture.[31]

What we have seen from these cases is that, in almost all cases, there is a serious mismatch between the information-technology infrastructure and the grand strategies of the multinational corporation. The information-technology function seems to be constantly behind the times, playing catch-up ball. The information-systems departments are coping with the new demands constantly being placed upon them, but it is a difficult challenge. The underlying problem is probably that the information-technology infrastructure of the multinational corporation can never anticipate changes in global strategy. The infrastructure is more rigid, takes longer to reform and revise than overall strategy, and the result is a permanent time-lag in responsiveness. Or is it? Perhaps there are strategies we can learn from these cases that are generally applicable to any organization.

---

[30] See John Leslie King, "Centralized Versus Decentralized Computing: Organizational Considerations and Management Options," *Computing Surveys,* 15 (4), December 1983, pp. 319–349.

[31] We cannot yet draw definitive conclusions on this point. It appears, however, that the study of the evolving relationship between centralization and decentralization in multinational corporations, and their use of information technology, will be an enduring question. What is the rationale for the different typologies we see? Is the tendency toward centralization or decentralization driven by technology, by business strategy, or by accident? MIS research must continue to investigate this relationship. In the case of United Technologies, it appears that the company's relationship with Ford determined the overall strategy. But what is the rationale for a weakening of centralization of the financial function? This clearly needs more research in light of the tendency toward centralization of financial functions in most corporations. What are the pressures for and the pressures against decentralization for *each* of the major applications within the portfolio of the multinational corporation?

SUMMARY

The general trend toward internationalization of all business competition also leads to greater interorganizational linkages, particularly between multinationals engaged in corporate alliances.

- Joint ventures, takeovers, mergers, and sharing or cooperative arrangements have been accelerating.
- Merging the information systems from allied companies can be traumatic and challenging, yet yield significant economies of scale.
- Environmental factors, mostly taking the form of different national regulations and conditions, always impinge on the implementation of this process.

The United Technologies Automotive case shows that building international manufacturing systems that also work in a multinational corporate alliance system provides many challenges at the practical level.

- The most detailed levels of the system are generally "un-exportable" to foreign environments unless heavily modified, particularly as regards language interfaces.
- The necessary telecommunications services cannot always be obtained at affordable prices.
- An adequate supply of trained human resources is not always available at affordable prices.

CHAPTER

18

Strategy #2: Develop International Systems Development Skills

At the heart of the information-technology function lies the critical skill base used to perform systems development. However, for major international projects a broader set of skills than just technical capabilities is needed. The ability to operate effectively with foreign cultures, sensitivity to the demands and intrigues of top management, and a comprehensive view of the real business of the business are examples of skills which are needed internationally from within the systems development function. There is, after all, an entirely different political dimension to international project management, and this manifests itself not only within the firm at the interdepartmental level, but also externally, as the information systems function is forced to deal with varying national authorities. The Philip Morris case demonstrates how many of these factors are successfully handled by the information systems function.

DISCUSSION

Developments in international business are driving the increasing pace of transnational systems development efforts. Many multinational corporations are suffering from organizational paralysis caused by the need to continue operation of systems which are most often broken down into many different "warring factions" strung around the world from location to location. In the past, this type of arrangement may have worked well, but now we are seeing an increased need for development of transnational systems. Within this context, transnational systems may be defined as developed applications that function throughout an international information system in a way that is oblivious to national borders. For example, the ability to check inventory levels from a central database located at the headquarters from terminals located in any of the countries where the multinational has business operations would be considered a global and transnational application.

Particularly with the improvements in international telecommunications, database technologies, and applications development strategies, it has become possible to extend the depth and reach of the information system in the multinational. This is done either through batch transfers of information between different sites, with an interactive system that allows geographically distributed users to access centralized or regional databases, or through use of electronic messaging systems, including electronic document interchange (EDI).[1] Rather than rely for international management control and reporting on occasional or informal reports, companies can use information technologies such as electronic mail and (more importantly) distributed databases and global applications, to coordinate the operations of subsidiaries better.

Financial control and reporting have long been centralized through information systems and may be the leading application in many multinationals, but it is by no means the only global application which is developing. Manufacturing control, inventory control, global sourcing, logistics, and interorganizational and strategic linkages with customers, suppliers and even competitors are changing the nature of the problem and putting greater emphasis on the need to build even more highly-integrated applications. Of course, these types of linkages and their associated strategies are well known at the domestic level,

---

[1] For a discussion of these alternatives and some guidelines for building good international telecommunications networks, see Geoff Wiggin, "The Golden Rules of Global Networking," *Datamation,* International Edition, 33 (19), October 1, 1987, pp. 68–73.

having been popularized in the early 1980s. However, some rethinking needs to be done to accomodate changes at the international level and any specific problems or challenges which must be addressed there.

Many examples of critical applications have been identified for use in the multinational corporations. The most famous and classic, so to speak, is financial control, the simple reporting of sales and income results from all of the various subsidiaries to the corporate headquarters, a necessary corporate function which dates back to the Middle Ages and nowadays is critical in filing the proper financial reports, particularly to the appropriate tax authorities. There are many other critical applications in areas such as inventory, human resources and personnel systems, manufacturing, distribution and general logistics, and so on. Each of these applications in most multinationals is actually a large conglomeration of related applications, all to support the overall function. For example, the "logistics application" in a multinational may actually be composed of dozens of different applications, many redundant, which have been created to support this function. This redundancy is present in most applications and represents an untold amount of wasted effort in terms of time, money, and human talent.

In general, the use of "global" systems to supplement the overall "global" corporate strategy is becoming widespread as a type of ad hoc ideology; and, like most ideologies, it has many different interpretations and schools of thought. But regardless of the particular ideology, or the specific strategy of the multinational, or even the application families under consideration, it is relatively easy to demonstrate that global systems development must be undertaken. What is *global systems development* in this context? It should not be thought of as simply the creation of a systems development task force to develop a single application that is distributed throughout the entire geographical scope of the multinational in such a way as to deliver equal functionality at each location, an application such as a global centralized inventory control or logistics systems. Instead, the definition or scope should be extended to consist more of a *global orientation* in conducting systems development. This does not necessarily mean that systems development must always result in global applications, but rather that the developers of all systems must keep in mind how they fit into the global strategy of the multinational. In some cases this may mean the development of large, globally operating applications; in other cases it may mean development or maintenance of small local applications, or interfacing of those local applications with the main corporate systems. However, in the latter case, the trade-offs made, the criteria for efficiencies, and so forth must be made with the overall multinational in mind, rather than with the local subsidiary in mind. This type of philosophy may run counter to the needs of developing countries because in some cases the global needs and efficiencies of the multinational corporation may be at odds with the development priorities of the host country. Under these circumstances, we typically see the emergence of various national barriers aimed at changing the nature of the applications development process so as to divert more resources to the developing country. This intervention by the government of the host country may be either overt or covert. Nontariff barriers—such as licensing of telecommunications, control over data bases, and control over equipment utilization and even importation—may be used in a more direct way to steer the applications development process of the multinational corporation. Although this no doubt raises the cost of operations of the multinational and lowers its ability to use information technology as a "firm-specific advantage" in the market of the host country, these types of actions can be justified for the public good insofar as they are consistent with overall economic development priorities.

One problem with this approach to systems development is that many skills in the information technology function of the multinational are based on the national model. In other words, talent pools with particular skills are isolated from each other behind national barriers, making it difficult to think or plan in terms of a consolidated human resources pool with a predictable and controllable group of talents that can be mobilized for a systems development project. Without a global approach to personnel management within the information technology function, it is impossible to manage and utilize the skill base adequately. This classic problem of personnel management and skills utilization exists throughout all functional areas of a large multinational firm and is not unique to the information technology function. However, given the highly skilled nature of the information systems professional, in some cases the consequences of bad management in this area can result in relatively greater harm than in any other areas, except perhaps finance.

A second factor in this regard is that the isolation of pools of information technology talent behind national borders within a global topology which is decentralized operationally in each national market should not be thought of in itself as being a symptom of poor management or planning. This situation, as explained earlier, is the result of the historical development of the multinational corporation and the limitations on international networking which were prevalent in the early 1970s and 1980s. Also, various national nontariff barriers and other regulations have tended to force or "encourage" the multinational to build separate data processing centers in each country where they are conducting business. Supply factors such as relatively high telecommunications costs have also encouraged a national model of data processing, for it was only at the very end of the 1980s and into the early 1990s that we saw a concerted effort being made to lower the excessive costs of international telecommunications to reflect true costs more accurately. Finally, the overall managerial policies in many multinationals encouraged a decentralized approach in matters of data processing. Within this context, the inevitable development toward national data processing centers was the result of the desire on the part of parties such as strong national managers to have autonomy apart from the headquarters and its various forms of control. The location of an independent data-processing center could serve this desire, and in addition support many of the essential operations functions necessary within each country.

As a generalization, we can say that the trend toward building global information systems and applications is an attempt to break with the decentralized legacy of the past and overcome the barriers that prevent the multinational from reaching overall efficiencies in its data processing activities.

In addition to these rather formidable *inherited* limitations on the building of global applications, there can be other barriers at the project management level. One of the most important of these is the need to get top management support for a global initiative.[2] Unfortunately, international projects often have no champion who is capable of ensuring that the systems development team will achieve the correct amount of both political and financial support to get its tasks done. In fact, it may be more common for a few of the individual national data processing establishments to resist global initiatives, particularly if they have not been adequately consulted and if they intuitively feel that the project is being imposed from headquarters. Even the most naive industrial psychologist recognizes that many persons have an inherent resistance to authority, particularly when they have built up a personal empire that they feel is under threat. If the idea of a global application is perceived to take away autonomy, possibly including a portion of the data processing budget which heretofore had been controlled at the local (i.e., national) level, then the reluctance of the data processing management at the local level to cooperate can be understood.

However, the local data processing management may not be the roadblock, but rather local line management. Even with acquiesce from the personnel in data processing, we might find that their hands are tied if the line

---

[2]Sullivan-Trainor's research, composed of interviews with managers of several large IS operations, focused on the problem of keeping top management sponsorship for critical information technology projects. He noted that management can "disappear" (i.e., get fired), the company can radically and suddenly change its priorities, and a divestiture or takeover can totally disrupt even the best-laid plans. He recommends getting user support, establishing benchmarks against competitors, focusing on showing broader rather than more specific benefits, and working hard to control both the funding and the execution of any project. See Michael L. Sullivan-Trainor, "Keep Management Hot about Technology," *Computerworld,* 24 (52, 53), December 24, 1990/January 1, 1991, pp. 2, 4.

management to which they report is against a global systems development effort. Political reality may not always result in the best economic reality. Why would local line management drag its feet in the face of a global project? To protect their local interests.[3] Perhaps they are being told that a portion of the cost for the systems development project is to come from their own budgets. If they are hard-pressed on the financial performance front, perhaps because the country in which they are operating is experiencing depressed sales, or is in an economic recession, or for any other reasons, they may be reluctant to allocate what they view as being scarce resources to the 'global' systems development effort. Yes, it is true that it may be easy to demonstrate that the systems development effort being contemplated is of great potential value to the multinational as a whole, but it may not be so easy to demonstrate that supporting its implementation will necessarily be of direct and tangible benefit to local line management.

A third problem with the efficient coordination of global systems development projects lies in availability of essential project management skills. In even some of the largest multinationals, the Chief Information Officer (CIO) can name only a handful of well-respected project managers who have developed a proven expertise in implementation of global projects.[4] One would imagine few organizations have a systematic way of identifying persons with these qualifications, and even if they did, it would be difficult to identify exactly what those qualifications are, apart from having a long proven track record in real global systems development. The inevitable question arises: What are some of the proven techniques that world-class project managers use in building global systems?

There are indications that taking a transnational approach can give advantages in developing global applications. Thus the focus of responsibility for systems development may not automatically be located in a single location, such as corporate headquarters. Rather, it will move about to those centers of excellence and expertise where it will be possible to take maximum advantage of the skills available. By implication, no assumption should be made regarding where the best talent is to be found for a specific project.

---

[3] Within the context of the multinational corporation, the term 'local' is used to refer to managers or assets associated with a subsidiary in a country away from the headquarters country.

[4] Much more research needs to be done to discover the nature and characteristics of successful global systems development project managers. How they operate, what their most critical skills are, how they make their basic decisions, how they succeed on the political front, and so on—these are all important questions which should be answerable in the future, given a significant amount of new research in this field.

One approach to managing international systems development projects involves the "Lead System," which allows the IT function to economize on systems development costs. It assumes that the necessary talent can be found anywhere throughout the information technology "empire" and seeks to take advantage of that assumption. Using this process, a lead team is assigned to the project. In contrast to a headquarters-driven approach, the lead is chosen from anywhere in the multinational organization. It is composed of the best persons for a job regardless of their nationality or where they are affiliated with the multinational. If several lead teams are chosen, each working on a different systems development project, then the managerial control over the process as a whole, having as it does several major project developments operating simultaneously, will become more complex, but still manageable because no one part of the organization has to bear the entire burden for managing all of the projects at once. The London operation may be handling all development for Europe, Atlanta for North America, and Tokyo for all Far East operations; and yet each of the different systems development teams would be building systems which are usable by and accessible to all of the other countries in the world where the multinational does business.

Given the need to develop a specific application that links together various subsidiaries of the multinational at the international level, an effort would be made to locate any talent within the multinational capable of solving the problem. Suppose that a smaller subsidiary in Western Europe has a team of data processing professionals who have developed a center of expertise in many important aspects of the application being considered. When a team such as this is found, then that group is empowered with the lead control over the global systems development effort. From that point onwards, the lead team is in charge of the application.[5] In this way, different lead teams could be empowered for many different global applications development efforts, all from different base locations throughout the multinational.

The main factor in developing new systems developments in MNCs is building up international skills specifically aimed at transnational computing. The efforts in doing this again should be decentralized because the skills appropriate to this type of effort are likely to be found in a variety of places. The goal of the information technology function should be to improve the total amount of skills inventory which can be called upon in order to carry out projects.

---

[5]Cash and McLeod discuss the concept of an "Emerging Technology group" which is responsible for working in team efforts for systems development in dependent companies. See James I. Cash, Jr. and Poppy L. McLeod, "Managing the Introduction of Information Systems Technology in Strategically Dependent Companies," *Journal of Management Information Systems*, I (4), Spring 1985, pp. 5–23.

THE SKILLS REQUIRED

What are these skills? Given the international and transcultural nature of many global systems development projects, good human relations skills are critical. This would include in many cases an ability to perform in a multilingual environment. The more different the culture is, the more critical these skills become. The United States and Western Europe have rather similar cultures. However, when Asia is involved, or Africa, or even parts of Latin America, the cultural and linguistic barriers rise in importance, thus placing considerably greater demands upon the project manager of a global systems development effort. Another important skill is cultural sensitivity on the part of the systems development team. This problem occurs when people must be managed. It is a well-known fact that persons of different cultures frequently offend one another without intention. Managing people in a complex operation over a long period of time under conditions of uncertainty with a lot of pressure is a situation where offending different persons can be highly counterproductive. Without a certain amount of cultural sensitivity, it is doubtful a project manager could operate at the international level and make significant progress.[6]

The following sections describe some of the critical skills which must be encouraged within the corporate environment.

Ability to Manage in Different Cultures

Much has been written about cultural differences and international management. In terms of development of international applications and the special project management skills required, there is probably nothing inherently different in the process which would not occur in the resulting human relations problems of activities in other functional areas of the multinational. There may even be a discoverable evidence which indicates that the *lingua franca* of the computer subculture, and the similarities of outlook brought about by use of similar operating systems and vendors, even if set in entirely different national environments, can all work together to provide a type of binding force making for a common view. This common view may bring cultures together rather than drive them apart. However, it may also be true that this type of common view derives from similar experiences at the technical and tactical level, but it may not automatically be present when project teams from different countries sit around a conference table in a planning session and begin to discuss their philosophies or approaches to systems

---

[6]There are two points in this regard: First, some cultures seem to be more different than others, and different combinations of cultures produce different mixes of volitility. Second, even when a multinational has a project manager who is highly successful within the home country, this does not guarantee automatic success at the international level.

development.[7] This type of brainstorming activity, which inevitably takes place in the beginning of an assignment during the problem definition phase of the systems development lifecycle, may tend to bring out and magnify any cultural differences which exist. It is still too early to come to a definitive answer to these questions because there is still a great amount of research which must be done.

Endurance and Proven Track Record in Complex Project Management

It appears from the interviews conducted in preparation of this monograph that the best international project managers are a special breed. Many times they are not of the same nationality as the headquarters multinational, particularly if the organization is an American one. The especially capable project manager typically has 8 to 15 years experience, with several overseas assignments under his belt.[8] From these interviews two distinctive characteristics seem to stand out. First, these people appear to be of a type that quickly heads to simplicity in a situation. Perhaps this is a notable characteristics of any rapid-fire problem solver. Second they are conscious of being culturally different, a consciousness brought about either by being different themselves, such as when a foreign national has worked his way up the career ladder in a multinational, or by having a keen awareness of national differences through being stationed in several overseas assignments. These two characteristics appear to describe the best candidate for management of global systems development projects. There also appears to be a type of "ease" in their personalities—the type of personality that makes one feel comfortable.

Ability to Work in Teams

Although the ability to work in teams is a well-accepted skill that must be taught in most of today's MBA programs and is a highly respected art, it is not

---

[7] For a look at how different organizations foster shared values and norms of cooperation in the systems development process, particularly as regards networking, see Kevin Barham, "Networking—the Corporate Way Around International Discord," *Multinational Business* (4), Winter 1990–1991, pp. 1–11. Barham believes that the critical task is to create a trust and mutual respect between the different teams in order to bring about the cooperation needed for successful planning, implementation, and follow-through.

[8] Things are changing, but I have not yet located an experienced female international project manager. By the end of the 1990s, if not sooner, this will no doubt have changed; but for this monograph, I was unable to obtain any females to interview. There may be some indications that the stereotypical female personality (if one believes in such sociological and psychological myths) is more capable of managing consensus and maintaining group cohesion; however, this is an entirely separate line of inquiry which I was unable to follow.

entirely clear whether the dynamics are the same when this way of working is taken into the international environment. Factors such as the language barrier and different cultural patterns may mean that some parts of a group become dominant even when their ideas are not particularly productive. This situation at best can lead to a poorer decision, at worst can lead to disaster. Only the skillful team leader can make sure that all points of view are taken into consideration and that even the weakest members of the group have their ideas taken up by the group. In this context the term "weakest" may mean "quietest" or "most polite," but in any case it is easy for groups to railroad over their more sensitive members. Therefore, the ability to work in *international* teams is a critical skill which must be nourished. Depending on the amount of money available for training, this ability can potentially be taught as a skill to fast track project managers, who will be in a position to attempt these types of projects in the future.

THE PHILIP MORRIS CORPORATION

Philip Morris Corporation (PM), a large consumer-oriented conglomerate, acquired General Foods in 1985. General Foods (GF) at the time had some excess fat, which was squeezed out two years later with a restructuring and the elimination of 1,000 positions to save $150 million per year.[9] The chairman of General Foods resigned a few years later, thus slowing down Philip Morris' plan to diversify out of the tobacco business. At that time tobacco, which accounted for 81 percent of its income, was under pressure from the U.S. Surgeon General.[10] Because of the worldwide nature of the cigarette business, PM had built up very large systems spanning the globe. The merger with General Foods and Kraft made Philip Morris the first $2-billion advertiser in the United States.[11] The takeover of Kraft had been hostile, and cost $12.9 billion; but after the bloodletting, management was confident that the combined Kraft–General Foods group could sustain growth of about 15 per cent per year in profits. Philip Morris remained 60 per cent dependent upon one brand, Marlboro.[12]

---

[9]Aimee L. Stern, "GF Tries the Old Restructure Ploy," *Business Month,* 130 (5), November 1987, pp. 36–39.

[10]Amy Dunkin, "Beyond Marlboro Country," *Business Week,* Industrial/Technology Edition (3064), August 8, 1988, pp. 54–58.

[11]Judann Dagnoli and Julie Liesse Erickson, "PM, Kraft Could Slice Promotions," *Advertising Age,* 59 (47), November 7, 1988, pp. 3, 74.

[12]Stratford P. Sherman, "How Philip Morris Diversified Right," *Fortune,* 120 (9), October 23, 1989, pp. 120–131.

When the merger with General Foods took place,[13] PM information systems management was fortunate in finding that GF has roughly similiar types of systems.[14] For example, in terms of the underlying communications infrastructure, the IS team at PM found that GF had a PROFS network.[15] At the time of the merger, PM had implemented a worldwide PROFS system, which was fully operational by September 1989. As the different parts of the PM businesses were patched together, IS management found that the tobacco section of the business also had a large PROFS installation operating. Tying together all of the different PROFS networks into a coherent system took approximately $1\frac{1}{2}$ years of development and programming effort. The major problems occurred in the consolidation and standards for electronic mail directories.

When deciding to undertake this project, the information technology function groups evaluated the inherent risk involved in several projects. After the review was completed, it was decided that trying to develop global applications which were infrastructure-oriented was less risky than trying to develop applications which touched too closely the Operational details of individual departments. In thinking through the longer term implications of undertaking the electronic mail initiative, the key managers in the information systems function observed that the implementation of the electronic mail

---

[13] Chandler describes the process of merger as follows: "First came legal consolidation, which gave a central office complete legal power over the activities of the constituent companies. Initially this took the form of creating a trust, and after the 1890s a holding company. Then came administrative centralization and industrial rationalization. Some of the manufacturing facilities of the constituent companies were enlarged, more were eliminated, and a few new ones built. Then the administration of these facilities was placed under control of a single production or operating department. Next the consolidated centralized enterprise normally embarked on a strategy of vertical integration by moving forward into marketing by setting up a branch office and distribution network, and backward by obtaining its own purchasing offices and sources of raw and semi-finished materials" (p. 403). Alfred D. Chandler, "The Growth of the Transnational Industrial Firm in the United States and the United Kingdom: A Comparative Analysis," pp. 396–409+. Given as the Tawney Memorial Lecture for 1979.

[14] It would be interesting to investigate a variety of mergers and acquisitions to learn the degree to which compatibility or incompatibility of information systems played a significant role in the final decision regarding the merging of the two companies. One could hypothesize that in cases where information technology obviously plays a great role in the business—airline reservation systems, timesharing systems, electronic document systems, or even noninformation but "information intensive" businessess such as banking and finance—there would be a greater probability that the compatibility of systems would play a relatively greater role than if this was not the case. The only way academic research could address this issue would be through interviews, surveys, or other methods to understand the track record for a sample of merger and acquisition actions across different sectors. One would suspect that in the majority of cases, the role of information systems' compatibility played virtually no part whatsoever.

[15] PROFS stands for Professional Office System, an IBM product that provides a variety of executive and managerial support functions for the individual manager. These functions include calendar, electronic mail, word processing, and others.

project, although relatively simple, would go far in helping to build international systems development skills which would no doubt be needed in the future for considerably more difficult projects.

Interviews revealed that the PM information technology management team was very global in its outlook and was constantly engaged in monitoring the international situation, particularly the many developments taking place in Eastern Europe.[16] However, they stressed that having a global outlook does not mean an automatic proclivity to build global information systems. I was suprised to learn that Philip Morris does not really believe in global information systems. They consider that only regional, domestic, or multidomestic information systems are suitable for the type of businesses they operate.

The changes taking place in Western Europe—lumped together under the term "1992"—should make it possible to develop Europe-wide regional applications. These *regional applications* will be confined to servicing customers and business functions with specific applications supporting a product line, rather than being aimed at developing a comprehensive Europe-wide information system that attempts to support all product lines simultaneously.

Such systems will be aimed at elimination of duplication in distribution systems and perhaps standardization of product lines. Higgins and Santalainen see evidence firms will be moving towards more "strategic information systems" which incorporate "integrated data networks."[17]

In Eastern Europe, however, the situation is quite different. The turbulent change taking place has caused the IS management at PM to adopt a very cautious approach to systems development. They note that many of the Eastern European countries do not have the infrastructure necessary to play a larger role in the European economy. They point to Poland's insufficient trucking capability as an example, where this insufficiency will make it impossible for Poland to handle the "large quantities of trailerloads" to keep pace with delivery requirements. Given this situation, the IS management sees no urgency in extending their complex information systems into Eastern Europe.

Even if they did, they would find that the telecommunications infrastructure of Poland is highly centralized around Warszawa, with spurs running out to each of the major cities including Gdańsk, Olsztyn, Szczecin, Poznan, Wrocław, Łodź, Lublin, Katowice, and Kraków. Studies have shown that

> The use of the telecommunication network for transborder-data-flows purposes is hindered by the relative lack of suitable informatics equipment. Production in Poland is not yet sufficient, and imports are restricted because they are treated as high-technology goods included in the lists established by the Co-ordinating

---

[16]Many of the interviews for this research took place during the months leading up to German reunification.

[17]James M. Higgins and Timo Santalainen, "Strategies for Europe 1992," *Business Horizons,* July/August 1989, pp. 54–58.

Committee for Multilateral Export Controls (COCOM). Only 8 percent of the computer systems can be used for remote services and, as a rule, only through dialogue terminals. Not more than half of those systems can connect more than a few terminals.[18]

In assessing the future development of international information systems strategies for PM, the IS management team has identified several barriers which pose a good chance of hindering efforts.

- *Language Barriers.* In the building of transaction systems, for example, PM frequently finds that although management may speak English well, the "information workers" who will actually be using the system do not have the same command of the language. The result is that the information system must make some type of adjustment for this. As systems cover more and more geographical and cultural locations, the maintenance and developmental overhead associated with making this adjustment increases. This may be particularly noticeable when system modifications that have an effect on what the actual end-user works with are needed. Calgon Carbon Corporation, for example, uses a type of "multinational integrated" software that allows end-user screens to send and receive information in local European languages, but still operate simultaneously in updating a centralized and standardized database.[19]
- *Regulations.* Many challenges posed to the information systems function arise *not* because of an intelligent corporate strategy but because national regulations *force* the multinational corporation to adopt a particular form of business in order to get market access. For example, many countries will not allow a multinational corporation to market its products in a country *unless it has a manufacturing plant located there.* There is, of course, no economic rationale for this from the corporate point of view. Typically the multinational corporation would not choose this route if left to its own estimation of economic rationality. One plant might serve an entire region of the world, instead of different plants in each country.
- *Lack of "global" suppliers.* Although PM finds it necessary to build large international systems, it finds it impossible to locate "global" suppliers.

---

[18]UNCTC, *Transborder Data Flows and Poland: Polish Case Study* (New York: United Nations, 1984). For more details on the status of telecommunications and computer systems in Eastern Europe, see Istvan Sebestyen, *Experimental and Operational East-West Computer Connections: The Telecommunication Hardware and Software, Data Communication Services, and Relevant Administrative Procedures* (Laxenburg: IIASA, 1983).

[19]The system is Tolas from GSI and runs on VAX equipment. This allows Calgon Carbon to have financial reporting functions in several different languages. See Jeanette Martin, "Software That Spans the Globe," *Datamation,* International Edition, 36 (21), November 1, 1990, pp. 96(5)–96(8).

Instead, it is forced to negotiate and sign separate agreements for the IS operations in different countries. This has been clearly identified as an unnecessary overhead.[20] It is particularly irritating to find that from country to country, the performance of equipment vendors may vary greatly, thus complicating planning.

- *Cultural problems.* Like language problems, but perhaps more severe, general cultural problems can inhibit the effectiveness of management teams engaged in intensive problem-solving exercises for solving information technology problems.[21]
- *Inadequate facilities.* IS management at PM has found that on a global basis, vendors of either services or equipment are many times *unable* to provide truly consistent global services. In terms of the PROFS network, for example, PM points out that the IBM international network being used has no mechanism for billing the entity being called—so-called "collect calls"—and, therefore, it cannot operate as a regular telephone system. Thus, a cost accounting element must be added to the management of the heavily used network.
- *Modification of accounting systems to cope with the variety of tax laws from country to country.* Within the IS function, the variances in tax laws are recognized as a problem simply because they add tremendous complication to the accounting conventions used in purchasing equipment. Like the cultural barrier question, variances in tax laws from country to country are *not specific* to information systems. However, since the bulk of purchases of information technology goes into the capital equipment acquisition budget, there can be some very large differences in the ultimate financial impact on the multinational depending on how the equipment is accounted for. From the point of view of IS research, these differences raise the question of *international locational economics,* that is, the development of methodologies to determine the optimum mix of satellite, peripheral and centralized equipment vis-à-vis the distribution of the capital impact. It is clear that different architectures, all of which might satisfy the actual applications demand, could have very large differences

---

[20] We have found examples of companies which have managed to develop a relationship with IBM based on a single point of contact for service throughout the world *through a single individual.* Kodak has found this approach provides numerous benefits. Interviews with representatives of other multinational corporations have indicated that this arrangement between Kodak and IBM is *not* a typical situation. Further probing uncovered that this arrangement is the result of the career decisions of a specific IBM employee and does not, therefore, represent a widely available option for multinationals.

[21] This, however, is by no means a problem which is specifically related to international IS management. It is a problem at all levels of the multinational corporation. A great deal of literature examines this issue.

in their ultimate financial impact. But what are the tools available to IS management in making these assessments? And how many organizations actually sit down and make these calculations?

- *Inadequate justification methods.* Interviews conducted with PM also pointed to the difficulty faced in collecting valid cost data on a worldwide basis. This problem makes it very difficult to analyze telecommunications infrastructure costs accurately. Not only does the analyst face a high variance in basic tariff rates from country to country, particularly within Europe, but also the analyst faces swings and changes in the *volume* of internal utilization. This uncertainty adds great complexity to any analysis and calls into question whether it is even worth the effort. For example, PM believes that they are unlikely to save money by implementing domestic, regional or global backbone systems. If this is the case, then the question immediately arises: *What type of utility are you getting from building a global information technology system?* The answer must lie in the *secondary efficiency effects* of information technology on the corporation. Information technology itself may not be efficient but it may greatly promote efficiency in other functional areas of the corporation. This is a basic distinction within IS strategy: Is the aim or rationalization or strategy to improve the IS function or is it to improve the function of line management and other functions within the multinational? The difficulty arises if there is a need to assess trade-offs between these two options. For example, how much inefficiency in the information technology area can be traded off against a presumption of efficiency in a functional area of the corporation? (It is highly unlikely that the trade-off could be made the other way around, for example, taking a "hit" in the efficiency of a line function in order to promote the efficiency of the information system.)

- *High domestic workloads and the place of international IS strategy.* The IS management at PM pointed out the existence of a conflict in work priorities between domestic operations and international operations. They stated that,"Most domestic IS groups are running lean, with a full plate of work, characterized by heavy maintenance requirements." They observed that if this is the case, then "Who will build the (international) system?" The implication of this observation is that, for the most part, *domestic* operations get priority over *international* operations. This result arises naturally because for the typical IS worker or manager, the domestic requirement appear much more pressing. Given this situation, it would seem even more difficult for the IS team to develop a strategic vision of its international operations if international frequently seem to get the short end of the stick in operational priorities. Should an international team or task force be created, then it is reasonable to suspect that it would face resistance on the part of managers and workers dominated

by domestic concerns. The international team might well be expected to get secondary priority in peoples' work activities. Thus a political battle might ensue. The international team might be asked to justify its international priorities against domestic priorities, which would be very much closer and better understood by both the "judges and the juries." Clearly the *role of the international IS manager vis-à-vis other managers* needs to be studied from the management perspective.
- *Skill shortage.* IS management at PM also mentioned an "eroding skill base threat." They observed that there is a shortage of people with the talent for designing and building complex systems at the international level. PM believes that one reason for this is that it is "in competition with software houses who pay higher salaries." As a result of this difficulty, PM has found it increasingly easy to out-source the most complex systems to external companies that provide programming services.

  Both the politics and economic rationale for out-sourcing are areas of growing concern. By the fall of 1989, Kodak and several other companies announced that they were out-sourcing large chunks of their information systems to vendors. Kodak out-sourced much of its operations to IBM. Part of the rationale lies in cost and complexity management. The skill shortage may be another part of it. (Can IBM attract talent more easily than Kodak?) The transference of risk is another important factor. Since this is a long-term process that is only now beginning to spread, the jury may still be out regarding the long-term effects. Many questions come to mind: What if there is a conflict over the contract? What happenss if changes in corporate strategy necessitate a change in the information technology infrastructure later on, but the out-source company demands much higher costs for implementing the changes than would have been the case internally? What if the company loses the critical human talent necessary to recover its systems if needed? Also, how are the contracts arranged? On the positive side, the rationale is that the IS function will be able to concentrate on *strategic systems* while the older base systems are being handled on the outside. At the time of this writing the outcome is unknown, but it is another important area to be studied, not only at the domestic level, but particlarly at the international level, since the tendency to use international services may be somewhat greater because of the cost and complexity involved.

  Although PM sees a risk in out-sourcing the most complex systems at the international level, the implication is that PM has no choice because of the skills shortage. It is clear that over-reliance on out-sourcing in the long run will weaken the multinational's ability to develop its own systems. The long-term implications of this strategy (or tactic) are not well investigated, but many, including PM, suspect that there may be a down side.

How Philip Morris Sees the Role of International Information Systems

For the most part, the IS management at Philip Morris does *not* see IS as taking a very great role in redesigning the way business works. Instead, they see the role of IS as being a map to the business—a process in which IS helps support business units in their operations. This supporting role is to take place on either a domestic or an international level. They do not believe that IS can create change. They say that "Information systems can *enable* change but not *drive* it (emphasis added)." They note that one of the difficulties in having a "flattened" organization is that it places a heavier burden on the president to be the change agent. This responsibility acts as an effective regulator on the amount of organizational change which can be handled.[22] The large scale of operations also poses a problem in this regard. PM has mentioned that senior management can lose touch with the market because the business is too large. Under these circumstances, it becomes more difficult to develop effective information systems.

To implement change more effectively on an international scale, the IS management is attempting to draw their executives *from the business units*. Doing so gives the IS department a direct connection with the business unit for which it might be developing an application or buiding a new system. It also ensures that the IS executive is very well versed in the details of the business unit being served.[23]

Another interesting difficulty mentioned by IS management at PM is that when there is an attempt to build or upgrade a new system in a business unit which is profitable, this *profitability acts as a barrier to innovation*. Under these circumstances, the line management team is busy maximizing profits and has little or no incentive to toy with either creating new systems or improving old ones. This is the famous "If it ain't broke, don't fix it" syndrome. The way the information systems are operating within the business unit may be right for that unit, but suboptimal for the company as a whole, and it may contradict

---

[22] This is an interesting observation because it goes against logic and common understanding regarding the supposed efficiency effects of adopting flatter organizations. The *flatter organization argument* holds that a simplified organization makes change easier, not harder: that having fewer levels of management to cope with gives the *change agent* better leverage to get work done. On the other hand, PM is arguing that this flatter organization means *less power to delegate* resulting in a cap on the amount of effective change which can of be implemented from the top. This would be an interesting area to study from the point of view of MIS research.

[23] As an aside, this same arrangement is used in Japanese government and industrial relations. Although the units of analysis are much larger, there is nevertheless a direct parallel. After leaving government at the mandatory retirement age, Japanese ministers and bureaucrats are placed in top-level industry jobs. This system helps to promote very close government and industry ties. See Chalmers Johnson, *MITI and the Japanese Miracle: The Growth of Industrial Policy, 1925–1975* (Stanford, CA: Stanford University Press, 1982).

the effort to develop common systems for the entire corporation. Generally, development of common systems requires some degree of business change—but *"business change is not wanted by successful business units."* Under some circumstances, this could lead to a conflict between the successful business unit and the IS function.[24]

As noted, PM is following a "multi-domestic" model or "regional integrative" model for their further development of international information systems. They are finding that it is easier to consolidate back-office rather than front-office systems. Their rule of thumb is that there is a tendency for the back office to take a more globalized structure than the front office. Why the "multi-domestic" model? IS management had tried to develop a worldwide data center. This centralized concept would have been the best solution to foster worldwide coordination and consolidation of many different critical functions in the organization. It immediately ran into problems. For example, a large number of requests for equipment purchases and funding for special projects started pouring in from data centers around the world, making it impossible to satisfy the demands. As a result of this experience, which occurred *before* a worldwide data center was built, Philip Morris adopted a "Triad" strategy for its data processing. It has concentrated its largest data centers in three locations: Europe, the United States, and Asia. It was simply impossible to build a comprehensive data processing facility.[25]

SUMMARY

As pressures rise for creation of ever more efficient and sophisticated international information systems, the information technology function must prepare to generate the needed skill base to build effectively.

---

[24] It does not take much guesswork to imagine who would win under these circumstances. It is almost certain that the IS function would find itself in a very difficult if not impossible situation. There is simply no argument it could make that would convince a line manager with P&L responsibility that it is worth risking profits to develop an unproven system innovation. One could hypothesize that only if the innovation were incremental in nature and had been proven to be both effective and nondisruptive to regular business operations would it stand a chance of not being crushed by opposition from the line management. Even under those circumstances, the justification would be difficult. Sheth and Ram call this phenomenon the *satisfaction with status quo,* and they discuss this in their book, *Bringing Innovation to Market: How to Break Corporate and Customer Barriers* (New York: John Wiley & Sons, Inc., 1987).

[25] There is a complex set of arguments regarding the balance between centralization and decentralization of data centers and the measurement and assessment of the efficiencies involved. In the case of Philip Morris, they found that the unexpected problems in coordination outweighed any advantages which might accrue from consolidation. This research has found several examples where the complexities of coordination on a global scale served as a powerful deterrent to consolidation.

- Systems development can maintain a global orientation without necessarily building global systems.
- The inherited system of repetitive national data processing centers will give way soon to more integrated data processing facilities with lower overall costs.
- Any type of consolidation or change in work habits in different countries may immediately raise serious political problems with which the information systems function must be prepared to cope.
- Use of the "lead system" can simplify matters and yield a more effective effort.
- Look for people who can work in different cultures, are team players, and already have a proven track record in international assignments.

The Philip Morris interviews demonstrate that companies can definitely build effective international systems if a careful approach is adopted.

- Projects which can be implemented quickly should be chosen to avoid giving the impression of ineffectiveness.
- Solutions which have a demonstrably favorable cost effect on the business have a better chance of winning.
- Any serious international systems should have a tested and well thought-out business case before it is fully accepted by the information systems function.
- It is better to pick projects which have the *least* effect on executive management, otherwise you risk getting your head chopped off by a strong country manager.
- Give priority to basic infrastructure projects before getting involved in detailed applications which will bring you into the specifics of the operations of individual functions.
- Develop the ability to model international data and design systems which bring about greater data homogeneity around the world throughout the multinational.

CHAPTER

19

Strategy #3: Build an Anticipative Infrastructure

If one is committing valuable resources toward a large international project, then build something with growth potential. Besides having built-in flexibility for the future, you may wish to allocate some of the savings achieved toward building further infrastructure. Expect to face many obstacles, including the "national manager" problem. "Covert infrastructure building" means adopting projects that both meet the short-term goals being set forth by management and yield benefits for long-term developments in infrastructure. Changing or merging data specifications and building transportable systems architectures are examples of this. The Syntex case shows what can happen when the best-laid plans are wrecked by a headstrong national manager.

DISCUSSION

Today's CIO faces great pressures in responding to the needs for change. The panoply of rapid technological change is well publicized. This change means, for example, that the information technology function must constantly plan for regular equipment replacement. In addition, the very rapid developments which have taken place in workstations and personal computers have turned into a very major challenge regarding traditional assumptions about distribution of computing resources.[1] In addition to hardware change, there is constant evolution in database technology, operating systems, telecommunications controls, and other related technologies. These place an even greater strain on the data processing infrastructure, because it must constantly adapt to new ways of doing things. The environment changes rapidly also, particularly at the international level. For example, the provision of international telecommunications has changed greatly over time. Circuits which in the past were unavailable or too expensive are now possible. Even some developing countries have broken down a number of the barriers in international telecommunications that made private networking impossible in the past. Very traditional and conservative organizations such as the Deutches Bundespost have started making changes in the availability of services, with greater flexibility than before. In general, infrastructures in various countries around the world have become friendlier and easier to work with in building up the information infrastructure of multinational corporations. All of these types of changes mean that the CIO and managerial team must work hard to continually adjust to circumstances. However, it is the changing nature of business strategies which do the most to place the information technology function under pressure.

Rapidly changing business strategies and structures can place severe pressures against the needs of the information system for several reasons. Although in some multinationals the CIO is involved in the top levels of strategic planning, this situation is more the exception than the rule; and the result is that for most organizations involved in formulating information technology strategy, there is more of a reactive mode. Strategy comes down from on high and the information technology is forced to respond. Under these conditions,

---

[1] As an analogy, we could say that the impact of the high-powered work station and personal computer on the infrastructure of computing in many organizations is similar to the impact of the development of the automobile on the future of the railroad industry.

Chapter 19   Strategy #3: Build an Anticipative Infrastructure

many of the most important initiatives may come after the fact. In the worst-case scenario, the strategic decision at the highest levels of the multinational is made with a dangerous disregard for the information technology implications, and the result may be an unpleasant discovery at a later time that the strategy cannot be realized because the information technology challenges are insurmountable. However, even when the consequences are not so disastrous, the problems faced by the CIO can be severe. Another factor complicating life lies in the underlying difference between a technological and business strategy.

The historical development of the information technology infrastructure of the multinational has a dynamic all its own, determined in large part by the various technology improvements and options that become available. As systems become larger, there is a natural sequence toward higher-powered machines. As user demands rise at the fringes of the "information empire" the introduction of high-powered work stations or minicomputer complexes can be used to put out the fires of rebellion among the users and their departments. However, business strategy is by no means driven by information technology and in fact moves in a different path, driven by different criteria and trade-offs. The logical development and upgrading of the information technology infrastructure in a part of the organization may be stifled because of business reasons (e.g., preparations may be under way to sell off those assets). The basics of the business strategy have a logic separate from information technology; and in all but the fewest multinationals it is the business strategy that dominates completely. Information technology is a submissive servant to corporate strategy, one of the many tools used to accomplish the ends.

These factors make it difficult for the information systems professionals to respond quickly to business strategy, and they make it *impossible* to control or drive it.

Other factors can throw monkey wrenches into the information systems plans for the multinational as well. National managers can hinder global plans since they are only interested in national or regional performance. In many if not most multinationals, the role of the national manager is very powerful. As seen from a few of the case studies and as confirmed by other interviews, the national manager is typically a line manager who rarely if ever has come up through the ranks of the information systems function. As a result the national manager may see information systems as more of a burden than an opportunity. In some multinationals, the emphasis on strict financial control is so great that information technology plans can be throttled severely. Thus, the information systems infrastructure is forced into a strategy of making a series of short-term tactical movements, rather than undertaking any significant strategic initiatives. The national manager may be undertaking the same type of strategy to pump up revenues for the year.[2] There is nothing to prevent the national manager from doing this, particularly if there are sound business reasons for halting any potential investment within that managerial jurisdiction. However, from the point of view of the multinational as a whole, the fact that a single national manager can have a tremendous effect on efforts being made on behalf of the entire global information system is indicative of a systematic problem in the managerial structure of the multinational that will not go away in the foreseeable future.

The final result of the "national manager" problem is that allocation of local resources for solving a corporate-wide problem may be difficult when the top priorities are usually local in nature. This problem is classical in the multinational corporation and is probably faced by many other functional areas of the multinational, but it is exacerbated by the different perceptions of the data processing professional and "all others" in the corporation. This problem complicates the political dimension for the information technology function. It must ask for resources at the local level (and many times systems development projects are quite expensive) and yet appeal to the interest of the "global dimension" of the multinational to get approval. This is at best shaky political ground upon which to stand.

In addition, managing the different parts of the information systems function can be difficult when local resources are used up in meeting global objectives without any clear benefit accruing to the local organization, particularly under conditions of resource scarcity. So besides having a political problem within the general line management of the multinational, the CIO may face a problem *within* the local data processing organizations. The hard-pressed data processing manager at the local level may be under considerable pressure from his constituency to meet user demands. To take resources away from meeting those efforts in order to satisy the "global imperative" may place the local management of the information technology function in a difficult position—having to make trade-offs between those higher up in their function, and the local line management which wants results at the national level.[3]

---

[2]In other words, the national manager may be acting rationally in seeking short-term goals, thereby crushing initiatives originating in the information technology function. The information technology function may not be the only group suffering from the rule of the national manager. One would imagine that perhaps all functions would suffer equally. Much has been written, however, about how because of a lack of understanding on the part of top management of the details and peculiar dynamics of information technology, that particular function can suffer more severely than others.

[3]The argument presented here places the question in a dichotomous dimension—either local or global orientation. In many organizations the distinction may not be so clear, particularly if there
(*continued*)

The information technology function under these difficult conditions must focus on building infrastructures that are able to adjust more rapidly to changing business strategies. From the very beginning, designs for different systems development projects must be made with flexibility in mind. Solutions that are specifically designed to allow modification should be placed at a premium. This idea of flexibility must also be implemented at the systems architecture level as well. In terms of human resources, many leading multinationals already place a premium upon flexibility, others are less future-oriented. However, in terms of the systems development effort, flexibility can help if implemented in this dimension as well.

In some of the interviews I conducted, it was possible to detect covert infrastructure building strategies on the part of the CIO. In this type of strategy, the information technology management continually seeks to meet the short-term goals of line management; but at the same time, while being engaged in these building initiatives, the information technology management makes a conscious decision to build in *excess capacity* or capability. This means that at a future time, some infrastructure capability can be drawn upon. It is like money in the bank, so to speak. Another related strategy is to take advantage of the savings that result from rationalization in the data processing infrastructure or operations.[4] For example, as systems are upgraded and made more efficient, a measurable savings accrues to the corporation. However, using this strategy, instead of returning all of the benefit to the corporation, the information technology function may capture some of the recovered value and use it for internal improvements in building up the infrastructure. Depending upon the size of the operation, this can provide a substantial resource.[5] In this way the CIO can covertly build in excess capacity while meeting the short-term goals of the multinational.

---

is a regional flavor to the operations, as many times there is. However, this distinction gives us a means to understand the polarities and dimensions of strategy. Being able to take a specific multinational corporation, measure it, assess its strategy, and then classify it according to this dimension is another matter. Like so many other management concepts, it breaks down when subjected to practice. This, however, does not mean it loses its effectiveness as an analytical tool. Conceptual tools such as this may not ever be operational but they are useful concepts nevertheless.

[4] I would like to thank Joseph Ferreira of the Index Group for his thoughts regarding this problem.

[5] It is difficult to predict exactly how such a process might work in individual multinational corporations. The variances in individual circumstances are so great, including the way resources are accounted for, that it is impossible to make a general rule. However, the general principle should be realizable by information technology management.

Examples of an anticipative information technology infrastructure might include (but not be limited to) the following:

- *International telecommunications.* Multinational corporations many times have dozens of separate networks, which have been put in place for a variety of reasons over time. Telecommunications linkages tend to grow as needed, and not to change very much once they are in place. New technologies such as multiplexing and fast-packet switching[6] with private networks are providing many opportunities for consolidation of many separate data circuits into single circuits, although it appears easier to do this at the national than the international level.[7] As this is done, it is possible for the information technology function to capture the surplus value from the savings and return only part of it to the multinational corporation, thereby keeping the rest for internal investment and improvement purposes. Pantages reported that in the case of Imperial Chemical Industrie's (ICI), there were four separate layers of information systems operating throughout the world, and the company was operating separate telecommunications networks within each country in which it was doing business.[8] The better to integrate its global operations, ICI concentrated on building a single worldwide network for document transfer, then worked to determine where it was possible to create common systems on an application-by-application basis.

- *Use of transportable systems architectures.* Many multinationals today are faced with carrying a large burden of incompatible equipment, even though in many cases the equipment is supplied by the same vendor. However, newer generations of technology are providing enhanced connectivity, and a considerably greater transferability of applications. This means, in effect, that applications can be moved to more powerful machines without too much trouble, and certainly without any fundamental rewriting of code. Making hardware and systems architecture investment decisions in such a way as to give priority to this type of architecture will yield future benefits that are not necessarily taken into account in a short-term perspective.

---

[6] Fast-packet technology allows data, voice, image, and video to be simultaneously carried on the backbone data network of the organization.

[7] This topic is specifically discussed with references to ISDN and the many services it will provide by Victoria A. Brown, "Calling the Shots with New Communications Networks," *The Journal of Business Strategy,* November/December 1988, pp. 46–49.

[8] Angeline Pantages, "The Right IS Chemistry," *Datamation,* 35 (16), August 15, 1989, pp. 61–62. The complexity of the Imperial Chemical Industries' computing and telecommunications environment made it impossible for them to search for or even attempt to create a worldwide integrated system. For companies such as ICI, the "global" system is more a myth than an attainable reality.

- *Globalization of data specifications.* One of the great inhibitors in development of global or more integrative strategies is the incompatibility that has grown up at the national (local) level in the design of databases and the specifications for data. The development of this type of variation is easy to understand as, in the absence of any strong incentive to build transnational applications, each national team will develop its own unique approach to different problems with which they are presented. As a result, any effort to consolidate and standardize databases and data definitions can quickly run into a massive amount of difficulty. One could generalize and say that it is at this level where one encounters much of the "local" nature of "local" data processing. Much of the variance may derive not so much from specific strategic and business requirements which exist at the local level as from minor variances which grew up with no particular reference to strategy, but just because of lack of central coordination. In other words, applications and systems that do most of their work at the national level can still serve as an effective part of the global information system if they are standardized correctly. When building new applications, even at the local level, the information technology functions should be required to the greatest amount feasible to ensure that details of data are set so that, should consolidation at the global level be required in the future, it can be built in without difficulty. Achieving this ability for local national applications to work effectively with the global information system may mean building extra definition tables into data dictionaries, or leaving holes which can be filled later. It may mean making a quick reference check to a central register that might be maintained somewhere in the multinational, but it is a step which will help ensure a smoother transition to globalization.

These, then, are some of the important dimensions which must be considered in building an *anticipative infrastructure* in the multinational corporation. There are political, managerial, and technical dimensions which must be considered. In some cases, the building of future capabilities may be in a sense covert in that it is made a part of short-term efforts. This may mean that the information technology function must appear to perform short-term while really acting long-term. It may be a piece of masterful deception, but after all, the long-term viability of the information technology infrastructure is at stake.

SYNTEX PHARMACEUTICAL

Syntex is a worldwide healthcare company. Its product focus is in human pharmaceuticals, diagnostics, and animal health. Backing all these businesses is a substantial research and development operation which is at work on the discovery, development, and registration of tomorrow's medicines. It has developed a forward-thinking human resources policy that encourages subordinate appraisals of their managers and public health awareness, all aimed at increasing general productivity.[9] Syntex is no stranger to inovation in management of the sales force. In the early 1980s it started using a modified Delphi technique to generate parameterized models for allocation of sales force personnel. The models told Syntex to increase its sales force size, which it did, and the result was a $25 million and 8 percent yearly increase in sales for much of the 1980s.[10] In packaging, Syntex created an easy-to-use, prefilled, disposable, one-dose applicator for applying antifungal cream, along with a new manufacturing line and set of procedures to manufacture the package.[11]

By 1988, Syntex was investing heavily in continued naproxen production and had patented more than 100 ways to manufacture the drug, hoping to continue its dominance in manufacturing of the drug after its patent expires in 1993.[12] It also manufactured ticlopidine, which helps to prevent the blood clots that cause strokes.[13] Its drug ganciclovir was the earliest approved drug for treating cytomegalovirus, which is a retinal tissue infection that attacks the vision of persons who are immunosuppressed.[14]

Information technology in Syntex is utilized and directed at a local level, mirroring the decentralized philosophy of the company.[15] In the late 1980s, the level of decentralization had reached such a point, with personal

---

[9]For the role of Syntex in subordinate appraisals, see H. John Bernardin and Richard W. Beatty, "Can Subordinate Appraisals Enhance Managerial Productivity?" *Sloan Management Review*, 28 (4), Summer 1987, pp. 63–73. It has also taken a strong position in supporting its employees who have the HIV virus, and in providing regular updates on breakthroughs in AIDS research. See Gwynn C. Akin, "Syntex Corporation Links Employee Education with AIDS Policy," *Business and Health*, 4 (11), September 1987, pp. 56–57. Syntex is presented as one of the leading-edge models for AIDS in the workplace in Martha McDonald, "How to Deal with AIDS in the Work Place," *Business and Health*, 8 (7), July 1990, pp. 12–22.

[10]Leonard M. Lodish, Ellen Curtis, Michael Ness, and M. Kerry Simpson, "Sales Force Sizing and Deployment Using a Decision Calculus Model at Syntex Laboratories," *Interfaces*, 18 (1), January/February 1988, pp. 5–20.

[11]Bruce R. Holmgren, "All-New Package Runs Well on All-New Line," *Packaging*, 33 (7), May 1988, pp. 44–48.

[12]It was reported that Syntex had sales of $941 million in 1987. The expiration of patent rights on a drug is a serious matter for pharmaceutical companies. The Syntex strategy was to build up its capabilities for mass production of the drug, and to patent the methods of manufacturing, so that even when naproxin lost patent protection, Syntex would still maintain an advantage in the market. See Gerald Parkinson, "Syntex Prepares for the Future," *Chemical Week*, 143 (3), July 20, 1988, pp. 40–41.

[13]See "Reginald Rhein, Jr., "Science Finally Strikes Back at Strokes," *Business Week*, Industrial/Technology Edition (3064), August 8, 1988, pp. 50–51.

[14]See Cynthia Starr, "Syntex Laboratories Sets Its Sights on CMV Retinitis," *Drug Topics*, 134 (21), November 5, 1990, pp. 19–20.

[15]Like all pharmaceutical companies, Syntex is forced to operate on a country-by-country basis because of the heavily regulated nature of the health care industry in most countries.

computers in the hands of end users, that most applications were being created with no control or coordination from the central information-technology management function. Syntex IS management had to work hard to set up coherent management of end-user computer utilization and applications development.[16] Another approach to the dangers of too much decentralization was to emphasize cross-functional systems, the creation of which required setting up centralized information systems groups to ensure that standards of some type were adhered to. Syntex used this approach in its laboratory unit.[17] In 1989, Syntex set up a joint venture with Procter & Gamble to distribute its drug Naprosyn. This drug, manufactured by Syntex, was the number 4 prescription drug in the United States and the top-selling antiarthritic. The 50-50 joint venture was estimated capable of producing sales of more than $200 million in its first year alone, as Naprosyn was transformed into an over-the-counter drug.[18]

The strategy of the company may be described as being highly research-intensive in searching for new products that will lead profitability in the future.[19] Syntex must continually make heavy investments into basic research and development to come up with breakthrough products that will earn revenues into the future. At the same time, it must defend its position as a manufacturer before its patents run out, and this is usually done by perfecting distribution and brand name recognition, and by developing manufacturing efficiencies which cannot be equalled by a competitor.

Syntex has pursued a policy of prudent tax management. It is incorporated in Panama and enjoys a tax status of a foreign-owned company through its use of offshore islands—such as the Bahamas—for residency, manufacture, and supply purposes.

Locating some operations away from the major industrial countries has cost advantages, but in terms of the information system, it can be a headache. Many of the places where Syntex has settled do not have the level of investment in the country infrastructure that we take for granted in America. Electricity and phones do not work efficiently, technology is slow to reach the countries, and technical support is hard to find.

Syntex's emphasis on decentralized decision-making challenges the concepts of central policy making, information sharing, and economy-of-scale negotiation and agreement with vendors.

---

[16]This is reported in Jeff Moad, "PCs: The Second Wave," *Datamation,* International Edition, 35 (3), February 1, 1989, pp. 14–20.

[17]See Jeff Moad, "Navigating Cross-Functional IS Waters," *Datamation,* 35 (5), March 1, 1989, pp. 73–75.

[18]Zachary Schiller, "Can P&G Commandeer More Shelves in the Medicine Chest?" *Business Week,* Industrial/Technology Edition (3099), April 10, 1989, pp. 64, 67.

[19]*Note:* It takes on average approximately 17 years to take a new drug from the initial discovery in the laboratory to full commercialization in the various markets around the world.

The Role of Information Technology

Syntex has in the past adopted several novel approaches to management of information technology within its corporation, including innovative maintenance programs for its IBM peripherals that created a savings of $400,000 in a three-year period. This self-maintenance program was based on a comprehensive risk analysis done *for each device* in the information technology infrastructure.[20]

A corporate decision was made to introduce a worldwide network for the purposes of transmitting messages among the companies. The selected platform was a system developed by Wang, using their product Mailway over dialed public telephone lines. The Mailway product is optimized for transmission of documents through an electronic mail facility. Documents and files can be easily transmitted from one location to another through the Mailway facility without any special conversion, formatting, or other transformations, such as compression, generally associated with data communication of documents. Documents, including mailing lists, source code programs, macros, and so on, which have been created on one Wang system, can be transmitted to another Wang system and used easily. All of their special characteristics, such as formatting, are also transmitted with them.

In 1987, it was reported that the international traffic volume between different sites was not enough to support leased international lines. The facilities around the world were in need of sharing data on only an hourly basis, not all the time. In the Palo Alto headquarters, Syntex was using 600 personal computers, 450 of which were connected to IBM mainframes through a Rolm CBX-II Model 9000 digital telephone switch. On a worldwide basis, Syntex had 50 Wang VS-100s working as mail servers and also supporting local electronic mail within each facility. In the SYVA diagnostic equipment division, Syntex was using 60 Apple MacIntosh computers. Syntex was experimenting with a system of "Electronic New Drug Applications" so as to enable them to use electronic forms to apply for drug approval from the FDA.[21]

By the early 1980s, the systems were in place and attempts were made to introduce automatic transmission using all the features of the Mailway package. The subsequent attempts to correct this situation and get a reliable system into production took a great deal of time on the part of the IS staff. A world-wide network was in place that was unreliable. The user community

---

[20] Alexia Martin, "Field Service: Firms Explore 'Help-Yourself' Attitude in Maintenance," *Computerworld*, 21 (33), August 17, 1987, p. S2. Syntex bought its own regular maintenance on its IBM mainframe, but started to provide maintenance on peripherals on a materials-and-time basis.

[21] Mark Stephens, "Syntex Global Network Based on Dial-Up Lines," *InfoWorld*, 9 (40), October 5, 1987, p. 16.

progressively began to bypass it by means of courier, telex, and, more recently, by the accelerating use of facsimile machines.

Two major technical needs figured in the solution which was found. The network had been based on dialed public telephone lines that were both unreliable and slow. The quality of public telephone circuits deteriorates quickly once the application must move away from the developed countries of the OECD area. In the case of Syntex, their use of countries such as Panama and of off-shore islands (as tax havens) ensured that the IS function would be unable to take advantage of the most advanced and highest quality telephone service. In addition, the data communication speeds associated with this type of arrangement are 1200 baud or 2400 baud, but rarely any faster. At 1200 baud, a 100-page document might take half an hour or more. Clearly, Syntex had a difficult problem.

As it became increasingly obvious that an improvement in the way of doing things was needed, Syntex began to search for a way either to upgrade or to replace the Wang system it had been using. As it began to think through the problem, two very important criteria emerged. First, it must protect the large investment it had already made in the Wang equipment. It was not going to consider any solution that would result in junking its installed base. Not only the investment in the installed base was involved. Syntex had come to rely on a certain way of working, and people were trained that way. Any vast change would surely disrupt business operations and cause a stink—something that the information systems function was determined to avoid.

Second, another important criterion which emerged was the need for the vendor to be able to service all of the geographical locations in which Syntex was operating data processing equipment. There was no doubt that only a major vendor could meet both of these requirements.

After consideration of several vendors, Syntex was impressed with the new Wang Office system. It was a vast improvement over the older-generation Mailway system and would be able to take advantage of the much less expensive X.25 public packet switched networks for data transmission, rather than requiring that Syntex continue to use the expensive dial-up methods it had grown accustomed to in the past. This feature would definitely protect the investment which had been made in Wang equipment. In addition, research indicated that X.25 networking was available from the PTT in each of the countries where Syntex operates, thus making it possible to build an international network quickly.[22]

---

[22] In most countries, all telephone, telex, and data communications services are operated by a national agency, called the PTT, which stands for Postal Telephone and Telegraph. Only in a handful of countries (United States, England, Japan, and a few others) have the PTTs oppened up to competition and privatization.

According to Syntex sources, a steering committee was formed to oversee the launch, testing, financing, and implementation of the project.[23] The information systems function created a very well-prepared presentation for the corporate vice president and vice chairman of the main board. The multimillion dollar project was approved at the corporate level.

In order to get going, Syntex started a pilot project to ensure that all of the details of the Office system would work as they were intended. Much effort went into planning the full-scale details of the project. However, as the project began to pick up steam, having as it did the full approval of the top levels of corporate management, some problems started to unravel the project.[24]

As the project gathered momentum, it was necesary to begin the process of bringing in the European side of Syntex's operations, a major part of its business. One of the first steps it took in this direction was to set up a European task force which reportedly did a very good job of identifying all of the critical information technology applications needed throughout the European offices of Syntex. As the plan for the worldwide electronic messaging and data transfer application began to take shape, it became obvious that the proportions of European needs varied depending on whether the observer was in the United States at Syntex headquarters or in Europe working at the local level.[25] What was the problem?

Although the project had been clearly approved at the corporate level, the way in which Syntex information systems was budgeted meant that each national manager had to pay for their systems. Even though the project had been agreed to by the top levels of the corporation, it took only one strong rejection from a regional manager to wreck the effort and bring the entire project to a halt.

---

[23] For a study of the use of steering committees in the insurance industry, see the study of The Hartford Insurance Group and its use of various committees in William Harrison, "How the Information Executive Can Promote Change," *Journal of Information Management*, 8 (2), Spring 1987, pp. 11–16.

[24] John Fayerweather has commented about the challenges of training local management, "LRP for International Operations," *California Management Review*, 1960/61, pp. 23–35. He notes: "In overseas executive development such assumptions about ... [common managerial culture] ... are not so broadly justified. Research into managerial organizations abroad emphasizes the prevalence of administrative attitudes which are substantially different from those of the U.S. managerial culture.... The codes which govern men's relations with others, the way they approach their work, their motivations, and other attitudes are in many societies significantly different from our own and strongly influence executive performance."

[25] *Note:* At one time, Tupperware had a similiar problem. It was solved by bringing in leaders from each of the overseas locations for several days of brainstorming to build consensus for the best course of action to take. According to Tupperware, this proved to be a very successful model for action. The IS team at Syntex did not take this approach.

In this case, the Syntex IS team was unable to solve the problem. This eventually led the IS team to curtail its international implementation efforts. As this case study is being written, the clock is ticking on the support for Mailway. Wang has come under increasing scrutiny as a vendor of choice because of their financial status, and a service which is unreliable will continue to receive less demand for its service.

The Syntex example is one of an information systems team that did everything right and yet faced considerable frustration of their plans. Perhaps in light of the state of affairs for Wang, Syntex may do well to adopt a completely different vendor. We might conclude that the problem is essentially political in nature. Did the IS team underestimate the power of the management team in place at individual national location? Yes, it certainly did. It failed to anticipate the veto power of a single regional manager in the Bahamas. After so much work, the rejection came as a bolt of lightning. It completely decimated the morale of the team. What can we learn from this case?

- *Need for agreement from the user community.* One of the problems in the strategy by the Syntex IS team is the failure to get agreement from the user community.[26] Before the development of the plan for upgrading the Mailway system, the users apparently had started developing, on their own, alternative systems of international communications that met their needs. The proposed solution was developed in response to the upgrading possibilities provided by the vendor. There is little indication that the IS team consulted the users or did any extensive analysis of what their needs were.

- *Need to assess the political power of the different players.* Another factor in this case is that the IS team failed to appreciate the political power of the various regional managers of the company. Because there was corporate approval and support for the project the assumption that it would automatically be approved was a serious error. It led to a tremendous psychological blow when the plan was rejected. It may be that Syntex, as a whole, does not have very formal chains of command for approval of such projects. If this is the case, then it is understandable that the IS team misjudged the situation. The obvious shock that was encountered

---

[26]This situation has been widely discussed in the MIS literature. Failure to get this type of agreement is not specifically an international problem, but rather is a problem which can occur in any type of implementation effort. In general, the importance of the study of this phenomenon began in the late 1970s as minicomputers and departmental systems began to acceleerate the spread of information technology access outside of the central installation to the end-user community. Particularly with regard to questions of office automation, where information technology was encountering users with little or no experience with computers, this problem became very important.

indicates that the highly decentralized nature of the company meant that corporate headquarters approval was not enough. In addition, it does not appear that top management at corporate headquarters was willing to go to bat for IS on a "global" basis.

- *Need to assess the long term prospects of the vendor before a major upgrade.* Wang as a computer company has been in trouble since the mid-1980s, and there were clear indications of this when the Syntex IS team was making its study and series of recommendations. For example, instead of working toward an upgrade, it might have used the opportunity to dump the vendor and move to a stronger player.[27]

- *Need to present different solutions based on mixed technologies and media.* There are indications from the interviews that the users had become used to working with alternative methods of communicating. The assumption on the part of the IS team appears to be that the reason for user defection from the Mailway system was due to the poor response and problems with international telecommunications. But what investigation was made into alternative media and ways of transmitting the data internationally? For example, what is the indication that with the proposed new system, the users would not continue to bypass in favor of facsimile systems?[28]

- *Need to resist being stampeded into a solution by a threat of no support.* To what extent did the Wang announcement that it was going to cease supporting its previous generation of software weigh in the decision? It is clear from the interviews that this factor was very important in pushing the IS team to accelerate their decision-making process. One also suspects that in order to bolster its obviously declining revenues from the user base, Wang had consciously taken this decision to *coax* its user base to switch over to the new—and more profitable for Wang—system.[29]

---

[27]There are obvious counter-arguments to this, but how strong would these arguments have to be to weigh against the prospects of a rapidly fading vendor? There are no indications form the interviews that the long-term prospects of Wang were taken into consideration; and one must ask, therefore, about the long-range "vision" of the IS team.

[28]It may be that the users would have continued to defect. Given the convenience and ease of use of facsimile systems, it is actually *easier* to imagine that the defections would continue rather than stop. Can we believe that the facsimile systems which had already been purchased outside the control of the IS function would be dismantled? There are obvious examples of facsimile solutions which would have worked well with X.25, for example, G-IV digital facsimile. However, there is no indication this type of solution, which could also have included options such as voice mail, was ever considered.

[29]This is not meant to be criticism of Wang. It is common for computer vendors to make various market moves which coax their user base into more advanced, and also more expensive, systems. Wang needed revenue, and also had developed a superior system. Want was and remains a superior provider of office automation systems, and its new alliance with IBM should strengthen it considerably.

If, however, the IS team had been giving serious consideration to other vendors, or if it was concerned about the long-term survivability of Wang, then the announcement regarding future withdrawal of support would have had little impact. It would have simply provided an extra argument to dump Wang. We cannot tell the degree of pressure this announcement had, on the Syntex decision, but it appears there is a lesson for everyone.

It is difficult to build an "anticipative" infrastructure when not everyone is willing to anticipate.

SUMMARY

Building the information technology infrastructure of the multinational has both a political and an economic dimension.

- Projects which concentrate at first more on "nonpolitical" solutions appear to fare better.
- Infrastructure should be built with both a long-term and short-picture in mind, even though local management can usually see only the short-term.
- The "national manager problem" should not be underestimated.

The Syntex example shows how subsidiary data processing organizations can wreck the prospects for building a global information system.

- Tracing the expenditure commitments for a global system gives important clues to where one might expect political problems.
- Well thought-out technical plans are only one of several factors which might explain success or failure.

CHAPTER

20

Strategy #4: Tear Down the "National" Model

Because of its administrative legacy, which ensures that its underlying structure was set before information technology came on the scene, the multinational corporation of today finds itself burdened with many different semi-autonomous data centers located in each major country where it does business. The tide has shifted, however, and the trend now is to connect them—to build integrated information systems that work as a single complex organism the world over and thereby control the operations of the multinational. The Caterpillar case is an example of such a system—a massively centralized system with points of presence throughout the world.

Chapter 20 Strategy #4: Tear Down the "National" Model   297

DISCUSSION

One goal of the regionalization of nationally organized data processing centers is to recover residual value in computing. For our purposes, residual value means the amount of excess costs which can be eliminated through consolidation of data processing centers, particularly when a national model is changed to either a regional or global (i.e., centralized) model in the distribution and operations of data centers. The reasons why different multinationals have been involved in setting up national data centers have been suggested by writers who examined transborder data flow and showed that many firms are forced to do so through national legislation.[1] This structure, which was inherited from the previous noncomputing age, has left a foundation of decentralization and strong national management that has provided a basis from which it is now possible to recover much of the initial investment. Although multinationals for a variety of reasons were once forced to adopt this type of decentralized approach, we now see that many of the assumptions have changed, thus uncovering new opportunities for the information technology function. While national regulations in the past required multinationals to build redundant data processing centers, these pressures have now been removed with the breaking down of national barriers.[2] Thus it is possible for the multinational to locate data centers according to more strict economic criteria. If the highly varied nature of national markets required multinationals to adopt a highly decentralized national strategy in the past, then once those barriers break down through homologation initiatives by[3] supranational authorities, such as the European Economic Community in Brussels, it becomes correspondingly possible for the multinational to achieve more economies of scale in market-oriented activities. Customization of products and services can be cut down; and the supporting information technology and applications infrastructure can be consolidated to reduce costs and potentially to improve servicing of business applications. In most organizations, this process of regionalization would proceed through several stages.

---

[1] See Edward M. Roche, Seymour Goodman, and Hsinchun Chen, "The Landscape of International Computing," *Advances in Computing,* Spring 1992.

[2] Robert Reich in *The Work of Nations: Preparing Ourselves for 21st-Century Capitalism* (New York: A. A. Knopf, 1991) has argued this process is almost complete and that national barriers are far less important compared to the early postwar period.

[3] The term *homologation* refers to the standardization of telecommunications service offerings and equipment standards.

First, many of the applications and systems which are hosted in the different national data processing locations would be transferred to the larger host at the regional headquarters. After this task is completed, the operations at the national area would be wound down, streamlined, and turned into a different type of operation involving more of an "information center" role for its activities. For a while, much of the local talent would be retained both to ensure a smooth transition and also to help in the retraining required.[4] Some of these employees might later be made redundant. For those kept on, their activities may remain much the same except that they will be working at a distance remote from the actual site of data processing.

Note that the primary economies of scale in data processing will come not from changing the nature of applications (at least in the early stages) but from the operational side as the number of main processors are operating efficiently.

Second, after these steps are completed, the multinational can then turn to exploitation of the data processing scale by consolidation of applications and also through redesigning much of the underlying workflow of the organization. In terms of application consolidation, the multinational will find that the adaptability of each individual application to regionalization will depend on the degree to which it is unique. There are some functions which will be better candidates than others for consolidation. Building maintenance and some aspects of human resources may be good candidates. In the manufacturing area, scheduling, inventory control, and manufacturing costs information accounting may also be good candidates for consolidation. However, the process of making applications work together in this manner typically takes a considerable amount of time. The reconciliation of the internal codes in an inventory or parts system may take years to work out, particularly if the different national practices over time have resulted in a highly specialized operation in each country. These types of fundamental problems of data conversion and

---

[4]The research of John Leslie King seems to suggest that the political issue may be more important than the economic one. "Centralized Versus Decentralized Computing: Organizational Considerations and Management Options," *Computing Surveys*, 15 (4), December 1983, pp. 319–349. He sees the debate about centralization versus decentralization as involving more than simply calculations about economic trade-offs. He goes so far as to say, "Computing should not be thought of as a tool by which the basic structures and behaviors of organizations can be changed." His research indicates, "Control must be recognized as the most important issue in making centralization/decentralization decisions." This idea would fit into the type of strategy I indicate here. The search for regionalization or centralization is part of the need for corporations to exercise more control over their operations and resources.

homogolation can be serious and require a great deal of effort. Of even more consequence is the number of problems which occur when "almost similar" programs and their data files are brought together into a basically similar structure, but with many small undocumented changes that have been made in the past to suit local conditions. When incompatible systems are merged together in this fashion, many unexpected and time-consuming incompatibilities between the "similar" applications that are being merged begin to appear. This type of problem is dangerous, because it is difficult to anticipate the total amount of time that will be required for the project as a whole and because of the inpredictable nature of undocumented changes. Under these circumstances, the benefits of having access to the considerable body of local talent which was responsible for maintaining the application is critical to success. Without this individual expertise, the consolidation effort will in most cases flounder.

Third, upon completion of this full consolidation process at the application level, the multinational should be able to enjoy two types of savings: savings from operation of fewer computing facilities along with the advantage of making use of very large computing and supercomputing facilities; and savings from more efficient processing of applications.

A vision of the integrated multinational computer environment is provided by Iyer and Schkade, who discuss the use of data management, decision support, and executive support within the context of the global management of a multinational corporation. They argue that their "holistic" or systemic view will afford many benefits to the multinational.[5]

When the organization has begun reaping these advantages, then the re-engineering of the firm and its work processes can take place. This should be started in the early stages of the process of consolidation, but it can only be implemented when the larger regional data processing data centers are operational. The essence of consoldation is looking for applications which can bridge the various functional processes from any of the national data processing centers of the multinational. It would be possible in the early stages of the process to plan for these eventual transformations in the functioning of the

---

[5]Raja K. Iyer and Lawrence L. Schkade, "Management Support Systems for Multinational Business," *Information and Management,* 12 (2), February 1987, pp. 59–64. My own personal opinion is that there may be a danger in placing too much emphasis on executive support systems because in organizations as large as today's multinational corporation, I am not sure how much difference an individual really makes. It may be better to concentrate on the entire underlying information infrastructure of the multinational. This opinion, however, is subjective and intuitive, rather than factual or experiential.

data processing operation; however, practical experience suggests that these plans will be modified so much as the real nature of the national differences in procedures is discovered that it might be just as well to wait until the consolidation process is more advanced.

These, then, are the three steps in regionalization of data processing. They are also phases which might be considered for a globalization effort, although in most cases this would be an even more complex undertaking, particularly if an intermediate step would involve regionalization efforts.

For the complex multinational, the steps towards globalization might involve first regionalization, then globalization (centralization); for a smaller firm, a straight move to globalization may be possible. What determines the path to take? The size of the organization; the extent of decentralization; the relative importance of the regional market to overall operations; the amount of experience with rationalization efforts—these might be a few of the factors. Some multinationals, for example, are finding that the use of consulting firms that specialize in these areas can go far in assessing the general background to the situation.

In accomplishing this process of consolidation—tearing down the walls that have isolated different data processing operations behind "Berlin Walls" of national barriers—many factors must be considered, including the human and managerial problems, the actual computer architecture, the continuing need to meet local data processing requirements, the match with corporate strategy, and the proper distribution of applications.

The human resources and managerial problems in this type of process can be substantial. In any change of this magnitude, the psychological and multicultural dimensions must be considered.[6] Not all countries of the world have the callous attitude toward labor found in the United States, where frequently people are treated as disposable dishtowels. For example, various labor practices in Europe may prohibit the most radical of consolidation efforts. Any initiative which is overtly aimed at head-count reductions is likely to run into serious problems, particularly when the data processing function is unionized. However, there are two aspects of this consolidation process which are positive, or at least not negative, for labor. First, the general consolidation of operations and data processing itself, (e.g., the transfer of the actual site of data processing) should not necessarily be interpreted to mean that jobs will be lost. Even when this occurs, there is a great need for the MNC to

---

[6] In their review of several large-scale international projects, Horwitch and Prahalad emphasized (p. 13) the need to "include individuals representing various backgrounds and views" as a critical element of a successful project. Mel Horwitch and C. K. Prahalad, Managing Multi-Organization Enterprises: The Emerging Strategic Frontier," *Sloan Management Review*, Winter 1981, pp. 3–16.

continue to tap the national expertise of the local data processing workers. The only difference is that their role may be enlarged by taking on more of a consulting-type profile vis-à-vis the central data processing core of the multinational. The transformation of the local (national) data processing center into a type of information center arrangement places more not fewer demands upon human resources. Second, there is always the question of staffing the new regional data processing operations, which have been heightened in profile and responsibility. In this connection, the best talent from each of the national organizations can be put together into the global applications development teams and, in fact, take on even more working responsibility. It is my view that as long as it is clear that human resources are not being abused, it will be possible to get cooperation for the benefit of the entire organization.[7]

Another major set of factors which must be managed involves the actual information architecture of the infrastructure. It is fortunate in this respect that major vendors such as IBM have been aggressively moving toward architectures which lend themselves to consolidation and greater integration in processing. The range of the System 390 series of machines with ES/9000 systems, for example, means that the movement of applications can be made from one machine to another, theoretically at least, with a minimum of rewriting of code because Systems Application Architecture (SAA) is available at all levels of the system from the small minicomputer up to the supercomputer level.[8] The movement of many European manufacturing firms toward the concept of "open systems" will provide many important opportunities to consolidate and relink the disparate parts of the information empire found in today's multinational corporation. Open systems will be based in large part upon the Unix operating system developed originally at Bell Laboratories, but they will pose more practical problems in terms of systems integration than environments which have IBM equipment. Much of the European effort in building up infor-

---

[7]Lawrence Franko showed how the managerial structure of the multinational firm changes as a function of where it was on the growth and maturity curve ("Who Manages Multinational Enterprises?" *Columbia Journal of World Business*, Summer 1973, pp. 30–42). His results may appear more appropriate to Western firms than for Japanese multinationals, which are so culturally different. He did not specifically study the data processing functions. If his observations are correct, then we can hypothesize the following: As the data processing center moves towards regionalization, a significant amount of headquarters involvement will be apparent, with managerial talent from the center dominating the process. As the data processing system stabilizes, this presence will diminish.

[8]The realities of this practical application of SAA are still unknown. SAA is more of a strategic direction for IBM rather than a specific family of specific products. Like its Systems Network Architecture (SNA), SAA will continue to evolve throughout the 1990s.

mation systems and European companies, similar in effort to the desire of the Japanese to build *hinomaru* companies,[9] has been to defeat the success of IBM in the European market. However, the demise of many of the European vendors has put a serious question mark on this effort.[10] As a result, multinationals may not be able to rely on European vendors for implementation of large global strategies. One would suspect that for global applications and very large multinationals, the market share of non-IBM vendors is even smaller than in the economies as a whole.

In any case, the movement toward regionalization or globalization (centralization) will open up a great variety of opportunities for transformation and accompanying updating of the installed base of computer and telecommunications equipment. This will require the information technology function to make a great number of decisions regarding replacement and upgrading of equpment. As the trade-offs are made, principles of information economics will have to be applied so that there is a mapping of business strategy against the selection of applications and supporting equipment infrastructure.[11] This

---

[9] A *hinomaru* company is one which is 100 percent Japanese. *Hinomaru* is the rising sun found in the center of the Japanese flag.

[10] At the beginning of the 1990s, Bull was facing massive losses and prospects for more than a 30 percent reduction in head count; ICL had been purchased by Fujitsu, although it had been a profitable company; Siemens was struggling with the Nixdorf acquisition and still losing money while at the same time depending upon the Japanese for mainframe and supercomputer technology. There were no other significant vendors of consequence in Europe. No realistic assessment would conclude that Europe is capable of building a world-class computer industry within the decade.

[11] Information economics is the discipline of making decisions regarding acquisition of equipment or development of new computer applications based on weighted assessments of both technology factors and business factors. The basic concepts of information economics are set forth by Marilyn M. Parker and Robert J. Benson with H. E. Trainor in *Information Economics: Linking Business Performance and Information Technology* (Englewood Cliffs, NJ: Prentice-Hall, 1988). They focus on balancing technological and business risk and on balancing quantitative versus qualitative factors in assessing investment priorities. See also Parker and Benson, *Information Economics: An Introduction*, working paper (Center for the Study of Data Processing, Washington University, 1987); *Advancing the State of the Art in Strategic Planning*, working paper (in same series, 1987); *Key Points in Strategic Planning*, working paper (in same series, 1988); "Information Economics," *Datamation,* December 1, 1987. On the topic of information technology, it is the view of Paul A. Strassman (from *The Business Value of Information,* in the ICIT Book), that under many cases, investments in information technology do not pay off at all. For an examination of the value of information technology investment at the national economy level, see the variety of studies by Stephen Roach, listed in the references. In terms of microeconomic efficiency, see Paul Osterman, "The Impact of Computers on the Employment of Clerks and Managers," *Industrial and Labor Relations Review,* 39 (2), January 1986. For an experimental study of information economics in the semiconductor industry, see Edward M. Roche et. al., *Experimental Applications of Group Decision Support Systems in an Information Economics Analysis of Competition in the Semiconductor Industry*, I–VI, working papers (MIS Department, University of Arizona, 1990).

is done by a weighted system of both tangible and intangible benefits all set within the context of business risk versus technological risk.[12]

As this process is taking place and the ensuing efficiencies are gained, it will still be necessary to continue to meet, and even expand, the local requirements for data processing. The migration of applications from the national to the regional or global level must not be at the sacrifice of those applications that have been built up over a great number of years at the local area and have been designed to meet the peculiar nature of the market in which they are operating.

The transfer of processing location theoretically should not affect applications at all, if telecommunications linkages are built which deliver the computer processing capacity to all needed locations without adding complex procedures. However, there may be a gradual pressure at the regional or global level to homogenize the structure and functioning of applications throughout the multinational. This change would be a great mistake, for it would risk losing the individual nature of the data processing in each national market. Instead of using regionalization and centralization as a way to eliminate local differences, the systems development process must act to preserve those differences which are important locally. This action does not mean that some standardization is not appropriate. One would expect that many of the variances in local data processing arrangements can be made to work well together throughout the multinational without losing their ability to meet the unique data processing requirements at each subsidiary. In this connection, a careful assessment of this balance between local data processing needs and the needs of the corporation as a whole must be made on a case-by-case basis as the process of consolidation takes place. There is no substitute for the careful examination of each point in choosing which applications or characteristics to eliminate and which to keep in the transfer process to the new data processing infrastructure.

In preserving the balance between global, regional, and local applications, the information technology function must ensure that a match is made between this strategy and the distribution of applications.[13] Applications which should be distributed throughout the entire organization must be built from

---

[12] The *technological* dimension of risk is associated with those failures in systems development which occur because improper assessment has been made of the technological feasibility of a project being attempted. *Business* risk occurs when a specific systems development effort does not meet the business objectives in spite of the investment which is made. Striking a balance between these two types of risk involves making sure that neither *line management* nor the *information systems function* is allowed to dominate decision-making and planning completely.

[13] Christian Koenig and Raymond-Alain Thietart ("Technology and Organization: The Mutual Organization in the European Aerospace Industry," *International Studies of Management and Organization*, XVII (4), pp. 6–30) analyze the "mutual organization" and the peculiar mix of centralization and decentralization that characterized four high-technology European industries: The Airbus

(continued)

a centralized point of view. There are exceptions to this. Some newer types of distributed processing allow databases to be distributed in many different locations. For example, a centralized inventory control data base may be "distributed" so that an updated version of it is kept in the various regional locations at all times. Technically, this is no longer a centralized architecture but a distributed one. This type of arrangement retains many of the essential features of a centralized system. In particular, a master copy of the data and information is kept at the center of the corporation. We must distinguish here between a computer science and a managerial orientation in analysis and classification of these matters. A computer science orientation would specify that this is a decentralized application set-up, whereas a managerial orientation would specify that it is a centralized application because the managerial control, planning, and original data are kept at the center of the organization. Within the context of the multinational, this type of application would still be considered global and essentially centralized in nature. These are fuzzy distinctions perhaps, but these types of managerial problems are not ones which lend themselves to sharp distinctions and fixed definitions. Management is not mathematics, and methodologies are not proofs of theorems.

On the other hand, regional and local applications must be identified, or re-identified, and set up in those locations in the most efficient manner. But what techniques can be used to classify the applications? A few rules of thumb might be suggested. Applications which tend toward globalization have a preponderance of similarities in all major data processing locations, regardless of the country they are in. They are built to support a series of information transactions which relate to the entire business structure of the multinational and not just to the business activities within a single nation-state. They support those internal transactions that are responsible for the core efficiencies of the multinational. They are probably composed of information and data that are minimally covered by the privacy laws which tend to limit transborder data flows of critical information and data being used by the applications. On the other hand, local applications and data functions have the opposite characteristics. They are characterized by limited domain applications, which are based on administrative procedures of an external nature that are unique to the nation state where they are operating. Many times these local applications are resistant to internationalization because they have no use whatsoever outside the national borders of the country in which they originate. They may be based on special sets of data which are not transportable outside the borders of the originating country, and they may have little if anything to do with the overall efficiency of the organization and its internalization of transactions. In

---

and Concorde jet aircraft projects, the ESRO (European Space Research Organization), and the ELDO (European Launcher Development Organization). They define the "mutual organization" as a "quasi-firm [which] relates a prime contractor as principal and a group of subcontractors as agents in a recurring relationship...a "network" since two or more organizations are involved in a long term relationship" (pp. 10–11).

this connection, it might be possible to construct a scale of "globalization versus localization" for each application under consideration in this type of effort. The types of variables which might be considered include the following: the ratio of the number of international transactions to the number of internal or local transactions; the location of key database; and the extent to which the same application exists at other parts of the corporation.

Another part of the problem involves matching the distribution of applications to corporate strategy. The starting point in most successful implementations of global strategic business applications is the identification of applications that are essential to the day-to-day operations of the business. These are the core applications, which should have the highest priorities at all levels, including planning, resource allocation, security, and disaster recovery. After they are implemented, then other "stringer" and "follower" applications can follow.

One of the most difficult challenges is management of the transition: how to manage the people involved in a transition such as this, including the need to rationalize data processing operations and cut overheads. The use of the "lead team" should do much in this respect. If the teams are led by project managers who have management experience from several years of activities, then at least for the skilled personnel who have been tapped for team activities, the transition should provide a great stimulus. There may, however, be a heightened risk of having conflicting lines of authority reporting to headquarters, regional data processing centers, and the local level. In a worst cast scenario, a fracture could develop between local line management and the lead team, which is taking its orders from headquarters. If those members of the local data processing infrastructure who have not been tapped to work on the global projects manage to build a psychological bridge with the local line management of the organization, and if they are determined to thwart the activities of the global team, then a highly disruptive confrontation may take place. To alleviate this problem, successful MNCs have adopted a type of democratic approach by using the national member of the team in each case to provide guidance for managing the situation and in not alienating labor from the business process.

The process of tearing down the national walls that have isolated different data processing centers in the multinational corporation may produce severe problems in management of human resources, including difficulties in team dynamics; in repositioning the data processing and telecommunications infrastructure; in searching for efficiencies; and in continuing to meet the peculiar nonsystemwide requirements of each national market.

CATERPILLAR LOGISTICS

Caterpillar is one of the largest industrial concerns in the world and is a household name in the construction sector in almost every part of the world.

Its bright yellow machines are copied by its many competitors, the toughest of which is the Japanese company Komatsu. Caterpillar manufactures and distributes heavy earthmoving equipment, large-scale turbine generators capable of powering entire cities, and engines, which are supplied to a variety of other companies. From the deserts of Kuwait to the Arctic environment of Prudhoe Bay, one finds Caterpillar heavy equipment in operation 24 hours per day.

Caterpillar was one of the earlier adopters of the Electronic Document Interchange (EDI), a standard for computerized exchange of trade documentation which it was reported to be using in the mid-1980s to link together more than 250 suppliers and 450 supplier locations into a single network using the EDI facilities of the General Electric Information Services Company (GEISCO).[14]

At that time, Caterpillar was in one of its worst financial and business crises, caused (1) by falling oil prices, which decreased the demand for Caterpillar equipment used in the oil industry; (2) by excessive debt in many countries of the developing world, which resulted in considerably less funds available to purchase the equipment for large infrastructure projects; (3) by tough competition at the smaller, lighter end of the market; and (4) by currency-conversion costs, through which shareholders lost about $800 million in value in 1986 alone due to the rise of the dollar.[15] Caterpillar was under constant pressure from its Japanese rival Komatsu, which had adopted as its corporate motto "Caterpillar Maru," or "Encircle Caterpillar." Komatsu attacked in the early 1980s with a strategy based on market segmentation and cost leadership. Caterpillar had done well until 1981, when it had year-end profits of $587 million; but during 1982–1985 Caterpillar reported losses in 4 of 14 quarters.[16] From 1982–1984, Caterpillar suffered almost $1 billion in losses. A turnaround started by 1987, although Caterpillar was forced to subsidize its dealers so they could meet the prices being offered by the competition.[17] It had cut costs by more than 25 percent since 1982 and was planning on cutting an additional 15 percent by 1990, a staggering amount by any reckoning. Nor was it satisfied with the $118 million profit it made the second quarter of 1987.[18] By 1988, Caterpillar's constant efforts in cutting costs in every corner, broadening its product line, and continuing to improve its quality

---

[14] Thomas F. Dillon, "Caterpillar Connects with EDI," *Purchasing World*, 30 (8), August 1986, pp. 62–64.

[15] Dexter Hutchins, "Caterpillar's Triple Whammy," *Fortune*, 114 (9), October 27, 1986, pp. 91–92.

[16] J. Taylor Sims, "Japanese Market Entry Strategy at Work: Komatsu vs. Caterpillar," *International Marketing Review*, 3 (3), Autumn 1986, pp. 21–32.

[17] Harlan S. Byrne, "Track of the Cat: Caterpillar Is Bulldozing Its Way to Higher Profits," *Barron's*, 67 (14), April 6, 1987, pp. 13, 70–71.

[18] Kathleen Deveny, "For Caterpillar, the Metamorphosis Isn't Over," *Business Week*, Industrial/Technology Edition (3014), August 31, 1987, pp. 72–74.

Chapter 20 Strategy #4: Tear Down the "National" Model   **307**

had started to pay off in terms of its rivalry with Komatsu, which was retrenching.[19] It had, for example, in spite of the financial hardships, introduced the new Challenger 65 agricultural tractor, which had a special new steel-reinforced rubber track and was the product of about seven years of research and development.[20] It introduced a new "low-swirl" air system for its new high-output 3116 six-cylinder mid-range diesel engine designed for trucking fleets.[21] Caterpillar also took advantage of the growth in demand for less than 200-horsepower crawler tractors and started integrating microprocessors, operator-friendly controls, air-conditioning, and other improvements to build a substantial presence in this market.[22] It is interesting that this is the precise type of market competitors like Komatsu would see as a good entry point, and it was assiduously blocked by Caterpillar. Caterpillar continued to introduce new models up throught 1990, when it introduced a line of crawler excavators based on high-pressure hydraulics, with reports of much higher reliability than previous models.[23] It continued its product innovation with continued improvements in its popular line of articulated haulers.[24]

On the finanicial side, by 1986 Caterpillar had suffered a 20 percent loss in value when it announced even poorer earnings. Although its market share in heavy equipment was up to 37 percent over 10 percent for Komatsu (which had to raise prices to dealers because of the shift in the yen to dollar rate), Caterpillar announced a five-year, $1 billion investment in factory automation and a very strong push to reduce costs.[25] It invested $7.5 million in three flexible machining cells in its Glasgow, Scotland, plant, designed to build nine types of carrier and case/frame assemblies. It was reportedly one of the most automated facilities in Europe.[26] Caterpillar was doing well in some parts

---

[19] Kathleen Deveny, Corie Brown, and William J. Hampton, "Going for the Lion's Share: The Time Is Right for U.S. Companies to Reclaim Lost Markets," *Business Week,* Industrial/Technology Edition (3061), July 18, 1988, pp. 70–72. For other financial information and reasons for Caterpillar's success, see Ronald Henkoff, "This Cat Is Acting Like a Tiger," *Fortune,* 118 (14), December 19, 1988, pp. 69–76.

[20] Anonymous, "Caterpillar: Challenging a 'Soft' Market," *Business Marketing,* 73 (8), August 1988, pp. 40, 42.

[21] Jim Mele, "Medium-Duty Diesels Go Heavy-Duty," *Fleet Owner,* Big Fleet Edition, August 1988, pp. 60–65.

[22] Bill Wagner, "New Trends in Smaller Crawler Tractors," *Equipment Management,* 18 (8), August 1990, pp. 50–54.

[23] Bill Wagner, "Crawler Excavators," *Equipment Management,* 18 (9), September 1990, pp. 42–50.

[24] John Koski, "Equipment Selection: Highly Articulate," *Equipment Management,* 19 (1), January 1991, pp. 20–25.

[25] Barry Stavro, "Digging Out," *Forbes,* 138 (10), November 3, 1986, pp. 127–128.

[26] Peter Mullins, "Four of Europe's Best 'Flex' Systems," *Production,* 98 (4), October 1986, pp. 78–85.

of the world, such as Asia, where it had teamed up with dynamic Chinese entrepreneurs.[27] For some, the reemergence of success for Caterpillar amounted to a reaffirmation that U.S. companies were competitive when they really wished to be.[28]

As the cost-cutting pressure mounted, Caterpillar closed its U.S.-based assembly plants for lift trucks and moved them to the Republic of Korea and to the United Kingdom. It also started working hard with its suppliers to control quality and delivery times for incoming materials. One example of this was its handling of incoming parts and steel, for which Caterpillar set up an information system for materials management and advance scheduling of all work loads.[29] Caterpillar set up a training institute to train suppliers; and by 1990 more than 1,000 individuals from 400 suppliers had passed through its classrooms, an important part of the 2,500 U.S. suppliers with which it was spending more than $6 billion on goods and services annually.[30] It also continued working with its suppliers to build strategic networks and even helped suppliers figure out ways to cut costs when this was possible.[31]

On the other side of the value-added chain, Caterpillar started a special carrier certification program to ensure that none of its equipment being shipped incurred any damage. This system was automated, and relied heavily on auditing of past records of shipments.[32] Caterpillar also formed a corporate transportation council to make sure that critical shipping decisions were made correctly and were the most efficient in meeting both customer needs and stringent cost and safety criteria.[33]

On the sales side, Caterpillar began to dissect its approach to marketing. For example, at a trade show in Las Vegas, it used time-lapse photography to analyze the movement of spectators through its exhibits, and also followed up with questionnaires to analyze customer response.[34] Catepillar was cited as the most outstanding exhibitor for 1987 at trade shows for spaces of more

---

[27]Philip Rennie, "Dynasty Buying with Lee Ming Tee," *Rydge's,* 59 (9), September 1986, pp. 38–40. Lee was aiming to be the Caterpillar distributor for the People's Republic of China, and was already active with Caterpillar in Papua New Guinea and Australia's Northern Territory.

[28]Robert S. Eckley, "Caterpillar's Ordeal: Foreign Competition in Capital Goods," *Business Horizons,* 32 (2), March/April 1989, pp. 80–86.

[29]Walter Weart, "Warehousing: Caterpillar," *Distribution,* 85 (12), December 1986, p. 16.

[30]Shirley Cayer, "Welcome to Caterpillar's Quality Institute," *Purchasing,* 109 (2), August 16, 1990, pp. 80–84.

[31]Jordan D. Lewis, "Using Alliances to Build Market Power," *Planning Review,* 18 (5), September/October 1990, pp. 4–9, 48.

[32]Peter Bradley, "Paving the Road to Quality Transportation," *Purchasing,* 106 (1), January 19, 1989, pp. 100–109.

[33]Thomas M. Rosenthal, "Shippers Call the Shots," *Global Trade,* 110 (1), January 1990, pp. 10–12.

[34]Kate Bertrand, "Talking Turkey on Trade Shows," *Business Marketing,* 72 (3), March 1987, pp. 94–103.

than 100,000 square feet. It had achieved a 78 percent recall percentage to its show, the highest ever recorded.[35] As part of this effort, Caterpillar had set up a comprehensive sales training program and was participating in up to 45 trade shows each year; these shows carried the marketing burden of Caterpillar's having doubled its product line since 1981.[36] In the fifth annual survey of sales forces, Caterpillar was ranked Number 1 in the United States for industrial and farm equipment based on criteria such as quality of training, product and technical knowledge demonstrated by salespeople, and other important factors.[37] In support of the sales effort, Caterpillar set up a separate finance company to help its customer purchase products, and it also began to offer special maintenance programs to ensure the equipment lasted as long as possible and cost the least to operate.[38] It used the same data it had collected on maintenance to beef up its Certified Rebuild Program of old machines, which were reconditioned by Caterpillar and then sold under a new serial number.[39] Its comprehensive data demonstrated that more than 80 percent of repairs on equipment are done after a catastrophic failure has occurred, but that much of the long-term cost could be avoided if preventive maintenance is performed.[40] The maintenance schedules for heavy equipment are very complex and are created only after analysis of years of data which have been collected through the corporate information system.

Caterpillar also worked on improving its system of remanufacturing of parts, which would carry the same guarantee but be less expensive for customers.[41] Caterpillar also informally took over the publication of a trade magazine, *Materials Handling News*, and used it as a vehicle for advertising and also for measuring the response to its different ads. Although competitor organizations were also advertising in the same outlet, only Caterpillar was able to measure sales response.[42]

---

[35] Richard K. Swandby, Ian K. Sequeira, and Lori L. Bock, "1987's Most Memorable Exhibits: Caterpillar, Allen-Bradley Zoom to Top," *Business Marketing,* 73 (6), June 1988, pp. 60–68.

[36] J. Edward Roberts, "Training Trade Show Salespeople: How Caterpillar Does It," *Business Marketing,* 73 (6), June 1988, pp. 70–73.

[37] Martin Everett, William Keenan, Jr., Bill Kelley, Arthur Bragg, Thayer C. Taylor, and Richard Kern, "America's Best Sales Forces," *Sales & Marketing Management,* 141 (7), June 1989, pp. 31–48.

[38] James Braham, "Marrying Goods & Services," *Industry Week,* 237 (9), November 7, 1988, pp. 69–71.

[39] Glenn A. Endicott, "Repair, Rebuild or Replace? Emergency!" *Equipment Management,* 17 (10), October 1989, pp. 62–64.

[40] John Koski, "Pay Me Now, or Pay Me Later," *Equipment Management,* 19 (3), March 1991, pp. 10–15.

[41] Jim Mele, "The Changing Market for Reman'ed Parts," *Fleet Owner,* Big Fleet Edition, 85 (9), September 1990, pp. 95–100.

[42] Bruce Whitehall, "How Caterpillar's 'Sponsored Circulation' Reaches Small Users," *Industrial Marketing Digest,* 14 (3), Third Quarter 1989, pp. 13–19.

Caterpillar also worked very hard to ensure that information technology was an integral part of the plan to cut costs, improve quality, and give better customer service on a worldwide basis. By 1987 it had reduced its telecommunications costs by more than one-third by installing a fiber-optic system linking five major corporate facilities to the world headquarters. The system involved a network arranged in a star topology using an AT&T System/85 at the center and four System/75 PBXs at each of the four branch locations. The system was based on about 600 miles of glass fiber (carrying traffic from 11,000 terminals and workstations), more than 400 voice lines, and engineering applications such as image transmission. Caterpillar planned on installing even more fiber-optics cables to link into another 24 facilities.[43] The new networks enabled engineers at distant sites to send pictures to each other along with audio when they had to communicate regarding manufacturing or other problems. Caterpillar used teleconferencing equipment and began linking together manufacturing and engineering centers, which many times were thousands of miles apart.[44] It started to adopt a more flexible attitude toward information technology standardization by letting in a number of Macintosh Apple computers for desktop publishing applications.[45] It eventually added a 3M FaxXchange system, which would deliver eight facsimiles simultaneously, thus cutting down on its costs for sending out market and financial information to the many financial analysts and institutional investors to whom it had to report on a regular basis. It also used it to communicate to 10–75 dealers as needed.[46] Caterpillar's use of information technology continued to increase rapidly, and by 1988 it announced that it was involved in running simulations of all computer-integrated manufacturing operations before committing.[47] Caterpillar knew that any potential manufacturing system had to be completely simulated before scarce resources were committed because the manufacturing and the coordination involved had become so complex.[48] It worked hard at using information technology to link together more closely its dealers through a "dealer information system," which linked all the offices together and also to Caterpillar headquarters. This was part of the "extended enterprise" model adopted by Caterpillar, made possible through information

---

[43]Bob Hamel, "Caterpillar Nets Savings," *Network World*, 4 (12), March 23, 1987, p. 7.

[44]John Cox, "Image Device Helps Firm Pool Resources," *Network World*, 5 (35), August 29, 1988, pp. 15, 17.

[45]Sally Cusack, "Apple's Macintosh Not Just a Toy," *Computerworld*, 22 (5), February 1, 1988, p. 69.

[46]Anonymous, "Fax Switch Broadcasts Financials for Public Company," *Networking Management*, 7 (7), July 1989, pp. 74–75.

[47]David Wortman, "CIM and Simulation," *Manufacturing Systems*, 6 (4), April 1988, pp. 44–50.

[48]Ira P. Krepchin, " 'We Simulate All Major Projects,' " *Modern Materials Handling*, 43 (9), August 1988, pp. 83–86.

technology.[49] It also fit in with Caterpillar's use of "functional shiftability," which is the process of contracting out certain functions or shifting them backward or forward through the marketing channel.[50]

Caterpillar's work with its suppliers was also brought into the picture as far as cost cutting was concerned. It was not content with the delivery charges of its steel suppliers, and through its traffic manager department began to work with its shippers to improve their efficiency, including automated linkages through the information system.[51]

It even built an information system to audit medical claims from doctors and ensure that costs did not go out of line. Through this system, it was able to shave 10 to 12 percent from its medical costs.[52] It issued guidelines stating how much it was willing to pay for certain medical procedures. [53] The system uses "CodeReview," a software package created by Health Payment Review, Inc. of Boston, Massachusetts.[54] Caterpillar spent $221 million in health claims in 1989 and was expecting to spend even more in 1990, the third year of having the system in place.[55] Without the system, claims would have been even higher.

By the end of the 1980s, Caterpillar had built flexible manufacturing systems (FMS) for its 3500 and 3600 series diesel engines, with four machining centers being operated by DEC VAX minicomputers and a DEC PDP computer. It was heading toward making parts for assembly only three to five days ahead of when they were ordered by customers.[56] Caterpillar's massive industrial reorganization effort was named "Plant With A Future." It represented an investment of $1.5 billion. The incoming parts for its H-Series tractors by 1989 were being manufactured on a just-in-time basis using three machine FMS units from Cincinnati Milacron, for a reduction of in-process inventory and lead times of more than 50 percent compared with other older

---

[49] Anonymous, "When It Pays to Think Big: The 'Extended Enterprise,' " *IBM Directions*, June 1988, pp. 2–5.

[50] Ronald D. Michman, "Managing Structural Changes in Marketing Channels," *Journal of Business & Industrial Marketing*, 5 (2), Summer/Fall 1990, pp. 5–14.

[51] E. J. Muller and Jay Gordon, "Caterpillar's Great Lakes' Strategy/Domino's Pushes Productivity," *Distribution*, 86 (9), September 1987, pp. 40–45.

[52] Don C. Holloway, Robert D. Hertenstein, and Richard H. Egdahl, "Correcting Surgical Claims Codes Yields Cost Savings," *Business & Health*, 5 (2), December 1987, pp. 26–30.

[53] Anonymous, "Companies Call the Shots on Transplant Coverage," *Employee Benefit Plan Review*, 42 (9), March 1988, pp. 13–14.

[54] Christine Woolsey, "Employer Spots Inflated Medical Bills," *Business Insurance*, 24 (26), June 25, 1990, pp. 3, 28.

[55] Mary Popa, "Back to Basics in Cost Containment," *Employee Benefit Plan Review*, 45 (9), March 1991, pp. 10–11.

[56] Clyde E. Witt, "Caterpillar Adds FMS to Engine Manufacturing," *Material Handling Engineering*, 44 (6), June 1989, pp. 78–82.

methods of manufacturing.[57] By early 1990, Caterpillar was reporting success with its Aurora, Illinois, plant, which was getting almost zero defect levels. In doing so it used an electric monorail to link storage and assembly areas for material handling to support the newly adopted "stack build" technique.[58] At its operation in Gosselies, Belgium, the "Plant With a Future" program—using automation, robots, and other types of facory systems—cut off 10 days from the time it took to build subassemblies, and resulted in a 30 percent increase in productivity for small-engine manufacturing. In its Grenoble, France, plant, it was using an unmanned crane and computerized flame cutter to reduce order fill time from 20 to only 8 days, and thereby to cut inventory levels by 50 percent, along with manufacturing space which was cut by 21 percent.[59] Caterpillar was getting into better position for 1992 in Europe.[60] However, European companies such as J. C. Bamford Excavators in England were very worried about Caterpillar taking a higher profile in Europe, particular as regards the strength of the latter's superior distribution system.[61] Caterpillar also worked hard at the more mundane aspects of manufacturing, such as development and utilization of the most automated work-holding and positioning equipment, which could also be responsible for substantial improvements in productivity.[62]

As the decade of the 1990s opened, Caterpillar was working harder at building a globally integrated information system that would link together its 32 manufacturing installations spread across 12 countries. Its manufacturing system was continuing the "Plants With a Future" program and working to get space savings, handle materials better, and automate wherever possible.[63] The original $1.5 billion investment in the modernization program had gone up to $2.3 billion by early 1990, and the high degree of vertical integration in Caterpillar had placed a premium on management of its information systems. Wall Street analysts believed the future was rosy for Caterpillar because of the great need in the United States for environmental cleanup, which

---

[57] Barbara Dutton, "Cat Climbs High with FMS," *Manufacturing Systems,* 7 (11), November 1989, pp. 16–22.

[58] Karen A. Auguston, "Caterpillar Slashes Lead Times from Weeks to Days," *Modern Materials Handling,* 45 (2), February 1990, pp. 48–51.

[59] Brian Bremner, "Can Caterpillar Inch Its Way Back to Heftier Profits?" *Business Week,* Industrial/Technology Edition (3125), September 25, 1989, pp. 75, 78. The same article reports, unfortunately, that the plant modernization process was over-budget and behind schedule at this point.

[60] Karen A. Auguston, "Caterpillar's Worldwide Strategy at Work in Belgium," *Modern Materials Handling,* 45 (8), July 1990, pp. 48–51.

[61] Matthew Lynn, "Digging for Victory," *Business,* October 1990, pp. 112–115.

[62] Paula M. Noaker, "Workholding: Firm and Flexible," *Manufacturing Engineering,* 105 (4), October 1990, pp. 37–40.

[63] Wes Iversen, "Information Systems: Tying It All Together," *Industry Week,* 239 (16), August 20, 1990, pp. 20–30.

uses heavy equipment, and also because of the growing and obvious need to rebuild the nation's infrastructure.[64] Writers such as Michael E. Porter were discussing how intense foreign competition was responsible for improvements in U.S. corporations, and how these improvements and turnarounds would not come under a system of market protection.[65] It was ranked as the highest of the industrials in its use of information technology by *Computerworld,* which cited the integration of its 32 manufacturing facilities around the world as being responsible for it getting such high marks.[66] By 1991, Caterpillar was using a 450-megahertz Allen-Bradley LAN/1 broadband local area network system to link together the total information flow of five different assembly lines into a continuous single process using its concept of the "Assembly Highway" at its plant in Decatur, Illinois.[67]

Another important part of the Plants With a Future modernization program involved the intensive use of Coordinate Measuring Machines (CMM), which were being used to greatly improve the throughput of metalworking operations. When CMM was mixed with Computer Integrated Manufacturing, Caterpillar was able to approach zero-defect manufacturing in some areas.[68]

Another critical application for the Caterpillar information system involved keeping exceedingly careful controls over costs. Caterpillar's cost information system was able to perform standard costing, monitor operational controls, and examine each product to determine its full costs.[69] By 1988, Caterpillar was operating a very aggressive program to benchmark their own internal performance against the costs of their competitors based on observation and analysis of their operations. This process alone had helped directly reduce Caterpillar's costs by 20 percent.[70]

Usually Caterpillar equipment represents a substantial investment on the part of the organization using it, and in many cases, the equipment performs a vital function which would cause a great amount of disruption if the equipment becomes inoperable. One can imagine the reaction of the operator of a small coal mine when one of the mine's three end-loaders is temporarily

---

[64]Thomas N. Cochran, "Cat Fancier," *Barron's,* 70 (28), July 9, 1990, p. 30.

[65]Michael E. Porter, "New Global Strategies for Competitive Advantage," *Planning Review,* 18 (3), May/June 1990, pp. 4–14.

[66]Michael Fitzgerald, "IS Helps 'Cat' Stay on Its Feet," *Computerworld,* October 8, 1990, pp. 58, 60.

[67]Bob Gilligan, "Caterpillar Grades Up Based on Broadband LAN," *Manufacturing Systems,* 9 (3), March 1991, p. 18–22.

[68]Don Stovicek, "CMMs Key to Plant with a Future," *Automation,* 37 (12), December 1990, pp. 24–25.

[69]Lou F. Jones, "Product Costing at Caterpillar," *Mangement Accounting,* 72 (8), February 1991, pp. 34–42.

[70]Lou Jones, "Competitor Cost Analysis at Caterpillar," *Management Accounting,* 70 (4), October 1988, pp. 32–38.

disabled. Until the machine comes back on line, production is reduced by a third, and usually employee time must be paid for as well. The same situation exists for a turbine generator supplying a small city or hospital complex with electrical power, or a diesel engine at a pumping station in the remote North Arctic or at a crude oil collection point in Plano, Texas. In any of these cases, it is critical that, should a breakdown occur, the Caterpillar equipment be made operational again within the shortest possible time.

The requirement that the equipment be kept running virtually at all times places a heavy burden upon the spare parts delivery system. Throughout the Caterpillar system, there are more than 250,000 individual parts which must be accounted for. Besides just the sheer number of parts involved, there is a tremendous range in size. Some parts are several feet or even yards long, and weigh thousands of pounds. Many parts are small and hand-sized, or even thimble-sized, one example being the numerous small filters that are placed inside the fuel lines of the machine. In addition, there is a large variability in where the spare parts are used. Obviously the type of equipment being used in the Arctic region is different from that in Texas, which in turn is different still from that found doing work in the Rainforest. Why is this variability important? Because in order to supply spare parts in a reasonable amount of time to each of the locations of the world where Caterpillar parts are being consumed (which includes almost every part of the world), Caterpillar is forced to calculate safety levels for stocking each of its part items.

The Caterpillar logistics and spare part supply operation is run from a central location in Morton, Illinois, in the heartland of the United States. This is also the manufacturing point for most of the spare parts. The logistics system is organized into roughly three tiers: the central organization in Morton, a handful of major regional supply centers, including several overseas locations such as Rotterdam and Sugano, Japan, and finally the individual dealers and service-point stations, each serviced by a regional supply center. Caterpillar guarantees that any part will be delivered anywhere in the world within 48 hours or the part is free of charge, and it uses this three-tiered logistics system to make good on this promise. The information technology supporting this 48-hour guarantee was developed with CASE technology. This development involved implementation of a new purchasing system, use of just-in-time inventory control, better scheduling, and a complete rethinking of how to work with both suppliers and customers.[71] Caterpillar also implemented a comprehensive training system for their dealers to help in the effort to improve parts availability and maintenance of equipment in the field.[72]

---

[71] Robert Knight, "Shop Floor Accepts CASE at a Caterpillar's Pace," *Software Magazine,* 10 (3), March 1990, pp. 72–73.

[72] S. Tamer Cavusgil, "The Importance of Distributor Training at Caterpillar," *Industrial Marketing Management,* 19 (1), February 1990, pp. 1–9.

The information system is completely centralized on a global basis and is run from a mainframe computer installation in Morton. Each of the regional distribution centers is connected into the Morton center with online computer linkages. Caterpillar uses a bar code system for much of its inventory control, and rigorously measures its performance in meeting customer demands for on-time delivery of spare parts. The system is set up so that in most cases the dealers are also linked in electronically, at least to the nearest regional distribution center. The system is capable of delivering a spare part in more than 80 percent of the time on an off-the-shelf basis. For those cases when the dealer does not have a part in stock (this occurs for parts which do not have so high a turnover rate), the dealer can consult the computer system linked to the regional center and order the part from that location. In the United States, most regional distribution centers are a maximum of eight hours' drive away from the dealer. Generally, the preparation and tear-down of the equipment being repaired take up a good deal of that time, and the part arrives within a reasonable time envelope.

In those cases, and they are relatively few, when the regional distribution center is temporarily without the part, the computer system is able to check the part's location within the nearest alternative dealer's stock, or is able to check the stocks of the next-closest regional distribution center. This search process is done automatically and is made possible because of the constant logging-in and logging-out of parts as they move through the logistics system from location to location. This type of checking for parts is "system wide," meaning that as the computer continues to check for parts, it can search through the entire Caterpillar system to cover all locations. When parts are unavailable, the search terminates at the giant Morton parts center, which has a special emergency order system operating around the clock to get orders filled in the shortest time.

The Catepillar operation at Morton is a very exciting place to visit. It is vast, and there are whirring red lights cautioning people against the dangers of the constantly moving loaders and delivery trucks. The performance percentages are posted daily and even hourly on the walls, and are always in the high 90s. Spare components are being shipped on a 24-hour-a-day basis to all parts of the world, using all types of services, including a nearby air strip. The central data processing function is constantly aware of the location of every part within the system as it moves from Morton, to the regional centers, to the dealers. In many cases, it has a record not only of the exact amount of each part held by the dealer, but also of the *shelf location* at the dealer's premises.

The solution that led to attaining such efficient delivery of spare parts came from an aggressive campaign that had spread over several years and involved constant comparison against competitors, breaking down the entire processing into the smallest components and analyzing the efficiency of each part, and working hard to simplify things where possible.[73] It can be argued that Caterpillar has reached a level of enviable success. This global system reaches all parts of the earth and allows Caterpillar to perform the complex safe-stocking-level calculations not only for each part, but also for each part *by location* as it is needed. This, of course, insures Caterpillar against overstocking tropical parts in the Arctic and Arctic parts in Kuwait.

SUMMARY

In most cases, it is necessary to break down the national model of data processing and consolidate or integrate matters into a global system, and doing this promises many benefits in terms of information technology costs as well as general cost savings for the corporation as a whole.

- Both historical tradition and limitations in technology made creation of "global" systems impossible or very difficult in the recent past.
- Consolidation of data centers will increase efficiency, particularly in regions such as Europe, where it is possible to run matters from a single location.
- There may be problems associated with consolidation, particularly as regards labor and workers within the data processing function, and in terms of national sovereignty and privacy legislation; and these may severely hinder the drive for efficiency and consolidation.
- It is not easy to choose how best to distribute applications and databases in the new environment.

The Caterpillar case shows many of the benefits of an efficiently operating globally centralized information system.

- It is possible to optimize performance of the logistics systems on a global basis, that is with global safe-stocking-level calculations.
- Even though the system is centralized from an architectural point of view, its "point of presence" is completely decentralized throughout all of the dealerships and regional distribution centers located in the world.
- In addition to the many benefits of being able to keep minimum stocking levels, the system helps provide superior customer service, which means that Caterpillar can keep its customer base loyal to its products and service.

---

[73] Neil S. Novich, "Leading-Edge Distribution Strategies," *Journal of Business Strategy*, 11 (6), November/December 1990, pp. 48–53.

CHAPTER

21

Strategy #5: Capture Residual Value

It is said that the data processing infrastructures of most multinational corporations are not set up in an efficient way and as a result cost the company millions in excess expenses yearly (or perhaps even monthly)! The process of capturing residual value from the information system involves working hard to eliminate as many duplicate facilities as possible. Competitive pressures for both cost reductions and performance increases will drive the multinationals to consolidate their data processing and soak up excess expenses associated with the old way of doing things. The Manufacturer's Hanover case demonstrates how some multinationals in financial services are taking what might appear at first to be radical steps to increase their overall efficiency in data processing.

DISCUSSION

In the past, because of the administrative heritage of the "pre-information society," the multinational corporation has developed a highly decentralized operational structure.[1] This structure was in place and well-entrenched long before the great advances in information technology of the 1970s and 1980s. As a result, information technology was "grafted" onto the top of the pre-existing managerial and operational infrastructure of the corporation. Information technology and its implementation followed the organization and not the other way around. If any re-engineering took place, it was the information technology function that was getting the short end of the stick.

The result of this administrative heritage is that most multinational corporations tend to have a decentralized structure, with strong, sometimes competing, national data processing organizations that are acting in the bulk of their operations as autonomous centers of information technology. Just as the line management responsible for a single country tended to grow in power and specialize, so too did the information technology function tend to grow specialized and self-contained behind national boundaries. Many actions taken by the host government also tended to encourage this trend. Controls on importation of information technology, labor regulations that determined staffing levels even for the data processing function, privacy legislation and other administrative controls that forced data processing of name-linked data to be done only within national borders, and other factors all tended to reinforce the decentralized national nature of the data processing infrastructures in multinational corporations. In most cases, these controls were not viewed as being too onerous, simply because the administrative heritage of the multinational was already strongly biased in the direction of strong national centers.

A discussion of the implications of computerized databanks is given by Laudon. He writes:

> From a technical and structural view, the central characteristic of the dossier society is the integration of distinct files serving unique programs and policies

---

[1] David F. Feeny, Brian R. Edwards, and Michael J. Earl mention "IT heritage" as one of the six variables that must be taken into consideration in assessing information technology in complex organizations. See "Complex Organizations and the Information Systems Function—a Research Study," Oxford Institute of Information Management, Research Paper Series RDP 87/7, p. 7.

into more or less permanent national data bases.... From a political and sociological view, the key feature of the dossier society is an aggregation of power in the federal government without precedent in peacetime America.... The technical means are now available and cheap enough to centralize and integrate the bits and pieces of American government and society into single, large, national constellations of power. As a result, these new technologies are increasingly important in determining how much and what kind of freedom, security, privacy, due process, and efficiency we will have.[2]

In any case, the result of the tendency to build separate data centers in each country where the MNC was doing business was the creation of a body of "warring feudal states" composed of different data processing operations run as a loose confederation within the global context of the multinational corporation.[3] If, for example, one were to have measured the total amount of data being processed at the local (national) level and compared it with the amount of data that was being transmitted to headquarters or to other subsidiaries and processed there, then the ratio would show that practically all but a very small percentage (less than 1%) was being processed locally. Particularly in the early stages of computerization, when batch processing was the predominant method of processing—and even later, when the concepts of telecommunications and networking meant little more than allowing batch uploads of information to a remote computer—the technology was just not there for the type of global transnational data processing that we see today.

What is the actual economic result of this administrative heritage of decentralized data processing centers? The most important result is that there

---

[2]Kenneth C. Laudon, *Dossier Society: Value Choices in the Design of National Information Systems* (New York: Columbia University Press, 1986). For a review of how privacy legislation was applied in Canada, which historically was one of the more sensitive countries as regards this issue, see Tom Riley, "Setting Standards—Data Privacy," *ComputerData*, 10 (12), December 1985, pp. 12–13. Riley reports on the standards set by IBM Canada Ltd.

[3]One wonders if the results found by David Dery will apply to the multinational corporation as it tries to consolidate its data processing centers. He writes: "Information technology is handicapped by structural arrangements. What information technology can do for management remains largely unrealized and, given the structures with which we dress information technology, its contributions remain largely unrealizable. We build large sizes so that information technology may be more efficiently used, but these bring together units which while sharing a desire to save, are in conflict with one another." See "Putting Information Technology to Work," *California Management Review*, XXII (2), Spring 1980, pp. 68–76.

is a significant amount of residual value left in the computing infrastructure. In other words, the potential for gaining efficiencies of scale and scope in data processing is very much greater now because there is stored-up value forced in the past by the negative effects of national regulations.

The answer to this is to move toward a consolidation of data centers. Depending on the structure of the multinational corporation and the nature of the national markets in which it is operating, it may have the opportunity to undergo a vast amount of reorganization, upgrade technology, and improve data processing efficiencies, all at the same time. A typical example might be a small multinational that is operating technology such as an IBM 3090 at its headquarters, with different small subsidiaries around the world operating System 36s or 38s for local processing. In smaller locations, it may have personal computer networks involved in limited data processing. For larger subsidiaries, the MNC may be operating larger machines such as IBM 4300 series. In these circumstances, it might be able to upgrade to AS/400 minicomputers, achieve efficiencies, consolidate many applications, and at the same time reduce the long-term costs of data processing. In considerably larger multinational corporations, the size of the information technology infrastructure is much greater, with more layers of equipment, more network connections, and probably a larger amount of residual value that can be recovered from the system.

Today's multinational corporation has a great deal of residual value left in its computing system, which can be squeezed out by transforming separate national data processing operations into regional data centers. The process of regionalization is appropriate for specific geographical areas of the world where many large-market nation-states are close together and share some type of synergy in terms of the market for the products of the multinational corporation. The most popular area of the world at the end of the 1980s to discuss in terms of regionalization of data processing was the European Economic Community. This was the most likely candidate for testing to see if it was possible to eliminate redundancies in national data processing and move to a more community-wide concept in which the new regionalized data processing infrastructure would serve the entire European market as a whole.

Grosse discusses the communications and information processing aspects of a regional solution for the multinational firm:

> [The multinational will receive a net benefit from]...placing the managers of the regional headquarters in a location with excellent communications, both to the home office and to affiliates...[and from] centralizing information at a manageable [i.e., regional] level, rather than overwhelming the home office with it, and rather than allowing excessive autonomy to each affiliate by not centralizing information at all....A regional headquarters...and its location is pri-

marily a function of passenger transportation and communication within the region.[4]

Although this process of consolidation is recognized widely to have a potential payoff in terms of data processing, there are remaining barriers to this process and these barriers are closely related to the national regulations that made it necessary in the first place to create a national model of data processing. Although a great amount has been printed regarding the effects of the creation of common market in 1992, still it is evident that this process will be a gradual one in which various trade barriers will be removed step-by-step over a period of time that extends beyond 1992. As late as 1989, multinationals were still complaining that getting leased private data circuits across Europe would take more than two years in waiting time because of the various conflicts between the different PTTs as monopoly carriers of data communications traffic. The unified Europe of 1992 will still likely have more than a dozen different national telephone companies. In spite of this, there are some estimates that from 1990 to 1995 many large European companies will increase the volume of data being telecommunicated over private networks by 40 percent to 100 percent per year, in spite of difficulties with standardization from country to country.[5] Much work still needs to be done in standardizing data-processing administrative procedures and requirements. There are clear differences among the different European states when it comes to privacy controls on computer-held databases, for example. There are also differences in standards for equipment, in national tax regimes (which determine the economic trade-offs for investments in computer equipment), and also in the cultural receptivity to information technology. The latter factor includes the role of white-collar labor organizations, which can prove to be an important determinant in "location economics" for the proper

---

[4] Robert E. Grosse, "Regional Offices in Multinational Firms," in Alan M. Rugman, ed., *New Theories of the Multinational Enterprise* (New York: St. Martin's Press, 1982). He notes (pp. 118–119), "Probably the single most important function of a regional office is *communication*. That is, gathering of information from customers, suppliers and affiliates in a region and communicating it to the firm's highest-level decision-makers, and vice versa. These decision-makers may include the regional office manager among them; the idea is that a better understanding of regional business conditions can be obtained through the regional office, and so home-office decision-making can be done by a reasonably manageable number of executives using already-screened information." [Emphasis added.]

[5] Jonathan B. Levine, "In Europe, the Next Walls to Fall Will Be Electronic," *Business Week*, Industrial/Technology Edition, December 3, 1990, pp. 158F. The report is based on estimates made by the Massachusetts-based consulting company Yankee Group from a survey it made of European corporations.

placing of data processing centers.[6] Efforts at data center consolidation can be influenced by the implementation of Codes of Conduct for the multinationals. Only when these national differences are eliminated and all of Europe is a level playing field will the conditions exist to make pure economic judgments regarding proper placement and consolidation of data processing facilities.

In the process of seeking regionalized scale economies in data processing, there are several ways in which the multinational can rationalize its operation. First, data processing power can be concentrated through the use of larger machines to service applications formerly served by different, smaller computers that were organized in the past around national borders. Second, duplication of personnel can be reduced, if the transition to a more consolidated data processing environment means that applications formerly processed separately can now be processed at single locations, thus using fewer human resources. Third, there can be a reduction in the use of duplicated computing resources, as well as the human resources and other factors of expense. For example, when several data processing centers and operations are consolidated into one, there is an immediate savings in terms of equipment, but there is a potentially greater savings in terms of personnel, particularly in reference to future systems development efforts that can now be consolidated. This latter savings alone can amount to more than any savings in capital equipment purchases. Finally, another great area of savings will occur in terms of reduction of redundant databases. In this connection, there are not only the direct savings that will come from maintenance and operation of the consolidated databases, but also the indirect savings that will occur as a result of the general reduction in complexity for the data processing establishment as a whole and for the databases and their operation and maintenance.

---

[6]For a discussion of the role of local labor organizations in connection with rationalization efforts in multinationals and how this affects the disclosure of information, see Richard L. Rowan and Duncan C. Campbell, "The Attempt to Regulate Industrial Relations through International Codes of Conduct," *Columbia Journal of World Business,* Summer 1983, pp. 64–72. They review the OECD *Declaration on International Investment and Multinational Enterprises,* which specifically mentions that employees should be able to get a great amount of detail regarding the global operations of the multinational for which they work. They also discuss the Vredeling proposal, which was adopted by the European Commission in October 1980. There is no specific mention made in any of these proposals for modifications of the information systems of the multinationals; however, it is obvious that the requirement that a great deal of detailed financial and operational information regarding the multinational be made available at the local level in each country would place a very different requirement upon the information technology function than would the absence of such a requirement. These proposals, and many like them, are a direct attack upon the headquarters/subsidiary relationship of dominance and submission that has been the historical pattern for management of multinationals. In the early stages of these debates, industry special interest groups in the United States resisted their implementation. However, toward the end of the 1980s, as more and more foreign investors bought into businesses in the United States, calls were raised for more detailed financial and operational reporting. The call for more reporting seems to come from the weak party. Regardless of the political dimension, this type of demand poses a challenge for the information technology function.

In carrying out this type of consolidation, the information-technology function must answer several questions. The replacement cycles for old equipment must be taken into consideration. If the bulk of the equipment located in the various national subsidiaries is old and near the end of its useful life, then the problem can be simplified by updating to newer equipment that is better designed to take advantage of more distributed processing, telecommunications intensity, and regionalization. However, if some of the national locations have relatively new equipment, then this fact will tend to force the information-technology function to slow its efforts in reaching consolidation while the useful life of the technology is used up. There are advantages and disadvantages to this action. Waiting can provide a better planning window in which to make sure that the gradual transition is smooth and that the various complex problems revolving around databases and applications development are solved. A disadvantage is that longer lead times give national authorities greater time to develop a counter-strategy, perhaps politically based, thus thwarting the globalization or regionalization effort. Another factor which complicates matters even more is that a careful estimation must be made of the economics of whether greater benefits are to be gained from riding the local (national) equipment through to the end of its useful life cycle, or seeking to capture efficiencies in the effort towards consolidation. This type of calculation is complex and is not amenable to a generalized formula.

In addition, any change of this magnitude in the way data processing is done in an organization will have a large effect upon managerial structures, including relationships of power, which exist not only within the data processing organization but extend out to line management.[7] Although this dimension of planning is frequently underestimated in its subtlety and complexity, in some cases, it can pose even more problems in carrying out information-technology strategy than arise from the technological dimension alone.

MANUFACTURERS HANOVER TRUST

Manufacturers Hanover Trust, affectionately abbreviated as "Manny-Hanny," is one of the older and perhaps more traditional commercial banks in the United States. Although the strength and power of the 1950s and 1960s for the U.S. banking sector is now little more than an ancient glorious past, Manny Hanny has continued to concentrate on innovation and the building of expertise

---

[7]For a discussion of the "foreign" manager in the host country, see Yoram Zeira and Ehud Harari, "Host-Country Organizations and Expatriate Managers in Europe," *California Management Review*, XXI (3), Spring 1979, pp. 40–50. Although this study does not discuss the question of hiring local managers within the data processing establishment per se, the same lessons could be applied. Their survey shows that "most respondents prefer to see host-country nationals rather than expatriates as top managers of foreign subsidiaries in their countries...."

in key product areas. It operates in many areas of the world, including Asia and Western Europe.

One of Manufacturers Hanover's largest lines of business is in providing letters of credit (LCs) to multinational firms involved in international trade. LCs provide the credit necessary for payments involved in shipping and purchasing internationally traded items. The LC is used when an importer and shipper agree on the specific terms for a trade. All parts of this contract must be settled before the money is actually released. Manufaturers Hanover was constantly trying to innovate in this line of business, and in the late 1980s was experimenting with providing customized multigrantor structures for a multibeneficiary Regulation 114 trust fund that would be targeted at affiliate or captive companies.[8]

Manny Hanny has also launched innovative programs such as the New York swingline credit facility, which operates a collateralized note-issuance facility (NIF), including a way to issue three-month Euronotes.[9] It also worked at increasing the intensity of its "multiple financial relationship" banking by introducing "One-For-All" Banking, a multiple-account product that puts together mutual funds and financial planning services and includes savings and checking, all supplemented by discounts on home mortgages.[10] An example of the wide-ranging types of activities it pursues is found in its participation in the restructuring of the Hong Kong-based Tung Shipping empire, the negotiations for which involved more than 200 banks and about $2.5 billion in assets.[11] Manny Hanny also worked in the leveraged buyout (LBO) market by handling much of the distribution for the R. J. Reynold's Nabisco deal, the distribution involving syndicates of $13.75 billion credit to cover the deal.[12]

Business conditions change continually for a bank such as Manny Hanny. Like many banks, it has been generous with the oil exploration industry. Many banks lent oil and gas companies up to 100 percent of the discounted net present value of their reserves without hesitation for much of the late 1970s and 1980s; but the massive drop in the price of oil in 1986 forced a complete rethinking of this important line of banking business, and a move towards more conservative lending.[13] Its London-based energy group was

---

[8] Victoria Lubbock, "Opening the Letters Market," *ReActions*, Banking Services Supplement, June 1987, pp. 18–22.

[9] Gavin Shreeve, "Capital Markets: NIFty Deal," *Banker*, 137 (738), August 1987, pp. 65–66.

[10] Robert J. Hutchinson, "'One Stop Banking' Cements Package Approach at Manufacturers Hanover," *Bank Marketing*, 19 (12), December 1987, pp. 18–21.

[11] Anonymous, "'The Reliable American' Renews Its Commitment," *Asian Finance*, 13 (12), December 15, 1987, pp. 80–81.

[12] Saul Hansell, "The Man Who Made the $14 Billion Loan," *Institutional Investor*, 23 (1), January 1989, pp. 247–250.

[13] Brian A. Toal, "Credit Where Credit Is Due," *Oil & Gas Investor*, 7 (9), April 1988, pp. 30–35.

forced to monitor oil and energy prices more carefully and make predictions on how these would be felt in the oil market, and on the bank's opportunities.[14]

In the consumer banking market in the harsh realities of the 1980s, Manny Hanny reduced the size of its branch network and continued to work aggressively at cutting expenses. The use of more branch office automation and better efficiency meant that its 1982 to 1987 restructuring operation was able to increase fee income by 80 percent, up to $84 million, and also accquire $12 billion in more deposits, an increase of 130 percent.[15] By the early 1990s, Manny Hanny, like most banks, was being forced to look to noninterest income from a variety of places, thus necessitating more thinking about how to increase its product line and generate more cash.[16] It was experimenting with electronic consolidation options for different customers who were always receiving a heavy load of regular payments from consumers, such as public utilities or other large service companies.[17] The new activities in the consolidation process were heavily based on data processing and involved a concerted effort to become a low-cost producer.[18] For example, Manufacturers Hanover Securities Corporation was working on beefing up its securities sales and trading operations, although its profits had slipped a great deal in 1989.[19] The rapid expansion of different types of services and financial instruments also brought a need to reassess which ones were losers and which ones winners. This called for the bank's leadership in 1991.[20]

The great number of different lines of business being conducted by Manufacturers Hanover, combined with the global scope of its operations, virtually guaranteed that management of information technology would require supreme effort on the part of the bank, in addition to the many factors involved with its smaller operations targeted at specific financial products. Manny Hanny was one of the first test sites for evaluation of a laser scanning system capable of examining the microscopic fibers within the paper of stock

---

[14] Interview with Joe Coneeny, of the London office of Manufacturers Hanover, in Nigel Bance, "Energy Finance: How the Bankers View the Future," *Euromoney*, Energy Finance Supplement, June/July 1990, pp. 29–34.

[15] William A. Buckingham, "A Winning Strategy for Branch Banking," *Bankers Magazine*, 171 (3), May/June 1988, pp. 14–18.

[16] Anonymous, "Some Ways to Generate Noninterest Income," *ABA Banking Journal*, 82 (6), June 1990, pp. 18, 20.

[17] George C. White, "Have You Heard? 'Check and List' Is Obsolete for Receiving Consumer Bill Payments," *Journal of Cash Management*, 10 (5), September/October 1990, pp. 52–53.

[18] Richard J. Matteis, "Operating Services—New Rules for the '90s," *Bank Management*, 67 (4), April 1991, pp. 24–27.

[19] Anonymous, "Beyond Section 20," *ABA Banking Journal*, 82 (6), June 1990, pp. 63–68.

[20] Andrea Green, "The Challenge of Hard Times," *Bank Marketing*, 23 (3), March 1991, pp. 18–21.

certificates to determine their validity.[21] When it was involved in a massive campaign to improve the efficiency of its branch network, automation played a critical part with the use of NCR 1773 automatic teller machines, which were engineered to sustain 6,500 transactions per month. These helped decrease rental and operating costs, double deposit rates, and halve staff in some branches.[22] Internally, in helping fire up the efficiency of the financial proposal writing process, Manny Hanny developed a Microsoft Windows–based interface to Wang 386 personal computers with special interface software, thus enabling account officers to book commercial loans much faster, with time required dropping from three weeks to three to four days.[23] It also experimented with setting up kiosks in one of its lobbys to operate a computerized interactive system designed to sell annuities and term life insurance.[24]

To sharpen its focus on the larger issues revolving around its global management of information technology, Manufacturers Hanover created a crack group of internal consultants. Named the Strategic Technology and Research (STAR) unit, it was set up in 1986. Within two years, in 1988, one of its first moves was to implement a Technical Analysis and Reasoning Assistant (TARA) system, which was used in the foreign exchange trading area.[25] The TARA system is used to monitor multiple currencies and bond and interest rates. It uses special algorithms to make buy and sell recommendations to the traders.[26] Other experiments included use of knowledge-based systems for analysis of consumer loan applications and margin credit accounts.[27] The STAR group was also responsible for choosing the Oracle relational database management system to run on its VAX clusters and help in the difficult planning process involving multiple products. This required supplying market data services to its foreign exchange trading and securities trading operations.[28] It also started

---

[21] Timothy C. Crane, "Shedding Light on Certificate Fraud," *ABA Banking Journal*, 80 (5), May 1988, pp. 22, 24.

[22] Kim Zimmermann, "Automation Helps Struggling Branch Double Deposits," *Bank Systems & Equipment*, 25 (9), September 1988, pp. 90–91.

[23] Arthur V. Block, "Automation with a Graphics Interface," *Personal Computing*, 12 (10), October 1988, pp. 132–134.

[24] Linda Koco, "N.Y. Bank Sells Annuities, Term Life via Kiosk," *National Underwriter*, Life/Health/Financial Services, 93 (42), October 16, 1989, p. 24.

[25] Katherine Burger, "MHT's STAR Consultants Raise Technology Consciousness," *Bank Systems & Equipment*, 26 (5), May 1989, pp. 45–46.

[26] Mark Arend, "AI: Expert Keeps Up with Bank's Currency Events," *Wall Street Computer Review*, 6 (9), June 1989, pp. 22–24, 91–92.

[27] Ivy Schmerken, "Wall Street's Elusive Goal: Computers That Think Like Pros," *Wall Street Computer Review*, 7 (9), June 1990, pp. 24–34, 74–76.

[28] Maryfran Johnson, "Bridging Tech, Functional Barriers," *Computerworld*, 24 (9), February 26, 1990, pp. 53, 58–59.

Chapter 21 Strategy #5: Capture Residual Value 327

working with expensive and complex image storage and retrieval products that would be used in support of its tax reporting, check processing, trade services and lockbox operations.[29]

However, one of its most significant ideas was to work at completely reengineering the corporation as a whole from an information technology point of view.[30] As the 1980s had passed by, it became clear that complexity of information processing was increasing dramatically, not decreasing. The development of 24-hours-per-day trading made it necessary for the bank to work at developing an automated risk management system with the capabilities of sharing information regarding currency exposures, histories of different major customers, and immediate cash position at many different locations around the world, to enable its traders to survive without getting completely wiped out of the market.[31] At the same time, it had to be able to work more closely with its global customers, provide a network of subcustodians throughout the world, process massive transactions in foreign exchange, and generally help its customers manage their holdings through such services as open-ended closings, accrual reporting, multicurrency accounting, and foreign exchange contracts and tax reclamations.[32] Part of this process involved the stunning recommendation to consolidate Manny Hanny's five major data centers into only two. Consolidation on such a large scale, involving such giant amounts of equipment, would involve using special software such as console automation tools to help with tape management, restarting, job scheduling, and particularly with job balancing.[33] There was absolutely no question of downsizing from mainframes in a firm with global 24-hour-per-day communications and very heavy volumes of transaction processing.[34] The proliferation of personal computers and other distributed processing systems had continued to raise concerns within the bank over security.[35] As the plan unfolded, eight

---

[29] Howard Cohen and Kenneth Silber, "MHT's Image Philosophy," *Bank Systems & Technology*, 27 (4), April 1990, pp. 44–56.

[30] Clinton Wilder, "Beyond Mere Automation," *Computerworld*, Section 1, 23 (45), November 6, 1989, pp. 79, 84.

[31] Ivy Schmerken, "Wall Street Struggles to Balance Global Risk," *Wall Street Computer Review*, 7 (11), August 1990, pp. 12–22, 48–56.

[32] Mark Arend, "Global Custodians Exhibit High-Tech Savvy," *Wall Street Computer Review*, 7 (11), August 1990, pp. 29–34, 57–58.

[33] Computer Intelligence Company reported that job scheduling tools are found in only 30 percent of 3,090 major installations. See Michael Feuche, "Data Center Automation: Consolidation Promotes Hands-Off Strategy," *Computerworld*, 24 (35), August 27, 1990, pp. 59–64, 69–70.

[34] Paul Pinella, "What PC Managers Need to Succeed," *Datamation*, 36 (18), September 15, 1990, pp. 87–92.

[35] Alan Radding, "Security Often Complex in Distributed Computing," *Bank Management*, 67 (3), March 1991, pp. 50–52.

data centers in the New York area were to be consolidated into only two, with projected annual savings of $10 million in 1992 and from $20 to $30 million total by 1993, to be complemented by a 7 percent reduction in overall workforce, or 1,400 people.[36] It was announced in late 1990 that the eight data centers would be reduced into a *single* data processing center, a complete reversal from the previous 15 years of data processing tradition at Manny Hanny, which had seen it work very hard at decentralization.[37]

This massive move toward centralization eventually extended to its European operations. As we go to press, it appears that Manny Hanny is planning on taking its London data center operation and moving it back into the United States, thereby moving the entire corporation much closer to being a completely centralized organization.

Manufacturers Hanover, like other financial services companies and banks, was stunned by the great proliferation in complexity of the variety of financial instruments that had grown up in the 1980s. It responded at first with moves toward distributed and departmental processing, and carried on many experiments with technologies in those areas. However, the growing demands of its worldwide customers called for greater *global* control over its many services that were being extended. The customers wished to understand their positions on a worldwide basis, and take advantage of services that could only be offered by centralized consolidation of information. At the same time, the move to a global system of 24-hour trading placed tremendous pressures upon the data processing establishment to be able to process the information required on a real-time basis. With around-the-clock trading, there is simply very little time remaining in the day to process information offline and calculate one's positions.

Underlying this entire situation was the question of consolidation and efficiency in global data-processing operations. Technology had moved to the point where it was possible to run much larger volumes of high-speed systems on single machine complexes, and at the same time telecommunications costs had dropped. There was a $10 million investment to make the transition, but that was little to pay for a $30 million savings. As the merger with Chemical Bank was announced, the data processing teams were no doubt engaged in seeking further consolidation through centralization. Using this technique, the information systems function could "uncover" large amounts of available monies which were now "surplus" because of the new possibilities being opened up with information technology.

---

[36] Elisabeth Horwitt, "Manny Hanny Downsizes," *Computerworld*, 24 (46), November 12, 1990, pp. 1, 4.

[37] David Freedman, "Bringing IT Back Home," *CIO*, 4 (3), December 1990, pp. 54–62.

SUMMARY

The administrative heritage of the multinational corporation has left many multinationals with a very decentralized structure for managing the bureaucracy of everyday trade and operations, but there is much value which may be recaptured from seeking greater economies of scale.

- The decentralized nature of many MNC operations grew up naturally in times of less information-intensity in global operations.
- The technologies available for centralization on a regional and global scale are only now, in the 1990s, becoming truly available.
- There is evidence which leads one to believe that most multinationals could capture significant value from a strong effort toward consolidation of data centers and movement toward global operations.
- Movement toward global operations is based on making assumptions regarding different national regulations, practices, and laws.

The Manufacturers Hanover Trust case demonstrates that servicing of global clients can be achieved better with centralized systems; and at the same time, the firm can save a big chunk of money through consolidation.

- Many corporations suffer from having jumped into the decentralization craze that swept through data processing circles in the late 1970s and 1980s.
- In the financial services sector, many of the key applications of global information systems are driven by customer demands.

CHAPTER

22

Strategy #6: Exploit the Coming Liberalization in International Telecommunications

Nations have for a variety of reasons taken actions at the economic and policy level that have tended to hinder the rapid development of telecommunications systems, particularly privately-held systems such as those operated by multinational corporations. In Europe, concerns regarding privacy of computer-held data were paramount in the development of restrictions on transborder data flow. In addition, there is broad agreement that the state-dominated mode of development of telecommunications infrastructure was appropriate in the early stages of the growth of telecommunications, as the bulk of the investment and effort went into basic infrastructure. It was not until radical changes had occurred in telecommunications and data processing technologies that certain assumptions had to be revised. The major item needing rethinking was the role of monopoly, usually exercised through the PTT. The assumptions regarding the benefits of monopoly in telecommunications are coming into question in many quarters, and the world is moving toward a greater liberalization of international telecommunications. The information technology function within today's multinational corporations needs to build capability to take advantage of the more liberal and potentially less expensive environment that may be emerging, and this includes being able to design higher quality networks. The situation in Eastern Europe will provide a completely new set of problems that must be faced by companies wishing to set up business there.

DISCUSSION

The story of international telecommunications and international business is a long one, starting first perhaps with Rothschilds' famous carrier pigeons. From its very beginning alongside the rapidly expanding railroad empire of Western Europe, the telecommunications system, first as telegraph lines, has been inextricably tied to international commerce; it continues this way today and will remain so in the foreseeable future. Telecommunications is the nervous system of global commerce. However, telecommunications has long been recognized as being close to the heart of government power. That is why cutoff of telecommunications circuits is one of the recognized sanctions available to the United Nations Security Council. It is also the reason why telecommunications has been treated until very recently as a natural monopoly controlled in most part by governments, except in the United States.

As technological changes in the 1970s began to open up the possibilities for MNCs to use international telecommunications to transmit important financial information and data across international borders, governments became concerned about this new form of activity. The reasons for their concern are recorded in history; but, acting primarily under the guise of protecting privacy, which in any case was a very real and valid concern, governments threatened to enact restrictions of transborder data flows. In some quarters, particularly the United States, these were considered to be far out of proportion to the remedy they were supposed to create.

The first contemplated limitations on transborder data flow were aimed at preventing private information on individual citizens from being telecommunicated out of the country, beyond the legal reach of the originating and protective state. There was an obvious and immediate problem with the operations of the MNC. With limitations on flows of personnel data, how could a company organize human resources on an international scale? If it was not possible to send sensitive financial information out of a country, how was a MNC going to achieve regional economies of scale?

There were several well reasoned arguments that sought to limit the effects and show the downside of transborder data flow regulations. It was argued, for example, that computer-controlled and -generated information was safer and more secure than paper-based information since computer security techniques had by that time become sophisticated. Another argument was that if only computer-generated and telecommunicated information was considered, but physical information was exempted, then abuses would not stop. Indeed, they would be less monitorable, and in addition the regulation would unfairly discriminate against the MNC.

These concerns were gradually addressed through the OECD Guidelines, which, although voluntary in nature, provided many safeguards to protect data and information on private citizens. The United States insisted that the international agreement was voluntary, without any legal power or sanctions. As a result, the Europeans pressed for creation of their own laws, which provided considerably stronger protection, particularly in Sweden and Germany.[1]

There was a problem with all of this, however. From the very beginning, many suspected that the feigned concerns about privacy were little more than excuses to keep the MNCs out of national markets, or at least to put in place yet another government-controllable lever that could be used to control the MNC. Some of the concerns—such as the problem with restricting only the flow of computer-based information over international borders and conveniently leaving out paper-based information; the evident unconcern on the part of many Europeans as to the economic impact or real cost of these restrictions; and the very great concern on the part of financial services companies, such as American Express, which saw these restrictions as a means to keep them locked out of various national markets—were in the background. Were issues regarding privacy and data protection being used to mask the real intentions of the lawmakers, aimed at keeping foreign competition out of Europe so as to leave the market to the domestic corporations?

Guynes and coworkers report that one of the most effective methods to deal with transborder data flow problems involved the cultivation of local liaisons with different host governments. They argue that it is important for a multinational corporation to recognize that different nations have legitimate concerns regarding privacy and sovereignty, and that these concerns should rightly be taken into consideration in building international networks and computer communication systems.[2]

As a result of these concerns, which surfaced in the political debates in the very early 1980s in various international forums, the questions raised by

---

[1] For example, Sweden created a Data Inspection Omsbudsman, who is responsible for investigating any abuse of databases. Other countries of Europe debated the creation of specific legal penalties for abuse of information in databases. Even in 1990, almost a quarter century after the issue first appeared, many Western European countries have very exacting restrictions about movement of data across national borders through computer communications systems.

[2] Jan L. Guynes, Stephen C. Guynes, and Ron G. Thorn, "The Impact of Transborder Data Flow Regulation," *Journal of Information Systems Management*, 7 (3), Summer 1990, pp. 70–73.

Chapter 22 Exploit Liberalization in International Telecommunications

limitations of the operations of international data processing networks started to bleed over into the GATT negotiations as applied to trade in services. Within this context, limitations on the international movement of data through computer systems came to be viewed in some circles as a very severe type of non-tariff barrier (NTB) to international trade. As this perception became more widespread, the protestations to the contrary became louder. Inevitably, the institutions responsible for hindering international data traffic came into focus—and this meant in most cases the PTTs.

Nevertheless, there are signs of liberalization in the air around the world, particulary in Western Europe and to some extent in Japan,[3] although in the case of Japan non-Japanese companies seem to be unable to take advantage of the liberalization as much as in other countries.[4] Hukill and Jussawalla show that the trend towards liberalization is also taking place in many ASEAN countries, and new innovative technologies are being installed.[5]

There were many arguments in favor of maintaining the strong centralized and controlling role of the PTT in telecommunications. Among them were the provision of jobs, the giving of universal service to rich and poor alike, the maintenance of quality throughout the entire telecommunications networks, the control over costs, and the ultimate control on use. All of these were strong arguments on the side of maintenance of the monopoly. But they were all arguments which eventually lost out. The world has moved in another direction, toward liberalization and increased flexibility for users of international telecommunications systems. The 1980s saw a wave of liberalization in telecommunications begin in the United States and spread to the United Kingdom and Japan. The most dramatic development in this respect was breakup of the Bell System in the United States and the privatization of Nippon Telephone and Telegraph in Japan, which was the largest company of its kind in

---

[3] Harumasa Sato and Rodney Stevenson, "Telecommunications in Japan: After Privatization and Liberalization," *Columbia Journal of World Business,* Spring 1989, pp. 31–41. The writers emphasize the unique characteristics of the Japanese situation: "If Japan's policy and communications businesses are to be fully understood, much more attention will have to be paid to the roles of culture and social context in the Japanese telecommunications market."

[4] In any case, foreign multinationals working in Japan tend to have data processing clustered in a single city, usually Tokyo.

[5] Mark A. Hukill and Meheroo Jussawalla, "Telecommunications Policies and Markets in the ASEAN Countries," *Columbia Journal of World Business*, Spring 1989, pp. 43–57. The ASEAN countries include Malaysia, Indonesia, Thailand, Singapore, and the Philippines.

the world, and perhaps the single largest company in the world, as judged by its market capitalization.

The effect of liberalization has been the proliferation of different networks and accompanying options for users. More networks,[6] more value-added services, and more flexibility in utilization of nonstandard equipment that in the past could not be interconnected into corporate networks mean that the MNC of today can build vastly more powerful and responsive networks than in the past. Net technologies such as voice mail, bandwidth managers, voice and data integration, teleconferencing, and digital (Group IV) facsimile can all be added to the networks without specific authorization in many cases from the PTT.

Walter Sweet reports, however, that Toyota Motor Corporation has found that even though much more flexibility is available in creating international telecommunications networks, it may achieve fastest implementation if it standardizes on one vendor's equipment and telecommunications protocol. However, this type of strategy can run into terrible problems when certain types of modems, or other telecommunications equipment are restricted by the host country.[7]

One of the many multinationals that has been taking advantage of the new liberalized environment is General Electric, which has been creating the GE Telecommunications Network (GETN). It is built upon high-capacity T-1 leased circuits, gives data circuits in multiples of 64 kbps units, and integrates voice, data and even teleconferencing.[8]

The different considerations that should be taken into account in building an international private network for the multinational corporation are discussed by Butkus and coworkers, who point out that different sophisticated operations research models are many times employed in assessing the best alternatives.[9]

---

[6]In Japan, after some liberalization had hit the market, there were more than 300 private value-added networks registered at a single time.

[7]Walter Sweet, "International Firms Strive for Uniform Nets Abroad," *Network World*, 7 (22), May 28, 1990, pp. 35–36, 62.

[8]Anonymous, "GE's Worldwide Network Integrates Voice, Data, Video," *Networking Management*, 8 (6), June 1990, pp. 99–100. The network was reportedly built in three steps: First, European connections were established, then the Far East, finally the network nodes in Latin America. The ability to have some flexibility in telecommunications equipment to be used gives GE the capacity to build a network which can offer "bandwidth on demand"–type services.

[9]Raymond T. Butkus, Mathilde Benveniste, and Richard W. Ross, Jr., "Linking the Global Corporation," *Network World*, 4 (51/v5n1), December 28, 1987/January 4, 1988, pp. 31–35. The key to their analysis lies in matching the necessary performance requirements with the overall business criteria, which must be derived from understanding the strategy and tactics of the business.

Chapter 22   Exploit Liberalization in International Telecommunications   335

Some countries have continued to resist this trend, arguing that it is necessary to maintain some type of state control so that investment priorities in a sector as important as telecommunications is can be made in the public interest, rather than being controlled completely by private interests and their supposed greed. France has been a strong proponent of this argument and has continued its habit of encouraging massive state intervention in the sector. Most developing countries tend to work hard at maintaining their respective monopolies over international telecommunications.

One result of these policies has been systematic overcharging for telecommunications services at the international level. In early 1990, for example, an investigation by the *Financial Times* revealed that users were being overcharged by more than $11 billion per year for international telecommunications services; and that such overcharges had little if anything to do with the actual costs of providing international telecommunications services. Instead, the charges were based on getting what the market would bear, given the inherent monopoly situation.[10]

Some of the problems with tariffs and costs for international telecommunications have been confirmed by an Arthur D. Little, Inc. study that emphasized the large variations in availability of services from country to country. The result is that most private international networks are a hodgepodge of networks pieced together to meet each national variation; and the situation seems to be worse in Latin America, Africa, and many parts of Asia.[11]

There are pressures by private companies for further liberalization, for example with private networks based on Very Small Aperture Terminals (VSATs).[12] The relatively new technology of the VSAT makes it much simpler

---

[10] It is interesting that in what was one of the most strongly protectionist markets, West Germany, the pressures for liberalization have come from the reunification with East Germany. As reunification approached with the December 2, 1990, elections, it became increasingly clear that the telecommunications legacy left behind by the former socialist government was a disaster. Much of the switching equipment was based on technology of the 1920s and 1930s—in fact, in many locations that vintage original equipment was still in place. To increase the rate of investment, the Bundespost began to allow private companies to operate, first in the data communications sector, and then in the voice sector. Without rapid alternative paths for voice communication being opened up, the process of economic reunification would be too slow.

[11] Stephanie McCann, "Potholes on the Global Data Highway," *Computerworld*, 24 (40), October 1, 1990, p. 100. On the positive side, the writer observes that many different national telecommunications authorities are beginning to work more together in creating services that can be used by multinational corporations.

[12] VSAT is one type of satellite-based telecommunications signalling system based on use of receiving and transmitting dishes of less than one meter in diameter. VSATs can be quickly installed and are capable of both voice and data traffic.

and quicker to build flexible private telecommunications networks than to go through public telephone companies located in many different jurisdictions and countries. VSAT technology in Europe, for example, would enable a company to put up a network in weeks or months instead of the customary years it takes in many locations because of foot-dragging by telecommunications authorities. Instead of having to wait for years to integrate information systems, technologies such as VSAT enable the MNC to accomplish this in coordination with global strategies, if the various national telecommunications authorities agree.

In addition to a movement around the world toward liberalization on the part of regulatory bodies, there have been several key technical advances in equipment that have made it easier to operate across national boundaries. The bandwidth manager, for example, is a technology which dynamically allocates leased circuit capacity between different protocols and between voice, image, and data. In the past, it would have been virtually impossible to set up similar pieces of equipment in different countries; but with the newer technologies, interfaces to the peculiarities of different national standards have been reduced to little more than a circuit card inserted into the body of the switching computer.

As a result of these developments both on the technology and on the regulatory side, MNCs must continue to be prepared to take advantage of an increasing array of opportunities as they appear. In many environments, preparedness will mean that management must change its assumptions about information technology and the degree to which it can play the activist role in business. The greater amount of flexibility being made apparent by these changes can yield some important strategies for the information technology management function.

Overall, the efficiency of the MNC can be improved in several important dimensions. The well-known tactic of improving inventory control through lower safety-stocking levels, made possible by rapid communication along different points in the supply chain, is demonstrated widely in several important sectors, such as spare parts in many large businesses. The increased speed at which a firm can clear its books at the end of the month for financial reporting and the resulting improvements in cash flow that can result are other proven ideas. There are other, more subtle ways in which this increased flexibility can add to efficiency. For example, in the realm of corporate intelligence—the systematic gathering and processing of heterogeneous types of environmental business data— advances in information systems can help the firm learn a great deal about its external environment, organize that information into a database, or present it to top-level management.

The largest immediate savings can come from adopting newer telecommunications technologies, particularly those that allow integration, that is, the bundling of different, heretofore, separate circuits into a single circuit. Over the years many corporations have built up many different telecommunications networks and circuits. Management of this complex infrastructure is often highly complex. Telecommunications managers are frequently unwilling to make changes in the architecture of circuits that are functioning without any major problems. Their conservatism and risk-avoidance are well understood. However, when managers are faced with the prospect of massive integration and cost cutting, eventually the argument for efficiency prevails over conservatism.

The largest benefits, however, are achieved in areas beyond the telecommunications area, primarily in the sphere of business operations. Rather than being able to estimate advantage in terms of only tangible benefits, one can now consider nontechnical, intangible benefits, which many times may outweigh the hard quantifiable benefits typical of cost-accounting approaches. Being able to use telecommunications to increase quality or customer service, for example, may produce enduring business benefits that will eventually far outweigh any investments required in the international telecommunications infrastructure.

Therefore, taking all of this into consideration, one can see clearly that the information technology management in the MNC must be prepared to take advantage of the opportunities being opened up by the gradual liberalization of international telecommunications and by the rapid advances in new telecommunications technologies. By taking advantage of these opportunities, MNCs can both gain significant efficiencies and develop important intangible business benefits.

TELE-VAULTING THE BERLIN WALL

The fall of the Iron Curtain at the beginning of the decade has opened up many business opportunities in Eastern Europe that did not exist during the reign of the Stalinist-oriented governments in that tormented part of the world.[13]

---

[13] Setting aside for the moment the political dimension of the immediate postwar period in Eastern Europe and focusing strictly on the business side, we note the large amount of international trade which has taken place, particularly in the area of raw materials. However, with the movement toward a stronger role for international trade, joint ventures, cooperative arrangements, all within the context of a move toward more consumer-oriented economies, we must recognize that information technology must play an increasing role, particularly in the areas of manufacturing automation, logistics, and inventory control.

Business relationships that had been dominated by state-orchestrated trading arrangements, many based on sophisticated barter and semi-barter deals, have in some cases started a process of liberalization that portends a considerably greater role for the private sector and the Western-style multinational corporation. In a simplified sense, the breakdown of the Stalinist system of managed market control and development closed one set of opportunities, yet opened others. The freeing of Soviet enterprises, such as they are, is a slow process, but has yielded a vast number of possibilities for new types of commercial arrangements such as joint ventures, licensing arrangements, subcontracting and even the creation of multinational corporations from the remains of economic organizations in the former USSR (although this is farther away than near-term).

Western-style and Japanese MNCs will have an active role to play in defining the new economic relationships that are emerging, and yet this role must be undertaken in the face of tremendous barriers hindering the development of full-scale trade with mother Russia. Inadequate legal protection for contracts and standard procedures for fact-finding and dispute settlement and the problems with the convertibility of the ruble all tend to complicate matters and slow down progress. In the early part of the 1990s the USSR was still working out the most basic level of understanding of the role of private enterprise and searching for a way of transforming the tired and crumbling socialist economy in such a way as not to create further economic chaos. The various ministries that had been in charge of different manufacturing enterprises quickly met economic chaos as their (what appeared to be relatively *stable*) lines of supply and delivery became irregular, thus practically crippling the economy. The fact that this type of disruption was happening to an entire economy rather than to a few isolated economic enterprises or sectors turned the economic transition into a massive sociological hodgepodge of jerk starts. Within this new context, the foreign multinational corporation must step into the scene and begin the process of cutting deals, for even the most hardened observer recognizes that with the supply of technology, manufacturing expertise, global coordination of foreign markets, operational excellence, and massive internal resources, both human and capital-based, the foreign multinational has much to bring to the table. It might not be too bullish to suppose that the foreign multinational may play the *dominant* role in the further economic development of many critical parts of the USSR's economy in the 1990s. Unfortunately, the instability of the economy and of its supporting legal and political infrastructure was bad enough at the beginning of the 1990s to elicit a seasoned pessimism even *without consideration* of the role of information technology, but when this too is considered, a serious alarm bell is sounded.

Regrettably, the telecommunications infrastructure of most of Eastern Europe is woefully inadequate to support sophisticated data processing applications and architectures, and the general utilization of computers there may be as much as a quarter of a century behind the times, if one measures such indicators as penetration. On the telecommunications side, only the most insignificant part of the networks is digital, and there is a reliance on mechanical switch technology that is in generally poor condition. The farther one moves from the main cities of the USSR, the more strained the situation becomes. The availability of leased lines, quick set-up of new services, public packet-switched networks, value-added services, and the like is simply out of the question for most of Eastern Europe. In many parts of the USSR, for example, the highest reliable baud rate that can be sent through the telephone system is 300 or perhaps 1200 baud.

Alberthal argues that, although in the developed Western cities the most efficient telecommunications investment would be in fiber optics systems, such as with metropolitan networks, in Eastern Europe it would be more logical and efficient to use satellite communications, since it would be impossible to rely on the infrastructure.[14]

A United Nations study of the informatics sector in Eastern Europe, including Bulgaria, Czechoslovakia, the German Democratic Republic, Hungary, Poland, Romania, and the Soviet Union, pointed out some of the problems:

> The data industries of these countries suffer from several weaknesses. One is a lagging development of materials and components. Another is a relatively poor development, both in terms of quantity as well as quality, of peripheral equipment. ... CMEA experience in the field of data industries indicates that their full utilization for the benefits of economic development depends on the parallel buildup of production and service capacities, as well as of an adequate telecommunication infrastructure. So far, both the service capacities and the telecommunication infrastructure in most of these countries seem to be lagging behind production capabilities. ... While a certain degree of international specialization in the production of data goods has already been achieved, data services and telecommunications are still predominantly locally oriented, resulting in relatively high costs and the inefficient use of resources.[15]

In addition, much of the information technology is behind the times and is in many cases incompatible with foreign equipment except at the most general level.[16] Although an interesting area of research in the future might

---

[14]Lester M. Alberthal, "Communications Leapfrog for East Europe's Infrastructure," *Financier*, 14 (4), April 1990, pp. 32–37.

[15]UNCTC, *Data Goods and Data Services in the Socialist Countries of Eastern Europe* (New York: United Nations, 1988).

[16]See the assessment by John B. Holt, "Decline of U.S. Computer Company Bargaining Power in Eastern Europe," *Columbia Journal of World Business*, Fall 1978, pp. 95–112. See also the seminal article of N. C. Davis and S. E. Goodman, "The Soviet Bloc's Unified System of Computers," *Computing Surveys*, 10 (2), June 1978.

involve studying the interface problems between Eastern European computer systems and their foreign counterparts, so far as we know this has not yet been done, even on a case-study basis. We can be sure, however, that the problems will be not inconsiderable in light of the fact that most of the operating systems being used, particularly on the larger machines, are outdated versions popular years ago in the West. Likewise, the technical characteristics of many of the specific hardware configurations preclude any hope of a "plug compatible" fit with Western equipment. Even if the problems were easier to solve, any multinational attempting such an operation on even a limited scale would find a shortage of trained personnel capable of completing the job.

This "technical Berlin wall" between the business data processing systems of the East and the West in Europe has been caused by national security restrictions and the general technology path followed within formerly Communist Europe. For years after World War II, the West, led by the United States, imposed a severe limitation on exports of all forms of technology to the USSR. Although this initial desire to curtail technology transfer started with the fear of atomic and later nuclear proliferation resulting from the Rosenbergs' aid in giving the secret of the atomic bomb to Stalin, it quickly spread to other related military sectors, including missile-related technology and all other forms of information technology that could be used to aid in the national security field. Since almost every general-purpose business computing system can have many military applications, if only to calculate trajectories of warheads through a Fortran program, the prohibition on exports of all significant forms of information technology to the Communist Bloc inevitably came into place and had a severe effect on the industrial infrastructure there.

The most significant effect was that the countries of the East had to build their own information technology and electronics industry. Although this form of externally imposed market protection did much to encourage general self-sufficiency in manufacturing of computers in the long run—a self-sufficiency that would at a later date be much admired in those Western countries unable to build their own industries—it did result in the East being locked into a semipermanent state of dependence on foreign technology and know-how that was impossible to escape. For example, in choosing the path of IBM compatibility and operating systems, the Soviet Union accepted a state of permanent inferiority. Their industries and supporters had to wait until each new improvement in the IBM way of doing things came along, then figure out how to copy it. Inevitably they eventually fell behind and were doomed to remain behind always. After each extension of the giant IBM operating system and portfolio of data processing concepts, a certain amount of time would have to pass by before the East Europeans were able to absorb the new development and integrate it into their own systems. How much time? Probably about half of a decade was the delay time for each major innovation. Inevitably the copies and jerry-rigging of the East European systems were imperfect, making further additions and modifications or improvements even more difficult to obtain at the same level of efficiency, thus resulting in a general overall deterioration of the ability to absorb the new concepts. All of this was happening on top of a technological infrastructure—microelectronics, micromechanics, advanced materials and related hardware technologies—that was increasingly less able to provide the proper platforms for innovation; for it too was falling behind the West because of inability to achieve economies of scale in manufacturing.

The grand result of this cycle of Western innovation followed by a delayed reaction of technological adaption in the East was the emergence of many fundamental incompatibilities between the East and the West. Although in the 1960s and perhaps 1970s many of the machines were similar, like mutating plants in different environments, from one generation to another they grew slowly apart and emerged as almost two different species.

Another important factor limiting the abilities of Western and Asian multinational corporations to enter rapidly into the business and associated information infrastructure of Eastern Europe lies in the shortage of human resources, and this fact is particularly evident in the computer programming and, more importantly, systems development area. Given the lack of a feasible telecommunications infrastructure in most of the Eastern countries, we would also expect that adequately trained talent in networking is missing. The practical effect of this human resources shortage is that talent must either be imported from abroad, or be "home grown" by concerned organizations. In the former case, it would be difficult to imagine the possibility of locating a significant number of experts in the West who understand the details of the operations of Eastern European telecommunications systems. These are some of the most secret and guarded installations in Eastern Europe; and information concerning the details of their operations, particularly at the highly technical level necessary for computer networking, is generally classified as a state secret (at least until recently). Therefore, should we search for qualified personnel in this regard we would more than likely pull a null set out from the basket.

The inevitable result of these factors is that the MNCs wishing to expand there will have to build networks from scratch without being able to draw upon the sophisticated infrastructure available in Western Europe, North America, and Japan: telecommunications, human resources, equipment availability. This fact will mean that the task of integrating large-scale information systems will be much more of a development effort than in developed countries. The World Bank report released in 1990, which made a sweeping assessment of the economic prospects for Eastern Europe, compared the situation there to conditions found in developing countries rather than in developed industrial countries. Using the experience that many multinational corporations have had in building information systems in developing countries as a guide, we would predict that many of the same challenges will come to the surface to inhibit rapid progress. These barriers all revolve around the inevitable shortages in human resources and general infrastructure that vastly increase the amount of work required to build a data center. Depending upon the economic sector being automated, even such basic supplies as electricity cannot always be guaranteed. Building a new data center in a developing country is bad enough; but when you must also build a reliable power supply, open a private internal school for training, and engineer a long-distance or city-wide telecommunications system, then the overall cost might easily slip out of hand and escalate wildly, particularly since each and every import must go through a certification process. Nevertheless, regardless of the types of barriers that might be encountered in the process of building infrastructure in Eastern Europe, this type of effort must be undertaken with zeal.

In setting up these networks, some innovative technologies will have to be considered. These new technologies might include VSATs or technologies such as the Motorola satellite-based telephone system. VSATs offer an inexpensive way to set up sophisticated voice and data networks without having to connect into the land-based network. Pelton calls the satellite a "revolutionary change agent."[17] In countries like the United States, such an approach may be made to avoid having to pay for the high cost of leased lines, particularly for circuits which are not fully utilized. However, in the nations of Eastern Europe the use of VSATs may be a way to set up a working and operational network *in the absence of* a well-functioning terrestrial alternative.

The iridium system from Motorola promises to make more nearly obsolete the idea of depending solely upon a terrestrial telecommunications network. This technology, which was emerging at the beginning of the 1990s, promised to make portable telephone service available anywhere in the world, independent of the standards disputes being waged in Western Europe by competing industrial conglomerates able to pull the strings of government policy makers. As the economic and social disaster resulting from 30 years of socialism and communism was unveiled in East Germany, it became evident that the telecommunications systems had been one of the greatest tragedies. As West German companies scrambled to build up their relationships with their Eastern brothers, mobile telephone services played a critical role in providing reliable telephone communications in the East. This solution was obviously much quicker in the implementation than the slow and deliberate development of a terrestrial infrastructure, which would take years. Both of these examples point to the need for the multinational seeking expansion into Eastern Europe to search for alternative means of telecommunications in order to get its system operational as quickly as possible. Unfortunately, the situation in Russia at present may not allow such creative solutions but should in the near future if the mild liberalization trends continue.

---

[17]Joseph N. Pelton, "The Communication Satellite: Revolutionary Change Agent?" *Columbia Journal of World Business,* Spring 1983, pp. 77–84.

There are, however, certain factors that will inhibit any effort to informatize relationships with Eastern European subsidiaries.[18] One of the greatest of these may be the continued imposition of various national security regulations, which tend to limit the sophistication of the information technologies that might be used. Restrictions on international technology transfer, administered through organizations such as COCOM (Coordinating Committee for Export Controls) have been designed to inhibit the technological development of Eastern Europe and have been moderately successful, at least up until the late 1980s when it was realized that much of the global spread of information technology was becoming unstoppable. Even with the current developments in Eastern Europe, many of these restrictions are still in place. The result on the planning for the technological infrastructure of the multinational hoping to set up shop in those countries can be devastating.

At one time COCOM strictly controlled exports of technology to the Soviet Bloc, but a wind of liberalization began in 1990 when approval was granted for Control Data Corporation to export 6 Cyber 962 supercomputers to the USSR and the ceiling on processing power for personal computers allowed for export was raised to 275 bits per second, equivalent to the new personal computers based on the Intel 80386 microprocessor. At the same time, IBM predicted that the East German market alone would be worth more than $21 billion in sales by the year 2000.[19]

As a result, we should expect that much of the applications software, particularly financial software, will have to be written on a customized basis to fit into the peculiar technology environment of Eastern Europe. Some of the major problems that will be encountered, apart from the many infrastructure challenges previously mentioned, include making basic decisions about whether to adopt East European technology, such as the Soviet Besm series computers, or forgo that option altogether and rely on the same type of information already used widely in the firm elsewhere. If the multinational is not working with an East European partner that already has in place a significant data processing capability, this option may be easier and perhaps preferable. Complications occur if the partner has a significant amount of data or applications that must be integrated into the data processing infrastructure of the multinational.

If a degree of interorganizational systems development is required, then the problem becomes more severe. There are two options in this respect. The multinational can either work with its new partner to take its data and convert it into the new data processing structure using the imported equipment, or

---

[18]Some writers use the verb "informate." Neither word exists in English as it is formally accepted in the early 1990s.

[19]Lothar Gries and Linda Lewis, "Eastern Bloc Trade Must Clear Financing Hurdles," *Computerworld,* 24 (34), August 20, 1990, p. 81.

attempt to build interfaces that give a type of transparency to the informational relationship. In this respect, use of batch-oriented technologies may be the most common path in the early stages.

Regardless of the particular path chosen, the cost and up-front investment will be well worth it, primarily because the economies, resources and peoples of Eastern Europe offer the best long-term possibilities for reaping economic advantages as well as for greatly expanding market opportunities in the future. This realization is sinking in around the world as we see investment capital for Latin America and some other regions of the world dry up as more resources are shifted towards Eastern Europe.

The information technology function of the multinational corporation will no doubt have to follow the grand strategy of movement to the East that is being adopted by the controlling business logic of the company. But as it copes with the implications that will arise from the need to get the data processing shop up and running smoothly, these problems, and even others perhaps, will continue to plague the operation throughout the 1990s.

SUMMARY

The movement toward liberalization in the international telecommunications field will provide the multinational with many options it has not experienced in the past.

- Investigations from the European Economic Community (EEC) and the U.S. Federal Communications Commission (FCC) have targeted overcharging on international telecommunications circuits, thus opening the door to a dropping of prices.
- Telecommunications costs have been regularly falling at a faster rate than computer hardware. From 1980 to 1990, semiconductor memory costs fell by 30 percent per year, but for telecommunications, as measured by cents per bit per second, the decline was 38 percent per year over the same period.
- New international telecommunications standards, such as the Synchronous Optical Network (SONET), will provide switched circuit speeds that were unimaginable at the end of the 1980s (Figure 22.1).

The situation in Eastern Europe is one in which multinational corporations hoping to build up their business will have to rethink their assumptions completely about availability of telecommunications infrastructure.

- In general, the Socialist economies of Eastern Europe were unable to modernize their telecommunications infrastructure.

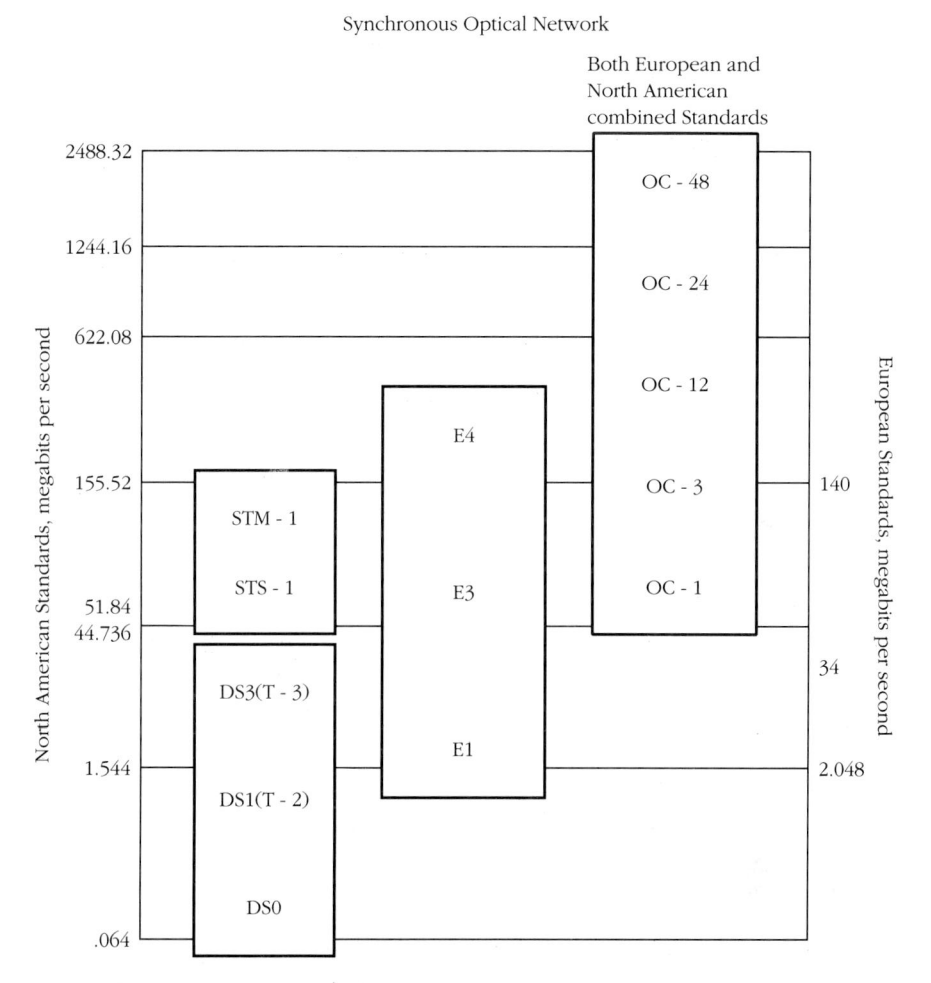

FIGURE 22.1 Speeds of the Synchronous Optical Network (SONET) compared with speeds achievable in North America and Western Europe in 1990.

- At the beginning of the 1990s, much of the infrastructure in Eastern Europe is more than one-half of a *century* out of date.
- New technologies such as digital cellular radio may be very useful in seeking innovative telecommunications solutions in Eastern European countries where the infrastructure is inadequate.
- Satellite-based telecommunications may prove to be more useful in Eastern Europe than elsewhere, because it will receive little competition from the terrestrial sector.

CHAPTER

23

Strategy #7: Homogenize Data Structures

In large geographically dispersed multinational corporations, the administrative heritage has left most MNCs with a number of pools of information technology. Instead of a globally integrated system, we usually find many different systems instead of one. With the growing internationalization and globalization of business these days, it is popular to speak about "building global systems," and this usually means the multinational must take steps to integrate all those pools of automation floating throughout the world. In doing so, one essential step is identification of that subset of data that is really needed on a global basis, and this step must be followed with standardization of data elements. However, the Imperial Chemical Industries case shows how difficult this can be, and how highly variable and changeable is the nature of the multinational corporation.

DISCUSSION

As a result of the national structure, most MNCs find they have different databases in each country. In most cases, almost the entire data processing structure, with the exception of headquarters, is reproduced on a national basis in each country in which the MNC operates, albeit at different levels of complexity. A good example of this is in the area of human resources applications such as payroll and taxation reporting.

This development is not entirely unexpected because in the past the MNC has been forced to deal with and adjust to highly variable national regulations, particularly as regards financial reporting. This requirement of necessity involved building different database structures and reporting mechanisms to handle the variety needed. This in turn leads to a type of optimization of systems architectures based on the national model.[1] The national model of data processing in turn can give rise to problems.

One of the most important problems that arises from having a national organization of data processing is the inability to get a global view of data. For example, if a company is to do a series of comparisons of sales or other matters on a international basis, then it must collect data from the field. In the majority of cases, standardized reporting from the subsidiaries is built into the normal working procedures of the MNC and its supporting information technology arrangements. However, in extraordinary circumstances, or for queries on an ad hoc basis, the relevant queries may take special programming efforts and associated resources because the systems are not flexible or standardized enough to provide the information quickly. It is in these cases where the disadvantages of the national model are most strongly felt. The difficulty for today's MNC is that the changing picture in international business is more than ever likely to require such quick access to data. This inevitably results in more emphasis being placed upon standardization of entire databases across national boundaries—the structure and elements of a database in one country should be, to the extent practicable, identical to databases in other countries. This type of arrangement allows considerably faster integration and querying of data.

---

[1] There are other factors involved in explaining this as well. Of particular concern is that, during the immediate post-war Period, the technologies for data processing available at the time did not allow working together on a wide-scale international basis. To have a major data processing center in each country tested the limits of the computing power available. As this situation gradually changed with the advent of higher forms of technology with considerably more and faster computing power, it became possible to complain of the lack of efficiencies found in the national model of data processing.

Examples of the type of rapid change that produces the need for a different and more consolidated view of data and corporate information on an international scale include inventory control, cash payments and assorted financial information, manufacturing data, and sales distribution data. Environmental factors that might induce a company to make repeated ad hoc assessments may be related to factors such as the merger and acquisitions climate that swept the corporate world in the late 1980s, including North America, Japan, and Western Europe.

MNCs need to make their data more consistent across national boundaries to get this better view of their day-to-day operations, but there are other important reasons as well. The most important is the ability to reach economies of scale in software and applications development. Gone are the days when scarce information systems professionals' time was spent reinventing the wheel in each country where an application had to be generated. The move toward consolidation and standardization of regional or international data processing centers has as its core the economic advantage that comes from making redundant many efforts that formerly would have been absolutely essential to continued operations of the MNC.

The new economies of scale in software and applications development mean that not only can effort be better spent, but it can also be spent in solving problems that are transnational in nature, rather than being bounded by the confines of the nation-state and the national operations of the subsidiary.

This is not to say that nationally focused efforts are going to disappear overnight. Nothing could be farther from the truth. As they are driven by differences in national conditions and regulations, they will continue to be necessary until national differences go away—that is not in the foreseeable future, except to a limited degree in Western Europe.[2]

---

[2] We do not yet know the results of the famous "1992" decision and its real effects on data processing. One can be sure that MNCs will be dealing with "1992" well after the year 1992 passes by. Nothing is going to happen magically overnight. In transport, telecommunications, customs regulations, and the massive piles of seemingly pointless paperwork that helps to regulate commerce in Western Europe, most people are searching for a simpler solution. But the efforts that are going to be required in so many areas of regulation—insurance, standards, and so on—are so great as to give hope only to a fool that a quick solution can be found. An additional problem involves the participation of the newly democratizing Central European countries, which have always looked to the West as trading partners. Are they to be kept out of the process? Surely, the desire of the East Europeans to join the European Economic Community will slow down the process of building a united Europe.

IMPERIAL CHEMICAL INDUSTRIES, PLC

The question of consolidating databases and in so doing making definitions for data standard across the multinational corporation is straightforward enough, and usually needs only the smallest amount of prompting to get general agreement even among the worst skeptics. But what happens when the corporation is so large, and so complex, and involved in so many different lines of business that it has historically operated very independent data centers, targeted at different purposes? To understand this type of situation, we turn to Imperial Chemical Industries, PLC, one of the largest industrial groups in Britain, and the fourth-largest chemical firm in the world. It was formed in 1926 by the merger of four different chemical companies in Britain. ICI concentrated on manufacturing commodity chemicals up until the 1980s, when we take up the story.[3] For it is here we shall see the massive practical problems involved in building effective global information systems.

ICI is by its very nature a highly decentralized operation, simply because it must be so active in so many different geographical regions of the world. A strong cadre of executive directors controls the top 200 positions of the firm, but each of the different operating units is responsible for its own activities to a great extent, including meeting overall corporate objectives.[4] A survey in 1990 found that ICI was one of the few hierarchical companies that provided very well for training and development of employees.[5] ICI has developed strong internal procedures for ensuring that the span of control for managers fits into the core management structure and can be implemented well with work groups and the general decision-making process.[6]

By the mid-1980s, the company had lived through the global decline in oil prices, which had been expected to benefit the company since petroleum is a key raw material. However, exports of chemicals had fallen by 6 percent in the first half of 1986, making foolishness of the earlier predictions that they would rise by 8 percent, and also calling into question the economic

---

[3] Anonymous, "Reshaping ICI: One Thing Leads to the Next," *Economist,* 315 (7652), April 28, 1990, pp. 21–23.

[4] Edgar Vincent, "Developing Managers for an International Business," *Journal of Management Development,* 7 (6), 1988, pp. 14–20.

[5] Edgar Wille, "Should Management Development Just Be for Managers?" *Personnel Management,* 22 (8), August 1990, pp. 34–37.

[6] George Pullan, "Organisation Design: Getting the Chemistry Right," *Personnel Management,* 22 (8), August 1990, pp. 46–50.

efficiency if ICI's ethane-based distillation of ethylene as compared with the older naphtha-based system, which had been in use when oil prices were lower.[7]

ICI persisted, however, in its continual development of new products and new ways to market them. In 1986, it introduced to the home gardener a self-contained weedkiller gun containing chemicals for lawns, vegetable gardens, and flowers all in one. It sold more than 1.5 million units in the first year in England alone.[8] In response to strong environmental concerns, ICI announced in 1990 that it had spent £200 million developing hydrofluorocarbon 134a, which would not deplete the ozone layer as do the standard chlorofluorocarbons (CFCs) used heavily in the refrigeration industry.[9] It announced a 10,000 metric ton per year facility to be set up at St. Gabriel, Louisiana, for the manufacture of 134a.[10]

In 1986 ICI made arrangements to purchase Glidden Coatings & Resins of Cleveland, Ohio. The acquisition would push ICI's sales in the United States to more than $3 billion per year and would enable it to focus on automotive finishes, and coatings, can finishes and different architectural coatings.[11] The acquisition, controlled by ICI in Wilmington, Delaware, was intended to help the company move away from the mature (i.e., no growth) markets of Europe and into the United States, which was growing and which (they were hoping) would account for more than a quarter of ICI's business by 1995. Eventually, the top executives of Glidden would be integrated into the ICI's worldwide paint operations. Through this purchase ICI now was the world's largest supplier of paint; and it controlled the $9.7 billion U.S. market, which was more than 35 percent of the world's total.[12] At the time, it was observed that running such a far-flung corporation required a matrix management system, which would allow a consolidated view of each product line on a global basis and yet provide very close corporate control within each geographical territory.[13] To make the acquisition pay off, ICI and Glidden started approx-

---

[7]Stephanie Cooke and Paula M. Block, "U.K. Chemicals: In the Shadow of the Oil Price Decline," *Chemical Week*, 139 (10), September 3, 1986, pp. 30–33.

[8]Louella Miles, "ICI Bug Gun Fires a Winning Round," *Marketing*, 26 (12), September 18, 1986, pp. 37–38.

[9]Richard Evans, "Ozone Savers," *International Management*, Europe Edition, 45 (3), April 1990, pp. 44–45.

[10]Emma Chynoweth, "ICI Unveils New Route to HFC-134a Production," *Chemical Week*, 1990.

[11]Kristine Portnoy and Langdon Brockinton, "ICI Moves in on U.S. Paints and Coatings," *Chemical Week*, 139 (9), August 27, 1986, pp. 13–14.

[12]Daniel J. McConville, "Glidden Maps Growth Plans Under ICI," *Chemical Week*, 141 (18), October 28, 1987, pp. 20–23.

[13]W. David Gibson, "ICI Americas: Sales Up 100% in Three Years, with More Acquisitions to Come," *Chemical Week*, 139 (19), November 5, 1986, pp. 22–25.

Chapter 23 Strategy #7: Homogenize Data Structures 351

imately 80 joint synergy projects aimed at tackling various large market segments by combining the skills of both ICI and its new partner, Glidden. Paint Technology was transferred to Glidden from ICI, resulting in annual savings of more than $400,000.[14]

The acquisition had been set up by Denys Henderson, who was operating ICI's acquisitions team and who went on to become the Chairman and Chief Executive Officer of the company in 1987. By then time more than 60 percent of ICI's sales were from outside the United Kingdom.[15] The total operations of the company were more than £912 million in pre-tax profits in 1985, which had grown from £284 million in 1980. Such growth confirmed the corporate direction of developing markets overseas.[16] For example, the Latin American operations of ICI were soon to account for 16 percent of *all* exports from the United Kingdom to that part of the world.[17] The logic of its action was clear: acquire companies which either had technology which ICI needed or could help it pump its products through to new markets.[18]

By the late 1980s, the strategy of ICI had come more clearly into focus. A tightly bonded executive team was set to continue the strategic thinking and planning for the company. With a special focus on possible acquisitions, the team was changing the role of the loose matrix structure that had been so dominant in the past. The new group was always to have a 10-year vision in pocket to guide itself.[19] ICI was moving away from production of primary chemicals, which were used by other companies for more value-added manufacturing, toward a new approach that emphasized product development in targeted segments and more intensive marketing. It did not, however, ignore developments in basic manufacturing costs, as shown by its Leading Concept Ammonia (LCA) process, which completely altered economies of scale toward more efficient miniturization.[20] Problems were reported with

---

[14]Garrod Whatley, "More Than a Merging of Colours," *Chief Executive,* December 1987, pp. 16–18.

[15]Herbert C. Short and David W. Gibson, "ICI's New Boss—His Precept: 'Keep Up the Momentum,'" *Chemical Week,* 140 (12), April 1, 1987, pp. 26–29.

[16]Ken Gofton, "Henderson Prepares for a New Era at ICI," *Marketing,* 26 (13), September 25, 1986, pp. 36–39.

[17]Hester Thomas, "A Market for Optimists Only," *Accountancy,* 103 (1149), May 1989, pp. 105–108.

[18]Jonathan Hunt, "The Final Peformance," *Chief Executive,* September 1986, pp. 30–31.

[19]Alan I. H. Pink, "Strategic Leadership Through Corporate Planning at ICI," *Long Range Planning,* 21 (1), February 1988, pp. 18–25.

[20]Herb Short, "NH$_3$ Break Thru: Small Plants," *Chemical Engineering,* 96 (7), July 1989, pp. 41–45.

this process several years later, in 1991.[21] However, in order to achieve this overall strategy of developing overseas markets, ICI had squeezed together into a single unit its chemical, fertilizer, paint, and plastics operations.[22] The stage for this type of expansion on an international scale had been set by the former chairman Sir John Harvey-Jones, who had reduced the board from 12 members to 9 and had added for the first time members from countries outside the United Kingdom—one from Germany, one from Japan, and one from the United States—thus ensuring that different directors would not simply be advocates for various UK-based portions of the company.[23] Although it was impossible to erase the British character of the company, many observers agreed that ICI had gone farther than any other company in becoming global in its orientation.[24] He had turned the giant company around from a loss in 1980 to eventual profits of more than £1 billion half a decade later, the first British industrial company to ever achieve this.[25] Nevertheless, the accounting system was set up so that each division was responsible for its own profits; and the role of accountants was very pronounced, even on corporate teams involving other functions such as marketing, production, research and development, and sales.[26]

Pettigrew's analysis of ICI during the period 1960 to 1983, based on about 150 interviews of executives, concluded that ICI made radical changes occasionally, but these were cushioned by long periods of incremental change in which the company digested its previous moves. He also observed that change emanating from the core of the organization was based on fundamental changes in the belief structure of the key corporate leaders.[27]

Another big move into the United States came in 1987, when ICI purchased Stauffer Chemical for $1.69 billion, thus expanding its influence into the giant corn and rice markets so as to increase its worldwide sales of agricultural chemicals to $1.5 billion. As a result of this acquisition, ICI's sales of agricultural chemicals in the United States rose from 19 percent of its sales to 32 percent.[28] ICI quickly shaved off the specialty parts of Stauffer's oper-

---

[21]Emma Chynoweth, "Ammonia Process Owners Knock Small-Scale Technology," *Chemical Week*, 148 (13), April 3, 1991, p. 13.

[22]Nicolas Travers, "ICI Prepares for a Hi-Tech Future," *Director*, 40 (6), January 1987, pp. 26–29.

[23]Geoffrey Foster, "The Legacy of Harvey-Jones," *Management Today*, January 1987, pp. 34–41, 86–88.

[24]Jeremy Main, "How to Go Global—and Why," *Fortune*, 120 (5), August 28, 1989, pp. 70–76.

[25]James Bredin, "Making Change Happen," *Industry Week*, 237 (2), July 18, 1988, pp. 47–48.

[26]Hester Thomas, "Business Accountants Are Team Players," *Accountancy*, 99 (1122), February 1987, pp. 103–104.

[27]Andrew M. Pettigrew, "Context and Action in the Transformation of the Firm," *Journal of Management Studies*, 24 (6), November 1987, pp. 649–670.

[28]Langdon Brockinton, "ICI Expands Its Interest in U.S. Agrichemicals," *Chemical Week*, 140 (23), June 17, 1987, pp. 6–7.

ation (hydraulic fluids, sulfur products, some catalysts, and flame retardants) and sold them to Akzo of the Netherlands for $625 million.[29] Next, it sold off Stauffer's inorganic chemical business to the French firm Rhône-Poulenc for $505 million, with an additional $17 million in debt that had to be assumed.[30] After the operation was complete, the exposure for Stauffer had been only $700 million; and ICI was standing as the fastest-growing company in the agricultural chemicals business in the United States market with sales of more than $1.5 billion per year and also as the world's third-largest producer.[31] A year or so after the merger, Stauffer was reporting plans for marketing 14 new chemicals within a few years, amid expanding business.[32] By the end of the 1980s, an OECD report was commenting on how mergers and acquisitions had made the international chemical industry become increasingly global, and that for each 1 percent increase in GNP, chemical sales increase by 2 percent, with only 10 multinationals expected to dominate the entire world chemicals industry.[33] One of those, of course, was destined to be ICI.

By the beginning of the 1990s, ICI was getting ready to dump its fertilizer business and move aggressively into East Asia. These actions were expected to generate 40 percent of the worldwide growth in the chemicals business in the 1990s.[34] One of the vehicles for doing this was a purified terephthalic acid plant in Thailand, where sales of its herbicide paraquat were going well.[35] The fertilizer operations were eventually sold to Kemira of Helsinki, Finland, for £75 million.[36] At about the same time, ICI jumped further into the peptides market by purchasing Cambridge Research Biochemicals, opening the door to antipeptide antibody technology, bulk peptides and high-purity peptides.[37]

ICI long experimented with different novel applications of information systems, particularly at the local level. In 1986, ICI was developing the "Coun-

---

[29] Herbert C. Short, Nel Slis, Iris Gomez, and Felice Mikelberg, "Akzo Wins Stauffer—Quickly," *Chemical Week,* 141 (1), July 1, 1987, pp. 10–11.

[30] David Hunger, "Buying a Piece of Stauffer," *Chemical Week,* 141 (14), September 30, 1987, pp. 8–9.

[31] Langdon Brockington, "ICI's Expanded Agchem Agenda," *Chemical Week,* 141 (24), December 9, 1987, pp. 41–43.

[32] Langdon Brockinton, "The ICI/Stauffer Marriage: A Year Later Progress Report," *Chemical Week,* 143 (24), December 14, 1988, pp. 17–18.

[33] Anonymous, "Chemicals. Staying on the Boil," *Economicst,* 311 (7599), April 22, 1989, p. 69.

[34] Anonymous, "Reshaping ICI: One Thing Leads to the Next," *Economist,* 315 (7652), April 28, 1990, pp. 21–23.

[35] Emma Chynoweth, "ICI Takes a Closer Look at Thailand," *Chemical Week,* 146 (21), May 30 1990, p. 15.

[36] Emma Chynoweth, "Kemira Outlines Plans for U.K. Fertilizers," *Chemical Week,* 147 (5), August 8, 1990, pp. 16–17.

[37] Ken Liddle, "The Cambridge Research Biochemicals Phenomenon," *Technovation,* 10 (4), June 1990, pp. 273–278.

sellor" system, which was used in the Plant Protection Division to enable farmers to connect online for advice on how to get the highest yields from their crops. This expert system helped to sell ICI chemicals, and ICI was predicting more growth in the utilization of expert systems.[38] Although the highly decentralized nature of its global operations made it impossible to think about a single system, ICI was busy developing new applications such as online services to be used internally for research on different chemical compounds, forecasting of economic and market developments in world trade, and analysis of different geographical areas of the world. Its office automation effort incorporated these options, and special care was taken to promote standardization of the formats for electronically transmitted messages so that they might be filed in a standard database.[39]

ICI has also experimented with manufacturing "digital paper," which is a way to use paper as an optical digital storage mechanism, that might be more durable (longer-lasting) than actual optical disks. ICI was working on expanding the shelf life to more than 20 years.[40]

In the Glidden Coatings and Resins operation it had purchased for penetration into the U.S. market, ICI began to experiment with the use of personal computers and the SMART system, provided by the Innovative Software company, to perform prototyping of a perpetual inventory control system.[41] It also experimented with novel marketing ideas, such as introducing "paint studios" within its various dealer distribution outlets, linked with point-of-sale terminals to monitor paint mix sales closely.[42]

In 1990, ICI announced it was working with a self-designed computer program to analyze fiber movement within compounds that are being processed into thermoplastics at its Tempe, Arizona plant.[43] ICI was also involved in extensive work with supercomputers to design new molecules to use across its entire product line and perform other research functions.[44]

The highly distributed nature of ICI's business immediately causes problems with "classic" strategies in the information systems world. For example,

---

[38]Richard Cheevers, "Technology at Work: Wired Up to an 'Expert,'" *Director,* 40 (3), October 1986, p. 27.

[39]Clive Weeks, "The Need for Integrated Management of Information," *Journal of Information Science Principles & Practice,* 12 (6), 1986, pp. 283–289.

[40]Anthony D. Vanker, "Digital Paper: Mass Storage Revolution?" *Laserdisk Professional,* 2 (1), January 1989, pp. 38–41.

[41]David M. Zenker, "The PC as Prototype Problem-Solver," *Management Accounting,* 68 (11), May 1987, pp. 30–33.

[42]David Gerrie, "Point of Sale: Paint Splash," *Marketing,* September 8, 1988, p. 43.

[43]Jack K. Rogers, "Laboratory Is Dedicated to Developing Composite Manufacturing Techniques," *Modern Plastics,* 67 (7), July 1990, pp. 14, 16.

[44]Emma Chynoweth, "Supercomputers Boost Product and Process R&D," *Chemical Week,* 148 (12), March 27, 1991, p. 39.

in the area of executive support systems, there is a serious problem with distribution of information.[45] In the case of ICI, the distribution of data is highly complex, and the types of data needed are highly varied. A wide range of management levels must be brought into the process.[46] For example, a single director of engineering at ICI might be reponsible for managing more than 1,200 employees and operations of over 200 plants located in various locations around the world, such as a polyester film plant in Japan, a pharmaceuticals plant in Puerto Rico, an ammonia production facility in the United Kingdom, a Louisiana polyurethane plant, and a methyl methacrylate plant in Taiwan.[47] Getting the correct information in a timely manner to this person would be quite a tricky matter. If there are hundreds of such persons of equal reponsibility throughout the multinational corporation, then imagine what a headache it would be to have to perform the systems analysis, and implement an effective executive support system!

All of the moves made during the late 1980s as ICI moved towards its new market-segment-oriented approach meant a great deal of reorganization in the way ICI did business. ICI was the classic case of the multinational corporation that had inherited a vast machinery of information systems, located in different parts of the world and in different sections of the company even within the same countries, that were not integrated and did not work with each other. ICI has attempted to restructure itself on a global basis so that it controls products as well as geographical areas and functions simultaneously. It had four separate layers of information systems, and each layer had several planning and operational groups involved in both day-to-day operations and strategic planning. The overall system was so complex that Lester argued that it was impossible for companies such as ICI to make decisions about whether to be "global" or "act local" because they had to do everything at the same time, and more.[48]

Building a single global information system was completely out of the question. It would be too complex and would take decades. Instead, ICI found a strategy which involved building bridges between different systems. These bridges would be responsible for moving and processing only that data which was needed on a firm-wide basis, or at least on a basis which was beyond the scope of the environment from whence it came. Pantages reports that ICI was constantly facing the problem of how to balance the desire for integrity of its computer architecture and standardization against the need for quick

---

[45] See section on corporate intelligence systems.

[46] Clive Lester, "EIS: Europe's Information Seekers," *Datamation*, 35 (13), July 1, 1989, pp. 68, (17–18).

[47] Eric Johnson, "The Priority of Engineering,"*Chemical Engineering*, 96 (8), August 1989, pp. 59, 61.

[48] Tom Lester, "A Structure for Europe," *Management Today*, January 1991, pp. 76–78.

solutions to business problems.[49] Clearly, the desire for effective global systems would not be enough to overcome the predelictions of division or product management to get on with their work. A crucial part of this work was to work out standard data definitions that could be interchanged throughout the firm. Just this process alone took a great deal of time and, according to persons who worked directly with this process, it lay at the very heart of the problems involved in building global information systems in a highly distributed company such as ICI.[50]

One example of the type of global application developed by ICI involved the research departments. The Chairman ordered that the 12,000 researchers working around the world in different ICI facilities be networked together to build up the chances for synergism for the intensive R&D needed to survive.[51] The network helps ensure that researchers do not lose sight of business objectives.

At some time in the future, ICI may develop a global information system. However, this would clearly be a process taking years, perhaps even a decade or more. There are as many systems as businesses, and the natures of the businesses are highly varied as well. It is inevitable that, rather than moving toward standardization and globalization, ICI's information systems will tend to take on the character of ICI's organization itself—decentralized, matrix-like, and highly varied. There will remain a large amount of work to do in creating effective integration of reporting functions, using small subsets of data that have to be "traded" internationally between different parts of the chemical empire; but no thought of global systems will ever be maintained. It isn't so much a question of "homogenizing all data structures" as it is choosing which ones are critical and important enough to merit the effort required.

SUMMARY

Building global systems may mean engaging in an elaborate process of tying together very separated systems designed with entirely different purposes in mind.

- It is not common to find a single multinational corporation that has an information system designed to be global in the first place.

---

[49] Angeline Pantages, "The Right IS Chemistry," *Datamation,* 35 (16), August 15, 1989, pp. 61–62.

[50] Alex Mayall, comments at International Conference on Information Systems conference panel on "Global Information Systems," Conference, Copenhagen, December 1990.

[51] David Hunter, "ICI Focuses on Leading-Edge R&D," *Chemical Week,* 146 (14), April 11, 1990, p. 22.

- It is probably almost always impossible to completely reengineer a multinational's information systems to make them completely integrated.
- One viable strategy appears to be to choose a subset of data that are critical for global decision-making, then work at building inter-system networks and data flow facilities that are designed to handle this subset.
- It is not easy to identify exactly which data are required for global decision-making, and even this process of identification can take a very long time and furthermore be subject to a vast amount of uncertainty and change.

The case of Imperial Chemical Industries, PLC shows why designing globally integrated information systems can be quite challenging.

- Large multiproduct and multidivisional corporations are in a state of constant change.
- It is not clear that a global solution is best in many cases, and there are various applications that by necessity must be handled at the local level.
- The bulk of operational matters are handled within widely dispersed plants and operational centers, and the local site is where the bulk of the data processing takes place.

CHAPTER
24

Strategy #8: Globalize Human Resources

Even though all multinational corporations have a vast network of human resources, within that pool of talent we find that the majority of persons are specialized and focused on their tasks within national boundaries. Not too many have a global view of the multinational and its activities. This narrow perspective is caused first of all by their corporate training and also by the inherent interests of individual divisions and subsidiaries, which are responsible for meeting their own profit objectives first, and serving other goals of the multinational second. Within the information systems function, the national focus can be a danger or at a minimum a hindrance to systems development efforts, particularly those which involve corporate-wide systems. Local interests may conflict with global interests. The key challenge, then, of human resources management must be to cultivate global thinking and global action so as to develop a corps of systems development specialists capable of operating truly at the international level.

DISCUSSION

There has been a substantial amount of research examining the management of human resources *in general* within the multinational corporation. For a view of the role of computer management of human resources see Wagner, who argues that massive computerization of human resources files is necessary because of the trend toward decentralization in many organizations.[1] The question of whether multinational firms create employment in the national economics where they operate is taken up by Harvey and Kerin[2] who conclude that the unemployment effects of MNCs are not significant, that other larger macroeconomic factors in the economy better explain changes in employment levels. Operations of foreign MNCs in domestic markets increase employment. Questions of the role of women in MNC subsidiaries are considered by Israeli, Banai, and Zeira,[3] however, they only address Western Europeans and do not cover other important parts of the world such as Asia or Latin America. The dangers of having what is termed an "ethnocentric" policy in human resources are emphasized by Zeira, who writes:

> The ethnocentric personnel policy limits the opportunity of HCN's [host country nationals] to be promoted to key managerial positions in the subsidiaries and at headquarters.... The staffing policy in ethnocentric MNC's creates extremely severe organizational and human problems, especially in their subsidiaries and regional headquarters. These dysfunctional elements are inherent in their structure and cannot be eliminated so long as headquarters is convinced that the ethnocentric structure has indispensable advantages.[4]

This danger was also found earlier by Simmonds: "About one-fifth of the total employment in these firms is foreign, yet only 1.6% of their top corporate management entered as foreigners after age 25 or remain outside the United

---

[1] L. G. Wagner, "Computers, Decentralization, and Corporate Control," *California Management Review*, Winter 1966, pp. 25–32.

[2] Michael G. Harvey and Roger A. Kerin, "Multinational Corporations Versus Organized Labor: Divergent Views on Domestic Unemployment," *California Management Review*, XVIII (3), Spring 1976, pp. 5–13.

[3] Dafna N. Israeli, Moshe Banai, and Yoram Zeira, "Women Executives in MNC Subsidiaries," *California Management Review*, XXIII (1), Fall 1980, pp. 53–63.

[4] Yoram Zeira, "Management Development in Ethnocentric Multinational Corporations," *California Management Review*, XVIII (4), Summer 1976, pp. 34–42.

States."[5] A practical examination of selection of top-level management is found in Teague, who writes, "It appears that, particularly at top management levels, the process of selecting managers remains a fundamentally judgmental, intuitive, and personal activity.... However, going through this process on an international scale is considerably more difficult than working with the same problem domestically."[6]

For the Japanese perspective, see Kono, who gives an interesting insight into Japanese attitudes regarding Western workers:

> The organization tends to be mechanistic because of the following characteristics. People do only what is ordered. Punishment plays a more important role than reward. People do not acknowledge the mistakes they have made, and they do not try to learn from them. People specialize, and are specialist-oriented. People compete with one another and do not teach one another, because of the merit system. Communication between colleagues is not good. The organization tends to be economic. The sense of identification with the organization is low and staff turnover is high. People leave the company when they acquire a certain skill. The status of blue-collar workers is lower than that of white-collar workers. The hierarchical differences are larger, and there is much less equality.[7]

On the other hand, Peterson and Schwind's survey of foreign managers operating in the Japanese environment found the following complaints about the Japanese: problems communicating, difficulty in receiving exact information and data, reluctance of Japanese to report failures, lack of initiative, and so on.[8] In addition, Sullivan and Nonaka found very sharp contrasts between Japanese and American managerial attitudes towards communication.[9] A classification of five forms of intercultural management structures between Japanese and

---

[5]Kenneth Simmonds, "Multinational? Well, Not Quite," *Columbia Journal of World Business*, Fall 1966, pp. 115–122.

[6]Frederick A. Teague, "International Management Selection and Development," *California Management Review*, XII (3), Spring 1970, pp. 1–6.

[7]Toyohiro Kono, "Multinational Management," *Japanese Economic Studies*, Fall/Winter 1984–85, pp. 3–44.

[8]Richard B. Peterson and Hermann F. Schwind, "A Comparative Study of Personnel Problems in International Companies and Joint Ventures in Japan," *Journal of International Business Studies*, September 1977, pp. 45–55.

[9]Jeremiah J. Sullivan and Ikujiro Nonaka, "The Application of Organizational Learning Theory to Japanese and American Management," *Journal of International Business Studies*, Fall 1986, pp. 127–147.

Chapter 24 Strategy #8: Globalize Human Resources   361

non-Japanese is found in Hayashi.[10] These cultural differences indicate that in organizations as large as multinational corporations, management of human resources presents a stiff challenge.

In addition to the general management problems encountered in the personnel area of the multinational, there is a subset of problems that relate specifically to the information systems function, where highly-qualified personnel are always difficult to find and sometimes harder to manage.

One of the important characteristics of today's multinational corporation and how it manages information technology involves the distribution and isolation of critical human resources. Even though every major systems development effort depends for its success upon effective utilization of human resources, this problem is difficult in even the most disciplined of organizations. Why else would the average systems development backlog be more than 12 months, or sometimes as much as three years or more? Clearly, when technology is evolving so quickly, development backlogs of such great distances into the future mean that the chance of implementing systems that are obsolete before they are ever completed is heightened.

The problem is made even more severe within the context of the multinational corporation. Not only are there a great many people to contend with, but also they are isolated, many times behind national borders, different cultures, and different languages. Some experiments have found that the complex human resources management problems of a multinational can be handled efficiently from a central location with relatively modest equipment, but there is no indication this type of approach is widespread in practice.[11] This lack of implementation is a reflection of the so-called "United Nations" model of the organization, in which semi-autonomous data processing centers have been created in most of the countries in which the multinational is conducting business. Although the excuse for this lies in how the multinational adapts to various restrictive government regulations in the host country, the effect for the information technology function remains the same—human resources are redundantly scattered throughout the information technology empire and are more difficult than ever to coordinate into an effective team. The duplication of data centers inevitably means the duplication of human

---

[10] Kichiro Hayashi, "Crosscultural Interface Management: The Case of Japanese Firms Abroad," *Japanese Economic Studies,* Fall 1986, pp. 3–41.

[11] For an analysis of more than 40,000 variables and 450,000 constraints for scheduling of personnel grouped into four different skill levels for 150 different jobs in a multinational corporation, see G. G. Hegde and Pandu R. Tadikamalla, "Interactive Workforce Management on a PC: An Industry-University Partnership," *European Journal of Operational Research,* 48 (2), 1990, pp. 275–280.

resources; and the larger the multinational, the greater the amount and degree of waste.

This duplication results in an overspecialization on the part of many data processing employees. This occurs because, rather than being concerned with the global issues of the multinational, the employees are focused almost exclusively on the operations within the national borders where they are operating. Probably only a small percentage of the employees of a multinational corporation spend a significant amount of time travelling to different locations in a professional capacity. It is therefore difficult to imagine that more than a few persons would have a truly global view of the multinational corporation and how it works. With the exception of the telecommunications function, which is concerned with linking the far-flung parts of the multinational empire together, even persons with the data processing function may have limited vision on global matters.

Even within the home country data processing establishment, we frequently find that the international section of the team is put off in a corner, away from the core of the data processing action.[12] For example, rather than being concerned with global inventory control, the operations staff will be focused only on the problems within their national territory. It is easy to see how this situation, driven as it is by individual priorities, could lead to a systemwide deoptimization even in such a basic area as safety-stocking-level calculations. Another example might be human resources and personnel applications specialists who in the absence of a global approach would have little incentive whatsoever to design open application systems capable of supporting the corporation as a whole, but who rather would tend to build applications that are more or less unique to each country in which they operate. This process of specialization in data processing application on a nation-by-nation basis is an example of the classic systems dynamics problem whereby the optimization of individual parts drags down the efficiency of the overall system.

To begin to remedy this situation, the human resources function within data processing can begin to maximize control over human resources by doing a comprehensive inventory of human resources and skills on a corporation-wide basis.[13] In addition to basic understanding of lower-level skills such as telecommunications expertise, or programming expertise, or small scale project management, and so on, it is important to maintain a good roster

---

[12] One wonders how many times troublesome project managers are shunted to overseas assignments simply to "get them out of the hair" of senior information technology function management at the headquarters.

[13] In some countries, there are problems with maintaining personnel files on citizens outside of the home country without permission. For example, Swedish privacy laws are very strict in this regard.

of more experienced persons who could possibly be tapped to solve the more difficult systemwide problems of the information system. With this initial inventory of human resources, the lead system (see below) can work more effectively, as the multinational can be assured that for any given global systems development project, only the very best of the human resources will be placed on the front line against the problem.

Another aspect of more careful human resources management on a global scale involves the search for efficiencies. There are two major aspects of this which should be brought out: elimination of redundancy and out-sourcing of noncore applications, both on the operational and systems development side.[14] In terms of redundancies, we have seen that the various forces that led multinationals to adopt the United Nations (distributed) model of data processing operations have resulted in duplication of human resources acquisition just as much as they have resulted in creation of redundant data processing centers in which these additional human resources are employed. A first-order effect of more effective global operations, insofar as they are achieved through *regionalization* of heretofore national data processing operations, is that they will automatically yield possibilities for elimination of surplus human talent. It is also reasonable to assume that use of the lead system or a modification of it may provide opportunities to get more horsepower from existing personnel. Through additional travel and added responsibilities that go beyond the traditional activities that have been confined to the borders of their host country, data processing personnel may be able to accomplish more in their field of expertise and thus cut down on the need to hire and retain redundant human resources. If this type of strategy does not place an overload on the personnel who have been tapped to take on more international activities, a savings should result.

The question of out-sourcing is more complex. Within the context of human resources management, the question of out-sourcing in many cases boils down to a trade-off between in-house wage costs and procurement of the equivalent resources outside the firm. There are many disadvantages of out-sourcing, and these have been discussed widely in the literature and trade press.[15] However, there is no doubt that out-sourcing can provide great advantages in terms of reducing the payroll. The typical strategy of out-sourcing

---

[14] *Out-sourcing* is a term that refers to the process of taking operational functions done within a firm and subcontracting them to an outside company to perform.

[15] Some of the principal disadvantages of out-sourcing include the following: that the multinational will over the medium and long term lose control over their data processing activities, thus placing their vendor in a more advantageous position that will eventually be reflected in substantially higher costs; that trade secrets or proprietary information regarding company business may leak out to competitors more readily; that the choice of vendors may be compromised in a way that may result in temporary savings but may lock the firm into a technological trajectory that
(*continued*)

involves the division of application in two categories: core/critical and non-core/critical, the latter being earmarked as a reasonable candidate for outsourcing. In theory, the firm should be able to retain only the most highly trained people in order to focus all of its effort on the most important mission-critical applications development. The other employees, who in the past have worked in the noncritical areas, can be dismissed. In terms of management of human resources, the message is clear: Firms must be able to identify both the mission-critical applications development projects and the mission-critical human resources that are going to be retained in order to bring them to fruition. To accomplish this, again it is necessary to have a global human resources roster of trained personnel, who have a great amount of experience and can make the first cut in the selection process.

It is reasonable to expect this need would require the creation of a comprehensive database on different personnel to keep track of in-house talent. This is a tricky proposition because the types of information that are used in making management selection decisions are many times illegal to keep on record because they may constitute slander or unfounded criticism. As a result of this, most personnel selection processes have a parallel informal character through which "background" information is obtained on the candidate for a specific task. This background information is typically word-of-mouth and in most cases not totally up-to-par in terms of being strictly legal (that is why it is obtained informally and off the record). Consequently, this information comes only through an informal management process that operates outside the formal personnel system. Thus, in most cases the selection will not be

---

forecloses future options (e.g., when a vendor introduces improvements to its product line), thus resulting in eventual higher costs. The problem relating to the guaranteed protection of proprietary company information may be one of the most severe. This issue has gained increasing importance in some sectors such as shared credit card processing, where companies engaged in a scrappy fight for credit card customers fear their competitors could get access to lists of their clients or their financial information and thus steal them away. Protection of this sort requires a large amount of legal involvement and any multinational is encouraged to take a very careful look at the protections that are involved. This question is becoming even more important as shared processing operations, which many times are already themselves subsidiaries of major credit card companies such as American Express, are done across national borders, in which case the firm allowing the out-sourcing must seek to acquire legal protection for its rights in a different country. An even more difficult problem occurs when the company allowing the out-sourcing is in the process of developing applications and systems that are proprietary in nature or that are aimed at giving it some type of competitive advantage in the market place. First, use of out-sourcing may hinder the systems development effort; second, the firm must seek guarantees that the in-house systems development employees of the firm providing the out-sourcing services do not at a later time use their knowledge of these proprietary systems for the benefit of the competition. Although this classic problem has taken place many times in the past in terms of the relationship between consulting firms and their clients, the problem also occurs in this data processing sector, and has not yet been satisfactorily resolved. There is a clear need to strike a balance of interests between the out-sourcer and the provider of the services.

made on a worldwide basis, but rather on the basis of the extent to which the selection team can draw upon its personal contacts to locate talent. There is nothing inherently wrong with this type of system, having as it does the type of both formal and informal nature that characterizes management decision-making in general; however, it contradicts directly the idea of setting up a global human resources database to make it possible to draw dispassionately upon the total human resources base of the multinational. It results in human resources decisions having a cliquish nature that inevitably results in locking out a significant amount of talent.

In any case, assuming the multinational is going to proceed with a new project to develop a better inventory of its base of specialized skills in the systems development area to be targeted at development of global mission-critical applications, it must keep in mind that its traditional categories of skills and information may be able to serve as only a starting point in selection and management of highly skilled and trained personnel. Special note must be made of multicultural skills, language skills, and some personality traits that form essential ingredients for successful implementation of global systems development projects.

SUMMARY

The critical factor in management of human resources in the information technology function involves developing and rewarding global skills in systems development.

- An incentive structure should be put in place to allow specialists to work for global, corporate-wide, objectives without being punished for "ignoring" their work at the local, subsidiary, level.
- Recruitment for international systems development projects should focus on persons with potential to handle multiple cultures, speak multiple languages, and with enough political sensitivity to avoid to the best extent possible political misunderstandings.
- The starting process in building these skills is to perform a global inventory of human skills throughout the entire multinational corporation with all of its different information systems functions.

PART V
POSTSCRIPT: MANAGING INTERNATIONAL INFORMATION

CHAPTER 25

The Multinational CIO

This chapter presents a brief summary of this entire monograph from the point of view of the Chief Information Officer. It reviews general trends and suggests steps the CIO can take to re-engineer his organization for the new global environment of the 1990s and beyond. Much of the insight in this concluding chapter is based on successful completion of consulting assignments for MNCs facing the challenge of international information systems management.

Note: Major parts of this chapter were written with Brad Power, Joseph Ferreira, and Adam Crescenzi of the CSC Index Group in Cambridge, Massachusetts, and London, England.

Chapter 25 The Multinational CIO

With the rapid changes taking place in today's world, it may be difficult for any Chief Information Officer to obtain a clear view of how to proceed in creating global systems. There is much reading to draw upon, and the endless series of case studies available, combined with the gradual but continual advances being made in available applications software, public services (particularly international telecommunications), and new, faster, improved platforms. All these can be relied upon to help the CIO set out the correct course of navigation through the global sea.

On the other hand, it is easy to be cynical and depressed at the prospects. There is a significant amount of literature and press information available, but it doesn't go deep enough. It does not satisfy, and the information strategist who goes through this information is left with the feeling of having imbibed a very shallow stream. After reading through much of the information, he or she would be able to write a scathing comment such as this:

> After having completed a somewhat wide-ranging review of both the international business literature and its poor cousin MIS literature, I have concluded three things. First, not very much is understood in the academic community about the use of information technology in multinational corporations, particularly at a level of detail found for domestic systems. Second, multinational corporations do not appear to be using information technology very well. Third, the second point is much more important than the first.
>
> It appears that global strategy in international business may have passed by the IS function, leaving it behind to ponder its massive strings of unwritten computer code and multi-year application backlogs. Business may have become international and global, but information technology has not—at least not intelligently, and certainly not to its fullest potential. It is still developing, and there is a need for a great amount of thinking about what the best solutions really are. It is a tricky business to make technological plans when they cannot possibly be implemented for half of a decade or more. In the rapidly crumbling ethos of the American corporation at least, infected and decaying as it is from the "fast buck" approach to strategic management, many people do not even plan on keeping their job that long. So who is to go to bat for something that will get a payoff when they are at another job? Yes, it is indeed a tricky business, but it may be even more tricky than you think.
>
> In addition to the fog of ambiguity that surrounds information technology and its use, there is the difficult question of the organizational form, that is, the question of how the business is to operate in its most detailed procedures. Information systems are designed around these detailed "standard operating procedures"—but what are these when your competitors are eating your lunch, forcing you into a massive restructuring and rethinking of your business? So here you are. The executive. It's tough, but "somebody's gotta do it," right? You have to participate in creating an information-technology strategy based on the standard operating procedures that will result from the adjustments you are making to the onslaughts of your competitors, and you have to do it with a view of five years or so into the future, when the applications will come "on-line." And there is a good chance that the technology you plan on using will be obsolete by that time.

If you are the Chief Information Officer, you have my sympathy. The strategic thinkers in the multinational are probably running circles around your office waving their little red books in the air like Mao Red Guards and chanting "globalization," "think globally, act locally," "strategic systems," and so on. You close the door to your office and the sound is decreased somewhat, but you see them through the window. The whir of the air-conditioning system soothes your failing nerves. "Another list of demands from end-users." You think of the massive work in systems and applications development underway, the limitations in technology, the problems with end-users, the pressures, the high turnover rates, the constant prodding of the narrow-minded bean counters who know nothing about technology management. The question is, "Who is the saint, and who is the devil?"

Unfortunately, there is no one around to throw you a line to pull you out of the storming sea, or, to use a computer metaphor, to remove your personal bio-unit from the growing silicon systems that have trapped it and threaten its existence. The academics certainly won't help you. This is not to say that they can't provide you with reading material while you wait for your ship to sink. The academic community has created an endless series of 20–30 page neatly packaged articles that can amuse you and perhaps help you figure out what to do, or at least what you should be doing. Academics have their own problems too. Most are trapped on a tenure-track schedule, continually facing short resources, a lack of reliable and comprehensive data, and the hundreds of Nintendo-generation students we are producing these days. Most academic writing, particularly in the information-systems area, as soon as it is released for review, immediately begins to receive SCUD missile attacks from The Gatekeepers. And who are they? The Gatekeepers are the academic equivalent of the bean counters you face in your own organization. They are the modern-day equivalent of Savonarola's Florentine clerics who spent months burning art and manuscripts because they glorified humanity, and not God; The Gatekeepers are protecting not God, but a heretical version of narrow-minded empiricism that sees all the world as a system of numbers, complete with elaborate statistical tests. Just as Savonarola reduced everything to God's will, so too do The Gatekeepers try to reduce studies of organizations and complex phenomena to neat systems of neo-Platonic logic, and bitterly resent other types of research. And what is the result?

The result is that there isn't much written on information technology in multinational corporations. This isn't going to help you with the true believers who are beating on the glass outside your door.

However, to offer a scathing critique of the available literature is not the purpose here. There *are* steps that can be taken by the CIO to develop winning strategies, and the mass of available literature from both the international business side as well as from the MIS area all point to a mosaic of possibilities. There is much evidence that many of the more successful corporations are involved in developing these winning strategies. There is also some evidence that many of the academics have learned a great deal more than they are sometimes given credit for.

A summary of the action steps that the CIO can take to develop these winning strategies is provided below. If readers wish to go deeper into the background of these observations, they are encouraged to read further into the theoretical work and the case studies.

Multinational corporations now account for most of the world's economic activity. They are active in virtually every sector of the economy from health care to finance, from information technology and mass media to transportation and energy. With the exception of a few areas such as craft industries, it is the MNC that accounts for the bulk of the world's economy. The MNC operates on an international scale that is unprecedented in history.[1]

There are indications that many MNCs are beginning to rely more and more on information technology.[2] Some are able to get and sustain competitive advantage in the overseas markets in which they operate. These global companies are able to use information technology to strike a balance between global management and the demands of individual national or regional markets. Companies are using IT to coordinate globally—in customer relations, product management, operations and logistics,[3] and infrastructure[4] —while simultaneously addressing local needs.

In customer relations, IT enables a company to present one consistent face to customers, view the total relationship with key customers, and mobilize worldwide resources quickly to meet customer needs. For example, Digital Equipment Corporation uses electronic mail and electronic conferencing to

---

[1] For a general history, see Mira Wilkins, "Modern European Economic History and the Multinationals," *Journal of Economic Literature,* pp. 575–595. See also Helga Nussbaum, "International Cartels and Multinational Enterprises," in Alice Teichova, Maurice Lévy-Leboyer, and Helga Nussbaum, eds., *Multinational Enterprise in Historical Perspective* (New York: Cambridge University Press, 1986). A comprehensive historical periodization of the MNC is found in John H. Dunning, ed., *Multinational Enterprises, Economic Structure and International Competitiveness* (New York: John Wiley & Sons, 1985); and John H. Dunning, ed., *The Multinational Enterprise* (London: George Allen & Unwin, Ltd., 1971). See also John H. Dunning, John A. Cantwell, and T. A. B. Corley, "The Theory of International Production: Some Historical Antecedents," in Peter Hertner and Geoffrey Jones, eds., *Multinationals: Theory and History* (Aldershot Harts, England: Gower Publishing Co., Ltd., 1986).

[2] Roach has argued that up to 48 percent of all capital investment in the United States is being put into information technology. Stephen Roach, *The New Technology Cycle* (New York: Morgan Stanley, September 11, 1985); see also *White-Collar Productivity: A Glimmer of Hope?* special economic study (New York: Morgan Stanley, September 16, 1988); see also *America's Technology Dilemma: A Profile of the Information Economy,* special economic study (New York: Morgan Stanley, April 22, 1987).

[3] For a study of a logistics and operation system for the international shipping industry, see David M. Miller, "An Interactive, Computer-Aided Ship Scheduling System," *European Journal of Operational Research,* 32 (3), December 1987, pp. 363–379, which reviews the work of the Ethyl Corporation.

[4] See Ralph Emmett Carlyle, "CIO: Misfit or Misnomer?" *Datamation,* August 1, 1988, pp. 50–56, who points out that investments in infrastructure may be hampered by short-term business strategies: "Such relentless pressure to perform in the short term usually precludes sustained executive commitment to long-term projects, killing a CIO's grand plans before they can materialize."

assemble service teams worldwide. Digital can locate service personnel for any problem and put them to work on it immediately. People are united in work groups by electronically linking them, not by physically moving them. Problem resolution can begin immediately. Teams can be modified quickly—experts added and subtracted—as the problem unfolds.

In product management, IT allows organizations to design customized products with mass-production economies, respond rapidly to changing conditions in consumer trends or product performance, and rapidly develop and launch products worldwide using international development teams. Apparel manufacturer Benetton mass-produces "half-garments" that are finished (e.g., dyed) according to local requirements for the week. The Italian-based clothier links its 4000 retail stores in a global communications network that provides daily updates on sales and inventory. Using the network, information systems, a CAD system linked to automatic cutting machines, and a highly automated warehouse, Benetton manufactures clothes according to local tastes in a worldwide market and responds to rapidly changing fashion trends. A pharmaceutical company links R&D labs in four sites in the United States and Europe, leveraging expertise globally via electronic mail and electronic conferencing. The company addresses local government approval requirements simultaneously in several countries instead of seeking drug approval on a sequential basis. In an industry marked by time-consuming approval cycles, this means capitalizing on foreign markets as quickly as possible and beating competitors to market.

In the area of operations and logistics, IT lets a firm source globally, flexibly allocating production activities across borders by optimizing internal production facilities and external purchasing of supplies. Dow Chemical uses a sophisticated sourcing and logistics system for juggling international production schedules. Using a computerized linear program, the company weighs everything from currency and tax rates to transportation and local production costs to identify its cheapest plant. For example, in making chloralkali and its derivatives, Dow's network chooses among factories on three continents to supply customers throughout the world.

In terms of the information-technology infrastructure, IT provides global access to proprietary data and specialist expertise, and collects and distributes global intelligence.[5] A multinational record company that collects information on a country basis on artists, records (including where the records can be sold), and costs in each country, links the information into a global catalogue to address local and specialized markets.

---

[5] At Mitsui the company motto is: "Information is the lifeblood of the company." The Japanese trading company uses a global network for competitive intelligence. Mitsui's satellite network connects 200 offices worldwide and carries 80,000 messages per day, many of them representing intelligence gathering. The Japanese train managers to make competitive intelligence everyone's business.

THE ADMINISTRATIVE HERITAGE OF THE MNC

In spite of these visible successes, our consulting experience has led us to conclude that for many other MNCs, the information-technology structures have not been very well organized and designed. For many MNCs, the present situation is not the result of a thought-out IT strategy; instead it appears to be more the result of inertia. Many MNCs seem burdened with an administrative heritage[6] that is preventing them from responding to changes. Their information systems appear to be lagging behind their business strategy.

The lack of a global IT strategy has its origin in the history of the multinational corporation itself. That structure was well in place *before* IT made its debut on the business scene. IT slipped into an already-established bureaucratic and organizational structure. This structure was present when IT was introduced, and it provided the conduits into which flowed the rivers of automation. Even new branches of MNCs appear to be modeled on the older patterns.

When most information technology was introduced—the early and mid-1960s—the typical MNC was set up on a country-by-country basis. An MNC was "global" only in the sense of ownership and some financial control and reporting. There was little global sourcing and few inter-subsidiary coordination problems to cope with. This type of organizational outcome was driven by the restrictive national legislation in the host countries.[7] Variations in tax regulations, rules of incorporation and ownership, product guidelines, and patent protection drove the multinational corporation to develop unique practices within each country where it did business. Although there are many explanations of why companies set up operations overseas instead of merely exporting from their home country, some of the major motivations are the need to overcome national barriers,[8] and to get access to raw materials. Some MNCs sought

---

[6]This term appears in Christopher A. Bartlett and Sumantra Ghoshal, "Managing Across Borders: New Strategic Requirements," *Sloan Management Review,* Summer 1987, pp. 7–17, which also develops the concept of "acting locally and managing globally within a general context, but not as regards information systems."

[7]For a discussion of the balance of power between the multinational corporation and the host country see Yves L. Doz, *Government Control and Multinational Strategic Management: Power Systems and Telecommunication Equipment* (New York: Praeger, 1979). Doz presents a bargaining power model in Yves Doz, *Strategic Management in Multinational Companies* (Oxford: Pergamon Press, 1986). A further discussion of this issue is found in José De La Torre, "Foreign Investment and Economic Development: Conflict and Negotiation," *Journal of International Business Studies,* Fall 1981, pp. 9–32. An analysis of political responsiveness on the part of the MNC is found in W. Chan Kim, "Competition and the Management of Host Government Intervention," *Sloan Management Review,* Spring 1987, pp. 33–39. See also Dennis J. Encarnation and Louis T. Wells, Jr., "Sovereignty en Garde: Negotiating with Foreign Investors," *International Organization,* 39 (1), Winter 1985, pp. 47–78.

[8]One of the pioneering works on national barriers is Joe S. Bain, *Barriers to New Competition: Their Character and Consequences in Manufacturing Industries* (Cambridge, MA: Harvard University Press, 1956).

to achieve economies of scale, others to wage a battle against their competitors in foreign markets in order to checkmate their expansion into third markets. However, the result was that the MNC was organized typically with a national headquarters around which orbited a constellation of semi-autonomous subsidiaries, and this structure was well in place before information technology had a major impact.[9]

As data processing was added into the MNC, however, it naturally tended to follow this same pattern and therefore created a string of semi-autonomous national data-processing centers. This was the result of the "administrative heritage" of the MNC. Other forces have influenced this outcome as well. Some national rules and regulations, such as rules on transborder data flow of personal data,[10] peculiarities of tax and accounting standards, and different requirements for information retention,[11] and so on — have driven the data-processing environment into a "national" model. Many applications that are unique to the national markets have also provided a further centrifugal pressure against the information-systems function, as purchasing, human resources, payroll, logistics, and other major applications are specific to the local level. The result of these forces is that in many cases, the only significant linkage with the headquarters is in the area of financial reporting. Within the organizational structure of each country operation, all of the basic business functions are replicated. Michael Angus, the chairman of Unilever PLC, for example,

---

[9]For a conceptual description of the historical evolution of data-processing arrangements in multinational corporations, showing change from an "empire" (centralized) model to a "U.N. Company" (decentralized around national data-processing centers) to a "global" arrangement, see CSC Index, "Engineering the New Global Corporation," *Insights,* Summer 1990, pp. 2–9. For a discussion of the Empire model, the United Nations model, and the global model of information processing within the multinational corporation, and how they relate to corporate strategy, see John M. Thompson, Ted W. Faigle, and James E. Short, "Competing Through Information Technology: We Are The World," *Information Strategy: The Executive's Journal,* 3 (4), Summer 1987, pp. 32–37.

[10]For one of the most comprehensive studies of this issue, see Karl P. Sauvant, *International Transactions in Services: The Politics of Transborder Data Flows* (Boulder, CO: Westview Press, 1986). See also Karl P. Sauvant, "Transborder Data Flows and the Developing Countries," *International Organization,* 37 (2), Spring 1983, pp. 359–371. For a discussion of possible taxation of transborder data flows in multinational corporations and what implications this will have, see Walter F. O'Connor, "The International Tax Implications of Transborder Data Flow," *International Tax Journal,* 15 (1), Winter 1989, pp. 73–85. See also Rajan Chandran, Arvind Phatak, and Rakesh Sambharya, "Transborder Data Flows: Implications for Multinational Corporations," *Business Horizons,* 30 (6), November/December 1987, pp. 74–82. Chandran et al. make a careful analysis of the different types of networks available to carry computer data including public and private networks. They argue that transborder data flow regulations will cause increased costs in the operations of multinationals. Similar material is provided by John Diebold, "Communications Bottlenecks Still Beset National Borders," *Network World,* 4 (22), June 1, 1987, pp. 1, 30–32. Diebold recommends that national leaders consider how to create a more "user-friendly" international environment to enable policies to keep up with changes in technology.

[11]It is interesting to note that although there has been a great deal of liberalization in areas such as international telecommunications, laws regarding personal data and record-keeping at the international level became even more strict in the 1980s.

has argued that the finance, research, and management development functions must be centrally controlled, but that other functions can be handled in a decentralized fashion.[12] On the other hand, a company like Boral of Australia gives a great deal of autonomy to its managers, in areas such as advertising, marketing, making decisions about production volumes, and even allocating capital for investment in new plant.[13]

As a result, many of today's CIOs have found they are sitting on top of an IT infrastructure that is broken up into almost as many pieces as there are countries in which the firm operates.[14] However, a great number of significant changes have rocked the nature of international business, and we seriously doubt that this type of arrangement will withstand the new competitive conditions of the 1990s.

NEW COMPETITIVE CONDITIONS

Although many MNCs have always been associated with the specific countries from which they originated, the trend is toward international cooperation and the emergence of the "stateless corporation" based on strategic alliances. There is a trend toward global alliances, many of which are technology-driven.[15] Particularly in R&D-intensive sectors—aerospace, microelectronics, pharmaceuticals—companies have taken up these alliances to pool resources. Matsushita of Japan, General Electric in the United States, MBB in Germany, and so on—are examples of companies entering into dramatic strategic alliances. MBB worked with General Electric in jet engines; Matsushita worked with Phillips of the Netherlands. The result is the creation of a type of "mega-company" composed of the alliances of giant multinationals.[16]

These strategic alliances have been further intensified by the rapid acceleration of global M&A activity. In sector after sector, companies are pooling

---

[12] See Preston Townley, "Globesmanship," *Across the Board,* 27 (1, 2), January/February 1990, pp. 24–34.

[13] See Anonymous, "Bottom Heavy Management for a Better Bottom Line at Boral," *Rydge's,* 59 (3), March 1986, pp. 42–43.

[14] The typical types of problems found are indicated in Charles E. Exley, Jr., "How Changes in MIS Affect the CFO and the CIO," *Financial Executive,* 6 (5), November/December 1990, p. 16, which mentions "lack of access to enterprise-wide data," "inability to integrate data spread around different applications and systems," "lack of application portability," "concern for data integrity," and "maintenance of monolithic systems," all linked together as "a variety of processors, files and databases, applications, and communications protocols, many of which are incompatible."

[15] The role of the CIO in take-over or acquisition situations is discussed in Mel Mandell, "The CIO: Myth or Reality," *Computer Decisions,* 19, March 23, 1987, p. 66.

[16] See Deigan Morris and Michael Hergert, "Trends in International Collaborative Agreements," *Columbia Journal of World Business,* Summer 1987, pp. 15–21. See also Kathryn Rudie Harrigan, "Strategic Alliances: Their New Role in Global Competition," *Columbia Journal of World Business,* Summer 1987, pp. 67–69+; Werner Feld, "Political Aspects of Transnational Business Collaboration in the Common Market," *International Organization,* 24 (2), 1970, pp. 209–238.

resources and talent to attack new markets. Many of these companies are so large, they can both cooperate and compete in different markets simultaneously. The threat of the intensified competition is pressing against all companies and their management strategists.

These alliances have been facilitated by the weakening of many national borders as a significant barrier to trade. A primary factor in this regard is the somewhat liberal international trade regime established after the second world war, through international organizations such as the General Agreement on Tariffs and Trade (GATT).[17] However, this process is accelerating dramatically in 1992 in Europe.[18] The post-1992 structure of the market may enable some MNCs to tear down the national walls that have separated their different data-processing centers and, in so doing, move to a centralized order-processing configuration on a Europe-wide basis.[19] This will replace the separate order fulfillment organizations for each country, which are the norm under the old model. In addition, the breakdown of the Iron Curtain and the resulting movement of the Eastern European countries toward free market economies and convertible currencies will further accelerate the expansion of international trading.

Any corporation that does not take steps to innovate in the way it organizes and operates its information-technology function is in danger. In light of these changes, the CIO must reexamine and question the traditional architectures that have characterized development and distribution of major data centers and the applications they support.[20] If the conditions—such as national regulations—that gave rise to this type of topology are removed, then what must be done to the IT function?

The answer lies in aligning more carefully with the changing corporate strategy.[21] This alignment must ensure that, as global strategies change and

---

[17] It is ironic that the GATT has worked hard to weaken many of the national barriers to commerce that initially played a large role in creating the modern MNC.

[18] For a review of top executives' views of 1992, see Booz-Allen & Hamilton, *Europe 1992: Threat or Opportunity* (New York: Booz-Allen & Hamilton, 1989).

[19] See CSC Index, "Europe in 1992: Winning Through Technology," *Indications*, 1988.

[20] This architecture has become increasingly complex as technology has advanced. The challenge for control over this expanding technology base has been, at least in part, responsible for the increased visibility of the CIO and perhaps even for the creation of the concept of the CIO itself. See Therese R. Welter, "The Chief Information Officer: What's Behind the Hype," *Industry Week*, June 29, 1987, pp. 45–48, who observes that "in reality the C.I.O. simply represents the changing human element in the broader corporate shift to elevate IS from a supportive tool...to a capital asset...[because] little by little, consolidation of the telecommunications, office automation, and data-processing departments occur, leading to a stronger and stronger executive, and, ultimately, to a very, very different [infra] structure."

[21] See Lew McCreary, "CIOs in the Spotlight," *CIO*, September 1989, pp. 62–68, who reports that "sixty-nine percent of respondents [CIOs] placed alignment at the top of the study's critical issues."

play themselves out, the information-technology infrastructure acts as a facilitator rather than an obstacle to corporate responsiveness.[22]

Such a harmonious match between the global strategy of the MNC and its information technology would ensure that strategy is reflected at all levels of the organization—because the information infrastructure of the corporation is the knowledge network supporting the organizational structure and its operations. This is a process that involves simultaneous redesigning of the MNC as well as redesigning and retrofitting of its information-technology infrastructure.

Most companies fail to have in place a coherent information-*technology* strategy.[23] Their IT infrastructure does not match or facilitate their emerging global *business* strategy. Few multinationals have discovered the potential of computer and communications technology to transform their operations on a global basis. A company may have a single product sold globally, but no globally rationalized product database. It may be fighting a battle for centralized control when the business strategy needs to be different for each national market. It most likely has many different national data centers when it could better serve strategy with regionalized data processing of selected applications and resources. There are other ways as well in which companies fail to map their information-technology infrastructure against their corporate strategy. We see that companies are only now beginning to develop sophisticated global *business* strategies, but few are developing serious parallel global IT strategies.[24]

These factors call for the MNC to re-engineer its business operations and the underlying information-technology systems that support them.

---

[22] See Peter G. W. Keen, *Shaping the Future: Business Design Through Information Technology* (Harvard: Harvard Business School Press, 1991). His section on "geographic positioning" discusses the MNC and how it should build a "transnational platform" (p. 73).

[23] In an Index survey of 384 information-systems executives in U.S. corporations, it was found that "the globalization of business... is an issue for business executives in less than half (43%) of the companies [surveyed]." See CSC Index, *Critical Issues of Information Systems Management for 1991* (Cambridge, MA: CSC Index, 1990), pp. 18–19. In a previous survey, it was found that "in about half the U.S. companies and 60% of the European corporations, business executives are addressing issues of globalization.... However, a much smaller percentage of companies are addressing the information systems issues related to globalization.... less than half (43%) were addressing the related I/S issues, and only one quarter (26%) said the I/S issues were clearly understood." See CSC Index, *Critical Issues of Information Systems Management for 1990* (Cambridge, MA: CSC Index, 1990), p. 37.

[24] It may be symptomatic that in many multinationals, the "international" section of the MIS function is shuttled off to the side as a type of after-thought. Many executives are so concerned with the day-to-day problems of their domestic operations, they have little time to worry about international questions. This raises questions for the CIO. Even the idea of an international information technology executive may imply, in some organizations, that they have fallen off from the path to top leadership and been delegated problem assignments overseas.

RE-ENGINEERING THE MNC FOR NEW COMPETITIVE CONDITIONS

There is every indication that the pace of change is increasing, not decreasing. These global transformations will inevitably change business strategies, but in perhaps unpredictable ways. As a result, the CIO must be on active stand-by and build up infrastructure ready to respond to rapidly developing strategy. The exceptional companies have begun to meet this challenge.

Our various assignments and implementations for more than 60 clients involved specifically in global projects have indicated the emergence of a new type of MNC that has been re-engineered to meet these new competitive conditions. This re-engineered global company produces tailored goods and services for a worldwide market, using resources anywhere in the world; it coordinates globally and acts locally.[25]

One example is the type of global inventory management being accomplished through integrated global IT systems, making possible general reduction in inventory levels on a worldwide basis. Companies such as American Express and DEC are finding that information technology is allowing them to deliver innovative services. Mitsui Corporation[26] and Manufacturer's Hanover Trust have developed the use of IT for building up global intelligence gathering systems.[27] Kodak has been able to use IT for global sourcing of components and supplies. General Electric, Texas Instruments, and Citicorp are using IT on a global scale to coordinate production and provision of services. Companies such as Boeing and Johnson & Johnson are using sophisticated IT networks to coordinate global R&D.[28]

---

[25] See Christopher Bartlett and Sumantra Ghoshal, *Managing Across Borders* (Cambridge, MA: Harvard Business School Press, 1989), for a discussion of this concept in general; however, their analysis is not focused specifically on information systems. For an analysis of this concept within the context of information technology, see Blake Ives and Sirkka L. Jarvenpaa, "Applications of Global Information Technology: Key Issues for Management," *MIS Quarterly*, March 1991, pp. 33–49.

[26] A general discussion of the information-processing characteristics of Japanese trading companies can be found in W. Chan Kim, "Global Diffusion of the General Trading Company Concept," *Sloan Management Review*, Summer 1986, pp. 35–43. See also I. Kojima and T. Ozawa, *Japan's General Trading Companies: Merchants of Economic Development* (Paris: OECD, 1984), and Ravi Sarathy, "Japanese Trading Companies: Can They Be Copied?" *Journal of International Business Studies*, Summer 1985, pp. 101–119.

[27] See Dominick B. Attanasio, "The Multiple Benefits of Competitor Intelligence," *The Journal of Business Strategy*, May/June 1988, pp. 16–19; Sumantra Ghoshal and Seok Ki Kim, "Building Effective Intelligence Systems for Competitive Advantage," *Sloan Management Review*, Fall 1986, pp. 49–58; Jan P. Herring, "Building a Business Intelligence System," *The Journal of Business Strategy*, May/June 1988, pp. 4–9. See also J. Alex Murray, "Intelligence Systems of the MNCs," *Columbia Journal of World Business*, September/October 1972, pp. 63–71.

[28] See Jack N. Behrman and William A. Fischer, *Overseas R&D Activities of Transnational Companies* (Cambridge, MA: Oelgeschlager, Gunn & Hain, Publishers, Inc., 1980).

As other MNCs view these successes and begin to transform their international information systems, we are finding that many CIOs are encountering serious internal barriers.

THE CHALLENGE OF BUSINESS RE-ENGINEERING

Most multinationals continue to operate as if people, plants, knowledge, and other corporate resources are oceans apart. Some multinationals struggle to develop an effective global business strategy because they do not understand the power of IT, and they cannot develop a global IT strategy because they do not have a global *business* strategy that sets overall direction.[29]

Even if they want to coordinate service on a worldwide basis like Digital, or orchestrate international operations like Benetton, they find this impossible. Their existing information systems, built for a different mode of operation, stand in the way.

The core of the problem lies in defining exactly what a "global IT strategy" really means. There are many questions which must be answered. Should the architecture be localized, regionalized, or centralized? Which applications, databases, and data centers should be internationalized? What are the basic economics of global information systems and what are the factors that keep them from being optimized? What tools are available to make intelligent cost/justification arguments and project screening on a global basis?

The most fundamental questions, however, are how the global MNC strategy maps against the IT infrastructure, and what the plausible and workable strategies for the CIO are.

The CIO must help build an infrastructure that will meet the present short-term needs but also serve as a prototype with the built-in flexibility needed to meet the longer-term strategies of the multinational. Defining this structure means knowing the potential of the technology and being able to take into consideration the unpredictability of the general business strategy of the multinational as a whole.

---

[29] See Peter G. W. Keen, *Shaping the Future: Business Design Through Information Technology* (Cambridge, MA: Harvard Business School Press, 1991), p. 73. He reports on a study done at Fordham University which concluded that "only a small fraction of firms are likely to learn how to think internationally about IT." Contrast this to the barriers faced by the CIO discussed by Alan Stanford, "The CIO Phenomenon," *SIM Network,* August/September 1986, pp. 1–3. Stanford mentions "misunderstanding of the CIO concept" as being a major problem, although "information technology success stories... are now well understood by senior executives."

The CIO must balance knowledge about information technology against the need to communicate with line and top level management.[30] A part of this process is the realization that rationalization can result in shared savings: some to the corporation and others to long-term investments in the IT infrastructure.[31] By carefully balancing these two savings, the CIO can develop a surplus value for the IT function that can be used for more effective expansion of capabilities.

The CIO must simultaneously manage several learning curves: the IS organization, the different national organizations, the corporation as a whole, and the country management. Doing all of this simultaneously requires bone-breaking work on the part of many persons, and it must be handled with consummate political skill.[32] Agreement in one sector of the organization does not automatically produce agreement in others.

The CIO cannot pretend to develop global business strategy independent of top management, but can in fact work toward building an infrastructure that can allow the corporation to change rapidly and adapt to new situations without too much shock.[33]

---

[30] See Alan Stanford, "The CIO Phenomenon," *SIM Network,* August/September 1986, pp. 1–3, who notes that "the practice of using information technology for competitive advantage can develop rapidly when the CIO maintains environmental and information technology scans to identify and seize opportunities in close teamwork with line managers." Keen divides the role of the CIO into four categories ("information executive," "whipping post missionary," "monopolist footdragger," and "information janitor") as a function of the balance between responsibility and authority given the CIO. Peter G. W. Keen, "Relationship of Senior Management and the IS Organization," in Sharlene Sue Jimenez, contributing ed., *Transforming the IS Organization* (Washington, D.C.: ICIT Press, 1988), pp. 41–54. Keen also writes that CIOs are "usually nothing more than lifeless implementers, operating on an island off the corporate mainland." Peter G. W. Keen, "What's Ailing Mr. Fix-It? Most Chief Information Officers Are Underqualified, and the Rest Don't Get Enough Respect," *Business Month,* 135, January 1990, p. 60. It may be easier for a Japanese CIO to operate effectively than a Western CIO. See Woody Horton, "Japan's View of the CIO," *CIO Magazine,* January/February 1989, pp. 50–51, who writes that "the Japanese apparently have a far lower threshold barrier to information sharing than Americans do.... If anything, the land of the Samurai is the original territory of the data junkie."

[31] Keefe writes that "an information officer thinks of the long term, since the technology he chooses will be with his company for many years. He may be responsible for the largest capital expenditures in the company." Lisa M. Keefe, "More Room at the Top," *Forbes,* 139, June 29, 1987, p. 102.

[32] The need for political skill in addition to mastery of technical details is given evidence in Edward J. Joyce, "In Search of the CIO," *Computer Decisions,* April 1989, pp. 52–55, who discusses "business savvy and organizational acumen" as critical qualities recruiters are looking for in placing CIOs. For a case study of a successful CIO-CEO collaboration, see the example of Lithonia Lighting Co. in Connie Winkler, "An Illuminating CEO-CIO Alliance," *Datamation,* 36, August 15, 1990, p. 79.

[33] For a summary of several interviews with CIOs who have faced the problem of working with top management in formulating an integrated strategy, see David Ludlum, "Adjusting to the Job of Strategist: Where the Air Is Thin and the View Is Big," *Computerworld,* 24 (30), July 23, 1990, pp. 81–83.

THE CHALLENGE OF GLOBAL SYSTEMS DEVELOPMENT

As the CIO starts to implement the changes that must be made, a number of barriers and problems come to the surface.

The biggest problem facing the CIO in developing a global IT strategy is that whereas senior management often recognizes the threat of global competition and the opportunities of increasingly global markets, they are not as clear on the new ways of operating required to address these threats and opportunities.[34]

In addition, many do not understand how IT can transform operations globally. Their entrenched, non-integrated business processes and systems naturally resist a global IT strategy since they were not designed to be cross-functional, much less cross-national.[35] Further, old systems carry the baggage of diverse technology and incompatible applications that makes it even more difficult to build common global systems. A major New York bank that began replacing incompatible systems with a global network in the mid-1970s is still working on it.

One major problem is the complexity and logistics of major international projects. Even for relatively straightforward projects, just the nature of international systems-development efforts makes them more expensive, more time-consuming, and more risky than they would be if they were only domestic. The fatigue of international travel, the expense, and the constant fight against time-zone differences makes coordination and planning of international projects very difficult and can wear down even the most energetic teams.

In addition, management of cultural and linguistic differences between different project leaders and team leaders can be a powder keg when tempers

---

[34] Freiser emphasizes the competitive nature of the CIO's position and argues that many CIOs fail to recognize change and cope with it. He writes that "Chief information officers also are moving from a strategy that relies on control to one that relies on added value." Theodore J. Freiser, "In the 1990s, I/S Will Take Center Stage in a Lead Business Role," *Chief Information Officer Journal*, Fall 1989, pp. 38–44. Rob Hard discusses the new role of CIOs as being "providers of access to data, not controllers of systems." Rob Hard, "CEOs Take a New Look at the CIO Function," *Hospitals*, 64, June 5, 1990, p. 64. This idea is also found in Ralph Carlyle, "The Out Of Touch CIO," *Datamation*, 36, August 15, 1990, p. 30, which reports on a Coopers and Lybrand, Inc., survey that found "many (CIOs) are still clinging to a paternalistic view of information systems users, seeing them as something to be controlled and manipulated rather than served." It concludes that "CIOs are dangerously disconnected from the business side of the house, customers, and the executive's own users."

[35] Keen makes a distinction between "range" and "reach" in the information system. He describes geographic reach as being equivalent to the physical distances linked together within the MNC's information system. Peter G. W. Keen, *Shaping the Future* (Cambridge, MA: Harvard Business School Press, 1991), pp. 39–40. The same concept is discussed in IBM Corporation, *IBM Announces System/390*, Videotape, September 5, 1990. However, the IBM definitions are slightly different and may appear broader; their definition of range includes interorganizational systems.

fly.[36] Robey and Rodriguez-Diaz have developed a case study involving a multinational corporation setting up in Latin America that demonstrates this.[37] Fear of job and power loss, resistance to relocation, and country-based reward and recognition systems are additional barriers. Project management under these circumstances calls for special skills that are easy neither to identify nor locate.

Another strong road-block may come from the country manager. Without a shared global vision of the business, the CIO will find it impossible to sustain a global IT strategy. The central problem is that people are generally responsible for their own turf and not for that of others. In most multinational corporations, the international dimension may be neglected because people's responsibilities are tied strongly to business performance in only one country. In these cases, "international" may be the poor boy on the block.

Finally, many CIOs find it difficult even to understand fully the scope of their international operations. Basic questions such as inventory of equipment, software installations, and human resources skills and talents available on a global basis many times go unanswered.[38]

HOW THE CIO CAN WIN

The CIO is uniquely positioned to understand global strategy and be a key driver—not only in IS, but across the organization. Since IS builds cross-functional systems for multiple business functions, the department is a natural to take on global systems that cross multiple countries. The CIO must seize

---

[36] The psychological dimension of personality types in tense project-management situations is discussed in Raymond E. Hill, "Managing the Human Side of Project Teams," in David I. Cleland and William R. King, eds., *Project Management Handbook* (New York: Van Nostrand Reinhold Company, 1983), pp. 581–604.

[37] Daniel Robey and Andres Rodriguez-Dias,"The Organizational and Cultural Context of Systems Implementation: Case Experience from Latin America,"*Information and Management,* 17 (4), November 1989, pp. 229–239. Their study, however, is limited to a single multinational corporation setting up operations in two of its Latin American subsidiaries, and therefore it is a very limited example. They argue that in different cultures, the concepts of information systems can greatly vary and cause misunderstandings unless carefully managed.

[38] See Raymond W. Bolek and Kathryn J. Hayley, "Developing Staff, Not Systems, Is Key Challenge to CIOs," *Chief Information Officer Journal,* Fall 1988, pp. 8–13, who reported survey results indicating that "the skills most needed now are those designed to integrate disjointed applications, including communications, strategic system planning, and project management.... CIOs hope to augment their current set of skills with those that offer new project delivery techniques, including artificial intelligence, expert systems, fourth generation languages and image processing." Unfortunately, the survey did not include any significant international issues. Fowler reports that even human resources for CIOs are in a shortage. Elizabeth M. Fowler, "Data Systems Managers Get Bigger Role," *New York Times,* Section 1, July 4, 1989, p. 44.

this leadership opportunity quickly to help his or her MNC avoid losing market opportunities and competitive advantage to other global competitors.

In working with CIOs on a variety of international assignments, management consultants have developed four strategic and tactical steps to enable the CIO to implement a global IT strategy: clarify direction, establish values, prototype yourself, and retool for global re-engineering.[39]

Some of the key factors for systems development in multinational corporations include the following:

- Centers of excellence can be set up in different countries from which the global effect can be directed.
- The design of the end-user interface should allow for different languages from the very beginning.
- Major areas of residual value may be found in consolidation of data centers in the new environment of fading national borders.
- Human resources must be managed on a global basis to avoid talent deficits in critical areas overseas.
- The least common denominator approach to standards will allow the maximum level of integration.

Clarify Direction

The CIO should determine global critical success factors and link them to the role of technology. The reasons for globalization must be clear and compelling. Ideally there is an obvious threat to survival, like the Japanese threat to Xerox 10 years ago. Then, the CIO must develop a global IS vision that clarifies both the company's global critical success factors and the role of technology in achieving new ways of operating. For example, if one of the critical success factors is to present one face to the customer, a global customer service system and worldwide network will be required. The IS vision should be powerful, measurable, and motivating. If there is no global business vision, the CIO should work with senior management to establish a vision and their sponsorship of global initiatives.

Establish Values

Overall values and guidelines must be formulated and agreed upon before tactical work begins. Globalization involves an array of complex strategic and technical issues. One way to help managers sort through the complexities is to establish global IT "principles." Principles are single-sentence statements

---

[39] For an alternative view, applicable to nonprofit institutions or educational institutions, see Carole A. Barone, "Planning and the Changing Role of the CIO in Higher Education," *Information Management Review,* Summer 1989, pp. 23–31.

with "will" or "must" that address infrastructure, data, applications, and the organization. For example: We *will* select vendors that provide global customer service and are committed to open systems. Or: The responsibility for deviations from common systems *must* lie with users. (This was one of the key factors at Ford Motor Company in orienting and motivating users toward common systems.) In developing principles, clarify values toward governance (central control versus local autonomy), risk (risk-tolerant versus risk-averse) and role of IT (innovation versus efficiency). The CIO should sponsor the development of global IT principles and then get senior management endorsement.

Prototype Your Global View

One way for the CIO to demonstrate the value of IT-enabled globalization is to globalize the IS department by encouraging IS employees to take on the same global orientation as top management. That means getting technical people around the world to use IT to share knowledge, cooperate in joint purchasing, and coordinate planning. IS should manage human resources globally to leverage key talent worldwide, establishing international career paths and identifying centers of excellence in different countries to leverage the best practices worldwide.

Retool for Global Re-engineering

To get on the way to globalization, the CIO must build a global information infrastructure.[40] The CIO should start by building a sophisticated global telecommunications network, identifying common systems and definitions for common data, determining global models and standards, and rationalizing data-center operations.[41]

BUILD A GLOBAL TELECOMMUNICATIONS NETWORK. In building a global telecommunications network,[42] the CIO's key challenge, as with other resources shared by

---

[40] In explaining the new role of the CIO, Meiklejohn writes: "Increasingly, therefore, the central IT department is concerned with provision of the underlying IT infrastructure and its strategy, expressed in terms of policies and standards." Ian Meiklejohn, "CIOs Search for a Role," *Management Today,* September 1989, p. 137.

[41] Stoll quotes Gruber: "At the present time, we have a situation of decentralized anarchy in information technology.... Every division is doing its own thing.... [and the CIO is needed to remedy the current] decentralized anarchy in information technology." Marilyn Stoll, "CIO Position Emerges as a New Strategic Force," *PC Week,* October 20, 1987, p. C1.

[42] The role of the CIO in enhancing the telecommunications infrastructure of the MNC is found in John J. Donovan, "Beyond Chief Information Officer to Network Manager," *Harvard Business*

(continued)

multiple business units, is getting funding. Lacking organization-wide approval, the CIO should consider starting simple and building up from there. Digital Equipment Corporation uses a three-step process:

- *Link up.* Connect simple business functions like electronic mail, word processing, and spreadsheets across departments and sites.
- *Build up.* Add more critical business applications like ordering, pricing, forecasting, and customer and product data.
- *Join up.* Expand the links to other units, customers, and suppliers.

O'Leary argues that one of the largest problems in creating efficient and strategic international networks for multinational corporations is insufficient attention to the widely different practices and regulatory requirements in different countries. This has been a problem with all industries, but O'Leary argues that the travel and financial services industries have been most vulnerable in this regard.[43]

There are technical and political challenges in building a global network. Decisions on whether to use local telecommunications authorities or independent value-added network providers must be made. Since lead time for circuits and equipment can be long—in some countries it can take months to get a high-speed digital circuit[44]—it is crucial to plan ahead. Central management from a single point requires 24-hour staffing to accommodate time zones; distributed management in several locations requires technical people who can effectively communicate with the local PTT and a central coordination point. In either case, maintenance activities must be coordinated over

---

Review, September/October 1988, p. 134: "Unless CIOs successfully transform themselves into network managers, they will be ill-equipped to confront the user dissatisfaction, organizational squabbles, and technological roadblocks invariably triggered by the advance of decentralized computing.... Network managers understand that in a world of accelerating decentralization, the most effective way to oversee a company's computer resources is to relinquish control of them and instead focus on the networks that connect them."

[43]Meghan O'Leary, "The World Is Your Oyster...Maybe," *CIO,* 2 (9), June 1989, pp. 42–50. She discusses the need for firms to create the ability to manage and build a distributed workstation environment that operates simultaneously in several different parts of the world.

[44]In our interviews, some MNCs reported delays of more than two *years* in arranging for a single modest capacity leased line from Spain to Germany. This type of problem has been recognized as one of the central issues in the transborder data flow debate. For a discussion of its effect on multinational corporations, see Eric J. Novotny, *Transborder Data Flows and World Public Order: Law and Policy Problems in Controlling Global Computer Communication Technology,* Doctoral thesis, Georgetown University, 1985. The results of a survey are found in Candace P. Deans et al., *Identification of Key International Information Systems Issues in the U.S.-Based Multinational Corporations,* working paper in Management Science DOR G-89-02, Division of Research, College of Business Administration, University of South Carolina, 1989.

long distances. On the other hand, some research has found that transborder data-flow restrictions have only a moderate effect on the operations of the multinational corporation.[45]

Anticipating increasing demand for global communication services, the CIO should build staff skills in global communications and ensure that IS can respond quickly to growing communication needs.

IDENTIFY COMMON SYSTEMS. The CIO must identify opportunities for common systems by examining common business practices, compatible applications and consistent data definitions. In general, there are three types of systems based on the level of customization needed: *single global systems* for global functions like finance or purchasing, *"mirrored" systems* for moderately global/moderately local functions like manufacturing, in which one common system is replicated and tailored for local markets; and *unique local systems* for local functions like sales and payroll.

Common systems and global standards promote global use of best practices and enable control of dispersed activities through access to global management information. Common systems facilitate global communication and information sharing, staff transfers, and new office start-ups. They streamline systems development and maintenance efforts and often drive decisions on common hardware and operating system software. However, common systems can reduce local flexibility and control, and can preclude the use of powerful new technologies that are not included in the standards. Other problems come from lack of common global business practices, and complexity in developing and supporting both common *and* local software.

ESTABLISH COMMON DATA DEFINITIONS. Global systems require business units around the world to use a common vocabulary. For example, many companies do not have one definition of sales. A sale may be an "order booked" in the United Kingdom, an "order scheduled" in Germany, and an "order produced" in France. One U.S. manufacturer with autonomous business units says, "We call the same customer 10 different things in different parts of the company." A corporate data-management task force is now developing common coding schemes. Resolving these issues will clear the way for the company's IS vision: a logical database, distributed worldwide.[46] "Data will live where it makes sense for it to live," the IS director of planning and development says. "We

---

[45]See Rakesh B. Sambharya and Arvind Phatak, "The Effect of Transborder Data Flow Restrictions on American Multinational Corporations," *Management International Review,* 30 (3), 1990, pp. 267–290. Sambharya and Phatak surveyed 455 U.S.-based multinational corporations, including 280 in manufacturing and 175 banks.

[46]This concept was discussed in depth by Mr. Alex Mayall at the ICIS conference in Copenhagen, 1990, in a panel presentation on Global Information Systems.

don't want to move data to the U.S. that should stay in the Asia-Pacific. But we want to be able to access it from the U.S. and put it together with data from Europe to get a sense of what's going on in the world."

DETERMINE GLOBAL IS MODELS AND STANDARDS. One of the CIO's biggest challenges is balancing the need for architectural consistency around the world with the business' desire to "get on with it" and develop the best local solution. The CIO should sponsor an international task force to define global technology models and standards that build on the global principles. Such models and standards might include selecting vendors who can provide support in dispersed locations.[47]

RATIONALIZE DATA CENTERS. Instead of operating data centers on a country basis, the CIO must optimize *across* the organization, consolidating data-center operations globally and regionally (e.g., in Europe and the Far East).[48]

The challenges facing the CIO in today's multinational corporation are complex and laden with technical, strategic, and political problems. In many organizations, it is clear that the rising importance of information technology has not reached the consciousness of the highest levels of management. It is, therefore, the role of the CIO to manage the complex process of building strategy-responsive global information systems. This management must operate in both directions: it must cope with the difficult implementation and project management issues; it must also take a proactive stance with top management. Our review of many cases indicates that although the task is potentially very difficult, the risks of failure can be quite severe for the MNC that is not led properly, and we fully expect to see big losers as well as occasional winners.

USE THE STRUCTURE OF ACCESS TO INTERNATIONAL DECISION-MAKING

Multinational corporations are influenced on every side by different regulations and national policies. Legal and regulatory barriers can inhibit or boost

---

[47] A discussion of problems of vendor support and different strategies companies are using to cope with this problem is found in Edward M. Roche, "Managing Systems Development in Multinational Corporations: Practical Lessons from Seven Case Studies" in Shailendra Palvia, Prasant Palvia, and Ronald Ziglir, eds., *Global Issues of Information Technology Management* (Harrisburg, PA: Idea Group Publishing, 1991).

[48] A discussion of the economic drivers of data-center consolidation in the international context is lacking in the literature, but should be developed in the future. A view of the psychological dimensions of the layoffs in DP this might entail is found in Martin Lasden, "It's Me Inc. vs. You Inc.," *Computer Decisions,* 18, December 16, 1986, p. 52.

operations; government encouragement and more overt forms of pressure can play a great role in structuring how a business operates and how much profit it is going to make. Policies regarding personnel that are legal and acceptable in one country may be abhorred or illegal in others. The steps a corporation can take to regain market share, to cut back operating costs when a financial squeeze appears, and the type of intellectual property rights a company can enjoy, are all examples of government-induced factors that can determine how a multinational corporation operates. Even as late as 1990, the European Community had not drafted legislation intended to protect databases, and some were even proposing legalization of reverse engineering for software.[49] It is often assumed that the lack of protection of intellectual property rights tends to discourage foreign direct investment (FDI) of the multinational corporations; however, this has not been completely confirmed:

> It is clear that, while a causal link may exist between intellectual property protection, on the one hand, and foreign investment and technology flows, on the other, this link may not be automatic and can only be confirmed through experience and empirical evidence. The perception that there is such a link makes the issue important in itself, as this perception can influence policy discussions and measures. But definitive conclusions on the actual existence of such a link and its nature require further empirical research.[50]

There are several levels at which the MNC is able significantly to influence policy. At the national level, that is, within the host country, the MNC must cope with the legal regime in place there. Since the various national regulations and conditions are so highly variable, particularly between developed and developing countries with their different historical traditions regarding government/business relations, these issues are most efficiently handled at the national level through the representative office, usually staffed with at least enough nationals to know their way around the governments concerned. In the old-standing, mature MNC, the legal and special planning staffs have been exposed to various forms of host governmental regulation, and the working procedures for exerting influence or at the very least getting a fair hearing for one's point of view are all well established. The gears have been pretty well greased for the mature corporations.[51] A great deal of study has been

---

[49]See Linda Bernier, "EC Rulings Open Door to Reverse Engineering," *Electronic Business*, 16 (16), August 20, 1990, p. 65.

[50]See UNCTC, *New Issues in the Uruguay Round of Multilateral Trade Negotiations*, UNCTC Current Studies, Series A, 19 (New York: United Nations, 1990), p. 6.

[51]It is interesting to observe the difficulties Japanese MNCs are having getting established in Western Europe. They have faced allegations over so-called "screw-driver" plants, as if they are the only MNCs in the world that engage in such activities, and over dumping, which in many cases means competitive pricing. How are companies in the Far East supposed to charge the
(*continued*)

devoted to understanding the relationship between the MNC and its host government. All these studies point to the mutuality of economic interests as being the single most important criterion in determining the "flavor" of the relationship.

The MNC finds that it interacts with host government officials at a variety of levels. It is at this social and business level of the relationship that impressions are made and important corporate intelligence is collected. An important vehicle for this is the business association. In many cases, particularly the United States, the business association has very strong input into government decision-making and policy making. It is, therefore, through these associations that the MNC can exert its interests at the national level.

At the international level, the picture is similar, but different. Many national associations are also associated with a parent international arm that operates in the same way to protect the interests of the membership at the international level, in the various international institutions that are in charge of setting one type of policy or another. For example, Chambers of Commerce are organized in almost every major industrial center; there is also an International Chamber of Commerce that acts as a type of "United Nations" for the various national organizations and represents interests at the international level to various concerned international organizations, such as the OECD in Paris.

The problems with technological change are immense and it is a paradox that the changes in the international regime or in the systems of relationship governing the establishment and operations of international computing facilities are always falling behind changes in technology. There is a permanent generation gap between law and technology, between reality and theory, and this reflects the tremendous complexity of generating highly detailed international agreements between competing and sovereign nation-states.[52] As a result of this, the individual MNC can find that it may be extremely time-consuming and difficult to get its interests represented at the highest international levels.

The role of the information-systems professional in all this political ambiguity is to manage "external relations" like a professional diplomat. The

---

same price for a product when their labor rates are much lower and productivity is much higher? For years in the post-war period, U.S. multinationals have been operating very extensive business networks in Western Europe. They have been "members of the club." But the Japanese have not been fortunate. They are not accepted as members. They are a different race, and this may lie at the heart of the problem at the deepest level.

[52] It also reflects the difference in legal philosophy between Roman and Common law. Jurists and legislators in the Roman tradition attempt to work out all the details and possible exceptions to a law when it is enacted. The Common law tradition, on the other hand, is built more on the setting of general principles and then allowing their gradual refinement over time through numerous decisions on different cases. France is a country, for example, which is oriented toward the Roman-law way of thinking.

decisions that will shape the development of the future regime will be taken elsewhere, and often with incomplete knowledge of the true effects on users. The CIO of the MNC must ensure that very careful communication between individual companies and the international organizations regulating them is maintained. At the same time, the CIO must encourage a relentless gathering of information on any and all international issues that might have a serious effect on the operations of the company, particularly the information-systems department and function.

In some cases, this monitoring can take place through the systematic gathering of information by a specialized staff. In some companies examined, a special international operations group handles this function. In other companies, a loose assortment of internationally skilled persons is assigned this function as a matter of course.

In most companies, however, the situation is very different. Normally, the company is represented at international organizations by a part of the corporate legal staff. In these cases, which are all too frequent, the legally oriented person in charge of the lobbying effort is not sufficiently familiar with all the technical issues to make a convincing case. In any case, they may not be familiar with the future strategies of the information-systems group at a detailed level. As a result, the MNC's needs at the information-technology level are not well-represented.

In order to countervail against this outcome, the CIO should ensure that, in all international fora and through various organizations that influence international outcomes, the interests of the information-technology function are taken into account.

APPENDIX

Notes and Sketches
for Understanding the
Dynamics of International
Information Systems

THE KEY VARIABLES

One of the interesting aspects of modeling international computing and telecommunications systems is the very large amount of information—factors and variables[1]—that must be taken into consideration. It is not simply a question of building a large distributed network using a system of exact measurements that will guarantee that the system will perform in an optimum manner. There are too many other factors that must be taken into consideration.

The first factor that might be considered is the actual type of information system you are trying to build. Is it centralized? Is it a decentralized processing system? This type of decision must be made with reference to the overall

---

[1] There are many ways in which to classify the variables associated with the entry of multinationals into host countries, and also to describe the general system dynamics of the growth of international information systems. For example, Yves L. Doz, *Government Control and Multinational Strategic Management: Power Systems and Telecommunications Equipment* (New York: Praeger, 1979) discusses several classes of factors through which governments exercise control over MNCs, including (1) influence over operating patterns, with such factors as different laws, licensing, taxation, regulation, trade barriers, and foreign investment screening; and (2) influence over management tools, including factors of informal socialization and incentives to have local nationals in management. These two sets of factors are a way to influence what he calls the "means" of the multinational corporation. As far as "contents" of the multinational's activities are concerned, Doz lists, in a parallel fashion, (1) factors concerning influence over operating patterns, such as investment incentives, regional subsidies, tax exemptions, training assistance, import duties, local content laws, hints on screening processes, and funding sources; and (2) (management tools) factors such as specifications and standards, socialization, purchasing processes, identity development, loyalty considerations, and transfer of human resources. A different but related list of factors is found in Stephen E. Guisinger, "A Comparative Study of Country Policies" in Stephen E. Guisinger and Associates, *Investment Incentives and Performance Requirements: Patterns of International Trade, Production, and Investment* (New York: Praeger, 1985). Guisinger divides the "incentives/discentives" into several classes and studies many factors under each. His overall categories are "affecting revenues," including tariffs, differential sales-excise taxes, export taxes/subsidies (including income tax credits), quotas, export minimums, price controls (or relief therefrom), multiple exchange rates, general overvaluation of currency, government procurement preference, production/capacity controls, guarantees against government competition, prior import deposits, and transfer price administration; "affecting inputs," including tariffs, differential sales taxes, export taxes/subsidies, quotas, price controls, multiple exchange rates, subsidy or tax for public-sector suppliers, domestic-content requirement (including R&D), prior import deposits, transfer price administration, limits on royalties and fees, multiple deductions for tax purposes, and cash or in-kind grants for R&D; "affecting components of value-added," encompassing several large categories with detailed variables in each, such as capital, cost of capital goods, cost of debt, cost of equity, corporate tax, labor (wage subsidies, training grants, minimum wage), relaxation of industrial relations laws, local labor requirements, land, and other factors such as limitations on foreign ownership, free-trade zones, general preinvestment assistance, countertrade requirements, and foreign exchange balancing requirements. His study then covers several industries across different countries.

strategy of your company. Perhaps your company is ethnocentric, or it may be a polycentric organization. Perhaps you are intending to rationalize different data centers located in different Western European countries into a single data-processing operation to be located in Brussels, in which case you are "regiocentric." But regardless of the type of architecture you are considering, the implementation of the details of the design will be done within the context of these many elements and external factors.

The architectural families in Table A.1 should be related to strategy, but as the preceding discussion indicates, to match architecture against strategy is not a straightforward matter. To these architectural families we have related a group of variables. Feel free to add your own.

An even more fundamental problem occurs with the distribution of applications. In the past, it was clear that the underlying architecture of the information-technology infrastructure would determine how applications were distributed throughout the multinational. However, this may no longer be the case, at least to the extent found in the past. Advances in telecommunications, including falling international data communications tariffs as well as better distributed processing designs, means that it is easier to move applications around—to centralize them or decentralize them—without having to make the same level of changes in the information-technology architecture.

The applications are also subject to decentralization or centralization, but this distinction is conveyed in the form of a string or combination to each of the variables in Table A.2.

These sets of factors or variables, however, are not sufficient to convey the dynamics of building international systems. International computing systems are built within the context of the international environment in which they operate. The most powerful set of factors influencing the systems development process, as well as the general operation of the computing system, are associated with the nation-state.

TABLE A.1 Architecture Variables

Architecture Family	Variable Symbol
Centralized	AR_{cent}
Decentralized	AR_{dcent}
Polycentric	AR_{plyc}
Regiocentric	AR_{regc}
Global	AR_{glo}
United Nations	AR_{UN}
Multinational	AR_{mnc}
Infrastructure	Inf
Centralized infrastructure	AR_{cent}^{Inf}
United Nations–style infrastructure	AR_{UN}^{Inf}

TABLE A.2 Application Variables

Applications in Multinational Corporations	Variable Symbol
Financial control	AP_{fin}
Human resources and personnel	AP_{hum}
Inventory control and logistics	AP_{log}
Marketing	AP_{mkt}
Research and development	$AP_{r\&d}$
Corporation intelligence	AP_{ci}

The many types of regulations and administrative controls can be considered, as they have a direct effect on the type of information-technology infrastructure one is allowed to build or operate. For example, privacy and transborder data flow regulations make it impossible to operate centralized architectures for human resources and personnel operations. On the other hand, privacy regulations and administrative controls should not have much of an effect on the centralization of non-name-linked data and information such as spare parts controls or inventory records.

The incomplete variable list in Table A.3 addresses a few of the regulatory and administrative-control factors at the nation-state level that influence

TABLE A.3 Regulatory and Administrative-Control Variables

Nation-State Factor	Variable Symbol
Privacy regulations	NS_{priv}
Transborder data flow controls	NS_{tdf}
Import controls on equipment	NS_{mprt}
Restrictive standards requirements	NS_{stnd}
Taxation	NS_{tax}
Licensing of databases	NS_{lic}^{Db}
Licensing of equipment	NS_{lic}^{Eq}
Auditing and financial reporting requirements	NS_{aud}
General legislation that is restrictive in nature	NS_{leg}
Industrial policy	NS_{ip}
Government purchasing requirements	NS_{ip}^{GP}
Subsidy to domestic industry	NS_{ip}^{SubDOM}
Subsidy to foreign industry	NS_{ip}^{SubFOR}
Subsidies to training and education	NS_{ip}^{Edu}
Discrimination in favor of domestic enterprises	NS_{dom}

how multinational corporations build their systems. (Compare to the Doz or Guisinger list in the footnote.)

Another set of variables or factors that must be considered, and that is more controversial and harder to study and even to comprehend in terms of building information systems, concerns the cultural factors at play in the locations where the information system is to be built and operated. It is indeed difficult to take into consideration these factors, particularly if one is wedded to the type of hard-core empiricism that provides the steel fist in so much academic work, but from both on-site travel and extensive interviews, it is clear that these factors are very important in building information systems at the international level. Only the most foolish CIO or project manager in the information-technology function would consider ignoring these factors.

Others can work out the details of the systems dynamics for the factors listed in Table A.4. Understanding these variables and factors involves a type of cross-cultural research in information systems and their implementation that does not yet exist in any significant part in the literature.

Another, final set of relationships and important factors *external to the information systems function* that influence how systems are built and whether they operate well, concerns the system of international organization and law set up in the immediate post–World War II period. The United Nations, the International Telecommunications Union, the International Standards Organisation—these types of international organizations, as well as the general open system of trade that was set up in the General Agreement on Tariffs and Trade (GATT), provided a stable environment that allowed technology to be used openly as it developed in sophistication.

Again, these variables or factors, listed in Table A.5, can be considered important elements in determining how international systems have developed. Some organizations have provided a safe haven for technology developments; others have tended to hinder its development and proliferation. For example, the ITU has done a great deal to help promote standards in international packet-switching technologies, and in this sense it has accelerated the develop-

TABLE A.4 Cultural Variables

General Cultural Considerations	Variable Symbol
Language barriers	NS_{cult}^{LB}
Tribal type	NS_{cult}^{Tr}
Asian type (Confucian)	NS_{cult}^{Conf}
Western type	NS_{cult}^{W}
Religious fanaticism	NS_{cult}^{Rel}
Islamic	NS_{cult}^{Moh}

TABLE A.5 International Organization and Law Variables

International Organization or Standard	Variable Symbol
International Telecommunications Union	IO_{ITU}
Technical standards for telecommunications	$IO_{ITU}^{standTEL}$
Frequency allocation	IO_{ITU}^{Freq}
Infrastructure development programs	IO_{ITU}^{Infr}
World Intellectual Property Organization	IO_{WIPO}
General treaty arrangements	IO_{gen}
Intergovernmental Bureau for Informatics	IO_{IBI}
United Nations Educational, Scientific and Culture Organization	IO_{ESCO}
World Bank	IO_{WB}

ment of global and international information systems. On the other hand, organizations such as UNESCO have aided in consideration of the New World Information Order, which sought—at least at one point in its development—to enforce a severe set of controls over the operations of the multinationals and their information-technology systems.

Another element in understanding how international systems have developed involves the dynamics of causal relations. These relations and corresponding symbols are listed in Table A.6.

TABLE A.6 Causal Relationships

Relation	Notation
Leads to (another set of relationships), "and therefore"	$\Rightarrow$
Is increased, becomes more powerful	$\uparrow$
Is decreased, becomes weakened	$\downarrow$
Changes to (the following situation)	$\rightarrow$
Is a subset of	$\subset$
Changes	Δ
Is more, stronger than	$>$
Is less, weaker than	$<$
Combined with	$\cup$
General family of variables	n
Inhibitor	$\vee$
Accelerator	$\wedge$
Unknown causal set	$[?]$
International homologation	$\equiv$

CAUSAL DYNAMICS AND SYSTEM-WIDE CHANGE

Based on a few of the observations in the research, we can suggest several items that are hypothetical and do not yet have any empirical foundation, but that offer a path along which one might tread in contemplating serious research on the issue.

The general relationship is that given $NS_n > IO_n$ and

$$\begin{bmatrix} NS_n \\ IO_n \end{bmatrix} \Delta \rightarrow AR$$

we do not know if

$$\begin{bmatrix} NS_n \\ IO_n \end{bmatrix} > AR$$

but this is assumed. Under the model, variations in AR, such as AR_{cent}, AR_{UN}, and AR_{cent}^{inf}, are determined by a specific causal set

$$[?] < \begin{bmatrix} NS_n \\ IO_n \end{bmatrix}$$

This means that each $AR_{(?)}$ is determined by a specific causal set $[?_n]$. The evidence suggests that [NS] AR_{UN}^{Inf} is composed of

$$\uparrow \begin{bmatrix} NS_{ip} \\ NS_{leg} \\ NS_{aud} \end{bmatrix} \Rightarrow AR_{UN}^{Inf}$$

Conversely, $\begin{bmatrix} AR_{UN}^{Inf} \rightarrow AR_{glo} \end{bmatrix}$ can only be possible with

$$\downarrow \begin{bmatrix} NS_{ip} \\ NS_{leg} \\ NS_{aud} \end{bmatrix}$$

provided $\downarrow NS_{leg}$ means homologation of international (INT) legislation $\left(\equiv \frac{leg}{INT} \right)$, and the same is true with NS_{ip} allowing $\equiv {}_{INT}$.

It appears[2] that

$$\begin{bmatrix} MNC_{AP_{fin}} \\ AP_{ci} \end{bmatrix} \Rightarrow AR_{cent}$$

---

[2] Based on general interviews of information systems professionals in multinational corporations.

but

$$\begin{bmatrix} AP_{hum} \\ AP_{mkt} \end{bmatrix} \Rightarrow \begin{bmatrix} AR_{dcent} \\ AR_{plyc} \\ AR_{regc} \end{bmatrix}$$

which many times is characterized by AR_{UN}. In other words, this agrees with the idea that

$$\uparrow \begin{bmatrix} NS_{priv} & NS_{tdf} \\ NS_{lic}^{Db} & NS_{aud} \\ NS_{leg} \end{bmatrix}$$

and especially $NS_{dom} \Rightarrow \uparrow AR_{UN}, \downarrow AR_{glo}$, and AR_{cent} and is therefore suboptimal for each of

$$\begin{bmatrix} AP_{log} & AP_{r\&d} \\ AP_{ci} & AP_{fin} \end{bmatrix}.$$

Defining conditions for strategy-induced transformations of international computing systems may be given by the generalized historical pattern and sequencing which appears to be

$$\begin{bmatrix} AR_{plyc} & AR_{UN} \\ AR_{dcent} & \end{bmatrix} \Rightarrow AR_{regc}$$

and later AR_{glo}, which is more characteristic of the late 1980s and possibly the early 1990s. The transition toward rationalization of functions such as

$$\begin{bmatrix} AR_{log} \\ AR_{mkt} \end{bmatrix}$$

through $\to AR_{glo}$ is both accelerated and inhibited as

$$\begin{bmatrix} IO_{gen} \\ IO_{wipo} \end{bmatrix} \Rightarrow \wedge AR_{glo}$$

and

$$\begin{bmatrix} NS_n \to \begin{pmatrix} NS_{priv} & NS_{leg} \\ NS_{tdf} & NS_{aud} \end{pmatrix} \end{bmatrix} \Rightarrow \vee AR_{glo}.$$

Understanding the Dynamics of International Information Systems

Generally, IO class variables tend to accelerate internationalization, whereas NS class variables tend to inhibit it.

In addition, when $\uparrow IO_{ITU}^{standTEL} \Rightarrow [AR_n] \rightarrow AR_{un}$ and, when $\uparrow IO_{ITU}^{standTEL} \Rightarrow [(AR_{un} \rightarrow AR_{glo})]$,

$$\uparrow NS(leg)_{priv} \Rightarrow \begin{bmatrix} \downarrow AR_{tr} \\ \uparrow AR_{un} \end{bmatrix}$$

Probably the family of NS_{cult}^n such as

$$\begin{bmatrix} NS_{cult}^{LB} & NS_{cult}^{Tr} \\ NS_{cult}^{Conf} & NS_{cult}^{Moh} \\ NS_{cult}^{Rel} & NS_{cult}^{W} \end{bmatrix}$$

create a great variety of differences in general receptivity. Putting aside the effects in less developed countries of

$$\begin{bmatrix} NS_{cult}^{Rel} & NS_{cult}^{Moh} \\ NS_{cult}^{Tr} & \end{bmatrix}$$

the strongest contrast in organization and cultural style in advanced societies is between NS_{cult}^{W} and NS_{cult}^{Conf}.

$IO(n)$ such as

$$\begin{bmatrix} IO_{ITU}^{Freq} \\ IO_{WIPO} \end{bmatrix} < [IO_{ITU}^{standTEL} \text{ as } \subset IO_{ITU}]$$

$$IO_{ESCO} \rightarrow \wedge \begin{bmatrix} AR_{un} \\ AR_{polyc} \end{bmatrix} \text{ and } \vee [AR_{glo}]$$

Finally, it appears that

$$\begin{bmatrix} NS_{ip}^{subDOM} & NS_{ip}^{Edu} \\ NS_{ip}^{GP} & NS_{dom} \end{bmatrix}$$

as $\subset [\mathrm{NS}_{\mathrm{ip}}^n]$ indicates that major utilization controls are

$$\begin{bmatrix} \mathrm{NS}_{\mathrm{lic}}^{\mathrm{DB}} & \mathrm{NS}_{\mathrm{lic}}^{\mathrm{Eq}} \\ \mathrm{NS}_{\mathrm{priv}} & \mathrm{NS}_{\mathrm{aud}} \\ \mathrm{NS}_{\mathrm{tdf}} & \end{bmatrix}$$

As different dynamics of international information systems are understood, then this experimental system of notation should prove useful in further theory–building regarding causal phenomena.

References

Adler, Emanuel. 1986. "Ideological 'Guerrillas' and the Quest for Technological Autonomy: Brazil's Domestic Computer Industry," *International Organization*, 40(3), Summer.

Agarwal, Robin. 1990. "TI-Acer DRAM Venture: Will This Marriage Survive?" *Electronic Business*, 16(8), April 30, pp. 67–68.

Akin, Gwynn C. 1987. "Syntex Corporation Links Employee Education with AIDS Policy," *Business and Health*, 4(11), September, pp. 56–57.

Alberding, Dick. 1987. "A Company Study: Exploiting Your Competitive Edge," *Journal of Business & Industrial Marketing*, 2(2), Spring, pp. 37–46.

Alberthal, Lester M. 1990. "Communications Leapfrog for East Europe's Infrastructure," *Financier*, 14(4), April, pp. 32–37.

Alchian, Armen A. and Harold Demsetz (nd). "Production, Information Costs, and Economic Organization," *The American Economic Review*, pp. 777–795.

Alpander, Guvenc G. 1978. "Multinational Corporations: Homebase-Affiliate Relations," *California Management Review*, XX(3), Spring, pp. 47–56.

Alper, Alan. 1986. "AT&T Focuses on Data Networking in Cost-Cutting Strategy," *Computerworld*, 20(45), November 10, pp. 98, 102.

Alper, Alan, James Connolly, and Clinton Wilder. 1987. "Honeywell Bull Born," *Computerworld*, 21(13), March 30, pp. 1, 102.

Anchordoguy, M. 1989. "Computer Inc.: Japan's Challenge to IBM," Harvard East Asian Monographs, 144 (Cambridge, MA: Harvard University Press).

Anonymous. 1986. "Bottom Heavy Management for a Better Bottom Line at Boral," *Rydge's*, 59(3), March, pp. 42–43.

Anonymous. 1986. "Financial Management: Micro Control in Large Corporations," *Business Software Review*, 5(9), September, pp. 17–19.

Anonymous. 1986. "Information Technology in Brazil—The National Firms Take the Lead," *Multinational Business* (3), pp. 33–35.

Anonymous. 1986. "Italy: Olivetti Is Reaching Out for the Apple," *Euromoney,* September, pp. 393, 397.

Anonymous. 1986. "More Market Reserves in Brazil," *Multinational Business* (4), pp. 25–27.

Anonymous. 1986. "Second 100 Leading National Advertisers: Wellcome Foundation/Whirlpool Corp./F. W. Woolworth Co./Zayre Corp.," *Advertising Age,* 57(56), November 3, pp. S64–S65.

Anonymous. 1987. "Alcatel—One Name, One Company," *Telecommunications,* International Edition, 21(10), October, pp. 146–147.

Anonymous. 1987. "Helping People Work More Effectively," *I/S Analyzer,* 25(12), December, pp. 1–12.

Anonymous. 1987. "Ideas & Applications: Intercontinental CAD/CAM," *Systems International,* 15(1), January, pp. 19–20.

Anonymous. 1987. "Italtel Keeps Her Suitors at Bay," *Telecommunications,* International Edition, 21(10), October, pp. 218, 220.

Anonymous. 1987. "Network Unites European Offices," *Systems International,* 15(6), June, p. 26.

Anonymous. 1987. "'The Reliable American' Renews Its Commitment," *Asian Finance,* 13(12), December 15, pp. 80–81.

Anonymous. 1987. "The Second 100 Leading National Advertisers: Whirlpool/Wickes Cos./Winn-Dixie Stores/F. W. Woolworth Co./Zayre Corp.," *Advertising Age,* 58(50), November 23, pp. S49–S50.

Anonymous. 1988. "A Well-Worn Road to Dominance," *Economist,* 308 (7568), September 17, p. 76.

Anonymous. 1988. "Can Fiber Slide Safely into Home?" *Telephone Engineer & Management,* 92(10), May 15, pp. 106–108.

Anonymous. 1988. "Caterpillar: Challenging a 'Soft' Market," *Business Marketing,* 73(8), August, pp. 40, 42.

Anonymous. 1988. "Companies Call the Shots on Transplant Coverage," *Employee Benefit Plan Review,* 42(9), March, pp. 13–14.

Anonymous. 1988. "Factories of the Future: Electrolux Corp.; General Dynamics Corp.; Whirlpool Corp.; Bader Meter, Inc.," *Industry Week,* 236(6), March 21, pp. 34–42.

Anonymous. 1988. "Gain Control of the Paper Environment," *Computer Data,* 13(2), February, pp. 12–13.

Anonymous. 1988. "Italian Economy: Privatisation in Fits and Starts; Rome Fiddles While the Economy Burns," *Economist,* 306(7539), February 27, pp. S28–S34.

Anonymous. 1988. "Nixdorf Bets on UNIX to Crack the U.S. Market," *Electronic Business,* 14(5), March 1, pp. 84, 86.

Anonymous. 1988. "The E.C.'s Research and Technology Development," *Europe* (282), December, pp. 28–30.

Anonymous. 1988. "When It Pays to Think Big: The 'Extended Enterprise,'" *IBM Directions,* June, pp. 2–5.

Anonymous. 1989. "Britannia Leads the Way," *IMC Journal,* 25(3), May/June, pp. 15–18.

References

Anonymous. 1989. "Chemicals. Staying on the Boil," *Economist,* 311(7599), April 22, p. 69.

Anonymous. 1989. "Computer Bureau: Beating the Odds," *Asian Finance,* 15(9), September 15.

Anonymous. 1989. "Fax Switch Broadcasts Financials for Public Company," *Networking Management,* 7(7), July, pp. 74–75.

Anonymous. 1989. "Managing Your Oyster," *Economist,* 313(7626), October 28, pp. 78–79.

Anonymous. 1989. "Rolm's New President Discusses IBM-Siemens Deal," *Business Communications Review,* 19(2), February, pp. 10, 12.

Anonymous. 1989. "Siemens and IBM Offer Each Other a Helping Hand," *Business Communications Review,* 19 (1), January, pp. 8–14.

Anonymous. 1989. "South Korea's Conglomerates: Do or Be Done For," *Economist,* 313(7632), December 9, pp. 74, 79.

Anonymous. 1989. "System Failure," *Economist,* 310(7593), March 11, p. 70.

Anonymous. 1990. "Beyond Section 20," *ABA Banking Journal,* 82(6), June, pp. 63–68.

Anonymous. 1990. "Can Carlo Come Back?" *Economist,* 315(7652), April 28, pp. 69–70.

Anonymous. 1990. "Europe's White-Goods Industry: Going Through the Wringer," *Economist,* 317(7680), November 10, pp. 80–81.

Anonymous. 1990. "GE's Worldwide Network Integrates Voice, Data, Video," *Networking Management,* 8(6), June, pp. 99–100.

Anonymous. 1990. "Going Solo: Olivetti," *Economist,* 317(7683), December 1, pp. 78, 80.

Anonymous. 1990. "Multinational Management Strategies," *Multinational Business* (3), Autumn, pp. 54–61.

Anonymous. 1990. "New Technologies," *European Trends* (3), pp. 56–60.

Anonymous. 1990. "Olivetti: Going for Broke," *Economist,* 314(7638), January 20, pp. 76, 78.

Anonymous. 1990. "Reshaping ICI: One Thing Leads to the Next," *Economist,* 315(7652), April 28, pp. 21–23.

Anonymous. 1990. "Some Ways to Generate Noninterest Income," *ABA Banking Journal,* 82(6), June, pp. 18, 20.

Anonymous. 1990. "The Strategic Alliance of AT&T and Italtel: Why Two Telecommunications Heavyweights Joined Forces," *Mergers & Acquisitions,* 24(4), January/February, pp. 70–71.

Anonymous. 1991. "The Solution from Down Under," *Management Accounting,* 69(4), April, p. 52.

Anonymous. 1991. "Spare the Rod and Spoil the Child," *Economist,* 319(7703), April 20, pp. 63–64.

Anonymous. 1991. "Tracking: Customers Call the Tune," *Financial Times,* Financial Times Survey, Courier, and Express Services, July 24, pp. iv–v.

Arend, Mark. 1989. "AI: Expert Keeps Up with Bank's Currency Events," *Wall Street Computer Review,* 6(9), June, pp. 22–24, 91–92.

Arend, Mark. 1990. "Global Custodians Exhibit High-Tech Savvy," *Wall Street Computer Review,* 7(11), August, pp. 29–34, 57–58.

Arensman, Russ. 1990. "PC Makers Look to Asia for the Next Surge in Sales," *Electronic Business,* 16(14), July 23, pp. 110–112.

Armstrong, John A. 1987. "Possible Dreams from IBM's Zurich Lab," *Across the Board,* 24(5), May, pp. 30–31.

Arrow, Kenneth J. 1974. *The Limits of Organization* (New York: Norton).

Arrow, Kenneth J. 1986. "Vertical Integration and Communication," in Walter P. Heller, Ross M. Starr, and David A. Starrett, eds., *Uncertainty, Information and Communication* (New York: Cambridge University Press), pp. 173–183.

Arthur, Charles and Sally Hamilton. 1990. "The Selling of STC," *Business,* November, pp. 72–77.

Arvai, Ernest Stephen. 1987. "Eliminating the Lag in International Reporting," *Information Strategy: The Executive's Journal,* 3(2), Winter, pp. 43–44.

Aryanpur, Sarah. 1988. "Olivetti Ups the Value of Its Resellers," *Systems International,* 16(8), August, p. 13.

Ashmore, G. Michael. 1988. "Bringing Information Technology to Life," *The Journal of Business Strategy,* May/June.

Attanasio, Dominick B. 1988. "The Multiple Benefits of Competitor Intelligence," *The Journal of Business Strategy,* May/June, pp. 16–19.

Auguston, Karen A. 1990a. "Caterpillar Slashes Lead Times from Weeks to Days," *Modern Materials Handling,* 45(2), February, pp. 48–51.

Auguston, Karen A. 1990b. "Caterpillar's Worldwide Strategy at Work in Belgium," *Modern Materials Handling,* 45(8), July, pp. 48–51.

Auster, Ellen R. 1987. *Columbia Journal of World Business,* Summer, pp. 3–6.

Azumi, K., D. Hickson, D. Horvath, and C. McMillan. 1984. "Structural Uniformity and Cultural Diversity in Organizations: A Comparative Study of Factors in Britain, Japan, and Sweden," in K. Sato and Y. Hoshino, eds., *The Anatomy of Japanese Business* (Armonk, NY: M. E. Sharpe, Inc.).

Bain, Joe S. 1956. *Barriers to New Competition: Their Character and Consequences in Manufacturing Industries* (Cambridge, MA: Harvard University Press).

Bance, Nigel. 1990. "Energy Finance: How the Bankers View the Future," *Euromoney,* Energy Finance Supplement, June/July, pp. 29–34.

Baranson, Jack. 1986. "Multinationals and Free Trade: The Implications of a U.S.-Canadian Agreement," *Multinational Business* (3), pp. 7–16.

Barham, Kevin. 1990–1991. "Networking—the Corporate Way Round International Discord," *Multinational Business* (4), Winter, pp. 1–11.

Barone, Carole A. 1989. "Planning and the Changing Role of the CIO in Higher Education," *Information Management Review,* Summer, pp. 23–31.

Barovick, Richard L. 1970. "Congress Looks at the Multinational Corporation," *Columbia Journal of World Business,* November/December, pp. 75–79.

Bartlett, Christopher A. and Hideki Yoshihara. 1988. "New Challenges for Japanese Multinationals: Is Organization Adaptation Their Achilles Heel?" *Human Resource Management,* 27(1), Spring, pp. 19–43.

References

Bartlett, Christopher A. and Sumantra Ghoshal. 1986. "Tap Your Subsidiaries for Global Reach," *Harvard Business Review,* November/December, pp. 87–94.

Bartlett, Christopher A. and Sumantra Ghoshal. 1987. "Managing Across Borders: New Strategic Requirements," *Sloan Management Review,* Summer, pp. 7–17.

Bartlett, Christopher A. and Sumantra Ghoshal. 1988. "Organizing for Worldwide Effectiveness: The Transnational Solution," *California Management Review,* Fall, pp. 54–74.

Bartlett, Christopher A. and Sumantra Ghoshal. 1989. *Managing Across Borders* (Cambridge, MA: Harvard Business School Press).

Barton, Ron and Richard Bobst. 1988. "How to Manage the Risks of Technology," *The Journal of Business Strategy,* November/December.

Batcha, Becky. 1987. "Three Vendors Give Cray Chase," *Computerworld,* 21(41), October 12, pp. 99–106.

Bates, Thomas H. 1973. "Management and the Multinational Business Environment," *California Management Review,* XV(3), Spring, pp. 37–45.

Beauvois, John J. 1960–1961. "International Intelligence for the International Enterprise," *California Management Review,* pp. 39–46.

Becker, Helmut. 1976. "Is There a Cosmopolitan Information Seeker?" *Journal of International Business Studies,* September, pp. 77–89.

Behrman, Jack N. 1969. "Multinational Corporations, Transnational Interests and National Sovereignty," *Columbia Journal of World Business,* March/April.

Behrman, Jack N. 1974. *Decision Criteria for Foreign Direct Investment in Latin America* (New York: Council of the Americas).

Behrman, Jack N. 1981. "Transnational Corporations in the New International Economic Order," *Journal of International Business Studies,* Spring/Summer, pp. 29–42.

Behrman, Jack N. and William A. Fischer. 1980a. *Overseas R&D Activities of Transnational Companies* (Cambridge, MA: Oelgeschlager, Gunn & Hain).

Behrman, Jack N. and William A. Fischer. 1980b. "Transnational Corporations: Market Orientations and R&D Abroad," *Columbia Journal of World Business,* Fall.

Belassa, Bela. 1974. "Trade Creation and Trade Diversion in the European Common Market: An Appraisal of the Evidence," *The Manchester School,* pp. 93–127.

Belitsos, Byron. 1989. "IBM's Rolm Deal: A Smart Move," *Computer Decisions,* 21(3), March, pp. 27–29.

Bello, Daniel C. and Nicholas C. Williamson. 1985. "The American Export Trading Company: Designing a New International Marketing Institution," *Journal of Marketing,* 49, Fall, pp. 60–69.

Benoit, Emile. 1972. "The Attack on the Multinationals," *Columbia Journal of World Business,* November/December, pp. 15–22.

Berger, Wolfram G. 1988. "Establishing the European Internal Market: Implications for Information Technology," *International Journal of Technology Management,* 3(6), pp. 631–641.

Berkman, Barbara N. 1989. "After AT&T, Olivetti Eyes U.S. Vertical Markets," *Electronic Business,* 15(15), July 24, pp. 17–18.

Berkman, Barbara N. 1990a. "Can the Barons of Jessi Save Europe's Chip Makers?" *Electronic Business,* 16(5), March 5, pp. 42–47.

Berkman, Barbara N. 1990b. "Europe's 1995 HDTV Goal: A Standard of Its Own," *Electronic Business,* 16(16), August 20, pp. 44–45.

Berkman, Barbara N. 1990c. "Istel: AT&T's Key to Open European Markets," *Electronic Business,* 16(14), July 23.

Berkman, Barbara N. 1990d. "Rebuilding the House of Siemens on a Worldwide Foundation," *Electronic Business,* 16(15), August 6, pp. 28–32.

Bernardin, H. John and Richard W. Beatty. 1987. "Can Subordinate Appraisals Enhance Managerial Productivity?" *Sloan Management Review,* 28(4), Summer, pp. 63–73.

Bernier, Linda. 1990. "EC Rulings Open Door to Reverse Engineering," *Electronic Business,* 16(16), August 20, p. 65.

Bertrand, Kate. 1987. "Talking Turkey on Trade Shows," *Business Marketing,* 72(3), March, pp. 94–103.

Blanden, Michael and Gavin Shreeve. 1990. "Minding the Business," *Banker,* 140(767), January, pp. 19–20.

Block, Arthur V. 1988. "Automation with a Graphics Interface," *Personal Computing,* 12(10), October, pp. 132–134.

Bock, Gordon, Thane Peterson, and Patrick Houston. 1986. "Honeywell Beats a Retreat from the Computer Wars," *Business Week,* Industrial/Technology Edition (2977), December 15, p. 30.

Boddewyn, J. J., Marsha Baldwin Halbrich, and A. C. Perry. 1986. "Service Multinationals: Conceptualization, Measurement and Theory," *Journal of International Business Studies,* Fall, pp. 41–57.

Boddewyn, Jean and Etienne F. Cracco. 1972. "The Political Game in World Business," *Columbia Journal of World Business,* January/February, pp. 45–56.

Bolek, Raymond W. and Kathryn J. Hayley. 1988. "Developing Staff, Not Systems, Is Key Challenge to CIOs," *Chief Information Officer Journal,* Fall, pp. 8–13.

Bonham-Yeaman, Doria. 1986. "The United States Leadership in Global Protection for Computer Chip Designs," *Columbia Journal of World Business,* Winter, pp. 81–87.

Booz-Allen & Hamilton. 1989. *Europe 1992: Threat or Opportunity,* New York.

Botkin, J., D. Dimancescu, and R. Stata. 1982. *Global Stakes: The Future of High Technology in America* (Cambridge, MA: Ballinger).

Boult, Raymond. 1990. "Competent Solutions," *Systems International,* 18(4), April, pp. 53–54.

Boult, Raymond, Alexander Dorozynski, Ted Katauskas, Skip Derra, Bob Keeler, Robert Cassidy, and Colleen Davis. 1990. "Salute to French Technology," *R&D,* 32(11), November, pp. 78–113.

Bozman, Jean S. 1987. "Will AT&T Hang It Up?" *Computerworld,* 21(28), July 13, pp. 95, 101.

Bradley, Peter. 1989. "Paving the Road to Quality Transportation," *Purchasing,* 106(1), January 19, pp. 100–109.

Braham, James. 1988. "Marrying Goods & Services," *Industry Week,* 237(9), November 7, pp. 69–71.

References

Brandt, Richard. 1987. "Seagate Goes East—And Comes Back a Winner," *Business Week,* Industrial/Technology Edition (2989), March 16, p. 94.

Brandt, William K. and James M. Hulbert. 1976. "Patterns of Communications in the Multinational Corporation: An Empirical Study," *Journal of International Business Studies,* September, pp. 57–64.

Bredin, James. 1988. "Making Change Happen," *Industry Week,* 237(2), July 18, pp. 47–48.

Breen, Michael and Erwin Shrader. 1990. "South Korea: Going Through a Rough Patch," *Asian Business,* 26(6), June, pp. 38–52.

Bremner, Brian. 1989. "Can Caterpillar Inch Its Way Back to Heftier Profits?" *Business Week,* Industrial/Technology Edition (3125), September 25, pp. 75, 78.

Bremner, Brian. 1990. "It's a New Day for ITT's Rand Araskog," *Business Week* (3167), July 2, pp. 50–51.

Brewer, Thomas L. 1983. "The Instability of Governments and the Instability of Controls on Funds Transfers by Multinational Enterprises: Implications for Political Risk Analysis," *Journal of International Business Studies,* Winter.

Brink, Victor Z. 1969. "Top Management Looks at the Computer," *Columbia Journal of World Business,* January/February.

Brockington, Langdon. 1987a. "ICI's Expanded Agchem Agenda," *Chemical Week,* 141(24), December 9, pp. 41–43.

Brockington, Langdon. 1987b. "ICI Expands Its Interest in U.S. Agrichemicals," *Chemical Week,* 140(23), June 17, pp. 6–7.

Brockington, Langdon. 1988. "The ICI/Stauffer Marriage: A Year Later Progress Report," *Chemical Week,* 143(24), December 14, pp. 17–18.

Brown, Bob. 1988. "IBM, Siemens Carve Up Rolm Operations; IBM/Siemens Deal Leaves Some Rolm Users Worried," *Network World,* 5(51), December 19, pp. 1, 6, 41.

Brown, Bob. 1988/1989. "IBM/Siemens Pact May Aid PBX Rivals," *Network World,* 5(52), December 26/January 2.

Brown, Victoria A. 1988. "Calling the Shots with New Communications Networks," *The Journal of Business Strategy,* November/December, pp. 46–49.

Brownell, Peter. 1987. "The Role of Accounting Information, Environment and Management Control in Multi-National Organizations," *Accounting and Finance,* May, pp. 1–16.

Bruce, Leigh. 1987a. "The New Alcatel Powerhouse: So Far, So Good," *International Management,* 42(10), October, pp. 45–53.

Bruce, Leigh. 1987b. "Corporate Turnaround: Bull Tackles the Yanks," *International Management,* 42(12), December, pp. 30–32.

Bucken, Mike. 1988. "Groundwork for the Future," *Software Magazine,* 8(14), November, p. 41.

Buckingham, William A. 1988. "A Winning Strategy for Branch Banking," *Bankers Magazine,* 171(3), May/June, pp. 14–18.

Buckley, Peter J. 1983. "Macroeconomic Versus International Business Approach to Direct Foreign Investment: A Comment on Professor Kojima's Interpretation," *Hitotsubashi Journal of Economics,* 24, pp. 95–100.

Buckley, Peter J. 1985a. "A Critical View of Theories of the Multinational Enterprise," in Peter J. Buckley and Mark Casson, eds., *The Economic Theory of the Multinational Enterprise* (New York: Macmillan).

Buckley, Peter J. 1985b. "The Economic Analysis of the Multinational Enterprise: Reading Versus Japan?" *Hitotsubashi Journal of Economics,* 26, pp. 117–124.

Burger, Katherine. 1989. "MHT's STAR Consultants Raise Technology Consciousness," *Bank Systems & Equipment,* 26(5), May, pp. 45–46.

Bush, Martin E. and Norman E. Fenton. 1990. "Software Measurement: A Conceptual Framework," *Journal of Systems & Software,* 12(3), July, pp. 223–231.

Butkus, Raymond T., Mathilde Benveniste, and Richard W. Ross, Jr. 1987/1988. "Linking the Global Corporation," *Network World,* 4(51)/5(1), December 28/January 4, pp. 31–35.

Butterworth, Robert. 1989. "Collection," in Roy Goodson, ed., *Intelligence Requirements for the 1990s: Collection, Analysis, Counterintelligence, and Covert Action* (Lexington, MA: Lexington Books), pp. 31–42.

Byrne, Harlan S. 1987. "Track of the Cat: Caterpillar Is Bulldozing Its Way to Higher Profits," *Barrons,* 67(14), April 6, pp. 13, 70–71.

Cao, A. D. 1980. "Non-Tariff Barriers to U.S. Manufactured Exports," *Columbia Journal of World Business,* Summer, pp. 93–102.

Calvert, A. L. 1981. "A Synthesis of Foreign Direct Investment Theories and Theories of the Multinational Firm," *Journal of International Business Studies,* Spring/Summer, pp. 43–59.

Campbell, Gordon. 1987. "In Conversation: John Kernick," *Computing Canada,* 13(10), May 14, p. 11.

Carlyle, Ralph Emmett. 1990. "The Out of Touch CIO," *Datamation,* 36, August 15, p. 30.

Carlyle, Ralph Emmett. 1988a. "CIO: Misfit or Misnomer?" *Datamation,* August 1, pp. 50–56.

Carlyle, Ralph Emmett. 1988b. "Managing IS at Multinationals," *Datamation,* 34(5), March 1, pp. 54–66.

Cash, James I., Jr. and Benn R. Konsynski. 1985. "IS Redraws Competitive Boundaries," *Harvard Business Review,* March/April, pp. 134–142.

Cash, James I., Jr. and Poppy L. McLeod. 1985. "Managing the Introduction of Information Systems Technology in Strategically Dependent Companies," *Journal of Management Information Systems,* I(4), Spring, pp. 5–23.

Casson, Mark. 1982. "Transaction Costs and the Theory of the Multinational Enterprise," in Alan M. Rugman, ed., *New Theories of the Multinational Enterprise* (New York: St. Martin's Press), p. 37.

Casson, Mark. 1985. "Transaction Costs and the Theory of the Multinational Enterprise," in Peter J. Buckley and Mark Casson, eds., *The Economic Theory of the Multinational Enterprise* (New York: Macmillan), pp. 20–38.

Casson, Mark. 1986. "General Theories of the Multinational Enterprise: Their Relevance to Business History," in Peter Hertner and Geoffrey Jones, eds., *Multinationals: Theory and History* (Aldershot Harts, England: Gower Publishing Co., Ltd.).

Caves, Richard E. 1971. "International Corporations: The Industrial Economics of Foreign Investment," *Economica,* February.

References

Caves, Richard E. 1974a. "Causes of Direct Investment: Foreign Firms' Shares in Canadian and United Kingdom Manufacturing Industries," *The Review of Economics and Statistics*, pp. 279–293.

Caves, Richard E. 1974b. "Multinational Firms, Competition, and Productivity in Host-Country Markets," *Economica*, May, pp. 176–193.

Caves, Richard E. 1982. "Multinational Enterprises and Technology Transfer," in Alan M. Rugman, ed., *New Theories of the Multinational Enterprise* (New York: St. Martin's Press).

Cavusgil, S. Tamer. 1990. "The Importance of Distributor Training at Caterpillar," *Industrial Marketing Management*, 19(1), February, pp. 1–9.

Cayer, Shirley. 1988a. "Building a World-Class Supplier Base Is the Number-One Priority," *Purchasing*, 104(4), April 14, pp. 52–55.

Cayer, Shirley. 1988b. "Buyers in the Appliance Industry Thrive in the New Global Market," *Purchasing*, 104 (4), April 14, pp. 46–51.

Cayer, Shirley. 1990. "Welcome to Caterpillar's Quality Institute," *Purchasing*, 109(2), August 16, pp. 80–84.

Cayer, Shirley. 1991. "Develop a Supplier; Own the Future," *Purchasing*, 110(8), May 2, pp. 57, 59.

Chakravarthy, Balaji S. and Howard V. Perlmutter. 1985. "Strategic Planning for a Global Business," *Columbia Journal of World Business*, Summer.

Chandler, Alfred D., Jr. 1979. "The Growth of the Transnational Industrial Firm in the United States and the United Kingdom: A Comparative Analysis," *American Economic Review*, pp. 396–409+.

Chandler, Alfred D., Jr. 1986. "Technological and Organizational Underpinnings of Modern Industrial Multinational Enterprise: The Dynamics of Competitive Advantage," in Alice Teichova, Maurice Lévy-Leboyer, and Helga Nussbaum, eds., *Multinational Enterprise in Historical Perspective* (New York: Cambridge University Press).

Chandran, Rajan, Arvind Phatak, and Rakesh Sambharya. 1987. "Transborder Data Flows: Implications for Multinational Corporations," *Business Horizons*, 30(6), November/December, pp. 74–82.

Cheevers, Richard. 1986. "Technology at Work: Wired Up to an 'Expert,'" *Director*, 40(3), October, p. 27.

Chereshkin, Dimitry, Wladyslow Turski, Tibor Vamos, A. Tomasz Jarmoszko, and Seymour Goodman. 1992. "National Information Technology Policies in East-Central Europe and the Soviet Union," *International Information Systems*, 1(1).

Chorafas, Dimitris N. 1970. "Computer Technology in Western and Eastern Europe," *Columbia Journal of World Business*, May/June, pp. 61–66.

Christodoulakis, D. N. and C. Tsalidis. 1990. "Design Principles of the ATHENA Software Maintainability Tool," *Microprocessing & Microprogramming*, 28(1–5), March, pp. 183–189.

Christodoulakis, D. P. Soupos and C. Zaroliagis. 1987. "The Implementation of a Software Engineering Database Using Desk-Size Computing Resources," *Microprocessing & Microprogramming*, 21(1–5), August, pp. 383–389.

Chynoweth, Emma. 1990a. "ICI Takes a Closer Look at Thailand," *Chemical Week*, 146(21), May 30, p. 15.

Chynoweth, Emma. 1990b. "ICI Unveils New Route to HFC-134a Production," *Chemical Week*.

Chynoweth, Emma. 1990c. "Kemira Outlines Plans for U.K. Fertilizers," *Chemical Week*, 147(5), August 8, pp. 16–17.

Chynoweth, Emma. 1991a. "Supercomputers Boost Product and Process R&D," *Chemical Week*, 148(12), March 27, p. 39.

Chynoweth, Emma. 1991b. "Ammonia Process Owners Knock Small-Scale Technology," *Chemical Week*, 148(13), April 3, p. 13.

Clark, R. 1979. *The Japanese Company* (New Haven and London: Yale University Press).

Clemons, Erik K. and Bruce W. Weber. 1990. "London's Big Bang: A Case Study of Information Technology, Competitive Impact, and Organizational Change," *Journal of Management Information Systems,* Spring, 6(4), pp. 41–60.

Clifford, Mark. 1987. "Corporate Democracy Pays Dividends," *Far Eastern Economic Review*, 138(47), November 19, pp. 84–85.

Clifford, Mark. 1990. "Friends in Need: South Korean–Soviet Trade Begins to Blossom," *Far Eastern Economic Review*, 149 (38), September 20, pp. 86–87.

Cochran, Thomas N. 1990. "Cat Fancier," *Barron's*, 70(28), July 9, p. 30.

Cochrane, Don. 1987. "Easing the Migration into the Future of Communications Technology," *Computer Networks & ISDN Systems*, 14(2–5), pp. 323–329.

Cohen, Howard and Kenneth Silber. 1990. "MHT's Image Philosophy," *Bank Systems & Technology*, 27(4), April, pp. 44–56.

Cole, Malcolm. 1986. "Olivetti Offers a System for the Busy Practice," *Accountancy*, 97(1113), May, pp. 139–141.

Colson, Frank. 1985. "New Perspectives on the Brazilian Computer," *Multinational Business* (4), pp. 1–9.

Commission on Transnational Corporations. 1991. "Impact of Transnational Service Corporations on Developing Countries: Report of the Secretary General," Doc. E/C.10/1991/6 (New York: United Nations).

Conde, David W. 1970. *CIA—Core of the Cancer* (New Delhi: Entente Private Limited).

Contractor, Farok J. 1986. "International Business: An Alternative View," *International Marketing Review*, Spring, pp. 74–84.

Cook, Stephanie. 1985. "Ireland Moving to Become Integral Part of Transatlantic Connection," *Data Communications*, 14(13), December, pp. 68, 70.

Cooke, Stephanie and Paula M. Block. 1986. "U.K. Chemicals: In the Shadow of the Oil Price Decline," *Chemical Week*, 139(10), September 3, pp. 30–33.

Cox, John. 1988. "Image Device Helps Firm Pool Resources," *Network World*, 5(35), August 29, pp. 15, 17.

Crane, Geoff. 1990. "Ailing Goldstar Needs Strong Medicine," *Electronic Business*, 16(16), August 20, pp. 67–70.

Crane, Timothy C. 1988. "Shedding Light on Certificate Fraud," *ABA Banking Journal*, 80(5), May, pp. 22, 24.

Cray, David. 1984. "Control and Coordination in Multinational Corporations," *Journal of International Business Studies*, Fall.

CSC Index. 1988. "Europe in 1992: Winning Through Technology," *Indications*.

References

CSC Index. 1990a. *Critical Issues of Information Systems Management for 1990* (Cambridge, MA: CSC Index), p. 37.

CSC Index. 1990b. *Critical Issues of Information Systems Management for 1991* (Cambridge, MA: CSC Index), pp. 18–19.

CSC Index. 1990c. "Engineering the New Global Corporation," *Insights,* Summer, pp. 2–9.

CSC Index. 1990d. "Managing Global Information Systems," *Meeting Summary,* Regional Forum (Cambridge, MA: CSC Index).

Cusack, Sally. 1988. "Apple's Macintosh Not Just a Toy," *Computerworld,* 22(5), February 1, p. 69.

Czinkota, Michael R. 1986. "International Trade and Business in the Late 1980's: An Integrated U.S. Perspective," *Journal of International Business Studies,* Spring, pp. 127–134.

Dagnoli, Judann and Julie Liesse Erickson. 1988. "PM, Kraft Could Slice Promotions," *Advertising Age,* 59(47), November 7, pp. 3, 74.

Dance, W. D. 1969. "An Evolving Structure for Multinational Operations," *Columbia Journal of World Business,* November/December.

Das, Ranjan. 1981. "Impact of Host Government Regulations on MNC Operation: Learning from Third World Countries," *Columbia Journal of World Business,* Spring, pp. 85–90.

Davidson, William H. 1982. "Small Group Activity at Musashi Semiconductor Works," *Sloan Management Review,* pp. 3–14.

Davidson, William H. 1984a. "Administrative Orientation and International Performance," *Journal of International Business Studies,* Fall.

Davidson, William H. 1984b. *The Amazing Race: Winning the Technorivalry with Japan* (New York: John Wiley & Sons).

Davis, N. C. and S. E. Goodman. 1978. "The Soviet Bloc's Unified System of Computers," in Association for Computer Machinery, *Computing Surveys,* 10(2), June, p. 111.

Dawkins, William. 1987. "E.E. Approves $6.2–Billion Plan for Research," *Europe* (271), November, pp. 22–23.

De Bony, Elizabeth. 1991. "Japan May Find Closed Doors in Europe," *Computerworld,* 25(9), March 4, p. 66.

De Groote, C. 1989. "PCTE—a Remarkable Platform," *Information & Software Technology,* 31(3), April, pp. 136–142.

De Jong, Ton, Robert de Hoog, and Guus Schreiber. 1988. "Knowledge Acquisition for an Integrated Project Management System," *Information Processing and Management,* 24(6), pp. 681–691.

De La Torre, José. 1981. "Foreign Investment and Economic Development: Conflict and Negotiation," *Journal of International Business Studies,* Fall, pp. 9–32.

De Man, Jozef A. 1988. "Designing Digital Systems with a Function Language," *Microprocessing & Microprogramming,* 24(1–5), August, pp. 227–232.

De Man, Jozef A., Johan Vanslembrouck. 1989. "Transformational Design of Digital Circuits," *Microprocessing & Microprogramming,* 27(1–5), August, pp. 273–278.

De Meyer, Arnoud. 1991. "Tech Talk: How Managers Are Stimulating Global R&D Communication," *Sloan Management Review,* 32(3), Spring, pp. 49–58.

De Sola Pool, I. 1983. *Technologies of Freedom* (Cambridge, MA: Harvard University Press).

Deans, Candace P. et al. 1989. *Identification of Key International Information Systems Issues in the U.S.-Based Multinational Corporations,* Working Paper in Management Science DOR G-89-02, Division of Research, College of Business Administration, University of South Carolina.

Deans, Candace P. et al. 1991. "Key International IS Issues in U.S.-Based Multinational Corporations," *Journal of Management Information Systems,* 7(4), Spring.

Dekker, Wisse. 1986. "Prospects for Collaboration and a Common Industrial Policy in Europe for the High-Technology Industries," *International Journal of Technology Management,* 1(3, 4), pp. 297–307.

DeLamarter, R. T. 1986. "Big Blue: IBM's Use and Abuse of Power" (New York: Dodd, Mead & Company).

Department of Industry (UK). 1982. "A Programme for Advanced Information Technology: The Report of the Alvey Committee" (London: Her Majesty's Stationery Office).

Department of Social and Economic Affairs. 1974. *The Acquisition of Technology from Multinational Corporations by Developing Countries,* Doc. No. ST/ESA/12 (New York: United Nations).

Derian, J. C. 1990. "America's Struggle for Leadership in Technology" (Cambridge, MA: The MIT Press).

Dery, David. 1980. "Putting Information Technology to Work," *California Management Review,* XXII(2), Spring, pp. 68–76.

Desmond, John. 1991. "Siemens, Bull Seeking Openness," *Software Magazine,* 11(6), May, pp. 23–25.

Desmond, Paul. 1990/1991. "T–1 Network Keeps Watch over Itself," *Network World,* 7(53)/8(1), December 31/January 7, pp. 1, 6.

Desmond, Paul and Bob Wallace. 1989. "IBM Refines Net View, Closes Siemens Deal," *Network World,* 6(33), August 21, pp. 1, 6, 58.

Deveny, Kathleen. 1987. "For Caterpillar, the Metamorphosis Isn't Over," *Business Week,* Industrial/Technology Edition (3014), August 31, pp. 72–74.

Deveny, Kathleen, Corie Brown, and William J. Hampton. 1988. "Going for the Lion's Share: The Time Is Right for U.S. Companies to Reclaim Lost Markets," *Business Week,* Industrial/Technology Edition (3061), July 18, pp. 70–72.

DeYoung, H. Garrett. 1990. "In Search of the New European Manager," *Electronic Business,* 16(23), December 10.

Diebold, John, ed. 1973. *The World of the Computer* (New York: Random House).

Diebold, John. 1987. "Communications Bottlenecks Still Beset National Borders," *Network World,* 4(22), June 1, pp. 1, 30–32.

Diebold, John. 1988. "The Changing Information Environment: Suggest Future Directions," *Vital Speeches,* 55(5), December 15, pp. 138–145.

Dillon, Thomas F. 1986. "Caterpillar Connects with EDI," *Purchasing World,* 30(8), August, pp. 62–64.

Dodsworth, Terry. 1987. "ITT Adopts New Role in Europe." *Europe,* March, pp. 22–23.

References

Donovan, John J. 1988. "Beyond Chief Information Officer to Network Manager, *Harvard Business Review,* September/October, p. 134.

Dordick, Herbert S. 1983. "The Emerging World Information Business," *Columbia Journal of World Business,* Spring, pp. 69–76.

Douglas, Alison. 1987. "Information: A New Multinational Industry?" *Multinational Business* (2), Summer, pp. 37–39.

Douglas, Susan P. and Yoram Wind. 1987. "The Myth of Globalization," *Columbia Journal of World Business,* Winter, pp. 19–29.

Doz, Yves L. 1979. *Government Control and Multinational Strategic Management: Power Systems and Telecommunications Equipment* (New York: Praeger).

Doz, Yves L. 1980. "Multinational Strategy and Structure in Government Controlled Businesses," *Columbia Journal of World Business,* Fall.

Doz, Yves L. 1986. *Strategic Management in Multinational Companies* (Oxford: Pergamon Press).

Doz, Yves L., Christopher A. Bartlett, and C. K. Prahalad. 1981. "Global Competitive Pressures and Host Country Demands: Managing Tensions in MNCs," *California Management Review,* XXIII(3), Spring, pp. 63–74.

Doz, Yves L. and C. K. Prahalad. 1984. "Patterns of Strategic Control Within Multinational Corporations," *Journal of International Business Studies,* Fall, pp. 55–72.

Dreyfuss, Joel. 1988. "IBM's Vexing Slide in Japan," *Fortune,* 117(7), March 28, pp. 73–77.

Dunkin, Amy. 1988. "Beyond Marlboro Country," *Business Week,* Industrial/Technology Edition (3064), August 8, pp. 54–58.

Dunning, John H. (nd). "United States Foreign Investment and the Technological Gap," in *Conflicts of Interest in Agricultural and Industrial Policies,* pp. 364–406.

Dunning, John H., ed. 1971. *The Multinational Enterprise* (London: George Allen & Unwin, Ltd.).

Dunning, John H. 1972. "The Determinants of International Production," first presented to a conference on "The Growth of Multinational Enterprises," Rennes, France, September.

Dunning, John H. 1977. "Trade, Location of Economic Activity and the MNE: A Search for an Eclectic Approach," in Bertil Ohlin, Per-Ove Hesselborn, and Per Magnus Wijkman, eds., *The International Allocation of Economic Activity: Proceedings of a Nobel Symposium Held at Stockholm* (London: The Macmillan Press, Ltd.).

Dunning, John H. 1980. "Toward an Eclectic Theory of International Production," *Journal of International Business Studies,* 11, Spring/Summer, pp. 9–31.

Dunning, John H., ed. 1985. *Multinational Enterprises, Economic Structure and International Competitiveness* (New York: John Wiley & Sons).

Dunning, John H. and Peter J. Buckley. 1977. "International Production and Alternative Models of Trade," in *The Manchester School,* pp. 392–403.

Dunning, John H., John A. Cantwell, and T. A. B. Corley. 1986. "The Theory of International Production: Some Historical Antecedents," in Peter Hertner and Geoffrey Jones, eds., *Multinationals: Theory and History* (Aldershot Harts, England: Gower).

Dunning, John H. and Matthew McQueen. 1982. "The Eclectic Theory of Multinational Enterprise and the International Hotel Industry," in A. M. Rugman, ed., *New Theories of the Multinational Enterprise* (New York: St. Martin's Press), pp. 79–106.

Dunning, John H. and George Norman. 1983. "The Theory of the Multinational Enterprise: An Application to Multinational Office Location," *Environment and Planning A*, pp. 675–692.

Dunning, John H. and Alan M. Rugman. 1985. "The Influence of Hymer's Dissertation on the Theory of Foreign Direct Investment," *AEA Papers and Proceedings*, 75(2), May, pp. 228–232.

Dutton, Barbara. 1989. "Cat Climbs High with FMS," *Manufacturing Systems*, 7(11), November, pp. 16–22.

Dyment, John J. 1987. "Strategies and Management Controls for Global Corporations," *Journal of Business Strategy*, 7 (4), Spring, pp. 20–26.

Dymsza, William A. 1982. "The Education and Development of Managers for Future Decades," *Journal of International Business Studies*, Winter.

Dymsza, William A. 1984a. "Global Strategic Planning: A Model and Recent Developments," *Journal of International Business Studies*, Fall, pp. 169–183.

Dymsza, William A. 1984b. "Trends in Multinational Business and Global Environments: A Perspective," *Journal of International Business Studies*, Winter.

Earl, Michael J. (nd). "Exploiting IT for Strategic Advantage—A Framework of Frameworks," Oxford Institute of Information Management, Research paper RDP 88/1.

Eberbach, Eugeniusz, Stephen C. McCabe, and Apostolos N. Refenes. 1989. "PARLE: A Language for Expressing Parallelism and Integrating Symbolic and Numeric Computations," *Microprocessing & Microprogramming*, 27(1–5), August, pp. 207–214.

Eckley, Robert S. 1989. "Caterpillar's Ordeal: Foreign Competition in Capital Goods," *Business Horizons*, 32(2), March/April, pp. 80–86.

Economic Commission for Europe. 1987. *The Telecommunication Industry: Growth and Structural Change* (New York: United Nations).

Eells, Richard. 1969. "Multinational Corporations: The Intelligence Function," *Columbia Journal of World Business*, November/December.

Egelhoff, William G. 1984. "Patterns of Control in U.S., UK, and European Multinational Corporations," *Journal of International Business Studies*, Fall, pp. 73–83.

Egelhoff, William G. 1988. "Strategy and Structure in Multinational Corporations: A Revision of the Stopford and Wells Model," *Strategic Management Journal*, 9(1–14).

Ekerson, Wayne. 1989. "EDS Sows Seeds of Future Profit in Post-1992 Europe," *Network World*, 6(38), September 25, pp. 33, 38.

Elam, Joyce, Dan Edwards, and Richard Mason. 1990. "How U.S. Cities Compete Through Information Technology: Securing an Urban Advantage," *Information Society*, 6, pp. 153–178.

Encarnation, Dennis J. and Louis T. Wells, Jr. 1985. "Sovereignty en Garde: Negotiating with Foreign Investors," *International Organization*, 39(1), Winter, pp. 47–78.

Endicott, Glenn A. 1989. "Repair, Rebuild or Replace? Emergency!" *Equipment Management*, 17(10), October, pp. 62–64.

References

Eom, Hyun B. and Sang M. Lee. 1987. "A Large-Scale Goal Programming Model-Based Decision Support for Formulating Global Financing Strategy," *Information and Management,* 12(1), January, pp. 33–44.

Etheridge, James and Peggy Trautman. 1990. "The Datamation 100: Groupe Bull; Siemens; Olivetti; NV Philips; Nixdorf," *Datamation,* 36(12), June 15, pp. 127–130.

Evans, Richard. 1990a. "Ozone Savers," *International Management,* Europe Edition, 45(3), April, pp. 44–45.

Evans, Richard. 1990b. "Takeovers: Japan Moves in at Dawn," *International Management,* Europe Edition, 45(8), September, pp. 44–47.

Evans, Richard. 1990c. "Parallel World of New Superpower," *International Management,* Europe Edition, 45(10), November, pp. 58–60.

Evans, Richard. 1991. "ESPRIT Evades the Soft Option," *International Management,* Europe Edition, 46(1), February, pp. 58–61.

Everett, Martin, William Keenan, Jr., Bill Kelley, Arthur Bragg, Thayer C. Taylor, and Richard Kern. 1989. "America's Best Sales Forces," *Sales & Marketing Management,* 141(7), June, pp. 31–48.

Exley, Charles E., Jr. 1990. "How Changes in MIS Affect the CFO and the CIO," *Financial Executive,* 6(5), November/December, p. 16.

Faden, Michael. 1988. "Olivetti: Biting the Hand That Feeds It?" *UNIX Review,* 6(2), February, pp. 14–23.

Fain, Tyrus G., Katharine C. Plant, and Ross Milloy, eds. 1977. *The Intelligence Community: History, Organization, and Issues* (New York & London: R. R. Bowker).

Fairlamb, David. 1986. "Multinationals Open In-House Banks," *Dun's Business Month,* 127(5), May, pp. 54–56.

Fannin, William R. and Arvin F. Rodrigues. 1986. "National or Global?—Control vs. Flexibility," *Long Range Planning,* 19(5), October, pp. 84–88.

Faucon, Michel. 1986. "A U.S. Multinational in Europe: Politics and Freedom of Operations," *Vital Speeches,* 52(22), September 1, pp. 695–698.

Faulhaber, G. R. 1987. "Telecommunications in Turmoil: Technology and Public Policy," (Cambridge, MA: Ballinger).

Fayerweather, John. 1960/1961. "LRP for International Operations," *California Management Review,* pp. 23–35.

Feeny, David F., Brian R. Edwards, Michael J. Earl. 1987. "Complex Organizations and the Information Systems Function—a Research Study," Oxford Institute of Information Management, Research paper series RDP 87/7.

Feld, Werner. 1970. "Political Aspects of Transnational Business Collaboration in the Common Market," *International Organization,* 24(2), pp. 209–238.

Ferguson, Charles H. 1990. "Computers and the Coming of the U.S. Keiretsu," *Harvard Business Review,* July/August (4).

Feuche, Michael. 1990. "Data Center Automation: Consolidation Promotes Hands-Off Strategy," *Computerworld,* 24(35), August 27, pp. 59–64, 69–70.

Finn, David. 1988. "High-Tech Woman at the Top," *Across the Board,* 25(7, 8), July/August, pp. 11–17.

Finn, David. 1990. "Good Design Is Good Business," *Marketing News*, 24(24), November 26, p. 9.

Fischer, William A. and Jack N. Behrman (nd). "The Coordination of Foreign R&D Activities by Transnational Corporations," *Journal of International Business Studies*, pp. 28–35.

Fitzgerald, Michael. 1990. "IS Helps 'Cat' Stay on Its Feet," *Computerworld*, Section 2, October 8, pp. 58, 60.

Flamm, K. 1987. "Targeting the Computer: Government Support and International Competition" (Washington, DC: The Brookings Institution).

Flamm, K. 1988. "Creating the Computer: Government, Industry, and High Technology" (Washington, DC: The Brookings Institution).

Foran, Marjorie. 1987/1988. "The Canadian Computer Industry: Factors Affecting Government Policy," *Optimum*, 18(4), pp. 79–99, 107.

Fornili, Sandro L. 1989. "You Don't Need Big Computers to Run Complex Simulations," *Research and Development*, 31(11), November, pp. 68–74.

Foster, Geoffrey. 1987. "The Legacy of Harvey-Jones," *Management Today*, January, pp. 34–41, 86–88.

Fowler, Elizabeth M. 1989. "Data Systems Managers Get Bigger Role," *New York Times*, Section 1, July 4, p. 44.

Fowler, Henry H. 1965. "National Interests and Multinational Business," *California Management Review*, Fall, pp. 3–12.

Franko, Lawrence G. (nd). "Patterns in the Multinational Spread of Continental European Enterprise," *Journal of International Business Studies*, pp. 41–53.

Franko, Lawrence G. 1973. "Who Manages Multinational Enterprises?" *Columbia Journal of World Business*, Summer, pp. 30–42.

Franko, Lawrence G. 1978. "Multinationals: The End of U.S. Dominance," *Harvard Business Review*, November/December, pp. 93–101.

Franko, Lawrence G. 1983. *The Threat of Japanese Multinationals: How the West Can Respond*, Wiley/IRM Series on Multinationals (Chichester & New York: John Wiley & Sons).

Franko, Lawrence G. 1987. "New Forms of Investment in Developing Countries by US Companies: A Five Industry Comparison," *Columbia Journal of World Business*, 22(2), Summer, pp. 39–56.

Franko, Lawrence G. 1989. "Use of Minority and 50–50 Joint Ventures by United States Multinationals During the 1970s: The Interaction of Host Country Policies and Corporate Strategies," *Journal of International Business Studies*, 20(1), Spring, pp. 19–40.

Frederick, William C. 1991. "The Moral Authority of Transnational Corporate Codes," *Journal of Business Ethics*, 10, pp. 165–177.

Freedman, David. 1990. "Bringing IT Back Home," *CIO*, 4(3), December, pp. 54–62.

Freiser, Theodore J. 1989. "In the 1990s, I/S Will Take Center Stage in a Lead Business Role," *Chief Information Officer Journal*, Fall, pp. 38–44.

Frenkel, K. A. 1990. "The European Community and Information Technology," *CACM*, 33(4), pp. 404–411.

Gabriel, Peter P. 1972. "Adaptation: The Name of the MNCs' Game," *Columbia Journal of World Business*, November/December, pp. 7–14.

Galbraith, J. R. and D. A. Nathanson. 1978. *Strategy Implementation: The Role of Structure and Process* (St. Paul, MN: West).

Ganley, Oswald Harold. 1982. *To Inform or to Control? The New Communications Network* (New York: McGraw-Hill).

Gardner, Richard N. and Robert G. Vambery. 1975. "Progress Towards a New World Economic Order," *Journal of International Business Studies,* Fall, pp. 5–14.

Garza, Victor R. and Tracey Capen. 1990. "Olivetti Is Tops in 25–MHz 386 Performance," *InfoWorld,* 12(33), August 13, p. 84.

Gatermann, Michael. 1986. "ITT's Empire in Decline?" *Director,* 40(3), October, pp. 67–72.

Gates, Stephen R. and William G. Egelhoff. 1986. "Centralization in Headquarters–Subsidiary Relationships," *Journal of International Business Studies,* Summer, pp. 71–92.

Gee, Jack. 1988. "The Bigger, the Better, Says Alcatel Chairman Suard," *Electronic Business,* 14(22), November 15, pp. 62–67.

Gemmell, Art. 1986. "Fujitsu's Cross-Cultural Style," *Management Review,* 75(6), June, pp. 7–8.

George, Joey F. and John Leslie King. 1990. *The Computing and Centralization Debate,* Working paper, Department of MIS, University of Arizona, April 9.

Geraghty, Coleen. 1986. "Computer Vendors Re-Shape Product Strategy for Asian Market," *Asian Finance,* 12(4), April 15.

Gerrie, David. 1988. "Point of Sale: Paint Splash," *Marketing,* September 8, p. 43.

Gessinger, Herald, Gunter W. Hasler, and Werner Hiller. 1988. "Technology Transfer Programme for the 5200 BCS Digital PABX," *International Journal of Technology Management,* 3(1, 2), pp. 196–204.

Ghoshal, Sumantra and Seok Ki Kim. 1986. "Building Effective Intelligence Systems for Competitive Advantage," *Sloan Management Review,* Fall, pp. 49–58.

Ghoshal, Sumantra. 1987. "Global Strategy: An Organizing Framework," *Strategic Management Journal,* 8, pp. 425–440.

Ghoshal, Sumantra. 1988. "Environmental Scanning in Korean Firms: Organizational Isomorphism in Action," *Journal of International Business Studies,* Spring, pp. 69–85.

Gibney, F. 1982. "Miracle by Design: The Real Reasons Behind Japan's Economic Success" (New York: Times Books).

Gibson, W. David. 1986. "ICI Americas: Sales Up 100% in Three Years, with More Acquisitions to Come," *Chemical Week,* 139(19), November 5, pp. 22–25.

Giddy, Ian H. 1978. "The Demise of the Product Cycle Model in International Business Theory," *Columbia Journal of World Business,* Spring, pp. 90–97.

Giddy, Ian H. and Stephen Young. 1982. "Conventional Theory and Unconventional MNEs," in Alan M. Rugman, ed., *New Theories of the Multinational Enterprise* (New York: St. Martin's Press).

Gillespie, G. Robert. 1988. "Auditing Concerns in Developing Countries," *Internal Auditor,* 45(5), October, pp. 27–30.

Gilligan, Bob. 1991. "Caterpillar Grades Up Based on Broadband LAN," *Manufacturing Systems,* 9(3), March, pp. 18–22.

Gittelshohn, John. 1988. "The Business Guide: Driving and Driven," *Business,* March, pp. 130–134.

Gofton, Ken. 1986. "Henderson Prepares for a New Era at ICI," *Marketing,* 26(13), September 25, pp. 36–39.

Goldberg, Eddy. 1987. "Users Call on WANs for Far-Reaching Business Needs," *Computerworld,* 21(13A), April 1, pp. 57–62.

Goldstein, Carl and Julian Baum. 1990. "Taiwan: Acer in the Hole; The Chips Are Down," *Far Eastern Economic Review,* 150(50), December 13, pp. 62–63.

Goldston, Terry. 1991. "Whirlpool's Whirlwind of Introductions," *Dealerscope Merchandising,* 33(2), February, pp. 68, 72.

Gomes-Casseres, Benjamin. 1990. "Firm Ownership Preferences and Host Government Restrictions: An Integrated Approach," *Journal of International Business Studies,* First quarter, pp. 1–22.

Goodman, S. E. 1985. "Technology Transfer and the Development of the Soviet Computer Industry," in B. Parrott, ed., *Trade, Technology and Soviet-American Relations* (Bloomington: Indiana University Press), pp. 117–140.

Goodwin, Candice. 1991. "Financial Software: Some Hard Choices," *Accountancy,* 107(1171), March, pp. 114–118.

Gouldson, Tim. 1987. "Olivetti Reveals Global Push," *Computing Canada,* 13(25), December 10, pp. 1, 6.

Gow, Kathleen A. 1990. "No Set Rules for Systems Design," *Computerworld,* 24(40), October 1, pp. 98–99.

Gray, H. Peter. 1985. "Multinational Corporations and Global Welfare: An Extension of Kojima and Ozawa," *Hitotsubashi Journal of Economics,* 26, pp. 125–133.

Gray, Harry J. 1985. "Forty Years of World Business," *Columbia Journal of World Business,* 20(4), pp. 7–8.

Green, Andrea. 1991. "The Challenge of Hard Times," *Bank Marketing,* 23(3), March, pp. 18–21.

Greene, Alice H. 1989. "Globalization: Reality or Trend?" *Production & Inventory Management Review & APICS News,* 9(12), December, pp. 24–25.

Gregory, G. 1985. "Japanese Electronics Technology: Enterprise and Innovation" (Chichester & New York: John Wiley & Sons).

Gremillion, Lee L. 1984. "Organization Size and Information System Use: An Empirical Study," *Journal of Management Information Systems,* I(2), pp. 4–17.

Grieco, Joseph M. 1982. "Between Dependency and Autonomy: India's Experience with the International Computer Industry," *International Organization,* 36(3), Summer, pp. 609–632.

Gries, Lothar and Linda Lewis. 1990. "Eastern Bloc Trade Must Clear Financing Hurdles," *Computerworld,* 24(34), August 20, p. 81.

Griffiths, Susan H. and Nigel J. Robertson. 1988. "Mexico: A Progress Report," *Journal of Cash Management,* 8(4), July/August, pp. 21–24.

Grigsby, Jefferson. 1989. "Europe: The Crisis of the Old Order," *Financial World,* 158(24), November 28, pp. 60–62.

Gross, Andrew C. 1974. "World Computer Markets," *Columbia Journal of World Business,* Spring, pp. 13–23.

References

Gross, Steve. 1988. "Will Honeywell Bull Survive Its Inheritance?" *Electronic Business,* 14(5), March 1, pp. 80, 82.

Grosse, Robert E. 1982. "Regional Offices in Multinational Firms," in Alan M. Rugman, ed., *New Theories of the Multinational Enterprise* (New York: St. Martin's Press).

Guichardaz, Philippe. 1989. "Europe's Challenge in HDTV," *Europe* (283), January/February, pp. 18–19.

Guillaume, Marnix L. K. 1990. "Risk Managers Face 'New Europe,'" *National Underwriter,* 94(28), July 9, pp. 9, 39–41.

Guisinger, Stephen E. 1985. "A Comparative Study of Country Policies," in Stephen E. Guisinger and Associates, eds., *Investment Incentives and Performance Requirements: Patterns of International Trade, Production, and Investment* (New York: Praeger).

Guterl, Fred V. 1989. "Goodbye, Old Matrix," *Business Month,* February, pp. 32–38.

Guynes, Jan L., Stephen C. Guynes, and Ron G. Thorn. 1990a. "Conquering International Boundaries That Restrict the Flow of Data," *Information Strategy: The Executives Journal,* 6(3), Spring, pp. 27–32.

Guynes, Jan L., Stephen C. Guynes, and Ron G. Thorn. 1990b. "The Impact of Transborder Data Flow Regulation," *Journal of Information Systems Management,* 7(3), Summer, pp. 70–73.

Hakam, A. N. and Zeph-Yun Chang. 1988. "Patterns of Technology Transfer in Singapore: The Case of the Electronics and Computer Industry," *International Journal of Technology Management,* 3(1, 2), pp. 181–188.

Hall, D., and M. Saias. 1980. "Strategy Follows Structure," *Strategic Management Journal,* 1(2).

Hamel, Bob. 1987. "Caterpillar Nets Savings," *Network World,* 4(12), March 23, p. 7.

Hamel, Gary and C. K. Prahalad. 1989. "Strategic Intent," *Harvard Business Review,* May/June, pp. 63–76.

Hampton, William J. and Zachary Schiller. 1987. "Why Image Counts: A Tale of Two Industries," *Business Week,* Industrial/Technology Edition (3002), June 8, pp. 138–140.

Hanada, Mitsuyo. 1987. "Management Themes in the Age of Globalization—Exploring Paths for the Globalization of the Japanese Corporation," *Management Japan,* 20(2), Autumn, pp. 19–26.

Hansell, Saul. 1989. "The Man Who Made the $14 Billion Loan," *Institutional Investor,* 23(1), January, pp. 247–250.

Hard, Rob. 1990. "CEOs Take a New Look at the CIO Function," *Hospitals,* 64, June 5, p. 64.

Harper, Tim, Paul Gannon, James Etheridge, and Johan Hallsenius. 1990. "The Datamation 100," *Datamation,* 36(12), June 15, pp. 130–134.

Harrigan, Kathryn Rudie. 1987. "Strategic Alliances: Their New Role in Global Competition," *Columbia Journal of World Business,* Summer, pp. 67–69+.

Harrington, Maura J. 1991. "Optical Discs Move into Reach," *Computerworld,* 25(17), April 29, p. 48.

Harrison, William. 1987. "How the Information Executive Can Promote Change," *Journal of Information Management,* 8(2), Spring, pp. 11–16.

Harvey, Michael G. and Ilkka A. Ronkainen. 1985. "International Counterfeiters: Marketing Success Without the Cost and the Risk," *Columbia Journal of World Business,* 20(3), Fall, pp. 37–45.

Harvey, Michael G. and Roger A. Kerin. 1976. "Multinational Corporations Versus Organized Labor: Divergent Views on Domestic Unemployment," *California Management Review,* XVIII(3), Spring, pp. 5–13.

Hax, Arnoldo C. 1973. "Planning a Management Information System for a Distributing and Manufacturing Company," *Sloan Management Review,* Spring, pp. 85–98.

Hayes, Robert H. 1974. "Europe's Computer Industry: Closer to the Brink," *Columbia Journal of World Business,* Summer, pp. 113–122.

Hayes, Robert H. and Steven C. Wheelwright. 1984. *Restoring Our Competitive Edge: Competing Through Manufacturing* (New York: John Wiley & Sons).

Head, Kenneth. 1990. "A SONET Milestone for the History Books," *Telephony,* 219(25), December 10, pp. 24–27.

Hedlund, Gunnar. 1984. "Organization In-Between: The Evolution of the Mother-Daughter Structure of Managing Foreign Subsidiaries in Swedish MNCs," *Journal of International Business Studies,* Fall.

Heenam, David A. and Warren J. Keegan. 1979. "The Rise of Third World Multinationals," *Harvard Business Review,* January/February, pp. 101–109.

Hegde, G. G., and Pandu R. Tadikamalla. 1990. "Interactive Workforce Management on a PC: An Industry-University Partnership," *European Journal of Operational Research,* 48(2), pp. 275–280.

Heininger, Horst. 1986. "Transnational Corporations and the Struggle for the Establishment of a New International Economic Order," in Alice Teichova, Maurice Lévy-Leboyer, and Helga Nussbaum, eds., *Multinational Enterprise in Historical Perspective* (New York: Cambridge University Press).

Heitkoetter, U. B. Helling, H. Nolte, and M. Kelly. 1990. "Design Metrics and Aids to Their Automatic Collection," *Information & Software Technology,* 32(1), January/February, pp. 79–87.

Heitzman, James. 1990. "Information Systems and Development in the Third World," *Information Processing and Management,* 26(4), pp. 489–502.

Henkoff, Ronald. 1988. "This Cat Is Acting Like a Tiger," *Fortune,* 118(14), December 19, pp. 69–76.

Hergert, Michael and Robin Hergert. 1987. "NEC Corporation's Entry into European Microcomputers," *Journal of Management Case Studies,* 3(2), Summer, pp. 109–135.

Herman, B. and B. van Holst. 1984. *International Trade in Services: Some Theoretical and Practical Problems* (Rotterdam: Netherlands Economic Institute).

Herring, Jan P. 1988. "Building a Business Intelligence System," *The Journal of Business Strategy,* May/June, pp. 4–9.

Hertner, Peter, and Geoffrey Jones. 1986. "Multinationals: Theory and History," in Peter Hertner and Geoffrey Jones, eds., *Multinationals: Theory and History* (Aldershot Harts, England: Gower Publishing Co., Ltd.).

Heuer, Richards J., Jr. 1978. "Content Analysis: Measuring Support for Brezhnev," in Richards J. Heuer, Jr., ed., *Quantitative Approaches to Political Intelligence: The CIA Experience* (Boulder, CO: Westview Press).

References

Hey, M. R. 1987. "Transputers and Computational Physics," *International Journal of Technology Management,* 2(3, 4), pp. 541–543.

Higgins, James M. and Timo Santalainen. 1989. "Strategies for Europe 1992," *Business Horizons,* July/August, pp. 54–58.

Hilborn, Cathy. 1986. "Honeywell, NEC, Bull Join Forces," *Computing Canada,* 12(26), December 29, pp. 1, 14.

Hill, Raymond E. 1983. "Managing the Human Side of Project Teams," in David I. Cleland and William R. King, eds., *Project Management Handbook* (New York: Van Nostrand Reinhold), pp. 581–604.

Hill, Roy. 1986. "Why Managers Today Have a Tougher Task—Of Managing Complexity," *International Management,* 41(8), August, pp. 22–24.

Hilsman, Roger. 1972. "Intelligence Through the Eyes of the Policy Maker," in *Surveillance and Espionage in a Free Society* (New York: Praeger), pp. 163–177.

Hird, E. V. 1991. "Transmission/T1: Sacrifices in the Name of Simplification," *Telephone Engineer and Management,* 95(1), January 1, pp. 43–47.

Hoffmann, Stanley. 1989. "The European Community and 1992," *Foreign Affairs,* 68(4), Fall, pp. 27–47.

Holloway, Don C., Robert D. Hertenstein, and Richard H. Egdahl. 1987. "Correcting Surgical Claims Codes Yields Cost Savings," *Business & Health,* 5(2), December, pp. 26–30.

Holmgren, R. Bruce. 1988. "All-New Package Runs Well on All-New Line," *Packaging,* 33(7), May, pp. 44–48.

Holmgren, R. Bruce. 1989. "All-New Line Automates Sample Packs for Doctors," *Packaging,* 34(8), June, pp. 66–71.

Holstein, W. J. 1990. "The Japanese Power Game: What It Means for America" (New York: Charles Scribner's Sons).

Holsti, Kal J. 1986. "Politics in Command: Foreign Trade as National Security Policy," *International Organization,* 40(3), Summer, pp. 643–671.

Holt, John B. 1978. "Decline of U.S. Computer Company Bargaining Power in Eastern Europe," *Columbia Journal of World Business,* Fall, pp. 95–112.

Honan, Patrick. 1988. "Alcatel's 386: A Systems Approach," *Personal Computing,* 12(5), May, pp. 219–220.

Horton, Woody (nd). "Japan's View of the CIO," *CIO Magazine,* January/February, pp. 50–51.

Horwitch, Mel and C. K. Prahalad. 1981. "Managing Multi-Organization Enterprises: The Emerging Strategic Frontier," *Sloan Management Review,* Winter, pp. 3–16.

Horwitt, Elisabeth. 1989a. "Rolm Users Look to Siemens," *Computerworld,* 23(3), January 23, p. 4.

Horwitt, Elisabeth. 1989b. "IBM Tweaks Rolm; No Siemens," *Computerworld,* 23(33), August 14, p. 10.

Horwitt, Elisabeth. 1990. "Manny Hanny Downsizes," *Computerworld,* 24(46), November 12, pp. 1, 14.

Hout, Thomas, Michael E. Porter, and Eileen Rudden. "How Global Companies Win Out," *Harvard Business Review,* September/October, pp. 98–108.

Huber, Roland. 1987. "The Role of Information Technology and Telecommunications in Promoting Economic Development in the European Community," *International Journal of Technology Management,* 2(3, 4), pp. 501–514.

Huggins, Lawrence P. 1988. "Does the Asian IS Market Already Belong to the Japanese?" *Information Strategy: The Executive's Journal,* 4(4), Summer, pp. 31–34.

Huitema, Christian. 1988. "The X.500 Directory Services," *Computer Networks & ISDN Systems,* 16(1, 2), September, pp. 161–166.

Hukill, Mark A. and Meheroo Jussawalla. 1989. "Telecommunications Policies and Markets in the ASEAN Countries," *Columbia Journal of World Business,* Spring, pp. 43–57.

Hunger, David. 1987. "Buying a Piece of Stauffer," *Chemical Week,* 141(14), September 30, pp. 8–9.

Hunt, Jonathan. 1986. "The Final Peformance," *Chief Executive,* September, pp. 30–31.

Hunter, David. 1990. "ICI Focuses on Leading-Edge R&D," *Chemical Week,* 146(14), April 11, p. 22.

Hurst, Rebecca. 1987. "Directing Communications at Warner," *Computerworld,* 21(36A), September 9, pp. 41–43.

Husian, Vincent P. 1972. "Rx for Top Management: A Periodic Checkup of EDP Operations," *California Management Review,* Spring, XIV(3), pp. 31–37.

Hutchins, Dexter. 1986. "Caterpillar's Triple Whammy," *Fortune,* 114(9), October 27, pp. 91–92.

Hutchinson, Robert J. 1987. "'One Stop Banking' Cements Package Approach at Manufacturers Hanover," *Bank Marketing,* 19(12), December, pp. 18–21.

Hymer, Stephen (nd). "The Multinational Corporation and the Law of Uneven Development," in *International Institutions,* pp. 113–139+.

IBM Corporation. 1990. *IBM Announces System/390,* Videotape, September 5.

Israeli, Dafna N., Moshe Banai, and Yoram Zeira. 1980. "Women Executives in MNC Subsidiaries," *California Management Review,* Fall, XXIII(1), pp. 53–63.

Iversen, Wes. 1990. "Information Systems: Tying It All Together," *Industry Week,* 239(16), August 20, pp. 20–30.

Ives, Blake and Sirkka L. Jarvenpaa. 1991. "Applications of Global Information Technology: Key Issues for Management," *MIS Quarterly,* March, pp. 33–49.

Iyer, Raja K. 1988. "Information and Modeling Resources for Decision Support in Global Environments," *Information and Management,* 14(2), February, pp. 67–73.

Iyer, Raja K., and Lawrence L. Schkade. 1987. "Management Support Systems for Multinational Business," *Information and Management,* 12(2), February, pp. 59–64.

Jackson, Colin. 1989. "Building a Competitive Advantage Through Information Technology," *Long Range Planning,* 22(4), August, pp. 29–39.

Jackson, Tim. 1990. "South Korea: An Impromptu Performance," *Economist,* 316(7668), August 18, pp. S5–S20.

Jacobson, G. and J. Hillkirk 1986. "Xerox: American Samurai" (New York: Macmillan).

Jaeger, Alfred M. 1983. "The Transfer of Organizational Culture Overseas: An Approach to Control in the Multinational Corporation," *Journal of International Business Studies,* Fall.

References

Jaeger, Alfred M. and B. R. Baliga. 1985. "Control Systems and Strategic Adaption: Lessons from the Japanese Experience." *Strategic Management Journal,* 6, pp. 115–134.

Jeffreys-Jones, Rhodri. 1977. *American Espionage: From Secret Service to CIA* (New York: The Free Press).

Jelinek, Miriann and Joel D. Golhar. 1983. "The Interface Between Strategy and Manufacturing Technology," *Columbia Journal of World Business,* Spring, pp. 26–36.

Jenkins, Avery. 1987. "Communications: Networks in a Strange Land," *Computerworld,* 21(36A), September 9, pp. 25–30.

Johanson, Jan and Jan-Erik Vahlne. 1977. "The Internationalization Process of the Firm—A Model of Knowledge Development and Increasing Foreign Market Commitments," *Journal of International Business Studies,* September, pp. 23–32.

Johanson, Jan and Lars-Gunnar Mattsson (nd). "Interorganizational Relations in Industrial Systems: A Network Approach Compared with the Transaction-Cost Approach," *International Studies of Management and Organization,* XVII(1), pp. 34–48.

Johnson, C. 1982. "MITI and the Japanese Miracle: The Growth of Industrial Policy, 1925–1975" (Stanford: Stanford University Press).

Johnson, Eric. 1989. "The Priority of Engineering," *Chemical Engineering,* 96(8), August, pp. 59, 61.

Johnson, Jan. 1987. "Users Laud Honey of an Alliance," *Computer Decisions,* 19(2), January 26, pp. 15–20.

Johnson, Maryfran. 1990. "Bridging Tech, Functional Barriers," *Computerworld,* 24(9), February 26, pp. 53, 58–59.

Johnston-Turner, Mary. 1990. "Strengthening the PBX-Computer Bond," *Network World,* 7(32), August 6, pp. 37–39, 49.

Johnstone, Bob. 1989. "Asia: Technology—Into the Next Generation," *Far Eastern Economic Review,* 145(35), August 31, pp. 48–54.

Jones, Lou F. 1988. "Competitor Cost Analysis at Caterpillar," *Management Accounting,* 70(4), October, pp. 32–38.

Jones, Lou F. 1991. "Product Costing at Caterpillar," *Management Accounting,* 72(8), February, pp. 34–42.

Joyce, Edward J. 1989. "In Search of the CIO," *Computer Decisions,* April, pp. 52–55.

Jurgen, Ronald K. 1988. "High-Definition Television Update," *IEEE Spectrum,* 25(4), April, pp. 56–62.

Jussawalla, Meheroo and C. W. Cheah. 1987. *The Calculus of International Communications: A Study in the Political Economy of Transborder Data Flows* (Littleton, CO: Libraries Unlimited, Inc.).

Jussawalla, Meheroo. 1984. *The Analytics of Transborder Data Flows,* Conference paper at Second World Conference on Transborder Data Flow Policies, Rome, June.

Kaczmarek, Mike. 1989. "SPC Express," *Quality,* 28(4), April, pp. 58–59.

Kaplinsky, Raphael and Kurt Hoffman. 1988. *Driving Force: The Global Restructuring of Technology, Labor and Investment in the Automobile and Components Industry* (Boulder, CO: Westview Press).

Karunaratne, Neil D. 1986. "Information Technology and the Developing Pacific," *Telecommunications Policy,* 10(2), June, pp. 83–87.

Kasparek, Wolfhart. 1987. "Applying Computer-Assisted Audit Techniques Overseas," *Internal Auditing,* 3(2), Fall, pp. 64–68.

Kasparek, Wolfhart. 1988a. "Auditing Multinational Operations: Foreign Commissions," *Internal Auditing,* 3(3), Winter, pp. 60–64.

Kasparek, Wolfhart. 1988b. "Interaction with Local Internal Auditors," *Internal Auditing,* 3(4), Spring, pp. 67–70.

Keefe, Lisa M. 1987. "More Room at the Top" *Forbes,* 139, June 29, p. 102.

Keefe, Sarah. 1989. "Into Low-Cost UNIX Through X-Windows," *Systems International,* 17(7), July/August, pp. 57–60.

Keegan, Warren J. 1968. "Acquisition of Global Business Information," *Columbia Journal of World Business,* March–April, pp. 35–41.

Keegan, Warren J. 1972. "A Conceptual Framework for Multinational Marketing," *Columbia Journal of World Business,* November/December, pp. 67–76.

Keen, Peter G. W. 1988. "Relationship of Senior Management and the IS Organization," in Sharlene Sue Jimenez, contributing ed., *Transforming the IS Organization* (Washington, DC: ICIT Press), pp. 41–54.

Keen, Peter G. W. 1990. "What's Ailing Mr. Fix-It? Most Chief Information Officers Are Underqualified, and the Rest Don't Get Enough Respect," *Business Month,* 135, January, p. 60.

Keen, Peter G. W. 1991a. *Shaping the Future: Business Design Through Information Technology* (Cambridge, MA: Harvard Business School Press).

Keen, Peter G. W. 1991b. "Telecommunications and Organizational Advantage," Conference paper, Global Competition and Telecommunications Colloquium, Harvard University, Graduate School of Business Administration, May 1–3.

Kendrick, John J. 1988. "Whirlpool's World Market," *Quality,* 27(12), December, pp. 18–20.

Kennedy, Charles R., Jr. 1984. "The External Environment-Strategic Planning Interface: U.S. Multinational Corporate Practices in the 1980s," *Journal of International Business Studies,* Fall, pp. 99–108.

Kenyon, Alfred and Shiv Sahai Mathur. 1987. "The Development of Strategies by International Commercial Banks," *Journal of General Management,* 13(2), Winter, pp. 56–73.

Keohane, Robert O. and Van Doorn Ooms. 1972. "The Multinational Enterprise and World Political Economy," *International Organization,* 26(1), Winter, pp. 84–120.

Keough, Lee. 1986. "Amdahl Steps Out," *Computer Decisions,* 18(25), November 4, pp. 34, 66.

Kerr, Susan. 1987. "Mergers: Are Three Heads Better than One?" *Datamation,* 33(2), January 15, pp. 19–23.

Kikuchi, M. 1983. *Japanese Electronics: A Worm's-Eye View of Its Evolution* (Tokyo: Simul Press).

Kille, Steve. 1988. "The THORN Large Scale Pilot Exercise,"*Computer Networks & ISDN Systems,* 16(1, 2), September, pp. 143–145.

Killen, M. 1988. *IBM: The Making of the Common View* (Boston: Harcourt Brace Jovanovich).

Kilmann, Ralph H. and Kyunjg-Il Ghymn. 1976. "The MAPS Design Technology: Designing Strategic Intelligence Systems for MNCs," *Columbia Journal of World Business,* Summer, pp. 35–47.

Kim, W. Chan. 1986. "Global Diffusion of the General Trading Company Concept," *Sloan Management Review,* Summer, pp. 35–43.

Kim, W. Chan. 1987. "Competition and the Management of Host Government Intervention," *Sloan Management Review,* Spring, pp. 33–39.

Kim, W. Chan and R. A. Mauborgne. 1988. "Becoming an Effective Global Competitor," *The Journal of Business Strategy,* January/February, pp. 33–37.

Kindel, Stephen. 1990. "World Washer: Why Whirlpool Leads in Appliances, Not Some Japanese Outfit," *Financial World,* 159(6), March 20, pp. 42–46.

King, John Leslie. 1983. "Centralized Versus Decentralized Computing: Organizational Considerations and Management Options," *Computing Surveys,* 15(4), December, pp. 319–349.

King, William R. 1985. "Information Technology and Corporate Growth," *Columbia Journal of World Business,* Summer, pp. 29–33.

Kirkpatrick, Lyman B., Jr. 1968. *The Real CIA* (New York: Macmillan).

Kirkpatrick, Lyman B., Jr. 1977. *The U.S. Intelligence Community: Foreign Policy and Domestic Activities* (Boulder and London: Westview Press).

Kitagawa, T. 1985. "Creation of Industry and Culture in Establishing Full-Scale Information Societies in Japan," in H. Sackman, ed., *Comparative Worldwide National Computer Policies,* Proceedings of the Third IFIP TC9 Conference on Human Choice and Computers (Amsterdam: North-Holland).

Knight, Robert. 1990. "Shop Floor Accepts CASE at a Caterpillar's Pace," *Software Magazine,* 10(3), March, pp. 72–73.

Kobayashi, K. 1986. "Computers and Communications: A Vision of C&C" (Cambridge, MA: The MIT Press).

Kobayashi, Noritake. 1990. "Comparison of Japanese and Western Multinationals—Part I," *Tokyo Business Today,* 58(10), October, p. 50.

Koco, Linda. 1989. "N.Y. Bank Sells Annuities, Term Life via Kiosk," *National Underwriter,* Life/Health/Financial Services, 93(42), October 16, p. 24.

Koenig, Christian and Raymond-Alain Thietart (nd). "Technology and Organization: The Mutual Organization in the European Aerospace Industry," *International Studies of Management and Organization,* XVII(4), pp. 6–30.

Koepfler, Edward R. 1989. "Keys to Growing a Global Strategy (Part 2)," *Systems/3X & AS World,* 17(5), May, pp. 141–142.

Kogut, Bruce. 1985. "Designing Global Strategies: Comparative and Competitive Value-Added Chains," *Sloan Management Review,* Summer, pp. 15–28.

Kogut, Bruce. 1987. Book review of *Competition in Global Industries* by M. Porter, in *Sloan Management Review,* Winter, pp. 73–76.

Kojima, I. and T. Ozawa. 1984. *Japan's General Trading Companies: Merchants of Economic Development* (Paris: OECD).

Kono, Toyohiro. 1984–85. "Multinational Management," *Japanese Economic Studies,* Fall/Winter, pp. 3–44.

Konstadt, Paul. 1990. "Into the Breach," *CIO,* 3(11), August, pp. 71–73.

Kornel, Amiel. 1990. "Fujitsu Move Rattles Europe," *Computerworld,* 24(32), August 6, pp. 1, 113.

Korzeniowski, Paul. 1987. "X.25 Connections: Variety Satisfied with INS Board," *Network World,* 4(12), March 23, pp. 17–18.

Korzeniowski, Paul. 1989. "International Software Trends: EDI—Overseas Signals Making More Sense," *Software Magazine,* 9(4), March, pp. 22–25.

Koski, John. 1991a. "Equipment Selection: Highly Articulate," *Equipment Management,* 19(1), January, pp. 20–25.

Koski, John. 1991b. "Pay Me Now, or Pay Me Later," *Equipment Management,* 19(3), March, pp. 10–15.

Kotkin, Joel. 1987. "The Chinese Way of Business," *Inc.,* 9(7), June, pp. 66–70.

Kraus, C. R. and A. W. Duerig. 1988. *The Rape of Ma Bell: The Criminal Wrecking of the Best Telephone System in the World* (Secaucus, NJ: Lyle Stuart, Inc.).

Kremer, Tony. 1988. "Europe 1992: Are Your Information Systems Going to Be Ready?" *Management Accounting,* 66(10), November, pp. 32–33.

Krepchin, Ira P. 1988. "We Simulate All Major Projects," *Modern Materials Handling,* 43(9), August, pp. 83–86.

Kuehn, Richard A. 1989. "Sorting Through the Siemens-IBM Deal," *Business Communications Review,* 19(2), February, pp. 91–92.

Kurita, Shohei. 1988. "The PC Market in Japan: Where's IBM?" *Electronic Business,* 14(10), May 15, pp. 56–57.

Kusumoto, S. 1989. *My Bridge to America: Discovering the New World for Minolta* (New York: E.P. Dutton).

Lukaszewicz, L. 1990. "On the Beginnings of Computer Development in Poland," *Annals of the History of Computing,* 12(2), pp. 103–108.

Lam, Danny Kin-Kong. 1991. "The Myth of State-Led Industrialization: The Origins of Electronics Manufacturing in Taiwan." Working paper, W. Paul Stillman School of Business, Seton Hall University.

Lam, Danny Kin-Kong and Ian Lee. 1991. "Guerrilla Capitalism and the Limits of Statist Theory: Comparing the Chinese NICs." Working paper, W. Paul Stillman School of Business, Seton Hall University.

Lamb, John. 1987. "Volvo's Net Gains," *Datamation,* International Edition, 33(19), October 1, pp. 76(1)–76(9).

Lascelles, David. 1991. "Banking on Boulevards to Build the Business," *Financial Times,* July 24, p. 8.

Lasden, Martin. 1986. "It's Me Inc. vs. You Inc.," *Computer Decisions,* 18, December 16, p. 52.

Laudon, Kenneth C. 1974. *Computers and Bureaucratic Reform* (New York: John Wiley & Sons).

Laudon, Kenneth C. 1985. "Environmental and Institutional Models of System Development: A National Criminal History System," *Communications of the ACM,* 28(7), July, pp. 728–740.

Laudon, Kenneth C. 1986. *Dossier Society: Value Choices in the Design of National Information Systems* (New York: Columbia University Press).

References

Leaversuch, Robert D. 1990. "Total Redesign of Refrigerators Now Is Inevitable," *Modern Plastics,* 67(10), October, pp. 68–73.

Lecht, Charles P. 1987. "IBM Japan, Superperformer, to the Rescue," *Computerworld,* 21(12), March 23, p. 17.

Lecraw, Donald J. 1983. "Performance of Transnational Corporations in Less Developed Countries," *Journal of International Business Studies,* Spring/Summer.

Leontiades, James C. 1985. *Multinational Corporate Strategy* (Lexington, MA: Lexington Books).

Lester, Clive. 1989. "EIS: Europe's Information Seekers," *Datamation,* 35(13), July 1, pp. 68(17–18).

Lester, Tom. 1991. "A Structure for Europe," *Management Today,* January, pp. 76–78.

Level, Leon J. 1986. "Meeting the Needs of Multinational Corporations," *Journal of Bank Research,* 16(4), pp. 254–257.

Levine, Jonathan B. 1990. "In Europe, the Next Walls to Fall Will Be Electronic," *Business Week,* Industrial/Technology Edition, December 3, p. 158F.

Lewis, Jordan D. 1990. "Using Alliances to Build Market Power," *Planning Review,* 18(5), September/October, pp. 4–9, 48.

Liddle, Ken. 1990. "The Cambridge Research Biochemicals Phenomenon," *Technovation,* 10(4), June, pp. 273–278.

Lindell, Erik. 1986. "Foreign Policy Export Controls and American Multinational Corporation," *California Management Review,* XXVIII(4), Summer, pp. 27–39.

Litell, Norman G. and Richard Munn. 1990. "Service Providers Expand Their Horizons," *Datamation,* 36(12), June 15, pp. 196–197.

Litvak, I. A. and C. J. Maule. 1968. "Guidelines for the Multinational Corporation," *Columbia Journal of World Business,* July/August, pp. 35–42.

Liu, Philip. 1988. "Emperor of Taiwan's Computer Industry," *Electronic Business,* 14(20), October 15, pp. 96, 98.

Lodge, George. 1989. "The American Corporation and Its New Relationships," *California Management Review,* Spring, pp. 9–24.

Lodish, Leonard M., Ellen Curtis, Michael Ness, and M. Kerry Simpson. 1988. "Sales Force Sizing and Deployment Using a Decision Calculus Model at Syntex Laboratories," *Interfaces,* 18(1), January/February, pp. 5–20.

Lubbock, Victoria. 1987. "Opening the Letters Market," *ReActions,* Banking Services Supplement, June, pp. 18–22.

Lucas, H. C. and R. A. Schwartz, eds. 1989. *The Challenge of Information Technology for the Securities Markets: Liquidity, Volatility & Global Trading* (Homewood, IL: Dow-Jones-Irwin).

Ludlum, David. 1990a. "The Value of Ad Hoc Partnerships," *Computerworld,* 24(16), April 16, p. 76.

Ludlum, David. 1990b. "Adjusting to the Job of Strategist: Where the Air Is Thin and the View Is Big," *Computerworld,* 24(30), July 23, pp. 81–83.

Lukow, Stephen, Nobuko Hara, Marcia Stepanek, and Lew Young. 1990. "The Datamation 100: Ricoh; Seiko Epson; C. Itoh; CSK; Acer," *Datamation,* 36(12), June 15, pp. 170–174.

Luvison, Angelo. 1988. "An Approach to Multi-Service Business Networks," *Telecommunications*, International Edition, 22(11), November, pp. 44–54.

Lynn, Matthew. 1990. "Digging for Victory," *Business*, October, pp. 112–115.

Macaulay, Stephen. 1987. "Cadillac: On Its Own—and Aggressive," *Production*, 99(10), October, pp. 74–76.

Maeght, Philippe E. and Anton W. Jolkovski. 1987. "Selective Facsimile: The Electronic Text Medium of the 21st Century?" *Computer Networks & ISDN Systems*, 14(2–5), pp. 155–158.

Magee, S. P. 1976. "Technology and the Appropriability Theory of the Multinational Corporation," in Jagdish Bhajwati, ed., *The New International Economic Order* (Cambridge, MA: The MIT Press).

Magee, S. P. 1977. "Multinational Corporation, the Industry Technology Cycle and Development," *Journal of World Trade Law*, July/August, pp. 399–421.

Mahoney, Eileen. 1987. "Negotiating New Information Technologies and National Development: The Role of the IBI," Ph.D. thesis, Temple University.

Maidique, Modesto A. and Robert H. Hayes. 1985. "The Art of High-Technology Management," *Sloan Management Review*, pp. 17–28+.

Main, Jeremy. 1989. "How to Go Global—and Why," *Fortune*, 120(5), August 28, pp. 70–76.

Maisonrouge, J. 1985. *Inside IBM: A Personal Story* (New York: McGraw-Hill).

Majumdar, Badiul A. 1988. "Industrial Policy in Action: The Case of the Electronics Industry in Japan," *Columbia Journal of World Business*, Fall, pp. 25–33.

Mandell, Mel. 1987. "The CIO: Myth or Reality," *Computer Decisions*, 19, March 23, p. 66.

Marcom, John, Jr. 1990. "First Europe, Then the World," *Forbes*, 146(10), October 29, pp. 134–135.

Margolis, Nell. 1990. "Computer Firms Set to Unite," *Computerworld*, 24(40), October 1, p. 131.

Martin, Alexia. 1987. "Field Service: Firms Explore 'Help-Yourself' Attitude in Maintenance," *Computerworld*, 21(33), August 17, p. S2.

Martin, Jeanette. 1988. "As Mini Supplier, Olivetti Recasts Its Identity—Again," *Datamation*, International Edition, 34(1), January 1, pp. 17–18.

Martin, Jeanette. 1990. "Software That Spans the Globe," *Datamation*, International Edition, 36(21), November 1, pp. 96(5)–96(8).

Mascarenhas, Briance. 1982. "Coping with Uncertainty in International Business," *Journal of International Business Studies*, Fall.

Mascarenhas, Briance. 1984. "The Coordination of Manufacturing Interdependence in Multinational Companies," *Journal of International Business Studies*, Winter, pp. 91–106.

Mascarenhas, Briance. 1989. "Transnational Linkages and Strategy," in Anant R. Negandhi and Savarta Arun, eds., *International Strategic Management* (Lexington, MA: Lexington Books).

Mason, R. Hal. 1974a. "The Selection of Technology: A Continuing Dilemma," *Columbia Journal of World Business*, Summer, pp. 29–34.

References

Mason, R. Hal. 1974b. "Conflicts Between Host Countries and the Multinational Enterprise," *California Management Review,* Fall, XVII(1), pp. 5–14.

Mason, R. Hal. 1980. "A Comment on Professor Kojima's 'Japanese Type versus American Type of Technology Transfer,' " *Hitotsubashi Journal of Economics,* February, pp. 42–52.

Mastanduno, Michael. 1988. "Trade as a Strategic Weapon: American and Alliance Export Control Policy in the Early Postwar Period," *International Organization,* 42(1), Winter, pp. 121–217.

Masuda, Y. 1985. "Computopia," *Agora,* 11, 1985/2, pp. 40–41.

Masuda, Y. 1988. *The Information Society as Post-Industrial Society,* (Tokyo: Institute for the Information Society).

Matsushita, Konosuke. 1988. *Quest for Prosperity: The Life of a Japanese Industrialist* (Tokyo, Kyoto, Singapore: PHP Institute, Inc.).

Matteis, Richard J. 1991. "Operating Services—New Rules for the '90s," *Bank Management,* 67(4), April, pp. 24–27.

Mayall, Alex. 1990. "Global Information Systems," Comments at ICIS Conference in Copenhagen, December.

McCaffery, Seligman & von Simson, Inc. 1979. *Impact of Transborder Data Flow Legislation: Corporate Case Studies,* Mimeo, August.

McCann, Stephanie. 1990. "Potholes on the Global Data Highway," *Computerworld,* 24(40), October 1, p. 100.

McClellan, S. T. 1984. *The Coming Computer Industry Shakeout: Winners, Losers, & Survivors* (New York: John Wiley & Sons).

McClelland, Stephen. 1990. "Face to Face: Telecommunications Talks to Bjarne Aamodt," *Telecommunications,* International Edition, 24(3), March, pp. 73–74.

McConville, Daniel J. 1987. "Glidden Maps Growth Plans Under ICI," *Chemical Week,* 141(18), October 28, pp. 20–23.

McCooey, Christopher. 1991. "From Competitor to European Insider," *Accountancy,* 107(1170), February, pp. 116–117.

McCreary, Lew. 1989. "CIOs in the Spotlight," *CIO,* September, pp. 62–68.

McDonald, Martha. 1990. "How to Deal with AIDS in the Work Place," *Business and Health,* 8(7), July, pp. 12–22.

McGovern, Patrick J. 1990. "The Networked Corporation," *Chief Executive* (57), April, pp. 46–49.

McLean, M., ed. 1982. "The Japanese Electronics Challenge," (New York: St. Martin's Press).

McLening, Maggie. 1986. "Big Blue Tiptoes into India," *Datamation,* 32(7), April 1, pp. 54–58.

McLeod, Raymond, Jr., and John C. Rogers. 1985. "Marketing Information Systems: Their Current Status in Fortune 1000 Companies," *Journal of Management Information Systems,* Spring, I(4). pp. 57–75.

Mead, Tim. 1991. "Siemens-Nixdorf's Wiedig: The Real Work Begins," *Datamation,* International Edition, 37(3), February 1, pp. 64(7)–64(8).

Means, Grady E. and Beverly Bugos. 1988. "Global Views: The Road to Rio," *CIO,* 1(7), June, pp. 16–19.

Meiklejohn, Ian. 1989. "CIOs Search for a Role," *Management Today*, September, p. 137.

Mele, Jim. 1988. "Medium-Duty Diesels Go Heavy-Duty," *Fleet Owner*, Big Fleet Edition, August, pp. 60–65.

Mele, Jim. 1990. "The Changing Market for Reman'ed Parts," *Fleet Owner*, Big Fleet Edition, 85(9), September, pp. 95–100.

Meyer, Richard and Sana Siwolop. 1990. "Fujitsu: The Samurai Have Landed," *Financial World*, 159(19), September 18, pp. 46–50.

Michman, Ronald D. 1990. "Managing Structural Changes in Marketing Channels," *Journal of Business & Industrial Marketing*, 5(2), Summer/Fall, pp. 5–14.

Mickolus, Edward F. 1978. "An Events Data Base for Analysis of Transnational Terrorism," in Richards J. Heuer, Jr., ed., *Quantitative Approaches to Political Intelligence: The CIA Experience* (Boulder, CO: Westview Press).

Miles, Louella. 1986. "ICI Bug Gun Fires a Winning Round," *Marketing*, 26(12), September 18, pp. 37–38.

Miller, David M. 1987. "An Interactive, Computer-Aided Ship Scheduling System," *European Journal of Operational Research*, 32(3), December, pp. 363–379.

Miller, Frederic A. 1986. "Siemens: A European Giant Comes Alive in the U.S.," *Business Week*, Industrial/Technology Edition, September 1, pp. 68H–68I.

Miller, Robert R. 1985. "Computers," in Stephen E. Guisinger and Associates, *Investment Incentives and Performance Requirements: Patterns of International Trade, Production, and Investment* (New York: Praeger Special Studies).

Miller, Robert R. and John A. Alic. 1986. "Financing Expansion in an International Industry: The Case of Electronics," *International Journal of Technology Management*, 1(1, 2), pp. 101–117.

Mintzberg, Henry. 1987. "Crafting Strategy," *Harvard Business Review*, July/August, pp. 66–75.

Moad, Jeff. 1988. "Japanese Pledge Allegiance to U.S. Information Systems Strategies," *Datamation*, 34(4), February 15, pp. 43–49.

Moad, Jeff. 1989a. "PCs: The Second Wave," *Datamation*, International Edition, 35(3), February 1, pp. 14–20.

Moad, Jeff. 1989b. "Navigating Cross-Functional IS Waters," *Datamation*, 35(5), March 1, pp. 73–75.

Moore, Jonathan. 1988. "Apple of Taiwan's Eye," *Far Eastern Economic Review*, 141(28), July 14, p. 62.

Morant, Adrian. 1990. "From ATM to ERBIUM in European Optics," *Telephone Engineer and Management*, 94(16), August 15, pp. 62–68.

Morgan, James. 1990. "Welcome Booklet Contest: Ten Ways to Tell Suppliers What They Need to Know," *Purchasing*, 109(3), September 13, pp. 80–84.

Morgan, Patrick V. 1986. "International HRM: Fact or Fiction?" *Personnel Administrator*, 31(9), September, pp. 42–47.

Moritani, M. 1982. *Japanese Technology: Getting the Best for the Least* (Tokyo: Simul Press).

Morris, Deigan and Michael Hergert. 1987. "Trends in International Collaborative Agreements," *Columbia Journal of World Business*, Summer, pp. 15–21.

References

Mosco, Vincent, and Janet Wasko, eds. 1988. *The Political Economy of Information* (Madison: University of Wisconsin).

Moto-Oka, T. 1982. "Fifth Generation Computer Systems," Proceeding of the International Conference on Fifth Generation Computer Systems, Tokyo, October 19–22, 1981 (Amsterdam: North-Holland).

Mounier-Kuhn, P. E. 1989. "Bull: A World-Wide Company Born in Europe," *Annals of the History of Computing*, 11(4), pp. 279–298.

Muller, E. J. and Jay Gordon. 1987. "Caterpillar's Great Lakes Strategy/Domino's Pushes Productivity," *Distribution*, 86(9), September, pp. 40–45.

Mullins, Peter. 1986. "Four of Europe's Best 'Flex' Systems," *Production*, 98(4), October, pp. 78–85.

Mulqueen, John T. 1988. "Research House Crosses Oceans and Continents to Track Drug Sales," *Data Communications*, 17(6), June, pp. 92–96.

Murphy, H. Lee. 1987. "Sears Bullish on Brands," *Advertising Age*, 58(47), November 2, p. 28.

Murray, J. Alex. 1972. "Intelligence Systems of the MNCs," *Columbia Journal of World Business*, September/October, pp. 63–71.

Myerson, Jeremy. 1990. "Ten Out of Ten," *Management Today*, June, pp. 96–101.

Mytelka, Lynn Kreiger, and Michel Delapierre. 1987. "The Alliance Strategies of European Firms in the Information Technology Industry and the Role of ESPRIT," *Journal of Common Market Studies*, XXVI(2), December, pp. 231–253.

Nakarmi, Laxmi and Robert Neff. 1990. "South Korea: Can This Tiger Burn Bright Again?" *Business Week*, Industrial/Technology Edition (3190), December 3, pp. 56–57.

Nakarmi, Laxmi. 1991. "At Lucky-Goldstar, the Koos Loosen the Reins," *Business Week*, Industrial/Technology Edition (3200), February 18, pp. 72–73.

Nanus, Burt. 1969. "The Multinational Computer," *Columbia Journal of World Business*, November/December.

Nanus, Burt. 1978. "Business, Government and the Multinational Computer," *Columbia Journal of World Business*, Spring, pp. 19–26.

Nanus, Burt, Leland M. Wooton, and Harold Borko. 1973. *The Social Implications of the Use of Computers Across National Boundaries* (Montvale, NJ: AFIPS Press), p. 3.

Narasimhan, Ram and Joseph R. Carter. 1990. "Organisation, Communication and Coordination of International Sourcing," *International Marketing Review*, 7(2), pp. 6–20.

Narjes, Karl-Heinz. 1989. "Policies and Experiences of International Organizations for the Promotion of Enhanced Interaction Between Industries, Universities and Other Research Organizations," *Technovation*, 9(2, 3), June, pp. 241–248.

Nau, H. R. 1990. *The Myth of America's Decline: Leading the World Economy into the 1990's* (New York: Oxford University Press).

Naylor, Thomas H. 1985. "The International Strategy Matrix," *Columbia Journal of World Business*, Summer.

Negandhi, Anant R. 1983. "Cross-Cultural Management Research: Trend and Future Directions," *Journal of International Business Studies*, Fall.

Noaker, Paula M. 1990. "Workholding: Firm and Flexible," *Manufacturing Engineering,* 105(4), October, pp. 37–40.

Novich, Neil S. 1990. "Leading-Edge Distribution Strategies," *Journal of Business Strategy,* 11(6), November/December, pp. 48–53.

Novotny, Eric J. 1985. *Transborder Data Flows and World Public Order: Law and Policy Problems in Controlling Global Computer Communication Technology,* Doctoral thesis, Georgetown University.

Nussbaum, Helga. 1986. "International Cartels and Multinational Enterprises," in Alice Teichova, Maurice Lévy-Leboyer, and Helga Nussbaum, eds., *Multinational Enterprise in Historical Perspective* (New York: Cambridge University Press).

Nye, Joseph S., Jr. (nd). "Multinational Corporations in World Politics," *Foreign Affairs,* pp. 153–175.

Nye, Joseph S., Jr., and Robert O. Keohane. 1971. "Transnational Relations and World Politics: An Introduction," *International Organization,* 25(3), pp. 329–349.

O'Connor, Walter F. 1989. "The International Tax Implications of Transborder Data Flow," *International Tax Journal,* 15(1), Winter, pp. 73–85.

O'Leary, Meghan. 1989. "The World Is Your Oyster...Maybe," *CIO,* 2(9), June, pp. 42–50.

OECD. 1985. *The Semiconductor Industry: Trade Related Issues* (Paris: Organisation for Economic Co-Operation and Development).

Office of Technology Assessment. 1983. *International Competitiveness in Electronics,* OTA-ISC-200 (Washington, DC: U.S. Government Printing Office).

Ohmae, Kenichi. 1987. "Japan's Role in the World Economy: A New Appraisal," *California Management Review,* XXIX(3), Spring, pp. 42–58.

Ohmae, Kenichi. 1989. "Managing in a Borderless World," *Harvard Business Review,* May/June, pp. 152–161.

Okimoto, Daniel I., T. Sugano, and F. B. Weinstein. 1984. *Competitive Edge: The Semiconductor Industry in the U.S. and Japan* (Stanford: Stanford Universty Press).

Oolman, H. M. Seutter and C. van Reeuwijk. 1989. "GLASS, a Language for Analog and Digital Circuit Description, and Its Environment," *Microprocessing & Microprogramming,* 27(1–5), August, pp. 267–271.

Osterman, Paul. 1986. "The Impact of Computers on the Employment of Clerks and Managers," *Industrial and Labor Relations Review,* 39(2), January.

Ozawa, Terutomo. "International Investment and Industrial Structure: New Theoretical Implications from the Japanese Experience," *Hitasubashi Journal of Economics,* pp. 72–92.

Pantages, Angeline. 1989. "The Right IS Chemistry," *Datamation,* 35(16), August 15, pp. 61–62.

Parker, Marilyn M. and Robert J. Benson. 1987a. *Advancing the State of the Art in Strategic Planning,* Working paper, Center for the Study of Data Processing, Washington University.

Parker, Marilyn M. and Robert J. Benson. 1987b. "Information Economics," *Datamation,* December 1.

Parker, Marilyn M. and Robert J. Benson. 1988. *Key Points in Strategic Planning,* Working paper, Center for the Study of Data Processing, Washington University.

References

Parker, Marilyn M. and Robert J. Benson with H. E. Trainor. 1987. *Information Economics: An Introduction,* Working paper, Center for the Study of Data Processing, Washington University.

Parker, Marilyn M. and Robert J. Benson with H. E. Trainor. 1988. *Information Economics: Linking Business Performance and Information Technology* (New York: Prentice-Hall).

Parkes, Christopher. 1990. "Unknown Warrior," *Business,* March, pp. 90–92.

Parkinson, Gerald. 1988. "Syntex Prepares for the Future," *Chemical Week,* 143(3), July 20, pp. 40–41.

Parsons, Talcott. 1956. "Suggestions for a Sociological Approach to the Theory of Organizations," *Administrative Science Quarterly,* June.

Patel, Bharat. 1989. "PROOF: Interconnecting ISDN and LANs," *Telecommunications,* International Edition, 23(10), October, pp. 49–54.

Patrick, H. and L. Meissner, eds., 1986. *Japan's High Technology Industries: Lessons and Limitations of Industrial Policy* (Seattle & London: University of Washington Press).

Pelton, Joseph N. 1983. "The Communication Satellite: Revolutionary Change Agent?" *Columbia Journal of World Business,* Spring, pp. 77–84.

Perakis, James A. 1986. "Consolidation Software," *FE: The Magazine for Financial Executives,* 2(9), September, pp. 31–32.

Perez, Michel. 1985. "Human Resources Policy in an Untraditional Company," *Benefits & Compensation International,* 15(6), December, pp. 19–20.

Perlmutter, Howard V. 1969. "The Tortuous Evolution of the Multinational Corporation," *Columbia Journal of World Business,* January/February.

Perry, Tekla S. 1987. "Semiconductors Go to Korea," *IEEE Spectrum,* 24(12), December, pp. 34–38.

Peterson, Richard B. and Hermann F. Schwind. 1977. "A Comparative Study of Personnel Problems in International Companies and Joint Ventures in Japan," *Journal of International Business Studies,* September, pp. 45–55.

Petroff, Jim and Marie Petroff. 1987. " 'Porsche Quality' in Application Design," *Systems/3X World,* 15(9), September, pp. 42–52.

Pettigrew, Andrew M. 1987. "Context and Action in the Transformation of the Firm," *Journal of Management Studies,* 24(6), November, pp. 649–670.

Picard, Jacques. 1980. "Organizational Structures and Integrative Devices in European Multinational Corporations," *Columbia Journal of World Business,* Spring.

Pinella, Paul. 1990. "What PC Managers Need to Succeed," *Datamation,* 36(18), September 15, pp. 87–92.

Pink, Alan I. H. 1988. "Strategic Leadership Through Corporate Planning at ICI," *Long Range Planning,* 21(1), February, pp. 18–25.

Pocock, Nancy. 1986. "Succeeding in the IBM-Compatible Market," *Data Processing,* 28(5), June, pp. 247–250.

Popa, Mary. 1991. "Back to Basics in Cost Containment," *Employee Benefit Plan Review,* 45(9), March, pp. 10–11.

Poppel, Harvey L. 1990. "Software Stays at the Cutting Edge," *Datamation,* 36(12), June 15, pp. 194–195.

Porter, Michael E. 1986. "Changing Patterns of International Competition," *California Management Review,* XXVIII(2), Winter, pp. 9–40.

Porter, Michael E. 1990. "New Global Strategies for Competitive Advantage," *Planning Review,* 18(3), May/June, pp. 4–14.

Portnoy, Kristine and Langdon Brockinton. 1986. "ICI Moves in on U.S. Paints and Coatings," *Chemical Week,* 139(9), August 27, pp. 13–14.

Powell, Dave. 1986. "Case Study: Implementing an International S/3X Network," *Systems/3X World,* 14(7), July, pp. 26–32.

Powers, Pam. 1987. "French Giant Alcatel Enters U.S. Picture," *Network World,* 4(43), October 26, pp. 11–12.

Poynter, Thomas A. 1982. "Government Intervention in Less Developed Countries: The Experience of Multinational Companies," *Journal of International Business Studies,* Spring/Summer.

Prestowitz, C. V., Jr., 1989. *Trading Places: How We are Giving Our Future to Japan and How to Reclaim It* (New York: Basic Books, Inc.).

Price, Chris. 1988. "Esprit de Corps," *Systems International,* 16(1), January, pp. 33–34.

Priel, Victor Z. 1974. "Some Management Aspects of Multinational Companies" (4, 5), pp. 45–68.

Pucik, Vladmir and Jan Hack Katz. 1986. "Information, Control, and Human Resource Management in Multinational Firms," *Human Resource Management,* 25(1), Spring, pp. 121–132.

Pullan, George. 1990. "Organisation Design: Getting the Chemistry Right," *Personnel Management,* 22(I), August, pp. 46–50.

Quatrepoint, J. M., J. Jublin, and D. Arnaud. 1976. *French Ordinateurs de l'affaire Bull à l'assassinat du Plan Calcul* (Paris: Editions Alain Moreau).

Rabino, Samuel and Elva Ellen Hubbard. 1984. "The Race of American and Japanese Personal Computer Manufacturers for Dominance of the US Market," *Columbia Journal of World Business,* Fall, pp. 18–31.

Radding, Alan. 1991. "Security Often Complex in Distributed Computing," *Bank Management,* 67(3), March, pp. 50–52.

Raimondi, Conna, Rosemary Hamilton, Clinton Wilder, and James Connolly. 1986. "Honeywell Surrenders Info Group/New Company Freed from Distractions of Honeywell Goals," *Computerworld,* 20(49), December 8, pp. 1, 6–7.

Raine, Eden. 1986. "Hardware Maintenance: Monitoring by Olivetti Gets Results," *Computing Canada,* 12(12), June 12, p. 17.

Raines, J. Patrick. 1985. "Common Market Competition Policy: The EC-IBM Settlement," *Journal of Common Market Studies,* 24(2), December, pp. 137–147.

Ramasastry, Jay. 1988. "The Road to HDTV," *Satellite Communications,* 12(4), April, pp. 33–35.

Ransom, Harry Howe. 1959. *Central Intelligence and National Security* (Cambridge, MA: Harvard University Press).

Raptis, George and Joanne Collins. 1986. "Managing Multinational Information Systems," *Management Accounting,* 67(7), January, pp. 14, 29, 81.

Rayner, Bruce C. P. and Linda Stallmann. 1990. "The Electronic Business International 100," *Electronic Business,* 16(21), November 12, pp. 86–91.

References

Reck, Robert H. 1989. "The Shock of Going Global," *Datamation,* 35(15), August 1, pp. 67–70.

Regan, Edward J. 1984. *Emerging Transborder Data Flow Issues and Their Impacts on International Banking,* Master's thesis, Stonier Graduate School of Banking.

Rehin, Adam. 1990. "Calling on CSTAs," *Telephony,* 219(23), November 26, pp. 26–34.

Reich, Robert B. 1991. "Who Is Them?" *Harvard Business Review,* 69(2), March/April, pp. 77–88.

Reich, Robert B. 1991. *The Work of Nations: Preparing Ourselves for 21st Century Capitalism* (New York: A. A. Knopf).

Reid, T. R. 1984. *The Chip: How Two Americans Invented the Microchip and Launched a Revolution* (New York: Simon and Schuster).

Remich, Norman E., Jr. 1991. "High Tech Wins Vote of Mature Consumers," *Appliance Manufacturer,* 39(3), March, pp. 62–63.

Rennie, Philip. 1986. "Dynasty Buying with Lee Ming Tee," *Rydge's,* 59(9), September, pp. 38–40.

Rhein, Reginald, Jr. 1988. "Science Finally Strikes Back at Strokes," *Business Week,* Industrial/Technology Edition (3064), August 8, pp. 50–51.

Rice, Valerie. 1989. "SGS-Thomson Hopes to Bring Life to Inmos' Transputer," *Electronic Business,* 15(17), August 21, p. 57.

Richelson, Jeffrey. 1984. *The U.S. Intelligence Community,* 2nd ed. (Cambridge, MA: Ballinger.)

Rifkin, Glenn. 1990. "Tight Lips, Laptops and Supers Help Merck Shine," *Computerworld,* Section 2, October 8, pp. 62–63.

Riley, Tom. 1985. "Setting Standards—Data Privacy," *ComputerData,* 10(12), December, pp. 12–13.

Roach, Stephen. 1985. *The New Technology Cycle* (New York: Morgan Stanley), September 11.

Roach, Stephen. 1987. *America's Technology Dilemma: A Profile of the Information Economy,* Special economic study (New York: Morgan Stanley), April 22.

Roach, Stephen. 1988. *White-Collar Productivity: A Glimmer of Hope?* Special economic study (New York: Morgan Stanley), September 16.

Roberts, J. Edward. 1988. "Training Trade Show Salespeople: How Caterpillar Does It," *Business Marketing,* 73(6), June, pp. 70–73.

Roberts, Robin and Anna Hickling. 1989. "Computer Integrated Management?" *Multinational Business* (2), Summer, pp. 18–25.

Robey, Daniel and Andres Rodriguez-Diaz. 1989. "The Organizational and Cultural Context of Systems Implementation: Case Experience from Latin America," *Information and Management,* 17(4), November, pp. 229–239.

Robinson, David. 1990. "Enhanced Environment," *Systems International,* 18(6), June, pp. 28–29.

Robinson, John. 1983. *Multinational and Political Control* (New York: St. Martin's Press).

Robinson, Richard D. 1981. "Background Concepts and Philosophy of International Business from World War II to the Present," *Journal of International Business Studies,* Spring/Summer, pp. 13–21.

Robock, Stefan H. 1974. "The Case for Home Country Controls over Multinational Firms," *Columbia Journal of World Business,* Summer, pp. 75–79.

Roche, Edward M. 1984a. "South Korea's Informatics Race," *Agora,* 9(3), pp. 12–14.

Roche, Edward M. 1984b. "Computer Communications in Korea," Mimeo.

Roche, Edward M. 1986. "The Computer Communications Lobby, the U.S. Department of State Working Group on Transborder Data Flows and Adoption of the OECD Guidelines on the Protection of Privacy and Transborder Data Flows of Personal Data," Ph.D. Thesis, Columbia University.

Roche, Edward M. 1990. "Korean Informatics Policy," Conference paper, presented at the Academic Symposium on the Impact of Recent Economic Developments on U.S./Korean Relations and the Pacific Basin, University of California at San Diego, Graduate School of International Relations and Pacific Studies, November 9–11.

Roche, Edward M. 1991a. "Managing Systems Development in Multinational Corporations: Practical Lessons from Seven Case Studies," in Shailendra Palvia, Prasant Palvia and Ronald Ziglir, eds., *Global Issues of Information Technology Management* (Harrisburg, PA: Idea Group).

Roche, Edward M. 1991b. *Telecommunications and Business Strategy* (Homedale, IL: Dryden Press).

Roche, Edward M. et al. 1990. "Experimental Applications of Group Decision Support Systems in an Information Economics Analysis of Competition in the Semiconductor Industry," I–VI, working papers, MIS Department, University of Arizona.

Rogers, Jack K. 1990. "Laboratory is Dedicated to Developing Composite Manufacturing Techniques," *Modern Plastics,* 67(7), July, pp. 14, 16.

Root, Franklin R. 1984. "Some Trends in the World Economy and Their Implications for International Business Strategy," *Journal of International Business Studies,* Winter.

Rosenbaum, Andy. 1989. "Siemens Restructures R&D to Be Closer to End Markets," *Electronic Business,* 15(6), March 20, pp. 60, 62.

Rosenthal, Thomas M. 1990. "Shippers Call the Shots," *Global Trade,* 110(1), January, pp. 10–12.

Ross, Donald E. 1987. "The Way to Handle Electronic Messages," *Infosystems,* 34(2), February, pp. 64, 66.

Rossant, John. 1990. "As Profits Plunge, De Benedetti Cries 'Basta,'" *Business Week,* Industrial/Technology Edition (3190), December 3, p. 52.

Rossant, John and Thame Peterson. 1989. "Can Cassoni Get Olivetti Off the Slippery Slope?" *Business Week,* Industrial/Technology Edition (3109), June 12, pp. 99, 102.

Rounce, Peter A., Ken Chan, Stuart Mackay, and Kevin Steptoe. 1989. "VLSI Architecture Research Within the ESPRIT SPAN Project," *Microprocessing & Microprogramming,* 26(2), June, pp. 139–152.

Roussel, Anne-Marie. 1990. "Top of the World," *International Management,* Europe Edition, 45(11), December, pp. 48–51.

References

Rowan, Richard L. and Duncan C. Campbell. 1983. "The Attempt to Regulate Industrial Relations Through International Codes of Conduct," *Columbia Journal of World Business,* Summer, pp. 64–72.

Roy, Barun. 1989. "Acer's Stan Shif: Against All Odds," *Asian Finance,* 15(11), November 15, pp. 17–23.

Ruggie, John Gerard, ed. 1983. *The Antinomies of Interdependence: National Welfare & the International Division of Labor* (New York: Columbia University Press).

Rugman, Alan M. 1980. "A New Theory of the Multinational Enterprise: Internationalization Versus Internalization," *Columbia Journal of World Business,* Spring.

Rugman, Alan. 1982. "Internalization and Non-Equity Forms of International Involvement," in Alan M. Rugman, ed., *New Theories of the Multinational Enterprise* (New York: St. Martin's Press).

Rugman, Alan M. 1985. "Multinationals and Global Competitive Strategy," *International Studies of Management and Organization,* XV(2), pp. 8–18.

Russell, Meg. 1990. "International Survey of Software Measurement Education and Training," *Journal of Systems & Software,* 12(3), July, pp. 233–241.

Saclé, Robert. 1968. "Coopérations-Concentrations et fusions d'entreprises dans la C.E.E.," *Revue du Marché Commun,* (109), January/February, p. 116.

Sahhafi, Massoud M. and Chin-Shu Davidson. 1989. "The New Age of Global Competition in the Semiconductor Industry: Enter the Dragon," *Columbia Journal of World Business,* Winter, pp. 60–70.

Sambharya, Rakesh B. and Arvind Phatak. 1990. "The Effect of Transborder Data Flow Restrictions on American Multinational Corporations," *Management International Review,* 30(3), pp. 267–290.

Samiee, Saeed. 1983. "Developments in Transnational Data Flows: Regulations and Perspectives," *Journal of International Business Studies,* Winter, pp. 159–162.

Samiee, Saeed. 1984. "Transnational Data Flow Constraints: A New Challenge for Multinational Corporations," *Journal of International Business Studies,* Spring/Summer.

Sarathy, Ravi. 1985. "Japanese Trading Companies: Can They Be Copied?" *Journal of International Business Studies,* Summer, pp. 101–119.

Sasseen, Jane. 1991. "Television Jousts with Japan," *International Management,* Europe Edition, 46(2), March, pp. 37–39.

Satchell, Stephen. 1987. "Acer 1100: 386 Machine Offers Super Support at Super Price," *InfoWorld,* 9(26), June 29, pp. 50–51.

Sato, Harumasa and Rodney Stevenson. 1989. "Telecommunications in Japan: After Privatization and Liberalization," *Columbia Journal of World Business,* Spring, pp. 31–41.

Sato, Sadayuki. 1980. "Japanese Multinational Enterprises: Potential and Limits," *Japanese Economic Studies,* Fall, pp. 68–85.

Sauvant, Karl P. 1983. "Transborder Data Flows and the Developing Countries," *International Organization,* 37(2), Spring, pp. 359–371.

Sauvant, Karl P. 1986. *International Transactions in Services: The Politics of Transborder Data Flows* (Boulder, CO: Westview Press).

Sauvant, Karl P. 1989. "Trade in Services: The Impact of Data Techniques," *Information Age,* 11(1), January, pp. 37–39.

Sauvant, Karl P. and Farid G. Lavipour, eds. 1976. *Controlling Multinational Enterprises: Problems, Strategies, Counterstrategies.* (Boulder, CO: Westview Press).

Schatz, Willie. 1986. "Communications: Airing the Issues," *Datamation,* 32(2), January 15, pp. 30–35.

Schiller, Herbert I. 1983. "The World Crisis and the New Information Technologies," *Columbia Journal of World Business,* Spring, pp. 86–89+.

Schiller, Zachary. 1986. "Appliances: Turning Up the Heat in the Kitchen," *Business Week,* Industrial/Technology Edition (2958), August 4, pp. 76, 78.

Schiller, Zachary. 1988. "Whirlpool Plots the Invasion of Europe," *Business Week,* Industrial/Technology Edition (3068), September 5, pp. 70, 72.

Schiller, Zachary. 1989. "Can P&G Commandeer More Shelves in the Medicine Chest?" *Business Week,* Industrial/Technology Edition (3099), April 10, pp. 64, 67.

Schirmer, Walter E. 1968. "American Alternatives in an Era of Free Trade," *Michigan Business Review,* March, pp. 8–19.

Schlender, Brenton R. 1990. "How Levi Strauss Did an LBO Right," *Fortune,* 121(10), May 7, pp. 105–107.

Schlosstein, S. 1989. *The End of the American Century* (New York, Chicago: Congdon & Weed, Inc.).

Schmerken, Ivy. 1990a. "Wall Street's Elusive Goal: Computers That Think Like Pros," *Wall Street Computer Review,* 7(9), June, pp. 24–34, 74–76.

Schmerken, Ivy. 1990b. "Wall Street Struggles to Balance Global Risk," *Wall Street Computer Review,* 7(11), August, pp. 12–22, 48–56.

Schollhammer, Hans. 1971a. "Organization Structures of Multinational Corporations," *Academy of Management Journal,* September, pp. 345–365.

Schollhammer, Hans. 1971b. "Long-Range Planning in Multinational Firms," *Columbia Journal of World Business,* September/October, pp. 79–86.

Schultz, Elizabeth. 1988a. "PBX Upgrades Travel the Bumpy Road to ISDN," *Telephony,* 215(22), November 28, pp. 36–39.

Schultz, Elizabeth. 1988b. "Siemens, IBM Join Forces to Tackle Tough PBX Problems," *Telephony,* 215(25), December 19, pp. 10–11.

Schware, Robert. 1989. "The World Software Industry and Software Engineering: Opportunities and Constraints for Newly Industrialized Economies," World Bank Technical Paper Number 104, Washington, D.C.

Scoville, Herbert, Jr. 1976. "The Role of Technology in Covert Intelligence Collection," in Robert L. Brorsage and John Marks, eds., *The CIA File* (New York: Grossman), pp. 109–124.

Scully, Sharon. 1986. "No Deal on EWSD," *Network World,* 3(8), April 28.

Sebestyen, Istvan, 1983. *Experimental and Operational East-West Computer Connections: the Telecommunication Hardware and Software, Data Communication Services, and Relevant Administrative Procedures* (Laxenburg: IIASA).

Seither, Mike. 1989. "Terminal Vendors Stake Out X Window Display Territories," *Mini-Micro Systems,* 22(2), February, pp. 24, 26.

References

Selwyn, Michael. 1990. "Sewing Up the World," *Asian Business,* 26(6), June, pp. 60–62.

Shaker, Frank. 1970. "The Multinational Corporation: The New Imperialism?" *Columbia Journal of World Business,* November/December, pp. 80–84.

Sharp, M., ed. 1985. "Europe and the New Technologies: Six Case Studies in Innovation and Adjustment" (London: Frances Pinter).

Sherman, Barbara. 1987. "This Database Has Visual Info on the U.K.," *Computing Canada,* 13(19), September 17, p. 28.

Sherman, Stratford P. 1989. "How Philip Morris Diversified Right," *Fortune,* 120(9), October 23, pp. 120–131.

Short, Herbert C. 1989. "NH3 Break Thru: Small Plants," *Chemical Engineering,* 96(7), July, pp. 41–45.

Short, Herbert C. and David W. Gibson. 1987. "ICI's New Boss—His Precept: 'Keep Up the Momentum,' " *Chemical Week,* 140(12), April 1, pp. 26–29.

Short, Herbert C., Nel Slis, Iris Gomez, and Felice Mikelberg. 1987. "Akzo Wins Stauffer—Quickly," *Chemical Week,* 141(1), July 1, pp. 10–11.

Shreeve, Gavin. 1987. "Capital Markets: NIFty Deal," *Banker,* 137(738), August, pp. 65–66.

Shrivastava, Paul. 1983. "Strategies for Coping with Telecommunications Technology in the Financial Services Industry," *Columbia Journal of World Business,* Spring, pp. 19–24.

Shrivastava, Paul. 1984. "Technological Innovation in Developing Countries," *Columbia Journal of World Business,* Winter, pp. 23–29.

Shure, Deborah Miller. 1986. "Upgraded Cash Management Fills Demand for Timely Info," *Bank Systems & Equipment,* 23(6), June.

Shutt, John. 1989. "SGS-Thomson's Ambitious Calendar," *International Management,* 44(6), June, pp. 55–57.

Simmonds, Kenneth. 1966. "Multinational? Well, Not Quite," *Columbia Journal of World Business,* Fall, pp. 115–122.

Sims, J. Taylor. 1986. "Japanese Market Entry Strategy at Work: Komatsu vs. Caterpillar," *International Marketing Review,* 3(3), Autumn, pp. 21–32.

Skagen, Anne E. 1989. "Nurturing Relationships and Enhancing Quality with Electronic Data Interchange," *Management Review,* February, pp. 28–32.

Skapinker, Michael. 1986. "Xerox Searches for Life Beyond Boxes," *International Management,* 41(6), June, pp. 24–30.

Skyrme, David J. 1990. "Developing Successful Marketing Intelligence: A Case Study," *Management Decision,* 28(1), pp. 54–61.

Slater, Robert. 1987. *Portraits in Silicon* (Cambridge, MA: The MIT Press).

Slofstra, Martin. 1990. "In Conversation: Harvey Coleman, Olivetti Canada," *Computing Canada,* 16(22), October 25, p. 13.

Smeaton, Alan F. 1987. "Information Retrieval Research and ESPRIT," *Journal of the ASIS,* 38(1), January, pp. 21–22.

Smith, Charles and Tony Major. 1990. "The Stakes Rise: Fujitsu Set to Put Heat on IBM with ICL Takeover," *Far Eastern Economic Review,* 149(31), August 2, pp. 46–47.

Smith, Robert M. 1986. "Overseeing Foreign Counsel: The In-House Lawyer's Role," *International Financial Law Review,* 5(9), September, pp. 24–25.

Snapp, Cheryl D. 1990. "EDI Aims High for Global Growth," *Datamation,* International Edition, 36(5), March 1, pp. 77–80.

Solomon, Steven. 1987. "More Rabbits, Please, Signor De Benedetti," *Forbes,* 139(5), March 9, pp. 114–118.

Spooner, Peter. 1987. "Management Hot House," *Chief Executive,* March, pp. 16, 18.

Stanford, Alan. 1986, "The CIO Phenomenon," *SIM Network,* August/September, pp. 1–3.

Starr, Cynthia. 1990. "Syntex Laboratories Sets Its Sights on CMV Retinitis," *Drug Topics,* 134(21), November 5, pp. 19–20.

Stavro, Barry. 1986. "Digging Out," *Forbes,* 138(10), November 3, pp. 127–128.

Stephens, Mark. 1987. "Syntex Global Network Based on Dial-Up Lines," *InfoWorld,* 9(40), October 5, p. 16.

Stern, Aimee L. 1987. "GF Tries the Old Restructure Ploy," *Business Month,* 130(5), November, pp. 36–39.

Stewart, Thomas A. 1990. "A Heartland Industry Takes On the World," *Fortune,* 121(6), March 12, pp. 110–112.

Stobaugh, Robert B. 1971. "The Multinational Corporation: Measuring the Consequences," *Columbia Journal of World Business,* January/February, pp. 59–64.

Stoll, Marilyn. 1987. "CIO Position Emerges as a New Strategic Force," *PC Week,* October 20, p. C1.

Stopford, John M. and Louis T. Wells, Jr. 1972. *Managing the Multinational Enterprise: Organization of the Firm and Ownership of the Subsidiaries* (New York: Basic Books, Inc.).

Stovicek, Don. 1990. "CMMs Key to Plant with a Future," *Automation,* 37(12), December, pp. 24–25.

Strassmann, Paul A. 1989. "The Business Value of Information," in Peter Keene, ed., *Measuring the Business Value of Information Technologies* (Washington, DC: International Center for Information Technology).

Sullivan, Jeremiah J. and Ikujiro Nonaka. 1986. "The Application of Organizational Learning Theory to Japanese and American Management," *Journal of International Business Studies,* Fall, pp. 127–147.

Sullivan-Trainor, Michael L. 1990/1991. "Keep Management Hot About Technology," *Computerworld,* 24(52, 53), December 24/January 1, pp. 2, 4.

Sullivan-Trainor, Michael L. and Joseph Maglitta. 1990. "Top IS Users Soar Above Tough Times," *Computerworld,* Section 2, October 8, pp. 6–9.

Svedberg, Peter. 1980. "Colonial Enforcement of Foreign Direct Investment," *The Manchester School,* pp. 21–38.

Swandby, Richard K., Ian K. Sequeira, and Lori L. Bock. 1988. "1987's Most Memorable Exhibits: Caterpillar, Allen-Bradley Zoom to Top," *Business Marketing,* 73(6), June, pp. 60–68.

Sweet, Walter. 1990. "International Firms Strive for Uniform Nets Abroad," *Network World,* 7(22), May 28, pp. 35–36, 62.

Symonds, William C., Thane Peterson, John J. Keller, and Marc Frons. 1987. "Dealmaker De Benedetti," *Business Week,* Industrial/Technology Edition (3013), August 24, pp. 42–47.

References

Symonds, William C., Thane Peterson, and Jonathan B. Levine. 1987. "An Italian Chipmaker Shows the Way," *Business Week,* Industrial/Technology Edition (3000), May 25, pp. 134, 136.

Taff, Anita. 1991. "Firms Unite to Form Plan for Broadband Offerings," *Network World,* 8(12), March 25, pp. 2, 47.

Tappan, David S., Jr. 1985. "Project Management of the Future," *Columbia Journal of World Business,* Twentieth Anniversary Issue, 20(4), pp. 27–29.

Tate, Paul and Linda Runyan. 1986. "Europe's Elite," *Datamation,* 32(15), August 1, pp. 34–39.

Teague, Frederick A. 1970. "International Management Selection and Development," *California Management Review,* XII(3), Spring, pp. 1–6.

Teece, David J. 1980. "Technological and Organisational Factors in the Theory of the Multinational Enterprise," in Mark Casson, ed., *The Growth of International Business* (London; Boston: Allen & Unwin), pp. 51–62.

Teece, David J. 1980. "Economies of Scope and the Scope of the Enterprise," *Journal of Economic Behavior and Organization,* 1, pp. 223–247.

Thomas, Hester. 1987. "Business Accountants Are Team Players," *Accountancy,* 99(1122), February, pp. 103–104.

Thomas, Hester. 1989. "A Market for Optimists Only," *Accountancy,* 103(1149), May, pp. 105–108.

Thompson, John M., Ted W. Faigle, and James E. Short. 1987. "Competing Through Information Technology: We Are the World," *Information Strategy: The Executive's Journal,* 3(4), Summer, pp. 32–37.

Thurow, Lester. 1984. "Revitalizing American Industry: Managing in a Competitive World Economy," *California Management Review,* XXVII(1), Fall, pp. 9–41.

Tiersten, Sylvia. 1989. "SGS-Thomson's Soup Cans Are 'M'm, M'm Good,'" *Electronic Business,* 15(4), February 20, pp. 30, 32.

Tilton, John E. 1979. *International Diffusion of Technology: The Case of Semiconductors* (Washington, DC: The Brookings Institution).

Toal, Brian A. 1988. "Credit Where Credit Is Due," *Oil & Gas Investor,* 7(9), April, pp. 30–35.

Tobias, Arthur J. 1988. "Multinationals Spearheading Worldwide Financial Thrust," *Software Magazine,* 8(7), May, pp. 64–70.

Townley, Preston. 1990. "Globesmanship," *Across the Board,* 27(1,2), January/February, pp. 24–34.

Travers, Nicolas. 1987. "ICI Prepares for a Hi-Tech Future," *Director,* 40(6), January, pp. 26–29.

Tunstall, J. 1986. *Communications Deregulation: The Unleashing of America's Communications Industry* (Oxford: Basil Blackwell).

Tutt, Nigel. 1989. "Europe's Computer Industry Prepares for 1992," *Europe,* (284), March, pp. 23–24.

UNCTC. 1983a. *Measures Strengthening the Negotiating Capacity of Governments in Their Relations with Transnational Corporations* (New York: United Nations).

UNCTC. 1983b. *Transnational Corporations in the International Auto Industry* (New York: United Nations).

UNCTC. 1984a. *Transborder Data Flows and Poland: Polish Case Study* (New York: United Nations).

UNCTC. 1984b. *Transborder Data Flows: Transnational Corporations and Remote-Sensing Data* (New York: United Nations).

UNCTC. 1984c. *Transnational Corporations in the Pharmaceutical Industry of Developing Countries* (New York: United Nations).

UNCTC. 1985a. *Transnational Corporations and International Trade: Selected Issues* (New York: United Nations).

UNCTC. 1985b. *Trends and Issues in Foreign Direct Investment and Related Flows* (New York: United Nations).

UNCTC. 1987. *Arrangements Between Joint Venture Partners in Developing Countries,* UNCTC Advisory Studies, Series B, No. 2 (New York: United Nations).

UNCTC. 1988a. *Data Goods and Data Services in the Socialist Countries of Eastern Europe* (New York: United Nations).

UNCTC. 1988b. *Joint Ventures as a Form of International Economic Co-operation* (New York: United Nations).

UNCTC. 1989a. *The Process of Transnationalization and Transnational Mergers,* UNCTC Current Studies, Series A, No. 8 (New York: United Nations).

UNCTC. 1989b. *Transnational Corporations in the Construction and Design Engineering Industry* (New York: United Nations).

UNCTC. 1989c. *Transnational Service Corporations and Developing Countries: Impact and Policy Issues,* UNCTC Current Studies, Series A, No. 10 (New York: United Nations).

UNCTC. 1990a. *New Approaches to Best-Practice Manufacturing: The Role of Transnational Corporations and Implications for Developing Countries,* UNCTC Current Studies, Series A, No. 12 (New York: United Nations).

UNCTC. 1990b. *The New Code Environment,* UNCTC Current Studies, Series A, No. 16 (New York: United Nations).

UNCTC. 1990c. *New Issues in the Uruguay Round of Multilateral Trade Negotiations,* UNCTC Current Studies, Series A, No. 19 (New York: United Nations).

UNCTC. 1990d. *Transnational Corporations in the Plastics Industry* (New York: United Nations).

UNCTC. 1990e. *Transnational Corporations, Services and the Uruguay Round* (New York: United Nations).

UNCTC. 1990f. *Transnational Corporations and the Transfer of New and Emerging Technologies to Developing Countries* (New York: United Nations).

UNCTC. 1991. *Transborder Data Flows and Mexico* (New York: United Nations).

UNIDO. 1980. *Global Study of the Pharmaceutical Industry* (Vienna: United Nations).

Van Maanen, John. 1989. "Some Notes on the Importance of Writing in Organization Studies," in James I. Cash and Paul R. Lawrence, eds., *The Information Systems Research Challenge: Qualitative Research Methods,* Vol. I (Boston: Harvard Business School).

Vanker, Anthony D. 1989. "Digital Paper: Mass Storage Revolution?" *Laserdisk Professional,* 2(1), January, pp. 38–41.

References

Vasilash, Gary S. 1991. "A Big Job. A Big Plant. An Enormous Challenge," *Production,* 103(2), February, pp. 42–46.

Verespej, Michael A. 1987. "Whirlpool's New Kitchen Recipe," *Industry Week,* 234(6), September 21, pp. 56, 58.

Vernay, J. 1989. "IBM France," *Annals of the History of Computing,* 11(4), pp. 299–312.

Verner, Liipfert, Bernhard and McPherson, Chartered. 1983. *The Effect of Government Targeting on World Semiconductor Competition: A Case History of Japanese Industrial Strategy and Its Costs for America* (Cupertino: Semiconductor Industry Association).

Vernon, Raymond. 1966. "International Investment and International Trade in the Product Cycle," *Quarterly Journal of Economics,* May, pp. 190–207.

Vernon, Raymond. 1976. "Multinational Enterprises and National Governments: Exploration of an Uneasy Relationship," *Columbia Journal of World Business,* Summer, pp. 9–16.

Vernon, Raymond. "The Product Cycle Hypothesis in a New International Environment," *Bulletin,* pp. 255–267.

Vernon-Wortzel, Heidi and Lawrence H. Wortzel. 1988. "Globalizing Strategies for Multinationals from Developing Countries," *Columbia Journal of World Business,* Spring, pp. 27–35.

Verrall, Malcolm. 1988. "PCTE—The Kernel of Software Engineering Environments," *Microprocessing & Microprogramming,* 24(1–5), August, pp. 161–165.

Vincent, Edgar. 1988. "Developing Managers for an International Business," *Journal of Management Development,* 7(6), pp. 14–20.

Vivian, Roy, H. 1987. "DPCM Studies Using Edge Prediction and Adaptive Quantisation Laws for the Transmission of Still Pictures over the ISDN," *Microprocessing & Microprogramming,* 21(1–5), August, pp. 141–150.

Vogel, E.F. 1985. *Comeback* (New York: Simon and Schuster).

Wagner, Bill. 1990a. "New Trends in Smaller Crawler Tractors," *Equipment Management,* 18(8), August, pp. 50–54.

Wagner, Bill. 1990b. "Crawler Excavators," *Equipment Management,* 18(9), September, pp. 42–50.

Wagner, L.G. 1966. "Computers, Decentralization, and Corporate Control," *California Management Review,* Winter, pp. 25–32.

Wang, N.T. 1986. "United States and China: Business Beyond Trade—An Overview," *Columbia Journal of World Business,* Spring, pp. 3–11.

Ward, Adele. 1991. "Practice Management: Geared Up for 1992?" *Accountancy,* 107(1171), March, pp. 119–120.

Warman, E. A. 1990. "Integration Revisited—An Appraisal of the State of the Integration of CAD," *Computers in Industry,* 14(1–3), May, pp. 59–65.

Warshofsky, F. 1989. "The Chip War: The Battle for the World of Tommorrow" (New York: Charles Scribner's Sons).

Waterman, Merwin H. 1968a. "Financial Management in Multinational Corporations: I," *Michigan Business Review,* January, pp. 10–15.

Waterman, Merwin H. 1968b. "Financial Management in Multinational Corporations: II," *Michigan Business Review,* March, pp. 26–32.

Watkins, Todd A. 1991. "A Technological Communications Costs Model of R&D Consortia as Public Policy," *Research Policy,* 20(2), April, pp. 87–107.

Weart, Walter. 1986. "Warehousing: Caterpillar," *Distribution,* 85(12), December, p. 16.

Weatherby, Dave. 1986. "Worldwide VANs," *Systems International,* 14(12), December, pp. 73–74.

Weber, Herbert. 1989. "From CASE to Software Factories," *Datamation,* 35(7), April 1, pp. 34–36, 52.

Weeks, Clive. 1986. "The Need for Integrated Management of Information," *Journal of Information Science Principles & Practice,* 12(6), pp. 283–289.

Weiner, Steve. 1990. "Growing Pains," *Forbes,* 146(10), October 29, pp. 40–41.

Wells, Louis T., Jr., 1972. "The Multinational Business Enterprise: What Kind of International Organization?" *International Organization,* XXV, pp. 447–464.

Welt, Robert G. S. 1987. "The Taiwan Computer Industry—a Market at the Peak of Evolution," *OEP Office Equipment & Products,* 16(109), Fall, pp. 36–37.

Welter, Therese R. 1987. "The Chief Information Officer: What's Behind the Hype," *Industry Week,* June 29, pp. 45–48.

Werner, Manuel. 1986. "Transborder Data Flows: A Cost Benefit Analysis," *Canadian Banker,* 93(5), October, pp. 36–39.

Whatley, Garrod. 1987. "More Than a Merging of Colours," *Chief Executive,* December, pp. 16–18.

Wheatman, Victor S. 1988. "Just Getting Started," *Software Magazine,* 8(4), March, pp. 52–58.

White, George C. 1990. "Have You Heard? 'Check and List' Is Obsolete for Receiving Consumer Bill Payments," *Journal of Cash Management,* 10(5), September/October, pp. 52–53.

Whitehall, Bruce. 1989. "How Caterpillar's 'Sponsored Circulation' Reaches Small Users." *Industrial Marketing Digest,* 14(3), pp. 13–19.

Whitty, Robin, Marin Bush, and Meg Russell. 1990. "METKIT and the ESPRIT Program," *Journal of Systems & Software,* 12(3), July, pp. 219–221.

Wiggin, Geoff. 1987. "The Golden Rules of Global Networking," *Datamation,* International Edition, 33(19), October 1, pp. 68–73.

Wilder, Clinton. 1989. "Beyond Mere Automation," *Computerworld,* Section 1, 23(45), November 6, pp. 79, 84.

Wilkins, Mira (nd). "Modern European Economic History and the Multinationals," *Journal of Economic Literature,* pp. 575–595.

Wilkinson, Mary. 1988. "State Cash Helps British Electronic R&D Catch Up," *Electronic Business,* 14(7), April 1, pp. 71–72.

Willard, Gary E. and Arnold C. Cooper. 1985. "Survivors of Industry Shake-Outs: The Case of the U.S. Color Television Set Industry," *Strategic Management Journal,* 6, pp. 299–318.

Wille, Edgar. 1990. "Should Management Development Just Be for Managers?" *Personnel Management,* 22(8), August, pp. 34–37.

Willems, Theo. 1986. "Mensgerichte Zakelijkheid" (Employee-Oriented Yet Business-Like), *Elan,* 1(3), March, pp. 41–43.

Williamson, John. 1990. "New Connections for the European PBX Industry," *Telephony,* 218(26A), June 25, pp. 22–23.

Williamson, O. E. 1975. *Markets and Hierarchies: Analysis and Anti-Trust Implications* (New York: Free Press).

Willner, Eric. 1988. "MIS in Banking: Keep Branch Systems Simple," *Computerworld,* 22(33), August 15, p. 70.

Wilson, Brent D. (nd). "The Propensity of Multinational Companies to Expand Through Acquisitions," *Journal of International Business Studies,* pp. 59–65.

Wilson, Dick. 1990. "Brother Ready to Raid Unified EC," *Asian Finance,* 16(10), October 15, pp. 22–23.

Winkler, Connie. 1990. "An Illuminating CEO-CIO Alliance," *Datamation,* 36, August 15, p. 79.

Wise, David and Thomas B. Ross. 1964. *The Invisible Government* (New York: Random House).

Witt, Clyde E. 1989. "Caterpillar Adds FMS to Engine Manufacturing," *Material Handling Engineering,* 44(6), June, pp. 78–82.

Wittig, T. and G. C. Koukoulis. 1986. "Expert Control," *Systems International,* 14(11), November, pp. 23, 26.

Wolf, M. J. 1983. *The Japanese Conspiracy: The Plot to Dominate Industry Worldwide—and How to Deal with It* (New York: Empire Books).

Womack, J. P., D. T. Jones, and D. Roos. 1990. *The Machine That Changed the World* (New York: Macmillan).

Woolsey, Christine. 1990. "Employer Spots Inflated Medical Bills," *Business Insurance,* 24(26), June 25, pp. 3, 28.

Wortman, David. 1988. "CIM and Simulation," *Manufacturing Systems,* 6(4), April, pp. 44–50.

Wortmann, Michael. 1990. "Multinationals and the Internationalization of R&D: New Developments in German Companies," *Research Policy,* 19(2), April, pp. 175–183.

Wotruba, Thomas R. 1990. "The Relationship of Job Image, Performance, and Job Satisfaction to Inactivity-Proneness of Direct Salespeople," *Journal of the Academy of Marketing Science,* 18(2), Spring, pp. 113–121.

Wright, Karen. 1990. "The Road to the Global Village," *Scientific American,* March, pp. 83–94.

Wright, Richard W. "Trends in International Business Research," *Journal of International Business Studies,* pp. 109–123.

Wrubel, Robert and Charles Gaffney. 1988. "Men of the Year: Philip E. Benton Jr.; Kaspar V. Cassani," *Financial World,* 157(25), November 29, pp. 34–40.

Wunder, Bernard J., Jr. 1983. "International Commerce in Telecommunications and Information Products," *Columbia Journal of World Business,* Spring, pp. 62–67.

Wyder, Rob. 1986. "Volvo Finds VTAM to Be the Key to Its In-House Electronic Mail," *Data Communications,* 15(10), September, pp. 193–199.

Yang, David C. 1990. "Machine Translators: Accounting Applications," *CPA Journal,* 60(11), November, pp. 8, 10.

Yannopoulos, G. N. 1983. "The Growth of Transnational Banking," in M. Casson, ed., *The Growth of International Business* (London: George Allen and Unwin).

Yoshino, M. Y. "Toward a Concept of Managerial Control for a World Enterprise," *Michigan Business Review,* XVIII(2), pp. 25–31.

Yoshino, M. Y. and T. B. Lifson. 1986. *The Invisible Link: Japan's Sogo Shosha and the Organization of Trade* (Cambridge, MA: The MIT Press).

Young, Stephen and Neil Hood. 1977. "Multinational and Host Governments: Lessons from the Case of Chrysler UK," *Columbia Journal of World Business,* Summer, pp. 97–106.

Zani, William M. 1970. "The Computer Utility," *California Management Review,* XIII(1), Fall, pp. 31–37.

Zeira, Yoram. 1976. "Management Development in Ethnocentric Multinational Corporations," *California Management Review,* XVIII(4), Summer, pp. 34–42.

Zeira, Yoram and Ehud Harari. 1979. "Host-Country Organizations and Expatriate Managers in Europe," *California Management Review,* XXI(3), Spring, pp. 40–50.

Zellner, Wendy. 1988. "A Tough Market Has Whirlpool in a Spin," *Business Week,* Industrial/Technology Edition (3050), May 2, pp. 121–122.

Zenker, David M. 1987. "The PC as Prototype Problem-Solver," *Management Accounting,* 68(11), May, pp. 30–33.

Zimmermann, Kim. 1988. "Automation Helps Struggling Branch Double Deposits," *Bank Systems & Equipment,* 25(9), September, pp. 90–91.

Zurawicki, Leon. 1975. "The Cooperation of the Socialist State with the MNCs," *Columbia Journal of World Business,* Spring, pp. 109–115.

Index

Index of Companies and Institutions

Ace-Telemail International, 193
Acer, 220
Acorn computers, 185
AEG, 207
AG Hasler, 210
Alcatel, 193, 206
Alvey research programme, 197
Amdahl, 212, 226
Application Specific Integrated Circuits (ASICs), 186, 223
Apricot Computers, 211
Asynchronous Transfer Mode (ATM), 198, 235
AT&T Network Systems International, 193
Ateliers de Constructions Électriques de Charleroi, 210
ATT consent decree, 176
Autophon S.A., 210

Basic Research in Industrial Technologies (BRITE), 198
Bell Telephone Manufacturing Company, 209
BESM series, 217
BMW, 207
Boeing Aerospace, 204
British Cable, 210
British Telecom, 189
Bunker Ramo, 184

Cable and Wireless, 207
Cables de Comunicaciones, 210
CACTUS, 200
CARLOS, 200
Cathedral system, 199
Centre National de la Recherche Scientifique, 197
China Postal and Telecommunications Industry Corporation, 209
Chung Cheony Group, 219
CIT Alcatel, 204
Compagnie des Machines Bull, 208
Compagnie Generale d'Electricité (CGE), 204, 206
Compagnie Lyonnaise de Transmission Optiques (CLTO), 210
Compañia Telefónica Nacional de España, 189, 209
Computer Integrated Telecommunications Systems (CITS), 227
Computer-Aided Design Interfaces (CAD*I), 202
Computer-Integrated Manufacturing Open Systems Architecture (CIM-OSA), 202
Control Data Corporation, 189
Convergent Technologies, 188
Corning Glass, 189, 210
Cray, 209, 228

Daimler-Benz, 207
Data General, 207
Datasaab, 210
Design Metrics Evaluator (DEMETER), 201
Digital Equipment Corporation (DEC), 207

Dornier, 207
DuPont, 189

Electronic Data Systems (EDS), 189
Electronic Intelligence (ELINT), 233
Ellemtel Utvecklings AB, 210
Enhanced Network Services (ENS) (Japan), 187
Eniac, 176
Ericsson, 210
ESPRIT, 197, 199
ETA Systems, 209
EUREKA, 197
European Strategic Programme of Research and Development in Information Technology (ESPRIT), 197
European Telecommunications Standards Institute (ETSI), 205

Fibres Optiques Industries, 210
Fujitsu, 187, 192, 211, 226

General Electric (computers), 176
General Language for System Semantics (GLASS), 200
Gold Star Fiber Optic, 187
Gold Star Semiconductor, 187
Groupe Bull, 196, 208

HDTV, 198
Hinomaru, 229
Honeywell-Ericsson Development Company, 210
Honeywell Information Systems, 208
Honeywell-NEC Supercomputers Inc. (HNSX), 209
Hong Kong Telephone, 207
Hughes Communications, 207

IBM, 189
IBM Italia, 192
IBM Japan Ltd., 191
IBM World Trade Organization, 178
ICO, 211
Inmos, 186
Intec, 193
Intel, 187
Intelsa, 210
International Computers Limited (ICL), 179, 234
International Consultative Radio Committee (CCIR), 198
ISC/Bunker Ramo, 185
Italcom, 192
Italtel Societa Italiana Telecomunicazioni SpA, 192
ITT, 209
ITT Dialcom, 189

Japan Communications Satellite Planning Company, 207
Japan Electronic Computer Corporation (JECC), 229

JESSI, 197, 203
Jeumont-Schneider, 192

Knowledge Acquisition Documentation and Structuring (KADS) methodology, 200
Kokusai Denshin Denwa, 189

Large Scale Pilot Exercise (LSPX), 200
Lucky-Goldstar, 187

Marconi Communication Systems Ltd., 207
Matra, 204
MBB, 207
McDonnell Douglas, 190
MCI Communications, 190
Mercury Communications, 207
Metrics Educational Toolkit (METKIT), 202
Microelectrónica de España, 189
Mitel, 190
Mitsubishi, 192
Mitsui, 207
Multiplex analog component standard (MAC), 198

NEC, 191, 208, 227
NHK, 198
Nippon Information and Communication (NI&C), 192
Nippon Telegraph & Telephone Corporation (NTT), 192
Nixdorf computer, 226
Nokia Data, 207
Northern Telecom, 190, 204, 207
Norwegian Telecommunications Administration, 205

Obviously Required Nameserver (THORN), 200
Olivetti, 183
Olivetti File-Net Document-Image processor, 186
Open Software Foundation, 196
Open System Architecture, 184

Parallel Architectures Research language (PARLE), 201
Philips (Netherlands), 188
Plan Calcul, 158, 196, 227
Plessey, 203, 210
Portable Common Tool Environment (PCTE), 200
Primary Rate ISDN OSI Office Facilities (PROOF), 201
Project Integrated Management System (PIMS), 200

Racal Electronics, 207
RACE, 198
RCA (computers), 176
Remington (computers), 176
Research for Advanced Communications in Europe (RACE), 198
Reynolds Metals, 210
Ricoh, 187
Robert Bosch GmbH, 193
Rolm, 190
RYAD series, 217

Satellite Business Systems, 190
Selenia Elsag, 192
SelFac, 200
Shanghai Bell Telephone Equipment Manufacturing Company, 209
Shrack Electronik AG, 210
Siemens, 190
Siemens Information Systems, 191
Siemens-Nixdorf Informationssysteme AG (SNI), 196, 227
Société Génerale de Belgique, 206
SONET, 189, 206
Special Systems Centre (CSS), 207
Sperry Univac, 207, 210
Standard Electrica SA, 209
Standard Electric Lorenz AG, 209
Standard Electric Puhelinteollisuus OY, 209
Standard Radio och Telefon AB, 209
Standard Telefon og Kabelfabrik A/S, 209
Standard Telephon und Radio AG, 209
Stromberg Carlson, 204
Sumitomo Corporation, 193
Sumitomo Electric, 207
Sun Microsystems, 212
Synchronous Optical Network, 189, 206
System X, 203
Sytek, 190

TDK, 189
TDX, 207
Telecommunications Technology Inc. (TTI), 208
Telefónica, 206
Telenokia, 204
Teletas, 209
Telettra, 192
Televerket, 210
Teli, 210
Tel Plus Communications, 191
Texas Instruments, 187
Texas Instruments Acer Semiconductor Ltd., 221
Thomson (France), 189
Thomson Télécommunications, 204
Thorn EMI, 186, 210
Thorn Ericsson, 210
Toshiba, 185
Transputers, 199
Triumph-Adler, 183

United Telecommunications, 193
Univac, 176
Universal Digital Computer Company, 219

Vitelic, 187

Wacker Chemitronic, 207

X-Windows, 221
Xerox, 183

Zaibatsu, 229
Zilog, 187

Subject Index

Absolute-cost barrier, 110
Accounting systems, 275
Administrative heritage, 318, 374

Administrative Legacy, 14, 16
American Century, 18
Ancient Regime, 16

Index

Anticipative infrastructure, 287
Appropriability theory, 133

Balanced flow of information, 153
Bandwidth management technology, 139
Bargaining power, 146, 149
Beggar-thy-neighbor policies, 157
Borderless world, 112
Brazilian informatics policies, 152
Bureaucratic control systems, 62
Business re-engineering, 379
Business structure (information structure), 50

CAD/CAM, 38, 77, 256
Capital-requirement barrier, 110
Centers of excellence, 76, 383
Central Intelligence Agency, 86
Centralization/decentralization, 8, 35, 42, 73, 78, 241, 260, 297
Centralized inventory control, 304
Chambers of Commerce, 389
Chief Information Officer (CIO), viii, 239
COCOM, 148, 343
Codes of conduct, 158, 322
Collaborative systems 34, 39
Comecon, 216
Common denominator, 102, 103
Common planning, 82
Common systems, 80
Configuration, 66. *See also* Coordination
Consolidation of applications, 298
Consolidation of data centers, 299
Cooperative systems, 39. *See also* Collaborative systems
Coordination, 61, 66
Core/critical applications, 364
Corporate Intelligence Systems, v, 62, 87
Cost justification methods, 276
Counterintelligence, 91
Cultural barriers, 269
Cultural control systems, 62
Customer-driven applications, 258
Customer relations, 371
Cybernetic control, 71

Database consolidation, 348
Data center consolidation, 321, 387
Data specifications, 287
Dependency Theory, 3, 151, 216
Developing countries, vii, 5, 151, 342
Direct access storage devices (DASDs), 161
Disembodied technology transfer, 145
Dual monitoring strategy, 93

East European telecommunications, 338
Economic imperatives, 48
Economic rent, 127
EDI, 39, 121, 248
EDI for Administration, Commerce and Transport (EDIFACT), 249
Electronic colonialism, 216
Embodied technology transfer, 145
End-user interfaces, 104, 383
Environmental data, 93
Environmental scanning, 56, 97
Ethnocentric organization, 52, 359
Europe 1992, 11, 259

European multinationals, 23
European networks, 141
Events database, 91
Excess capacity, 285
External environment, 50

FDI, 57
Financial information, 43
Financial reporting, 101
Financial systems, 256
Firm Specific Advantages (FSAs), v, 64, 110
Flattened organization, 278
Foreign Direct Investment, 6, 110, 133
Four Dragons, 219
Functional access, 36

GATT, 57, 181, 333, 376
Geocentric organization, 27, 52
Global Inventory Management, 20, 378
Globalization, 300
Global scanner multinational, 115
Global supplier database, 81
Global systems, 34, 37, 40
Global vendors, 274
Golden Age, 17
Governance costs, 133
Group of 77, 111

Headquarters/subsidiary coordination, v
Historical autonomy, 103
Horizontal investments, 111
Host country facilities, 275
Host country/MNC relations, vi
Human fabric, 124
Human resources, 362, 383

IBM and India, 147
Imperfect information, 98
Imperialistic organization, 26
Index of internalization, 161
India and IBM, 147
Informational transaction space, 36
Information arbitrage, 67, 112
Information center role, 298
Information economics, 302
Information flows, 42
Information Network System (INS) (Japan), 251
Information structure, 50
Information technology infrastructure, 48, 51
Information-based comparative advantage, 116
Innovation-based oligopoly, 113
Intelligence coordinator, 86
Intelligence cycle, 89
Interface to common standards, 123
Inter-firm linkages, 243
Internalization (definition), vi, 127
International corporate linkages (ICLs), 244–245
International systems, 34, 40
International telecommunications, 286
ISDN, 32
IT-based FSAs, 110

Japanese language employees, 106

Keiretsu, 252
Korean *Chaebols*, 24

Index

Language barrier, 253, 259, 274
Lead system, 268
Learning curves, 380
Least common denominator, 383
Lesser developed countries (LDCs), 116. *See also* Developing countries
Line management, 104
Lingua franca, 248, 269
Local applications, 304
Location economics, 31, 321
Location-specific (L-type) advantages, 129
Location theory, 68
Logistics applications, 263–264
London Stock Exchange, 116

Manufacturing systems, 256
Market-driven strategy, 116
Marketing intelligence, 96
Market-monitoring systems, v, 56
Mega centers, 53
Mergers & acquisitions, 15, 59
Millions of instructions per second (MIPS), 161
Mind matrix, 70
Mirrored systems, 386
Multicultural skills, 365
Multicurrency software, 108
Multi-domestic model, 279
Multidomestic organization, 26, 100
Multilanguage interfaces, 104
Multilingual applications, 106
Multinational systems, 34, 36
Multipolar System, 18
Multivariate analysis, participation, and structure methodology (MAPS), 88

National data processing centers, 318–319
National identity, 149
National managers, 283
National sovereignty, 48
Network-type organizations, 70
New international economic order, 155
Newly industrializing countries (NICs), 181, 223
Non-tariff barriers (NTBs), vii, 10, 159, 333

Object-oriented languages, 254
OECD guidelines on transborder data flow, 160, 332
Operations and logistics, 372
Order processing, 120
Out-sourcing, 363
Ownership-specific (O-type) advantages, 129

Physical access, 36
Political barriers to implementation, 247
Political imperatives, 48
Political power, 293
Polycentric organization, 24, 27, 52
Pride of ownership, 122
Product cycle model (PCH), 113
Product-differentiation barrier, 110
Product management, 372
Project management, 267, 270, 381
Proprietary knowledge, 113
PTT, 330

Quality control, 128

R&D, 60
R&D coordination, 21
Re-engineering, 12
Reach of information technology, 130
Reaction space, 141
Redundant databases, 322
Regiocentric organization, 25, 27, 52
Regional applications, 273
Regionalization, 300
Regional managers, 292
Regional systems, 40
Remote sensing, 154
Residual value, 297, 320, 383
Resistance to internationalization, 167

Satellite managers, 123
Scale economy barrier, 110
Screw-driver plants, 211
Semi-autonomous data centers, 120, 297
Senior management, 381
Silicon Utopianism, 216
Skill requirements, 269, 277
Sogo shosha, 131
SONET, 32, 345
Specialization in market-making, 128
Specialization in risk-bearing, 128
Stand-alone data centers, 120
Standardization, 83
Stateless corporation, 375
Strategic alliances, 244, 246, 375
Strategic intelligence, 91
Structured Query Language (SQL), 249
Supply of skills, 259
SWIFT, 39, 248
System documentation, 253
Systems Development, vii
Systems development life-cycle, 245
Systems missionaries, 121

Tactical intelligence, 91
Technology-driven strategy, 116
Technology transfer, 145
Telecommunications, 384
Telecommunications infrastructure, 152
Telecommunications problems, 257
Trade creation, 131
Trade in services, 58
Training of users, 80
Transborder Data Flow (TDF), vii, 44, 105, 110, 159, 331–332
Transnational intrafirm division of labor, 152
Transnational systems, 34, 36, 41
Transportable systems architectures, 286
Type-Z companies, 63

United Nations model, 36, 100
Uruguay Round, 57

Value-added chain, 240
Value of information, 94
Vendor assessment, 294
Vertical integration, 115, 244
Very Small Aperature Terminals (VSATs), 128, 335–336
Vision, 382

Worldwide sourcing, 21